Lecture Notes in Computer Science 8483

Commenced Publication in 1973
Founding and Former Series Editors:
Gerhard Goos, Juris Hartmanis, and Jan van Leeuwen

T0236430

Marco Bernardo Ferruccio Damiani
Reiner Hähnle Einar Broch Johnsen
Ina Schaefer (Eds.)

Formal Methods for Executable Software Models

14th International School on Formal Methods
for the Design of Computer, Communication,
and Software Systems, SFM 2014
Bertinoro, Italy, June 16-20, 2014
Advanced Lectures

 Springer

Volume Editors

Marco Bernardo
Università di Urbino, Dipartimento di Scienze di Base e Fondamenti
Piazza della Republica 13, 61029 Urbino, Italy
E-mail: marco.bernardo@uniurb.it

Ferruccio Damiani
Università di Torino, Dipartimento di Informatica
Corso Svizzera 185, 10149 Torino, Italy
E-mail: damiani@di.unito.it

Reiner Hähnle
Technische Universität Darmstadt, Fachbereich Informatik
Hochschulstraße 10, 64289 Darmstadt, Germany
E-mail: haehnle@cs.tu-darmstadt.de

Einar Broch Johnsen
University of Oslo, Department of Informatics
P.O. Box 1080 Blindern, 0316 Oslo, Norway
E-mail: einarj@ifi.uio.no

Ina Schaefer
Technische Universität Braunschweig
Institut für Softwaretechnik und Fahrzeuginformatik
Mühlenpfordtstraße 23, 38106 Braunschweig, Germany
E-mail: i.schaefer@tu-braunschweig.de

ISSN 0302-9743   e-ISSN 1611-3349
ISBN 978-3-319-07316-3   e-ISBN 978-3-319-07317-0
DOI 10.1007/978-3-319-07317-0
Springer Cham Heidelberg New York Dordrecht London

Library of Congress Control Number: 2014939047

LNCS Sublibrary: SL 2 – Programming and Software Engineering

Typesetting: Camera-ready by author, data conversion by Scientific Publishing Services, Chennai, India

Printed on acid-free paper

Springer is part of Springer Science+Business Media (www.springer.com)

Preface

This volume presents a set of papers accompanying the lectures of the 14th International School on Formal Methods for the Design of Computer, Communication and Software Systems (SFM). This series of schools addresses the use of formal methods in computer science as a prominent approach to the rigorous design of the above-mentioned systems. The main aim of the SFM series is to offer a good spectrum of current research in foundations as well as applications of formal methods, which can be of help for graduate students and young researchers who intend to approach the field. SFM 2014 was devoted to executable software models and covered topics such as variability models, automated analysis techniques, deductive verification, and run-time assessment and testing. The eight papers collected in the two parts of this volume represent the broad range of topics of the school.

The first part is concerned with modeling and verification; it consists of five papers. The paper by Bubel, Flores Montoya, and Hähnle focusses on ABS, the Abstract Behavioral Modeling (ABS) language, and shows how resource consumption analysis, deadlock detection, and functional verification work on ABS models. Giachino and Laneve address recursive programs that admit dynamic resource creation and define a deadlock-detection algorithm based on a generalization to mutations of the theory of permutations of names. The paper by Ábrahám, Becker, Dehnert, Jansen, Katoen, and Wimmer surveys explicit and symbolic techniques for the computation and representation of probabilistic counterexamples for discrete-time Markov chains and probabilistic automata. Gmeiner, Konnov, Schmid, Veith, and Widder illustrate how to integrate parametric data and counter abstraction, finite-state model checking, and abstraction refinement in the setting of threshold-based fault-tolerant distributed algorithms. The paper by Amighi, Blom, Darabi, Huisman, Mostowski, and Zaharieva-Stojanovski discusses the VerCors approach to concurrent software verification, by showing the use of permission-based separation logic to reason about multithreaded Java programs as well as kernel programs following the Single Instruction Multiple Data paradigm.

The second part is on run-time assessment and testing; it contains three papers. De Boer and De Gouw present a method for preventing, isolating, and fixing software bugs, which is based on automated run-time checking of a combination of protocol- and data-oriented properties of object-oriented programs. The paper by Albert, Arenas, Gómez-Zamalloa, and Rojas overviews white-box test-case generation techniques relying on symbolic execution, with emphasis on an implementation in constraint logic programming and an extension to actor-based concurrent software. Finally Lochau, Peldszus, Kowal, and Schaefer describe the activity of model-based testing for single systems and then review techniques specific to software product lines such as sample-based testing and variability-aware product line testing.

We believe that this book offers a useful view of what has been done and what is going on worldwide in the field of formal methods for executable software models. This school was organized in collaboration with the EU FP7 project Envisage, whose support we gratefully acknowledge. We wish to thank all the speakers and all the participants for a lively and fruitful school. We also wish to thank the entire staff of the University Residential Center of Bertinoro for the organizational and administrative support.

June 2014

Marco Bernardo
Ferruccio Damiani
Reiner Hähnle
Einar Broch Johnsen
Ina Schaefer

Table of Contents

Modeling and Verification

Run-Time Assessment and Testing

Analysis of Executable Software Models*

Richard Bubel, Antonio Flores Montoya, and Reiner Hähnle

TU Darmstadt, Dept. of Computer Science, Germany
{bubel,aeflores,haehnle}@cs.tu-darmstadt.de

Abstract. In this tutorial we focus on the *Abstract Behavioral Modeling* (ABS) language, a highly modular, executable modeling language for concurrent systems. We show how three analyses for ABS models are working: resource consumption, deadlock detection, and functional verification. The acceptance of incomplete ABS models together with the capability to analyse them makes ABS extremely useful as a precise modeling language to be used in the design phases of software development.

1 Introduction

Modern software is complex, often runs in a concurrent or distributed environment, and undergoes frequent evolutionary changes driven by rapid changes stemming from business and technological factors. Software is an essential and integral part of most contemporary consumer products, machinery, communication systems, transport systems, etc. The growing ubiquity of software in commodities, but also in safety- and security-critical applications implies that software defects more and more have direct consequences for end users and are of central importance for the acceptance, quality, and safety of many products.

Recall the well-known cost increase for fixing defects during successive software development phases [14]. IBM Systems Sciences Institute estimates that a defect that costs one unit to fix in design, costs 15 units to fix in testing (system/acceptance) and 100 units or more to fix in production (see Fig. 1), and this cost estimation does not even consider the *impact cost* due to, for example, delayed time to market, lost revenue, lost customers, and bad public relations. Together with the ubiquity of software, the penalty for late discovery of defects makes a very powerful case for software development methods and tools that permit to analyze the consequences of design choices, and possibly erroneous decisions, at an as early stage as possible.

Conventional, informal and semi-formal notations, such as the UML or feature diagrams, however, are not rich and formal enough to admit simulation, automated analysis, or rapid prototyping. It is with this gap in mind that in the past years there has been a lot of interest in *executable modeling languages*.

In this tutorial we focus on the *Abstract Behavioral Specification* (ABS) language [25,1], a highly modular, executable modeling language for concurrent

---

* Partly funded by the EU project FP7-610582 ENVISAGE.

M. Bernardo et al. (Eds.): SFM 2014, LNCS 8483, pp. 1–25, 2014.

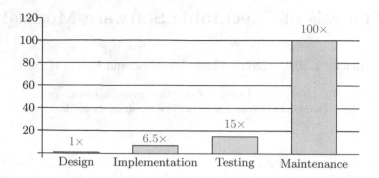

Fig. 1. Relative costs to fix software defects for static infrastructure (source: IBM Systems Sciences Institute). The columns indicate the phase of the software development at which the defect is found and fixed.

systems that exhibit a high degree of product variability. ABS is a rich, object-oriented language with strong typing, strong encapsulation, abstract data types, a simple, but powerful concurrency model. What sets it apart from mainstream programming languages are three aspects: first, ABS comes with a formal, operational semantics [17]; second, ABS has been carefully designed so as to make automated analyses of various kinds feasible; third, ABS models can be partially specified. Because of the first two features, it is possible to construct a range of automatic and semi-automatic analysis tools for the *full ABS language*. In the present tutorial we show how three analyses of particular importance are working: resource consumption (Sect. 3.1), deadlock detection (Sect. 3.2), and functional verification (Sect. 3.3). The acceptance of incomplete ABS models together with the capability to analyse them makes ABS extremely useful as a precise modeling language to be used in the design phases of software development.

To make this chapter self-contained, we include a very concise introduction into the ABS language in Sect. 2, however, we strongly recommend to read the tutorial [23] as a background. To make the content of this chapter manageable, we focus on two analysis methods for ABS, but we stress that a whole range of tools is available for ABS [34]. In the present volume, the interested reader can find more information on an alternative approach to *deadlock analysis* in the chapter by Laneve et al., on *test generation* in the chapter of Albert et al., and on *runtime assertion checking* in the chapter of de Boer et al.

2   Setting the Context: Abstract Behavioral Modeling

2.1   The Abstract Behavioral Specification (ABS) Language

In this section we briefly introduce the *Abstract Behavioral Specification* (ABS) language [25,1]. The text is based on the ABS introduction given in [35]. For readers unfamiliar with ABS, we recommend the tutorial [23].

ABS is an abstract, executable, object-oriented modeling language [25]. It has been designed as a modeling language that is in particular well equipped for the modeling needs of distributed systems with a high degree of variability.

Formal treatment of ABS models is possible, because the ABS modeling language is properly defined in terms of a formal SOS-style semantics. In particular, all design decisions are carefully crafted to ensure that ABS models are amenable to formal analyses. ABS is under active development and current research targets modeling and analysis of cloud-based services with respect to service contracts [16].

Fig. 2 shows the layered architecture of ABS. The base are functional abstractions around a standard notion of parametric algebraic data types (ADTs). Next we have an object-oriented imperative layer similar but much simpler than JAVA. The concurrency model of ABS is two-tiered: at the lower level it is similar to that of JCoBox [32] that generalizes the concurrency model of Creol [26] from single concurrent objects to concurrent object groups (COGs). COGs encapsulate synchronous, multi-threaded, shared state computation on a single processor. On top of this is an actor-based model with asynchronous calls, message passing, active waiting, and future types. An essential difference to thread-based concurrency is that task scheduling is *cooperative*, i.e., switching between tasks of the same object happens only at specific scheduling points during the execution, which are explicit in the source code and can be syntactically identified. This allows to write concurrent programs in a much less error-prone way than in a thread-based model and makes ABS models suitable for static analysis. Specifically, the ABS concurrency model excludes race conditions on shared data.

| Delta Modeling Language |
| Local Contracts, Assertions |
| Asynchronous Communication |
| Concurrent Object Groups (COGs) |
| Imperative Language |
| Object Model |
| Pure Functional Programs |
| Algebraic (Parametric) Data Types |

Fig. 2. Layered Architecture of ABS

Local contracts and assertions allow to specify a wide variety of functional properties about ABS programs in a Design-by-Contract [28] style. The top layer *Delta Modeling Language (DML)* adds delta-oriented programming [31] to ABS. Although being a central feature in ABS, delta modeling and variability-aware analyses are out of scope for this paper. The contribution of Clarke et al. in this volume contains more information on variability modeling.

2.2 ABS Example

In this tutorial we use a simple banking system as a running example. Fig. 3 shows some of its interfaces.

```
interface Account {
  Int getAid();
  Int deposit(Int x);
  Int withdraw(Int x);
  Bool transfer(Int amount, Account target);
}

interface DB {
  Unit insertAccount(Account a);
  Maybe<Account>getAccount(Int aid);
}
```

Fig. 3. Banking example: Interfaces

The interface Account models a bank account with the expected services such as deposit and withdrawal of money. The interface DB models the bank database used to manage accounts. In particular, it provides means to query for an account using its unique account number.

```
class AccountImpl(Int aid, Int balance) implements Account {
  Int getAid() { return aid; }

  Int deposit(Int x) {
    balance = balance + x;
    return balance;
  }

  Int withdraw(Int x) {
    if (balance - x >= 0) {
      balance = balance - x;
    }
    return balance;
  }

  Bool transfer(Int amount, Account target) { ... }
}
```

Fig. 4. Banking example: Account implementation

```
class DBImpl implements DB {
  List<Account> as = Nil;
  Account getAccount(Int aid) {
    Account result = null;
    Int n = length(as);
    Int cnt = 0;
    while (cnt < n) {
      Account a = nth(as,cnt);
      Fut<Int>idFut = a!getAid();
      Int id=idFut.get;
      if (aid == id) {
        result = a;
      }
      cnt = cnt+1;
    }
    return result;
  }
  ...
}
```

Fig. 5. Simplified example of bank database query

In Fig. 4 an implementing class of interface `Account` is shown. A major design decision is that the balance of accounts must never be negative. Hence, in case of a withdrawal it is checked, whether the account has a sufficient balance to perform the withdrawal. Otherwise, no money is withdrawn and the method returns the unchanged balance.

Fig. 5 shows how class `DatabaseImpl` implements the `DB` interface. The method `getAccount(Int)` implements the lookup for a given account number `aid` as follows: it iterates through the list of all accounts managed by the database. For each managed account it looks up the account number via an asynchronous method call `a!getAid()`. In case of success, the found account is returned, otherwise **null** is returned.

3 Analysis Methods

3.1 Resource Analysis

Automatic resource analysis attempts to infer safe upper bounds on the amount of resources that might be consumed by a program or model during its execution as a function of its input variables. A resource can be any magnitude that we are interested to measure for a given model execution. Time or memory consumption are typical examples of resources. There is an extensive literature on program resource analysis, both for the functional and imperative paradigm [5,22,21,24,10,36,33,15]. However, most approaches are focused on sequential programs and do not treat concurrent programs. This is not a coincidence, given that concurrency adds both inherent and accidental complexity to a resource analysis. Inherent complexity stems mainly from the increased non-determinism that comes with concurrency. Accidental complexity is a consequence of the choice of concurrency models that derive from low-level primitives that are prevalent in current mainstream programming languages. Collaborative scheduling, as realized in ABS, reduces the inherent complexity of the analysis as it reduces the number of possible interleavings that might occur. On the other hand, the use of future variables and synchronization on guards reduces its accidental complexity. As a consequence, in contrast to languages such as JAVA or C/C++, it is possible to automatically analyze concurrent ABS models and obtain resource consumption upper bounds for many interesting and realistic examples.

Basic Approach. We introduce the basic approach to resource analysis of sequential programs [6,5] that we later adapt to concurrent ABS models. Before analyzing a program we abstract away from all information that is not relevant for resource consumption. An abstract representation that turns out to be useful is based on *cost equations*. Cost equations are a specific kind of non-deterministic recurrence relations enriched with a constraint φ that relates the variables that appear in the cost equation and imposes applicability conditions on it. A cost equation $\langle c(\bar{x}) = e, \varphi \rangle$ represents a fragment of code (typically a method or a loop) with integer variables $\bar{x}$, where e represents the cost of executing the fragment of code as a function of $\bar{x}$ and might contain references to other cost equations.

Example 1. The (simplified) cost equations of the method `getAccount` from Fig. 5 are:

$$\text{getAccount}(as, aid) = 3 + \text{length}(as) + \text{while}(0, n, aid, as) \quad n = as$$
$$\text{while}(cnt, n, aid, as) = 4 + \text{nth}(as, cnt) + \text{getAid}(a) +$$
$$\quad \text{if}(cnt, n, aid, a) + \text{while}(cnt + 1, n, aid, as) \quad cnt < n$$
$$\text{while}(cnt, n, aid, as) = 0 \quad cnt \geq n$$
$$\text{if}(cnt, n, aid, a) = 1 \quad a = aid$$
$$\text{if}(cnt, n, aid, a) = 0 \quad a \neq aid$$

The cost equations of length, nth and getAid have been omitted.

The cost expression e is obtained by applying a *cost model* to the ABS model. Intuitively, a cost model maps each instruction to a cost. The choice of the cost model determines the resources that we want to observe. For example, if our cost model maps every instruction to a cost of 1, we will infer an upper bound on the number of executed instructions. Or we could assign a different cost to each **new** C instruction according to the type of object created (and 0 to any other instruction) to measure the heap memory consumption.

Example 2. The cost model applied in our example counts the number of assignments. The cost equation

$$\langle \text{getAccount}(as, aid) = 3 + \text{length}(as) + \text{while}(0, n, aid, as), \quad n = as \rangle \quad (1)$$

contains the constant 3, because of the assignments `Account result = null;`, `Int n = length(as);`, and `Int cnt = 0;` in `getAccount`.

To obtain the constraint φ of a cost equation, each variable is abstracted to its "size" according to a chosen *size measure* and the instructions are substituted by constraints that represent the effect of the instructions on the size of the variables. The set of constraints obtained in this way for a code fragment are then conjoined to a single predicate φ. A typical size measure for arrays and lists is their length. The constraint φ can be enriched with invariants generated using abstract interpretation techniques.

Example 3. The constraint of cost equation (1) reflects the use of size measures and invariants. The list as has been abstracted to its length and through invariant generation techniques we obtain that the result value n of length(as) is the length of the list as, that is $n = as$.

There are multiple techniques to solve systems of cost equations [4,9,11]. In general, the strongly connected components (SCCs) in a system of cost equations are determined and incrementally solved. For each SCC, we look for a ranking function that bounds the number of its possible iterations. Then, we approximate the cost of each iteration as a function of the initial variables.

Example 4. We compute the cost of while following the approach of [4]. Assume the cost of nth(as, cnt) is cnt and the cost of getAid(a) and if(cnt, n, aid, a) are 0 and 1, respectively. The cost of one iteration of while is $4 + cnt + 1$. The value of cnt changes in each iteration, but we can use the invariant $cnt \leq n$ to infer that cnt is bounded by n. Now we can approximate any iteration by $5 + n$. Finally, the function $n - cnt$ is a valid ranking function of while, because it is always non-negative and it decreases with each iteration. A valid upper bound of while is, therefore, $(n - cnt) * (5 + n)$.

Concurrency. ABS's concurrency model poses additional challenges to resource analysis [3]. During the execution of a task, other interleaving tasks can modify the values of the shared variables (that is, object fields). This has to be taken into account when generating a suitable abstraction of ABS models. A safe approximation consists in "forgetting" all the information related to object fields every time when an interleaving might occur (at **await** and **suspend** instructions). This loss of information can reduce the precision of the analysis or even prevent obtaining upper bounds.

Example 5. In Fig. 6 we consider a small modification of the code in Fig. 5. We have removed the auxiliary variable n and we do not block the complete database each time we want to obtain an account's id. In the cost equation abstraction of instruction `await idFut?;` we lose the information about the object's fields. The resulting cost expressions of while are:

$$\text{while}(cnt, n, aid, as) = 4 + \text{length}(as) + \text{nth}(as, cnt) + \text{getAid}(a) + $$
$$+ \text{if}(cnt, n, aid, a) + \text{while}(cnt + 1, n, aid, as') \qquad cnt < as$$
$$\text{while}(cnt, n, aid, as) = \text{length}(as) \qquad cnt \geq as$$

```
class DBImpl implements DB {
  List<Account> as = Nil;
  Account getAccount(Int aid) {
    Account result = null;
    Int cnt = 0;
    while (cnt < length(as)) {
      Account a = nth(as,cnt);
      Fut<Int>idFut = a!getAid();
      await idFut?;
      Int id = idFut.get;
      if (aid == id) {
        result = a;
      }
      cnt = cnt + 1;
    }
    return result;
  }
  ...
}
```

Fig. 6. Bank database query with concurrency

In these new cost equations we are not able to find a ranking function, because as can vary at every iteration. Therefore, no upper bound is found.

This approximation can be improved using *class invariants*. A class invariant in ABS is a predicate on the object fields that holds not only at the beginning and end of each method, but also at every release point.

Example 6. If we can infer the class invariant $as \leq as_{max}$, we can include this invariant after each release point:

$$\text{while}(cnt, n, aid, as) = \quad 4 + \text{length}(as) + \text{nth}(as, cnt) + \text{getAid}(a) + $$
$$\text{if}(cnt, n, aid, a) + \text{while}(cnt + 1, n, aid, as')$$
$$cnt < as \wedge as' \leq as_{max}$$

With that invariant, we can find the ranking function $as_{max} - cnt$ and obtain an upper bound.

A more advanced technique for proving termination and for inferring upper bounds of loops with interleavings was presented in [8]. That technique follows a rely-guarantee style of reasoning. Assume we have a loop whose termination proof fails because of the information lost at the release points. First, we assume that the shared variables are not modified at the release points, but we do not assume any initial value. Given this assumption we try to prove termination again using standard techniques. If we fail to prove termination, the interleavings were not the cause of the failure. If we succeed, we know that without interleavings the loop terminates. We can also conclude that if the number of interleavings that modify the fields involved in the termination proof is finite, then the loop will also terminate. As we did not assume any initial value on the fields to prove termination, after any modification, the loop is still terminating. If the modifications are finite, the overall system will terminate.

In addition, one has to prove the assumption, that is, the number of times the fields are modified during execution of the loop is finite. To this end, examine the program points that modify fields. These points can be filtered through a May-Happen-in-Parallel (MHP) analysis [7] (see also Sect. 3.2) to keep only those points that can possibly be executed during the execution of the loop. Then try to prove that the remaining program points are executed a finite number of times by proving termination of all the loops that can reach these program points. If we find a circular dependency, that is, the need to prove termination of a loop to prove its own termination, the process terminates with a failure.

Cost Centers. Distributed systems are usually composed of multiple machines, each with its own resources. But traditionally the output of a resource analysis consists only of a single cost expression of the overall cost. This is not appropriate for distributed systems. It is more interesting to obtain separate cost expressions for each distributed component. This can be achieved with the notion of *cost centers* [3].

A cost center is a part of a distributed system with resources whose consumption we want to measure independently from other parts of the system. For example, in ABS cost centers might correspond to COGs or single objects. We can generate cost equations where each part of the cost is multiplied by a constant that represents the cost center where that cost is incurred. For example, the cost equation $\langle C(\bar{x}) = 2 * c_1 + 3 * c_2, \varphi \rangle$ represents code that consumes 2 resource units in cost center c_1 and 3 units in cost center c_3. Once a set of cost equations parameterized with cost centers $c_1, c_2, \ldots, c_n$ is obtained, we can compute the resources consumed by a cost center c_i. We set $c_i = 1$ and $c_j = 0$ for every $j \neq i$ and solve the cost equations as usual.

3.2 Deadlock Analysis

As explained in Sect. 2.1, ABS models use a high-level concurrency model that does not deal explicitly with primitives such as locks or semaphores. This allows us to implement static deadlock analyses that are both precise *and* efficient. In general, deadlock situations are produced when a concurrent model reaches a state in which one or more tasks are waiting for each others' termination and none of them can make any progress. The combination of blocking (**get**) and non-blocking (**await**) operations in ABS can result in complex deadlock situations.

To realize a deadlock analysis we have to identify the elements that can contribute to a deadlock situation and their mutual dependencies. In the case of ABS, these elements can be tasks and COGs. There can be three kinds of dependencies among tasks and COGs:

1. *task-task* dependencies, when a task waits for the termination of another task with a non-blocking operation (**await**);
2. *COG-task* dependencies, when a task waits for the termination of another task but keeps the COG's lock (using **get**);
3. *task-COG* dependencies that occur between each task and the COG they belong to.

The set of these dependencies form a *dependency graph*, where the nodes of the graph are the tasks and COGs involved. A deadlock can occur if, at some point during the execution, there is circular dependency in the active dependencies at that point. Given a concrete state, we can extract a dependency graph. If such graph is cyclic, the state is a deadlock state.

Example 7. Given the following code:

```
1   class AImp() implements A {
2     Unit syncMessage(A x,String m) {
3        Fut<Unit> f=x!recv(m);
4        f.get
5     }
6
7     Unit AsyncMessage(A x,String m) {
8        Fut<Unit> f=x!recv(m);
9        await f?;
10    }
11
12    Unit recv(String m){ }
13  }
14
15  {
16    A a1=new cog AImp();
17    A a2=new cog AImp();
18    a1!syncMessage(a2,''ping'');
19    a2!AsyncMessage(a2,''ping'');
20  }
```

The corresponding dependency graph is:

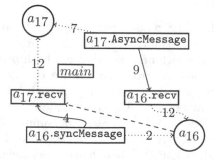

One possible approach for statically detecting deadlock situations is to infer a safe, abstract dependency graph. That is, we want to infer a dependency graph such that any cycle in the dependency graph of any concrete execution can be mapped to a cycle in the abstract dependency graph. If the abstract graph has no cycles, no cycle will be possible in any concrete execution of the model.

We can approximate the dependency graphs with a points-to analysis, similar to the one of [29]. A points-to analysis generates a set of abstract objects that belong to abstract COGs forming an *abstract configuration*. Each object is abstracted by a sequence of allocation points of a fixed length that determines the precision of the analysis. For each abstract object o and method in that kind of object m, we have an abstract task $o.m$. The points-to analysis also provides information on which objects may be pointed to by each reference at any program point. Here, future variables are considered as special references that point to abstract tasks. The dependency graph can be constructed as follows: The nodes of the graph are the abstract COGs and the abstract tasks formed from the method names and abstract objects. The edges can be obtained by examining the points-to information of the future variables at the synchronization points (the **await** and **get** instructions).

An important source of imprecision is the fact that we infer a single dependency graph that "covers" all the possible concrete graphs. In the abstract graph there might be dependencies that form a cycle but that cannot be active simultaneously in any concrete execution state. Such a situation would generate a false positive. We can discard some of these unfeasible cycles with a *May-Happen-in-Parallel* (MHP) analysis [7]. A MHP analysis tells us, given two program points, whether there can be any concrete state in which those two points are being executed in parallel. A dependency cycle is feasible if all the synchronization points that generated its dependencies can happen in parallel.

This approach has shown to be efficient and precise enough for many practical cases. The major source of imprecision is the abstraction performed by the points-to analysis which fixes the set of possible abstract objects beforehand. In particular, all objects created inside a loop are abstracted to a single abstract object. Whenever there are dependencies among these objects' tasks, we will get spurious deadlock alerts. The latter are handled better by contract-based approaches, such as the one of Cosimo et al [19,20] (see also the Chapter by Laneve at al. in this volume).

3.3 Deductive Verification

For real-world programming languages like JAVA, deductive verification of distributed and concurrent programs is hard. A major reason for this are concurrency models that are not well-defined, platform-dependent or too liberal. These weaknesses cause a proliferation of the possible interleavings that have to be checked for a given property. Hence, much research effort has been directed towards techniques that allow to restrict the number of possible interleavings, for example, symmetry reductions.

As explained in Sect. 2.1, the ABS language was *designed* around a concurrency model whose analysis stays manageable. Shared memory communication is only possible within a concurrent object group (COG), for which ABS permits only cooperative scheduling. Hence, all interleaving points occur syntactically explicit in an ABS program in form of an **await** statement which releases control. Communication between different COGs (which are executed in parallel on distributed nodes) is restricted to message passing.

The limitations of the ABS concurrency model makes it possible to define a *compositional* specification and verification method. This is essential for being able to scale verification to non-trivial programs, because it is possible to specify and verify each ABS method separately, without the need for a global invariant. During formal verification of ABS, we do *not* model threads or process queues explicitly, and hence, stay in an essentially sequential setting. This makes it possible to largely reuse a well-understood specification approach for sequential, imperative programs. We follow the *Design-by-Contract* [28] paradigm with an emphasis on specification of interface and class invariants.

The ABS verification method instantiates a combination of the *rely-guarantee* and assumption/commit paradigms [27,30]. The workflow is as follows: For each interface and each implementing class appropriate invariants are specified:

Interface invariants express mostly restrictions on the control-flow, i.e., constraints on the order of asynchronous method calls.

Class invariants are mainly used to relate the state of an object to the local *history* of the system. The history is a sequence of events such as method invocations, method completions, or object creations. For instance, a method invocation event is implicitly generated and recorded in the object-local history whenever a method is called asynchronously.

To verify an ABS model we prove that for each class an arbitrarily chosen object preserves its interface and its class invariants. The compositionality of our method then gives the guarantee that these invariants are preserved by *all* objects of the system.

To specify history properties we use a formalisation of histories that was developed in [18]. For the purpose of this tutorial, we restrict ourselves to the four event types depicted in Fig. 7.

(1) Object s invokes asynchronously method m on object r. This asynchronous invocation results in the creation of a future and is also recorded as an *invocation event* in the history of the caller object s.

(2) Once the method invocation is scheduled for execution in r, an *invocation reaction event* is created and recorded in the history of the callee r.

(3) After the execution of method m completes and resolves the future, an accompanying *completion event* is created and recorded in the history of r.

(4) When the future gets finally queried for the return value (usually by the invoking object) a *completion reaction event* is added to the history of the caller s.

Specification and verification of ABS models is done in ABS dynamic logic (ABS DL). ABS DL is a typed first-order logic with the addition of a box modality: Let ϕ denote an ABS DL formula, and p be a sequence of executable ABS statements, then

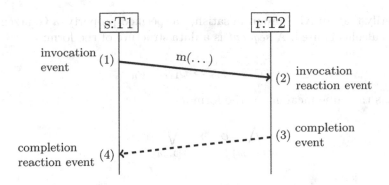

Fig. 7. History events and when they occur

– [p]ϕ (spoken: box p ϕ) is an ABS DL formula with the (informal) meaning:
If p terminates then ϕ hold in its final state.

In addition, ABS DL uses updates (taken from [13]) to capture state changes.
An *elementary update* has the form $x:=t$ where x is a program variable and t a
term. Updates can be applied to formulas or terms: Let u be an update and ξ a
term (formula), then $\{u\}\xi$ is a term (formula).

Example 8. Given a program variable i and the formula i > 0. Then evaluating
the formula

$$\{i:=3\}(i > 0)$$

In a program state s means that i > 0 is evaluated in a state s' which coincides
with s on all program variables except for i, which has the value 3. The meaning
of an update is identical to the meaning of an assignment whose only side-effect
is the actual update of the value stored in the location on the left-hand side.
The above formula is this equivalent to

$$[i=3;](i > 0) \ .$$

To express properties of a system in terms of histories, ABS DL uses a dedicated, globally defined program variable **history**, which contains the union of all
object-local histories as a sequence of events. The history events themselves are
elements of datatype *Event*, which defines for each event type a constructor function. For instance, an invocation event is represented as invocEv($s, r, fut, m, args$)
where s is the caller, r the callee, fut the created future, m the asynchronously
called method and *args* the method arguments.

In addition to the history formalization as a sequence of events, there are a
number of auxiliary and convenience predicates that allow to express common
properties concerning histories. For example, predicates like wfHist(*History*),
beginsWith(*History*, *Event*), endsWith(*History*, *Event*), etc., are used to specify
wellformedness of histories, etc.

To verify that an ABS program satisfies a specified property, a Gentzen-style sequent calculus is used. A *sequent* is a data structure of the form:

$$\phi_1, \ldots, \phi_m \Rightarrow \psi_1, \ldots, \psi_n$$

which has the same meaning as the formula

$$\bigwedge_{i \in \{1 \ldots m\}} \phi_i \rightarrow \bigvee_{j \in \{1 \ldots n\}} \psi_j \ .$$

A sequent rule

$$\text{name} \ \frac{\overbrace{s_1 \quad \cdots \quad s_n}^{\text{premise}}}{\underbrace{s}_{conclusion}}$$

$(s, s_i, i \in \{1 \ldots n\}$ are sequents) has a name, a premise consisting of a possibly empty sequence of sequents and a conclusion. A sequent rule is called *correct* if the validity of the premise implies the validity of the rule's conclusion. An *axiom* is a sequent rule without premise.

A sequent *proof* is a tree where each node is labelled with a sequent and there exists a sequent rule r for each inner node such that the conclusion of r matches the node's sequent and the rule's premises match the sequents of the node's children. A branch (of the proof tree) is called closed if the last rule application was an axiom. A proof is called *closed* if and only if all its branches are closed.

The sequent calculus as realized in ABS DL essentially simulates a symbolic interpreter for ABS. The assignment rule for a local program variable is:

$$\text{assign} \ \frac{\varGamma \Rightarrow \{v := e\} \, [\text{rest}]\phi, \varDelta}{\varGamma \Rightarrow [v=e;\text{rest}]\phi, \varDelta}$$

where v is a local program variable and e a pure (side effect free) expression. The rule rewrites the formula by moving the assignment from the program into an update. During symbolic execution the updates accumulate in front of the modality containing the executed program. Once the program to be verified has been completely executed and the modality is empty, these updates are applied to the formula after the modality, resulting in a pure first-order formula (assuming there are no nested modalities). An example for a rule that causes the proof tree to split is

$$\text{ifSplit} \ \frac{\varGamma, e \doteq \text{True} \Rightarrow [\text{p};\text{rest}]\phi, \varDelta \qquad \varGamma, e \doteq \text{False} \Rightarrow [\text{q};\text{rest}]\phi, \varDelta}{\varGamma \Rightarrow [\text{if (e) \{ p \} else \{ q \} rest}]\phi, \varDelta}$$

where for each branch of the conditional statement a corresponding proof branch is created. Each of the two branches has to be considered and closed to prove that the property ϕ holds after the ABS program terminates.

We conclude this section with the rules for asynchronous method invocation and the **await** statement:

asyncMC

$$\frac{\begin{array}{l} \Gamma \Rightarrow o \neq \text{null} \wedge \text{wfHist}(\text{history}), \Delta \\ \Gamma \Rightarrow \{\mathcal{U}\}(\text{futureUnused}(\textit{frc}, \text{history}) \rightarrow \\ \{\text{fr} := \textit{frc} \,\|\, \text{history} := \text{append}(\text{history}, \text{invocEv}(\text{this}, o, \textit{frc}, m, \bar{e}))\}[\text{rest}]\phi) \end{array}}{\{\mathcal{U}\}[\text{r = o!m(args); rest}]\phi}$$

In case of an asynchronous method invocation the proof splits into two branches: the first branch (displayed on top) ensures that the callee is not **null** and that the history is wellformed. The second branch introduces a new constant *frc* which represents the future (placeholder for the method's return value). The left side of the implication ensures that the future is new and it has not yet been used (futureUnused) and updates the history by appending the invocation event for the asynchronous method call. Afterwards, execution continues with the remaining program **rest**. The sequent rule for the **await** statement is:

awaitComp

$$\frac{\begin{array}{l} \Gamma \Rightarrow \textit{Cinv}(C)(\text{heap}, \text{history}, \text{this}), \Delta \\ \Gamma \Rightarrow \{\text{heap} := \text{newHeap} \,\| \\ \quad \text{history} := \text{append}(\text{history}, \text{append}(\text{newHist}, \text{compREv}(\ldots)))\} \\ \quad (\textit{Cinv}(C)(\text{heap}, \text{history}, \text{this}) \wedge \text{wfHist}(\text{history}) \rightarrow [\text{rest}]\phi), \Delta \end{array}}{\Gamma \Rightarrow [\text{await r?; rest}]\phi, \Delta}$$

where **newHist**, **newHeap** are fresh Skolem constants; C is the class in which the ABS code in the premise's modality is executed.

The **await** statement releases control allowing other threads to take over. Once the await guard is satisfied (here: the future is resolved), the waiting thread can be rescheduled. As control of the COG is released by the currently executed code, we must ensure that a state has been reached in which the invariant of class C is satisfied, because the continuing thread will rely on it. The fulfillment of that class invariant is checked by the first branch.

The second branch assumes that the **await** condition is satisfied and continues the execution in a state where the completion reaction event has been appended to the extended history. This means that the value of the **history** variable before execution of the **await** statement has been some event sequence (modeled with the Skolem constant **newHist**), representing those events that occurred between control release and control resume. In our rely-guarantee-based setting, we can safely assume that upon resume of control, the class invariant has been established by the previous thread and holds again. But the heap might have been changed and all previously accumulated knowledge about it must be removed. This is achieved by assigning to the heap an unknown value (modeled with the Skolem constant **newHeap**).

4   Application Examples

4.1   Resource Analysis

We explore the possibilities of the different cost models, size measure, and cost center definitions. We will analyze the example from Fig. 8. The resource and termination analysis is part of the SACO tool [2] available at `http://costa.ls.fi.upm.es/web/saco.php`. Once the SACO plugin has been installed, please create an ABS project with the code of our example. To analyze the program, we select the method `getAccount` in the `Outline` view. Then, we select `SACO->Analyze with SACO`. A dialog will appear showing the different analyses available in SACO. We check `Resource Analysis` and click on `Analyze`. Unfortunately, the result we obtain contains the term `c(maximize_failed)` which indicates a failure in the maximization process. This is, because even if there are no concurrent interleavings, we need an invariant for the initial value of the field `as`. So we add an invariant at the beginning of the method:

```
[as <= max(as)]
Account getAccount(Int aid) {
  Account result = null;
  ...
}
```

Once the invariant is added we obtain a valid upper bound. Instead of analyzing directly, we can select `SACO->Analyze with SACO`, check `Resource Analysis` and click on `Configure+Analyze`. Now we can select the parameters of the analysis. Some of the options are:

Cost Model: indicates the type of resource that we are interested in measuring. Some of the cost models are: `Steps` (counts the number of executed instructions), `Tasks` (counts the number of asynchronous calls to methods), `Memory` (measures the size of the created data structures).

Cost Centers: allows to decide whether we want to use cost centers or not. If we decide to use cost centers, we can choose between `class` and `object`. The option `class` associates a cost center to each class, whereas `object` associates a cost center to each abstract object inferred in the points-to analysis.

Size Abstraction: allows choosing how data structures are abstracted into an integer number. Two possibilities are provided: `Size`, which counts all nodes in the structure, and `Depth`, which counts the length of the longest path.

Now we analyze the number of tasks that are created during the execution of `getAccount` in total. We set the cost model to `Tasks`, no cost centers and size abstraction `Depth` (Our main data structure is a list and `Depth` corresponds to the length of the list). We obtain that the number of tasks is $max(as)$ which corresponds to the number of calls to `getAid`.

Next we perform an analysis with cost centers. We select the option cost center `class` and the cost model `Steps`. The result is:

$$12 + 6 * \text{nat}(\max(\text{as}) - 1) + \text{nat}(\max(\text{as}) - 1) * (20 + 9 * \text{nat}(\max(\text{as}) - 2))$$
```
                    within cost-center 'DBImpl'
nat(max(as) - 1) within cost-center 'AccountImpl'
```

Here we can see how the cost in `AccountImpl` is linear but is quadratic in `DBImpl`. This quadratic cost is due to the function `nth` that has linear cost and is executed a linear number of times. Knowing that, we could try to improve the method to avoid the quadratic cost.

Rely-Guarantee Termination. We try to prove termination of the example with interleavings in Fig. 6. To apply the rely-guarantee method, we need a complete model with a main block (termination depends on which other methods can be executed in parallel). We add the the following main block:

```
{
  Account a;
  DB db = new cog DBImpl();
  Int max = 10;
  Int i = 1;
  while(i <= max){
    a = new cog AccountImpl(i,0);
    Fut<Unit> aFut = db!insertAccount(a);
    await aFut?;
    i = i+1;
  }
  db!getAccount(3);
}
```

In this main block we create a database, then add 10 new accounts with account ids ranging from 1 to 10, and finally we query the database with the account 3.

To analyze the resulting program, we select the main block in the `Outline` view, select `SACO->Analyze with SACO`, check `Termination Analysis` and click on `Analyze`. The result is a list of strongly connected components (SCCs) and the information whether they are terminating or not. In this case, all the SCCs turn out to be terminating. The termination of `getAccount` depends on `as`. However, when `getAccount` is executed, all the `insertAccount` calls must have terminated. That is detected by the MHP analysis and thus termination is proven.

If we remove the instruction **await aFut?;**, this is not the case any more. Several instances of `insertAccount` might execute in parallel with `getAccount`. But we can prove termination of the loop in the main block, and this implies that `as` can be modified in parallel only a finite number of times (10 times) and, therefore, `getAccount` is still guaranteed to terminate.

4.2 Deadlock Analysis

We illustrate the behavior of the analysis with the example code of Fig. 8. The example has a **main** method (line 44) that creates a server and a client. Then, it

```
19   ...//Module and Interface declarations have been omitted
20
21   class ClientI(Server server) implements Client {
22   Config config = null;
23   Unit setConfig(Config co) {
24   config=co;
25   }
26   Unit syncSend(String m) {
27     //await config!=null;
28
29     Fut<Unit> f = server!recv(m);
30     f.get;
31   }
32   }
33   class ServerI implements Server{
34   Config co = null;
35   Unit ini(Client client) {
36     co = new ConfigI();
37     Fut<Unit> f = client!setConfig(co);
38     f.get;
39   }
40    Unit recv(String message) {
41   }
42   }
43
44   {
45   Server s = new cog ServerI();
46   Client c = new cog ClientI(s);
47   s!ini(c);
48   c!syncSend("hello");
49   }
50   }
```

Fig. 8. Client-server deadlock example

initializes the server with a reference to the client at line 47. The method ini()
(line 35) creates a Config object and passes it to the client using the method
setConfig() (line 23). The server should not do anything until the client has
received the configuration so it waits holding the lock at line 38. Finally, the
main method calls syncSend() in line 48. Method syncSend() (line 26) sends
a message to the server by calling recv() (line 40) and blocks the client until
recv() is completed in line 30.

A deadlock can occur if syncSend() (line 26) starts before setConfig()
(line 23). The server will stay blocked at line 38 waiting for setConfig() to finish. At the same time the client will stay blocked at line 30 waiting for recv().
Neither setConfig() nor recv() is able to start as their COGs are blocked by
other methods.

The deadlock analysis proceed as follows. First, is uses the points-to information to identify the objects, COGs and tasks that can be created: c (the client), s (the server) and their respective tasks: $c.\texttt{setConfig}$, $c.\texttt{syncSend}$, $s.\texttt{ini}$, and $s.\texttt{recv}$. Second, it identifies the synchronization points and extracts their dependencies: line 30 generates $c \xrightarrow{line\ 30} s.\texttt{recv}$ and $c.\texttt{syncSend} \xrightarrow{line\ 30} s.\texttt{recv}$; line 38 generates $s \xrightarrow{line\ 38} c.\texttt{setConfig}$ and $s.\texttt{ini} \xrightarrow{line\ 38} c.\texttt{setConfig}$; also the dependencies from each task to its COG: $s.\texttt{recv} \xrightarrow{line\ 40} s$, $s.\texttt{ini} \xrightarrow{line\ 35} s$, $c.\texttt{setConfig} \xrightarrow{line\ 23} c$, and $c.\texttt{syncSend} \xrightarrow{line\ 26} c$.

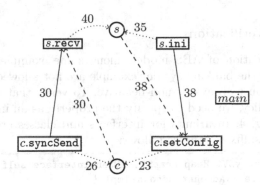

Fig. 9. Deadlock dependency graph of example from Fig.8

In the thus constructed dependency graph (see Fig. 9), we look for cycles. There is one cycle: $c \xrightarrow{line\ 30} s.\texttt{recv} \xrightarrow{line\ 40} s \xrightarrow{line\ 38} c.\,\texttt{setConfig} \xrightarrow{line\ 23} c$. Finally, we check whether all program points involved in the cycle can happen in parallel using the MHP analysis. In this case, all the involved points (line 30, line 40, line 38 and line 23) can happen in parallel to each other and the tool will report the deadlock cycle. If we uncomment line 27, $\texttt{setConfig()}$ is forced to finish before proceeding to line 30. Therefore, no deadlock is possible. The dependency graph is the same, but the MHP analysis reports that line 30 and line 23 now cannot happen in parallel and the cycle is discarded.

This deadlock analysis is part of the SACO tool (See Sec. 4.1). Lets use the Eclipse plugin interface to analyze the example from Fig. 8. Once the SACO plugin has been installed, we create a ABS project with the code of our example. In order to analyze the program, we select the **Main Block** in the **Outline** view. Then, we select **SACO->Analyze with SACO**. A dialog will appear showing the different analyses of SACO. Check the option **Deadlock Analysis** and click **Analyze**. Shortly after, a report of the possible deadlocks will appear in the Eclipse console (See Fig. 10) and the synchronization instructions involved in the deadlocks will appear highlighted. Again, if we uncomment line 27 and repeat the analysis, we will see a new message in the console indicating that the program has no deadlocks.

```
cog ServerI(45,main) blocked in object ServerI(45,main) at ServerI.ini Line 38
                    |
            (Waiting for)
                   \/
task ClientI.setConfig in object ClientI(46,main) in cog ClientI(46,main)
                    |
               (MHP)
                \/
cog ClientI(46,main) blocked in object ClientI(46,main) at ClientI.syncSend Line 30
                    |
            (Waiting for)
                \/
task ServerI.recv in object ServerI(45,main) in cog ServerI(45,main)
```

Fig. 10. Output of the deadlock analysis for the example of Fig. 8

4.3 Deductive Verification

We illustrate verification of ABS models along some examples. The account types supported by the banking system example are not allowed to be in debt, i.e., their balance must always be non-negative. To verify that our ABS model implements this policy, we need to specify the property as an invariant of class AccountImpl in Fig. 4. Invariants for interfaces and classes are specified in a separate file whose suffix is .inv as follows:

```
\invariants(Seq historySV, Heap heapSV, ABSAnyInterface self) {
  nonNegativeBalance : Account.AccountImpl {
    int::select(heapSV, self, Account.AccountImpl::balance) >= 0
  };
}
```

The keyword **invariants** opens a section wherein invariants can be specified. Its parameters declare program variables that can be used to refer to the history (historySV), the heap (heapSV), and the current object (self, similar as JAVA's this). These program variables can be used in the specification of class invariants.

The section declares an invariant with the name nonNegativeBalance for class AccountImpl. The class invariant states that the value of field balance for the current object must be non-negative. The built-in function int::select is the standard heap selection function for return type Int.

Loading the problem in KeY-ABS opens the proof obligation selection dialog shown in Fig. 11. On selection of the proof obligation *Preserves Class Invariant* for method withdraw(Int) of class AccountImpl, a proof obligation of the following (slightly simplified) form is generated:

$$\{history := append(history, invocREv(...))\}$$
$$((CInv(heap, history, self) \land wfHist(history)) \to [mb;]CInv(...))$$

where mb denotes the body of method withdraw(Int). In this example the proof obligation can be proven automatically with a few steps.

The attempt to prove that the invariant is preserved as well by method deposit(Int) fails with one open goal. Inspecting the goal reveals that the

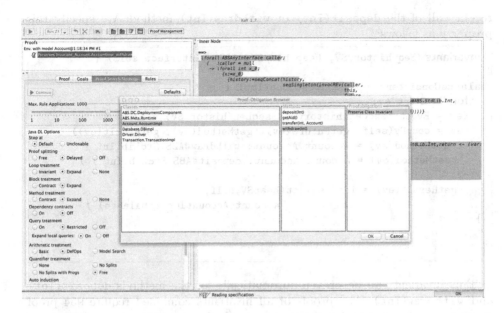

Fig. 11. Proof-Obligation selection dialog

method cannot be proven for negative arguments of `deposit(Int)`. This is not
an issue for method `withdraw` which has an explicit check, but for `deposit(Int)`
negative arguments need to be excluded using either a precondition or an invariant. An invariant is more appropriate, because it reflects the design decision that
accounts never run a negative balance. Moreover, an invariant lets one reuse the
restriction also in other contexts.

```
\invariants(Seq historySV, Heap heapSV, ABSAnyInterface self) {
  amountOfDepositNonNegative : Account.AccountImpl {
    \forall Event ev; (
    \forall int i; ( i >= 0 & i < seqLen(historySV) ->
    ( ev = Event::seqGet(historySV, i) &
    ( isInvocationEv(ev) | isInvocationREv(ev)) &
    getMethod(ev) = Account.Account::deposit#ABS.StdLib.Int ->
      int::seqGet(getArguments(ev), 0) >= 0 ) ) )
};
```

This invariant ensures that method `deposit(Int)` is in any event history
always invoked with a non-negative argument by inspecting the associated invocation (reaction) events. With this additional invariant we can close the proof
for `deposit(Int)`, requiring to instantiate the second quantifier in the invariant
once by hand.

As a final example, we specify how the value of field `balance` of class `Account`
relates to the history: it always coincides with the value returned by the most

recent call of the `deposit(Int)` or `withdraw(Int)` method. We specify this property as follows:

```
\invariants (Seq historySV, Heap heapSV, ABSAnyInterface self) {

balanceConsistent : Account.AccountImpl {
  \forall  Event ev;(
  (ev = Event::seqGet(historySV, seqLen(historySV) - 1) &
   ev = compEv(self, getFuture(ev), getMethod(ev), getResult(ev)) &
   ( getMethod(ev) = Account.Account::withdraw#ABS.StdLib.Int |
     getMethod(ev) = Account.Account::deposit#ABS.StdLib.Int ) )
  ->
     getResult(ev) = int::select(heapSV,self,
                                 Account.AccountImpl::balance) )
};

}
```

This invariant can be proven automatically for the methods `deposit(Int)` and `withdraw(Int)`. The proofs of all invariants combined require 954 proof steps with only two user interactions for method `deposit(Int)` and 1700 proof steps for method `withdraw(Int)` with no user interactions (see Fig. 12).

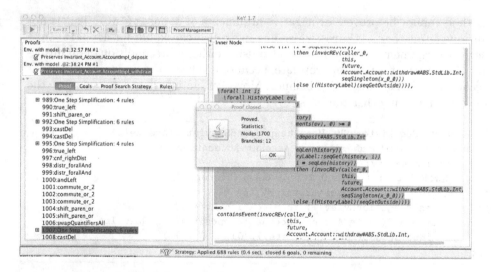

Fig. 12. Proof that method `withdraw` preserves the invariants

5   Conclusion and Future Perspectives

We discussed three complementary analyses techniques for the ABS modeling language: deadlock detection, resource consumption, and deductive verification.

None of the analyses in this tutorial would have been possible with the same degree of automation and precision in implementation languages such as JAVA or C/C++. It is a crucial insight that ABS was developed from the start with analyzability in mind. As the ABS examples demonstrate (and, even more so, industrial case studies [34]), it is nevertheless possible to create rich and realistic software models.

The three presented analyses differ in difficulty of usage and in precision: easiest to use is the deadlock detection analysis, which is fully automatic and does not require any configuration. If the analysis finds a problem, the call chain leading to the potential deadlock is shown and the involved statements are highlighted in the Eclipse IDE. The deadlock analysis is correct, i.e., when no deadlocks are reported, the analyzed ABS program is deadlock-free. But, as a consequence of abstraction and over-approximation, not all reported deadlocks need actually occur, so one has to carefully check the analysis report to reject false positives.

The resource consumption analysis requires that a cost model was specified or at least an *a priori* specified cost model needs to be selected. The actual analysis is again fully automatic and the derived costs for the ABS model are shown. The analysis might, however, not always return with a result. If it returns with an upper bound, then this is sound, that is, no concrete run of the ABS model will exceed the computed worst case. It is, however, possible that *no* concrete run reaches the upper bound, that is, the analysis might not be tight.

Deductive verification clearly is the most difficult to use analysis presented in this paper. It requires to specify invariants of the system and the verification process requires some amount of user interaction. Both activities require considerable expertise with formal specification and verification. On the positive side, the deductive verification is precise and highly expressive with respect to the properties that can be specified. It allows to verify data dependent, functional properties of ABS models. An in-depth discussion of the trade-offs of various verification scenarios can be found in [12].

References

1. The ABS Language Specification, ABS version 1.2.0 edition (April 2013), http://tools.hats-project.eu/download/absrefmanual.pdf
2. Albert, E., Arenas, P., Flores-Montoya, A., Genaim, S., Gómez-Zamalloa, M., Martin-Martin, E., Puebla, G., Román-Díez, G.: SACO: Static Analyzer for Concurrent Objects. In: Ábrahám, E., Havelund, K. (eds.) TACAS 2014 (ETAPS). LNCS, vol. 8413, pp. 562–567. Springer, Heidelberg (2014)
3. Albert, E., Arenas, P., Genaim, S., Gómez-Zamalloa, M., Puebla, G.: Cost Analysis of Concurrent OO programs. In: Yang, H. (ed.) APLAS 2011. LNCS, vol. 7078, pp. 238–254. Springer, Heidelberg (2011)
4. Albert, E., Arenas, P., Genaim, S., Puebla, G.: Closed-form upper bounds in static cost analysis. Journal of Automated Reasoning 46(2), 161–203 (2011)
5. Albert, E., Arenas, P., Genaim, S., Puebla, G., Zanardini, D.: Cost analysis of Java bytecode. In: De Nicola, R. (ed.) ESOP 2007. LNCS, vol. 4421, pp. 157–172. Springer, Heidelberg (2007)

6. Albert, E., Arenas, P., Genaim, S., Puebla, G., Zanardini, D.: COSTA: Design and implementation of a cost and termination analyzer for Java bytecode. In: de Boer, F.S., Bonsangue, M.M., Graf, S., de Roever, W.-P. (eds.) FMCO 2007. LNCS, vol. 5382, pp. 113–132. Springer, Heidelberg (2008)

7. Albert, E., Flores-Montoya, A.E., Genaim, S.: Analysis of May-Happen-in-Parallel in Concurrent Objects. In: Giese, H., Rosu, G. (eds.) FMOODS/FORTE 2012. LNCS, vol. 7273, pp. 35–51. Springer, Heidelberg (2012)

8. Albert, E., Flores-Montoya, A., Genaim, S., Martin-Martin, E.: Termination and cost analysis of loops with concurrent interleavings. In: Van Hung, D., Ogawa, M. (eds.) ATVA 2013. LNCS, vol. 8172, pp. 349–364. Springer, Heidelberg (2013)

9. Albert, E., Genaim, S., Masud, A.N.: More precise yet widely applicable cost analysis. In: Jhala, R., Schmidt, D. (eds.) VMCAI 2011. LNCS, vol. 6538, pp. 38–53. Springer, Heidelberg (2011)

10. Alias, C., Darte, A., Feautrier, P., Gonnord, L.: Multi-dimensional rankings, program termination, and complexity bounds of flowchart programs. In: Cousot, R., Martel, M. (eds.) SAS 2010. LNCS, vol. 6337, pp. 117–133. Springer, Heidelberg (2010)

11. Alonso-Blas, D.E., Arenas, P., Genaim, S.: Precise cost analysis via local reasoning. In: Van Hung, D., Ogawa, M. (eds.) ATVA 2013. LNCS, vol. 8172, pp. 319–333. Springer, Heidelberg (2013)

12. Beckert, B., Hähnle, R.: Reasoning and verification. IEEE Intelligent Systems (to appear, 2014)

13. Beckert, B., Hähnle, R., Schmitt, P.H. (eds.): Verification of Object-Oriented Software. LNCS (LNAI), vol. 4334. Springer, Heidelberg (2007)

14. Boehm, B.W., Papaccio, P.N.: Understanding and controlling software costs. IEEE Trans. Software Eng. 14(10), 1462–1477 (1988)

15. Brockschmidt, M., Emmes, F., Falke, S., Fuhs, C., Giesl, J.: Alternating runtime and size complexity analysis of integer programs. In: Ábrahám, E., Havelund, K. (eds.) TACAS 2014 (ETAPS). LNCS, vol. 8413, pp. 140–155. Springer, Heidelberg (2014)

16. de Boer, F.S., Hähnle, R., Johnsen, E.B., Schlatte, R., Wong, P.Y.H.: Formal modeling of resource management for cloud architectures: An industrial case study. In: De Paoli, F., Pimentel, E., Zavattaro, G. (eds.) ESOCC 2012. LNCS, vol. 7592, pp. 91–106. Springer, Heidelberg (2012)

17. Report on the Core ABS Language and Methodology: Parts A and B. Deliverable 1.1 of project FP7-231620 (HATS) (March 2010), http://www.hats-project.eu

18. Din, C.C., Dovland, J., Johnsen, E.B., Owe, O.: Observable behavior of distributed systems: Component reasoning for concurrent objects. Journal of Logic and Algebraic Programming 81(3), 227–256 (2012)

19. Giachino, E., Grazia, C.A., Laneve, C., Lienhardt, M., Wong, P.Y.H.: Deadlock analysis of concurrent objects: Theory and practice (2013), http://www.cs.unibo.it/~laneve (submitted)

20. Giachino, E., Laneve, C.: A beginner's guide to the deadLock Analysis Model. In: Palamidessi, C., Ryan, M.D. (eds.) TGC 2012. LNCS, vol. 8191, pp. 49–63. Springer, Heidelberg (2013)

21. Gulavani, B.S., Gulwani, S.: A numerical abstract domain based on expression abstraction and max operator with application in timing analysis. In: Gupta, A., Malik, S. (eds.) CAV 2008. LNCS, vol. 5123, pp. 370–384. Springer, Heidelberg (2008)

22. Gulwani, S., Mehra, K.K., Chilimbi, T.M.: Speed: Precise and efficient static estimation of program computational complexity. In: Principles of Programming Languages (POPL 2009), pp. 127–139. ACM (2009)
23. Hähnle, R.: The Abstract Behavioral Specification Language: A Tutorial Introduction. In: Giachino, E., Hähnle, R., de Boer, F.S., Bonsangue, M.M. (eds.) FMCO 2012. LNCS, vol. 7866, pp. 1–37. Springer, Heidelberg (2013)
24. Jan Hoffmann, M.H., Aehlig, K.: Multivariate amortized resource analysis. In: Principles of Programming Languages (POPL 2011), pp. 357–370. ACM (2011)
25. Johnsen, E.B., Hähnle, R., Schäfer, J., Schlatte, R., Steffen, M.: ABS: A core language for abstract behavioral specification. In: Aichernig, B.K., de Boer, F.S., Bonsangue, M.M. (eds.) FMCO 2010. LNCS, vol. 6957, pp. 142–164. Springer, Heidelberg (2011)
26. Johnsen, E.B., Owe, O.: An asynchronous communication model for distributed concurrent objects. Software and System Modeling 6(1), 35–58 (2007)
27. Jones, C.B.: Development Methods for Computer Programs including a Notion of Interference. PhD thesis, Oxford University, jun, Printed as: Programming Research Group, Technical Monograph 25 (1981)
28. Meyer, B.: Applying "design by contract". IEEE Computer 25(10), 40–51 (1992)
29. Milanova, A., Rountev, A., Ryder, B.G.: Parameterized object sensitivity for points-to analysis for java. ACM Trans. Softw. Eng. Methodol. 14, 1–41 (2005)
30. Misra, J., Chandy, K.M.: Proofs of networks of processes. IEEE Transactions on Software Engineering 7(4), 417–426 (1981)
31. Schaefer, I., Bettini, L., Bono, V., Damiani, F., Tanzarella, N.: Delta-oriented programming of software product lines. In: Bosch, J., Lee, J. (eds.) SPLC 2010. LNCS, vol. 6287, pp. 77–91. Springer, Heidelberg (2010)
32. Schäfer, J., Poetzsch-Heffter, A.: JCoBox: Generalizing active objects to concurrent components. In: D'Hondt, T. (ed.) ECOOP 2010. LNCS, vol. 6183, pp. 275–299. Springer, Heidelberg (2010)
33. Sinn, M., Zuleger, F., Veith, H.: A simple and scalable static analysis for bound analysis and amortized complexity analysis. CoRR, abs/1401.5842 (2014)
34. Wong, P.Y.H., Albert, E., Muschevici, R., Proença, J., Schäfer, J., Schlatte, R.: The ABS tool suite: modelling, executing and analysing distributed adaptable object-oriented systems. Journal on Software Tools for Technology Transfer 14(5), 567–588 (2012)
35. Wong, P.Y.H., Bubel, R., de Boer, F.S., Gómez-Zamalloa, M., de Gouw, S., Hähnle, R., Meinke, K., Sindhu, M.A.: Testing abstract behavioral specifications. Software Tools for Technology Transfer (to appear, 2014)
36. Zuleger, F., Gulwani, S., Sinn, M., Veith, H.: Bound analysis of imperative programs with the size-change abstraction. In: Yahav, E. (ed.) Static Analysis. LNCS, vol. 6887, pp. 280–297. Springer, Heidelberg (2011)

Deadlock Detection
in Linear Recursive Programs*

Elena Giachino and Cosimo Laneve

Università di Bologna, Dept. of Computer Science and Egineering – INRIA FOCUS,
Italy
{giachino,laneve}@cs.unibo.it

Abstract. Deadlock detection in recursive programs that admit dynamic resource creation is extremely complex and solutions either give
imprecise answers or do not scale.

We define an algorithm for detecting deadlocks of *linear recursive
programs* of a basic model. The theory that underpins the algorithm
is a generalization of the theory of permutations of names to so-called
mutations, which transform tuples by introducing duplicates and fresh
names.

Our algorithm realizes the back-end of deadlock analyzers for object-
oriented programming languages, once the association programs/basic-
model-programs has been defined as front-end.

1 Introduction

Modern systems are designed to support a high degree of parallelism by ensuring that as many system components as possible are operating concurrently.
Deadlock represents an insidious and recurring threat when such systems also
exhibit a high degree of resource and data sharing. In these systems, deadlocks
arise as a consequence of exclusive resource access and circular wait for accessing
resources. A standard example is when two processes are exclusively holding a
different resource and are requesting access to the resource held by the other. In
other words, the correct termination of each of the two process activities *depends*
on the termination of the other. Since there is a *circular dependency*, termination
is not possible.

The techniques for detecting deadlocks build graphs of dependencies (x, y)
between resources, meaning that the release of a resource referenced by x depends on the release of the resource referenced by y. The absence of cycles in the
graphs entails deadlock freedom. The difficulties arise in the presence of infinite
(mutual) recursion: consider, for instance, systems that create an unbounded
number of processes such as server applications. In such systems, process interaction becomes complex and either hard to predict or hard to be detected during
testing and, even when possible, it can be difficult to reproduce deadlocks and
find their causes. In these cases, the existing deadlock detection tools, in order

---

* Partly funded by the EU project FP7-610582 ENVISAGE: Engineering Virtualized
  Services.

M. Bernardo et al. (Eds.): SFM 2014, LNCS 8483, pp. 26–64, 2014.

to ensure termination, typically lean on finite models that are extracted from the dependency graphs.

The most powerful deadlock analyzer we are aware of is TYPICAL, a tool developed for pi-calculus by Kobayashi [20,18,16,19]. This tool uses a clever technique for deriving inter-channel dependency information and is able to deal with several recursive behaviors and the creation of new channels without using any pre-defined order of channel names. Nevertheless, since TYPICAL is based on an inference system, there are recursive behaviors that escape its accuracy. For instance, it returns false positives when recursion is mixed up with *delegation*. To illustrate the issue we consider the following deadlock-free pi-calculus factorial program

```
*factorial?(n,(r,s)).
  if n=0 then r?m. s!m else new t in
                     (r?m. t!(m*n)) | factorial!(n-1,(t,s))
```

In this code, factorial returns the value (on the channel s) by *delegating* this task to the recursive invocation, if any. In particular, the initial invocation of factorial, which is r!1 | factorial!(n,(r,s)), performs a synchronization between r!1 and the input r?m in the continuation of factorial?(n,(r,s)). In turn, this may delegate the computation of the factorial to a subsequent synchronization on a new channel t. TYPICAL signals a deadlock on the two inputs r?m because it fails in connecting the output t!(m*n) with them.

The technique we develop in this paper allows us to demonstrate the deadlock freedom of programs like the one above.

To ease program reasoning, our technique relies on an abstraction process that extracts the dependency constraints in programs

- by dropping primitive data types and values;
- by highlighting dependencies between pi-calculus actions;
- by overapproximating statement behaviors, namely collecting the dependencies and the invocations in the two branches of the conditional (the set union operation is modeled by &).

This abstraction process is currently performed by a formal inference system that does not target pi-calculus, but it is defined for a JAVA-like programming language, called ABS [17], see Section 6. Here, pi-calculus has been considered for expository purposes. The ABS program corresponding to the pi-calculus factorial may be downloaded from [15]; readers that are familiar with JAVA may find the code in the Appendix A. As a consequence of the abstraction operation we get the function

$$\text{factorial}(r,s) = (r,s)\&(r,t)\&\text{factorial}(t,s)$$

where (r,s) shows the dependency between the actions r?m and s!m and (r,t) the one between r?m and t!(m*n). The semantics of the abstract factorial is defined operationally by unfolding the recursive invocations. In particular, the unfolding of $\text{factorial}(r,s)$ yields the sequence of abstract states (free names in the definition of factorial are replaced by fresh names in the unfoldings)

```
factorial(r, s) ⟶ (r, s)&(r, t)&factorial(t, s)
              ⟶ (r, s)&(r, t)&(t, s)&(t, u)&factorial(u, s)
              ⟶ (r, s)&(r, t)&(t, s)&(t, u)&(u, s)&(u, v)
                 &factorial(v, s)
              ⟶  ⋯
```

We demonstrate that the abstract `factorial` (and, therefore, the foregoing pi-calculus code) never manifests a circularity by using a *model checking* technique. This despite the fact that the model of `factorial` has infinite states. In particular, we are able to decide the deadlock freedom by analyzing finitely many states – precisely three – of `factorial`.

Our Solution. We introduce a basic recursive model, called *lam programs* – lam is an acronym for *deadLock Analysis Model* – that are collections of function definitions and a main term to evaluate. For example,

$$\big(\ \texttt{factorial}(r, s) = (r, s)\&(r, t)\&\texttt{factorial}(t, s)\ ,\texttt{factorial}(r, s)\ \big)$$

defines `factorial` and the main term $\texttt{factorial}(r, s)$. Because lam programs feature recursion and dynamic name creation – *e.g.* the free name t in the definition of `factorial` – the model is not finite state (see Section 3).

In this work we address the

Question 1. Is it decidable whether the computations of a lam program will ever produce a circularity?

and the main contribution is the positive answer when programs are *linear recursive*.

To begin the description of our solution, we notice that, if lam programs are non-recursive then detecting circularities is as simple as unfolding the invocations in the main term. In general, as in case of `factorial`, the unfolding may not terminate. Nevertheless, the following two conditions may ease our answer:

(i) the functions in the program are *linear recursive*, that is (mutual) recursions have at most one recursive invocation – such as `factorial`;
(ii) function invocations do not show duplicate arguments and function definitions do not have free names.

When (i) and (ii) hold, as in the program

$$\big(\texttt{f}(x, y, z) = (x, y)\&\texttt{f}(y, z, x),\ \texttt{f}(u, v, w)\big)\ ,$$

recursive functions may be considered as *permutations of names* – technically we define a notion of *associated (per)mutation* – and the corresponding theory [8] guarantees that, by repeatedly applying a same permutation to a tuple of names, at some point, one obtains the initial tuple. This point, which is known as the *order* of the permutation, allows one to define the following algorithm for Question 1:

1. compute the order of the permutation associated to the function in the lam and
2. correspondingly unfold the term to evaluate.

For example, the permutation of f has order 3. Therefore, it is possible to stop the evaluation of f after the third unfolding (at the state $(u, v)\&(v, w)\&(w, u)$ & $f(u, v, w)$) because every dependency pair produced afterwards will belong to the relation $(u, v)\&(v, w)\&(w, u)$.

When the constraint (ii) is dropped, as in factorial, the answer to Question 1 is not simple anymore. However, the above analogy with permutations has been a source of inspiration for us.

$$(g(x_0, x_1, x_2, x_3, x_4, x_5, x_6) = (x_3, x_1)\&(x_0, x_8)\&(x_8, x_7)\&g(x_2, x_0, x_1, x_5, x_6, x_7, x_8),$$

$$g(x_0, x_1, x_2, x_3, x_4, x_5, x_6))$$

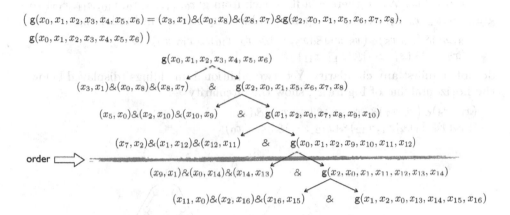

Fig. 1. A lam program and its unfolding

Consider the main term factorial(r, s). Its evaluation will never display factorial(r, s) twice, as well as any other invocation in the states, because the first argument of the recursive invocation is free. Nevertheless, we notice that, from the second state – namely $(r, s)\&(r, t)\&$factorial(t, s) – onwards, the invocations of factorial are not identical, but *may be identified by a map* that

– associates names created in the last evaluation step to past names,
– is the identity on other names.

The definition of this map, called *flashback*, requires that the transformation associated to a lam function, called *mutation*, also records the name creation. In fact, the theory of mutations allows us to map factorial(t, s) back to factorial(r, s) by recording that t has been created after r, *e.g.* $r<t$.

We generalize the result about permutation orders (Section 2):

> *by repeatedly applying a same mutation to a tuple of names, at some point we obtain a tuple that is identical, up-to a flashback, to a tuple in the past.*

As for permutations, this point is the *order* of the mutation, which (we prove) it is possible to compute in similar ways.

However, unfolding a function as many times as the order of the associated mutation may not be sufficient for displaying circularities. This is unsurprising because the arguments about mutations and flashbacks focus on function invocations and do not account for dependencies. In the case of lams where (i) and (ii) hold, these arguments were sufficient because permutations reproduce *the same* dependencies of past invocations. In the case of mutations, this is not true anymore as displayed by the function g in Figure 1. This function has order 3 and the first three unfoldings of $g(x_0, x_1, x_2, x_3, x_4, x_5, x_6)$ are those above the horizontal line. While there is a flashback from $g(x_0, x_1, x_2, x_9, x_{10}, x_{11}, x_{12})$ to $g(x_0, x_1, x_2, x_3, x_4, x_5, x_6)$, the pairs produced up-to the third unfolding

$$(x_3, x_1)\&(x_0, x_8)\&(x_8, x_7)\&(x_5, x_0)\&(x_2, x_{10})\&(x_{10}, x_9)$$
$$\&(x_7, x_2)\&(x_1, x_{12})\&(x_{12}, x_{11})$$

do not manifest any circularity. Yet, two additional unfoldings (displayed below the horizontal line of Figure 1), show the circularity

$$(x_0, x_8)\&(x_8, x_7)\&(x_7, x_2)\&(x_2, x_{10})\&(x_{10}, x_9)$$
$$\&(x_9, x_1)\&(x_1, x_{12})\&(x_{12}, x_{11})\&(x_{11}, x_0) \, .$$

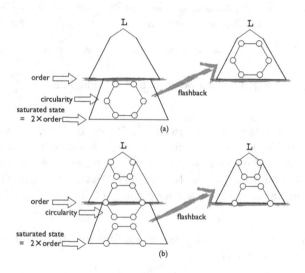

Fig. 2. Flashbacks of circularities

In Section 4 we prove that a sufficient condition for deciding whether a lam program as in Figure 1 will ever produce a circularity is to unfold the function g *up-to two times* the order of the associated mutation – this state will be called *saturated*. If no circularity is manifested in the saturated state then the lam is "circularity-free". This supplement of evaluation is due to the existence of two alternative ways for creating circularities. A first way is when the circularity is given by the dependencies produced by the unfoldings from the order to the saturated state. Then, our theory guarantees that the circularity is also present in the unfolding of g till the order – see Figure 2.a. A second way is when the dependencies of the circularity are produced by (1) the unfolding till the order *and* by (2) the unfolding from the order till the saturated state – these are the so-called *crossover circularities* – see Figure 2.b. Our theory allows us to map dependencies of the evaluation (2) to those of the evaluation (1) and the flashback may break the circularity – in this case, the evaluation till the saturated state is necessary to collect enough informations. Other ways for creating circularities are excluded. The intuition behind this fact is that the behavior of the function (the dependencies) repeats itself following the same pattern every order-wise unfolding. Thus it is not possible to reproduce a circularity that crosses more than one order without having already a shorter one. The algorithm for detecting circularities in linear recursive lam programs is detailed in Section 5, together with a discussion about its computational cost.

We have prototyped our algorithm [15]. In particular, the prototype (1) uses a (standard but not straightforward) *inference system* that we developed for deriving behavioral types with dependency informations out of **ABS** programs [13] and (2) has an add-on translationg these behavioral types into lams. We have been able to verify an industrial case study developed by SDL Fredhoppper – more than 2600 lines of code – in 31 seconds. Details about our prototype and a comparison with other deadlock analysis tools can be found in Section 6. There is no space in this contribution to discuss the inference system: the interested readers are referred to [13].

2 Generalizing Permutations: Mutations and Flashbacks

Natural numbers are ranged over by a, b, i, j, m, n, ..., possibly indexed. Let V be an infinite set of names, ranged over by $x, y, z, \cdots$. We will use partial order relations on names – relations that are reflexive, antisymmetric, and transitive –, ranged over by V, V', I, $\cdots$. Let $x \in V$ if, for some y, either $(x, y) \in V$ or $(y, x) \in V$. Let also $var(V) = \{x \mid x \in V\}$. For notational convenience, we write $\widetilde{x}$ when we refer to a list of names $x_1, \ldots, x_n$.

Let $V \oplus \widetilde{x} < \widetilde{z}$, with $\widetilde{x} \in V$ and $\widetilde{z} \notin V$, be the least partial order containing the set $V \cup \{(y, z) \mid x \in \widetilde{x} \text{ and } (x, y) \in V \text{ and } z \in \widetilde{z}\}$. That is, $\widetilde{z}$ become *maximal names* in $V \oplus \widetilde{x} < \widetilde{z}$. For example,

- $\{(x, x)\} \oplus x < z = \{(x, x), (x, z), (z, z)\}$;
- if $V = \{(x, y), (x', y')\}$ (the reflexive pairs are omitted) then $V \oplus y < z$ is the reflexive and transitive closure of $\{(x, y), (x', y'), (y, z)\}$;
- if $V = \{(x, y), (x, y')\}$ (the reflexive pairs are omitted) then $V \oplus x < z$ is the reflexive and transitive closure of $\{(x, y), (x, y'), (y, z), (y', z)\}$.

Let $x \leqslant y \in V$ be $(x, y) \in V$.

Definition 1. *A* mutation *of a tuple of names, denoted $(\![a_1, \cdots, a_n]\!)$ where $1 \leqslant a_1, \cdots, a_n \leqslant 2 \times n$, transforms a pair $\langle V, (x_1, \cdots, x_n) \rangle$ into $\langle V', (x'_1, \cdots, x'_n) \rangle$ as follows. Let $\{b_1, \cdots, b_k\} = \{a_1, \cdots, a_n\} \setminus \{1, 2, \cdots, n\}$ and let $z_{b_1}, \cdots, z_{b_k}$ be k pairwise different fresh names. [That is names not occurring either in $x_1, \cdots, x_n$ or in V.] Then*

- *if $1 \leqslant a_i \leqslant n$ then $x'_i = x_{a_i}$;*
- *if $a_i > n$ then $x'_i = z_{a_i}$;*
- $\mathbb{V}' = \mathbb{V} \oplus x_1, \cdots, x_n < z_{i_1}, \cdots, z_{i_k}$.

The mutation $(\!(a_1, \cdots, a_n)\!)$ of $\langle \mathbb{V}, (x_1, \cdots, x_n) \rangle$ is written $\langle \mathbb{V}, (x_1, \cdots, x_n) \rangle$ $\xrightarrow{(\!(a_1, \cdots, a_n)\!)} \langle \mathbb{V}', (x'_1, \cdots, x'_n) \rangle$ and the label $(\!(a_1, \cdots, a_n)\!)$ is omitted when the mutation is clear from the context. Given a mutation $\mu = (\!(a_1, \cdots, a_n)\!)$, we define the application of μ to an index i, $1 \leqslant i \leqslant n$, as $\mu(i) = a_i$.

Permutations are mutations $(\!(a_1, \cdots, a_n)\!)$ where the elements are pairwise different and belong to the set $\{1, 2, \cdots, n\}$ (e.g. $(\!(2, 3, 5, 4, 1)\!)$). In this case the partial order $\mathbb{V}$ never changes and therefore it is useless. Actually, our terminology and statements below are inspired by the corresponding ones for permutations. A mutation differs from a permutation because it can exhibit repeated elements, or even new elements (identified by $n + 1 \leqslant a_i \leqslant 2 \times n$, for some a_i). For example, by successively applying the mutation $(\!(2, 3, 6, 1, 1)\!)$ to $\langle \mathbb{V}, (x_1, x_2, x_3, x_4, x_5) \rangle$, with $\mathbb{V} = \{(x_1, x_1), \cdots, (x_5, x_5)\}$ and $\tilde{x} = x_1, x_2, x_3, x_4, x_5$, we obtain

$$\langle \mathbb{V}, (x_1, x_2, x_3, x_4, x_5) \rangle \quad \longrightarrow \quad \langle \mathbb{V}_1, (x_2, x_3, y_1, x_1, x_1) \rangle$$
$$\longrightarrow \quad \langle \mathbb{V}_2, (x_3, y_1, y_2, x_2, x_2) \rangle$$
$$\longrightarrow \quad \langle \mathbb{V}_3, (y_1, y_2, y_3, x_3, x_3) \rangle$$
$$\longrightarrow \quad \langle \mathbb{V}_4, (y_2, y_3, y_4, y_1, y_1) \rangle$$
$$\longrightarrow \quad \cdots$$

where $\mathbb{V}_1 = \mathbb{V} \oplus \tilde{x} < y_1$ and, for $i \geqslant 1$, $\mathbb{V}_{i+1} = \mathbb{V}_i \oplus y_i < y_{i+1}$. In this example, 6 identifies a new name to be added at each application of the mutation. The new name created at each step is a maximal one for the partial order.

We observe that, by definition, $(\!(2, 3, 6, 1, 1)\!)$ and $(\!(2, 3, 7, 1, 1)\!)$ define a same transformation of names. That is, the choice of the natural between 6 and 10 is irrelevant in the definition of the mutation. Similarly for the mutations $(\!(2, 3, 6, 1, 6)\!)$ and $(\!(2, 3, 7, 1, 7)\!)$.

Definition 2. *Let $(\!(a_1, \cdots, a_n)\!) \approx (\!(a'_1, \cdots, a'_n)\!)$ if there exists a bijective function f from $[n + 1 .. 2 \times n]$ to $[n + 1 .. 2 \times n]$ such that:*

1. *$1 \leqslant a_i \leqslant n$ implies $a'_i = a_i$;*
2. *$n + 1 \leqslant a_i \leqslant 2 \times n$ implies $a'_i = f(a_i)$.*

We notice that $(\!(2, 3, 6, 1, 1)\!) \approx (\!(2, 3, 7, 1, 1)\!)$ and $(\!(2, 3, 6, 1, 6)\!) \approx (\!(2, 3, 7, 1, 7)\!)$. However $(\!(2, 3, 6, 1, 6)\!) \not\approx (\!(2, 3, 6, 1, 7)\!)$; in fact these two mutations define different transformations of names.

Definition 3. *Given a partial order $\mathbb{V}$, a $\mathbb{V}$-flashback is an injective renaming ρ on names such that $\rho(x) \leqslant x \in \mathbb{V}$.*

In the above sequence of mutations of $(x_1, x_2, x_3, x_4, x_5)$ there is a $\mathbb{V}_4$-flashback from $(y_2, y_3, y_4, y_1, y_1)$ to $(x_2, x_3, y_1, x_1, x_1)$. In the following, flashbacks will be also applied to tuples: $\rho(x_1, \cdots, x_n) \overset{def}{=} (\rho(x_1), \cdots, \rho(x_n))$.

In case of mutations that are permutations, a flashback is the identity renaming and the following statement is folklore. Let μ be a mutation. We write μ^m for the application of μ m times, namely $\langle \mathbb{V}, (x_1, \cdots, x_n) \rangle \xrightarrow{\mu^m} \langle \mathbb{V}', (y_1, \cdots, y_n) \rangle$ abbreviates $\underbrace{\langle \mathbb{V}, (x_1, \cdots, x_n) \rangle \xrightarrow{\mu} \cdots \xrightarrow{\mu} \langle \mathbb{V}', (y_1, \cdots, y_n) \rangle}_{m \text{ times}}$.

Proposition 1. *Let $\mu = (\!(a_1, \cdots, a_n)\!)$ and*

$$\langle \mathbb{V}, (x_1, \cdots, x_n) \rangle \xrightarrow{\mu} \langle \mathbb{V}', (x_1', \cdots, x_n') \rangle$$
$$\xrightarrow{\mu^m} \langle \mathbb{V}'', (y_1, \cdots, y_n) \rangle$$
$$\xrightarrow{\mu} \langle \mathbb{V}''', (y_1', \cdots, y_n') \rangle$$

If there is a $\mathbb{V}''$ flashback ρ such that $\rho(y_1, \cdots, y_n) = (x_1, \cdots, x_n)$ then there is a $\mathbb{V}'''$-flashback from $(y_1', \cdots, y_n')$ to $(x_1', \cdots, x_n')$.

Proof. Let ρ' be the relation $y_i' \mapsto x_i'$, for every i. Then

1) ρ' is a mapping: $y_i' = y_j'$ implies $x_i' = x_j'$. In fact, $y_i' = y_j'$ means that either (i) $1 \leqslant a_i, a_j \leqslant n$ or (ii) $a_i, a_j > n$. In subcase (i) $y_{a_i} = y_{a_j}$, by definition of mutation. Therefore $\rho(y_{a_i}) = \rho(y_{a_j})$ that in turn implies $x_{a_i} = x_{a_j}$. From this last equality we obtain $x_i' = x_j'$. In subcase (ii), $a_i = a_j$ and the implication follows by the fact that $(\!(a_1, \cdots, a_n)\!)$ is a mutation.

2) ρ' is injective: $x_i' = x_j'$ implies $y_i' = y_j'$. If $x_i' \in \{x_1, \cdots, x_n\}$ then $1 \leqslant a_i, a_j \leqslant n$. Therefore, by the definition of mutation, $x_{a_i} = x_{a_j}$ and, because ρ is a flashback, $y_{a_i} = y_{a_j}$. By this last equation $y_i' = y_j'$. If $x_i' \notin \{x_1, \cdots, x_n\}$ then $a_i > n$ and $a_i = a_j$. Therefore $y_i' = y_j'$ by definition of mutation.

3) ρ' is a flashback: $x_i' \neq y_i'$ implies $x_i' \leqslant y_i' \in \mathbb{V}'''$. If $1 \leqslant a_i \leqslant n$ then $y_i' = y_{a_i}$ and $x_i' = x_{a_i}$. Therefore $y_{a_i} \neq x_{a_i}$ and we conclude by the hypothesis about ρ that $\rho'(y_{a_i})$ satisfies the constraint in the definition of flashback. If $a_i > n$ then $x_1, \cdots, x_n \leqslant x_i' \in \mathbb{V}'$. Since $\rho(y_i) = x_i$, by the hypothesis about ρ, $x_i \leqslant y_i \in \mathbb{V}''$. Therefore, by definition of mutation, $x_i' \leqslant y_i \in \mathbb{V}''$. We derive $x_i' \leqslant y_i' \in \mathbb{V}'''$ by transitivity because $\mathbb{V}'' \subseteq \mathbb{V}'''$ and $y_i \leqslant y_i' \in \mathbb{V}'''$.

The following Theorem 1 generalizes the property that every permutation has an *order*, which is the number of applications that return the initial tuple. In the theory of permutations, the order is the least common multiple, in short *lcm*, of the lengths of the cycles of the permutation. This result is clearly false for mutations because of the presence of duplications and of fresh names. The generalization that holds in our setting uses flashbacks instead of identities. We begin by extending the notion of cycle.

Definition 4 (Cycles and sinks). *Let $\mu = (\!(a_1, \cdots, a_n)\!)$ be a mutation and let $1 \leqslant a_{i_1}, \cdots, a_{i_\ell} \leqslant n$ be pairwise different naturals. Then:*

i. *the term $(a_{i_1} \cdots a_{i_\ell})$ is a cycle of μ whenever $\mu(a_{i_j}) = a_{i_{j+1}}$, with $1 \leqslant j \leqslant \ell - 1$, and $\mu(a_{i_\ell}) = a_{i_1}$ (i.e., $(a_{i_1} \cdots a_{i_\ell})$ is the ordinary permutation cycle);*
ii. *the term $[a_{i_1} \cdots a_{i_{\ell-1}}]a_{i_\ell}$ is a bound sink of μ whenever $a_{i_1} \notin \{a_1, \cdots, a_n\}$, $\mu(a_{i_j}) = a_{i_{j+1}}$, with $1 \leqslant j \leqslant \ell - 1$, and a_{i_ℓ} belongs to a cycle;*

iii. the term $[a_{i_1} \cdots a_{i_\ell}]_a$, *with* $n < a \leqslant 2 \times n$, *is a free sink of* μ *whenever* $a_{i_1} \notin \{a_1, \cdots, a_n\}$ *and* $\mu(a_{i_j}) = a_{i_{j+1}}$, *with* $1 \leqslant j \leqslant \ell - 1$ *and* $\mu(a_{i_\ell}) = a$.

The length *of a cycle is the number of elements in the cycle; the* length *of a sink is the number of the elements in the square brackets.*

For example the mutation $(\!\!(5, 4, 8, 8, 3, 5, 8, 3, 3)\!\!)$ has cycle $(3, 8)$ and has bound sinks $[1, 5]_3$, $[6, 5]_3$, $[9]_3$, $[2, 4]_8$, and $[7]_8$. The mutation $(\!\!(6, 3, 1, 8, 7, 1, 8)\!\!)$ has cycle $(1, 6)$, has bound sink $[2, 3]_1$ and free sinks $[4]_8$ and $[5, 7]_8$.

Cycles and sinks are an alternative description of a mutation. For instance $(3, 8)$ means that the mutation moves the element in position 8 to the element in position 3 and the one in position 3 to the position 8; the free sink $[5, 7]_8$ means that the element in position 7 goes to the position 5, whilst a fresh name goes in position 7.

Theorem 1. *Let* μ *be a mutation,* ℓ *be the lcm of the length of its cycles,* ℓ' *and* ℓ'' *be the lengths of its longest bound sink and free sink, respectively. Let also* $k \stackrel{def}{=} \max\{\ell + \ell', \ell''\}$. *Then there exists* $0 \leqslant h < k$ *such that* $\langle \mathbb{V}, (x_1, \cdots, x_n) \rangle \xrightarrow{\mu^h}$ $\langle \mathbb{V}', (y_1, \cdots, y_n) \rangle \xrightarrow{\mu^{k-h}} \langle \mathbb{V}'', (z_1, \cdots, z_n) \rangle$ *and* $\rho(z_1, \cdots, z_n) = (y_1, \cdots, y_n)$, *for some* $\mathbb{V}''$-*flashback* ρ. *The value* k *is called* order *of* μ *and denoted by* $\mathfrak{o}_\mu$.

Proof. Let $\mu = (\!\!(a_1, \cdots, a_n)\!\!)$ be a mutation, and let $A = \{1, 2, \ldots, n\} \backslash \{a_1, \cdots, a_n\}$.

If $A = \varnothing$, then μ is a permutation; hence, by the theory of permutations, the theorem is immediately proved taking ρ as the identity and $h = 0$.

If $A \neq \varnothing$ then let $a \in A$. By definition, a must be the first element of (i) a bound sink or (ii) a free sink of μ. We write either $a \in A_{(i)}$ or $a \in A_{(ii)}$ if a is the first element of a bound or free sink, respectively.

In subcase (i), let ℓ'_a be the length of the bound sink with subscript a' and $\ell_{a'}$ be the length of the cycle of a'. We observe that in $\langle \mathbb{V}, (x_1, \cdots, x_n) \rangle \xrightarrow{\mu^{\ell'_a}}$ $\langle \mathbb{U}, (x'_1, \cdots, x'_n) \rangle \xrightarrow{\mu^{\ell_{a'}}} \langle \mathbb{W}, (x''_1, \cdots, x''_n) \rangle$ we have $x'_{a'} = x''_{a'}$.

In subcase (ii), let ℓ''_a be the length of the free sink. We observe that in $\langle \mathbb{V}, (x_1, \cdots, x_n) \rangle \xrightarrow{\mu^{\ell''_a}} \langle \mathbb{U}, (x'_1, \cdots, x'_n) \rangle$ we have $x_a \leqslant x'_a \in \mathbb{U}$, by definition of mutation.

Let ℓ, ℓ' and ℓ'' as defined in the theorem. Then, if $\ell + \ell' \geqslant \ell''$ we have that $\langle \mathbb{V}, (x_1, \cdots, x_n) \rangle \xrightarrow{\mu^{\ell'}} \langle \mathbb{V}', (y_1, \cdots, y_n) \rangle \xrightarrow{\mu^\ell} \langle \mathbb{V}'', (z_1, \cdots, z_n) \rangle$ and $\rho(z_1, \cdots, z_n) = (y_1, \cdots, y_n)$, where $\rho = [z_1 \mapsto y_1, \cdots, z_n \mapsto y_n]$ is a $\mathbb{V}''$-flashback. If $\ell + \ell' < \ell''$ then $\langle \mathbb{V}, (x_1, \cdots, x_n) \rangle \xrightarrow{\mu^{\ell'' - \ell}} \langle \mathbb{V}', (y_1, \cdots, y_n) \rangle \xrightarrow{\mu^\ell} \langle \mathbb{V}'', (z_1, \cdots, z_n) \rangle$ and $\rho(z_1, \cdots, z_n) = (y_1, \cdots, y_n)$, where $\rho = [z_1 \mapsto y_1, \cdots, z_n \mapsto y_n]$ is a $\mathbb{V}''$-flashback.

For example, $\mu = (\!\!(6, 3, 1, 8, 7, 1, 8)\!\!)$, has a cycle $(1, 6)$, bound sink $[2, 3]_1$ and free sinks $[4]_8$ and $[5, 7]_8$. Therefore $\ell = 2$, $\ell' = 2$ and $\ell'' = 2$. In this case, the values k and h of Theorem 1 are 4 and 2, respectively. In fact, if we apply the mutation μ four times to the pair $\langle \mathsf{V}, (x_1, x_2, x_3, x_4, x_5, x_6, x_7) \rangle$, where $\mathsf{V} = \{(x_i, x_i) \mid 1 \leqslant i \leqslant 7\}$ we obtain

$$
\begin{aligned}
\langle \mathsf{V}, (x_1, x_2, x_3, x_4, x_5, x_6, x_7) \rangle &\xrightarrow{\mu} \langle \mathsf{V}_1, (x_6, x_3, x_1, y_1, x_7, x_1, y_1) \rangle \\
&\xrightarrow{\mu} \langle \mathsf{V}_2, (x_1, x_1, x_6, y_2, y_1, x_6, y_2) \rangle \\
&\xrightarrow{\mu} \langle \mathsf{V}_3, (x_6, x_6, x_1, y_3, y_2, x_1, y_3) \rangle \\
&\xrightarrow{\mu} \langle \mathsf{V}_4, (x_1, x_1, x_6, y_4, y_3, x_6, y_4) \rangle
\end{aligned}
$$

where $\mathsf{V}_1 = \mathsf{V} \oplus x_1, x_2, x_3, x_4, x_5, x_6, x_7 < y_1$ and, for $i \geqslant 1$, $\mathsf{V}_{i+1} = \mathsf{V}_i \oplus y_{i-1} < y_i$. We notice that there is a V_4-flashback ρ from $(x_1, x_1, x_6, y_4, y_3, x_6, y_4)$ (produced by μ^4) to $(x_1, x_1, x_6, y_2, y_1, x_6, y_2)$ (produced by μ^2).

3   The Language of Lams

We use an infinite set of *function names*, ranged over f, f', g, $\mathsf{g}', \ldots$, which is disjoint from the set V of Section 2. A *lam program* is a tuple $\big(\mathsf{f}_1(\widetilde{x_1}) = \mathsf{L}_1, \cdots, \mathsf{f}_\ell(\widetilde{x}_\ell) = \mathsf{L}_\ell, \mathsf{L}\big)$ where $\mathsf{f}_i(\widetilde{x}_i) = \mathsf{L}_i$ are *function definitions* and L is the *main lam*. The syntax of L_i and L is

$$
\mathsf{L} \quad ::= \quad 0 \quad | \quad (x, y) \quad | \quad \mathsf{f}(\widetilde{x}) \quad | \quad \mathsf{L} \& \mathsf{L} \quad | \quad \mathsf{L} + \mathsf{L}
$$

Whenever parentheses are omitted, the operation "$\&$" has precedence over "$+$". We will shorten $\mathsf{L}_1 \& \cdots \& \mathsf{L}_n$ into $\&_{i \in 1..n} \mathsf{L}_i$. Moreover, we use T to range over lams that do not contain function invocations.

Let $var(\mathsf{L})$ be the set of names in L. In a function definition $\mathsf{f}(\widetilde{x}) = \mathsf{L}$, $\widetilde{x}$ are the *formal parameters* and the occurrences of names $x \in \widetilde{x}$ in L are *bound*; the names $var(\mathsf{L}) \backslash \widetilde{x}$ are *free*.

In the syntax of L, the operations "$\&$" and "$+$" are associative, commutative with 0 being the identity. Additionally the following axioms hold (T does not contain function invocations)

$$
\mathsf{T} \& \mathsf{T} = \mathsf{T} \qquad \mathsf{T} + \mathsf{T} = \mathsf{T} \qquad \mathsf{T} \& (\mathsf{L}' + \mathsf{L}'') = \mathsf{T} \& \mathsf{L}' + \mathsf{T} \& \mathsf{L}''
$$

and, in the rest of the paper, we will never distinguish equal lams. For instance, $\mathsf{f}(\widetilde{u}) + (x, y)$ and $(x, y) + \mathsf{f}(\widetilde{u})$ will be always identified. These axioms permit to rewrite a lam without function invocations as a *collection* (operation $+$) of *relations* (elements of a relation are gathered by the operation $\&$).

Proposition 2. *For every* T, *there exist* $\mathsf{T}_1, \cdots, \mathsf{T}_n$ *that are dependencies composed with* $\&$, *such that* $\mathsf{T} = \mathsf{T}_1 + \cdots + \mathsf{T}_n$.

Remark 1. Lams are intended to be abstract models of programs that highlight the resource dependencies in the reachable states. The lam $\mathsf{T}_1 + \cdots + \mathsf{T}_n$ of Proposition 2 models a program whose possibly infinite set of states $\{\mathsf{S}_1, \mathsf{S}_2, \cdots\}$ is such that the resource dependencies in S_i are a subset of those in some T_{j_i}, with $1 \leqslant j_i \leqslant n$. With this meaning, generic lams $\mathsf{L}_1 + \cdots + \mathsf{L}_m$ are abstractions of transition systems (a standard model of programming languages), where transitions are ignored and states record the resource dependencies and the function invocations.

Remark 2. The above axioms, such as $\mathsf{T}\&(\mathsf{L}' + \mathsf{L}'') = \mathsf{T}\&\mathsf{L}' + \mathsf{T}\&\mathsf{L}''$ are restricted to terms T that do not contain function invocations. In fact, $\mathsf{f}(\widetilde{u})\&((x,y) + (y,z)) \neq (\mathsf{f}(\widetilde{u})\&(x,y)) + (\mathsf{f}(\widetilde{u})\&(y,z))$ because the two terms have a different number of occurrences of invocations of f, and this is crucial for linear recursion – see Definition 6.

In the paper, we always assume lam programs $\big(\mathsf{f}_1(\widetilde{x_1}) = \mathsf{L}_1, \cdots, \mathsf{f}_\ell(\widetilde{x_\ell}) = \mathsf{L}_\ell, \mathsf{L}\big)$ to be *well-defined*, namely *(1)* all function names occurring in L_i and L are defined; *(2)* the arity of function invocations matches that of the corresponding function definition.

Operational Semantics. Let a *lam context*, noted $\mathfrak{L}[\ ]$, be a term derived by the following syntax:

$$\mathfrak{L}[\ ] \quad ::= \quad [\ ] \quad | \quad \mathsf{L}\&\mathfrak{L}[\ ] \quad | \quad \mathsf{L} + \mathfrak{L}[\ ]$$

As usual $\mathfrak{L}[\mathsf{L}]$ is the lam where the hole of $\mathfrak{L}[\ ]$ is replaced by L. The operational semantics of a program $\big(\mathsf{f}_1(\widetilde{x_1}) = \mathsf{L}_1, \cdots, \mathsf{f}_\ell(\widetilde{x_\ell}) = \mathsf{L}_\ell, \mathsf{L}_{\ell+1}\big)$ is a transition system whose *states* are pairs $\langle \mathsf{V}, \mathsf{L}\rangle$ and the *transition relation* is the least one satisfying the rule:

(RED)
$$\frac{\mathsf{f}(\widetilde{x}) = \mathsf{L} \qquad var(\mathsf{L})\backslash\widetilde{x} = \widetilde{z} \qquad \widetilde{w} \text{ are fresh}}{\langle \mathsf{V}, \mathfrak{L}[\mathsf{f}(\widetilde{u})]\rangle \longrightarrow \langle \mathsf{V} \oplus \widetilde{u} < \widetilde{w}, \mathfrak{L}[\mathsf{L}']\rangle}\quad \mathsf{L}[\widetilde{w}/\widetilde{z}][\widetilde{u}/\widetilde{x}] = \mathsf{L}'$$

By (RED), a lam L is evaluated by successively replacing function invocations with the corresponding lam instances. Name creation is handled with a mechanism similar to that of mutations. For example, if $\mathsf{f}(x) = (x,y)\&\mathsf{f}(y)$ and $\mathsf{f}(u)$ occurs in the main lam, then $\mathsf{f}(u)$ is replaced by $(u,v)\&\mathsf{f}(v)$, where v is a *fresh maximal name* in some partial order. The initial state of a program with main lam L is $\langle \mathbb{I}_\mathsf{L}, \mathsf{L}\rangle$, where $\mathbb{I}_\mathsf{L} \stackrel{def}{=} \{(x,x) \mid x \in var(\mathsf{L})\}$.

To illustrate the semantics of the language of lams we discuss three examples:

1. $\big(\mathsf{f}(x,y,z) = (x,y)\&\mathsf{g}(y,z) + (y,z), \ \mathsf{g}(u,v) = (u,v) + (v,u), \ \mathsf{f}(x,y,z)\big)$ and $\mathbb{I} = \{(x,x),(y,y),(z,z)\}$. Then

$$\langle \mathbb{I}, \mathsf{f}(x,y,z)\rangle \longrightarrow \langle \mathbb{I}, (x,y)\&\mathsf{g}(y,z) + (y,z)\rangle$$
$$\longrightarrow \langle \mathbb{I}, (x,y)\&(y,z) + (x,y)\&(z,y) + (y,z)\rangle$$

The lam in the final state *does not contain function invocations.* This is because the above program is not recursive. Additionally, the evaluation of $\mathsf{f}(x,y,z)$ *has not created names.* This is because names in the bodies of $\mathsf{f}(x,y,z)$ and $\mathsf{g}(u,v)$ are bound.

2. $\big(\mathsf{f}'(x) = (x,y)\&\mathsf{f}'(y), \ \mathsf{f}'(x)\big)$ and $\mathsf{V}_0 = \{(x_0,x_0)\}$. Then

$$\langle \mathsf{V}_0, \mathsf{f}'(x_0)\rangle$$
$$\longrightarrow \langle \mathsf{V}_1, (x_0,x_1)\&\mathsf{f}'(x_1)\rangle$$
$$\longrightarrow \langle \mathsf{V}_2, (x_0,x_1)\&(x_1,x_2)\&\mathsf{f}'(x_2)\rangle$$
$$\longrightarrow^n \langle \mathsf{V}_{n+2}, (x_0,x_1)\&\cdots\&(x_{n+1},x_{n+2})\&\mathsf{f}'(x_{n+2})\rangle$$

where $V_{i+1} = V_i \oplus x_i < x_{i+1}$. In this case, the states grow in the number of dependencies as the evaluation progresses. This growth *is due to the presence of a free name* in the definition of f' that, as said, corresponds to generating a fresh name at every recursive invocation.

3. $\big(f''(x) = (x, x') + (x, x')\&f''(x'), \ f''(x_0)\big)$ and $V_0 = \{(x_0, x_0)\}$. Then

$$\langle V_0, f''(x_0) \rangle$$
$$\longrightarrow \ \langle V_1, (x_0, x_1) + (x_0, x_1)\&f''(x_1) \rangle$$
$$\longrightarrow \ \langle V_2, (x_0, x_1) + (x_0, x_1)\&(x_1, x_2) + (x_0, x_1)\&(x_1, x_2)\&f''(x_2) \rangle$$
$$\longrightarrow^n \ \langle V_{n+2}, (x_0, x_1) + \cdots + (x_0, x_1)\&\cdots\&(x_{n+1}, x_{n+2})\&f''(x_{n+2}) \rangle$$

where V_{i+1} are as before. In this case, the states grow in the number of " $+$ "-terms, which become larger and larger as the evaluation progresses.

The semantics of the language of lams is nondeterministic because of the choice of the invocation to evaluate. However, lams enjoy a diamond property *up-to bijective renaming of (fresh) names.*

Proposition 3. *Let $\imath$ be a bijective renaming and $\imath(V) = \{(\imath(x), \imath(y)) \mid (x, y) \in V\}$. Let also $\langle V, \ L \rangle \longrightarrow \langle V', \ L' \rangle$ and $\langle \imath(V), \ L[\imath(\widetilde{x})/\widetilde{x}] \rangle \longrightarrow \langle V'', \ L'' \rangle$, where $\widetilde{x} = var(V)$. Then*

(i) either there exists a bijective renaming $\imath'$ such that

$$\langle V'', \ L'' \rangle = \langle \imath(V'), \ L'[\imath(\widetilde{x'})/\widetilde{x'}] \rangle,$$

where $\widetilde{x'} = var(V')$,

(ii) or there exist L''' and a bijective renaming $\imath'$ such that $\langle V', \ L' \rangle \longrightarrow \langle V''', \ L''' \rangle$ and $\langle V'', \ L'' \rangle \longrightarrow \langle \imath'(V'''), \ L'''[\imath'(\widetilde{z})/\widetilde{z}] \rangle$, where $\widetilde{z} = var(V''')$.

The Informative Operational Semantics. In order to detect the circularity-freedom, our technique computes a lam till every function therein has been adequately unfolded (up-to twice the order of the associated mutation). This is formalized by switching to an "informative" operational semantics where basic terms (dependencies and function invocations) are labelled by so-called *histories*.

Let a *history*, ranged over by $\alpha, \beta, \cdots$, be a sequence of function names $f_{\ell_1} f_{\ell_2} \cdots f_{\ell_n}$. We write $f \in \alpha$ if f occurs in α. We also write α^n for $\underbrace{\alpha \cdots \alpha}_{n \text{ times}}$

Let $\alpha \leq \beta$ if there is α' such that $\alpha\alpha' = \beta$. The symbol ε denotes the empty history.

The informative operational semantics is a transition system whose states are tuples $\langle V, {}^\flat F, \ \mathbb{L} \rangle$ where ${}^\flat F$ is a set of function invocations with histories and $\mathbb{L}$, called *informative lam*, is a term as L, except that pairs and function invocations are indexed by histories, i.e. ${}^\alpha(x, y)$ and ${}^\alpha f(\widetilde{u})$, respectively.

Let

$$addh(\alpha, L) \stackrel{def}{=} \begin{cases} {}^\alpha(x, y) & \text{if } L = (x, y) \\[2mm] {}^\alpha f(\widetilde{x}) & \text{if } L = f(\widetilde{x}) \\[2mm] addh(\alpha, L')\&addh(\alpha, L'') & \text{if } L = L'\&L'' \\[2mm] addh(\alpha, L') + addh(\alpha, L'') & \text{if } L = L' + L'' \end{cases}$$

For example $addh(\mathtt{f}1, (x_4, x_2)\&\mathtt{f}(x_2, x_3, x_4, x_5)) = {}^{\mathtt{f}1}(x_4, x_2)\& {}^{\mathtt{f}1}\mathtt{f}(x_2, x_3, x_4, x_5)$.
Let also ${}^{\flat}\mathfrak{L}[\ ]$ be a lam context with histories (dependency pairs and function invocations are labelled by histories, the definition is similar to $\mathfrak{L}[\ ]$).

The informative transition relation is the least one such that

(RED+)

$$\frac{\mathtt{f}(\tilde{x}) = L \qquad var(L)\backslash\tilde{x} = \tilde{z} \qquad \tilde{w} \text{ are fresh}}{L[\tilde{w}/\tilde{z}][\tilde{u}/\tilde{x}] = L'}$$

$$\langle \mathtt{V}, {}^{\flat}\mathbb{F}, {}^{\flat}\mathfrak{L}[{}^{\alpha}\mathtt{f}(\tilde{u})]\rangle \quad\longrightarrow\quad \langle \mathtt{V} \oplus \tilde{u} <\tilde{w}, {}^{\flat}\mathbb{F} \cup \{{}^{\alpha}\mathtt{f}(\tilde{u})\}, {}^{\flat}\mathfrak{L}[addh(\alpha\mathtt{f}, L')]\rangle$$

When $\langle \mathtt{V}, {}^{\flat}\mathbb{F}, \mathtt{L}\rangle \longrightarrow \langle \mathtt{V}', {}^{\flat}\mathbb{F}', \mathtt{L}'\rangle$ by applying (RED+) to ${}^{\alpha}\mathtt{f}(\tilde{u})$, we say that the term ${}^{\alpha}\mathtt{f}(\tilde{u})$ *is evaluated in the reduction*. The initial informative state of a program with main lam L is $\langle \mathbb{0}_L, \varnothing, addh(\varepsilon, L)\rangle$.

For example, the flh-program

$$\left(\ \begin{array}{ll}
\mathtt{f}(x, y, z, u) & = (x, z)\&\mathtt{l}(u, y, z)\,, \\
\mathtt{l}(x, y, z) & = (x, y)\&\mathtt{f}(y, z, x, u)\,, \\
\mathtt{h}(x, y, z, u) & = (z, x)\&\mathtt{h}(x, y, z, u)\&\mathtt{f}(x, y, z, u)\,, \\
\mathtt{h}(x_1, x_2, x_3, x_4)\ )
\end{array}\right.$$

has an (informative) evaluation

$$\langle \mathbb{0}_L, \varnothing, {}^{\varepsilon}\mathtt{h}(x_1, x_2, x_3, x_4)\rangle$$
$$\longrightarrow \langle \mathbb{0}_L, {}^{\flat}\mathbb{F}, \mathbb{L}\& {}^{\mathtt{h}}\mathtt{f}(x_1, x_2, x_3, x_4)\rangle$$
$$\longrightarrow \langle \mathbb{0}_L, {}^{\flat}\mathbb{F}_1, \mathbb{L}\& {}^{\mathtt{hf}}(x_1, x_3)\& {}^{\mathtt{hf}}\mathtt{l}(x_4, x_2, x_3)\rangle$$
$$\longrightarrow \langle \mathbb{0}_L \oplus x_4 <x_5, {}^{\flat}\mathbb{F}_2, \mathbb{L}'\& {}^{\mathtt{hfl}}(x_4, x_2)\& {}^{\mathtt{hfl}}\mathtt{f}(x_2, x_3, x_4, x_5)\rangle,$$

where

$$\begin{array}{ll}
\mathbb{L} & = {}^{\mathtt{h}}(x_3, x_1)\& {}^{\mathtt{h}}\mathtt{h}(x_1, x_2, x_3, x_4) \\
\mathbb{L}' & = \mathbb{L}\& {}^{\mathtt{hf}}(x_1, x_3) \\
{}^{\flat}\mathbb{F} & = \{{}^{\varepsilon}\mathtt{h}(x_1, x_2, x_3, x_4)\} \\
{}^{\flat}\mathbb{F}_1 & = {}^{\flat}\mathbb{F} \cup \{{}^{\mathtt{h}}\mathtt{f}(x_1, x_2, x_3, x_4)\} \\
{}^{\flat}\mathbb{F}_2 & = {}^{\flat}\mathbb{F}_1 \cup \{{}^{\mathtt{hf}}\mathtt{l}(x_4, x_2, x_3)\}.
\end{array}$$

There is a strict correspondence between the non-informative and informative semantics that is crucial for the correctness of our algorithm in Section 5. Let $[\![\cdot]\!]$ be an *eraser map* that takes an informative lam and removes the histories. The formal definition is omitted because it is straightforward.

Proposition 4. *1. If* $\langle \mathtt{V}, {}^{\flat}\mathbb{F}, \mathtt{L}\rangle \longrightarrow \langle \mathtt{V}', {}^{\flat}\mathbb{F}', \mathtt{L}'\rangle$ *then* $\langle \mathtt{V}, [\![\mathtt{L}]\!]\rangle \longrightarrow \langle \mathtt{V}', [\![\mathtt{L}']\!]\rangle$;

2. If $\langle \mathtt{V}, [\![\mathtt{L}]\!]\rangle \longrightarrow \langle \mathtt{V}', \mathtt{L}'\rangle$ *then there are* ${}^{\flat}\mathbb{F}, {}^{\flat}\mathbb{F}', \mathtt{L}'$ *such that* $[\![\mathtt{L}']\!] = \mathtt{L}'$ *and* $\langle \mathtt{V}, {}^{\flat}\mathbb{F}, \mathtt{L}\rangle \longrightarrow \langle \mathtt{V}', {}^{\flat}\mathbb{F}', \mathtt{L}'\rangle$.

Circularities. Lams record sets of relations on names. The following function $\flat(\cdot)$, called *flattening*, makes explicit these relations

$$\begin{array}{ll}
\flat(0) = 0, \qquad \flat((x, y)) = (x, y), \qquad \flat(\mathtt{f}(\tilde{x})) = 0, \\
\flat(L\&L') = \flat(L)\&\flat(L'), \qquad \flat(L + L') = \flat(L) + \flat(L').
\end{array}$$

For example, if $L = \mathtt{f}(x, y, z) + (x, y)\&\mathtt{g}(y, z)\&\mathtt{f}(u, y, z) + \mathtt{g}(u, v)\&(u, v) + (v, u)$ then $\flat(L) = (x, y) + (u, v) + (v, u)$. That is, there are three relations in L: $\{(x, y)\}$

and $\{(u, v)\}$ and $\{(v, u)\}$. By Proposition 2, $\flat(\mathsf{L})$ returns, up-to the lam axioms, sequences of (pairwise different) &-compositions of dependencies. The operation $\flat(\cdot)$ may be extended to informative lams $\mathbb{L}$ in the obvious way: $\flat(^{\alpha}(x, y)) = {}^{\alpha}(x, y)$ and $\flat(^{\alpha}\mathbf{f}(\tilde{x})) = 0$.

Definition 5. *A lam* L *has a circularity if*

$$\flat(\mathsf{L}) = (x_1, x_2)\&(x_2, x_3)\&\cdots\&(x_m, x_1)\&\mathsf{T}' + \mathsf{T}''$$

for some $x_1, \cdots, x_m$. *A state* $\langle \mathsf{V}, \mathsf{L} \rangle$ *has a circularity if* L *has a circularity. Similarly for an informative lam* $\mathbb{L}$.

The final state of the $\mathbf{fgh}$-program computation has a circularity; another function displaying a circularity is $\mathbf{g}$ in Section 1. None of the states in the examples 1, 2, 3 at the beginning of this section has a *circularity*.

4   Linear Recursive Lams and Saturated States

This section develops the theory that underpins the algorithm of Section 5. In order to lightening the section, the technical details have been moved in Appendix B.

We restrict our arguments to (mutually) recursive lam programs. In fact, circularity analysis in non-recursive programs is trivial: it is sufficient to evaluate all the invocations till the final state and verify the presence of circularities therein. A further restriction allows us to simplify the arguments without loosing in generality (*cf.* the definition of saturation): we assume that every function is (mutually) recursive. We may reduce to this case by expanding function invocation of non (mutually) recursive functions (and removing their definitions).

Linear Recursive Functions and Mutations. Our decision algorithm relies on interpreting recursive functions as mutations. This interpretation is not always possible: the recursive functions that have an associated mutation are the linear recursive ones, as defined below.

The technique for dealing with the general case is briefly discussed in Section 8 and is detailed in Appendix C.

Definition 6. *Let* $\left(\mathbf{f}_1(\widetilde{x_1}) = \mathsf{L}_1, \cdots, \mathbf{f}_\ell(\widetilde{x_\ell}) = \mathsf{L}_\ell, \mathsf{L}\right)$ *be a lam program. A sequence* $\mathbf{f}_{i_0}\mathbf{f}_{i_1}\cdots\mathbf{f}_{i_k}$ *is called a recursive history of* $\mathbf{f}_{i_0}$ *if (a) the function names are pairwise different and (b) for every* $0 \leqslant j \leqslant k$, L_{i_j} *contains one invocation of* $\mathbf{f}_{i_{j+1\%k}}$ *(the operation* % *is the remainder of the division).*

The lam program is linear recursive *if (a) every function name has a unique recursive history and (b) if* $\mathbf{f}_{i_0}\mathbf{f}_{i_1}\cdots\mathbf{f}_{i_k}$ *is a recursive history then, for every* $0 \leqslant j \leqslant k$, L_{i_j} *contains exactly one invocation of* $\mathbf{f}_{i_{j+1\%k}}$.

For example, the program

$$\left(\; \mathbf{f}_1(x, y) = (x, y)\&\mathbf{f}_1(y, z)\&\mathbf{f}_2(y) + \mathbf{f}_2(z)\, , \mathbf{f}_2(y) = (y, z)\&\mathbf{f}_2(z)\, , \mathsf{L}\;\; \right)$$

is linear recursive. On the contrary

$$\big(\mathtt{f}(x) = (x,y)\&\mathtt{g}(x)\,,\ \mathtt{g}(x) = (x,y)\&\mathtt{f}(x) + \mathtt{g}(y)\,,\ \mathtt{L}\,\big)$$

is not linear recursive because g has two recursive histories, namely g and gf.

Linearity allows us to associate a *unique* mutation to every function name. To compute this mutation, let H range over sequences of function invocations. We use the following two rules:

$$\frac{\mathtt{f}_i\alpha \models \varepsilon \quad \mathtt{f}_i(\widetilde{x}_i) = \mathtt{L}_i}{\alpha \models \mathtt{f}_i(\widetilde{x}_i)}
\qquad
\frac{\begin{array}{c}\mathtt{f}_j\alpha \models \mathtt{Hf}_i(\widetilde{x}) \quad \mathtt{f}_i(\widetilde{x}_i) = \mathtt{L}_i \\ var(\mathtt{L}_i)\backslash\widetilde{x}_i = \widetilde{z} \quad \widetilde{w}\ \text{are fresh} \\ \mathcal{L}[\mathtt{f}_j(\widetilde{y})] = \mathtt{L}_i[\widetilde{w}/\widetilde{z}][\widetilde{x}/\widetilde{x}_i]\end{array}}{\alpha \models \mathtt{Hf}_i(\widetilde{x})\mathtt{f}_j(\widetilde{y})}$$

Let $\varepsilon \models \mathtt{f}(x_1,\cdots,x_n)\cdots\mathtt{f}(x'_1,\cdots,x'_n)$ be the final judgment of the proof tree with leaf $\mathtt{f}\alpha\mathtt{f} \models \varepsilon$, where $\mathtt{f}\alpha$ is the recursive history of $\mathtt{f}$. Let also $x'_1,\cdots,x'_n\backslash x_1$, $\cdots,x_n = z_1,\cdots,z_k$. Then the *mutation of* $\mathtt{f}$, written $\mu_\mathtt{f} = (\!| a_1,\cdots,a_n |\!)$ is defined by

$$a_i = \begin{cases} j & \text{if } x'_i = x_j \\[1em] n+j & \text{if } x'_i = z_j \end{cases}$$

Let $\mathtt{o}_\mathtt{f}$, called *order of the function* $\mathtt{f}$, be the order of $\mu_\mathtt{f}$. For example, in the flh-program, the recursive history of $\mathtt{f}$ is $\mathtt{fl}$ and, applying the algorithm above to $\mathtt{flf} \models \varepsilon$, we get $\varepsilon \models \mathtt{f}(x,y,z,u)\mathtt{l}(u,y,z)\mathtt{f}(y,z,u,v)$. The mutation of $\mathtt{f}$ is $(\!| 2,3,4,5 |\!)$ and $\mathtt{o}_\mathtt{f} = 4$. Analogously we can compute $\mathtt{o}_\mathtt{l} = 3$ and $\mathtt{o}_\mathtt{h} = 1$.

Saturation. In the remaining part of the section we assume a fixed linear recursive program $\big(\mathtt{f}_1(\widetilde{x_1}) = \mathtt{L}_1,\cdots,\mathtt{f}_\ell(\widetilde{x}_\ell) = \mathtt{L}_\ell, \mathtt{L}\big)$ and let $\mathtt{o}_{\mathtt{f}_1},\cdots,\mathtt{o}_{\mathtt{f}_\ell}$ be the orders of the corresponding functions.

Definition 7. *A history* α *is*

f-*complete*
> *if* $\alpha = \beta^{\mathtt{o}_\mathtt{f}}$, *where* β *is the recursive history of* $\mathtt{f}$. *We say that* α *is* complete *when it is* f-complete, *for some* $\mathtt{f}$.

f-*saturating*
> *if* $\alpha = \beta_1\cdots\beta_{n-1}\alpha_n^2$, *where* $\beta_i \leq (\alpha_i)^2$, *with* α_i *complete, and* α_n *f-complete. We say that* α *is* saturating *when it is* f-saturating, *for some* $\mathtt{f}$.

In the flh-program, $\mathtt{o}_\mathtt{f} = 4$, $\mathtt{o}_\mathtt{l} = 3$, and $\mathtt{o}_\mathtt{h} = 1$, and the recursive histories of f, l and h are equal to fl, to lf and to h, respectively. Then $\alpha = (\mathtt{fl})^4$ is the f-complete history and $\mathtt{h}^2(\mathtt{fl})^8$ and $\mathtt{h}(\mathtt{fl})^8$ are f-saturating.

The following proposition is an important consequence of the theory of mutations (Theorem 1) and the semantics of lams (and their axioms). In particular, it states that, if a function invocation $\mathtt{f}_0(\widetilde{u_0})$ is unfolded up to the order of $\mathtt{f}_0$ then (i) the last invocation $\mathtt{f}_0(\widetilde{v})$ may be mapped back to a previous invocation by a flashback and (ii) the same flashback also maps back dependencies created by the unfolding of $\mathtt{f}_0(\widetilde{v})$.

Proposition 5. *Let* $\beta = \mathtt{f}_0\mathtt{f}_1\cdots\mathtt{f}_n$ *be* $\mathtt{f}_0$-*complete and let*

$$\langle \mathbb{V}, {}^{\flat}\mathbb{F}, {}^{\flat}\mathcal{L}_0[{}^{\alpha}\mathtt{f}_0(\widetilde{u_0})]\rangle \longrightarrow^{n+1} \langle \mathbb{V}', {}^{\flat}\mathbb{F}', {}^{\flat}\mathcal{L}_0[{}^{\flat}\mathcal{L}_1[\cdots{}^{\flat}\mathcal{L}_n[{}^{\alpha\mathtt{f}_0\cdots\mathtt{f}_n}\mathtt{f}_0(\widetilde{u_{n+1}})]\cdots]]\rangle$$

where ${}^{\flat}\mathbb{F}' = {}^{\flat}\mathbb{F} \cup \{{}^{\alpha}\mathtt{f}_0(\widetilde{u_0}), {}^{\alpha\mathtt{f}_0}\mathtt{f}_1(\widetilde{u_1}), \cdots, {}^{\alpha\mathtt{f}_0\cdots\mathtt{f}_{n-1}}\mathtt{f}_n(\widetilde{u_n})\}$ *and* $\mathtt{f}_i(\widetilde{u_i}) = \mathtt{L}'_i$ *and* $addh(\alpha\mathtt{f}_0\cdots\mathtt{f}_i, \mathtt{L}'_i) = {}^{\flat}\mathcal{L}_i[{}^{\alpha\mathtt{f}_0\cdots\mathtt{f}_i}\mathtt{f}_{i+1}(\widetilde{u_{i+1}})]$ *(unfolding of the functions in the complete history of* $\mathtt{f}_0$*). Then there is a* ${}^{\alpha\mathtt{f}_0\cdots\mathtt{f}_{h-1}}\mathtt{f}_h(\widetilde{u_h}) \in {}^{\flat}\mathbb{F}'$ *and a* $\mathbb{V}'$*-flashback* ρ *such that*

1. $\mathtt{f}_0(\rho(\widetilde{u_{n+1}})) = \mathtt{f}_h(\widetilde{u_h})$ *(hence* $\mathtt{f}_0 = \mathtt{f}_h$*);*
2. *let* $\mathtt{f}_0(\widetilde{u_{n+1}}) = \mathtt{L}$ *and* $\flat(\mathtt{L}) = \mathtt{T}_1 + \cdots + \mathtt{T}_k$ *and*
   $\flat({}^{\flat}\mathcal{L}_0[{}^{\flat}\mathcal{L}_1[\cdots{}^{\flat}\mathcal{L}_n[{}^{\alpha\beta}\mathtt{f}_0(\widetilde{u_{n+1}})]\cdots]]) = {}^{\flat}\mathtt{T}'_1 + \cdots + {}^{\flat}\mathtt{T}'_{k'}$. *Then, for every* $1 \leqslant i \leqslant k$, *there exists* $1 \leqslant j \leqslant k'$ *such that* ${}^{\flat}\mathtt{T}'_j = addh(\alpha\mathtt{f}_0\cdots\mathtt{f}_{h-1}, \mathtt{T}_i) \& {}^{\flat}\mathtt{T}''_j$, *for some* ${}^{\flat}\mathtt{T}''_j$.

The notion of $\mathtt{f}$-saturating will be used to define a "saturated" state, i.e., a state where the evaluation of programs may safely (as regards circularities) stop.

Definition 8. *An informative lam* $\langle \mathbb{V}, {}^{\flat}\mathbb{F}, \mathbb{L}\rangle$ *is saturated when, for every* ${}^{\flat}\mathcal{L}[\,]$ *and* $\mathtt{f}(\widetilde{u})$ *such that* $\mathbb{L} = {}^{\flat}\mathcal{L}[{}^{\alpha}\mathtt{f}(\widetilde{u})]$, α *has a saturating prefix.*

It is easy to check that the following informative lam generated by the computation of the $\mathtt{flh}$-program is saturated:

$$\langle \mathbb{V}_7, {}^{\flat}\mathbb{F}, {}^{\mathtt{h}^2}\mathtt{h}(x_1, x_2, x_3, x_4) \,\&\, \&_{0 \leqslant i \leqslant 8}{}^{\mathtt{hf}(\mathtt{lf})^i}(x_{i+1}, x_{i+3})$$
$$\&\, \&_{0 \leqslant i < 8}{}^{\mathtt{h}(\mathtt{f1})^i}(x_{i+3}, x_{i+1})$$
$$\&\, {}^{\mathtt{h}(\mathtt{f1})^8}\mathtt{f}(x_9, x_{10}, x_{11}, x_{12})\rangle,$$

where $\mathbb{V}_{i+1} = \mathbb{V}_i \oplus x_{i+4} < x_{i+5}$, and

$${}^{\flat}\mathbb{F} = \{{}^{\varepsilon}\mathtt{h}(x_1, x_2, x_3, x_4), {}^{\mathtt{h}}\mathtt{h}(x_1, x_2, x_3, x_4)\}$$
$$\cup \{{}^{\mathtt{h}(\mathtt{f1})^i}\mathtt{f}(x_{i+1}, x_{i+2}, x_{i+3}, x_{i+4}) \mid 0 \leqslant i \leqslant 7\}$$
$$\cup \{{}^{\mathtt{hf}(\mathtt{lf})^i}\mathtt{l}(x_{i+4}, x_{i+2}, x_{i+3}) \mid 0 \leqslant i \leqslant 7\}.$$

Every preliminary statement is in place for our key theorem that details the mapping of circularities created by transitions of saturated states to past circularities.

Theorem 2. *Let* $\langle \mathbb{I}_L, \varnothing, addh(\varepsilon, \mathtt{L})\rangle \longrightarrow^* \langle \mathbb{V}, {}^{\flat}\mathbb{F}, \mathbb{L}\rangle$ *and* $\langle \mathbb{V}, {}^{\flat}\mathbb{F}, \mathbb{L}\rangle$ *be a saturated state. If* $\langle \mathbb{V}, {}^{\flat}\mathbb{F}, \mathbb{L}\rangle \longrightarrow \langle \mathbb{V}', {}^{\flat}\mathbb{F}', \mathbb{L}'\rangle$ *then*

1. $\langle \mathbb{V}', {}^{\flat}\mathbb{F}', \mathbb{L}'\rangle$ *is saturated;*
2. *if* $\mathbb{L}'$ *has a circularity then* $\mathbb{L}$ *has already a circularity.*

Proof. *(Sketch)* Item 1. directly follows from Proposition 5. However, this proposition is not sufficient to guarantee that circularities created in saturated states are mapped back to past ones. In particular, the interesting case is the one of *crossover circularities*, as discussed in Section 1. Therefore, let

$$\alpha_1(x_1, x_2), \cdots, \alpha_{h-1}(x_{h-1}, x_h), \alpha_h(x_h, x_{h+1}), \cdots, \alpha_n(x_n, x_1)$$

be a circularity in $\mathbb{L}'$ such that $\alpha_h(x_h, x_{h+1}), \cdots, \alpha_n(x_n, x_1)$ were already present in $\mathbb{L}$. Proposition 5 guarantees the existence of a flashback ρ that maps $\alpha_1(x_1, x_2)$

$\&\cdots\&^{\alpha_{h-1}}(x_{h-1},x_h)$ to $^{\alpha_1}(\rho(x_1),\rho(x_2))\&\cdots\&^{\alpha_{h-1}}(\rho(x_{h-1}),\rho(x_h))$. However, it is possible that

$$^{\alpha_1}(\rho(x_1),\rho(x_2))\&\cdots\&^{\alpha_{h-1}}(\rho(x_{h-1}),\rho(x_h))\&^{\alpha_h}(x_h,x_{h+1})\&\cdots\&^{\alpha_n}(x_n,x_1)$$

is no more a circularity because, for example, $\rho(x_h) \neq x_h$ (assume that $\rho(x_1) = x_1$). Let us discuss this issue. The hypothesis of saturation guarantees that transitions produce histories $\alpha^2\beta$, where α is complete. Additionally, $\alpha_1, \cdots, \alpha_{h-1}$ must be equal because they have been created by $\langle V, {}^\flat F, \mathbb{L}\rangle \longrightarrow \langle V', {}^\flat F', \mathbb{L}'\rangle$. For simplicity, let $\beta = \mathbf{f}$ and $\alpha = \mathbf{f}\alpha'$. Therefore, by Proposition 5, ρ maps $^{\alpha^2\mathbf{f}}(x_1,x_2)\&\cdots\&\,^{\alpha^2\mathbf{f}}(x_{h-1},x_h)$ to $^{\alpha\mathbf{f}}(\rho(x_1),\rho(x_2))\&\cdots\&^{\alpha\mathbf{f}}(\rho((x_{h-1}),\rho(x_h))$ and, $\rho(x_h) \neq x_h$ when x_h is created by the computation evaluating functions in α'.

To overcome this problem, it is possible to demonstrate using a statement similar to (but stronger than) Proposition 5 that ρ maps $^{\alpha_h}(x_h, x_{h+1})\ \&\ \cdots\ \&^{\alpha_n}(x_n,x_1)$ to $^{[\alpha_h]}(\rho(x_h),\rho(x_{h+1}))\&\cdots\&^{[\alpha_n]}(\rho(x_n),\rho(x_1))$ where $[\alpha_i]$ are "kernels" of α_i where every γ^k in α_i, with γ a complete history and $k \geqslant 2$, is replaced by γ. The proof terminates by demonstrating that the term

$$^{\alpha\mathbf{f}}(\rho(x_1),\rho(x_2))\&\cdots\&^{\alpha\mathbf{f}}(\rho((x_{h-1}),\rho(x_h))$$
$$\&^{[\alpha_h]}(\rho(x_h),\rho(x_{h+1}))\&\cdots\&^{[\alpha_n]}(\rho(x_n),\rho(x_1))$$

is in $\mathbb{L}$ (and it is a circularity).

5 The Decision Algorithm for Detecting Circularities in Linear Recursive Lams

The algorithm for deciding the circularity-freedom problem in linear recursive lam programs takes as input a lam program $(\mathbf{f}_1(\widetilde{x_1}) = L_1, \cdots, \mathbf{f}_\ell(\widetilde{x_\ell}) = L_\ell, L)$ and performs the following steps:

STEP 1: *find recursive histories.* By parsing the lam program we create a graph where nodes are function names and, for every invocation of $\mathbf{g}$ in the body of $\mathbf{f}$, there is an edge from $\mathbf{f}$ to $\mathbf{g}$. Then a standard depth first search associates to every node its recursive histories (the paths starting and ending at that node, if any). The lam program is linear recursive if every node has at most one associated recursive history.

STEP 2: *computation of the orders.* Given the recursive history α associated to a function $\mathbf{f}$, we compute the corresponding mutation by running $\alpha \models \varepsilon$ (see Section 4). A straightforward parse of the mutation returns the set of cycles and sinks and, therefore, gives the order $\mathbf{o_f}$.

STEP 3: *evaluation process.* The main lam is unfolded till the the saturated state. That is, every function invocation $\mathbf{f}(\widetilde{x})$ in the main lam is evaluated up-to twice the order of the corresponding mutation. The function invocation of $\mathbf{f}$ in the saturated state is erased and the process is repeated on every other function invocation (which, therefore, does not belong to the recursive history of $\mathbf{f}$), till no function invocation is present in the state. At this stage we use the lam axioms that yield a term $T_1 + \cdots + T_n$.

STEP 4: *detection of circularities.* Every T_i in $T_1 + \cdots + T_n$ may be represented as a graph where nodes are names and edges correspond to dependency pairs. To detect whether T_i contains a circular dependency, we run Tarjan algorithm [31] for connected components of graphs and we stop the algorithm when a circularity is found.

Every preliminary notion is in place for stating our main result; we also make few remarks about the correctness of the algorithm and its computational cost.

Theorem 3. *The problem of the circularity-freedom of a lam program is decidable when the program is linear recursive.*

The algorithm consists of the four steps described above. The critical step, as far as correctness is concerned, is the third one, which follows by Theorem 2 and by the diamond property in Proposition 3 (whatever other computation may be completed in such a way the final state is equal up-to a bijection to a saturated state).

As regards the computational complexity STEPS 1 and 2 are linear with respect to the size of the lam program and STEP 4 is linear with respect to the size of the term $T_1 + \cdots + T_n$. STEP 3 evaluates the program till the saturated state. Let

o_{max} be the largest order of a function;
m_{max} be the maximal number of function invocations in a body, apart the one in the recursive history.

Without loss of generality, we assume that recursive histories have length 1 and that the main lam consists of m_{max} invocations of the same function. Then an upper bound to the length of the evaluation till the saturated state is

$$(2 \times o_{max} \times m_{max}) + (2 \times o_{max} \times m_{max})^2 + \cdots + (2 \times o_{max} \times m_{max})^\ell$$

Let k_{max} be the maximal number of dependency pairs in a body. Then the size of the saturated state is $O(k_{max} \times (o_{max} \times m_{max})^\ell)$, which is also the computational complexity of our algorithm.

6 Assessments

The algorithm defined in Section 5 has been prototyped [15]. As anticipated in Section 1, our analysis has been applied to a concurrent object-oriented language called ABS [17], which is a JAVA-like language with futures and an asynchronous concurrency model (ASP [6] is another language in the same family).

The prototype is part of a bigger framework for the deadlock analysis of ABS programs called DF4ABS (Deadlock Framework for ABS). It is a modular framework which includes two different approaches for analysing lams: DF4ABS/model-check (which is the one described in the current paper) and DF4ABS/fixpoint (which is the one described in [13,14]).

The technique underpinning the DF4ABS/fixpoint tool derives the dependency graph(s) of lam programs by means of a standard fixpoint analysis. To circumvent the issue of the infinite generation of new names, the fixpoint is computed on models with a limited capacity of name creation. This introduces overapproximations that in turn display false positives (for example, DF4ABS/fixpoint returns a false positive for the lam of factorial). In the present work, this limitation of finite models is overcome (for linear recursive programs) by recognizing patterns of recursive behaviors, so that it is possible to reduce the analysis to a finite portion of computation without losing precision in the detection of deadlocks.

The derivation of lams from ABS programs is defined by an *inference system* [13,14]. The inference system extracts behavioral types from ABS programs and feeds them to the analyzer. These types display the resource dependencies and the method invocations while discarding irrelevant (for the deadlock analysis) details. There are two relevant differences between inferred types and lams: (i) methods' arguments have a record structure and (ii) behavioral types have the union operator (for modeling the if-then-else statement). To bridge this gap and have some initial assessments, we perform a basic *automatic* transformation of types into lams.

We tested our prototype on a number of medium-size programs written for benchmarking purposes by ABS programmers and on an industrial case study based on the Fredhopper Access Server (FAS) developed by SDL Fredhopper [9]. This Access Server provides search and merchandising IT services to e-Commerce companies. The (leftmost three columns of the) following table reports the experiments: for every program we display the number of lines, whether the analysis has reported a deadlock (D) or not (✓), the time in seconds required for the analysis. Concerning time, we only report the time of the analysis (and not the one taken by the inference) when they run on a QuadCore 2.4GHz and Gentoo (Kernel 3.4.9):

program	lines	DF4ABS/model-check result time	DF4ABS/fixpoint result time	DECO result time
PingPong	61	✓ 0.311	✓ 0.046	✓ 1.30
MultiPingPong	88	D 0.209	D 0.109	D 1.43
BoundedBuffer	103	✓ 0.126	✓ 0.353	✓ 1.26
PeerToPeer	185	✓ 0.320	✓ 6.070	✓ 1.63
FAS Module	2645	✓ 31.88	✓ 39.78	✓ 4.38

The rightmost column of the above table reports the results of another tool that have also been developed for the deadlock analysis of ABS programs: DECO [11]. The technique in [11] integrates a point-to analysis with an analysis returning (an over-approximation of) program points that may be running in parallel. As for other model checking techniques, the authors use a finite amount of (abstract) object names to ensure termination of programs with object creations underneath iteration or recursion. For example, DECO (as well as DF4ABS/fixpoint) signals a deadlock in programs containing methods whose lam is[1] $m(x, y) = (y, x)\&m(z, x)$ that our technique correctly recognizes as deadlock-free.

As highlighted by the above table, the three tools return the same results as regards deadlock analysis, but are different as regards performance. In particular DF4ABS/model-check and DF4ABS/fixpoint are comparable on small/midsize programs, DECO appears less performant (except for PeerToPeer, where DF4ABS/fixpoint is quite slow because of the number of dependencies produced by the fixpoint algorithm). On the FAS module, DF4ABS/model-check and DF4ABS/fixpoint are again comparable – their computational complexity is exponential – DECO is more performant because its worst case complexity is cubic in the dimension of the input. As we discuss above, this gain in performance is payed by DECO in a loss of precision.

Our final remark is about the proportion between linear recursive functions and nonlinear ones in programs. This is hard to assess and our answer is perhaps not enough adequate. We have parsed the three case-studies developed in the European project HATS [9]. The case studies are the FAS module, a Trading System (TS) modeling a supermarket handling sales, and a Virtual Office of the Future (VOF) where office workers are enabled to perform their office tasks seamlessly independent of their current location. FAS has 2645 code-lines, TS has 1238 code-lines, and VOF has 429 code-lines. In none of them we found a nonlinear recursion, TS and VOF have respectively 2 and 3 linear recursions (there are recursions in functions on data-type values that have nothing to do with locks and control). This substantiates the usefulness of our technique in these programs; the analysis of a wider range of programs is matter of future work.

7 Related Works

The solutions in the literature for deadlock detection in infinite state programs either give imprecise answers or do not scale when, for instance, programs also admit dynamic resource creation. Two basic techniques are used: type-checking and model-checking.

Type-based deadlock analysis has been extensively studied both for process calculi [19,30,32] and for object-oriented programs [3,10,1]. In Section 1 we have thoroughly discussed our position with respect to Kobayashi's works; therefore we omit here any additional comment. In the other contributions about deadlock analysis, a type system computes a partial order of the deadlocks in a program and a subject reduction theorem proves that tasks follow this order. On the contrary, our technique does not compute any ordering of deadlocks, thus being more flexible: a computation may acquire two deadlocks in different order at different stages, thus being correct in our case, but incorrect with the other techniques. A further difference with the above works is that we use behavioral types, which are terms in some simple process algebras [21]. The use of simple

---

[1] The code of a corresponding ABS program is available at the DF4ABS tool website [15], *c.f.* UglyChain.abs.

process algebras to guarantee the correctness (= deadlock freedom) of interacting parties is not new. This is the case of the exchange patterns in SSDL [27], which are based on CSP [4] and pi-calculus [23], of session types [12], or of the terms in [26] and [7], which use CCS [22]. In these proposals, the deadlock freedom follows by checking either a dual-type relation or a behavioral equivalence, which amounts to model checking deadlock freedom on the types.

As regards model checking techniques, in [5] circular dependencies among processes are detected as erroneous configurations, but dynamic creation of names is not treated. An alternative model checking technique is proposed in [2] for multi-threaded asynchronous communication languages with futures (as ABS). This technique is based on vector systems and addresses infinite-state programs that admit thread creation but not dynamic resource creation.

The problem of verifying deadlocks in infinite state models has been studied in other contributions. For example, [28] compare a number of unfolding algorithms for Petri Nets with techniques for safely cutting potentially infinite unfoldings. Also in this work, dynamic resource creation is not addressed. The techniques conceived for dealing with dynamic name creations are the so-called *nominal techniques*, such as nominal automata [29,25] that recognize languages over infinite alphabets and HD-automata [24], where names are explicit part of the operational model. In contrast to our approach, the models underlying these techniques are finite state. Additionally, the dependency relation between names, which is crucial for deadlock detection, is not studied.

8   Conclusions and Future Work

We have defined an algorithm for the detection of deadlocks in infinite state programs, which is a decision procedure for linear recursive programs that feature dynamic resource creation. This algorithm has been prototyped [15] and currently experimented on programs written in an object-oriented language with futures [17]. The current prototype deals with nonlinear recursive programs by using a source-to-source transformation into linear ones. This transformation *may introduce fake dependencies* (which in turn may produce false positives in terms of circularities). To briefly illustrate the technique, consider the program

$$\big(\,\mathrm{h}(t) = (t,x)\&(t,y)\&\mathrm{h}(x)\&\mathrm{h}(y)\,,\ \mathrm{h}(u)\,\big),$$

Our transformation returns the linear recursive one:

$$\big(\,\mathrm{h}^{aux}(t,t') = (t,x)\&(t,x')\&(t',x)\&(t',x')\&\mathrm{h}^{aux}(x,x')\,,$$
$$\mathrm{h}(u) = \mathrm{h}^{aux}(u,u)\,,\ \mathrm{h}(u)\,\big)\,.$$

To highlight the fake dependencies added by h^{aux}, we notice that, after two unfoldings, $\mathrm{h}^{aux}(u,u)$ gives

$$(u,v)\&(u,w)\&(v,v')\&(v,w')\&(w,v')\&(w,w')\&\mathrm{h}^{aux}(v',w')$$

while $\mathrm{h}(u)$ has a corresponding state (obtained after four steps)

$$(u,v)\&(u,w)\&(v,v')\&(v,v'')\&(w,w')\&(w,w'')$$
$$\&\mathrm{h}(v')\&\mathrm{h}(v'')\&\mathrm{h}(w')\&\mathrm{h}(w'')\,,$$

and this state has no dependency between names created by different invocations. It is worth to remark that these additional dependencies cannot be completely eliminated because of a cardinality argument. The evaluation of a function invocation $f(\tilde{u})$ in a linear recursive program may produce at most one invocation of f, while an invocation of $f(\tilde{u})$ in a nonlinear recursive program may produce two or more. In turn, these invocations of f may create names (which are exponentially many in a nonlinear program). When this happens, the creations of different invocations must be *contracted* to names created by one invocation and explicit dependencies must be *added* to account for dependencies of each invocation. [Our source-to-source transformation is sound: if the transformed linear recursive program is circularity-free then the original nonlinear one is also circularity-free. So, for example, since our analysis lets us determine that the saturated state of h^{aux} is circularity-free, then we are able to infer the same property for h.] We are exploring possible generalizations of our theory in Section 4 to nonlinear recursive programs that replace the notion of mutation with that of *group of mutations*. This research direction is currently at an early stage.

Another obvious research direction is to apply our technique to deadlocks due to process synchronizations, as those in process calculi [23,19]. In this case, one may take advantage of Kobayashi's inference for deriving inter-channel dependency informations and manage recursive behaviors by using our algorithm (instead of the one in [20]).

There are several ways to develop the ideas here, both in terms of the language features of lams and the analyses addressed. As regards the lam language, [13] already contains an extension of lams with union types to deal with assignments, data structures, and conditionals. However, the extension of the theory of mutations and flashbacks to deal with these features is not trivial and may yield a weakening of Theorem 2. Concerning the analyses, the theory of mutations and flashbacks may be applied for verifying properties different than deadlocks, such as state reachability or livelocks, possibly using different lam languages and different notions of saturated state. Investigating the range of applications of our theory and studying the related models (corresponding to lams) are two issues that we intend to pursue.

References

1. Abadi, M., Flanagan, C., Freund, S.N.: Types for safe locking: Static race detection for Java. TOPLAS 28 (2006)
2. Bouajjani, A., Emmi, M.: Analysis of recursively parallel programs. In: POPL 2012, pp. 203–214. ACM (2012)
3. Boyapati, C., Lee, R., Rinard, M.: Ownership types for safe program.: preventing data races and deadlocks. In: OOPSLA, pp. 211–230. ACM (2002)
4. Brookes, S.D., Hoare, C.A.R., Roscoe, A.W.: A theory of communicating sequential processes. J. ACM 31, 560–599 (1984)
5. Carlsson, R., Millroth, H.: On cyclic process dependencies and the verification of absence of deadlocks in reactive systems (1997)
6. Caromel, D., Henrio, L., Serpette, B.P.: Asynchronous and deterministic objects. In: POPL, pp. 123–134. ACM (2004)

7. Chaki, S., Rajamani, S.K., Rehof, J.: Types as models: model checking message-passing programs. SIGPLAN Not. 37(1), 45–57 (2002)
8. Comtet, L.: Advanced Combinatorics: The Art of Finite and Infinite Expansions, Dordrecht, Netherlands (1974)
9. Requirement elicitation. Deliverable 5.1 of project FP7-231620 (HATS) (August 2009), http://www.hats-project.eu/sites/default/files/Deliverable51_rev2.pdf.
10. Flanagan, C., Qadeer, S.: A type and effect system for atomicity. In: PLDI, pp. 338–349. ACM (2003)
11. Flores-Montoya, A.E., Albert, E., Genaim, S.: May-happen-in-parallel based deadlock analysis for concurrent objects. In: Beyer, D., Boreale, M. (eds.) FMOODS/-FORTE 2013. LNCS, vol. 7892, pp. 273–288. Springer, Heidelberg (2013)
12. Gay, S.J., Nagarajan, R.: Types and typechecking for communicating quantum processes. MSCS 16(3), 375–406 (2006)
13. Giachino, E., Grazia, C.A., Laneve, C., Lienhardt, M., Wong, P.Y.H.: Deadlock analysis of concurrent objects: Theory and practice. In: Johnsen, E.B., Petre, L. (eds.) IFM 2013. LNCS, vol. 7940, pp. 394–411. Springer, Heidelberg (2013)
14. Giachino, E., Laneve, C., Lienhardt, M.: A Framework for Deadlock Detection in ABS (2013), http://www.cs.unibo.it/~laneve (submitted)
15. Giachino, E., Laneve, C., Lienhardt, M.: Deadlock Framework for ABS (DF4ABS) - online interface (2013), http://www.cs.unibo.it/~giachino/siteDat/
16. Igarashi, A., Kobayashi, N.: A generic type system for the pi-calculus. Theor. Comput. Sci. 311(1-3), 121–163 (2004)
17. Johnsen, E.B., Hähnle, R., Schäfer, J., Schlatte, R., Steffen, M.: ABS: A core language for abstract behavioral specification. In: Aichernig, B.K., de Boer, F.S., Bonsangue, M.M. (eds.) Formal Methods for Components and Objects. LNCS, vol. 6957, pp. 142–164. Springer, Heidelberg (2011)
18. Kobayashi, N.: A partially deadlock-free typed process calculus. TOPLAS 20(2), 436–482 (1998)
19. Kobayashi, N.: A new type system for deadlock-free processes. In: Baier, C., Hermanns, H. (eds.) CONCUR 2006. LNCS, vol. 4137, pp. 233–247. Springer, Heidelberg (2006)
20. Kobayashi, N.: TyPiCal (2007), http://www.kb.ecei.tohoku.ac.jp/~koba/typical/
21. Laneve, C., Padovani, L.: The *must* preorder revisited. In: Caires, L., Vasconcelos, V.T. (eds.) CONCUR 2007. LNCS, vol. 4703, pp. 212–225. Springer, Heidelberg (2007)
22. Milner, R.: A Calculus of Communication Systems. LNCS, vol. 92. Springer, Heidelberg (1980)
23. Milner, R., Parrow, J., Walker, D.: A calculus of mobile processes, ii. Inf. and Comput. 100, 41–77 (1992)
24. Montanari, U., Pistore, M.: An introduction to history dependent automata. Electr. Notes Theor. Comput. Sci. 10, 170–188 (1997)
25. Neven, F., Schwentick, T., Vianu, V.: Towards regular languages over infinite alphabets. In: Sgall, J., Pultr, A., Kolman, P. (eds.) MFCS 2001. LNCS, vol. 2136, pp. 560–572. Springer, Heidelberg (2001)
26. Nielson, H.R., Nielson, F.: Higher-order concurrent programs with finite communication topology. In: POPL, pp. 84–97. ACM (1994)
27. Parastatidis, S., Webber, J.: MEP SSDL Protocol Framework (April 2005), http://ssdl.org

28. Schrter, C., Esparza, J.: Reachability analysis using net unfoldings. In: CS&P 2000, pp. 255–270 (2000)
29. Segoufin, L.: Automata and logics for words and trees over an infinite alphabet. In: Ésik, Z. (ed.) CSL 2006. LNCS, vol. 4207, pp. 41–57. Springer, Heidelberg (2006)
30. Suenaga, K.: Type-based deadlock-freedom verification for non-block-structured lock primitives and mutable references. In: Ramalingam, G. (ed.) APLAS 2008. LNCS, vol. 5356, pp. 155–170. Springer, Heidelberg (2008)
31. Tarjan, R.E.: Depth-first search and linear graph algorithms. SIAM J. Comput. 1(2), 146–160 (1972)
32. Vasconcelos, V.T., Martins, F., Cogumbreiro, T.: Type inference for deadlock detection in a multithreaded polymorphic typed assembly language. In: PLACES. EPTCS, vol. 17, pp. 95–109 (2009)

A   Java Code of the Factorial Function

There are several JAVA programs implementing `factorial` in Section 1. However our goal is to convey some intuition about the differences between TYPICAL and our technique, rather than to analyze the possible options. One option is the code

```
synchronized void fact(final int n,final int m,final Maths x)
                           throws InterruptedException {
    if (n==0) x.retresult(m) ;
    else {
        final Maths y = new Maths() ;
        Thread t = new Thread(new Runnable() {
            public void run() {
                try { y.fact(n-1,n*m,x) ;
                } catch (InterruptedException e) { }
            } }) ;
        t.start();
        t.join() ;
    }
}
```

Since `factorial` is `synchronized`, the corresponding thread acquires the lock of its object – let it be *this* – before execution and releases the lock upon termination. We notice that `factorial`, in case n>0, delegates the computation of factorial to a separate thread on a new object of `Maths`, called y. This means that no other synchronized thread on *this* may be scheduled until the recursive invocation on y terminates. Said formally, the runtime Java configuration contains an object dependency $(this, y)$. Repeating this argument for the recursive invocation, we get configurations with chains of dependencies $(this, y), (y, z), \cdots$, which are finite by the well-foundedness of naturals.

B   Proof of Theorem 2

This section develops the technical details for proving Theorem 2.

Definition 9. *A history α is*

f-*yielding*
if $\alpha = \alpha_1^{h_1} \beta_1 \cdots \alpha_n^{h_n} \beta_n$ such that, for every i, α_i is a recursive history, $\beta_i \leq \alpha_i$, and $\alpha = \alpha' f_i$ implies the program has the definition $f_i(\tilde{x}_i) = \mathfrak{L}[f(\tilde{u})]$, for some $\tilde{u}$. The kernel of α, denoted $[\alpha]$, is $\alpha_1^{h'_1} \beta_1 \cdots \alpha_n^{h'_n} \beta_n$, where $h'_i = \min(h_i, 1)$.

By definition, if α is f-saturating then it is also f-yielding. In this case, the kernel $[\alpha]$ has a suffix that is f-complete. In the flh-program, $o_f = 4$, $o_1 = 3$, and $o_h = 1$, and the recursive histories of f, l and h are equal to fl, to lf and to h, respectively. Then $\alpha = (fl)^4$ is the f-complete history and $\alpha' = h^2f$ is l-yielding, with $[\alpha'] = hf$.

We notice that every history of an informative lam (obtained by evaluating $\langle \mathbb{0}_L, \varnothing, addh(\varepsilon, L)\rangle$) is a yielding sequence. We also notice that, for every f, ε is f-yielding. In fact, ε is the history of every function invocation in the initial lam, which may concern every function name of the program. As regards the kernel, in Lemma 1, we demonstrate that, if $\alpha = \alpha_1^{h_1} \beta_1 \cdots \alpha_n^{h_n} \beta_n$ is a f-yielding history such that every $h_i \geq 2$, then every term ${}^{\alpha}f(\widetilde{u})$ may be mapped by a flashback ρ to a term ${}^{[\alpha]}f(\rho(\widetilde{u}))$; similarly for dependencies. This is the basic property that allows us to map circularities to past circularities (see Theorem 2).

Next we introduce an ordering relation over renamings, (in particular, flashbacks) and the operation of renaming composition. The definitions are almost standard:

- $\rho \leq^{\text{fb}} \rho'$ if, for every $x \in dom(\rho)$, $\rho(x) = \rho'(x)$.
- $\rho \circ \rho'$ be defined as follows:

$$(\rho \circ \rho')(x) \overset{def}{=} \begin{cases} \rho'(x) & \text{if } \rho'(x) \notin dom(\rho) \\ \rho(\rho'(x)) & \text{otherwise} \end{cases}$$

We notice that, if both

1. ρ and ρ' are flashbacks and
2. for every $x \in dom(\rho)$, $\rho'(x) = x$

then $\rho \leq^{\text{fb}} \rho \circ \rho'$ holds. In the following, lams $\flat(L)$ and $\flat(\mathbb{L})$, being $+$ of terms that are dependencies composed with $\&$, will be written $T_1 + \cdots + T_m$ and ${}^{\flat}T_1 + \cdots + {}^{\flat}T_m$, for some m, respectively, where T_i and ${}^{\flat}T_i$ contain dependencies (x, y) and ${}^{\alpha}(x, y)$. Let also $\rho(\&_{i \in I}(x_i, y_i)) = \&_{i \in I}(\rho(x_i), \rho(y_i))$.

With an abuse of notation, we will use the set operation "$\in$" for L and $\flat L$. For instance, we will write $L' \in L$ when there is $\mathcal{L}[\ ]$ such that $L = \mathcal{L}[L']$. Similarly, we will write $T \in T_1 + \cdots + T_n$ when there is T_i such that $T \in T_i$.

A consequence of the axiom $T\&(L' + L'') = T\&L' + T\&L''$ is the following property of the informative operational semantics.

Proposition 6. *Let* $\langle V_1, {}^{\flat}F, {}^{\flat}\mathcal{L}_0[{}^{\alpha}f_1(\widetilde{u_1})]\rangle$ *be a state of an informative operational semantics. For every* $1 \leq i \leq n$, *let* $f_i(\widetilde{u_i}) = L_i'$ *and* $addh(\alpha f_0 \cdots f_i, L_i')$ *be* ${}^{\flat}\mathcal{L}_i[{}^{\alpha f_1 \cdots f_i}f_{i+1}(\widetilde{u_{i+1}})]$. *Finally, let*

$$\flat({}^{\flat}\mathcal{L}_1[\cdots {}^{\flat}\mathcal{L}_n[{}^{\alpha f_1 \cdots f_n}f_{n+1}(\widetilde{u_{n+1}})]\cdots]) = {}^{\flat}T_1 + \cdots + {}^{\flat}T_r$$
$$\flat({}^{\flat}\mathcal{L}_n[{}^{\alpha f_1 \cdots f_n}f_{n+1}(\widetilde{u_{n+1}})]) = {}^{\flat}T_1' + \cdots + {}^{\flat}T_{r'}' \,.$$

If ${}^{\alpha f_1 \cdots f_n}(x, y)\&addh(\alpha', T) \in {}^{\flat}T_1 + \cdots + {}^{\flat}T_r$ *then, for every* $1 \leq j \leq r'$, ${}^{\flat}T_j'\&addh(\alpha', T) \in {}^{\flat}T_1 + \cdots + {}^{\flat}T_r$.

The next lemma allows us to map, through a flashback, terms in a saturated state to terms that have been produced in the past. The correspondence is defined by means of the (regular) structure of histories.

Lemma 1. *Let* $\langle \mathbb{0}_L, \varnothing, addh(\varepsilon, L)\rangle \longrightarrow^* \langle V, {}^{\flat}F, \mathbb{L}\rangle$ *and* $\langle V, {}^{\flat}F, \mathbb{L}\rangle$ *be saturated and* $\flat(\mathbb{L}) = {}^{\flat}T_1 + \cdots + {}^{\flat}T_m$. *Then*

1. *if* ${}^{\beta\alpha^{n+2}\beta'}f(\widetilde{u}) \in \mathbb{L}$, *where* $\beta\alpha^{n+2}\beta'$ *is* f-*yielding, then there are* $n + 1$ V-*flashbacks* $\rho_{\beta, \alpha, \beta'}^{(2)}, \cdots, \rho_{\beta, \alpha, \beta'}^{(n+2)}$ *such that:*

(a) $^{\beta\alpha^{n+1}\beta'}\mathbf{f}(\rho_{\beta,\alpha,\beta'}^{(n+2)}(\widetilde{u})) \in {}^{\flat}\mathbb{F}$;

(b) $\&_{j\in J}\,addh(\beta\alpha^{k+1}\beta_j, T'_j) \in {}^{\flat}T_1 + \cdots + {}^{\flat}T_m$ where, for every j, $\beta_j \leq \alpha$, implies $\&_{j\in J}\,addh(\beta\alpha^k\beta_j, \rho_{\beta,\alpha,\beta'}^{(k+1)}(T'_j)) \in {}^{\flat}T_1 + \cdots + {}^{\flat}T_m$;

(c) $^{\beta\alpha^{k+1}\beta'}\mathbf{f}(\widetilde{u}) \in {}^{\flat}\mathbb{F}$ implies $^{\beta\alpha^k\beta'}\mathbf{f}(\rho_{\beta,\alpha,\beta'}^{(k+1)}(\widetilde{u})) \in {}^{\flat}\mathbb{F}$.

2. if $\alpha_1, \cdots, \alpha_k$ are $\mathbf{f}_1$-yielding, $\cdots$, $\mathbf{f}_k$-yielding, respectively, then there are flashbacks $\rho_{\alpha_1}, \cdots, \rho_{\alpha_k}$ such that

(a) if $^{\alpha_1}\mathbf{f}_1(\widetilde{u}) \in \mathbb{L}$ or $^{\alpha_1}\mathbf{f}_1(\widetilde{u}) \in {}^{\flat}\mathbb{F}$ then $^{[\alpha_1]}\mathbf{f}_1(\rho_{\alpha_1}(\widetilde{u})) \in {}^{\flat}\mathbb{F}$;

(b) if $\&_{1\leq j\leq k}\,addh(\alpha_j, T_j) \in {}^{\flat}T_1 + \cdots + {}^{\flat}T_m$ then $\&_{1\leq j\leq k}\,addh([\alpha_j], \rho_{\alpha_j}(T)) \in {}^{\flat}T_1 + \cdots + {}^{\flat}T_m$;

(c) if $\alpha_1 \leq \alpha_2$ then $\rho_{\alpha_1} \leq^{\mathbf{fb}} \rho_{\alpha_2}$.
   (In particular, if $\alpha_1 = \beta\alpha^{n+2}\beta'$, with $\beta' \leq \alpha$, and $\alpha_2 = \beta\alpha^{n+3}$ then $\rho_{\alpha_1} \leq^{\mathbf{fb}} \rho_{\alpha_2}$).

Proof. (Sketch) As regards item 1, let $\alpha = \beta'\beta''$ and let $\beta''\beta' = \mathbf{ff}_1\cdots\mathbf{f}_m$ (therefore the length of α is $m+1$). The evaluation $\langle \mathbb{I}_L, \varnothing, addh(\varepsilon, L)\rangle \longrightarrow^*$ $\langle \mathbb{V}, {}^{\flat}\mathbb{F}, \mathbb{L}\rangle$ may be decomposed as follows

$$\langle \mathbb{I}_L, \varnothing, addh(\varepsilon, L)\rangle \longrightarrow^* \langle \mathbb{V}', {}^{\flat}\mathbb{F}', {}^{\flat}\mathfrak{L}[^{\beta\alpha^{n+1}\beta'}\mathbf{f}(\widetilde{u'})]\rangle$$
$$\longrightarrow^* \langle \mathbb{V}, {}^{\flat}\mathbb{F}, \mathbb{L}\rangle$$

By definition of the operational semantics there is the *alternative* evaluation

$$\langle \mathbb{V}', {}^{\flat}\mathbb{F}', {}^{\flat}\mathfrak{L}[^{\beta\alpha^{n+1}\beta'}\mathbf{f}(\widetilde{u'})]\rangle$$
$$\longrightarrow \langle \mathbb{V}'', {}^{\flat}\mathbb{F}'', {}^{\flat}\mathfrak{L}[^{\flat}\mathfrak{L}'[^{\beta\alpha^{n+1}\beta'\mathbf{f}}\mathbf{f}_1(\widetilde{u_1})]]\rangle$$
$$\longrightarrow^* \langle \mathbb{V}''', {}^{\flat}\mathbb{F}''', {}^{\flat}\mathfrak{L}[^{\flat}\mathfrak{L}'[^{\flat}\mathfrak{L}_1[\cdots {}^{\flat}\mathfrak{L}_m[^{\beta\alpha^{n+1}\beta'\mathbf{ff}_1\cdots\mathbf{f}_m}\mathbf{f}(\widetilde{u''})]\cdots]]]\rangle$$

[notice that $\beta\alpha^{n+1}\beta'\mathbf{ff}_1\cdots\mathbf{f}_m = \beta\alpha^{n+2}\beta'$]. Property (1.a) is an immediate consequence of Proposition 5; let $\varrho_{\beta,\alpha,\beta'}^{(n+2)}$ be the flashback for the last state. The property (1.b), when $k = n$, is also an immediate consequence of Propositions 5 and of 6. In the general case, we need to iterate the arguments on shorter histories and the arguments are similar for (1.c). In order to conclude the proof of item 1, we need an additional argument. By Proposition 3, there exists an evaluation

$$\langle \mathbb{V}''', {}^{\flat}\mathbb{F}''', {}^{\flat}\mathfrak{L}[^{\flat}\mathfrak{L}'[^{\flat}\mathfrak{L}_1[\cdots {}^{\flat}\mathfrak{L}_m[^{\beta\alpha^{n+1}\beta'\mathbf{ff}_1\cdots\mathbf{f}_m}\mathbf{f}(\widetilde{u''})]\cdots]]]\rangle$$
$$\longrightarrow^* \langle \mathbb{V}^{\sharp}, {}^{\flat}\mathbb{F}^{\sharp}, \mathbb{L}^{\sharp}\rangle$$

such that $\langle \mathbb{V}^{\sharp}, {}^{\flat}\mathbb{F}^{\sharp}, \mathbb{L}^{\sharp}\rangle$ and $\langle \mathbb{V}, {}^{\flat}\mathbb{F}, \mathbb{L}\rangle$ are identified by a bijective renaming, let it be $\jmath$. We define the $\rho_{\beta,\alpha,\beta'}^{(n+2)}$ corresponding to the evaluation $\langle \mathbb{I}_L, \varnothing, addh(\varepsilon, L)\rangle$ $\longrightarrow^* \langle \mathbb{V}, {}^{\flat}\mathbb{F}, \mathbb{L}\rangle$ as $\rho_{\beta,\alpha,\beta'}^{(n+2)} \overset{def}{=} \jmath \circ \varrho_{\beta,\alpha,\beta'}^{(n+2)} \circ \jmath^{-1}$. Similarly for the other $\rho_{\beta,\alpha,\beta'}^{(k+1)}$. The properties of item 1 for $\langle \mathbb{V}, {}^{\flat}\mathbb{F}, \mathbb{L}\rangle$ follow by the corresponding ones for

$$\langle \mathbb{V}''', {}^{\flat}\mathbb{F}''', {}^{\flat}\mathfrak{L}[^{\flat}\mathfrak{L}'[^{\flat}\mathfrak{L}_1[\cdots {}^{\flat}\mathfrak{L}_m[^{\beta\alpha^{n+1}\beta'\mathbf{ff}_1\cdots\mathbf{f}_m}\mathbf{f}(\widetilde{u''})]\cdots]]]\rangle .$$

We prove item 2. We observe that a term with history $\beta_0(\alpha'_1)^{h_1}\beta_1\cdots\beta_{n-1}$ $(\alpha'_n)^{h_n}\beta_n$ in ${}^{\flat}\mathbb{F}$ or in $\mathbb{L}$ may have no corresponding term (by a flashback) with history $\beta_0(\alpha_1')^{h_1-1}\beta_1\,(\alpha_2')^{h_2}\cdots\beta_{n-1}\,(\alpha_n')^{h_n}\beta_n$. This is because the evaluation to the saturated state may have not expanded some invocations. It is however true that terms with histories $[\beta_0(\alpha_1')^{h_1}\beta_1\cdots\beta_{n-1}(\alpha_n')^{h_n}\beta_n]$ (kernels) are either in $^\flat\mathsf{F}$ or in L and the item 2 is demonstrated by proving that a flashback to terms with histories that are kernels does exist.

Let $\alpha_1 = \beta_0(\alpha_1')^{h_1}\beta_1\cdots\beta_{n-1}(\alpha_n')^{h_n}\beta_n$ be a f-yielding sequence. We proceed by induction on n. When $n = 1$ there are two cases: $h_1 \leqslant 1$ and $h_1 \geqslant 2$. In the first case there is nothing to prove because $[\alpha] = \alpha$. When $h_1 \geqslant 2$, since α fits with the hypotheses of Item 1, there exist $\rho^{(2)}_{\beta_0,\alpha_1',\beta_1}, \cdots, \rho^{(h_1)}_{\beta_0,\alpha_1',\beta_1}$. Let $\delta^{(2)}_{\beta_0,\alpha_1',\beta_1} = \rho^{(2)}_{\beta_0,\alpha_1',\beta_1}$ and $\delta^{(i+1)}_{\beta_0,\alpha_1',\beta_1} = \rho^{(i+1)}_{\beta_0,\alpha_1',\beta_1}[x \mapsto x \mid x \in dom(\delta^{(i)}_{\beta_0,\alpha_1',\beta_1})]$. We also let $\rho_{\alpha_1} = \delta^{(2)}_{\beta_0,\alpha_1',\beta_1} \circ \cdots \circ \delta^{(h_1)}_{\beta_0,\alpha_1',\beta_1}$ and we observe that, by definition of renaming composition, if $\alpha_1 \leq \alpha_2$ then $\rho_{\alpha_1} \leq^{fb} \rho_{\alpha_2}$. In this case, the items 2.a and 2.b follow by item 1, Proposition 6 and the diamond property of Proposition 3.

We assume the statement holds for a generic n and we prove the case $n + 1$. Let $\alpha_1 = \beta\beta_n(\alpha_{n+1}')^{h_{n+1}}\beta_{n+1}$ and $h_{n+1} > 0$ (because $[\beta_n(\alpha_{n+1}')^1\beta_{n+1}] = \beta_n\alpha_{n+1}'\beta_{n+1}$). We consider the map

$$\rho_{\alpha_1} \stackrel{def}{=} \rho_\beta \circ \delta^{(2)}_{\beta_n,\alpha_{n+1}',\beta_{n+1}} \circ \cdots \circ \delta^{(h_{n+1})}_{\beta_n,\alpha_{n+1}',\beta_{n+1}}$$

where $\delta^{(i)}_{\beta_n,\alpha_{n+1}',\beta_{n+1}}$, $2 \leqslant i \leqslant h_{n+1}$ are defined as above. As before, the items 2.a and 2.b follow by item 1 for $\delta^{(2)}_{\beta_n,\alpha_{n+1}',\beta_{n+1}} \circ \cdots \circ \delta^{(h_n|1)}_{\beta_n,\alpha_{n+1}',\beta_{n+1}}$ and by Proposition 6 and the diamond property of Proposition 3. Then we apply the inductive hypothesis for ρ_β. The property (2.c) $\alpha_1 \leq \alpha_2$ implies $\rho_{\alpha_1} \leq^{fb} \rho_{\alpha_2}$ is an immediate consequence of the definition.

Every preliminary statement is in place for our key theorem that details the mapping of circularities created by transitions of saturated states to past circularities. For readability sake, we restate the theorem.

Theorem 2. *Let $\langle \mathbb{I}_L, \varnothing, addh(\varepsilon, \mathsf{L})\rangle \longrightarrow^* \langle \mathsf{V}, {}^\flat\mathsf{F}, \mathsf{L}\rangle$ and $\langle \mathsf{V}, {}^\flat\mathsf{F}, \mathsf{L}\rangle$ be a saturated state. If $\langle \mathsf{V}, {}^\flat\mathsf{F}, \mathsf{L}\rangle \longrightarrow \langle \mathsf{V}', {}^\flat\mathsf{F}', \mathsf{L}'\rangle$ then*

1. $\langle \mathsf{V}', {}^\flat\mathsf{F}', \mathsf{L}'\rangle$ *is saturated;*
2. *if L' has a circularity then L has already a circularity.*

Proof. The item 1. is an immediate consequence of Proposition 5. We prove 2. Let

- $\mathsf{L} = {}^\flat\mathcal{L}[{}^\alpha\mathsf{f}(\tilde{u})]$;
- $\mathsf{f}(\tilde{u}) = \mathsf{L}'$;
- $\mathsf{L}' = {}^\flat\mathcal{L}[addh(\alpha\mathsf{f}, \mathsf{L}')]$;
- $\flat(\mathsf{L}) = \flat({}^\flat\mathcal{L}[{}^\alpha\mathsf{f}(\tilde{u})]) = {}^\flat\mathsf{T}_1 + \cdots + {}^\flat\mathsf{T}_p$;
- $\flat(\mathsf{L}') = \mathsf{T}_1' + \cdots + \mathsf{T}_{p'}'$;
- $\flat(\mathsf{L}') = {}^\flat\mathsf{T}_1'' + \cdots + {}^\flat\mathsf{T}_q''$;

$- \, {}^{\alpha_0}(x_0, x_1) \& \cdots \& {}^{\alpha_n}(x_n, x_0) \in {}^{\flat}T_1'' + \cdots + {}^{\flat}T_q''$ (it is a circularity).

Without loss of generality, we may reduce to the following case (the general case is demonstrated by iterating the arguments below).

Let $\alpha\mathsf{f} = \beta(\alpha')^{m+2}\beta'$ and let

$$
\begin{aligned}
{}^{\alpha_0}(x_0, x_1)\& \cdots \& {}^{\alpha_n}(x_n, x_0) = \; & \&_{0 \leqslant j \leqslant n'} \, {}^{\beta(\alpha')^{m+1}\beta'\beta_j}(x_j, x_{j+1}) \\
& \& \, {}^{\alpha_{n'+1}}(x_{n'+1}, x_{n'+2}) \\
& \& \cdots \& {}^{\alpha_n}(x_n, x_0)
\end{aligned}
$$

with $\varepsilon \lneq \beta_j \leq \beta''\beta'$, where $\beta'\beta'' = \alpha'$, and $n' < n$ (otherwise 2 is straightforward because the circularity may be mapped to a previous circularity by $\rho_{\beta,\alpha',\beta'}^{(m+2)}$, see Lemma 1(1.b), or it is already contained in $\mathbb{L}$). This is the case of crossover circularities, as discussed in Section 1.

By Lemma 1,

$$
\begin{aligned}
& {}^{\beta(\alpha')^m\beta'\beta_0}(\rho_{\beta,\alpha,\beta'}^{(m+2)}(x_0), \rho_{\beta,\alpha,\beta'}^{(m+2)}(x_1)) \& \cdots \\
& \& \, {}^{\beta(\alpha')^{m+1}\beta'\beta_{n'}}(\rho_{\beta,\alpha,\beta'}^{(m+2)}(x_{n'}), \rho_{\beta,\alpha,\beta'}^{(m+2)}(x_{n'+1}))
\end{aligned} \tag{1}
$$

is in some ${}^{\flat}T_i''$. There are two cases.

Case 1: for every $n' + 1 \leqslant i \leqslant n$, $\alpha_i \lneq \beta(\alpha')^{m+1}\beta'$. Then, by Lemma 1(1), we have $\rho_{\beta,\alpha,\beta'}^{(m+2)}(x_0) = \rho_{\beta,\alpha,\beta'}^{(m+1)}(x_0)$ and $\rho_{\beta,\alpha,\beta'}^{(m+2)}(x_{n'+1}) = \rho_{\beta,\alpha,\beta'}^{(m+1)}(x_{n'+1})$. Therefore, by Lemma 1(2),

$$
\begin{aligned}
(1) \& \; & {}^{\alpha'_{n'+1}}(\rho_{\beta,\alpha,\beta'}^{(m+1)}(x_{n'+1}), \rho_{\beta,\alpha,\beta'}^{(m+1)}(x_{n'+2})) \\
& \& \cdots \& {}^{\alpha'_n}(\rho_{\beta,\alpha,\beta'}^{(m+1)}(x_n), \rho_{\beta,\alpha,\beta'}^{(m+1)}(x_0))
\end{aligned}
$$

with suitable $\alpha'_{n'+1}, \cdots, \alpha'_n$, is a circularity in ${}^{\flat}T_1'' + \cdots + {}^{\flat}T_q''$. In particular, whenever, for every $n' + 1 \leqslant i \leqslant n$, $\alpha_i = \beta(\alpha')^m\beta'\beta_i$ with $\varepsilon \lneq \beta_i \leq \beta''\beta'$, the flashback $\rho_{\beta,\alpha,\beta'}^{(m+1)}$ maps dependencies ${}^{\alpha_i}(x_i, x_{i+1})$ to dependencies

$$
{}^{\beta(\alpha')^{m-1}\beta'\beta_i}(\rho_{\beta,\alpha,\beta'}^{(m+1)}(x_i), \rho_{\beta,\alpha,\beta'}^{(m+1)}(x_{i+1}))
$$

if $m > 0$. It is the identity, if $m = 0$.

Case 2: there is $n' + 1 \leqslant i \leqslant n$ such that $\alpha_i \nleq \beta(\alpha')^{m+2}\beta'$. Let this i be $n' + 1$. For instance, $\beta = \beta_1'(\alpha'')^{m'}\beta_1''$ and $\alpha_{n'+1} = \beta_1'(\alpha'')^{m'+1}\beta_1''(\alpha''')^{m''}\beta_1'''$ with $m' \geqslant 2$ and $m'' \geqslant 2$. In this case it is possible that there is no pair ${}^{\gamma}(y, y')$, with $\gamma \geq \beta_1'(\alpha'')^{m'}$, to which map ${}^{\alpha_{n'+1}}(x_{n'+1}, x_{n'+2})$ by means of a flashback. To overcome this issue, we consider the flashbacks $\rho_{\alpha_0}, \cdots, \rho_{\alpha_{n'}}, \rho_{\alpha_{n'+1}}$ and we observe that

$$
\begin{aligned}
& {}^{[\alpha_0]}(\rho_{\alpha_0}(x_0), \rho_{\alpha_0}(x_1)) \& \cdots \& {}^{[\alpha_{n'}]}(\rho_{\alpha_{n'}}(x_{n'}), \rho_{\alpha_{n'}}(x_{n'+1})) \\
& \& \, {}^{[\alpha_{n'+1}]}(\rho_{\alpha_{n'+1}}(x_{n'+1}), \rho_{\alpha_{n'+1}}(x_{n'+2})) \& \cdots \\
& \& \, {}^{[\alpha_n]}(\rho_{\alpha_n}(x_n), \rho_{\alpha_n}(x_1))
\end{aligned} \tag{2}
$$

verifies

(a) for every $0 \leqslant i < n$, $\rho_{\alpha_i}(x_{i+1}) = \rho_{\alpha_{i+1}}(x_{i+1})$ and $\rho_{\alpha_n}(x_0) = \rho_{\alpha_0}(x_0)$;

(b) the term (2) is a subterm of ${}^\flat T_1'' + \cdots + {}^\flat T_q''$.

As regards (a), the property derives by definition of the flashbacks ρ_{α_i} and $\rho_{\alpha_{i+1}}$ in Lemma 1. As regards (b), it follows by Lemma 1(2.b) because ${}^{\alpha_0}(x_0, x_1)\& \cdots \&$ ${}^{\alpha_n}(x_n, x_1) \in {}^\flat T_1'' + \cdots + {}^\flat T_q''$.

C   Nonlinear Programs: Technical Aspects

When the lam program is not linear recursive, it is not possible to associate a unique mutation to a function. In the general case, our technique for verifying circularity-freedom consists of transforming a nonlinear recursive program into a linear recursive one and then running the algorithm of the previous section. As we will see, the transformation introduces inaccuracies, e.g. dependencies that are not present in the nonlinear recursive program.

C.1   The Pseudo-linear Case

In nonlinear recursive programs, recursive histories are no more adequate to capture the mutations defined by the functions. For example, in the nonlinear recursive program (called $f'g'$-program)

$$\bigl(f'(x, y, z) = (x, y)\&g'(y, z), \ g'(x, y) = g'(x, z)\&f'(z, y, y), \ L\bigr)$$

the recursive history of f' is $f'g'$. The sequence $f'g'g'$ *is not* a recursive history because it contains multiple occurrences of the function g'. However, if one computes the sequences of invocations $f'(x, y, z) \cdots f'(\widetilde{u})$, it is possible to derive the two sequences $f'(x, y, z)g'(y, z)f'(z', z, z)$ and $f'(x, y, z)g'(y, z)\,g'(y, u)f'(u', u, u)$ that define two different mutations $(\!(4, 3, 3)\!)$ and $(\!(6, 5, 5)\!)$ (see the definition of mutation of a function).

Definition 10. *A program* $(f_1(\widetilde{x_1}) = L_1, \cdots, f_\ell(\widetilde{x}_\ell) = L_\ell, L)$ *is* pseudo-linear recursive *if, for every* f_i, *the set of functions* $\{f \mid closure(f) = closure(f_i)\}$ *contains at most one function with a number of recursive histories greater than* 1.

The $f'g'$-program above is pseudo-linear recursive, as well as the fibonacci program in Section 1 and the following $1'$-program

$$\bigl(1'(x, y, z) = (x, y)\&1'(y, z, x) + (x, u)\&1'(u, u, y), \ L\bigr) \ .$$

In these cases, functions have a unique recursive history but there are multiple recursive invocations. On the contrary, the $f''g''$-program below

$$\bigl(\ f''(x, y) = (x, z)\&f''(y, z) + g''(y, x) \ ,$$
$$g''(x, y) = (y, x)\&f''(y, z)\&g''(z, x) \ ,$$
$$f''(x_1, x_2) \ \bigr)$$

is not pseudo-linear recursive.

Pseudo-linearity has been introduced because of the easiness of transforming them into linear recursive programs. The transformation consists of the three

Table 1. Pseudo-linear to linear transformation

$$\frac{rechis(\mathbf{f}_i) = \{\mathbf{f}_i\mathbf{f}_k\alpha, \mathbf{f}_i\beta_0, \cdots, \mathbf{f}_i\beta_n\} \quad \{head(\beta_0), \cdots, head(\beta_n)\}\backslash \mathbf{f}_k \neq \varnothing}{\mathbf{L}_i = \mathcal{L}[\mathbf{f}_k(\widetilde{u})] \quad var(\mathbf{L}_k)\backslash\widetilde{x_k} = \widetilde{z} \quad \widetilde{w} \text{ are fresh}}$$

$$(\cdots \mathbf{f}_i(\widetilde{x}_i) = \mathbf{L}_i, \cdots, \mathbf{L}) \overset{\text{pl}\mapsto\text{l}}{\Longmapsto}_1 (\cdots \mathbf{f}_i(\widetilde{x}_i) = \mathcal{L}[\mathbf{L}_k[\widetilde{w}/\widetilde{z}][\widetilde{u}/\widetilde{x}_i]], \cdots, \mathbf{L})$$

$$\frac{\begin{array}{c} rechis(\mathbf{f}_i) = \{\mathbf{f}_i\alpha\} \quad \mathbf{f}_k = head(\alpha) \\ \mathbf{L}_i = \mathcal{L}[\mathbf{f}_k(\widetilde{u_0})]\cdots[\mathbf{f}_k(\widetilde{u_{n+1}})] \quad \mathbf{f}_k \notin \mathcal{L} \\ var(\mathbf{L}_k)\backslash\widetilde{x_k} = \widetilde{z} \quad \widetilde{w_0}, \cdots, \widetilde{w_{n+1}} \text{ are fresh} \\ \mathcal{L}[\mathbf{L}_k[\widetilde{w_0}/\widetilde{z}][\widetilde{u_0}/\widetilde{x_k}]]\cdots[\mathbf{L}_k[\widetilde{w_{n+1}}/\widetilde{z}][\widetilde{u_{n+1}}/\widetilde{x_k}]] = \mathbf{L}_i' \end{array}}{(\cdots \mathbf{f}_i(\widetilde{x}_i) = \mathbf{L}_i, \cdots, \mathbf{L}) \overset{\text{pl}\mapsto\text{l}}{\Longmapsto}_2 (\cdots \mathbf{f}_i(\widetilde{x}_i) = \mathbf{L}_i', \cdots, \mathbf{L})}$$

$$\frac{\begin{array}{c} \mathbf{L}_i = \mathcal{L}[\mathbf{f}_i(\widetilde{u_0})]\cdots[\mathbf{f}_i(\widetilde{u_{n+1}})] \quad \mathbf{f}_i \notin \mathcal{L} \quad \widetilde{w_0}, \cdots, \widetilde{w_{n+1}} \text{ are fresh} \\ \mathbf{L}_i^{aux} = \mathbf{f}_i^{aux}(\widetilde{u_0}[\widetilde{w_0}/\widetilde{x}_i], \cdots, \widetilde{u_{n+1}}[\widetilde{w_{n+1}}/\widetilde{x}_i])\&(\&_{j\in 0..n+1}\flat_{\mathbf{f}_i}(\mathbf{L}_i)[\widetilde{w_j}/\widetilde{x}_i]) \end{array}}{\begin{array}{c} (\cdots \mathbf{f}_i(\widetilde{x}_i) = \mathbf{L}_i, \cdots, \mathbf{L}) \overset{\text{pl}\mapsto\text{l}}{\Longmapsto}_3 \\ (\cdots \mathbf{f}_i(\widetilde{x}_i) = \mathbf{f}_i^{aux}(\underbrace{\widetilde{x}_i, \cdots, \widetilde{x}_i}_{n+2 \text{ times}}), \mathbf{f}_i^{aux}(\widetilde{w_0}, \cdots, \widetilde{w_{n+1}}) = \mathbf{L}_i^{aux}, \cdots, \mathbf{L}) \end{array}}$$

steps specified in Table 1, which we discuss below. Let $(\mathbf{f}_1(\widetilde{x_1}) = \mathbf{L}_1, \cdots, \mathbf{f}_\ell(\widetilde{x}_\ell) = \mathbf{L}_\ell, \mathbf{L})$ be a lam program, let $rechis(\mathbf{f}_i)$ be the set of recursive histories of $\mathbf{f}_i$, and let $head(\varepsilon) = \varepsilon$ and $head(\mathbf{f}\alpha) = \mathbf{f}$.

Transformation $\overset{\text{pl}\mapsto\text{l}}{\Longmapsto}_1$: Removing multiple recursive histories. We repeatedly apply the rule defining $\overset{\text{pl}\mapsto\text{l}}{\Longmapsto}_1$. Every instance of the rule selects a function $\mathbf{f}_i$ with a number of recursive histories greater than one – the hypotheses $rechis(\mathbf{f}_i) = \{\mathbf{f}_i\mathbf{f}_k\alpha, \mathbf{f}_i\beta_0, \cdots, \mathbf{f}_i\beta_n\}$ and $\{head(\beta_0), \cdots, head(\beta_n)\}\backslash\mathbf{f}_k \neq \varnothing$ – and expands the invocation of $\mathbf{f}_k$, with $\mathbf{f}_k \neq \mathbf{f}_i$. By definition of pseudo-linearity, the other function names in $rechis(\mathbf{f}_i)$ have one recursive history. At each application of the rule the sum of the lengths of the recursive histories of $\mathbf{f}_i$ decreases. Therefore we eventually unfold the (mutual) recursive invocations of $\mathbf{f}_i$ till the recursive history of $\mathbf{f}_i$ is unique. For example, the program

$$\big(\mathbf{f}(x) = (x, y)\&\mathbf{g}(x), \ \mathbf{g}(x) = (x, y)\&\mathbf{f}(x) + \mathbf{g}(y), \ \mathbf{L}\big)$$

is transformed into

$$\big(\mathbf{f}(x) = (x, y)\&\mathbf{g}(x), \ \mathbf{g}(x) = (x, y)\&(x, z)\&\mathbf{g}(x) + \mathbf{g}(y), \ \mathbf{L}\big).$$

Transformation $\overset{\text{pl}\mapsto\text{l}}{\Longmapsto}_2$: Reducing the histories of pseudo-linear recursive functions. By $\overset{\text{pl}\mapsto\text{l}}{\Longmapsto}_1$, we are reduced to functions that have one recursive history. Yet, this is not enough for a program to be linear recursive, such as the $\mathbf{1}'$-program or the following $\mathbf{h}''\mathbf{1}''$-program

$$\big(\ \mathbf{h}''(x, y) = (x, z)\&\mathbf{1}''(y, z) + \mathbf{1}''(y, x),$$
$$\mathbf{1}''(x, y) = (y, x)\&\mathbf{h}''(y, z)\&\mathbf{h}''(z, x),$$
$$\mathbf{h}''(x_1, x_2)\ \big)$$

(the reason is that the bodies of functions may have different invocations of a same function). Rule $\overset{\text{pl}\mapsto\text{l}}{\Longrightarrow}_2$ expands the bodies of pseudo-linear recursive functions till the histories of nonlinear recursive functions have length one. In this rule (and in the following), we use lam contexts with multiple holes, written $\mathcal{L}[]\cdots[]$. We write $f \notin \mathcal{L}$ whenever there is no invocation of f in $\mathcal{L}$.

By the hypotheses of the rule, it applies to a function f_i whose next element in the recursive history is f_k (by definition of the recursive history, $f_i \neq f_k$) and whose body L_i contains *at least* two invocations of f_k. The rule transforms L_i by expanding every invocation of f_k. For example, the functions h'' and $1''$ in the $h''1''$-program are transformed into

$$h''(x,y) = (x,z)\&1''(y,z) + 1''(y,x) \,,$$
$$1''(x,y) = (y,x)\&((y,z')\&1''(z,z') + 1''(z,y))$$
$$\&((z,z'')\&1''(x,z'') + 1''(x,z)).$$

The arguments about the termination of the transformation $\overset{\text{pl}\mapsto\text{l}}{\Longrightarrow}_2$ are straightforward.

Transformation $\overset{\text{pl}\mapsto\text{l}}{\Longrightarrow}_3$: *Removing nonlinear recursive invocations.* By $\overset{\text{pl}\mapsto\text{l}}{\Longrightarrow}_2$ we are reduced to pseudo-linear recursive programs where the nonlinearity is due to recursive, but not mutually-recursive functions (such as fibonacci). The transformation $\overset{\text{pl}\mapsto\text{l}}{\Longrightarrow}_3$ removes multiple recursive invocations of nonlinear recursive programs. This transformation is the one that introduces inaccuracies, e.g. pairs that are not present in the nonlinear recursive program.

In the rule of $\overset{\text{pl}\mapsto\text{l}}{\Longrightarrow}_3$ we use the auxiliary operator $\flat_f(L)$ defined as follows:

$$\flat_f(0) = 0, \qquad\qquad \flat_f((x,y)) = (x,y),$$
$$\flat_f(f(\tilde{x})) = 0, \qquad\qquad \flat_f(g(\tilde{x})) = g(\tilde{x}), \text{ if } (f \neq g),$$
$$\flat_f(L\&L') = \flat_f(L)\&\flat_f(L'), \quad \flat_f(L + L') = \flat_f(L) + \flat_f(L').$$

The rule of $\overset{\text{pl}\mapsto\text{l}}{\Longrightarrow}_3$ selects a function f_i whose body contains multiple recursive invocations and extracts all of them – the term $\flat_{f_i}(L_i)$. This term is put in parallel with an auxiliary function invocation – the function f_i^{aux} – that collects the arguments of each invocation f_i (with names that have been properly renamed). The resulting term, called L_i^{aux} is the body of the new function f_i^{aux} that is invoked by f_i in the transformed program. For example, the function fibonacci

$$\texttt{fibonacci}(r,s) = (r,s)\&(t,s)\&\texttt{fibonacci}(r,t)\&\texttt{fibonacci}(t,s)$$

is transformed into

$$\texttt{fibonacci}(r,s) \qquad = \texttt{fibonacci}^{aux}(r,s,r,s),$$
$$\texttt{fibonacci}^{aux}(r,s,r',s') = (r,s)\&(r',s')$$
$$\&\texttt{fibonacci}^{aux}(r,t,t,s')$$

where different invocations ($\texttt{fibonacci}(r,s)$ and $\texttt{fibonacci}(r',s')$) in the original program are contracted into one auxiliary function invocation ($\texttt{fibonacci}^{aux}(r,s,r',s')$). As a consequence of this step, the creations of names performed by different invocations are contracted to names created by one invocation. This leads to merging dependencies, which, in turn, reduces the precision of the analysis. (As discussed in Section 1, a cardinality argument prevents the inaccuracies introduced by $\overset{\text{pl}\mapsto 1}{\Longmapsto}_3$ from being totally eliminated.)

As far as the correctness of the transformations in Table 1 is concerned, we begin by defining a correspondence between states of a pseudo-linear program and those of a linear one. We focus on $\overset{\text{pl}\mapsto 1}{\Longmapsto}_3$ because the proofs of the correctness of the other transformations are straightforward.

Definition 11. *Let $\mathcal{L}_2$ be the linear program returned by the Transformation 3 of Table 1 applied to $\mathcal{L}_1$. A state $\langle \mathbb{V}_1, \mathsf{L}_1 \rangle$ of $\mathcal{L}_1$ is linearized to a state $\langle \mathbb{V}_2, \mathsf{L}_2 \rangle$ of $\mathcal{L}_2$, written $\langle \mathbb{V}_1, \mathsf{L}_1 \rangle \sqsupseteq_{\text{lin}} \langle \mathbb{V}_2, \mathsf{L}_2 \rangle$, if there exists a surjection σ such that:*

1. *if $(x, y) \in \mathbb{V}_1$ then $(\sigma(x), \sigma(y)) \in \mathbb{V}_2$.*
2. *if $\flat(\mathsf{L}_1) = \mathsf{T}_1 + \cdots + \mathsf{T}_m$ and $\flat(\mathsf{L}_2) = \mathsf{T}'_1 + \cdots + \mathsf{T}'_n$, then for every $1 \leqslant i \leqslant m$, there exists $1 \leqslant j \leqslant n$, such that $\sigma(\mathsf{T}_i) \in \mathsf{T}'_j$;*
3. *if $\mathtt{f}(\widetilde{x}_1) \in \mathsf{L}_1$ then either (1) $\mathtt{f}(\sigma(\widetilde{x}_1))$ in L_2 or (2) there are $\mathtt{f}(\widetilde{x}_2) \cdots \mathtt{f}(\widetilde{x}_k)$ in L_1 and $\mathtt{f}^{aux}(\widetilde{y}_1, \cdots, \widetilde{y}_h)$ in L_2 such that, for every $1 \leqslant k' \leqslant k$ there exists h' with $\sigma(\widetilde{x}_{k'}) = \widetilde{y}_{h'}$;*

In the following lemma we use the notation $\mathfrak{L}[\mathsf{L}_1] \cdots [\mathsf{L}_n]$ defined in terms of standard lam context by $(\cdots ((\mathfrak{L}[\mathsf{L}_1])[\mathsf{L}_2]) \cdots)[\mathsf{L}_n]$.

Lemma 2. *Let $\langle \mathbb{V}_1, \mathsf{L}_1 \rangle \sqsupseteq_{\text{lin}} \langle \mathbb{V}_2, \mathsf{L}_2 \rangle$. Then, $\langle \mathbb{V}_2, \mathsf{L}_2 \rangle \longrightarrow \langle \mathbb{V}'_2, \mathsf{L}'_2 \rangle$ implies there exists $\langle \mathbb{V}_1, \mathsf{L}_1 \rangle \longrightarrow^* \langle \mathbb{V}'_1, \mathsf{L}'_1 \rangle$ such that $\langle \mathbb{V}'_1, \mathsf{L}'_1 \rangle \sqsupseteq_{\text{lin}} \langle \mathbb{V}'_2, \mathsf{L}'_2 \rangle$*

Proof. Base case. Initially $\mathsf{L}_1 = \mathsf{L}_2$ because the main lam is not affected by the transformation. Therefore the first step can only be an invocation of a standard function belonging to both programs. We have two cases:

1. the function was linear already in the original program, thus it was not modified by the transformation. In this case the two programs performs the same reduction step and end up in the same state.
2. the function has been *linearized* by the transformation. In this case the invocation at the linear side will reduce to an invocation of an *aux*-function and it will not produce new pairs nor new names. The corresponding reduction in $\langle \mathbb{V}_1, \mathsf{L}_1 \rangle$ is a zero-step reduction. It is easy to verify that $\langle \mathbb{V}_1, \mathsf{L}_1 \rangle \sqsupseteq_{\text{lin}} \langle \mathbb{V}'_2, \mathsf{L}'_2 \rangle$.

Inductive case. We consider only the case in which the selected function is an *aux*-function. The other case is as in the base case. Let

$$\langle \mathbb{V}_1^{(n)}, \mathfrak{L}_1^{(n)}[\mathtt{f}(\widetilde{v}_1)] \cdots [\mathtt{f}(\widetilde{v}_k)] \rangle$$
$$\sqsupseteq_{\text{lin}} \quad \langle \mathbb{V}_2^{(n)}, \mathfrak{L}_2^{(n)}[\mathtt{f}^{aux}(\widetilde{u}_1, \cdots, \widetilde{u}_h)] \rangle$$

Without loss of generality we can assume that $\mathfrak{L}_1^{(n)}$ does not contain other invocations to $\mathtt{f}$ and the "linearized to" relationship makes $\mathtt{f}(\widetilde{v}_1) \& \cdots \& \mathtt{f}(\widetilde{v}_k)$ correspond to $\mathtt{f}^{aux}(\widetilde{u}_1, \cdots, \widetilde{u}_h)$. Then we have

$$\langle \mathbb{V}_2^{(n)}, \mathfrak{L}_2^{(n)}[\mathtt{f}^{aux}(\widetilde{u}_1, \cdots, \widetilde{u}_h)] \rangle \longrightarrow$$
$$\langle \mathbb{V}_2^{(n)} \oplus \widetilde{u}_1, \cdots, \widetilde{u}_h {<} \widetilde{w}, \mathfrak{L}_2^{(n)}[\mathsf{L}_{\mathtt{f}^{aux}}[\widetilde{w}/\widetilde{z}][\widetilde{u}_1, \cdots, \widetilde{u}_h/\widetilde{y}_1, \cdots, \widetilde{y}_h]] \rangle$$

where, $\mathbf{f}^{aux}(\widetilde{y}_1, \cdots, \widetilde{y}_h) = \mathtt{L}_{\mathbf{f}^{aux}}$, $var(\mathtt{L}_{\mathbf{f}^{aux}}) \backslash \widetilde{y}_1 \cdots \widetilde{y}_h = \widetilde{z}$ and $\widetilde{w}$ are fresh names. By construction,

$$\mathtt{L}_{\mathbf{f}^{aux}} = \mathbf{f}^{aux}(\widetilde{y}_1'[\widetilde{y}_1/\widetilde{y}], \cdots, \widetilde{y}_k'[\widetilde{y}_k/\widetilde{y}]) \, \& \, \&_{i \in 1..k}(\flat_{\mathbf{f}}(\mathtt{L}_{\mathbf{f}})[\widetilde{y}_i/\widetilde{y}])$$

where $\mathbf{f}(\widetilde{y}) = \mathcal{L}_{\mathbf{f}}[\mathbf{f}(\widetilde{y}_1')] \cdots [\mathbf{f}(\widetilde{y}_k')] = \mathtt{L}_{\mathbf{f}}$ and $\mathbf{f} \notin \mathcal{L}_{\mathbf{f}}$.

The corresponding reduction steps of $\langle \mathtt{V}_1^{(n)}, \mathfrak{L}_1^{(n)}[\mathbf{f}(\widetilde{v}_1)] \cdots [\mathbf{f}(\widetilde{v}_k)] \rangle$ are the following ones:

$$\langle \mathtt{V}_1^{(n)}, \mathfrak{L}_1^{(n)}[\mathbf{f}(\widetilde{v}_1)] \cdots [\mathbf{f}(\widetilde{v}_k)] \rangle \xrightarrow{\mathbf{f}(\widetilde{v}_1)} \cdots \xrightarrow{\mathbf{f}(\widetilde{v}_k)}$$
$$\langle \mathtt{V}_1^{(n)} \oplus \widetilde{v}_1 < \widetilde{w}_1 \oplus \cdots \oplus \widetilde{v}_k < \widetilde{w}_k, \; \mathfrak{L}_1^{(n)}[\mathtt{L}_{\mathbf{f}}[\widetilde{v}_1/\widetilde{y}]] \cdots [\mathtt{L}_{\mathbf{f}}[\widetilde{v}_k/\widetilde{y}]] \rangle$$

and $\widetilde{w}_i$ are the fresh names created by the invocation $\mathbf{f}(\widetilde{v}_i)$, $1 \leqslant i \leqslant k$. We need to show that:

$$\langle \mathtt{V}_1^{(n)} \oplus \widetilde{v}_1 < \widetilde{w}_1 \oplus \cdots \oplus \widetilde{v}_k < \widetilde{w}_k, \; \mathfrak{L}_1^{(n)}[\mathtt{L}_{\mathbf{f}}[\widetilde{v}_1/\widetilde{y}]] \cdots [\mathtt{L}_{\mathbf{f}}[\widetilde{v}_k/\widetilde{y}]] \rangle$$
$$\sqsupseteq_{\mathtt{lin}}$$
$$\langle \mathtt{V}_2^{(n)} \oplus \widetilde{u}_1, \cdots, \widetilde{u}_h < \widetilde{w}, \; \mathfrak{L}_2^{(n)}[\mathtt{L}_{\mathbf{f}}^{aux}] \rangle$$

where

$$\mathtt{L}_{\mathbf{f}}^{aux} = \mathbf{f}^{aux}(\widetilde{y}_1'[\widetilde{u}_1/\widetilde{y}], \cdots, \widetilde{y}_k'[\widetilde{u}_k/\widetilde{y}]) \, \& \, \mathtt{L}^{aux} \text{ and } \mathtt{L}^{aux} = \&_{i \in 1..k}(\flat_{\mathbf{f}}(\mathtt{L}_{\mathbf{f}})[\widetilde{u}_i/\widetilde{y}])[\widetilde{w}/\widetilde{z}].$$

To this aim we observe that:

- for every $1 \leqslant k' \leqslant k$ there exists h' such that $\sigma(\widetilde{v}_{k'}) = \widetilde{u}_{h'}$; moreover $\widetilde{w} = \sigma(\widetilde{w_1}) = \cdots = \sigma(\widetilde{w_k})$. This satisfies condition _1_ of Definition 11;
- if $(a, b) \in \mathtt{L}_{\mathbf{f}}[\widetilde{v}_i/\widetilde{y}]$, with $a, b \in \widetilde{w}_i, \widetilde{v}_i$, then $(\sigma(a), \sigma(b)) \in \flat_{\mathbf{f}}(\mathtt{L}_{\mathbf{f}})[\widetilde{u}_i/\widetilde{y}][\widetilde{w}/\widetilde{z}]$, being σ defined as in the previous item, therefore $\sigma(a), \sigma(b) \in \widetilde{w}, \widetilde{u}_i$. Notice that, due to the $\&_{i \in 1..k}$ composition in the body of $\mathbf{f}^{aux}$, two pairs sequentially composed in $\mathtt{L}_{\mathbf{f}}$ may end up in parallel (through σ). The converse never happens. Therefore condition _2_ of Definition 11 is satisfied.
- if $\mathbf{g}(\widetilde{a}) \in \mathtt{L}_{\mathbf{f}}$ we can reason as in the previous item. We notice that function invocations $\mathbf{g}(\widetilde{u})$ that have no counterpart (through σ) in $\mathtt{L}_{\mathbf{f}}[\widetilde{v}_i/\widetilde{y}]$ may be cointained in $\&_{i \in 1..k}(\flat_{\mathbf{f}}(\mathtt{L}_{\mathbf{f}})[\widetilde{u}_i/\widetilde{y}])[\widetilde{w}/\widetilde{z}]$. We do not have to mind about them because the lemma guarantees the converse containment.
- in $\mathtt{L}_{\mathbf{f}}[\widetilde{v}_i/\widetilde{y}]$ we have k new invocations of $\mathbf{f}(\widetilde{b}_{i,1}) \cdots \mathbf{f}(\widetilde{b}_{i,k})$, where $\widetilde{b}_{i,j} = \widetilde{y}_j'[\widetilde{v}_i/\widetilde{y}][\widetilde{w}_j/\widetilde{z}]$. Therefore in the pseudolinear lam we have k^2 invocations of $\mathbf{f}$, while in the corresponding linear lam we find just one invocation of $\mathbf{f}^{aux}(\widetilde{y}_1'[\widetilde{u}_1/\widetilde{y}][\widetilde{w}/\widetilde{z}], \cdots, \widetilde{y}_k'[\widetilde{u}_k/\widetilde{y}][\widetilde{w}/\widetilde{z}])$. We notice that the surjection σ is such that $(\widetilde{y}_j'[\widetilde{u}_j/\widetilde{y}][\widetilde{w}/\widetilde{z}] = \sigma(\widetilde{b}_{1,j}) = \cdots = \sigma(\widetilde{b}_{k,j})$, with $1 \leqslant j \leqslant k$. This, together with the previous item, satisfies condition _3_ of Definition 11.

Lemma 3. _Let_ $\langle \mathtt{V}_1, \mathtt{L}_1 \rangle \sqsupseteq_{\mathtt{lin}} \langle \mathtt{V}_2, \mathtt{L}_2 \rangle$ _and_ $\langle \mathtt{V}_1, \mathtt{L}_1 \rangle \longrightarrow^* \langle \mathtt{V}_1', \mathtt{L}_1' \rangle$. _Then there are_ $\langle \mathtt{V}_1', \mathtt{L}_1' \rangle \longrightarrow^* \langle \mathtt{V}_1'', \mathtt{L}_1'' \rangle$ _and_ $\langle \mathtt{V}_2, \mathtt{L}_2 \rangle \longrightarrow^* \langle \mathtt{V}_2', \mathtt{L}_2' \rangle$ _such that_ $\langle \mathtt{V}_1'', \mathtt{L}_1'' \rangle \sqsupseteq_{\mathtt{lin}} \langle \mathtt{V}_2', \mathtt{L}_2' \rangle$

Proof. A straightforward induction on the length of $\langle \mathbb{V}_1, L_1 \rangle \longrightarrow^* \langle \mathbb{V}_1', L_1' \rangle$. In the inductive step, we need to expand the recursive invocations "at a same level" in order to mimic the behavior of functions f^{aux}.

Theorem 4. *Let $\mathcal{L}_1$ be a pseudo-linear program and $\mathcal{L}_2$ be the result of the transformations in Table 1. If a saturated state of $\mathcal{L}_2$ has no circularity then no state of $\mathcal{L}_1$ has a circularity.*

Proof. The transformations $\overset{pl \mapsto l}{\Longmapsto}_1$ and $\overset{pl \mapsto l}{\Longmapsto}_2$ perform expansions and do not introduce inaccuracies. By Lemma 2, for every $\langle \mathbb{V}_2, L_2 \rangle$ reached by evaluating $\mathcal{L}_2$, there is $\langle \mathbb{V}_1, L_1 \rangle$ that is reached by evaluating $\mathcal{L}_1$ such that $\langle \mathbb{V}_1, L_1 \rangle \ni_{lin} \langle \mathbb{V}_2, L_2 \rangle$. This guarantees that every circularity in $\langle \mathbb{V}_1, L_1 \rangle$ is also present in $\langle \mathbb{V}_2, L_2 \rangle$. We conclude by Lemma 3 and Theorem 2.

We observe that, our analysis returns that the `fibonacci` program is circularity-free.

C.2   The General Case

In non-pseudo-linear recursive programs, more than one mutual recursive function may have several recursive histories. The transformation $\overset{npl \mapsto pl}{\Longmapsto}$ in Table 2 takes a non-pseudo-linear recursive program and returns a program where the "non-pseudo-linearity" is simpler. Repeatedly applying the transformation, at the end, one obtains a pseudo-linear recursive program.

More precisely, let $\left(f_1(\widetilde{x_1}) = L_1, \cdots, f_\ell(\widetilde{x_\ell}) = L_\ell, L\right)$ be a non-pseudo-linear recursive program. Therefore, there are at least two functions with more than one recursive history. One of this function is f_j, which is the one that is being explored by the rule $\overset{npl \mapsto pl}{\Longmapsto}$. Let also f_i be another function such that $closure(f_j) = closure(f_i)$ (this f_i must exists otherwise the program would be already pseudo-linear recursive). These constraints are those listed in the first line of the premises of the rule. The idea of this transformation is to defer the invocations of the functions in $\{head(\alpha_1 f_j), \cdots, head(\alpha_{h+1} f_j)\} \backslash f_i$, i.e., the functions different from f_i that can be invoked within f_j's body, to the body of the function f_i. The meaning of the second and third lines of the premises of the rule is to identify the p_k different invocations of these m functions ($k \geqslant m$). Notice that every $\alpha_1, \cdots, \alpha_{h+1}$ could be empty, meaning that f_j is directly called. At this point, what we need to do is (1) to store the arguments of each invocation of $f_{i_1}, \cdots, f_{i_m}$ into those of an invocation of f_i – actually, a suitable tuple of them, thus the arity of f_i is augmented correspondingly – and (2) to perform suitable expansions in the body of f_i. In order to augment the arguments of the invocations of f_i that occur in the other parts of the program, we use the auxiliary rule $\overset{f_i, n}{\Longmapsto}$ that extends every invocation of f_i with n additional arguments that are always fresh names. The fourth line of the premises calculates the number n of additional arguments, based on the number of arguments of the functions that are going to be moved into f_i's body. The last step, described in the last

Table 2. Non-pseudo-linear to pseudo-linear transformation

$$\frac{\mathtt{f} \notin \mathcal{L} \qquad \widetilde{z_1}, \cdots, \widetilde{z_m} \ \textit{are n-tuple of fresh names}}{\mathcal{L}[\mathtt{f}(\widetilde{u_1})] \cdots [\mathtt{f}(\widetilde{u_m})] \xLongrightarrow{\mathtt{f}, n} \mathcal{L}[\mathtt{f}(\widetilde{u_1}, \widetilde{z_1})] \cdots [\mathtt{f}(\widetilde{u_m}, \widetilde{z_m})]}$$

$$\frac{\begin{array}{c} rechis(\mathtt{f}_j) = \{\mathtt{f}_j \mathtt{f}_i \alpha_0, \mathtt{f}_j \alpha_1, \cdots, \mathtt{f}_j \alpha_{h+1}\} \qquad \mathtt{f} \in \mathtt{f}_i \alpha_0 \qquad \sharp(rechis(\mathtt{f})) > 1 \\ \{\mathtt{f}_{i_1}, \cdots, \mathtt{f}_{i_m}\} = \{head(\alpha_1 \mathtt{f}_j), \cdots, head(\alpha_{h+1} \mathtt{f}_j)\} \backslash \mathtt{f}_i \\ \mathtt{L}_j = \mathcal{L}[\mathtt{f}_{p_1}(\widetilde{u_1})] \cdots [\mathtt{f}_{p_k}(\widetilde{u_k})] \qquad \{\mathtt{f}_{p_1}, \cdots, \mathtt{f}_{p_k}\} = \{\mathtt{f}_{i_1}, \cdots, \mathtt{f}_{i_m}\} \qquad \mathtt{f}_{i_1}, \cdots, \mathtt{f}_{i_m} \notin \mathcal{L} \\ n = \sharp(\widetilde{u_1} \cdots \widetilde{u_k}) \qquad (\mathtt{L}_h \xLongrightarrow{\mathtt{f}_i, n} \mathtt{L}_h')^{h \in \{1, \cdots, \ell+1\}} \qquad \mathtt{L}_j' = \mathcal{L}'[\mathtt{f}_{i_1}(\widetilde{u_1})] \cdots [\mathtt{f}_{i_m}(\widetilde{u_k})] \\ \widetilde{z_1^1}, \cdots, \widetilde{z_k^1}, \cdots, \widetilde{z_1^k}, \cdots, \widetilde{z_k^k}, \widetilde{z_1}, \cdots, \widetilde{z_k}, \ \textit{are fresh} \\ \mathtt{L}_j'' = \mathcal{L}'[\mathtt{f}_i(\widetilde{z_1^1}, \widetilde{u_1}, \widetilde{z_2^1}, \cdots, \widetilde{z_1^1})] \cdots [\mathtt{f}_i(\widetilde{z_1^k}, \cdots, \widetilde{z_k^k}, \widetilde{u_k})] \end{array}}{\begin{array}{c}(\mathtt{f}_1(\widetilde{x_1}) = \mathtt{L}_1, \cdots \mathtt{f}_i(\widetilde{x_i}) = \mathtt{L}_i, \cdots, \mathtt{f}_j(\widetilde{x_j}) = \mathtt{L}_j, \cdots, \mathtt{f}_\ell(\widetilde{x_\ell}) = \mathtt{L}_\ell, \mathtt{L}_{\ell+1}) \xLongrightarrow{\text{npl} \mapsto \text{pl}} \\ (\mathtt{f}_1(\widetilde{x_1}) = \mathtt{L}_1', \cdots \mathtt{f}_i(\widetilde{x_i}, \widetilde{z_1}, \cdots, \widetilde{z_k}) = \mathtt{L}_i' \& (\&_{q \in 1..k} \mathtt{f}_{p_q}(\widetilde{z_q})), \cdots, \mathtt{f}_j(\widetilde{x_j}) = \mathtt{L}_j'', \cdots, \mathtt{f}_\ell(\widetilde{x_\ell}) = \mathtt{L}_\ell', \mathtt{L}_{\ell+1}')\end{array}}$$

line of the premises of the rule, is to replace the invocations of the functions $\mathtt{f}_{i_1}, \cdots, \mathtt{f}_{i_m}$ with invocations of $\mathtt{f}_i$. Notice that, in each invocation, the position of the actual arguments is different. In the body of $\mathtt{f}_i$, after the transformation, the invocations of those functions will be performed passing the right arguments. For example, the $\mathtt{f}''\mathtt{g}''$-program

$$\left(\begin{array}{l} \mathtt{f}''(x, y) = (x, z) \& \mathtt{f}''(y, z) + \mathtt{g}''(y, x), \\ \mathtt{g}''(x, y) = (y, x) \& \mathtt{f}''(y, z) \& \mathtt{g}''(z, x), \\ \mathtt{f}''(x_1, x_2) \end{array}\right)$$

is rewritten into

$$\left(\begin{array}{l} \mathtt{f}''(x, y) = (x, z) \& \mathtt{g}''(x', y', y, z) + \mathtt{g}''(y, x, z', z''), \\ \mathtt{g}''(x, y, u, v) = (y, x) \& \mathtt{f}''(y, z) \& \mathtt{g}''(z, x, x', y') \& \mathtt{f}''(u, v), \\ \mathtt{f}''(x_1, x_2) \end{array}\right).$$

The invocation $\mathtt{f}''(y, z)$ is moved into the body of $\mathtt{g}''$. The function $\mathtt{g}''$ has an augmented arity, so that its first two arguments refer to the arguments of the invocations of $\mathtt{g}''$ in the original program, and the last two arguments refer to the invocation of $\mathtt{f}''$. Looking at the body of $\mathtt{g}''$, the unchanged part (with the augmented arity of $\mathtt{g}''$) covers the first two arguments; whilst the last two arguments are only used for a new invocation of $\mathtt{f}''$.

The correctness of $\xLongrightarrow{\text{npl} \mapsto \text{pl}}$ is demonstrated in a similar way to the proof of the correctness of $\xLongrightarrow{\text{pl} \mapsto 1}_3$. We begin by defining a correspondence between states of a non-pseudo-linear program and those of a pseudo-linear one.

Definition 12. *Let $\mathcal{L}_2$ be the pseudo-linear program returned by the transformation of Table 2 applied to $\mathcal{L}_1$. A state $\langle \mathsf{V}_1, \mathsf{L}_1 \rangle$ of $\mathcal{L}_1$ is pseudo-linearized to a state $\langle \mathsf{V}_2, \mathsf{L}_2 \rangle$ of $\mathcal{L}_2$, written $\langle \mathsf{V}_1, \mathsf{L}_1 \rangle \ni_{\text{pl}} \langle \mathsf{V}_2, \mathsf{L}_2 \rangle$, if there exists a surjection σ such that:*

1. if $(x, y) \in \mathsf{V}_1$ then $(\sigma(x), \sigma(y)) \in \mathsf{V}_2$.
2. if $\flat(\mathsf{L}_1) = \mathsf{T}_1 + \cdots + \mathsf{T}_m$ and $\flat(\mathsf{L}_2) = \mathsf{T}_1' + \cdots + \mathsf{T}_n'$, then for every $1 \leqslant i \leqslant m$, there exists $1 \leqslant j \leqslant n$, such that $\sigma(\mathsf{T}_i) \in \mathsf{T}_j'$;

3. *if* $f(\tilde{x}) \in L_1$ *then either (1)* $f(\sigma(\tilde{x}))$ *in* L_2 *or (2) there is* $f(\tilde{y}_1 \cdots \tilde{y}_k)$ *in* L_2 *such that, for some* $1 \leqslant i \leqslant k$, $\sigma(\tilde{x}) = \tilde{y}_i$;

We use the same notational convention for contexts as in Lemma 2.

Lemma 4. *Let* $\langle V_1, L_1 \rangle \ni_{pl} \langle V_2, L_2 \rangle$. *Then,* $\langle V_1, L_1 \rangle \longrightarrow \langle V_1', L_1' \rangle$ *implies there exists* $\langle V_2, L_2 \rangle \longrightarrow^+ \langle V_2', L_2' \rangle$ *such that* $\langle V_1', L_1' \rangle \ni_{pl} \langle V_2', L_2' \rangle$

Proof. Base case. L_1 is the main lam of the nonlinear program, and L_2 its pseudolinear transformation.

$$L_1 = \mathcal{L}_1[f_1(\tilde{u}_1)] \cdots [f_m(\tilde{u}_k)],$$

where $\mathcal{L}_1$ does not contain any other function invocations, and $m \leqslant k$, meaning that some of the f_i, $1 \leqslant i \leqslant m$, can be invoked more than once on different parameters.

After the transformation, L_2 contains the same pairs as L_1 and the same function invocations, but with possibly more arguments:

$$L_2 = \mathcal{L}_1[f_1(\tilde{u}_1, \tilde{z}_1)] \cdots [f_m(\tilde{u}_k, \tilde{z}_k)].$$

Notice that some of the $\tilde{z}_j$, $1 \leqslant j \leqslant k$, may be empty if the corresponding function has not been expanded during the transformation. Moreover V_1 and V_2 contains only the identity relations on the arguments, so we have $V_1 \subseteq V_2$. Therefore, all conditions of definition 12 are trivially verified.

Inductive case. We have

$$L_1 = \mathcal{L}_1[f_1(\tilde{u}_1)] \cdots [f_m(\tilde{u}_k)],$$

where $\mathcal{L}_1$ does not contain any other function invocations, and $m \leqslant k$, meaning that some of the f_i, $1 \leqslant i \leqslant m$, can be invoked more than once on different parameters.

We have

$$L_2 = \mathcal{L}_2[f_1(\tilde{u}_1, \tilde{z}_1)] \cdots [f_m(\tilde{u}_k, \tilde{z}_k)].$$

where $\mathcal{L}_2$ may contain other function invocations, but by inductive hypothesis we know that Definition 12 is verified. In particular condition *3* guarantees that at least the invocations of $f_1, \ldots, f_m$, with suitable arguments, are in L_2.

Now, let us consider the reduction

$$\langle V_1, L_1 \rangle \longrightarrow \langle V_1', L_1' \rangle.$$

Without loss of generality, we can assume the reduction step performed an invocation of function $f_1(\tilde{u}_1)$.

We have different cases:

1. the function's lam L_{f_1} has not been modified by the transformation. In this case the result follows trivially.

2. the function's lam L_{f_1} has been affected only in that some function invocations in it have an updated arity. Meaning that it was only trasformed by $\overset{g,l}{\Longmapsto}$, for some g and l, as a side effect of other function expansions. It follows that $b(L_{f_1}) = b(L'_{f_1})$, where L'_{f_1} is the body of f_1 after the transoformation has been applied. This satisfies condition 2 of Definition 12. Those function invocations that have not been modified satisfy trivially the condition 3 of Definition 12. Regarding the other function invocations we have, by construction, that if $g(\tilde{x}) \in L_{f_1}$ then $g(\tilde{x}, \tilde{y}) \in L'_{f_1}$, where $\tilde{y}$ are fresh names. This satisfies condition 3 of Definition 12, as well. As for condition 1, we have

$$V'_1 = V_1 \oplus (\tilde{u}_1 < \tilde{w}_1),$$

where $\tilde{w}$ are fresh names created in L_{f_1}, and

$$V'_2 = V_2 \oplus (\tilde{u}_1, \tilde{z}_1 < \tilde{w}_1, \tilde{y}_1, \cdots, \tilde{y}_s),$$

where $\tilde{y}_1, \cdots, \tilde{y}_s$ are the fresh names augmenting the function arities within L'_{f_1}. We choose the same fresh names $\tilde{w}_1$ and condition 1 is satisfied.

3. the function's lam L_{f_1} has been subject of the expansion of a function. Let

$$L_{f_1} = \mathcal{L}_{f_1}[g_1(\tilde{v}_1)] \cdots [g_h(\tilde{v}_n)],$$

where $\mathcal{L}_{f_1}$ contains only pairs, then, assuming without loss of generality that g_1 was expanded:

$$L'_{f_1} = \mathcal{L}_{f_1}[g_1(\tilde{v}_1, \tilde{z}_1^1, \ldots, \tilde{z}_r^1)] \cdots [g_1(\tilde{v}_n, \tilde{z}_1^r, \ldots, \tilde{z}_r^r)],$$

where r is obtained by subtracting from the number of invocations n the number of occurrences of invocations of g_1 in L'_{f_1}.

Now, the psedulinear program has to perform the r invocations of g_1 that were not present in the original program, since they have been replaced r invocations of $g_2 \cdots g_h$, in order to reveal the actual invocations $g_2 \cdots g_h$ that has been delegated to g_1 body. By construction, the arguments of the invocations where preserved by the transformation, so that if $g_2(\tilde{x})$ is produced by reduction of the nonlinear program, then the pseudolinear program will produce $g_2(\tilde{x}, \tilde{y})$, with $\tilde{y}$ fresh and possibily empty. This satisfy condition 3 of Definition 12.

However the body of g_1 may have been transformed in a similar way by expanding another method, let us say g_2. Then all the invocations of g_2 in g_1's body that corresponds to the previously delegated function invocations $g_2 \cdots g_h$ have to be invoked as well. This procedure has to be iterated until all the corresponding invocations are encountered. Each step of reduction will produce spurious pairs and function invocations, but all of these will be on different new names.

Lemma 5. *Let* $\langle V_1, L_1 \rangle \sqsupseteq_{pl} \langle V_2, L_2 \rangle$ *and* $\langle V_1, L_1 \rangle \longrightarrow^* \langle V'_1, L'_1 \rangle$. *Then there are* $\langle V'_1, L'_1 \rangle \longrightarrow^* \langle V''_1, L''_1 \rangle$ *and* $\langle V_2, L_2 \rangle \longrightarrow^* \langle V'_2, L'_2 \rangle$ *such that* $\langle V''_1, L''_1 \rangle \sqsupseteq_{pl} \langle V'_2, L'_2 \rangle$

Proof. A straightforward induction on the length of $\langle \mathbb{V}_1, L_1 \rangle \longrightarrow^* \langle \mathbb{V}_1', L_1' \rangle$.

Every preliminary result is in place for the correctness of the transformation $\overset{\mathrm{npl} \mapsto \mathrm{pl}}{\Longrightarrow}$.

Theorem 5. *Let $\mathcal{L}_1$ be a non-pseudo-linear program and $\mathcal{L}_2$ be the result of the transformations in Table 2. If $\mathcal{L}_2$ is circularity-free then $\mathcal{L}_1$ is circularity-free.*

Proof. By Lemma 4, for every $\langle \mathbb{V}_1, L_1 \rangle$ reached by evaluating $\mathcal{L}_1$, there is $\langle \mathbb{V}_2, L_2 \rangle$ that is reached by evaluating $\mathcal{L}_2$ such that $\langle \mathbb{V}_1, L_1 \rangle \ni_{\mathrm{pl}} \langle \mathbb{V}_2, L_2 \rangle$. This guarantees that every circularity in $\langle \mathbb{V}_1, L_1 \rangle$ is also present in $\langle \mathbb{V}_2, L_2 \rangle$. We conclude by Lemma 5.

Counterexample Generation
for Discrete-Time Markov Models:
An Introductory Survey

Erika Ábrahám[1], Bernd Becker[2], Christian Dehnert[1], Nils Jansen[1],
Joost-Pieter Katoen[1], and Ralf Wimmer[2]

[1] RWTH Aachen University, Germany
{abraham,dehnert,nils.jansen,katoen}@cs.rwth-aachen.de
[2] Albert-Ludwigs-University Freiburg, Germany
{becker,wimmer}@informatik.uni-freiburg.de

Abstract. This paper is an introductory survey of available methods for the computation and representation of probabilistic counterexamples for discrete-time Markov chains and probabilistic automata. In contrast to traditional model checking, probabilistic counterexamples are sets of finite paths with a critical probability mass. Such counterexamples are not obtained as a by-product of model checking, but by dedicated algorithms. We define what probabilistic counterexamples are and present approaches how they can be generated. We discuss methods based on path enumeration, the computation of critical subsystems, and the generation of critical command sets, both, using explicit and symbolic techniques.

1 Introduction

The importance of counterexamples. One of the main strengths of model checking is its ability to automatically generate a *counterexample* in case a model refutes a given temporal logic formula [1]. Counterexamples are the most effective feature to convince system engineers about the value of formal verification [2]. First and foremost, counterexamples provide essential diagnostic information for *debugging* purposes. A counterexample-guided simulation of the model at hand typically gives good insight into the reason of refutation. The same applies when using counterexamples as witnesses showing the reason of fulfilling a property. Counterexamples are effectively used in *model-based testing* [3]. In this setting, models are used as blueprint for system implementations, i.e., the conformance of an implementation is checked against a high-level model. Here, counterexamples obtained by verifying the blueprint model act as test cases that, after an adaptation, can be issued on the system-under-test. Counterexamples are at the core of obtaining feasible *schedules* in planning applications. Here, the idea is to verify the negation of the property of interest—it is never possible to reach a given target state (typically the state in which all jobs have finished their execution) within k steps—and use the counterexample as an example schedule

M. Bernardo et al. (Eds.): SFM 2014, LNCS 8483, pp. 65–121, 2014.

illustrating that all jobs can complete within k steps. This principle is exploited in e. g., task scheduling in timed model checking [4]. A more recent application is the synthesis of *attacks* from counterexamples for showing how the confidentiality of programs can be broken [5]. These so-called refinement attacks are important, tricky, and are notorious in practice. Automatically generated counterexamples act as attacks showing how multi-threaded programs under a given scheduler can leak information. Last but not least, counterexamples play an important role also in *counterexample-guided abstraction refinement (CEGAR)* [6], a successful technique in software verification. Spurious counterexamples resulting from verifying abstract models are exploited to refine the (too coarse) abstraction. This abstraction-refinement cycle is repeated until either a concrete counterexample is found or the property can be proven.

Counterexample generation. For these reasons, counterexamples have received considerable attention in the model checking community. Important issues have been (and to some extent still are) how counterexamples can be *generated* efficiently, preferably in an on-the-fly manner during model checking, how memory consumption can be kept small, and how counterexamples themselves can be kept succinct, and be *represented* at the model description level (rather than in terms of the model itself). The *shape* of a counterexample depends on the property specification language and the checked formula. The violation of *linear-time safety* properties is indicated by finite paths that end in a "bad" state. Therefore, for logics such as LTL, typically finite paths through the model suffice. Although LTL model checking is based on (nested) depth-first search, LTL model checkers such as SPIN incorporate breadth-first search algorithms to generate *shortest* counterexamples, i. e., paths of minimal length. The violation of *liveness* properties, instead, require infinite paths ending in a cyclic behavior under which something "good" will never happen. These lassos are finitely represented by concatenating the path until reaching the cycle with a single cycle traversal. For *branching-time* logics such as CTL, such finite paths suffice as counterexamples for a subclass of universally quantified formulas. To cover a broader spectrum of formulas, though, more general shapes are necessary, such as tree-like counterexamples [7]. As model-checking suffers from the combinatorial growth of the number of states—the so-called state space explosion problem—various successful techniques have been developed to combat this. Most of these techniques, in particular *symbolic* model checking based on binary decision diagrams (BDDs, for short), have been extended with symbolic counterexample generation algorithms [8]. Prominent model checkers such as SPIN and NuSMV include powerful facilities to generate counterexamples in various formats. Such counterexamples are typically provided at the modeling level, like a diagram indicating how the change of model variables yields a property violation, or a message sequence chart illustrating the failing scenario. Substantial efforts have been made to generate succinct counterexamples, often at the price of an increased time complexity. A survey of practical and theoretical results on counterexample generation in model checking can be found in [2].

Probabilistic model checking. This paper surveys the state of the art in counterexample generation in the setting of *probabilistic* model checking [9–11]. Probabilistic model checking is a technique to verify system models in which transitions are equipped with random information. Popular models are discrete- and continuous-time Markov chains (DTMCs and CTMCs, respectively), and variants thereof which exhibit non-determinism such as probabilistic automata (PA). Efficient model-checking algorithms for these models have been developed, implemented in a variety of software tools, and applied to case studies from various application areas ranging from randomized distributed algorithms, computer systems and security protocols to biological systems and quantum computing. The crux of probabilistic model checking is to appropriately combine techniques from numerical mathematics and operations research with standard reachability analysis and model-checking techniques. In this way, properties such as "the (maximal) probability to reach a set of bad states is at most 0.1" can be automatically checked up to a user-defined precision. Markovian models comprising millions of states can be checked rather fast by dedicated tools such as PRISM [12] and MRMC [13]. These tools are currently being extended with counterexample generation facilities to enable the possibility to provide useful diagnostic feedback in case a property is violated. More details on probabilistic model checking can be found in, e. g., [9, 14, 15].

Counterexamples in a probabilistic setting. Let us consider a finite DTMC, i. e., a Kripke structure whose transitions are labeled with discrete probabilities. Assume that the property "the (maximal) probability to reach a set of bad states is at most 0.1" is violated. That means that the accumulated probability of all paths starting in the initial state s_0 and eventually reaching a bad state exceeds 10%. This can be witnessed by a set of finite paths all starting in s_0 and ending in a bad state whose total probability exceeds 0.1. Counterexamples are thus *sets of finite paths*, or viewed differently, a finite tree rooted at s_0 whose leafs are all bad. Evidently, one can take all such paths (i.e, the complete tree) as a counterexample, but typically succinct diagnostic information is called for. There are basically two approaches to accomplish this: *path enumeration* and *critical subsystems*. In contrast to standard model checking, these algorithmic approaches are employed after the model-checking phase in which the refutation of the property at hand has been established. Up to now, there is no algorithm to generate probabilistic counterexamples during model checking.

Path enumeration. For DTMCs, a counterexample can be obtained by explicitly enumerating the paths comprising a counterexample. A typical strategy is to start with the most probable paths and generate paths in order of descending probability. This procedure stops once the total probability of all generated paths exceeds the given bound, ensuring minimality in terms of number of paths. Algorithmically, this can be efficiently done by casting this problem as a *k shortest path* problem [16, 17] where k is not fixed a priori but determined on the fly during the computation. This method yields a *smallest* counterexample whose probability mass is maximal—and thus most discriminative—among all minimal counterexamples. This approach can be extended to until properties, bounded versions thereof, ω-regular properties, and is applicable to non-strict upper and lower bounds on the admissible probability. Whereas [16, 17] exploit existing k shortest path algorithms with pseudo-polynomial complexity (in k), [18] uses *heuristic search* to obtain most probable paths. Path enumeration techniques have also been tackled with *symbolic* approaches like *bounded model checking* [19] extended with *satisfiability modulo theories (SMT)* techniques [20], and using *BDD-techniques* [21]. The work [22] proposes to compute and represent counterexamples in a succinct way by *regular expressions*. Inspired by [23], these regular expressions are computed using a state elimination approach from automata theory that is guided by a k shortest paths search. Another compaction of counterexamples is based on the abstraction of *strongly-connected components* (SCCs, for short) of a DTMC, resulting in an acyclic model in which counterexamples can be determined with reduced effort [24]. An approach to compute counterexamples for non-deterministic models was proposed in [25].

Critical subsystems. Alternatively to generating paths, here a fragment of the discrete-time Markov model at hand is determined such that in the resulting submodel a bad state is reached with a likelihood exceeding the threshold. Such a fragment is called a *critical subsystem*, which is *minimal* if it is minimal in terms of number of states or transitions, and *smallest* if it is minimal and has a maximal probability to reach a bad state under all minimal critical subsystems. A critical subsystem induces a counterexample by the set of its paths. Determining smallest critical subsystems for probabilistic automata is an NP-complete problem [26], which can be solved using mixed integer linear programming techniques [27, 28]. Another option is to exploit k *shortest path* [29] and *heuristic search* [30] methods to obtain (not necessarily smallest or minimal) critical subsystems. *Symbolic* approaches towards finding small critical subsystems have been developed in [31, 32]. The approach [24] has been pursued further by doing SCC reduction in a hierarchical fashion yielding *hierarchical counterexamples* [29].

Modeling-language-based counterexamples. Typically, huge and complex Markov models are described using a *high-level modeling language*. Having a human-readable specification language, it seems natural that a user should be pointed to the part of the high-level model description which causes the error, instead of getting counterexamples at the state-space level. This has recently initiated finding *smallest critical command sets*, i. e., the minimal fragment of a model description such that the induced (not necessarily minimal) Markov model violates the property at hand, thereby maximizing the probability to reach bad states. For PRISM, models are described in a stochastic version of Alur and Henzinger's reactive modules [33]. In this setting, a probabilistic automaton is typically specified as a parallel composition of modules. The behavior of a single module is described using a set of probabilistic guarded commands. Computing a smallest critical command set amounts to determining a minimal set of guarded commands that together induce a critical subsystem, with maximal probability to reach bad states under all such minimal sets. This NP-complete problem has been tackled using mixed integer linear programming [34]. This approach is not restricted to PRISM's input language, but it is also applicable to other modeling formalisms for probabilistic automata such as process algebras [35].

Tools and applications. DiPRO [36] and COMICS [37] are the only publicly available tools supporting counterexample generation for Markov models.[1] DiPRO applies directed path search to discrete- and continuous-time Markov models to compute counterexamples for the violation of PCTL or CSL properties. Although the search works on explicit model representations, the relevant model parts are built on the fly, which makes DiPRO very efficient and highly scalable. COMICS computes hierarchically abstracted and refinable critical subsystems for discrete-time Markov models. Strongly connected components are the basis for the abstraction, whereas methods to compute k shortest paths are applied in different contexts to determine critical subsystems. Probabilistic counterexamples have been used in different applications. Path-based counterexamples have been applied to guide the refinement of too coarse abstractions in CEGAR-approaches for probabilistic programs [38]. Tree-based counterexamples have been used for a similar purpose in the setting of assume-guarantee reasoning on probabilistic automata [39]. Other applications include the identification of failures in FMEA analysis [40] and the safety analysis of an airbag system [41]. Using the notion of causality, [42, 43] have developed techniques to guide the user to the most responsible causes in a counterexample once a DTMC violates a probabilistic CTL formula, whereas [44] synthesizes fault trees from probabilistic counterexamples.

Organization of this paper. This paper surveys the existing techniques for generating and representing counterexamples for discrete-time Markov models. We cover both explicit as well as symbolic techniques, and also treat the recent development of generating counterexamples at the level of model descriptions, rather than for models themselves. The focus is on a tutorial-like presentation with various illustrative examples. For a full-fledged presentation of all technical aspects as well as formal proofs we refer to the literature. Section 2 provides the necessary background on discrete-time Markov models as well as their reachability analysis. Section 3 defines what counterexamples are. Section 4 is devoted to path-based counterexamples and their applications, whereas Section 5 deals with critical subsystems. Section 6 presents the generation of smallest critical command sets in terms of the model description language. A brief description and comparison of the available tools is given in Section 7. Finally, Section 8 concludes the survey.

2   Foundations

In this section we introduce discrete-time Markov models (Section 2.1) along with probabilistic reachability properties for them (Section 2.2). For further reading we refer to, e. g., [9, 14, 15, 45].

---

[1] DiPRO is available from http://www.inf.uni-konstanz.de/soft/dipro/ and COMICS from http://www-i2.informatik.rwth-aachen.de/i2/comics/

2.1 Models

When modeling real systems using formal modeling languages, due to the complexity of the real world, we usually need to abstract away certain details of the real system. For example, Kripke structures specify a set of model states representing the states of the real-world system, and transitions between the model states modeling the execution steps of the real system. However, the model states do not store any specific information about the real system state that they represent (e. g., concrete variable values in a program). To be able to specify and analyze properties that are dependent on information not included in the model, we can define a set of *atomic propositions* and label each model state with the set of those propositions that hold in the given state.

Example 1. Assume a program declaring two Boolean variables b_1 and b_2, both with initial value *false*, and executing $b_1 := true$ and $b_2 := true$ in parallel. We use $S = \{s_0, s_1, s_2, s_3\}$ as model state set with the following encoding:

Model state	Program variable values	
s_0	$b_1 = false$	$b_2 = false$
s_1	$b_1 = true$	$b_2 = false$
s_2	$b_1 = false$	$b_2 = true$
s_3	$b_1 = true$	$b_2 = true$

We are interested in the equality of b_1 and b_2. We define an atomic proposition set $AP = \{a\}$, where a encodes the equality of b_1 and b_2, and a state labeling function $L : \{s_0, s_1, s_2, s_3\} \to 2^{\{a\}}$ mapping the set $\{a\}$ to s_0 and s_3 and the empty set $\emptyset$ to the other two states.   ■

In the following we fix a finite set AP of atomic propositions.

In systems that exhibit probabilistic behavior, the outcome of an executed action is determined probabilistically. When modeling such systems, the transitions must specify not only the successors but also the probabilities with which they are chosen, formalized by *probability distributions*.

Definition 1 (Sub-distribution, distribution, support). *A sub-distribution over a countable set S is a function $\mu : S \to [0, 1]$ such that $\sum_{s \in S} \mu(s) \leq 1$; μ is a (probability) distribution if $\sum_{s \in S} \mu(s) = 1$. The set of all sub-distributions over S is denoted by* $\mathrm{SDistr}(S)$, *the set of probability distributions by* $\mathrm{Distr}(S)$. *By* $\mathrm{supp}(\mu) = \{s \in S \mid \mu(s) > 0\}$ *we denote the support of a (sub-)distribution* μ.

Example 2. Consider again the program from Example 1 and assume that in the initial state s_0 the statement $b_1 := true$ is executed with probability 0.6 and $b_2 := true$ with probability 0.4. This is reflected by the distribution $\mu_0 : \{s_0, s_1, s_2, s_3\} \to [0, 1]$ with $\mu_0(s_1) = 0.6$, $\mu_0(s_2) = 0.4$, and $\mu_0(s_0) = \mu(s_3) = 0$. The support of the distribution is $\mathrm{supp}(\mu_0) = \{s_1, s_2\}$.

After executing $b_1 := true$, the system is in state s_1 and $b_2 := true$ will be executed with probability 1. The corresponding distribution is specified by

$\mu_1(s_3) = 1$ and $\mu_1(s_0) = \mu_1(s_1) = \mu_1(s_2) = 0$. Such a distribution, mapping the whole probability 1 to a single state, is called a *Dirac* distribution.

For state s_2, the distribution μ_2 equals μ_1. Finally for s_3, the Dirac distribution μ_3 defines a self-loop on s_3 with probability 1, modeling idling. ∎

Discrete-time Markov chains. Discrete-time Markov chains are a widely used formalism to model probabilistic behavior in a discrete-time model. State changes are modeled by discrete transitions whose probabilities are specified by (sub-)distributions as follows.

Definition 2 (Discrete-time Markov chain). *A discrete-time Markov chain (DTMC) over atomic propositions* AP *is a tuple* $\mathcal{D} = (S, s_{\mathrm{init}}, P, L)$ *with S being a countable set of states, $s_{\mathrm{init}} \subset S$ the initial state, $P : S \to \mathrm{SDistr}(S)$ the transition probability function, and L a labeling function with $L : S \to 2^{\mathrm{AP}}$.*

We often see the transition probability function $P : S \to (S \to [0,1])$ rather as being of type $P : (S \times S) \to [0,1]$ and write $P(s, s')$ instead of $P(s)(s')$.

Example 3. The system from Example 2 can be modeled by the DTMC $\mathcal{D} = (S, s_0, P, L)$, where S and L are as in Example 1 and P assigns μ_i (defined in Example 2) to s_i for each $i \in \{0, \ldots, 3\}$. This DTMC model can be graphically depicted as follows:

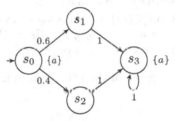

∎

Please note that in the above definition of DTMCs we generalize the standard definition and allow sub-distributions. Usually, $P(s)$ is required to be a probability distribution for all $s \in S$. We can transform a DTMC $\mathcal{D} = (S, s_{\mathrm{init}}, P, L)$ with sub-distributions into a DTMC $\alpha_{s_\perp}(\mathcal{D}) = (S', s_{\mathrm{init}}, P', L')$ with distributions using the transformation $\alpha_{s_\perp}$ with

- $S' = S \,\dot{\cup}\, \{s_\perp\}$ for a fresh sink state $s_\perp \notin S$,

- $P'(s, s') = \begin{cases} P(s, s'), & \text{for } s, s' \in S, \\ 1 - \sum_{s'' \in S} P(s, s''), & \text{for } s \in S \text{ and } s' = s_\perp, \\ 1, & \text{for } s = s' = s_\perp, \\ 0, & \text{otherwise (for } s = s_\perp \text{ and } s' \in S), \end{cases}$ and

- $L'(s) = L(s)$ for $s \in S$ and $L'(s_\perp) = \emptyset$.

According to the DTMC semantics below, the reachability probabilities in $\mathcal{D}$ and $\alpha_{s_\perp}(\mathcal{D})$ are equal for the states from S. The advantage of allowing sub-stochastic distributions is that a *subsystem* of a DTMC, determined by a subset of its states, is again a DTMC.

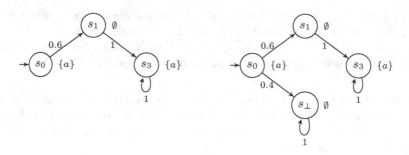

Fig. 1. Completing sub-distributions of a DTMC (cf. Example 4)

Example 4. Consider again the DTMC from Example 3. If we are only interested in the behavior for executing the statement $b_1 := true$ first, then the transition from s_0 to s_2 can be neglected. The DTMC model in this case has a sub-distribution assigned to s_0, as shown in Figure 1 on the left. We can transform this DTMC with a sub-distribution into a reachability-equivalent DTMC with distributions as shown in Figure 1 on the right.   ∎

Assume in the following a DTMC $\mathcal{D} = (S, s_{\text{init}}, P, L)$. We say that there is a *transition* (s, s') from the *source* $s \in S$ to the *successor* $s' \in S$ iff $s' \in \text{supp}(P(s))$. We say that the states in $\text{supp}(P(s))$ are the *successors* of s.

We sometimes refer to the *underlying graph* $\mathcal{G_D} = (S, E_\mathcal{D})$ of $\mathcal{D}$, with nodes S and edges $E_D = \{(s, s') \in S \times S \,|\, s' \in \text{supp}(P(s))\}$.

Example 5. The underlying graph of the DTMC from Example 3 on page 71 can be visualized as follows:

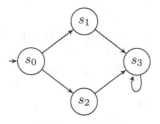

∎

A *path* of $\mathcal{D}$ is a finite or infinite sequence $\pi = s_0 s_1 \ldots$ of states $s_i \in S$ such that $s_{i+1} \in \text{supp}(P(s_i))$ for all $i \geq 0$. We say that the transitions (s_i, s_{i+1}) are *contained* in the path π, written $(s_i, s_{i+1}) \in \pi$. Starting with $i = 0$, we write $\pi[i]$ for the $(i+1)^{\text{th}}$ state s_i on path π. The *length* $|\pi|$ of a finite path $\pi = s_0 \ldots s_n$ is the number n of its transitions. The last state of π is denoted by $\text{last}(\pi) = s_n$.

By $\text{Paths}^{\mathcal{D}}_{\text{inf}}(s)$ we denote the set of all infinite paths of $\mathcal{D}$ starting in $s \in S$. Similarly, $\text{Paths}^{\mathcal{D}}_{\text{fin}}(s)$ contains all finite paths of $\mathcal{D}$ starting in $s \in S$, and $\text{Paths}^{\mathcal{D}}_{\text{fin}}(s, t)$ those starting in $s \in S$ and ending in $t \in S$. For $T \subseteq S$ we also use the notation $\text{Paths}^{\mathcal{D}}_{\text{fin}}(s, T)$ for $\bigcup_{t \in T} \text{Paths}^{\mathcal{D}}_{\text{fin}}(s, t)$. A state $t \in S$ is *reachable* from another state $s \in S$ iff $\text{Paths}^{\mathcal{D}}_{\text{fin}}(s, t) \neq \emptyset$.

Example 6. The DTMC model $\mathcal{D}$ from Example 3 on page 71 has two infinite paths starting in s_0, specified by $\text{Paths}^{\mathcal{D}}_{\inf}(s_0) = \{s_0 s_1 s_3^{\omega}, s_0 s_2 s_3^{\omega}\}$. The finite paths starting in s_0 are $\text{Paths}^{\mathcal{D}}_{\text{fin}}(s_0) = \{s_0, s_0 s_1, s_0 s_1 s_3^+, s_0 s_2, s_0 s_2 s_3^+\}$. The finite paths starting in s_0 and ending in s_3 are $\text{Paths}^{\mathcal{D}}_{\text{fin}}(s_0, s_3) = \{s_0 s_1 s_3^+, s_0 s_2 s_3^+\}$. ∎

To be able to talk about the probabilities of certain behaviors (i. e., path sets), we follow the standard way [46] to define for each state $s \in S$ a probability space $(\Omega^{\mathcal{D}}_s, \mathcal{F}^{\mathcal{D}}_s, \Pr^{\mathcal{D}}_s)$ on the infinite paths of the DTMC $\mathcal{D}$ starting in s. The sample space $\Omega^{\mathcal{D}}_s$ is the set $\text{Paths}^{\mathcal{D}}_{\inf}(s)$. The *cylinder set* of a finite path $\pi = s_0 \dots s_n$ of $\mathcal{D}$ is defined as $\text{Cyl}(\pi) = \{\pi' \in \text{Paths}^{\mathcal{D}}_{\inf}(s_0) \mid \pi \text{ is a prefix of } \pi'\}$. The set $\mathcal{F}^{\mathcal{D}}_s$ of events is the unique smallest σ-algebra that contains the cylinder sets of all finite paths in $\text{Paths}^{\mathcal{D}}_{\text{fin}}(s)$ and is closed under complement and countable union. The unique probability measure $\Pr^{\mathcal{D}}_s$ (or short $\Pr$) on $\mathcal{F}^{\mathcal{D}}_s$ specifies the probabilities of the events recursively, for cylinder sets by

$$\Pr\big(\text{Cyl}(s_0 \dots s_n)\big) = \prod_{i=0}^{n-1} P(s_i, s_{i+1}),$$

for the complement $\bar{\Pi}$ of a set $\Pi \in \mathcal{F}^{\mathcal{D}}_s$ by $\Pr^{\mathcal{D}}_s(\bar{\Pi}) = 1 - \Pr^{\mathcal{D}}_s(\Pi)$, and for the countable union $\Pi = \bigcup_{i=1}^{\infty} \Pi_i$ of pairwise disjoint sets $\Pi_i \in \mathcal{F}^{\mathcal{D}}_s$, $i \in \mathbb{N}$, by $\Pr^{\mathcal{D}}_s(\Pi) = \sum_{i=1}^{\infty} \Pr^{\mathcal{D}}_s(\Pi_i)$.

For finite paths π we set $\Pr_{\text{fin}}(\pi) = \Pr\big(\text{Cyl}(\pi)\big)$. For sets of finite paths $R \subseteq \text{Paths}^{\mathcal{D}}_{\text{fin}}(s)$ we define $\Pr_{\text{fin}}(R) = \sum_{\pi \in R'} \Pr_{\text{fin}}(\pi)$ with $R' = \{\pi \in R \mid \forall \pi' \in R. \pi' \text{ is not a proper prefix of } \pi\}$.

Example 7. Consider again the DTMC from Example 3 on page 71. For the initial state s_0, the probability space $(\Omega^{\mathcal{D}}_{s_0}, \mathcal{F}^{\mathcal{D}}_{s_0}, \Pr^{\mathcal{D}}_{s_0})$ is given by the following components:

- The sample space is $\Omega^{\mathcal{D}}_{s_0} = \text{Paths}^{\mathcal{D}}_{\inf}(s_0) = \{s_0 s_1 s_3^{\omega}, s_0 s_2 s_3^{\omega}\}$.
- The event set $\mathcal{F}^{\mathcal{D}}_{s_0}$ contains the cylinder sets of all finite paths starting in s_0 and the empty set, i. e.,

$$\begin{aligned}
\mathcal{F}^{\mathcal{D}}_{s_0} = \{ &\emptyset, \\
&\text{Cyl}(s_0) = \text{Paths}^{\mathcal{D}}_{\inf}(s_0) = \{s_0 s_1 s_3^{\omega}, s_0 s_2 s_3^{\omega}\}, \\
&\text{Cyl}(s_0 s_1) = \text{Cyl}(s_0 s_1 s_3^+) = \{s_0 s_1 s_3^{\omega}\}, \\
&\text{Cyl}(s_0 s_2) = \text{Cyl}(s_0 s_2 s_3^+) = \{s_0 s_2 s_3^{\omega}\} \qquad \}.
\end{aligned}$$

The empty set is added as the complement of $\text{Cyl}(s_0)$. The other cylinder set complements and all countable unions over these elements are cylinder sets themselves and therefore already included.

- The probability measure $\Pr^{\mathcal{D}}_{s_0}$ is defined by

$$\begin{aligned}
\Pr^{\mathcal{D}}_{s_0}(\emptyset) &= 0, & \Pr^{\mathcal{D}}_{s_0}(\text{Cyl}(s_0)) &= 1, \\
\Pr^{\mathcal{D}}_{s_0}(\text{Cyl}(s_0 s_1)) &= 0.6, & \Pr^{\mathcal{D}}_{s_0}(\text{Cyl}(s_0 s_2)) &= 0.4.
\end{aligned}$$

∎

Besides using explicit model representations enumerating states and transitions, a DTMC can be represented *symbolically* using (ordered) binary decision diagrams (BDDs) and multi-terminal BDDs (MTBDDs). For an introduction to (MT)BDDs we refer to, e. g., [9]. In a symbolic representation, states are encoded using a set of Boolean variables such that each state is uniquely represented by an assignment to the Boolean variables. State sets, like the state space, the initial state or a set of states having a certain label of interest, are represented by some BDDs such that the variable evaluations along the paths leading to the leaf with label 1 encode those states that belong to the given set. Additionally, an MTBDD $\hat{P}$ stores the transition probabilities. This MTBDD uses two copies of the Boolean variables, one to encode the source states and one to encode the successor states of transitions. The evaluation along a path encodes the source and successor states, where the value of the leaf to which a path leads specifies the transition probability. Operations on (MT)BDDs can be used to compute, e. g., the successor set of a set of states or the probabilities to reach a certain set of states in a given number of steps.

Example 8. The four system states of the DTMC $\mathcal{D}$ from Example 3 on page 71 can be encoded by two Boolean variables x and y:

	s_0	s_1	s_2	s_3
x	0	0	1	1
y	0	1	0	1

The symbolic representation of $\mathcal{D}$ together with the state set $T = \{s_3\}$ of special interest would involve the following (MT)BDDs:

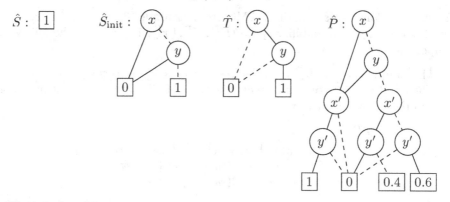

Though for this toy example the explicit representation seems to be more convenient, for large models the symbolic representation can be smaller by orders of magnitude. ∎

Markov Decision Processes and Probabilistic Automata. DTMCs behave deterministically, i. e., the choice of the next transition to be taken is purely probabilistic. Enriching DTMCs by nondeterminism leads to *Markov decision processes* and *probabilistic automata*.

Definition 3 (Probabilistic automaton [47]). *A probabilistic automaton (PA) is a tuple $\mathcal{M} = (S, s_{\text{init}}, \text{Act}, \hat{P}, L)$ where S is a finite set of states, $s_{\text{init}} \in S$ is the initial state, Act is a finite set of actions, $\hat{P} : S \to (2^{\text{Act} \times \text{SDistr}(S)} \setminus \emptyset)$ is a probabilistic transition relation such that $\hat{P}(s)$ is finite for all $s \in S$, and $L : S \to 2^{\text{AP}}$ is a labeling function.*

$\mathcal{M}$ is a Markov decision process (MDP) if for all $s \in S$ and all $\alpha \in \text{Act}$ $\left|\{\mu \in \text{SDistr}(S) \mid (\alpha, \mu) \in \hat{P}(s)\}\right| \leq 1$ holds.

Intuitively, the evolution of a probabilistic automaton is as follows. Starting in the initial state s_{init}, a pair $(\alpha, \mu) \in \hat{P}(s_{\text{init}})$ is chosen nondeterministically. Then, the successor state $s' \in S$ is determined probabilistically according to the distribution μ. A *deadlock* occurs in state s_{init} with probability $1 - \sum_{s' \in S} \mu(s')$. Repeating this process in s' yields the next state and so on.

The actions $\text{Act}_s = \{\alpha \in \text{Act} \mid \exists \mu \in \text{SDistr}(S). (\alpha, \mu) \in \hat{P}(s)\}$ are said to be *enabled* at state $s \in S$.

Note that DTMCs constitute a subclass of MDPs (apart from the fact that the actions are not relevant for DTMC and are therefore typically omitted) and MDPs build a subclass of PAs.

Example 9. To illustrate the difference between the different model classes, consider the following probabilistic models:

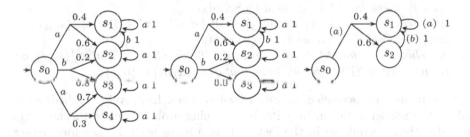

The involved distributions are

$$\mu_1(s) = \begin{cases} 0.4, & \text{if } s=s_1, \\ 0.6, & \text{if } s=s_2, \\ 0, & \text{else,} \end{cases} \quad \mu_2(s) = \begin{cases} 0.2, & \text{if } s=s_2, \\ 0.8, & \text{if } s=s_3, \\ 0, & \text{else,} \end{cases} \quad \mu_3(s) = \begin{cases} 0.7, & \text{if } s=s_3, \\ 0.3, & \text{if } s=s_4, \\ 0, & \text{else} \end{cases}$$

and the Dirac distributions d_i, $i = 1, 2, 3, 4$, assigning probability 1 to s_i and 0 to all other states.

The model on the left is a PA. In state s_0 there are two enabled actions a and b, where a appears in combination with two different distributions. Therefore, this model is not an MDP.

In contrast, the model in the middle is an MDP, since in each state and for each enabled action there is a single distribution available.

The model on the right is a DTMC, because a single distribution is mapped to each state. ∎

An *infinite path* in a PA $\mathcal{M}$ is an infinite sequence $\pi = s_0(\alpha_0, \mu_0)s_1(\alpha_1, \mu_1) \ldots$ such that $(\alpha_i, \mu_i) \in \hat{P}(s_i)$ and $s_{i+1} \in \text{supp}(\mu_i)$ for all $i \geq 0$. A *finite path* in $\mathcal{M}$ is a finite prefix $\pi = s_0(\alpha_0, \mu_0)s_1(\alpha_1, \mu_1) \ldots s_n$ of an infinite path in $\mathcal{M}$ with last state by $\text{last}(\pi) = s_n$. Let $\pi[i]$ denote the $(i+1)^{\text{th}}$ state s_i on path π. The sets of all infinite and finite paths in $\mathcal{M}$ starting in $s \in S$ are denoted by $\text{Paths}_{\text{inf}}^{\mathcal{M}}(s)$ and $\text{Paths}_{\text{fin}}^{\mathcal{M}}(s)$, respectively, whereas $\text{Paths}_{\text{fin}}^{\mathcal{M}}(s, t)$ is the set of all finite paths starting in s and ending in t. For $T \subseteq S$ we also use the notation $\text{Paths}_{\text{fin}}^{\mathcal{M}}(s, T)$ for $\bigcup_{t \in T} \text{Paths}_{\text{fin}}^{\mathcal{M}}(s, t)$.

Example 10. The sequence $s_0 (a, \mu_1) s_1 ((a, d_1) s_1)^\omega$ is an infinite path in all three models from Example 9 on page 75. (To be precise, the path of the DTMC does not contain the action-distribution pairs.)   ∎

To define a suitable probability measure on PAs, the nondeterminism has to be resolved by a *scheduler* first.

Definition 4 (Scheduler, deterministic, memoryless)

– A scheduler *for a PA* $\mathcal{M} = (S, s_{\text{init}}, \text{Act}, \hat{P}, L)$ *is a function*

$$\sigma \colon \text{Paths}_{\text{fin}}^{\mathcal{M}}(s_{\text{init}}) \to \text{Distr}(\text{Act} \times \text{SDistr}(S))$$

such that $\text{supp}(\sigma(\pi)) \subseteq \hat{P}(\text{last}(\pi))$ *for each* $\pi \in \text{Paths}_{\text{fin}}^{\mathcal{M}}(s_{\text{init}})$. *The set of all schedulers for* $\mathcal{M}$ *is denoted by* $\text{Sched}_{\mathcal{M}}$.
– *A scheduler* σ *for* $\mathcal{M}$ *is* memoryless *iff for all* $\pi, \pi' \in \text{Paths}_{\text{fin}}^{\mathcal{M}}(s_{\text{init}})$ *with* $\text{last}(\pi) = \text{last}(\pi')$ *we have that* $\sigma(\pi) = \sigma(\pi')$.
– *A scheduler* σ *for* $\mathcal{M}$ *is* deterministic *iff for all* $\pi \in \text{Paths}_{\text{fin}}^{\mathcal{M}}(s_{\text{init}})$ *and* $(\alpha, \mu) \in \text{Act} \times \text{SDistr}(S)$ *we have that* $\sigma(\pi)((\alpha, \mu)) \in \{0, 1\}$.

Schedulers are also called *policies* or *adversaries*. Intuitively, a scheduler resolves the nondeterminism in a PA by assigning probabilities to the nondeterministic choices available in the last state of a finite path. It therefore reduces the nondeterministic model to a fully probabilistic one.

Example 11. Consider the PA depicted on the left-hand-side in Example 9 on page 75. We define a scheduler σ_0 by specifying for all $\pi \in \text{Paths}_{\text{fin}}^{\mathcal{M}}(s_{\text{init}})$ and for all $(\alpha, \mu) \in \hat{P}(\text{last}(\pi))$

$$\sigma_0(\pi)(\alpha, \mu) = \begin{cases} 0.25, & \text{if } \text{last}(\pi) = s_0 \text{ and } \alpha = a, \\ 0.5, & \text{if } \text{last}(\pi) = s_0 \text{ and } \alpha = b, \\ 1, & \text{if } \text{last}(\pi) \in \{s_1, s_3, s_4\}, \\ 0.9, & \text{if } \pi = \pi' (\alpha', \mu') s_2 \text{ and } \alpha' = \alpha, \\ 0.1, & \text{if } \pi = \pi' (\alpha', \mu') s_2 \text{ and } \alpha' \neq \alpha, \end{cases}$$

and $\sigma_0(\pi)(\alpha, \mu) = 0$ for all $\pi \in \text{Paths}_{\text{fin}}^{\mathcal{M}}(s_{\text{init}})$ and $(\alpha, \mu) \in (\text{Act} \times \text{SDistr}(S)) \setminus \hat{P}(\text{last}(\pi))$. The above scheduler σ_0 is not memoryless, since the schedule for paths with last state s_2 depends on the last action on the path. This scheduler is also not deterministic, since it assigns also probabilities different from 0 and 1 to action-distribution pairs.

Let scheduler σ_1 be defined for all $\pi \in \mathrm{Paths}_{\mathrm{fin}}^{\mathcal{M}}(s_{\mathrm{init}})$ and for all $(\alpha, \mu) \in \hat{P}(\mathrm{last}(\pi))$ by

$$
\sigma_1(\pi)(\alpha, \mu) = \begin{cases}
0.25, & \text{if } \mathrm{last}(\pi) = s_0 \text{ and } \alpha = a, \\
0.5, & \text{if } \mathrm{last}(\pi) = s_0 \text{ and } \alpha = b, \\
1, & \text{if } \mathrm{last}(\pi) \in \{s_1, s_2, s_3, s_4\} \text{ and } \alpha = a, \\
0, & \text{else (if } \mathrm{last}(\pi) = s_2 \text{ and } \alpha = b),
\end{cases}
$$

and $\sigma_1(\pi)(\alpha, \mu) = 0$ for all $\pi \in \mathrm{Paths}_{\mathrm{fin}}^{\mathcal{M}}(s_{\mathrm{init}})$ and $(\alpha, \mu) \in (\mathrm{Act} \times \mathrm{SDistr}(S)) \setminus \hat{P}(\mathrm{last}(\pi))$. The scheduler σ_1 is memoryless but not deterministic.

Finally, the following scheduler σ_2 is deterministic and memoryless:

$$
\sigma_2(\pi)(\alpha, \mu) = \begin{cases}
1, & \text{if } \mathrm{last}(\pi) = s_0 \text{ and } (\alpha, \mu) = (a, \mu_1), \\
1, & \text{if } \mathrm{last}(\pi) = s_2 \text{ and } (\alpha, \mu) = (b, d_1), \\
1, & \text{if } \mathrm{last}(\pi) = s_i \text{ and } (\alpha, \mu) = (a, d_i) \text{ for } i \in \{1, 3, 4\}, \\
0, & \text{else.}
\end{cases}
$$

∎

Definition 5 (Induced DTMC). *Let* $\mathcal{M} - (S, s_{\mathrm{init}}, \mathrm{Act}, \hat{P}, L)$ *be a PA and* σ *a scheduler for* $\mathcal{M}$. *We define the DTMC* $\mathcal{M}^\sigma = (\mathrm{Paths}_{\mathrm{fin}}(s_{\mathrm{init}}), s_{\mathrm{init}}, P', L')$ *with*

$$
P'(\pi, \pi') = \begin{cases}
\sigma(\pi)((\alpha, \mu)) \cdot \mu(s), & \text{if } \pi' = \pi\, (\alpha, \mu)\, s, \\
0, & \text{otherwise,}
\end{cases}
$$

and $L'(\pi) = L(\mathrm{last}(\pi))$ *for all* $\pi, \pi' \in \mathrm{Paths}_{\mathrm{fin}}(s_{\mathrm{init}})$. *We call* $\mathcal{M}^\sigma$ *the DTMC induced by* $\mathcal{M}$ *and* σ.

Example 12. The scheduler σ_2 from Example 11 (on page 76) for the PA depicted on the left in Example 9 (on page 75) induces the following DTMC:

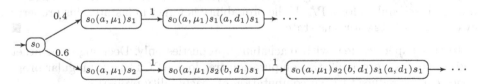

Since the scheduler σ_2 is memoryless, each pair of states π and π' with $\mathrm{last}(\pi) = \mathrm{last}(\pi')$ are equivalent (*bisimilar*) in the sense that the set of all label sequences (*traces*) along paths starting in those states are equal. (Note that the labeling is not depicted in the above picture.) Since the logics we consider can argue about the labelings only, such state pairs satisfy the same formulas. We say that the *observable behavior* of our models is given by the their trace sets.

Based on this observation, we can build an abstraction of the above induced DTMC by introducing abstract states $s \in S$ (the states of the inducing PA) representing all states π with $\text{last}(\pi) = s$ of the induced DTMC. For the above example, the scheduler is not only memoryless but also deterministic. For those schedulers this abstraction defines a DTMC containing the states of the PA and all distributions selected by the scheduler. For σ_2 the result is the DTMC depicted on the right in Example 9 on page 75.

In the following, when talking about the DTMC induced by a PA and a *memoryless deterministic* scheduler, we mean this abstraction. ∎

For the probability measure on paths of a PA $\mathcal{M}$ under a scheduler σ for $\mathcal{M}$, we use the standard probability measure on paths of the induced DTMC $\mathcal{M}^\sigma$, as described previously. We denote this probability measure by $\text{Pr}_{s_{\text{init}}}^{\mathcal{M},\sigma}$ (or, briefly, $\text{Pr}^{\mathcal{M},\sigma}$).

2.2   Reachability Properties

As specification for both DTMCs and PAs we consider so-called *reachability properties*. We are interested in a quantitative analysis such as:

"What is the probability to reach a certain set of states T starting in state s?"

Such a set of *target* states T might, e. g., model *bad* or *safety-critical* states, for which the probability to visit them should be kept below a certain upper bound. Formally, we identify target states by labeling them with some dedicated label $\text{target} \in \text{AP}$ such that $T = \{s \in S \mid \text{target} \in L(s)\}$. Instead of depicting target labels, in the following we illustrate target states in figures as double-framed gray-colored nodes.

We formulate reachability properties like $\mathbb{P}_{\bowtie\lambda}(\Diamond\text{target})$ for $\bowtie \in \{<, \leq, \geq, >\}$ and $\lambda \in [0,1] \cap \mathbb{Q}$. For simplicity, we will sometimes also write $\mathbb{P}_{\bowtie\lambda}(\Diamond T)$. Such a property holds in a state s of a DTMC $\mathcal{D}$ iff the probability to reach a state from T when starting in s in $\mathcal{D}$ satisfies the bound $\bowtie \lambda$. The DTMC satisfies the property iff it holds in its initial state. For a PA $\mathcal{M}$ we require the bound to be satisfied under all schedulers.

Example 13. For instance, $\mathbb{P}_{\leq 0.1}(\Diamond\text{target})$ states that the probability of reaching a state labeled with target is less or equal than 0.1, either for a DTMC or under all schedulers for a PA. If the probability is larger in a state, this property evaluates to false for this state. ∎

In this paper we deal with reachability properties only. Deciding some other logics like, e. g., probabilistic computation tree logic (PCTL) or ω-regular properties can be reduced to the computation of reachability properties.

Furthermore, in the following we restrict ourselves to reachability properties of the form $\mathbb{P}_{\leq\lambda}(\Diamond\text{target})$. Formulas of the form $\mathbb{P}_{<\lambda}(\Diamond\text{target})$ can be handled similarly. The cases $\geq$ and $>$ can be reduced to $<$ and $\leq$, respectively, using negation, e. g., $\mathbb{P}_{>\lambda}(\Diamond\text{target})$ is equivalent to $\mathbb{P}_{\leq 1-\lambda}(\Diamond\neg\text{target})$.

At some places we will also mention *bounded* reachability properties of the form $\mathbb{P}_{\leq\lambda}(\Diamond^{\leq h}T)$ for a natural number h. The semantics of such formulas is similar to the unbounded case $\mathbb{P}_{\leq\lambda}(\Diamond T)$, however, here the probability to reach a state in T via paths of length at most h should satisfy the bound.

Reachability for DTMCs. Assume a DTMC $\mathcal{D} = (S, s_{\text{init}}, P, L)$, a label target $\in$ AP and a target state set $T = \{t \in S \mid \text{target} \in L(t)\}$. We want to determine whether $\mathcal{D}$ satisfies the property $\mathbb{P}_{\leq\lambda}(\Diamond T)$, written $\mathcal{D} \models \mathbb{P}_{\leq\lambda}(\Diamond T)$. This is the case iff the property holds in the initial state of $\mathcal{D}$, denoted by $\mathcal{D}, s_{\text{init}} \models \mathbb{P}_{\leq\lambda}(\Diamond T)$.

Let $s \in S \setminus T$. The set of paths contributing to the probability of reaching T from s is given by

$$\Diamond T(s) = \{\pi \in \text{Paths}_{\text{inf}}^{\mathcal{D}}(s) \mid \exists i. \text{target} \in L(\pi[i])\}$$

where we overload $\Diamond T$ to both denote a set of paths and a property, and also write simply $\Diamond T$ if s is clear from the context.

The above set $\Diamond T(s)$ equals the union of the cylinder sets of all paths from $\text{Paths}_{\text{fin}}^{\mathcal{D}}(s, T)$:

$$\Diamond T(s) = \bigcup_{\pi \in \text{Paths}_{\text{fin}}^{\mathcal{D}}(s,T)} \text{Cyl}(\pi).$$

Note that $\text{Paths}_{\text{fin}}^{\mathcal{D}}(s, T)$ contains in general also prefixes of other contained paths (if there are paths of length at least 1 from T to T). When computing the probability mass of $\Diamond T(s)$, such extensions are not considered. We can remove those extensions by restricting the finite paths to visit T only in their last state: $\Diamond T(s) = \bigcup_{\pi \in \Diamond T_{\text{fin}}(s)} \text{Cyl}(\pi)$ with

$$\Diamond T_{\text{fin}}(s) = \{\pi \in \text{Paths}_{\text{fin}}^{\mathcal{D}}(s, T) \mid \forall 0 \leq i < |\pi|. \pi[i] \notin T\}.$$

As no path in the set $\Diamond T_{\text{fin}}(s)$ is a prefix of another one, the probability of this set can be computed by the sum of the probabilities of its elements:

$$\begin{aligned}
\text{Pr}_s^{\mathcal{D}}(\Diamond T(s)) &= \text{Pr}_s^{\mathcal{D}}\Big(\bigcup_{\pi \in \Diamond T_{\text{fin}}(s)} \text{Cyl}(\pi)\Big) \\
&= \sum_{\pi \in \Diamond T_{\text{fin}}(s)} \text{Pr}_s^{\mathcal{D}}(\text{Cyl}(\pi)) \\
&= \sum_{s' \in S \setminus T} P(s, s') \cdot \text{Pr}_{s'}^{\mathcal{D}}(\Diamond T(s')) + \sum_{s' \in T} P(s, s').
\end{aligned}$$

Therefore, we can compute for each state $s \in S$ the probability of reaching T from s by solving the equation system consisting of a constraint

$$p_s = \begin{cases} 1, & \text{if } s \in T, \\ 0, & \text{if } T \text{ is not reachable from } s, \\ \sum_{s' \in S} P(s, s') \cdot p_{s'}, & \text{otherwise} \end{cases}$$

for each $s \in S$. The unique solution $\nu : \{p_s \mid s \in S\} \to [0, 1]$ of this linear equation system assigns to p_s the probability of reaching T from s for each state $s \in S$. That means, $\mathcal{D} \models \mathbb{P}_{\leq\lambda}(\Diamond T)$ iff $\nu(p_{s_{\text{init}}}) \leq \lambda$.

We can simplify the above equation system if we first remove all states from the model from which T is not reachable.

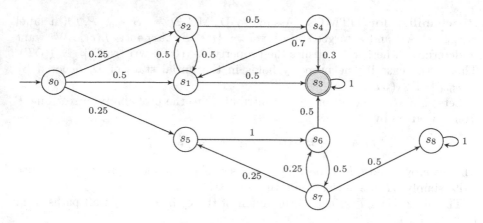

Fig. 2. An example DTMC (cf. Example 14)

Definition 6 (Relevant states of DTMCs). *Let*

$$S_{\mathcal{D}}^{\mathrm{rel}(T)} = \{s \in S \mid \mathrm{Paths}_{\mathrm{fin}}^{\mathcal{D}}(s, T) \neq \emptyset\}$$

and call its elements relevant *for T (or for* target*). States $s \notin S_{\mathcal{D}}^{\mathrm{rel}(T)}$ are called* irrelevant *for T (or for* target*).*

The set of relevant states can be computed in linear time by a backward reachability analysis on $\mathcal{D}$ [9, Algorithm 46].

If a model does not contain any irrelevant states, the above equation system reduces to the constraints

$$p_s = \begin{cases} 1, & \text{if } s \in T, \\ \sum_{s' \in S} P(s, s') \cdot p_{s'}, & \text{otherwise} \end{cases}$$

for each $s \in S$.

Example 14. Consider the DTMC illustrated in Figure 2 with target state set $T = \{s_3\}$. State s_8 is irrelevant for T and can be removed. The probabilities to reach s_3 can be computed by solving the following equation system:

$$
\begin{aligned}
p_{s_0} &= 0.5 \cdot p_{s_1} + 0.25 \cdot p_{s_2} + 0.25 \cdot p_{s_5} & p_{s_1} &= 0.5 \cdot p_{s_2} + 0.5 \cdot p_{s_3} \\
p_{s_2} &= 0.5 \cdot p_{s_1} + 0.5 \cdot p_{s_4} & p_{s_3} &= 1 \\
p_{s_4} &= 0.7 \cdot p_{s_1} + 0.3 \cdot p_{s_3} & p_{s_5} &= 1 \cdot p_{s_6} \\
p_{s_6} &= 0.5 \cdot p_{s_3} + 0.5 \cdot p_{s_7} & p_{s_7} &= 0.25 \cdot p_{s_5} + 0.25 \cdot p_{s_6}
\end{aligned}
$$

The unique solution ν defines $\nu(p_{s_0}) = {}^{11}\!/_{12}$, $\nu(p_{s_1}) = \nu(p_{s_2}) = \nu(p_{s_3}) = \nu(p_{s_4}) = 1$, $\nu(p_{s_5}) = \nu(p_{s_6}) = {}^2\!/_3$ and $\nu(p_{s_7}) = {}^1\!/_3$. ∎

Reachability for PAs. Assume a PA $\mathcal{M} = (S, s_{\text{init}}, \text{Act}, \hat{P}, L)$, a label $\texttt{target} \in$ AP and a target state set $T = \{t \in S \mid \texttt{target} \in L(t)\}$. Intuitively, a reachability property holds for $\mathcal{M}$ if it holds under all possible schedulers. Formally, $\mathcal{M} \models \mathbb{P}_{\leq\lambda}(\Diamond T)$ if for all schedulers σ of $\mathcal{M}$ we have that $\mathcal{M}^\sigma \models \mathbb{P}_{\leq\lambda}(\Diamond T)$.

It can be shown that there always exists a *memoryless deterministic* scheduler that maximizes the reachability probability for $\Diamond T$ among all schedulers. Therefore, to check whether $\mathcal{M}^\sigma \models \mathbb{P}_{\leq\lambda}(\Diamond T)$ holds for all schedulers σ, it suffices to consider a memoryless deterministic scheduler σ^* which maximizes the reachability probability for $\Diamond T$ under all memoryless deterministic schedulers, and check the property for the induced DTMC $\mathcal{M}^{\sigma^*}$. For the computation of σ^* we need the notion of *relevant* states.

Definition 7 (Relevant states of PAs). *We define*

$$S_{\mathcal{M}}^{\text{rel}(T)} = \{s \in S \mid \exists \sigma \in \text{Sched}_{\mathcal{M}}.\, s \in S_{\mathcal{M}^\sigma}^{\text{rel}(T)}\}$$

and call its elements relevant *for T (or for $\texttt{target}$). States $s \notin S_{\mathcal{M}}^{\text{rel}(T)}$ are called* irrelevant *for T (or for $\texttt{target}$).*

Again, the set of relevant states can be computed in linear time by a backward reachability analysis on $\mathcal{M}$ [9, Algorithm 46].

The maximal probabilities $p_s = \text{Pr}_s^{\mathcal{M}^{\sigma^*}}(\Diamond T(s))$, $s \in S$, can be characterized by the following equation system:

$$p_s = \begin{cases} 1, & \text{if } s \in T, \\ 0, & \text{if } s \notin S_{\mathcal{M}}^{\text{rel}(T)}, \\ \max\{\sum_{s' \in S} \mu(s, s') \cdot p_{s'} \mid (\alpha, \mu) \in \hat{P}(s)\}, & \text{otherwise} \end{cases}$$

for each $s \in S$. This equation system can be transformed into a linear optimization problem that yields the maximal reachability probability together with an optimal scheduler [9, Theorem 10.105].

Example 15. Consider the left-hand-side PA model from Example 9 on page 75. The probability to reach s_1 from s_0 is maximized by the deterministic memoryless scheduler σ_2 choosing (a, μ_1) in state s_0, (b, d_1) in state s_2, and (a, d_i) in all other states $s_i \in \{s_1, s_3, s_4\}$. ∎

3 Counterexamples

When a DTMC $\mathcal{D}$ violates a reachability property $\mathbb{P}_{\leq\lambda}(\Diamond T)$ for some $T \subseteq S$ and $\lambda \in [0, 1] \cap \mathbb{Q}$, an explanation for this violation can be given by a set of paths, each of them leading from the initial state to some target states, such that the probability mass of the path set is larger than λ. Such path sets are called *counterexamples*. For a PA $\mathcal{M}$, a counterexample specifies a deterministic memoryless scheduler σ and a counterexample for the induced DTMC $\mathcal{M}^\sigma$.

Counterexamples are valuable for different purposes, e. g., for the correction of systems or for counterexample-guided abstraction refinement. However, counterexamples may contain a very large or even infinite number of paths (note that for a DTMC $\mathcal{D}$ the whole set $\mathrm{Paths}_{\mathrm{fin}}^{\mathcal{D}}(s_{\mathrm{init}}, T)$ is the largest counterexample). Therefore, it can increase the practical usefulness if we aim at the computation of counterexamples satisfying certain properties. Some important aspects are:

- The *size of the counterexample*, i. e., the number of paths in it.
- The *probability mass* of the counterexample.
- The *computational costs*, i. e., the time and memory required to obtain a counterexample.
- Counterexamples can be given using *representations* at different language levels.
  - At the level of paths, besides path enumeration, a counterexample can be represented by, e. g., computation trees or regular expressions. Path-based representations will be discussed in Section 4.
  - At the model level, a part of the model can represent a counterexample by all paths leading inside the given model part from s_{init} to T. Such representations are the content of Section 5.
  - At a higher level, a fragment of a probabilistic program, for which a PA or a DTMC was generated as its semantics, can also represent a counterexample. We discuss such counterexamples in Section 6.
  Important in our considerations will be the *size of the representation*.

We first formalize counterexamples and measures regarding the first two points, and will discuss representation issues and computational costs in the following sections.

Definition 8 (DTMC evidence and counterexample, [17]). *Assume a DTMC $\mathcal{D} = (S, s_{\mathrm{init}}, P, L)$ violating a reachability property $\mathbb{P}_{\leq\lambda}(\Diamond T)$ with $T \subseteq S$ and $\lambda \in [0,1] \cap \mathbb{Q}$.*

An evidence (for $\mathcal{D}$ and $\mathbb{P}_{\leq\lambda}(\Diamond T)$) is a finite path $\pi \in \mathrm{Paths}_{\mathrm{fin}}^{\mathcal{D}}(s_{\mathrm{init}}, T)$. A counterexample is a set C of evidences such that $\mathrm{Pr}_{s_{\mathrm{init}}}^{\mathcal{D}}(C) > \lambda$. A counterexample C is minimal if $|C| \leq |C'|$ for all counterexamples C'. It is a smallest counterexample if it is minimal and $\mathrm{Pr}_{s_{\mathrm{init}}}^{\mathcal{D}}(C) \geq \mathrm{Pr}_{s_{\mathrm{init}}}^{\mathcal{D}}(C')$ for all minimal counterexamples C'.

Example 16. Consider the DTMC from Example 3 on page 71 and the reachability property $\mathbb{P}_{\leq 0.3}(\Diamond\{s_3\})$. The path sets $\Pi_1 = \{s_0 s_1 s_3, s_0 s_1 s_3 s_3\}$, $\Pi_2 = \{s_0 s_1 s_3, s_0 s_2 s_3\}$, $\Pi_3 = \{s_0 s_1 s_3\}$, and $\Pi_4 = \{s_0 s_2 s_3\}$ are all counterexamples (with probability mass 0.6, 1, 0.6, and 0.4, respectively). Only Π_3 and Π_4 are minimal, where only Π_3 is a smallest counterexample. ∎

For reachability properties of the form $\mathbb{P}_{\leq\lambda}(\Diamond\mathtt{target})$ with a non-strict upper bound on the admissible reachability property, a finite counterexample always exists, if the property is violated. For strict upper bounds $\mathbb{P}_{<\lambda}(\Diamond\mathtt{target})$, however, an infinite number of paths can be required if the actual reachability probability equals λ [17].

Example 17. Consider the following DTMC:

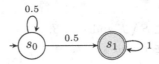

The probability to reach s_1 is 1, i.e., the property $\mathbb{P}_{<1}(\lozenge\{s_1\})$ is violated. However, a counterexample must contain all the infinite number of paths $s_0 s_1$, $s_0 s_0 s_1$, $s_0 s_0 s_0 s_1$ etc. ■

Even if the counterexample is finite, the number of required paths can be very large. Han *et al.* [17] determine for the case study of a probabilistic synchronous leader election protocol that the number of evidences is double exponential in the system parameters.

Definition 9 (PA counterexample). *Assume a PA $\mathcal{M} = (S, s_{\text{init}}, \text{Act}, \hat{P}, L)$ violating a reachability property $\mathbb{P}_{\leq\lambda}(\lozenge T)$ with $T \subseteq S$ and $\lambda \in [0,1] \cap \mathbb{Q}$.*

A counterexample (for $\mathcal{M}$ and $\mathbb{P}_{\leq\lambda}(\lozenge T)$) is a pair (σ, C) such that σ is a scheduler for $\mathcal{M}$ and C is a counterexample for $\mathcal{M}^\sigma$. A counterexample (σ, C) is minimal if $|C| \leq |C'|$ for all counterexamples (σ', C'). It is a smallest counterexample if it is minimal and $\text{Pr}^{\mathcal{M}}_{s_{\text{init}}}(C) \geq \text{Pr}^{\mathcal{M}}_{s_{\text{init}}}(C')$ for all minimal counterexamples (σ', C').

Example 18. Consider the left-hand-side PA model from Example 9 on page 75 and the reachability property $\mathbb{P}_{\leq 0.9}(\lozenge\{s_1\})$. A smallest counterexample is $(\sigma_2, \{s_0 s_1, s_0 s_2 s_1\})$ with σ_2 as defined in Example 11 on page 76. ■

4   Path-Based Counterexamples

After having introduced discrete-time probabilistic models and counterexamples for reachability properties, in the following we discuss how we can *compute* such counterexamples for the different model classes in different representations. We start with methods that are based on the search for paths at the state-space level.

4.1   Path-Based Counterexamples for DTMCs

Smallest Counterexamples. For DTMCs, Han, Katoen and Damman show in [17] how the computation of a smallest counterexample can be reduced to the computation of k *shortest paths* in a directed weighted graph for a suitable $k \in \mathbb{N}$.

We need in the following the property that the DTMC $\mathcal{D} = (S, s_{\text{init}}, P, L)$ we consider has a *single absorbing target state*. If it is the case, we define $\mathcal{D}' = \mathcal{D}$. Otherwise, the DTMC $\mathcal{D}$ is first transformed by adding a new, absorbing target state $t \notin S$ and redirecting all transitions starting in former target states to lead to the new one. This transformation yields the DTMC $\mathcal{D}' = (S', s_{\text{init}}, P', L')$ with $S' = S \,\dot\cup\, \{t\}$ and

$$P'(s,s') = \begin{cases} P(s,s'), & \text{if } s \in S \setminus T \text{ and } s' \in S, \\ 1, & \text{if } s \in T \text{ and } s' = t, \\ 1, & \text{if } s = s' = t, \\ 0, & \text{otherwise,} \end{cases} \qquad L'(s) = \begin{cases} \{\texttt{target}\}, & \text{if } s = t, \\ \emptyset, & \text{otherwise.} \end{cases}$$

Note that the probability to reach t from $s \in S$ in $\mathcal{D}'$ equals the probability to reach T from s in $\mathcal{D}$.

As the next step, a *directed weighted graph* $G_\mathcal{D} = (V, E, w)$ with nodes V, edges E and edge weights $w : E \to \mathbb{R}^{\geq 0}$ is obtained from $\mathcal{D}'$ as follows: $V = S'$, $(s, s') \in E$ iff $P'(s, s') > 0$, and $w(s, s') = -\log P'(s, s')$ (one could take any basis, we take the natural logarithm with basis e).

We define the weight $w(\pi)$ of a path π in $G_\mathcal{D}$ as the sum of the weights of the transitions in π. The relation between the weight of a finite path $\pi = s_0 \ldots s_n$ in $G_\mathcal{D}$ and the probability of the same path in $\mathcal{D}$ is as follows:

$$\begin{aligned} w(\pi) &= \textstyle\sum_{i=0}^{n-1} w(s_i, s_{i+1}) &= \textstyle\sum_{i=0}^{n-1} -\log P'(s_i, s_{i+1}) \\ &= -\textstyle\sum_{i=0}^{n-1} \log P'(s_i, s_{i+1}) = -\log \textstyle\prod_{i=0}^{n-1} P'(s_i, s_{i+1}) \\ &= -\log \Pr_{s_0}^{\mathcal{D}'}(\pi). \end{aligned}$$

Note that we can also compute the probabilities from the weights by $\Pr_{s_0}^{\mathcal{D}'}(\pi) = e^{-w(\pi)}$. Since the negative logarithm is monotonically decreasing in the interval $(0, 1]$, more probable paths in $\mathcal{D}'$ have smaller weights in $G_\mathcal{D}$, i.e., $\Pr_s^{\mathcal{D}'}(\pi) \geq \Pr_s^{\mathcal{D}'}(\pi')$ iff $w(\pi) \leq w(\pi')$ for all states $s \in S$ and paths $\pi, \pi' \in \text{Paths}_{\text{fin}}^{\mathcal{D}}(s)$.

That means, the problem to find a sufficient number of most probable paths in $\mathcal{D}$ can be solved by finding a sufficient number of shortest paths in $G_\mathcal{D}$. The main advantage of this problem transformation, besides the lower complexity of the addition operation compared to multiplication, is that we can apply shortest path search algorithms without modification.

Definition 10 (k shortest path problem, [17]). *Given a directed weighted graph $G = (V, E, w)$, nodes $s, t \in V$, and $k \in \mathbb{N}$, the k shortest path problem (KSP) is to find k different paths $\pi_1, \ldots, \pi_k$ from s to t in G (if they exist) such that for all $1 \leq i < j \leq k$, $w(\pi_i) \leq w(\pi_j)$ and for all paths π from s to t either $\pi \in \{\pi_1, \ldots, \pi_k\}$ or $w(\pi) \geq w(\pi_k)$.*

Theorem 1 ([17]). *A smallest counterexample C for $\mathcal{D}$ contains $|C|$ shortest paths in $G_\mathcal{D}$ from s_{init} to t.*

Example 19. Consider the DTMC $\mathcal{D}$ from Example 14 on page 80, depicted in Figure 2, which already has a single absorbing target state. The corresponding directed weighted graph $G_\mathcal{D}$ is shown in Figure 3 (with rounded weights).

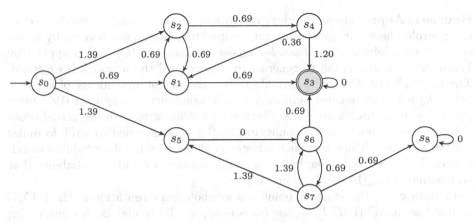

Fig. 3. The directed weighted graph for the DTMC from Figure 2 (cf. Example 19)

We would like to compute a counterexample for $\mathbb{P}_{\leq 0.4}(\Diamond\{s_3\})$. Thus we search for k shortest paths $\pi_1,\ldots,\pi_k$ in $G_{\mathcal{D}}$ for an appropriate k such that $\sum_{i=1}^{k} e^{-w(\pi_i)} > 0.4$. The four shortest paths in $G_{\mathcal{D}}$, with their (rounded) weights in $G_{\mathcal{D}}$ and probabilities in $\mathcal{D}$ are as follows:

Path	Weight (rounded)	Probability
$\pi_1 = s_0 s_1 s_3$	1.39	$1/4$
$\pi_2 = s_0 s_5 s_6 s_3$	2.08	$1/8$
$\pi_3 = s_0 s_2 s_1 s_3$	2.77	$1/16$
$\pi_4 = s_0 s_1 s_2 s_1 s_3$	2.77	$1/16$

Since $\sum_{i\in\{1,2,3\}} e^{-w(\pi_i)} = \sum_{i\in\{1,2,4\}} e^{-w(\pi_i)} = 1/4 + 1/8 + 1/16 = 0.4375 > 0.4$, both path sets $\{\pi_1,\pi_2,\pi_3\}$ and $\{\pi_1,\pi_2,\pi_4\}$ are smallest counterexamples. ∎

As the size of a smallest counterexample is not known in advance, we need k shortest paths computation algorithms that can determine the value of k *on the fly*. Examples of such algorithms are Eppstein's algorithm [48], the algorithm by Jiménez and Marzal [49], and the K* algorithm [50] by Aljazzar and Leue. While the former two methods require the whole graph to be placed in memory in advance, the *K* algorithm* (see also Section 4.2) expands the state space on the fly and generates only those parts of the graph that are needed. Additionally, it can apply directed search, i. e., it exploits heuristic estimates of the distance of the current node to a target node in order to speed up the search. The heuristic has thereby to be admissible, i. e., it must never over-estimate the distance.

For *bounded* reachability properties $\mathbb{P}_{\leq\lambda}(\Diamond^{\leq h}T)$, a *hop-constrained k shortest paths problem (HKSP)* can be used to determine a smallest counterexample. In this case the additional constraint that each evidence may contain at most h transitions must be imposed. In [17] an adaption of Jiménez and Marzal's algorithm to the HKSP problem is presented.

Heuristic Approaches. Besides the above methods to compute smallest counterexamples, heuristic approaches can be used to compute not necessarily smallest or even minimal ones. *Bounded model checking (BMC)* [51] is applied by Wimmer *et al.* in [19, 20] to generate evidences until the bound λ is exceeded. The basic idea of BMC is to formulate the existence of an evidence of length k (or $\leq k$) for some natural number k as a satisfiability problem. In [19] purely propositional formulas are used, which does not allow to take the actual probability of an evidence into account; in [20] this was extended to SMT formulas over linear real arithmetic, which allows to enforce a minimal probability of evidences. Using strategies like binary search, evidences with high probability (but still bounded length) can be found first.

In both cases, the starting point is a symbolic representation of the DTMC at hand as an MTBDD $\hat{P}$ for the transition probability matrix. For generating propositional formulas, this MTBDD is abstracted into a BDD $\hat{P}_{\mathrm{BDD}}$ by mapping each leaf labeled with a positive probability to 1. Hence, the BDD $\hat{P}_{\mathrm{BDD}}$ stores the edges of the underlying graph. The generation of propositional formulas is done by applying Tseitin's transformation [52] to this BDD, resulting in a predicate trans such that $\mathsf{trans}(v, v')$ is satisfied for an assignment of the variables v and v' if and only if the assignment corresponds to a transition with positive probability in the DTMC. The same is done for the initial state, resulting in a predicate init such that $\mathsf{init}(v)$ is satisfied if the assignment of v corresponds to the initial state of the DTMC and a predicate $\mathsf{target}(v)$ for the set of target states. With these predicates at hand, the BMC-formula is given as follows:

$$\mathsf{BMC}(k) = \mathsf{init}(v_0) \wedge \bigwedge_{i=0}^{k-1} \mathsf{trans}(v_i, v_{i+1}) \wedge \mathsf{target}(v_k). \tag{1}$$

This formula is satisfied by an assignment ν iff $\nu(v_i)$ corresponds to a state s_i for $i = 1, \ldots, k$ such that $s_0 s_1 \ldots s_k$ is an evidence for the considered reachability property.

Starting at $k = 0$, evidences are collected and excluded from further search by adding new clauses to the current formula, until either the set of collected paths forms a counterexample or the current formula becomes unsatisfiable. In the latter case we increase k and continue the search.

During the BMC search, loops on found paths can be identified. A found path containing a loop can be added to the collection of evidences with arbitrary unrollings of the loop. However, since loop unrollings lead to longer paths, attention must be payed to exclude those paths when k reaches the length of previously added paths with unrolled loops.

The propositional BMC approach yields a counterexample consisting of evidences with a minimal number of transitions, but the drawback is that the actual probabilities of the evidences are ignored. This issue can be solved by using a SAT-modulo-theories formula instead of a purely propositional formula [20]. Thereby the transition predicate trans is modified to take the probabilities into account: $\mathsf{trans}(v_i, p_i, v_{i+1})$ is satisfied by an assignment ν iff $\nu(v_i)$ corresponds to state s_i, $\nu(v_{i+1})$ to state s_{i+1}, $P(s_i, s_{i+1}) > 0$, and $\nu(p_i) = \log P(s_i, s_{i+1})$. By adding the constraint $\sum_{i=0}^{k-1} p_i \geq \log \delta$ for some constant $\delta \in (0, 1]$, we can enforce that only paths with probability at least δ are found.

Additionally, using an SMT formulation allows us to take *rewards* into account: we can extend the DTMC by a function $\rho : S \times S \rightarrow \mathbb{R}$, which specifies the reward of a transition. Rewards can—depending on the context—either represent *costs* (e. g., energy consumption, computation time, etc.) or *benefits* (number of packets transmitted, money earned, etc). Similar to constraints on the probability of an evidence, we can enforce that the accumulated reward along an evidence satisfies a linear constraint [20, 53].

Symbolic Methods. For a DTMC $\mathcal{D} = (S, s_{\text{init}}, P, L)$ together with a set of target states T that are represented *symbolically* in the form of BDDs $\hat{I}$ and $\hat{T}$ for the initial state and the target states, respectively, and an MTBDD $\hat{P}$ for the transition probability matrix, Günther, Schuster and Siegle [21] propose a BDD-based algorithm for computing the k most probable paths of a DTMC. They use an adaption of Dijkstra's shortest path algorithm [54], called *flooding Dijkstra*, to determine the most probable path. Then they transform the DTMC such that the most probable path of the transformed system corresponds to the second-most-probable path in the original DTMC. For this they create two copies of the DTMC: The new initial state is the initial state of the first copy, the new target states are the target states in the second copy. The transitions of the second copy remain unchanged. In the first copy, all transitions on the already found most probable path also remain unchanged. All other transitions lead from the first copy to the corresponding state in the second copy. Thus, to reach a target state from the initial state, at least one transition has to be taken which is not contained in the most probable path. The corresponding function has as input BDDs the symbolic representation of the DTMC as well as a BDD SP representing the current most probable path. Returned is a new symbolic DTMC:

$$(\hat{P}, \hat{I}, \hat{T}) := \texttt{Change}(\hat{P}, \hat{I}, \hat{T}, SP)$$

We illustrate this process using an example.

Example 20. Consider again the DTMC in Figure 2 on page 80. The first application of Dijkstra's algorithm yields the most probable path $s_0 s_1 s_3$ with probability $1/2 \cdot 1/2 = 1/4$ from the initial state s_0 to the target state s_3. To obtain the second-most-probable path, the DTMC in Figure 4 is constructed. In the modified DTMC, the initial state is s_0^0, the target state is s_3^1. The most probable path from s_0^0 to s_3^1 is $s_0^0 s_5^1 s_6^1 s_3^1$ with probability $1/4 \cdot 1 \cdot 1/2 = 1/8$. This path corresponds to $s_0 s_5 s_6 s_3$ in the original DTMC, which is the second-most probable path there. ∎

To obtain the next path, the same transformation is applied again. After k paths the underlying graph has increased exponentially in k. Each transformation step requires to introduce two new BDD-variables and typically increases

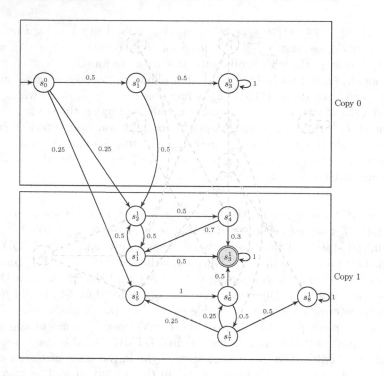

Fig. 4. Exclusion of the most probable path (the states and transitions which are not reachable from the initial state s_0^0 have been colored grey to improve readability)

the size of the symbolic representation. Therefore this methods scales well to large state spaces, but not for large values of k.

Compact Representations. Alone the mere number of evidences in a counterexample can render the counterexample unusable for debugging purposes. Therefore a number of approaches have been proposed to obtain smaller, better understandable *representations* of counterexamples. Typically they exploit the fact that many paths in a counterexample differ only in the number and order of unrollings of loops.

Building upon ideas by Daws [55] for model checking parametric DTMCs, Han, Katoen and Damman [17, 22] proposed the representation of counterexamples as regular expressions: First the DTMC is turned into a deterministic finite automaton (DFA), whose transitions are labeled with (state, probability) pairs: Essentially, a transition from s to s' with probability $p = P(s, s') > 0$ in the DTMC is turned into the transition $s \xrightarrow{(s',p)} s'$ of the DFA. State elimination is used to turn the DFA into a regular expression. The state elimination removes states iteratively, and for each removed state it connects its predecessors with its successors by direct transitions. These new transitions are labeled with regular expressions describing the inputs read on the possible path from a predecessor

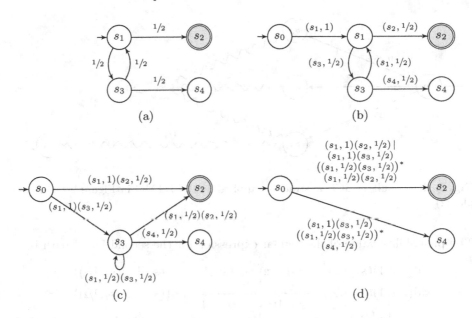

Fig. 5. Representing counterexamples as regular expressions (cf. Example 21)

via the removed state to a successor. In order to obtain a small regular expression for a counterexample, the authors proposed to iterate the following steps:

1. Find a most probable path in the remaining automaton using Dijkstra's shortest path algorithm.
2. Eliminate all states (except the first and last one) on this path; the order of elimination is determined according to a heuristics like [56], well known from the literature on automata theory. This gives a regular expression describing the considered most probable path.
3. Evaluate the set of regular expressions generated so far and check whether the joint probability mass of the represented paths is already beyond the given bound λ. If this is the case, terminate and return the regular expressions. Otherwise start a new iteration of the elimination loop.

Example 21. Consider the DTMC in Figure 5 (a) with target state s_2. Its DFA is depicted under (b). The first most probable path is $s_0 s_1 s_2$, i.e., we eliminate s_1, resulting in the DFA (c). The probability value of the regular expression generated for the found path is

$$\mathrm{val}\big((s_1,1)(s_2,{}^1\!/_2)\big) = \mathrm{val}\big((s_1,1)\big) \cdot \mathrm{val}\big((s_2,{}^1\!/_2)\big) = 1 \cdot {}^1\!/_2 = {}^1\!/_2 \,.$$

If this mass is not yet sufficient to violate the bound, we search for the most probable path in (c), which is $s_0 s_3 s_2$. We eliminate s_3 resulting in the DFA (d).

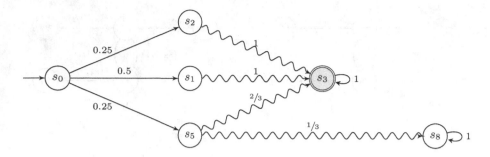

Fig. 6. The result of SCC abstraction applied to the DTMC in Figure 2 (cf. Example 22)

The probability value of the regular expression for the second found path is

$$\text{val}\big((s_1,1)(s_3,1/2)\quad ((s_1,1/2)(s_3,1/2))^* \quad (s_1,1/2)(s_2,1/2)\big) =$$
$$\text{val}\big((s_1,1)(s_3,1/2)\big) \cdot \frac{1}{1-\text{val}\big((s_1,1/2)(s_3,1/2)\big)} \cdot \text{val}\big((s_1,1/2)(s_2,1/2)\big) =$$
$$1 \cdot 1/2 \qquad\qquad 4/3 \qquad\qquad 1/2 \cdot 1/2 =$$
$$1/6.$$

Since there are no more paths from the initial state s_0 to s_2, the total probability to reach s_2 from s_0 is the value $1/2 + 1/6 = 2/3$ of the regular expression $(s_1,1)(s_2,1/2) \mid (s_1,1)(s_3,1/2)((s_1,1/2)(s_3,1/2))^*(s_1,1/2)(s_2,1/2)$. ∎

The same can also be applied for *bounded* reachability properties $\mathbb{P}_{\leq\lambda}(\lozenge^{\leq h}T)$. The only changes are the usage of a hop-constraint shortest path algorithm and a different method for determining the probability of the represented path, such that only the probability of those paths represented by the regular expressions is counted whose length is at most h.

A different compaction of counterexamples is described by Andrés, D'Argenio and van Rossum in [24]. As many paths only differ in the number and order of unrollings of *loops* in the system, the non-trivial *strongly connected components*[2] (*SCCs*) of the DTMC under consideration, i. e., those SCCs which contain more than one state, are abstracted into direct edges from the input to the output states of the SCC. Input states are states in the SCC which have an incoming edge from outside the SCC, and output states are outside of the SCC, but have an incoming edge from inside the SCC. The probability of these edges is determined using model checking as the probabilities to reach the output states from the input states. After this abstraction, counterexamples as sets of paths can be easily determined in the resulting acyclic model.

Example 22. In the DTMC from Figure 2 on page 80, there are two non-trivial SCCs consisting of the states (i) $\{s_5, s_6, s_7\}$ with input state s_5 and output states

---

[2] A strongly connected component (SCC) is a maximal set of states such that for all s and s' in the SCC, s' can be reached from s inside the SCC.

s_3 and s_8, and (ii) $\{s_1, s_2, s_4\}$ with input states s_1 and s_2 and output state s_3. Eliminating these SCCs results in the DTMC shown in Figure 6. The wave-like edges represent paths through SCCs that have been abstracted. ■

4.2   Path-Based Counterexamples for PA

The simplest way to generate path-based counterexamples for a PA $\mathcal{M}$ [25, 38] is to first generate a *memoryless deterministic scheduler* σ^* which *maximizes* the reachability probability. Such a scheduler can be obtained as a by-product from model checking. This scheduler σ^* induces a DTMC $\mathcal{M}^{\sigma^*}$, such that $\mathrm{Pr}^{\mathcal{M}^{\sigma^*}}_{s_{\mathrm{init}}}(\lozenge T) = \max_{\sigma \in \mathrm{Sched}_{\mathcal{M}}} \mathrm{Pr}^{\mathcal{M}^{\sigma}}_{s_{\mathrm{init}}}(\lozenge T) > \lambda$. In a second step, the methods for counterexample generation described above are applied to $\mathcal{M}^{\sigma^*}$, resulting in a counterexample C for $\mathcal{M}^{\sigma^*}$. Then (σ^*, C) is a counterexample for $\mathcal{M}$.

However, as the computation of a maximizing scheduler requires to have the whole state space of $\mathcal{M}$ residing in memory, the advantage of using an algorithm like K* [50] which expands the state space on the fly when necessary, is lost. Therefore, Aljazzar and Leue [25] proposed a method which allows to not only compute the paths but also the scheduler on the fly as follows.

The problem when applying K* to a PA is that the generated paths are in general not compatible to the same scheduler. Therefore all paths are kept and clustered according to the scheduler choice made in each state. To do so an AND/OR-tree is maintained, which is initially empty. The OR-nodes correspond to the state nodes, in which the scheduler makes a decision. The AND-nodes correspond to the probabilistic decisions after an action-distribution pair has been chosen by the scheduler. Applying the K* algorithm to the PA $\mathcal{M}$, the next most probable path is determined. The new path π is inserted into the tree by first determining the longest prefix which is already contained in the tree. The remainder of the path becomes a new sub-tree, rooted at the node where the longest prefix ends. By a bottom-up traversal, a counterexample and a (partial) scheduler can be determined from the AND/OR-tree.

Example 23. Assume the MDP in Figure 7 left, which violates the reachability property $\mathbb{P}_{\leq 0.75}(\lozenge\{s_4\})$. Assume furthermore that the path search gives us the following paths in this order:

Path	Path probability
$\pi_1 = s_0 s_1 s_4$	0.5
$\pi_2 = s_0 s_2 s_4$	0.4
$\pi_3 = s_0 s_2 s_0 s_1 s_4$	0.25
$\pi_4 = s_0 s_1 s_0 s_1 s_4$	0.2
$\pi_5 = s_0 s_2 s_0 s_2 s_4$	0.2
$\pi_6 = s_0 s_1 s_0 s_2 s_4$	0.16
$\pi_7 = s_0 s_2 s_0 s_2 s_0 s_1 s_4$	0.125
$\pi_8 = s_0 s_1 s_0 s_2 s_0 s_1 s_4$	0.1

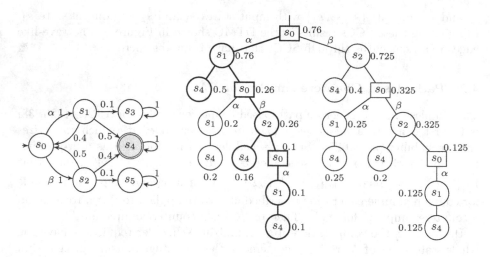

Fig. 7. Example MDP (cf. Example 23)

The generated path tree is depicted in Figure 7 on the right-hand side. The rectangular nodes are OR-nodes, the circles are AND-nodes. The value attached to a leaf is the probability of the path from the root to the leaf. The value attached to an inner AND-node is the sum of the values of its children, whereas the value of an OR-node is the maximum of all children values. Thus the value of the root specifies the maximal probability of found compatible paths, which are possible under a common scheduler.

After having added the last path, the probability of the root is above 0.75; the boldface subtree specifies a suitable scheduler to build a counterexample with the path set $\{\pi_1, \pi_6, \pi_8\}$. Note that this scheduler is deterministic but not memoryless. ∎

4.3   Applications of Path-Based Counterexamples

Path-based counterexamples are mostly used in two main areas: Firstly, for extracting the actual causes why a system fails. This information can be used for *debugging* an erroneous system [42–44]. Secondly, for *counterexample-guided abstraction refinement* of probabilistic automata [38]. We briefly sketch the main ideas of these works.

The extraction of reasons why a system fails is based on the notion of *causality* [57]. The idea behind that is that an event A is *critical* for event B, if A had not happened, then B would not have happened either. However, this simple notion of criticality is sometimes too coarse to be applicable. Therefore Halpern and Pearl [57] have refined it to take a *side-condition* into account: Essentially, if the events in some set E did not have happened, then A would be critical for the occurrence of B. In this case A is a *cause* of B.

Example 24 (taken from [57]). Assume Suzy and Billy are both throwing stones at a bottle, and both throw perfectly, so each stone would shatter the bottle. But Suzy throws a little harder such that her stone reaches the bottle first.

Clearly we would say that the cause of the shattering of the bottle is Suzy throwing a stone. However, Suzy throwing is not critical, since if she did not throw, the bottle would be shattered anyway (by Billy's stone). But under the side-condition that Billy does not throw, Suzy's throw becomes critical.[3]   ■

For details on this notion of causality, its formal definition, and a series of examples we refer the reader to [57].

Chockler and Halpern [58] use a quantitative notion regarding causes, given by the *degree of responsibility* $dR(A)$ of a cause A: Essentially $dR(A) = \frac{1}{1+k}$ where k is the size of the smallest side-condition needed to make A critical.

Debbi and Bourahla [42, 43] consider *constrained reachability properties* of the form $\mathbb{P}_{\leq\lambda}(\varphi_1 \cup \varphi_2)$ where φ_1 and φ_2 are arbitrary Boolean combinations of atomic propositions from the set AP, and $\mathbb{U}$ is the temporal until operator. As potential causes for the violation of the property they consider propositions of certain states, i.e., pairs $\langle s, a\rangle$ for $s \in S$ and $a \in$ AP: If the value of such a proposition is switched (under some side-condition), some paths in the considered counterexample no longer satisfy the formula $\varphi_1 \cup \varphi_2$, and the probability mass of the remaining paths is no longer above the bound λ. They assign weights to the causes as follows: The probability $\Pr(s, a)$ of a cause (s, a) is the sum of the probabilities of all paths π in the counterexample which contain state s. The weight $w(s, a)$ of a cause (s, a) is given by $w(s, a) = \Pr(s, a) \cdot dR(s, a)$. The causes are presented to the user with decreasing weight.

A different approach, also based on the notion of causality of [57], is described by Leitner-Fischer and Leue in [44, 59]. The authors proposed to extract *fault trees* from path-based probabilistic counterexamples. For this they do not consider just evidences of the underlying DTMC, but they rather keep track of the events which caused the transitions along an evidence. Since the order of events along the evidences can be crucial for the failure, they extend the notion of causality to also take the event order into account. Hence, a cause is a sequence of events together with restrictions on the order of the events. Additionally, the joint probability of the evidences which correspond to such a cause is computed. A fault tree is generated from the causes by using the undesired behavior as the root, which has one subtree per cause. Each cause is turned into a tree by using an AND gate over those events whose order does not matter, and an ordered-AND gate if the order does matter. Additionally the subtree corresponding to a cause is annotated by the probability of the corresponding evidences.

An interactive *visualization* technique is proposed by Aljazzar and Leue in [60] to support the user-guided identification of causal factors in large counterexamples. The authors apply this visualization technique to debug an embedded control system and a workstation cluster.

---

[3] The precise formal definition encompasses more constraints in order to avoid Billy throwing being a cause.

Failure mode and effects analysis (FMEA) allows to analyze potential system hazards resulting from system (component) failures. An extension of the original FMEA method can also handle probabilistic systems. In this context, path-based probabilistic counterexamples were used by Aljazzar *et al.* in [41] to facilitate the redesign of a potentially unsafe airbag system.

A different application of path-based counterexamples is described by Hermanns, Wachter and Zhang in [38] for *counterexample-guided abstraction refinement (CEGAR)*: The starting point is an abstraction of a PA, over-approximating the behavior of a concrete PA model. If this abstraction is too coarse, it might violate a property even if the concrete system satisfies it. In this case counterexamples are used to refine the abstraction.

A PA is abstracted by defining a finite partitioning of its state space and representing each block of the partition by an abstract state; all transitions targeting a concrete state are redirected to its abstract state, and similarly all outgoing transitions of a concrete state start in the abstract state to which it belongs.

Starting with an initial abstraction, model checking is performed to check whether the property at hand is satisfied. If this is the case, one can conclude that it is also satisfied in the concrete model. However, if the property is violated by the abstraction, the optimal scheduler, obtained from the model checking process, is used to compute the induced DTMC. Therein a path-based counterexample is determined. Now two cases are possible: Either the counterexample of the abstract system corresponds to a counterexample in the concrete model, in which case the property is also violated by the concrete model. Or the counterexample is *spurious*, i. e., it exists only in the abstraction due to the over-approximating behavior, in which case the abstraction needs to be refined. This is done by *predicate abstraction*, splitting the abstract states according to a predicate P into a subset satisfying P and one violating it. The predicate P is obtained from the counterexample evidences via interpolation.

Experimental results show that in some cases a definite statement about the satisfaction of the property at hand can be made on a very coarse approximation. This speeds up the model checking process and allows to handle much larger systems than with conventional methods.

5   Critical Subsystems

Path-based representations of counterexamples, as discussed in the previous Section 4, have some major drawbacks: The number of paths needed might be very large (or even infinite), leading to high memory requirements. As a consequence, the number of search iterations in terms of path-searches is equally high, leading to high computational costs. Finally, a counterexample consisting of a high number of potentially long paths is hard to understand and analyze, therefore its usefulness is restricted.

An alternative is to use *critical subsystems*, which are fractions of DTMC, MDP or PA models violating a property, such that the behavior of the models restricted to the critical subsystems already violates the property. It is often possible to generate critical subsystems whose size is smaller by orders of magnitude in comparison to the input system. Thereby, the *critical part* of the original system leading to the violation is highlighted.

Definition 11 (Critical subsystems of DTMCs). *Assume a DTMC $D = (S, s_{init}, P, L)$, a target state set $T \subseteq S$ and some $\lambda \in [0, 1] \cap \mathbb{Q}$ such that $D \not\models \mathbb{P}_{\leq \lambda}(\Diamond T)$.*

A subsystem D' of D, written $D' \sqsubseteq D$, is a DTMC $D' = (S', s_{init}, P', L')$ such that $S' \subseteq S$, $s_{init} \in S'$, $P'(s, s') > 0$ implies $P'(s, s') = P(s, s')$ for all $s, s' \in S'$, and $L'(s) = L(s)$ for all $s \in S'$.

Given $S' \subseteq S$ with $s_{init} \in S'$, the subsystem $D_{S'} = (S', s_{init}, P', L')$ of D with $P'(s, s') = P(s, s')$ and $L'(s) = L(s)$ for all $s, s' \in S'$ is called the subsystem of D induced by S'.

A subsystem D' of D is critical *for $\mathbb{P}_{\leq \lambda}(\Diamond T)$ if $T \cap S' \neq \emptyset$ and $D' \not\models \mathbb{P}_{\leq \lambda}(\Diamond (T \cap S'))$.*

Example 25. For the DTMC in Figure 2 on page 80 and the reachability property $\mathbb{P}_{\leq 0.3}(\Diamond \{s_3\})$, the following DTMC is a critical subsystem, since the probability to reach s_3 from s_0 is $\frac{1}{2} \cdot \frac{1}{1 - \frac{1}{2} \cdot \frac{1}{2}} \cdot \frac{1}{2} = \frac{1}{3} > 0.3$:

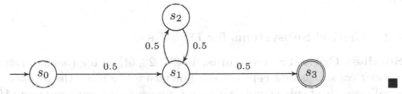

The above definition of critical subsystems of DTMCs is a special case of the following definition generalized for PAs:

Definition 12 (Critical subsystems for PAs). *Assume a PA $M = (S, s_{init}, Act, \hat{P}, L)$, a target state set $T \subseteq S$ and some $\lambda \in [0, 1] \cap \mathbb{Q}$ such that $M \not\models \mathbb{P}_{\leq \lambda}(\Diamond T)$.*

A subsystem M' of M, written $M' \sqsubseteq M$, is a PA $M' = (S', s_{init}, Act, \hat{P}', L')$ such that $S' \subseteq S$, $s_{init} \in S'$, $L'(s) = L(s)$ for all $s \in S'$, and for each $s \in S'$ there is an injective function $f : \hat{P}'(s) \to \hat{P}(s)$ such that for all $(\alpha', \mu') \in \hat{P}'(s)$ with $f((\alpha', \mu')) = (\alpha, \mu)$ if it holds that $\alpha' = \alpha$ and $\mu'(s') = \mu(s')$ for all $s' \in supp(\mu')$.

A subsystem M' of M is critical *for $\mathbb{P}_{\leq \lambda}(\Diamond T)$ if $T \cap S' \neq \emptyset$ and $M' \not\models \mathbb{P}_{\leq \lambda}(\Diamond (T \cap S'))$.*

To have well-understandable explanations for the property violation, for PAs we are interested in their critical subsystems induced by deterministic memoryless schedulers. Therefore, in the context of counterexamples in the following we consider only DTMCs (as deterministic PAs) as critical subsystems.

The set of those paths of a critical subsystem D' which are evidences for a reachability property form a counterexample in the classical sense as in Definition 8, i.e.,

$$C := \mathrm{Paths}_{fin}^{D'}(s_{init}, T)$$

is a counterexample. Therefore, a critical subsystem can be seen as a *symbolic representation* of a counterexample.

We define minimality of critical subsystems in terms of their state space size: A critical subsystem is *minimal* if it has a minimal set of states under all critical subsystems. Analogously to counterexamples, we can also define a *smallest* critical subsystem to be a minimal critical subsystem in which the probability to reach a target state is maximal under all minimal critical subsystems. Note that even if a critical subsystem is smallest or minimal, this does not induce a smallest or minimal counterexample in the sense of [17].

Critical subsystems can be generated in various ways. In this section, we first discuss the generation of critical subsystems for DTMCs: We start by describing how solver technologies can be used to compute *smallest critical subsystems* of DTMCs. This powerful method is also applicable to arbitrary ω-regular properties [27, 28, 61]. Afterward we describe heuristic algorithms which determine a (small) critical subsystem by means of *graph algorithms* as presented by Aljazzar and Leue in [30] and by Jansen *et al.* in [29]. We also give the intuition of an *extension to symbolic graph representations* [32]. The second part of this section is devoted to the computation of smallest critical subsystems for MDPs and PAs.

5.1   Critical Subsystems for DTMCs

Smallest Critical Subsystems. In [27, 28, 61] an approach to compute *smallest critical subsystems* is proposed. The idea is to encode the problem of finding a smallest critical subsystem as a *mixed integer linear programming (MILP)* problem (see, e.g., [62]). It is also possible to give an SMT-formulation over linear real arithmetic, but the experiments in [27] clearly show that the MILP formulation is much more efficiently solvable. We therefore restrict our presentation here to the MILP formulation.

Definition 13 (Mixed integer linear program). *Let $A \in \mathbb{Q}^{m \times n}$, $B \in \mathbb{Q}^{m \times k}$, $b \in \mathbb{Q}^m$, $c \in \mathbb{Q}^n$, and $d \in \mathbb{Q}^k$. A mixed integer linear program (MILP) consists in computing $\min c^T x + d^T y$ such that $Ax + By \leq b$ and $x \in \mathbb{R}^n$, $y \in \mathbb{Z}^k$.*

In the following let $\mathcal{D} = (S, s_{\text{init}}, P, L)$ be a DTMC and $\mathbb{P}_{\leq \lambda}(\Diamond T)$ a reachability property that is violated by $\mathcal{D}$. We assume that $\mathcal{D}$ does not contain any state that is irrelevant for reaching T from s_{init}.

We want to determine a minimal set $S' \subseteq S$ of states such that $\mathcal{D}_{S'}$ is a critical subsystem. To do so, we introduce for each state $s \in S$ a decision variable $x_s \in \{0, 1\} \subseteq \mathbb{Z}$, which should have the value 1 iff s is contained in the selected subsystem, i.e., if $s \in S'$. Additionally we need for each $s \in S$ a variable $p_s \in [0, 1] \cap \mathbb{Q}$ which stores the probability to reach T from s within the selected subsystem $\mathcal{D}_{S'}$. The following MILP then yields a smallest critical subsystem of $\mathcal{D}$ and $\mathbb{P}_{\leq \lambda}(\Diamond T)$:

$$\text{minimize} \quad -\frac{1}{2} \cdot p_{s_{\text{init}}} + \sum_{s \in S} x_s \tag{2a}$$

such that

$$\forall s \in T : \quad p_s = x_s \tag{2b}$$

$$\forall s \in S \setminus T : \quad p_s \leq x_s \tag{2c}$$

$$\forall s \in S \setminus T : \quad p_s \leq \sum_{s' \in \mathrm{supp}(P(s))} P(s,s') \cdot p_{s'} \tag{2d}$$

$$p_{s_{\mathrm{init}}} > \lambda . \tag{2e}$$

If ν is a satisfying assignment of this MILP, then $\mathcal{D}_{S'}$ with $S' = \{s \in S \mid \nu(x_s) = 1\}$ is a smallest critical subsystem. Constraint (2b) states that the probability of a target state is 1 if it is contained in the subsystem, and 0 otherwise. Constraint (2c) ensures that the probability contribution of states not contained in the subsystem is 0. Constraint (2d) bounds the probability contribution of each non-target state by the sum of the probabilities to go to a successor state times the probability contribution of the successor state. Finally, (2e) encodes that the subsystem is critical.

The objective function (2a) ensures (i) that the subsystem is minimal by minimizing the number of x_s-variables with value 1 and (ii) that the subsystem is smallest by minimizing $-1/2 \cdot p_{s_{\mathrm{init}}}$.

Example 26. Consider again the DTMC $\mathcal{D}$ in Figure 2 on page 80 and the violated reachability property $\mathbb{P}_{\leq 0.3}(\Diamond \{s_3\})$. Note that s_8 is irrelevant and can therefore be ignored together with all its incident transitions. The constraints to compute a smallest critical subsystem are as follows:

minimize $-1/2 \cdot p_{s_0} + x_{s_0} + x_{s_1} + x_{s_2} + x_{s_3} + x_{s_4} + x_{s_5} + x_{s_6} + x_{s_7}$
such that

$$p_{s_3} = x_{s_3}$$

$$p_{s_0} \leq x_{s_0} \qquad p_{s_0} \leq 0.5 p_{s_1} + 0.25 p_{s_2} + 0.25 p_{s_5}$$

$$p_{s_1} \leq x_{s_1} \qquad p_{s_1} \leq 0.5 p_{s_2} + 0.5 p_{s_3}$$

$$p_{s_2} \leq x_{s_2} \qquad p_{s_2} \leq 0.5 p_{s_1} + 0.5 p_{s_4}$$

$$p_{s_4} \leq x_{s_4} \qquad p_{s_4} \leq 0.7 p_{s_1} + 0.3 p_{s_3}$$

$$p_{s_5} \leq x_{s_5} \qquad p_{s_5} \leq 1.0 p_{s_6}$$

$$p_{s_6} \leq x_{s_6} \qquad p_{s_6} \leq 0.5 p_{s_3} + 0.5 p_{s_7}$$

$$p_{s_7} \leq x_{s_7} \qquad p_{s_7} \leq 0.25 p_{s_5} + 0.25 p_{s_6}$$

$$p_{s_0} > 0.3$$

Solving this MILP yields the following assignment:

Variable	x_{s_0}	p_{s_0}	x_{s_1}	p_{s_1}	x_{s_2}	p_{s_2}	x_{s_3}	p_{s_3}	x_{s_4}	p_{s_4}	x_{s_5}	p_{s_5}	x_{s_6}	p_{s_6}	x_{s_7}	p_{s_7}
Value	1	$5/12$	1	$2/3$	1	$1/3$	1	1	0	0	0	0	0	0	0	0

This solution corresponds to the DTMC $\mathcal{D}_{S'}$ with $S' = \{s_0, s_1, s_2, s_3\}$, shown in Figure 11(b) on page 102. ∎

The solution of this MILP is rather costly (solving MILPs in general is NP-complete). However, the solution process can be accelerated by adding redundant

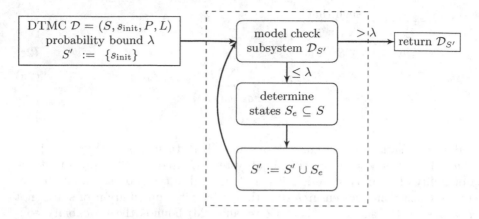

Fig. 8. Incremental generation of critical subsystems

constraints which exclude non-optimal solutions from the search space [27, 61]. For example, one can require that each state $s \notin T$ contained in the subsystem has a successor state which is also contained in the subsystem:

$$\forall s \in S \setminus T: \quad x_s \leq \sum_{s' \in \text{supp}(P(s))} x_{s'} \ .$$

The described approach has been generalized to arbitrary ω-regular properties [28, 61].

Heuristic Approaches. An alternative approach to determine critical subsystems is to use the classical path search algorithms as presented in Section 4 to search for evidences and use the states or transitions of these evidences to incrementally build a subsystem until it becomes critical. Here we focus on building critical subsystems using the states in evidences. Analogously, we could also use the transitions to build a subsystem with a similar approach.

Assume in the following a DTMC $\mathcal{D} = (S, s_{\text{init}}, P, L)$, a set $T \subseteq S$ of target states and an upper probability bound $\lambda \in [0, 1] \cap \mathbb{Q}$ of reaching target states from T. We assume this probability to be exceeded in $\mathcal{D}$.

The process of computing a critical subsystem is depicted in Figure 8. We start with the smallest possible subsystem containing just the initial state (see Definition 11 for the definition of $\mathcal{D}_{S'}$). As long as the subsystem is not yet critical, we iteratively determine a new state set and extend the previous subsystem with these states. Thereby the method that determines the state sets must assure progress, i.e., that new states are added to the subsystem after a finite number of iterations. Under this condition, the finiteness of the state space guarantees termination.

Calling a model checker in every iteration is quite costly. Therefore, all approaches based on this framework use some heuristics to avoid this. For instance, one might think of performing model checking only after a certain number of iterations or only start to check the system after a certain size of the subsystem is reached.

We will now shortly discuss what approaches have been proposed to determine the state sets to incrementally extend subsystems.

Extended best-first search. The first method to compute critical subsystems using graph-search algorithms was given in [30] by Aljazzar and Leue. The authors extend the *best-first* (*BF*) search method [63] to what they call *eXtended Best-First* (*XBF*) search, implemented in [36]. Below we describe the XBF search, without highlighting the differences to the BF search, which are discussed in [30].

For the XBF search, the system does not need to be given explicitly in the beginning but is explored *on the fly*, which is a great advantage for very large systems where a counterexample might be reasonably small. Instead, a symbolic model representation can be used.

Starting from the initial state, new states are discovered by visiting the successors of already discovered states. Two state lists open and closed store the states discovered so far. The ordered list open contains discovered states whose successors have not been expanded yet. In each step, one (with respect to the ordering maximal) state s from open is chosen, its not yet discovered successors are added to open, and s is moved from open to closed. To have all relevant information about the explored part of the model, for all states in the above two lists we also store all incoming transitions through which the state was visited.

The list open is ordered with respect to an evaluation function $f : S \to \mathbb{Q}$ which estimates for each discovered state s the probability of the most probable path from the initial state to a target state through s. The estimation

$$f(s) = g(s) \cdot h(s)$$

is composed by two factors: Firstly, $g(s)$ estimates the probability of the most probable path from s_{init} to s by the probability of the most probable such path found so far. Secondly, $h(s)$ uses further knowledge about the system at hand (if available) to estimate the probability of the most probable path from s to T. If the latter function is not constant, the search is called *informed search*.

Initially, $g(s_{\text{init}}) = 1$. When expanding the successor s' of a state s, we define $g(s')$ to be $g(s) \cdot P(s, s')$ if s' is encountered the first time, and the maximum of $g(s) \cdot P(s, s')$ and the old $g(s')$ value else. When in the latter case $g(s')$ is updated to a larger value, if s' was already in the closed set, it is moved back to the open set to propagate the improvement.

The algorithm maintains an initially empty subsystem $\mathcal{D}'$ of the already discovered model part. Each time a state s is visited, such that s is either a target state or it is included in $\mathcal{D}'$, the subsystem $\mathcal{D}'$ gets extended with the fragment of the currently known model part that is backward reachable from s. The algorithm terminates if this subsystem becomes critical ([30] calls it a *diagnostic subgraph*).

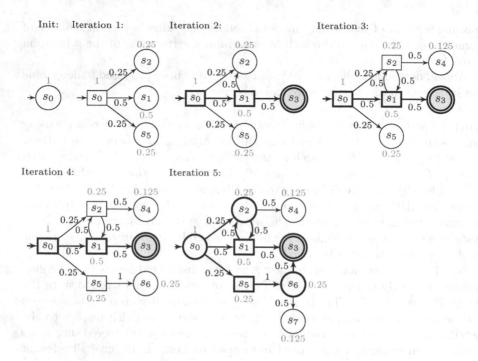

Fig. 9. Illustration of the XBF search (cf. Example 27)

Example 27. For the DTMC in Figure 2 on page 80 and the reachability property
$\mathbb{P}_{\leq 0.5}(\lozenge\{s_3\})$, the computation of the XBF search is illustrated in Figure 9.
Rectangular nodes are stored in the closed list, circles in the open list. For
simplicity we assume $h(s) = 1$ for all states $s \in S$. Thus the current estimate
values $f(s) = g(s) \cdot 1$ (shown beside the states in gray color) equal the highest
known path probability from s_0 to s. The boldface fraction of the discovered
model part is the current subsystem, which is critical after the fifth iteration
(with probability $^{13}/_{24}$ to reach s_3 from s_0). ∎

Search based on k shortest paths. In [29] two different graph search algorithms
are utilized. We distinguish the *global search* and *local search* approach.

The *global search* is an adaption of the k shortest paths search as described
in Section 4. However, paths are collected not until a counterexample as a list of
paths is formed, but until the subsystem $\mathcal{D}_{S'}$ induced by the states S' on found
paths has enough probability mass, i. e., until it becomes critical.

Example 28. For the DTMC $\mathcal{D}$ in Figure 2 on page 80 and the violated property
$\mathbb{P}_{\leq 0.4}(\lozenge\{s_3\})$, three most probable paths are:

Path	Probability
$\pi_1 = s_0 s_1 s_3$	0.25
$\pi_2 = s_0 s_5 s_6 s_3$	0.125
$\pi_3 = s_0 s_2 s_1 s_3$	0.0625

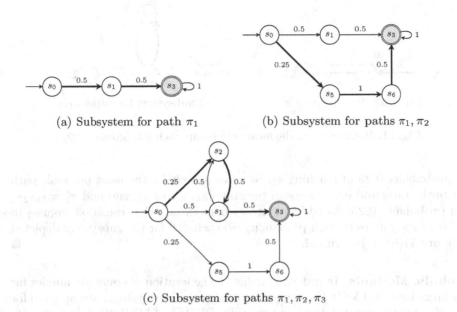

(a) Subsystem for path π_1 (b) Subsystem for paths π_1, π_2

(c) Subsystem for paths π_1, π_2, π_3

Fig. 10. Illustration of the global search approach (cf. Example 28)

Now, we subsequently add these paths to an initially empty subsystem, until inside this system the probability to reach the state s_3 exceeds 0.4. We highlight the latest paths by thick edges in the subsystem. Starting with π_1, the initial subsystem consists of the states of this path, see Figure 10(a), with the reachability probability $0.25 < 0.4$. In the next iteration, the subsystem is extended by the states of path π_2, see Figure 10(b). The probability is now 0.375 which is still not high enough. Adding path π_3 in the next iteration effectively extends the subsystem by state s_2 as the other states are already part of the subsystem. Note that we add to the subsystem not only the states and transitions along found paths, but all transitions connecting them in the full model. The model checking result is now $13/24 \approx 0.542$, so the subsystem depicted in Figure 10(c) is critical and the search terminates.   ∎

The *local search* also searches for most probable paths to form a subsystem, however, not the most probable paths from the initial to target states, but the most probable paths connecting fragments of already found paths. Intuitively, every new path to be found has to be the most probable one that both starts and ends in states that are already contained in the current subsystem while the states in between are new.

Example 29. Reconsider the DTMC in Figure 2 on page 80 and the violated property $\mathbb{P}_{\leq 0.4}(\Diamond s_3)$ as in Example 28. Initially, we search for the most probable path that connects the initial state and target states, i. e., again path $\pi_1 = s_0 s_1 s_3$ is found and added to the subsystem, depicted in Figure 11(a). The subsystem

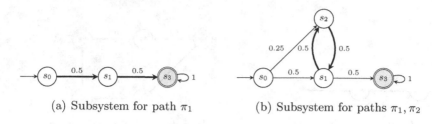

(a) Subsystem for path π_1 (b) Subsystem for paths π_1, π_2

Fig. 11. Illustration of the local search approach (cf. Example 29)

has probability 0.25 of reaching s_3. Now, we search for the most probable path that both starts and ends in one of the states s_0, s_1, or s_3, and find $\pi_2' = s_1 s_2 s_1$ with probability 0.25. As adding state s_2 induces also the transition from s_0 to s_2 this already gives enough probability $5/12 \approx 0.416$ for the subsystem depicted in Figure 11(b) to be critical.   ∎

Symbolic Methods. In order to enable the generation of counterexamples for very large input DTMCs, the computation of critical subsystems was adapted for *symbolic graph representations*, in particular BDDs and MTBDDs, see Section 2.

The framework for the symbolic method is the same as depicted in Figure 8, while special attention is required regarding certain properties of BDDs. As methods to find new states to extend a subsystem, symbolic versions of the *global search* and the *local search* were devised. This was done for both *bounded model checking* and *symbolic graph search algorithms*; for an introduction to the underlying concepts see Section 4. The adaptions were first proposed in [31] and improved and extended in [32].

Recall, that a DTMC $\mathcal{D} = (S, s_{\text{init}}, P, L)$ together with a set of target states $T \subseteq S$ is symbolically represented by a BDD $\hat{I}$ representing the initial state s_{init}, a BDD $\hat{T}$ representing the target states T and an MTBDD $\hat{P}$ representing the transition probability matrix P. In the symbolic algorithms, an MTBDD *SubSys* is maintained which stands for the current subsystem. The goal of all methods given in the following is to compute a set of states that is used to extend the current subsystem, saved in a BDD *NewStates*. The subsystem is verified by a symbolic version of the standard DTMC model checking procedure, see [64, 65]. This is also used in PRISM [12].

Bounded Model Checking. Using the bounded model checking approach from [19] for DTMCs in combination with the incremental generation of subsystems, this directly yields a global search approach for symbolic graph structures. Recall Formula 1 from Section 4.1, where from the (MT)BDDs $\hat{I}$, $\hat{T}$ and $\hat{P}$ predicates init, target and trans are created. In every iteration, the SAT solver computes a path of the DTMC starting at $\hat{I}$ and ending in a state of $\hat{T}$ using transitions of $\hat{P}$. This is achieved by satisfaction of the corresponding predicates. *NewStates* is assigned the states of this path and *SubSys* is extended accordingly. This goes on until model checking reports that the subsystem has enough probability mass.

In contrast to adapting the global search, for the *local search*, also referred to as *fragment search*, we need predicates that are changed *dynamically*. This is due to the fact that in each iteration a path starting at any state of the current subsystem and ending in such a state is to be searched for. As *SubSys* is changed all throughout the process, we need a predicate K that captures this changing set of states. This is technically achieved by utilizing the *assumption* functionality of the SAT solver in the sense that in every iteration the predicate K is satisfied if the SAT solver assigns its variables such that a state of the current subsystem corresponds to these variable values. The goal is now to find paths of arbitrary but bounded length n by assigning the variable sets $v_0, \ldots, v_n$ such that they correspond to such a path. The formula reads as follows:

$$\mathsf{K}(v_0) \;\wedge\; \mathsf{trans}(v_0, v_1) \;\wedge \neg\mathsf{K}(v_1) \;\wedge\; \bigvee_{i=2}^{n} \mathsf{K}(v_i)$$

$$\wedge \bigwedge_{j=1}^{n-1} [(\neg\mathsf{K}(v_j) \to \mathsf{trans}(v_j, v_{j+1})) \;\wedge\; (\mathsf{K}(v_j) \to v_j = v_{j+1})]$$

Intuitively, every path starts in a state of K ($\mathsf{K}(v_0)$). From this state, a transition ($\mathsf{trans}(v_0, v_1)$) has to be taken to a state that is *not* part of K ($\neg\mathsf{K}(v_1)$). One of the following states has to be part of K again ($\bigvee_{i=2}^{n} \mathsf{K}(v_i)$). For all states it has to hold that as long as a state is not part of K, a transition is taken to another state ($\neg\mathsf{K}(v_j) \to \mathsf{trans}(v_j, v_{j+1})$). As soon as a state is inside K, all following variables are assigned the same values creating an implicit self-loop on this state ($\mathsf{K}(v_{j-1}) \to v_j = v_{j+1}$). For more technical details such as the handling of the initial path starting in the initial state s_{init} and ending in a target state or how to actually form the set K, we refer to the original publications. In addition, a heuristic was given guiding the SAT solver to assign variables such that more probable paths are found.

Symbolic Graph Search. In Section 4.1 we described how the k shortest path search was implemented symbolically [21]. The key ingredients were a symbolic version of Dijkstra's shortest path, called *flooding Dijkstra*, and the method $\mathsf{Change}(\hat{P}, \hat{I}, \hat{T}, SP)$ which transformed the input system given by $\hat{P}, \hat{I}$ and $\hat{T}$ with respect to the current shortest path SP such that SP is not found any more by the flooding Dijkstra. Instead, the second most probable path in the context of the original system is returned in this modified system. This process is iterated until the sufficient number of paths is achieved. For the shortest path algorithm we write

$$\mathsf{ShortestPath}(\hat{P}, \hat{I}, \hat{T})$$

for paths that have transitions out of $\hat{P}$, start in $\hat{I}$ and end in $\hat{T}$.

Although this is conceptually working, the transition MTBDD $\hat{P}$ is basically doubled in each step by the graph transformation. This causes an exponential blow-up of the MTBDD-size which renders this approach not applicable for relevant benchmarks. Therefore, a straightforward adaption to the generation of critical subsystems is not feasible.

In modification called the *adaptive global search*, the method for changing the graph was used in a different way. Instead of incrementally changing the system according to the current shortest path, in each step the *original system* $(\hat{P}, \hat{I}, \hat{T})$ is transformed such that the new shortest path will have only states that are not already part of *SubSys*:

$$(\hat{P}, \hat{I}, \hat{T}) := \texttt{Change}(\hat{P}, \hat{I}, \hat{T}, SubSys)$$

Thereby, the size of the system only increases linearly in each step. Additionally, the flooding Dijkstra computes not only one shortest path but actually the set of all shortest paths that have the same probability and length. All of these paths are added to the current subsystem at once. If the probability mass is exceeded extensively, the *adaptive* algorithm performs a backtracking.

An adaption of the fragment search to symbolic graph algorithms was also done. Consider a BDD *SubSysStates* which represents the states of the current subsystem. Then, in every iteration the shortest path starting and ending in states of the subsystem via transitions from the original system without the subsystem is computed:

$$\texttt{ShortestPath}(\hat{P} \setminus SubSys, SubSysStates, SubSysStates)$$

These symbolic graph algorithms enabled the generation of counterexamples for input DTMCs with billions of states in their explicit representation.

Compact Representations. Based on a hierarchical SCC abstraction presented in [66], the authors of [29] proposed a method for generating *hierarchical counterexamples* for DTMCs. The starting point is an abstract model, for which a critical subsystem is computed (in [29] the local and global search from Section 5.1 are used, but any other approach could be also applied). In order to explore the system in more detail, important parts of the critical subsystem can be concretized and, to reduce its size, in this concretized system again a critical subsystem can be determined. This allows to search for counterexamples on very large input graphs, as the abstract input systems are both very small and simply structured. As concretization up to the original system can be done only in certain parts of interest, no information is lost while only a fraction of the whole system has to be explored.

We first describe the basic idea of the *SCC abstraction* from [66], which can also be used for model checking. The underlying graph of the DTMC gets hierarchically decomposed first into its SCCs, then the SCCs into sub-SCCs not containing the input states and so on, until at the inner-most levels no further non-trivial sub-SCCs exist.

Example 30. The hierarchical SCC decomposition of the DTMC in Figure 2 on page 80 is illustrated in Figure 12, where the SCCs and sub-SCCs are indicated by rectangles. When neglecting its input states, the SCC $S_1 = \{s_1, s_2, s_4\}$ does

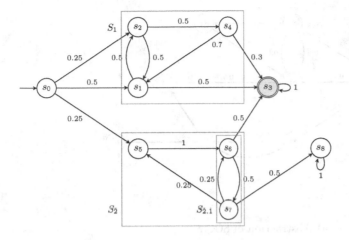

Fig. 12. The SCC decomposition of a DTMC $\mathcal{D}$ (cf. Example 30)

not have any sub-SCCs. The SCC $S_2 = \{s_5, s_6, s_7\}$ contains a sub-SCC $S_{2.1} = \{s_6, s_7\} \subseteq S_2$. ∎

In a bottom-up traversal starting at the inner-most sub-SCCs, the reachability probabilities $p_{\mathrm{abs}}(s, s')$ from each input state s to each output state s' inside the given sub-SCC are computed by utilizing certain properties of DTMCs. This computation was inspired by the work of Andrés, D'Argenio and van Rossum [24]. All non-input nodes and all transitions inside the sub-SCC are removed and abstract transitions are added from each input state s to each output state s' carrying the whole probability mass $p_{\mathrm{abs}}(s, s')$. Note that the probability to reach target states from the initial state in the resulting DTMC equals the probability in the DTMC before the transformation.

Example 31. Consider the hierarchically decomposed DTMC $\mathcal{D}$ in Figure 12. In Figure 13(a), the abstraction of the sub-SCC $S_{2.1}$ is shown. Basically, the sub-SCC is abstracted by a single abstract state s_6. We denote such abstract states by a rectangular shape, and abstract transitions by thick lines. The abstract probabilities are:

$$p_{\mathrm{abs}}(s_6, s_3) = \,^4/_7 \quad p_{\mathrm{abs}}(s_6, s_5) = \,^1/_7 \quad p_{\mathrm{abs}}(s_6, s_8) = \,^2/_7 \,.$$

At the next outer level, now the SCC S_2 can be abstracted. After abstracting also SCC S_1, an acyclic graph remains which is depicted in Figure 13(b). Note that SCC S_1 results in two abstract states as it has two input states, i. e., states that have an incoming transitions from outside the SCC.

It is easy to compute the abstract probabilities therein, e. g., by solving the simple linear equation system as explained in Section 2. The resulting abstract graph is depicted in Figure 13(c). Here, only transitions from the initial state s_0 to all absorbing states including the target state s_3 are contained. As this

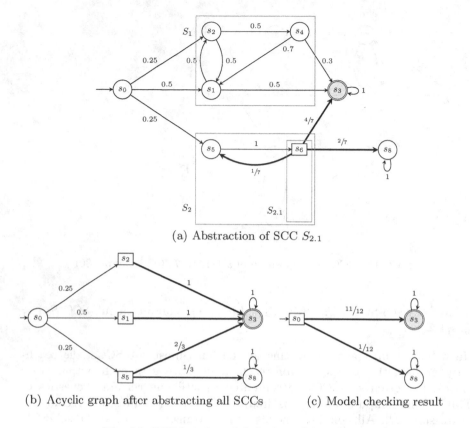

(a) Abstraction of SCC $S_{2.1}$

(b) Acyclic graph after abstracting all SCCs   (c) Model checking result

Fig. 13. SCC-based model checking (cf. Example 31)

corresponds to the probability of reaching state s_3 in the original DTMC $\mathcal{D}$, we have the model checking result for the reachability property:

$$\mathrm{Pr}^{\mathcal{D}}(\lozenge\{s_3\}) = p_{\mathrm{abs}}(s_1, s_3) = {}^{11}/_{12} \approx 0.9167\,.$$

∎

The key idea of the hierarchical counterexample generation is now to start the search on the abstract graph. Following the general procedure as depicted in Figure 8, states are collected using path search algorithms until the subsystem has enough probability mass to be critical. If the resulting critical subsystem gives enough debugging information, the process terminates, otherwise certain abstract states, i. e., abstracted SCCs or sub-SCCs, inside the abstract critical subsystem can be *concretized* with respect to the former SCC abstraction and a new search can be started on this more detailed system. The choice of one or more states to be concretized can either be done interactively by user input or guided by certain heuristics.

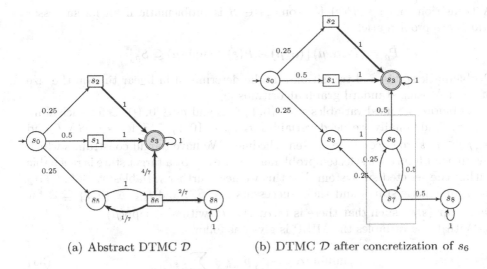

(a) Abstract DTMC $\mathcal{D}$ (b) DTMC $\mathcal{D}$ after concretization of s_6

Fig. 14. Concretizing state s_6 (cf. Example 32)

Example 32. To explain the procedure of concretizing states, consider a partially abstracted version of the DTMC from Figure 12 depicted in Figure 14(a), where states s_0 and s_5 are concretized, but s_1, s_2 and s_6 are still abstract. Assume now, s_6 is chosen to be concretized. All abstract transitions leaving s_6 are removed and the SCC which was abstracted by them is inserted. The result of the concretization step is depicted in Figure 14(b).   ∎

5.2 Critical Subsystems for PAs

Let $\mathcal{M} = (S, s_{\text{init}}, \text{Act}, \hat{P}, L)$ be a PA and $\mathbb{P}_{\leq\lambda}(\lozenge T)$ be a reachability property which is violated by $\mathcal{M}$. We want to compute a smallest critical subsystem for PA, which is an NP-hard problem. The approach below [27] is formalized for reachability properties, but it can be extended to ω-regular properties.

The main difference to DTMCs is that the MILP has to be enriched by the computation of an appropriate scheduler. Please note that a scheduler that maximizes the reachability probability does not necessarily induce a DTMC having a critical subsystem which is minimal among all critical subsystems of the PA. Hence, we cannot compute a scheduler beforehand, but have to integrate the scheduler computation into the MILP.

Doing so we have to take into account that, for some state $s \in S$, under some schedulers the target states T can be unreachable from s, but reachable for other schedulers. Such states are called *problematic*. Let

$$S_p = \{s \in S \mid \exists \sigma \in \text{Sched}_{\mathcal{M}} : \text{Pr}_s^{\mathcal{M}^\sigma}(\lozenge T) = 0\}$$

be the set of all problematic states and let S_p^+ the set of all problematic states and their successors. If $s \notin S_p$ then s is called *unproblematic* for T.

A transition $(\alpha, \mu) \in \hat{P}(s)$ for some $s \in S$ is problematic if all its successor states are problematic:

$$\hat{P}_p = \{(s, \alpha, \mu) \mid (\alpha, \mu) \in \hat{P}(s) \wedge \operatorname{supp}(\mu) \subseteq S_p\} .$$

Problematic states and transitions can be determined in linear time in the size of the PA using standard graph algorithms [9].

As before, we need variables $x_s \in \{0, 1\} \subseteq \mathbb{Z}$ and $p_s \in [0, 1] \cap \mathbb{Q}$ for each state $s \in S$. Additionally we need variables $\sigma_{s,\alpha,\mu} \in \{0, 1\} \subseteq \mathbb{Z}$ for $s \in S \setminus T$ and $(\alpha, \mu) \in \hat{P}(s)$ to encode the chosen scheduler. We have to add constraints which ensure that from each selected problematic state $s \in S_p$ a target state is reachable within the selected subsystem. For this we need further variables: $r_s \in [0, 1] \cap \mathbb{Q}$ for problematic states and their successors $s \in S_p^+$, and $t_{s,s'} \in \{0, 1\} \subseteq \mathbb{Z}$ for each pair (s, s') such that there is $(s, \alpha, \mu) \in \hat{P}_p$ with $s' \in \operatorname{supp}(\mu)$.

With these variables the MILP is given as follows:

$$\text{minimize} \quad -\frac{1}{2} p_{s_{\text{init}}} + \sum_{s \in S} x_s \tag{3a}$$

such that

$$p_{s_{\text{init}}} > \lambda \tag{3b}$$

$$\forall s \in T: \quad p_s = x_s \tag{3c}$$

$$\forall s \in S \setminus T: \quad p_s \leq x_s \tag{3d}$$

$$\forall s \in S \setminus T: \quad \sum_{(\alpha, \mu) \in \hat{P}(s)} \sigma_{s,\alpha,\mu} = x_s \tag{3e}$$

$$\forall s \in S \setminus T \; \forall (\alpha, \mu) \in \hat{P}(s): \quad p_s \leq (1 - \sigma_{s,\alpha,\mu}) + \sum_{s' \in \operatorname{supp}(\mu)} \mu(s') \cdot p_{s'} \tag{3f}$$

$$\forall (s, \alpha, \mu) \in \hat{P}_p \; \forall s' \in \operatorname{supp}(\mu): \quad t_{s,s'} \leq x_{s'} \tag{3g}$$

$$\forall (s, \alpha, \mu) \in \hat{P}_p \; \forall s' \in \operatorname{supp}(\mu): \quad r_s < r_{s'} + (1 - t_{s,s'}) \tag{3h}$$

$$\forall (s, \alpha, \mu) \in \hat{P}_p: \quad (1 - \sigma_{s,\alpha,\mu}) + \sum_{s' \in \operatorname{supp}(\mu)} t_{s,s'} \geq x_s . \tag{3i}$$

The objective function (3a) and the constraints (3b), (3c), and (3d) are the same as for DTMCs. Constraint (3e) takes care that the scheduler selects exactly one pair $(\alpha, \mu) \in P(s)$ for each state $s \in S$ that is contained in the subsystem, and none for states not in the subsystem. Constraint (3f) is the pendant to constraint (2d) of the MILP for DTMCs. The difference is the term $(1 - \sigma_{s,\alpha,\mu})$. It ensures that the constraint is trivially satisfied for all transitions that are not selected by the scheduler. The remaining constraints (3g)–(3i) take care that from each problematic state a non-problematic (and therefore a target) state is reachable within the selected subsystem. For details on these reachability constraints we refer the reader to [61].

Example 33. Consider the same MDP in Figure 7 (page 92) and the reachability property $\mathbb{P}_{\leq 0.75}(\lozenge\{s_4\})$ as in Example 23 (page 91). To compute a smallest critical subsystem, we first remove the irrelevant states s_3 and s_5 from the model. Note that the resulting MDP has no problematic states. Since the considered model is an MDP, for readability we write $\sigma_{s,\alpha}$ instead of $\sigma_{s,\alpha,\mu}$ for the scheduler choices in the following MILP formulation:

$$\text{minimize} \quad -\tfrac{1}{2}p_{s_0} + (x_{s_0} + x_{s_1} + x_{s_2} + x_{s_4}) \text{ such that}$$

$$p_{s_4} = x_{s_4}$$
$$p_{s_0} \leq x_{s_0}$$
$$p_{s_0} > 0.75 \qquad p_{s_1} \leq x_{s_1}$$
$$p_{s_2} \leq x_{s_2}$$

$$p_{s_0} \leq (1 - \sigma_{s_0,\alpha}) + p_{s_1}$$
$$\sigma_{s_0,\alpha} + \sigma_{s_0,\beta} = x_{s_0} \qquad p_{s_0} \leq (1 - \sigma_{s_0,\beta}) + p_{s_2}$$
$$\sigma_{s_1,\tau} = x_{s_1} \qquad p_{s_1} \leq (1 - \sigma_{s_1,\tau}) + 0.4p_{s_0} + 0.5p_{s_4}$$
$$\sigma_{s_2,\tau} = x_{s_2} \qquad p_{s_2} \leq (1 - \sigma_{s_2,\tau}) + 0.5p_{s_0} + 0.4p_{s_4}$$

The assignment mapping (i) 1 to x_{s_0}, x_{s_1}, x_{s_4}, p_{s_4}, $\sigma_{s_0,\alpha}$ and $\sigma_{s_1,\tau}$, (ii) $5/6 \approx$ 0.83 to p_{s_0} and p_{s_1}, and (iii) 0 to all other variables is a solution to the above constraint system, specifying a scheduler choosing action α in state s_0, and determining a smallest critical subsystem of the induced DTMC with state set $\{s_0, s_1, s_4\}$. ∎

Example 34. To illustrate the need for the special handling of problematic states, consider again the example MDP in Figure 7 on page 92, but assume that at state s_0 there would be an additional distribution with action γ, looping on s_0 with probability 1.

Without the constraints (3g)–(3i), the assignment mapping (i) 1 to x_{s_0}, p_{s_0} and $\sigma_{s_0,\gamma}$ and (ii) 0 to all other variables would satisfy the remaining MILP constraints, however, it would specify a subsystem containing the single state s_0, i.e., having the probability 0 to reach the target state s_4.

The MILP with the constraints (3g)–(3i) exclude this possibility. Intuitively, (3g)–(3i) exclude subsystems that have a bottom SCC containing problematic states only. ∎

6 Description-Language-Based Counterexamples

Typically, probabilistic models are not explicitly given at the state space level, but rather in a symbolic format that is able to succinctly capture large and complex system behavior.

Prism's Guarded Command Language. One example of such a symbolic modeling formalism is the *guarded-command language* employed by the well-known probabilistic model checker `Prism` [12]. It is a stochastic variant of Alur and Henzinger's reactive modules [33].

In this language, a *probabilistic program* consists of a set of *modules*. Each module declares a set of module *variables* and a set of *guarded commands*. A module has read and write access to its own variables, but only read access to the variables of other modules. The guarded commands have the form

$$[\alpha]\ g\ \rightarrow\ p_1 : f_1 + \ldots + p_n : f_n$$

where α is a *command label* being either an action name or τ, the *guard* g is a predicate over the variables in the program, f_i are the *variable update functions* that specify how the values of the module's variables are changed by the command, and the p_i are the *probabilities* with which the corresponding updates happen. A command with action label τ is executed asynchronously in the sense that no other command is executed simultaneously. In contrast, commands labeled with an action name $\alpha \neq \tau$ synchronize with all other modules that also have a command with this label, i.e., each of them executes a command with label α simultaneously.

Example 35. The top of Figure 15 shows an example guarded-command program in `Prism`'s input language. The program involves two modules `coin` and `processor`.

Initially the module `coin` can (asynchronously) do a coin flip (command c_1). The variable f stores the fact whether the coin has been already flipped ($f = 1$) or not ($f = 0$). After the coin flip, the variable c stores whether the coin shows tails ($c = 0$) or heads ($c = 1$)

After the coin flip, both modules can process some data by synchronizing on the `proc` action (c_3 and c_4). The variable p is used to make a bookkeeping whether processing has taken place ($p = 1$) or not ($p = 0$). However, the processing step can by mistake set the coin to show heads with probability 0.01 (c_3).

Additionally, if the coin is flipped and it shows tails, the coin flip can be undone by the synchronizing `reset` action (c_2 and c_6), leading the system back to its initial state.

Finally, if data has been processed the system may loop forever (c_5).   ∎

Several modules can be casted to a single module using *parallel composition*. The variable set of the composition is the union of the variable sets of the composed modules. Each non-synchronizing command is also a command in the composition. For each combination of synchronizing commands, the composition contains a single command whose guard is the conjunction of the involved guards, and whose updates are all possible combinations of joint updates with the product of the involved probabilities.

Example 36. The parallel composition of the two modules of the example probabilistic program at the top of Figure 15 is given at the bottom of the same figure.   ∎

```
module coin
    f: bool init 0; c: bool init 0;
    [τ] ¬f → 0.5 : (f′ = 1)&(c′ = 1) + 0.5 : (f′ = 1)&(c′ = 0);          (c₁)
    [reset] f ∧ ¬c → 1 : (f′ = 0);                                        (c₂)
    [proc] f → 0.99 : (f′ = 1) + 0.01 : (c′ = 1);                         (c₃)
endmodule
module processor
    p: bool init 0;
    [proc] ¬p → 1 : (p′ = 1);                                            (c₄)
    [τ] p → 1 : (p′ = 1);                                                (c₅)
    [reset] true → 1 : (p′ = 0)                                          (c₆)
endmodule
```

```
module coin ∥ processor
    f: bool init 0; c: bool init 0; p: bool init 0;
    [τ] ¬f → 0.5 : (f′ = 1)&(c′ = 1) + 0.5 : (f′ = 1)&(c′ = 0);          (ĉ₁)
    [reset] f ∧ ¬c → 1 : (f′ = 0)&(p′ = 0);                              (ĉ₂)
    [proc] f ∧ ¬p → 0.99 : (f′ = 1)&(p′ = 1) + 0.01 : (c′ = 1)&(p′ = 1); (ĉ₃)
    [τ] p → 1 : (p′ = 1);                                                (ĉ₄)
endmodule
```

Fig. 15. Top: The probabilistic program from Example 35, specified in **Prism**'s guarded-command language; Bottom: The parallel composition of the two modules

The *semantics* of a module is given in terms of a probabilistic automaton [47]. The state space of the automaton is the set of all valuations of the variables that appear in the program. The transitions between states are determined by the module's commands. More specifically, for every state and every guarded command with label α whose guard evaluates to true in the given state, the transition relation contains a pair (α, μ) such that μ defines for each update a transition to the state after the update with the probability of the update.

Example 37. The (reachable part of the) probabilistic automaton specifying the meaning of the probabilistic program in Figure 15 is depicted in Figure 16.

Note that the coin will finally show heads with probability 1 for all schedulers which choose the **reset** action with a non-zero probability if it is enabled. This behavior can be modified by, e.g., defining a scheduler with memory, which bounds the number of **reset** executions by some finite bound. ∎

A probabilistic program satisfies a reachability property iff the PA specifying its semantics does so. Thus explanations for the violation could be given by path- and subsystem-based counterexamples at the state-space level. However, such counterexamples tend to be too large and structureless to be easily interpretable in the probabilistic program, and therefore they are not well suited to help the designer to eliminate the unwanted behavior at the command level of modules.

Therefore, [34] proposed to naturally extend the computation of smallest critical subsystems to probabilistic programs by determining a *subset of the commands* that gives rise to a sub-PA that still violates the property in question.

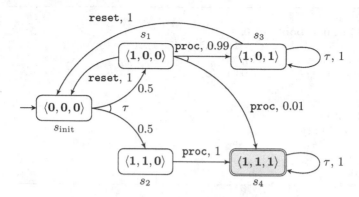

Fig. 16. The PA specifying the semantics of the probabilistic program in Figure 15 (cf. Example 37)

More precisely, the task is to compute a minimal number of commands such that the reachability probability in the semantics of the restricted program exceeds the threshold λ. Moreover, we aim at finding a *smallest critical command set* which maximizes the reachability probability under all subsets of the commands. It thus acts as a counterexample by pointing to a set of commands that already generate erroneous behavior. Additionally, to increase usefulness, the commands in a smallest critical command set can be further reduced by removing some of their update branches without which the property is still violated.

Example 38. Consider our example probabilistic program from Figure 15 and a reachability property $\mathbb{P}_{\leq\lambda}(\lozenge\{s_4\})$ (where s_4 describes the state in which all variables evaluate to 1).

If $0 < \lambda < 0.5$, at the level of the composed module $\mathtt{coin} \parallel \mathtt{processor}$ (at the bottom of Figure 15), the commands $\hat{c}_1$ and $\hat{c}_3$ would build a smallest critical command set. At the level of the modules $\mathtt{coin}$ and $\mathtt{processor}$, we need to include c_1, c_3 and c_4.

For $\lambda \geq 0.5$, a smallest critical command set would be $\{\hat{c}_1, \hat{c}_2, \hat{c}_3\}$ at the composed level $\mathtt{coin} \parallel \mathtt{processor}$. At the level of the modules, we can only exclude c_5.   ∎

Linear Programming Approach. In [34], the authors show the problem of finding a smallest critical command set to be NP-hard and present a *mixed integer linear programming (MILP)* approach to solve it. The basic idea is to describe the PA semantics of a smallest critical command set of a probabilistic program, together with a maximal scheduler, by an MILP formulation. This MILP formulation can be disposed to a state-of-the-art MILP solver to get an optimal solution.

Assume a probabilistic program and let $\mathcal{M} = (S, s_{\text{init}}, \text{Act}, \hat{P}, L)$ be the PA generated by it after removing all irrelevant states, and assume that the reachability property $\mathbb{P}_{\leq\lambda}(\lozenge T)$ is violated by $\mathcal{M}$. For each state $s \in S$ and transition

$(\alpha, \mu) \in \hat{P}(s)$ let $L(s, \alpha, \mu)$ denote the set of commands that generate the given transition.[4] Note that in case of synchronization several commands together create a certain transition.

The idea to encode the selection of smallest critical command sets as an MILP problem is similar to the MILP encoding of smallest critical subsystems for PAs (see Section 5.1). However, now we want to select a minimal number of commands of a probabilistic program instead of a minimal number of states of a PA. The selected commands should induce a PA, for which there is a memoryless deterministic scheduler inducing a critical subsystem of the PA.

Additionally to the variables used for the smallest critical subsystem encoding for PAs, we encode the selection of a smallest critical command set using a variable $x_c \in \{0, 1\}$ for each command c, which is 1 iff c is part of the smallest critical command set. Using these variables, the MILP for a smallest critical command set is as follows:

$$\text{minimize} \quad -\frac{1}{2} \cdot p_{s_{\text{init}}} + \sum_c x_c \tag{4a}$$

such that

$$p_{s_{\text{init}}} > \lambda \tag{4b}$$

$$\forall s \in S \setminus T: \quad \sum_{(\alpha,\mu) \in P(s)} \sigma_{s,\alpha,\mu} \leq 1 \tag{4c}$$

$$\forall s \in S \ \forall (\alpha, \mu) \in P(s) \ \forall c \in L(s, \alpha, \mu): \quad x_c \geq \sigma_{s,\alpha,\mu} \tag{4d}$$

$$\forall s \in T: \quad p_s = 1 \tag{4e}$$

$$\forall s \in S \setminus T: \quad p_s \leq \sum_{(\alpha,\mu) \in P(s)} \sigma_{s,\alpha,\mu} \tag{4f}$$

$$\forall s \in S \setminus T \ \forall (\alpha, \mu) \in P(s): \quad p_s \leq \sum_{s' \in \text{supp}(\mu)} \mu(s') \cdot p_{s'} + (1 - \sigma_{s,\alpha,\mu}) \tag{4g}$$

$$\forall (s, \alpha, \mu) \in \hat{P}_p: \quad \sigma_{s,\alpha,\mu} \leq \sum_{s' \in \text{supp}(\mu)} t_{s,s'} \tag{4h}$$

$$\forall s \in S_p \ \forall (\alpha, \mu) \in P(s) \ \forall s' \in \text{supp}(\mu): \quad r_s < r_{s'} + (1 - t_{s,s'}) . \tag{4i}$$

By (4b) we ensure that the the subsystem induced by the selected scheduler is critical. For reachability properties, we can restrict ourselves to memoryless deterministic schedulers. So for each state at most one action-distribution pair is selected by the scheduler (4c). Note that there may be states where no such pair is chosen, which we call deadlocking. If the scheduler selects an action-distribution pair, all commands involved in its generation have to be chosen (4d). For all target states $s \in T$ the probability p_s is set to 1 (4e), while the probability is set

---

[4] If several command sets generate the same transition, we make copies of the transition.

to zero for all deadlocking non-target states (4f). Constraint (4g) is responsible for assigning a valid probability to p_s under the selected scheduler. The constraint is trivially satisfied if $\sigma_{s,\alpha,\mu} = 0$. If (α, μ) is selected, the probability p_s is bounded from above by the probability to go to one of the successor states of (α, μ) and to reach the target states from there.

For non-deadlocking problematic states, the reachability of at least one unproblematic state is ensured by (4h) and (4i). First, for every state s with a selected (α, μ) that is problematic regarding T, at least one transition variable must be activated. Second, for a path according to these transition variables, an increasing order is enforced for the problematic states. Because of this order, no problematic states can be revisited on an increasing path which enforces the final reachability of a non-problematic or deadlocking state.

These constraints enforce that each satisfying assignment corresponds to a critical command set. By minimizing the number of the selected commands we obtain a size-minimal critical command set. By the additional term $-\frac{1}{2} \cdot p_{s_{\text{init}}}$ we obtain a smallest critical command set. The coefficient $-\frac{1}{2}$ is needed to ensure that the benefit from maximizing the probability is smaller than the loss by adding an additional command.

Example 39. We want to compute a smallest critical command set for the example probabilistic program in Figure 15 and $\mathbb{P}_{\leq 0.4}(\lozenge\{s_4\})$. Since the induced PA is an MDP, for readability we write $\sigma_{s,\alpha}$ instead of $\sigma_{s,\alpha,\mu}$ for the scheduler choices in the following MILP formulation:

$$\text{minimize} \quad -\tfrac{1}{2}p_{s_{\text{init}}} + (x_{c_1} + x_{c_2} + x_{c_3} + x_{c_4} + x_{c_5} + x_{c_6}) \text{ such that}$$

$$p_{s_{\text{init}}} > 0.4$$

$$\sigma_{s_{\text{init}},\tau} \leq 1 \qquad\qquad \sigma_{s_{\text{init}},\tau} \leq x_{c_1} \quad \sigma_{s_2,\text{proc}} \leq x_{c_3}$$
$$\sigma_{s_1,\text{proc}} + \sigma_{s_1,\text{reset}} \leq 1 \qquad \sigma_{s_1,\text{proc}} \leq x_{c_3} \quad \sigma_{s_2,\text{proc}} \leq x_{c_4}$$
$$\sigma_{s_2,\text{proc}} \leq 1 \qquad\qquad \sigma_{s_1,\text{proc}} \leq x_{c_4} \quad \sigma_{s_3,\text{reset}} \leq x_{c_2}$$
$$\sigma_{s_3,\text{reset}} + \sigma_{s_3,\tau} \leq 1 \qquad \sigma_{s_1,\text{reset}} \leq x_{c_2} \quad \sigma_{s_3,\text{reset}} \leq x_{c_6}$$
$$\sigma_{s_1,\text{reset}} \leq x_{c_6} \quad \sigma_{s_3,\tau} \leq x_{c_5}$$

$$p_{s_4} = 1 \qquad\qquad p_{s_{\text{init}}} \leq 0.5p_{s_1} + 0.5p_{s_2} + (1 - \sigma_{s_{\text{init}},\tau})$$
$$p_{s_1} \leq 0.99p_{s_3} + 0.01p_{s_4} + (1 - \sigma_{s_1,\text{proc}})$$
$$p_{s_{\text{init}}} \leq \sigma_{s_{\text{init}},\tau} \qquad p_{s_1} \leq p_{s_{\text{init}}} + (1 - \sigma_{s_1,\text{reset}})$$
$$p_{s_1} \leq \sigma_{s_1,\text{proc}} + \sigma_{s_1,\text{reset}} \qquad p_{s_2} \leq p_{s_4} + (1 - \sigma_{s_2,\text{proc}})$$
$$p_{s_2} \leq \sigma_{s_2,\text{proc}} \qquad p_{s_3} \leq p_{s_{\text{init}}} + (1 - \sigma_{s_3,\text{reset}})$$
$$p_{s_3} \leq \sigma_{s_3,\text{reset}} + \sigma_{s_3,\tau} \qquad p_{s_3} \leq p_{s_3} + (1 - \sigma_{s_3,\tau})$$

$$\sigma_{s_3,\tau} \leq t_{s_3,s_3}$$
$$r_{s_3} < r_{s_3} + (1 - t_{s_3,s_3})$$

It is easy to check that the assignment mapping 1 to $\sigma_{s_{\mathrm{init}},\tau}$, $\sigma_{s2,\mathrm{proc}}$, x_{c_1}, x_{c_3}, x_{c_4} and p_{s_4}, 0.5 to $p_{s_{\mathrm{init}}}$ and p_{s_2}, and 0 to all other variables is a satisfying solution, encoding the smallest critical command set $\{c_1, c_3, c_4\}$.   ∎

7   Tools and Implementations

In this section we give a short overview on public tools and prototype implementations for some of the approaches that were presented in this paper. We report on the scalability of the different approaches as far as there were comparisons made in the corresponding papers. We first present the publicly available tools.

7.1   DiPro — A Tool for Probabilistic Counterexample Generation

DiPro [36] was the first official tool for the counterexample generation of probabilistic systems. Basically, most of the implemented approaches are based on variations of *best-first search*. An *extended best-first search* is used to generate critical subsystems of DTMCs and CTMCs, see Section 5 and the corresponding paper [30]. Moreover a K^* search [67] for finding the k most probable paths of a DTMC together with some optimizations is implemented, see Section 4. Finally, DiPro is able to compute a path-based counterexample together with a scheduler for MDPs, see Section 5 and [25].

Technically, the best-first search approaches of DiPro are implemented using the simulation engine of a previous version of the probabilistic model checker PRISM [12]. Thereby, the state space is built incrementally and in many cases not to its full extend. That enables the generation of counterexamples for rather large graphs for many benchmarks.

In order to help the user understand the process of finding a counterexample, the tool offers a graphical user interface [60] where the search process is illustrated.

7.2   COMICS — Computing Smallest Counterexamples for DTMCs

COMICS [37] implements the approaches of [29], namely the *hierarchical counterexample generation* and the two search approaches called *global search* and *local search*, see Section 5. The core functionality is to offer the computation of counterexamples for reachability properties of DTMCs either automatically or user-guided. A graphical user-interface offers to depict every stage of the hierarchical counterexample generation. The user can interactively choose certain states of interest to be concretized, while there are also several heuristics available to automate this choice. Furthermore, several heuristics can be used for the search process, e. g., how many states to concretize in one step or how often model checking is performed. Moreover, the tool has a mere command-line version in order to perform benchmarking. It is always possible to compute smallest critical subsystems without the hierarchical concretization. Finally, the k shortest path approach, see Section 4 and [17], was implemented in order to provide comparisons regarding scalability.

7.3   Other Implementations

Basically, we did not have access to the implementations on foreign approaches as presented in this paper.

We are able to report on the implementations of the several approaches concerning the computation of *smallest critical subsystems*, see Sections 5 and 6. Parts of these implementations are summarized in a tool called LTLSUBSYS. The high-level approaches are mainly implemented into the framework of a successor of the probabilistic model checker MRMC [13]. These still prototypical implementations utilize the SMT-solver Z3 [68] and the MILP solvers SCIP [69], CPLEX [70] and GUROBI [71].

Moreover, we describe the scalability of the approaches to symbolic counterexample generation, see Section 5 and the publications [31, 32].

7.4   Comparison of the Tools

We will now shortly report on comparisons of DiPRO, COMICS and LTLSUBSYS that were made in previous publications.

First, COMICS and DiPRO were directly compared for reachability properties of DTMCs in [32, 37, 61]. Summarizing the results we observe that for benchmarks with up to one million states COMICS performs better in terms of running times and of the size of the generated subsystem. However, for larger benchmarks DiPRO might be the better choice, as the state space is generated on the fly. Thus, if the critical subsystem generated by DiPRO is of moderate size, a result is obtained even for very large graphs. Please keep in mind that each tool has its own advantages such as the animated search process of DiPRO or the user-guided hierarchical counterexample search of COMICS.

LTLSUBSYS was compared to both publicly available tools in [61]. In terms of running times, the creation of a *smallest* critical subsystem is almost always worse than the heuristical tools. In terms of the system size, LTLSUBSYS naturally always generates the smallest possible critical subsystem. For the benchmarks tested in the paper, the *local search* approach in some cases generated critical subsystems that were only around 10% larger than the actual minimal subsystem while the running time was considerably lower. Note finally, that within an MILP solver such as GUROBI, an intermediate solution and a lower bound on the value of the optimal solution is maintained at every time. In many cases, the minimal solution is obtained within seconds while it is a very hard case to actually prove minimality. Thereby, if the intermediate result is already sufficiently small, the search process can be stopped at any time.

The symbolic counterexample generation based on graph algorithms as presented in [32] and Section 5 was compared to COMICS and DiPRO. As expected, on smaller benchmarks the other tools perform better in terms of running times. The size of the subsystems was comparable to the results as obtained by COMICS as the same approaches were used only on the one hand for explicit graph representations and on the other hand for symbolic graph representations. For benchmarks with millions of states, DiPRO and the symbolic algorithms were the only ones to obtain results while the latter obtained better running times the larger the benchmarks were. Finally, the symbolic algorithms were able to generate counterexamples for systems with billions of states while all other approaches failed.

8 Conclusion

This paper surveyed state-of-the-art methods for counterexample generation for discrete-time Markov models. Three techniques have been covered: path-based representations, minimal critical subsystems, and high-level representations of counterexamples. In addition to techniques using explicit model representations, we addressed methods that use symbolic BDD based model representations and symbolic computations.

It is fair to say, that probabilistic counterexamples are still at their infancy. Although dedicated tools such as DiPro and Comics support (some of) the techniques presented in this survey, the integration into mainstream probabilistic model checkers is still open. This could make the usage of probabilistic counterexamples more popular in other application domains like, e. g., robotics or security. Besides, it is a challenging task to consider counterexamples for continuous-time or hybrid probabilistic models, in particular for time-constrained reachability properties.

References

1. Clarke, E.M.: The birth of model checking. In: Grumberg, O., Veith, H. (eds.) 25 Years of Model Checking. LNCS, vol. 5000, pp. 1–26. Springer, Heidelberg (2008)
2. Clarke, E.M., Veith, H.: Counterexamples revisited: Principles, algorithms, applications. In: Dershowitz, N. (ed.) Verification: Theory and Practice. LNCS, vol. 2772, pp. 208–224. Springer, Heidelberg (2004)
3. Fraser, G., Wotawa, F., Ammann, P.: Issues in using model checkers for test case generation. Journal of Systems and Software 82(9), 1403–1418 (2009)
4. Behrmann, G., Larsen, K.G., Rasmussen, J.I.: Optimal scheduling using priced timed automata. SIGMETRICS Performance Evaluation Review 32(4), 34–40 (2005)
5. Ngo, T.M., Stoelinga, M., Huisman, M.: Effective verification of confidentiality for multi-threaded programs. Journal of Computer Security 22(2), 269–300 (2014)
6. Clarke, E.M., Grumberg, O., Jha, S., Lu, Y., Veith, H.: Counterexample-guided abstraction refinement for symbolic model checking. J. ACM 50(5), 752–794 (2003)
7. Clarke, E.M., Jha, S., Lu, Y., Veith, H.: Tree-like counterexamples in model checking. In: Proc. of LICS, pp. 19–29. IEEE Computer Society Press (2002)
8. Clarke, E.M., Grumberg, O., McMillan, K.L., Zhao, X.: Efficient generation of counterexamples and witnesses in symbolic model checking. In: Proc. of DAC, pp. 427–432 (1995)
9. Baier, C., Katoen, J.P.: Principles of Model Checking. The MIT Press (2008)
10. Baier, C., Haverkort, B.R., Hermanns, H., Katoen, J.P.: Performance evaluation and model checking join forces. Commun. ACM 53(9), 76–85 (2010)

11. Kwiatkowska, M.Z.: Model checking for probability and time: From theory to practice. In: Proc. of LICS, pp. 351–360. IEEE Computer Society Press (2003)
12. Kwiatkowska, M.Z., Norman, G., Parker, D.: PRISM 4.0: Verification of probabilistic real-time systems. In: Gopalakrishnan, G., Qadeer, S. (eds.) CAV 2011. LNCS, vol. 6806, pp. 585–591. Springer, Heidelberg (2011)
13. Katoen, J.P., Zapreev, I.S., Hahn, E.M., Hermanns, H., Jansen, D.N.: The ins and outs of the probabilistic model checker MRMC. Perform. Eval. 68(2), 90–104 (2011)
14. Kwiatkowska, M.Z., Norman, G., Parker, D.: Stochastic model checking. In: Bernardo, M., Hillston, J. (eds.) SFM 2007. LNCS, vol. 4486, pp. 220–270. Springer, Heidelberg (2007)
15. Katoen, J.P.: Model checking meets probability: A gentle introduction. In: Engineering Dependable Software Systems. NATO Science for Peace and Security Series - D: Information and Communication Security, vol. 34, pp. 177–205. IOS Press, Amsterdam (2013)
16. Han, T., Katoen, J.P.: Counterexamples in probabilistic model checking. In: Grumberg, O., Huth, M. (eds.) TACAS 2007. LNCS, vol. 4424, pp. 72–86. Springer, Heidelberg (2007)
17. Han, T., Katoen, J.P., Damman, B.: Counterexample generation in probabilistic model checking. IEEE Transactions on Software Engineering 35(2), 241–257 (2009)
18. Aljazzar, H., Leue, S.: Extended directed search for probabilistic timed reachability. In: Asarin, E., Bouyer, P. (eds.) FORMATS 2006. LNCS, vol. 4202, pp. 33–51. Springer, Heidelberg (2006)
19. Wimmer, R., Braitling, B., Becker, B.: Counterexample generation for discrete-time markov chains using bounded model checking. In: Jones, N.D., Müller-Olm, M. (eds.) VMCAI 2009. LNCS, vol. 5403, pp. 366–380. Springer, Heidelberg (2009)
20. Braitling, B., Wimmer, R., Becker, B., Jansen, N., Ábrahám, E.: Counterexample generation for markov chains using SMT-based bounded model checking. In: Bruni, R., Dingel, J. (eds.) FMOODS/FORTE 2011. LNCS, vol. 6722, pp. 75–89. Springer, Heidelberg (2011)
21. Günther, M., Schuster, J., Siegle, M.: Symbolic calculation of k-shortest paths and related measures with the stochastic process algebra tool CASPA. In: Proc. of DYADEM-FTS, pp. 13–18. ACM Press (2010)
22. Damman, B., Han, T., Katoen, J.P.: Regular expressions for PCTL counterexamples. In: Proc. of QEST, pp. 179–188. IEEE Computer Society Press (2008)
23. Daws, C.: Symbolic and parametric model checking of discrete-time Markov chains. In: Liu, Z., Araki, K. (eds.) ICTAC 2004. LNCS, vol. 3407, pp. 280–294. Springer, Heidelberg (2005)
24. Andrés, M.E., D'Argenio, P., van Rossum, P.: Significant diagnostic counterexamples in probabilistic model checking. In: Chockler, H., Hu, A.J. (eds.) HVC 2008. LNCS, vol. 5394, pp. 129–148. Springer, Heidelberg (2009)
25. Aljazzar, H., Leue, S.: Generation of counterexamples for model checking of Markov decision processes. In: Proc. of QEST, pp. 197–206. IEEE Computer Society Press (2009)
26. Chadha, R., Viswanathan, M.: A counterexample-guided abstraction-refinement framework for Markov decision processes. ACM Transactions on Computational Logic 12(1), 1–45 (2010)
27. Wimmer, R., Jansen, N., Ábrahám, E., Becker, B., Katoen, J.-P.: Minimal critical subsystems for discrete-time Markov models. In: Flanagan, C., König, B. (eds.) TACAS 2012. LNCS, vol. 7214, pp. 299–314. Springer, Heidelberg (2012)

28. Wimmer, R., Becker, B., Jansen, N., Ábrahám, E., Katoen, J.P.: Minimal critical subsystems as counterexamples for ω-regular DTMC properties. In: Proc. of MBMV, pp. 169–180. Verlag Dr. Kovač (2012)
29. Jansen, N., Ábrahám, E., Katelaan, J., Wimmer, R., Katoen, J.P., Becker, B.: Hierarchical counterexamples for discrete-time Markov chains. In: Bultan, T., Hsiung, P.-A. (eds.) ATVA 2011. LNCS, vol. 6996, pp. 443–452. Springer, Heidelberg (2011)
30. Aljazzar, H., Leue, S.: Directed explicit state-space search in the generation of counterexamples for stochastic model checking. IEEE Transactions on Software Engineering 36(1), 37–60 (2010)
31. Jansen, N., Ábrahám, E., Zajzon, B., Wimmer, R., Schuster, J., Katoen, J.P., Becker, B.: Symbolic counterexample generation for discrete-time Markov chains. In: Păsăreanu, C.S., Salaün, G. (eds.) FACS 2012. LNCS, vol. 7684, pp. 134–151. Springer, Heidelberg (2013)
32. Jansen, N., Wimmer, R., Ábrahám, E., Zajzon, B., Katoen, J.P., Becker, B., Schuster, J.: Symbolic counterexample generation for large discrete-time Markov chains. In: Science of Computer Programming (2014) (accepted for publication)
33. Alur, R., Henzinger, T.A.: Reactive modules. Formal Methods in System Design 15(1), 7–48 (1999)
34. Wimmer, R., Jansen, N., Vorpahl, A., Ábrahám, E., Katoen, J.-P., Becker, B.: High-level counterexamples for probabilistic automata. In: Joshi, K., Siegle, M., Stoelinga, M., D'Argenio, P.R. (eds.) QEST 2013. LNCS, vol. 8054, pp. 39–54. Springer, Heidelberg (2013)
35. Katoen, J.P., van de Pol, J., Stoelinga, M., Timmer, M.: A linear process-algebraic format with data for probabilistic automata. Theor. Comput. Sci. 413(1), 36–57 (2012)
36. Aljazzar, H., Leitner-Fischer, F., Leue, S., Simeonov, D.: DiPro - A tool for probabilistic counterexample generation. In: Groce, A., Musuvathi, M. (eds.) SPIN Workshops 2011. LNCS, vol. 6823, pp. 183–187. Springer, Heidelberg (2011)
37. Jansen, N., Ábrahám, E., Volk, M., Wimmer, R., Katoen, J.-P., Becker, B.: The COMICS tool – Computing minimal counterexamples for DTMCs. In: Chakraborty, S., Mukund, M. (eds.) ATVA 2012. LNCS, vol. 7561, pp. 349–353. Springer, Heidelberg (2012)
38. Hermanns, H., Wachter, B., Zhang, L.: Probabilistic CEGAR. In: Gupta, A., Malik, S. (eds.) CAV 2008. LNCS, vol. 5123, pp. 162–175. Springer, Heidelberg (2008)
39. Komuravelli, A., Păsăreanu, C.S., Clarke, E.M.: Assume-guarantee abstraction refinement for probabilistic systems. In: Madhusudan, P., Seshia, S.A. (eds.) CAV 2012. LNCS, vol. 7358, pp. 310–326. Springer, Heidelberg (2012)
40. Grunske, L., Winter, K., Yatapanage, N., Zafar, S., Lindsay, P.A.: Experience with fault injection experiments for FMEA. Softw. Pract. Exper. 41(11), 1233–1258 (2011)
41. Aljazzar, H., Fischer, M., Grunske, L., Kuntz, M., Leitner-Fischer, F., Leue, S.: Safety analysis of an airbag system using probabilistic FMEA and probabilistic counterexamples. In: Proc. of QEST, pp. 299–308. IEEE Computer Society Press (2009)
42. Debbi, H., Bourahla, M.: Generating diagnoses for probabilistic model checking using causality. Journal of Computing and Information Technology 21(1), 13–23 (2013)
43. Debbi, H., Bourahla, M.: Causal analysis of probabilistic counterexamples. In: Proc. of MEMOCODE, pp. 77–86. IEEE (2013)

44. Leitner-Fischer, F., Leue, S.: Probabilistic fault tree synthesis using causality computation. Int'l Journal of Critical Computer-Based Systems 4(2), 119–143 (2013)
45. Bernardo, M., Hillston, J. (eds.): SFM 2007. LNCS, vol. 4486. Springer, Heidelberg (2007)
46. Kemeney, J.G., Snell, J.L., Knapp, A.W.: Denumerable Markov Chains. Springer (1976)
47. Segala, R., Lynch, N.A.: Probabilistic simulations for probabilistic processes. Nordic Journal on Computing 2(2), 250–273 (1995)
48. Eppstein, D.: Finding the k shortest paths. SIAM Journal on Computing 28(2), 652–673 (1998)
49. Jiménez, V.M., Marzal, A.: Computing the k shortest paths: A new algorithm and an experimental comparison. In: Vitter, J.S., Zaroliagis, C.D. (eds.) WAE 1999. LNCS, vol. 1668, pp. 15–29. Springer, Heidelberg (1999)
50. Aljazzar, H., Leue, S.: K*: A heuristic search algorithm for finding the k shortest paths. Artificial Intelligence 175(18), 2129–2154 (2011)
51. Biere, A., Cimatti, A., Clarke, E.M., Strichman, O., Zhu, Y.: Bounded model checking. Advances in Computers 58, 118–149 (2003)
52. Tseitin, G.S.: On the complexity of derivation in propositional calculus. Studies in Constructive Mathematics and Mathematical, Logic Part 2, 115–125 (1970)
53. Braitling, B., Wimmer, R., Becker, B., Ábrahám, E.: Stochastic bounded model checking: Bounded rewards and compositionality. In: Proc. of MBMV, pp. 243–254. Universität Rostock, ITMZ (2013)
54. Dijkstra, E.W.: A note on two problems in connexion with graphs. Numerische Mathematik 1, 269–271 (1959)
55. Daws, C.: Symbolic and parametric model checking of discrete-time Markov chains. In: Liu, Z., Araki, K. (eds.) ICTAC 2004. LNCS, vol. 3407, pp. 280–294. Springer, Heidelberg (2005)
56. Han, Y.S., Wood, D.: Obtaining shorter regular expressions from finite-state automata. Theoretical Computer Science 370(1-3), 110–120 (2007)
57. Halpern, J.Y., Pearl, J.: Causes and explanations: A structural approach. Part I: Causes. British Journal on the Philosophy of Science 56, 843–887 (2005)
58. Chockler, H., Halpern, J.Y.: Responsibility and blame: A structural-model approach. Journal of Artificial Intellelligence Research (JAIR) 22, 93–115 (2004)
59. Leitner-Fischer, F., Leue, S.: On the synergy of probabilistic causality computation and causality checking. In: Bartocci, E., Ramakrishnan, C.R. (eds.) SPIN 2013. LNCS, vol. 7976, pp. 246–263. Springer, Heidelberg (2013)
60. Aljazzar, H., Leue, S.: Debugging of dependability models using interactive visualization of counterexamples. In: Proc. of QEST, pp. 189–198. IEEE Computer Society Press (2008)
61. Wimmer, R., Jansen, N., Ábrahám, E., Katoen, J.P., Becker, B.: Minimal counterexamples for refuting ω-regular properties of Markov decision processes (extended version). Reports of SFB/TR 14 AVACS 88 (2012) ISSN: 1860-9821,
    http://www.avacs.org/fileadmin/Publikationen/Open/
    avacs_technical_report_088.pdf
62. Schrijver, A.: Theory of Linear and Integer Programming. Wiley (1986)
63. Pearl, J.: Heuristics: Intelligent Search Strategies for Computer Problem Solving. Addison-Wesley Longman Publishing Co. Inc., Boston (1984)
64. Baier, C., Clarke, E.M., Hartonas-Garmhausen, V., Kwiatkowska, M.Z., Ryan, M.: Symbolic model checking for probabilistic processes. In: Degano, P., Gorrieri, R., Marchetti-Spaccamela, A. (eds.) ICALP 1997. LNCS, vol. 1256, pp. 430–440. Springer, Heidelberg (1997)

65. Parker, D.: Implementation of Symbolic Model Checking for Probabilistic Systems. PhD thesis, University of Birmingham (2002)
66. Ábrahám, E., Jansen, N., Wimmer, R., Katoen, J.P., Becker, B.: DTMC model checking by SCC reduction. In: Proc. of QEST, pp. 37–46. IEEE Computer Society Press (2010)
67. Aljazzar, H., Leue, S.: K*: A directed on-the-fly algorithm for finding the k shortest paths. Technical report, Chair of Software Engineering, University of Konstanz, Germany (2008)
68. de Moura, L.M., Bjørner, N.: Z3: An efficient SMT solver. In: Ramakrishnan, C.R., Rehof, J. (eds.) TACAS 2008. LNCS, vol. 4963, pp. 337–340. Springer, Heidelberg (2008)
69. Achterberg, T.: SCIP: Solving constraint integer programs. Mathematical Programming Computation 1(1), 1–41 (2009)
70. IBM CPLEX optimization studio, version 12.4 (2012), http://www-01.ibm.com/software/integration/optimization/cplex-optimization-studio/
71. Gurobi Optimization, Inc.: Gurobi optimizer reference manual (2013), http://www.gurobi.com

Tutorial on Parameterized Model Checking of Fault-Tolerant Distributed Algorithms*

Annu Gmeiner, Igor Konnov, Ulrich Schmid, Helmut Veith, and Josef Widder

Vienna University of Technology (TU Wien), Austria

Abstract. Recently we introduced an abstraction method for parameterized model checking of threshold-based fault-tolerant distributed algorithms. We showed how to verify distributed algorithms without fixing the size of the system a priori. As is the case for many other published abstraction techniques, transferring the theory into a running tool is a challenge. It requires understanding of several verification techniques such as parametric data and counter abstraction, finite state model checking and abstraction refinement. In the resulting framework, all these techniques should interact in order to achieve a possibly high degree of automation. In this tutorial we use the core of a fault-tolerant distributed broadcasting algorithm as a case study to explain the concepts of our abstraction techniques, and discuss how they can be implemented.

1   Introduction

Distributed systems are crucial for today's computing applications, as they enable us to increase performance and reliability of computer systems, enable communication between users and computers that are geographically distributed, or allow us to provide computing services that can be accessed over the Internet. Distributed systems allow us to achieve that by the use of distributed algorithms. In fact, distributed algorithms have been studied extensively in the literature [62,11], and the central problems are well-understood. They differ from the fundamental problems in sequential (that is, non-distributed) systems. The central problems in distributed systems are posed by the inevitable uncertainty of any local view of the global system state, originating in unknown/varying processor speeds, communication delays, and failures. Pivotal services in distributed systems, such as mutual exclusion, routing, consensus, clock synchronization, leader election, atomic broadcasting, and replicated state machines, must hence be designed to cope with this uncertainty.

As we increasingly depend on the correct operation of distributed systems, the ability to cope with failures becomes particularly crucial. To do so, one actually has to address two problem areas. On the one hand, one has to design

---

* Some of the presented material has been published in [53,52]. Supported by the Austrian National Research Network S11403 and S11405 (RiSE) of the Austrian Science Fund (FWF) and by the Vienna Science and Technology Fund (WWTF) through grants PROSEED.

M. Bernardo et al. (Eds.): SFM 2014, LNCS 8483, pp. 122–171, 2014.

algorithms that can deal with partial failure that is outside the control of a system designer. Typical examples are temporary disconnections of the network (e.g., due to mobility), power outages, bit-flips due to radiation in space, or hardware faults. On the other hand, we have to prevent, or rather find and remove, design faults, which are often termed as bugs. The former area of fault tolerance is classically addressed by means of replication and fault-tolerant distributed algorithms [62,11,25], while the latter is dealt with by rigorous software engineering methods such as model checking [31,12,47]. In order to maximize the reliability, one should deploy fault-tolerant distributed algorithms that have been verified.

We prefer model checking to verification using proof checkers such as PVS or Isabelle, as model checking promises a higher degree of automation, and still allows us to verify designs and implementation. Testing, on the other hand, can be completely automated and it allows us to validate large systems. However, there are still many research challenges in testing of distributed systems, and in general, testing suffers from being incomplete. Hence, model checking strikes a good balance between automatization and completeness. In verification of fault-tolerant distributed algorithms we are not looking for a push-button technology: First, as we will see below, distributed algorithms are naturally parameterized, and parameterized model checking is undecidable even for very simple systems [10,77]. Second, distributed algorithms are typically only given in natural language or pseudo code. Hence, in contrast to software model checking where the input is given as a program in, e.g., C, currently the input for the verification of distributed algorithms is not machine readable, and we require expert knowledge from the beginning. Finally, a method where the user (or rather the system designer) guides the model checking tool is acceptable if we can check automatically that the user input does not violate soundness.

Only very few fault-tolerant distributed algorithms have been automatically verified. We think that this is because many aspects of distributed algorithms still pose research challenges for model checking:

– The inherent concurrency and the uncertainty caused by partial failure lead to many sources of non-determinism. Thus, fault-tolerant distributed algorithms suffer from combinatorial explosion in the state-space and in the number of behaviors.
– For many applications, the size of the distributed system, that is, the number of participants is a priori unknown. Hence, the design and verification of distributed algorithms should work for all system sizes. That is, distributed systems are parameterized by construction.
– Distributed algorithms are typically only correct in certain environments, e.g., when there is only a certain fraction of the processes faulty, when the interleaving of steps is restricted, or when the message delays are bounded.
– Faults change the semantics of primitives (send, receive, FIFO, access object), classic primitives such as handshake may be impossible or impractical to implement.
– There is no commonly agreed-upon distributed computing model, but rather many variants, which differ in subtle details. Moreover, distributed

algorithms are usually described in pseudocode, typically using different (alas unspecified) pseudocode languages, which obfuscates the relation to the underlying computing model.

In this tutorial we discuss practical aspects of parameterized model checking of fault-tolerant distributed algorithms. We use Srikanth and Toueg's broadcasting primitive [76] as a case study, and discuss various aspects using encodings in PROMELA and YICES. The reader is thus expected to have basic knowledge of of SPIN and YICES [2,5,49,38].

Srikanth and Toueg's broadcasting primitive is an example for threshold-based fault-tolerant algorithms, and our methods are tailored for this kind of distributed algorithms. We thus capture important mechanisms in distributed algorithms like waiting for messages from a majority of processes. Section 2 contains more detailed discussion on our motivations. We will discuss in detail the formalization of such algorithms in a parametric variant of Promela in Section 3. We then show in Section 4 how to use abstraction to reduce the parameterized model checking problem to a finite state model checking problem, and discuss how to deal with many practical issues that are due to abstraction. We show the efficiency of our method by experimental evaluation in Section 6.

2   Context

2.1   Parameterized Model Checking

In its original formulation [30], Model Checking was concerned with efficient procedures for the evaluation of a temporal logic specification φ over a finite Kripke structure K, i.e., decision procedures for $K \models \varphi$. Since K can be extremely large, a multitude of logic-based algorithmic methods including symbolic verification [64,18] and predicate abstraction [46] were developed to make this decidable problem tractable for practical applications. Finite-state models are, however, not always an adequate modeling formalism for software and hardware.

(i) Infinite-state models. Many programs and algorithms are naturally modeled by unbounded variables such as integers, lists, stacks etc. Modern model checkers are using predicate abstraction [46] in combination with SMT solvers to reduce an infinite-state model I to a finite state model $h(I)$ that is amenable to finite state model checking. The construction of h assures soundness, i.e., for a given specification logic such as ACTL*, we can assure by construction that $h(I) \models \varphi$ implies $I \models \varphi$. The major drawback of abstraction is incompleteness: if $h(I) \not\models \varphi$ then it does in general not follow that $I \not\models \varphi$. (Note that ACTL* is not closed under negation.) Counterexample-guided abstraction refinement (CEGAR) [27,13] addresses this problem by an adaptive procedure, which analyzes the abstract counterexample for $h(I) \not\models \varphi$ on $h(I)$ to find a concrete counterexample or obtain a better abstraction $h'(I)$. For abstraction to work in practice, it is crucial that the abstract domain from which h and h' are chosen is tailored to the problem class and possibly the specification. Abstraction thus is a semi-decision procedure whose usefulness has to be demonstrated by practical examples.

(ii) An orthogonal modeling and verification problem is parameterization: Many software and hardware artifacts are naturally represented by an infinite class of structures $\mathbf{K} = \{K_1, K_2, \dots\}$ rather than a single structure. Thus, the verification question is $\forall i.\, K_i \models \varphi$, where i is called the parameter. In the most important examples of this class, the parameter i is standing for the number of replications of a concurrent component, e.g., the number of processes in a distributed algorithm, or the number of caches in a cache coherence protocol. It is easy to see that even in the absence of concurrency, parameterized model checking is undecidable [10]; more interestingly, undecidability even holds for networks of constant size processes that are arranged in a ring and that exchange a single token [77,41]. Although several approaches have been made to identify decidable classes for parameterized verification [41,40,81], no decidable formalism has been found which covers a reasonably large class of interesting problems. The diversity of problem domains for parameterized verification and the difficulty of the problem gave rise to many approaches including regular model checking [6] and abstraction [70,28] — the method discussed here. The challenge in abstraction is to find an abstraction $h(\mathbf{K})$ such that $h(\mathbf{K}) \models \varphi$ implies $K_i \models \varphi$ for *all* i.

Most of the previous research on parameterized model checking focused on concurrent systems with $n + c$ processes where n is the parameter and c is a *constant*: n of the processes are *identical* copies; c processes represent the non-replicated part of the system, e.g., cache directories, shared memory, dispatcher processes etc. [45,50,65,28]. Most of the work on parameterized model checking considers only safety. Notable exceptions are [56,70] where several notions of fairness are considered in the context of abstraction to verify liveness.

2.2 Fault-Tolerant Distributed Algorithms

In this tutorial we are not aiming at the most general approach towards parameterized model checking, but we are addressing a very specific problem in the field, namely, parameterized verification of fault-tolerant distributed algorithms (FTDA). This work is part of an interdisciplinary effort by the authors to develop a tool basis for the automated verification, and, in the long run, deployment of FTDAs [51,57]. FTDAs constitute a core topic of the distributed algorithms community with a rich body of results [62,11]. FTDAs are more difficult than the standard setting of parameterized model checking because *a certain number t of the n processes can be faulty*. In the case of e.g. Byzantine faults, this means that the faulty processes can send messages in an unrestricted manner. Importantly, the upper bound t for the faulty processes is also a parameter, and is essentially a fraction of n. The relationship between t and n is given by a *resilience condition*, e.g., $n > 3t$. Thus, one has to reason about all systems with $n - f$ non-faulty and f faulty processes, where $f \le t$ and $n > 3t$.

From a more operational viewpoint, FTDAs typically consist of multiple processes that communicate by message passing over a completely connected communication graph. Since a sender can be faulty, a receiver cannot wait for a message from a specific sender process. Therefore, most FTDAs use counters to reason about their environment. If, for instance, a process receives a certain message m from more than t distinct processes, it can conclude that at least one of the senders is non-faulty. A large class of FTDAs [39,75,44,37,36] expresses these counting arguments using *threshold guards:*

```
if received <m> from t+1 distinct processes
then action(m);
```

Note that threshold guards generalize existential and universal guards [40], that is, rules that wait for messages from at least one or all processes, respectively. As can be seen from the above example, and as discussed in [51], existential and universal guards are not sufficient to capture advanced FTDAs.

2.3   The Formalization Problem

In the literature, the vast majority of distributed algorithms is described in pseudo code, for instance, [75,8,79]. The intended semantics of the pseudo code is folklore knowledge among the distributed computing community. Researchers who have been working in this community have intuitive understanding of keywords like "send", "receive", or "broadcast". For instance, inside the community it is understood that there is a semantical difference between "send to all" and "broadcast" in the context of fault tolerance. Moreover, the constraints on the environment are given in a rather informal way. For instance, in the authenticated Byzantine model [39], it is assumed that faulty processes may behave arbitrarily. At the same time, it is assumed that there is some authentication service, which provides unbreakable digital signatures. In conclusion, it is thus assumed that faulty processes send any messages they like, *except* ones that look like messages sent by correct processes. However, inferring this kind of information about the behavior of faulty processes is a very intricate task.

At the bottom line, a close familiarity with the distributed algorithms community is required to adequately model a distributed algorithm in preparation of formal verification. When the essential conditions are hidden between the lines of a research paper, then one cannot be sure that the algorithm being verified is the one that is actually intended by the authors. With the current state of the art, we are thus forced to do *verification of a moving target.*

We conclude that there is need for a versatile specification language which can express distributed algorithms along with their environment. Such a language should be natural for distributed algorithms researchers, but provide unambiguous and clear semantics. Since distributed algorithms come with a wide range of different assumptions, the language has to be easily configurable to these situations. Unfortunately, most verification tools do not provide sufficiently expressive languages for this task. Thus, it is hard for researchers from the distributed computing community to use these tools out of the box. Although distributed algorithms are usually presented in a very compact form, the "language primitives" (of pseudo code) are used without consideration of implementation issues and computational complexity. For instance sets, and operations on sets are often used as they ease presentation of concepts to readers, although fixed size vectors would be sufficient to express the algorithm and more efficient to implement. Besides, it is not unusual to assume that any local computation on a node can be completed within one step. Another example is the handling of messages. For instance, how a process stores the messages that have been received in the past is usually not explained in detail. At the same time, quite complex operations are performed on this information.

2.4 Verified Fault-Tolerant Distributed Algorithms

Several distributed algorithms have been formally verified in the literature. Typically, these papers have addressed specific algorithms in fixed computational models. There are roughly two lines of research. On the one hand, the semi-manual proofs conducted with proof assistants that typically involve an enormous amount of manual work by the user, and on the other hand automatic verification, e.g., via model checking. Among the work using proof assistants, Byzantine agreement in the synchronous case was considered in [61,73]. In the context of the heard-of model with message corruption [15] Isabelle proofs are given in [24]. For automatic verification, for instance, algorithms in the heard-of model were verified by (bounded) model checking [78]. Partial order reductions for a class of fault-tolerant distributed algorithms (with "quorum transitions") for fixed-size systems were introduced in [19]. A broadcasting algorithm for crash faults was considered in [43] in the context of regular model checking; however, the method has not been implemented so it is not clear how practical it is. In [9], the safety of synchronous broadcasting algorithms that tolerate crash or send omission faults has been verified. Another line of research studies decidability of model checking of distributed systems under different link semantics [7,32].

Model checking of fault-tolerant distributed algorithms is usually limited to small instances, i.e., to systems consisting of only few processes (e.g., 4 to 10). However, distributed algorithms are typically designed for parameterized systems, i.e., for systems of arbitrary size. The model checking community has created interesting results toward closing this gap, although it still remains a big research challenge. For specific cache coherence protocols, substantial research has been done on model checking safety properties for systems of arbitrary size, for instance, [65,26,68]. Since these protocols are usually described via message passing, they appear similar to asynchronous distributed algorithms. However, issues such as faulty components and liveness are not considered in the literature. The verification of large concurrent systems by reasoning about suitable small ones has also been considered [41,29,32,70].

3 Modeling Fault-Tolerant Distributed Algorithms

3.1 Threshold-Guarded Distributed Algorithms

Processes, which constitute the distributed algorithms we consider, exchange messages, and change their state predominantly based on the received messages.

In addition to the standard execution of actions, which are guarded by some predicate on the local state, most basic distributed algorithms (cf. [62,11]) add existentially or universally guarded commands involving received messages:

if received <m>	**if** received <m>
from some process	from all processes
then action (m);	**then** action (m);
(a) existential guard	(b) universal guard

Depending on the content of the message <m>, the function `action` performs a local computation, and possibly sends messages to one or more processes. Such constructs can be found, e.g., in (non-fault-tolerant) distributed algorithms for constructing spanning trees, flooding, mutual exclusion, or network synchronization [62]. Understanding and analyzing such distributed algorithms is already far from being trivial, which is due to the partial information on the global state present in the local state of a process. However, faults add another source of nondeterminism. In order to shed some light on the difficulties faced a distributed algorithm in the presence of faults, consider Byzantine faults [69], which allow a faulty process to behave arbitrarily: Faulty processes may fail to send messages, send messages with erroneous values, or even send conflicting information to different processes. In addition, faulty processes may even collaborate in order to increase their adverse power.

Fault-tolerant distributed algorithms work in the presence of such faults and provide some "higher level" service: In case of distributed agreement (or consensus), e.g., this service is that all non-faulty processes compute the same result even if some processes fail. Fault-tolerant distributed algorithms are hence used for increasing the system-level reliability of distributed systems [71].

If one tries to build such a fault-tolerant distributed algorithm using the construct of Example (a) in the presence of Byzantine faults, the (local state of the) receiver process would be corrupted if the received message <m> originates in a faulty process. A faulty process could hence contaminate a correct process. On the other hand, if one tried to use the construct of Example (b), a correct process would wait forever (starve) when a faulty process omits to send the required message. To overcome those problems, fault-tolerant distributed algorithms typically require assumptions on the maximum number of faults, and employ suitable thresholds for the number of messages that can be expected to be received by correct processes. Assuming that the system consists of n processes among which at most t may be faulty, *threshold-guarded commands* such as the following are typically used in fault-tolerant distributed algorithms:

if received <m> from n−t distinct processes
then action (m);

Assuming that thresholds are functions of the parameters n and t, threshold guards are just a generalization of quantified guards as given in Examples (a) and (b): In the above command, a process waits to receive $n - t$ messages from distinct processes. As there are at least $n - t$ correct processes, the guard cannot be blocked by faulty processes, which avoids the problems of Example (b). In the distributed algorithms literature, one finds a variety of different thresholds: Typical numbers are $\lceil n/2+1 \rceil$ (for majority [39,67]), $t+1$ (to wait for a message from at least one correct process [76,39]), or $n - t$ (in the Byzantine case [76,8] to wait for at least $t + 1$ messages from correct processes, provided $n > 3t$).

In the setting of Byzantine fault tolerance, it is important to note that the use of threshold-guarded commands implicitly rests on the assumption that a receiver can distinguish messages from different senders. This can be achieved, e.g., by using point-to-point links between processes or by message authentication. What is important here is that Byzantine faulty processes are only allowed to exercise control on their own messages and computations, but not on the messages sent by other processes and the computation of other processes.

3.2   Reliable Broadcast and Related Specifications

The specifications considered in the field of fault tolerance differ from more classic fields, such as concurrent systems where dining philosophers and mutual exclusion are central problems. For the latter, one is typically interested in local properties, e.g., if a philosopher i is hungry, then i eventually eats. Intuitively, dining philosophers requires us to trace indexed processes along a computation, e.g., in LTL, $\forall i.\ \mathbf{G}\,(\text{hungry}_i \rightarrow (\mathbf{F}\,\text{eating}_i))$, and thus to employ *indexed* temporal logics for specifications [21,28,29,41].

In contrast, fault-tolerant distributed algorithms are typically used to achieve *global* properties. Reliable broadcast is an ongoing "system service" with the following informal specification: Each process i may invoke a primitive called broadcast by calling $bcast(i, m)$, where m is a unique message content. Processes may deliver a message by invoking $accept(i, m)$ for different process and message pairs (i, m). The goal is that all correct processes invoke $accept(i, m)$ for the same set of (i, m) pairs, under some additional constraints: all messages broadcast by correct processes must be accepted by all correct processes, and $accept(i, m)$ may not be invoked, unless i is faulty or i invoked $bcast(i, m)$. Our case study is to verify that the algorithm from [76] implements these primitives on top of point-to-point channels, in the presence of Byzantine faults. In [76] the specifications where given in natural language as follows:

(U) Unforgeability. If correct process i does not broadcast (i, m), then no correct process ever accepts (i, m).

(C) Correctness. If correct process i broadcasts (i, m), then every correct process accepts (i, m).

(R) Relay If a correct process accepts (i, m), then every other correct process accepts (i, m).

In [76], the instances for different (i, m) pairs do not interfere. Therefore, we will not consider i and m. Rather, we distinguish the different kinds of invocations of $bcast(i, m)$ that may occur, e.g., the cases where the invoking process is faulty or correct. As we focus on the core functionality, we do not model the broadcaster explicit. We observe that correct broadcasters will either send to all, or to no other correct processes. Hence, we model this by initial values V1 and V0 at correct processes that we use to model whether a process has received the message by the broadcaster or not, respectively. Then the precondition of correctness can be modeled that all correct processes initially have value V1, while the precondition of unforgeability that all correct processes initially have value V0. Depending on the initial state, we then have to check whether every/no correct process accepts (that is, changes the status to AC). To capture this kind of properties, we have to trace only existentially or universally quantified properties, e.g., a part of the broadcast specification (relay) states that if some correct process accepts a message, then all (correct) processes accept the message, that is, $\mathbf{G}\left((\exists i.\ \mathrm{accept}_i) \rightarrow \mathbf{F}\left(\forall j.\ \mathrm{accept}_j\right)\right)$.

We are therefore considering a temporal logic where the *quantification over processes is restricted to propositional formulas*. We will need two kinds of quantified propositional formulas that consider (i) the finite control state modeled as a single status variable sv, and (ii) the possible unbounded data. We introduce the set AP_{SV} that contains propositions that capture comparison against some status value Z from the set of all control states, i.e., $[\forall i.\ sv_i = Z]$ and $[\exists i.\ sv_i = Z]$.

This allows us to express specifications of distributed algorithms:

$$\mathbf{G}\left([\forall i.\ sv_i \neq \mathrm{V1}] \rightarrow \mathbf{G}\left[\forall j.\ sv_j \neq \mathrm{AC}\right]\right) \tag{U}$$

$$\mathbf{G}\left([\forall i.\ sv_i = \mathrm{V1}] \rightarrow \mathbf{F}\left[\exists j.\ sv_j = \mathrm{AC}\right]\right) \tag{C}$$

$$\mathbf{G}\left([\exists i.\ sv_i = \mathrm{AC}] \rightarrow \mathbf{F}\left[\forall j.\ sv_j = \mathrm{AC}\right]\right) \tag{R}$$

We may quantify over all processes as we only explicitly model those processes that follow their code, that is, correct or benign faulty processes. More severe faults that are unrestricted in their internal behavior (e.g., Byzantine faults) are modeled via non-determinism in message passing.

In order to express comparison of data variables, we add a set of atomic propositions AP_D that capture comparison of data variables (integers) x, y, and constant c; AP_D consists of propositions of the form $[\exists i.\ x_i + c < y_i]$. The labeling function of a system instance is then defined naturally as disjunction or conjunction over all process indices.

Observe that the specifications (C) and (R) are conditional liveness properties. Intuitively, a process has to find out that the condition is satisfied a run, and in distributed systems this is only possible by receiving messages. Specification (C) can thus only be achieved if some messages are received. Indeed, the algorithm in [76] is based on a property called *reliable communication* which ensures that every message sent by a correct process to a correct process is eventually received by the latter. Such properties can be expressed by justice requirements [70], which is a specific form of fairness. We will express justice as an $\mathsf{LTL} \setminus \mathsf{X}$ formula ψ over AP_D. Then, given an $\mathsf{LTL} \setminus \mathsf{X}$ specification φ over AP_{SV}, a process description P in PROMELA, and the number of (correct) processes N, the parameterized model checking problem is to verify whether

$$\underbrace{P \parallel P \parallel \cdots \parallel P}_{N\,times} \models \psi \rightarrow \varphi.$$

Algorithm 1. Core logic of the broadcasting algorithm from [76].

Code for processes i if it is correct:
Variables
1: $v_i \in \{\text{FALSE}, \text{TRUE}\}$
2: $accept_i \in \{\text{FALSE}, \text{TRUE}\} \leftarrow \text{FALSE}$

Rules
3: **if** v_i **and** not sent $\langle echo \rangle$ before **then**
4:     send $\langle echo \rangle$ to all;
5: **if** *received* $\langle echo \rangle$ from at least $t + 1$ *distinct* processes
        and not sent $\langle echo \rangle$ before **then**
6:     send $\langle echo \rangle$ to all;
7: **if** *received* $\langle echo \rangle$ from at least $n - t$ *distinct* processes **then**
8:     $accept_i \leftarrow \text{TRUE}$;

3.3 Threshold-Guarded Distributed Algorithms in Promela

Algorithm 1 is our case study for which we also provide a complete PROMELA implementation later in Listing 3. To explain how we obtain this implementation, we proceed in three steps where we first discuss asynchronous distributed algorithms in general, then explain our encoding of message passing for threshold-guarded fault-tolerant distributed algorithms. Algorithm 1 belongs to this class, as it does not distinguish messages according to their senders, but just counts received messages, and performs state transitions depending on the number of received messages; e.g., line 7. Finally we encode the control flow of Algorithm 1. The rationale of the modeling decisions are that the resulting PROMELA model (i) captures the assumptions of distributed algorithms adequately, and (ii) allows for efficient verification either using explicit state enumeration or by abstraction.

Computational Model for Asynchronous Distributed Algorithms. We recall the standard assumptions for asynchronous distributed algorithms. A system consists of n processes, out of which at most t may be faulty. When considering a fixed computation, we denote by f the actual number of faulty processes. Note that f is not "known" to the processes. It is assumed that $n > 3t \wedge f \leq t \wedge t > 0$. Correct processes follow the algorithm, in that they take steps that correspond to the algorithm. Between every pair of processes, there is a bidirectional link over which messages are exchanged. A link contains two message buffers, each being the receive buffer of one of the incident processes.

A step of a correct process is *atomic* and consists of the following three parts. (i) The process possibly receives a message. A process is not forced to receive a message even if there is one in its buffer [42]. (ii) Then, it performs a state transition depending on its current state and the (possibly) received message. (iii) Finally, a process may send at most one message to each process, that is, it puts a message in the buffers of the other processes.

Computations are asynchronous in that the steps can be arbitrarily interleaved, provided that each correct process takes an infinite number of steps.

Algorithm 1 has runs that never accept and are infinite. Conceptually, the standard model requires that processes executing terminating algorithms loop forever in terminal states [62]. Moreover, if a message m is put into process p's buffer, and p is correct, then m is eventually received. This property is called *reliable communication*.

From the above discussion we observe that buffers are required to be unbounded, and thus sending is non-blocking. Further, the receive operation does never block the execution; even if no message has been sent to the process. If we assume that for each message type, each correct process sends at most one message in each run (as in Algorithm 1), non-blocking send can in principle natively be encoded in PROMELA using message channels. In principle, non-blocking receive also can be implemented in PROMELA, but it is not a basic construct. We discuss the modeling of message passing in more detail in Section 3.3.

Fault types. In our case study Algorithm 1 we consider *Byzantine* faults, that is, faulty processes are not restricted, except that they have no influence on the buffers of links to which they are not incident. Below we also consider restricted failure classes: *omission faults* follow the algorithm but may fail to send some messages, *crash faults* follow the algorithm but may prematurely stop running. Finally, *symmetric faults* need not follow the algorithm, but if they send messages, they send them to all processes. The latter restriction does not apply to Byzantine faults which may send conflicting information to different processes.

Verification goal in the concrete (non-parameterized) case. Recall that there is a condition on the parameters n, t, and f, namely, $n > 3t \land f \le t \land t > 0$. As these parameters do not change during a run, they can be encoded as constants in PROMELA. The verification problem for a distributed algorithm with fixed n and t is then the composition of model checking problems that differ in the actual value of f (satisfying $f \le t$).

Efficient Encoding of Message Passing. In threshold-guarded distributed algorithms, the processes (i) count how many messages of the same type they have received from *distinct* processes, and change their states depending on this number, (ii) always send to *all* processes (including the sender), and (iii) send messages only for a fixed number of types (only messages of type ⟨echo⟩ are sent in Algorithm 1).

Fault-free communication. We discuss in the following that one can model such algorithms in a way that is more efficient in comparison to a straightforward implementation with PROMELA channels. In our final modeling we have an approach that captures both message passing and the influence of faults on correct processes. However, in order not to clutter the presentation, we start our discussion by considering communication between correct processes only (i.e., $f = 0$), and add faults later in this section.

In the following code examples we show a straightforward way to implement "received ⟨echo⟩ from at least x distinct processes" and "send ⟨echo⟩ to all" using PROMELA channels: We declare an array p2p of n^2 channels, one per pair of processes, and then we declare an array rx to record that at most one ⟨echo⟩ message from a process j is received by a process i:

```
mtype = { ECHO }; /* one message type */
chan p2p[NxN] = [1] of { mtype }; /* channels of size 1 */
bit  rx[NxN]; /* a bit map to implement "distinct" */
active[N] proctype STBcastChan() {
  int i, nrcvd = 0; /* nr. of echoes */
```

Then, the receive code iterates over n channels: for non-empty channels it receives an ⟨echo⟩ message or not, and empty channels are skipped; if a message is received, the channel is marked in rx:

```
i = 0; do
:: (i < N) && nempty(p2p[i * N + _pid]) ->
   p2p[i * N + _pid]?ECHO; /* retrieve a message */
   if
   :: !rx[i * N + _pid] ->
      rx[i * N + _pid] = 1; /* mark the channel */
      nrcvd++; break; /* receive at most one message */
   :: rx[i * N + _pid];   /* ignore duplicates */
   fi; i++;
:: (i < N) ->
   i++;   /* channel is empty or postpone reception */
:: i == N -> break;
od
```

Finally, the sending code also iterates over n channels and sends on each:

```
for (i : 1 .. N) { p2p[_pid * N + i]!ECHO; }
```

Recall that threshold-guarded algorithms have specific constraints: messages from all processes are processed uniformly; every message is carrying only a message type without a process identifier; each process sends a message to all processes in no particular order. This suggests a simpler modeling solution. Instead of using message passing directly, we keep only the numbers of sent and received messages in integer variables:

```
int nsnt; /* one shared variable per a message type */
active[N] proctype STBcast() {
  int nrcvd = 0, next_nrcvd = 0; /* nr. of echoes */
  ...
  step: atomic {
    if /* receive one more echo */
    :: (next_nrcvd < nsnt) ->
       next_nrcvd = nrcvd + 1;
    :: next_nrcvd = nrcvd; /* or nothing */
    fi;
    ...
    nsnt++; /* send echo to all */
  }
```

```
active[F] proctype Byz() {           active[F] proctype Symm(){
step: atomic {                       step: atomic {
  i = 0; do                            if
  :: i < N -> sendTo(i);i++;           :: /* send to all */
  :: i < N -> i++; /*skip*/               for (i : 1 .. N)
  :: i == N -> break;                     { sendTo(i); }
  od                                   :: skip; /* or none */
}; goto step;                          fi
}                                    }; goto step;
                                     }

active[F] proctype Omit() {
step: atomic {
 /* receive as a correct */          active[F] proctype Clean(){
 /* compute as a correct */          step: atomic {
 if :: correctCodeSendsAll ->         /* receive as a correct */
  i = 0; do                           /* compute as a correct */
  :: i < N -> sendTo(i);i++;          /* send as a correct */
  :: i < N -> i++; /*omit*/           };
  :: i == N -> break;                 if
  od                                    :: goto step;
 :: skip;                               :: goto crash;
 fi                                   fi;
}; goto step;                        crash:
}                                    }
```

Fig. 1. Modeling faulty processes explicitly: Byzantine (Byz), symmetric (Symm), omission (Omit), and clean crashes (Clean)

As one process step is executed atomically (indivisibly), concurrent reads and updates of $nsnt$ are not a concern to us. Note that the presented code is based on the assumption that each correct process sends at most one message. We show how to enforce this assumption when discussing the control flow of our implementation of Algorithm 1 in Section 3.3.

Recall that in asynchronous distributed systems one assumes communication fairness, that is, every message sent is eventually received. The statement $\exists i.\ rcvd_i < nsnt$ describes a global state where messages are still in transit. It follows that a formula ψ defined by

$$\mathbf{G}\,\mathbf{F} \neg [\exists i.\ rcvd_i < nsnt] \qquad \text{(RelComm)}$$

states that the system periodically delivers all messages sent by (correct) processes. We are thus going to add such fairness requirements to our specifications.

Faulty processes. In Figure 1 we show how one can model the different types of faults (discussed on page 132) using channels. The implementations are direct consequences of the fault types description. Figure 2 shows how the impact of faults on processes following the algorithm can be implemented in the shared

```
/* N > 3T ∧ T ≥ F ≥ 0 */          /* N > 2T ∧ T ≥ Fp ≥ Fs ≥ 0 */
active[N-F] proctype ByzI() {      active[N-Fp] proctype SymmI(){
step: atomic {                     step: atomic {
  if                                 if
  :: (next_nrcvd < nsnt + F)         :: (next_nrcvd < nsnt + Fs)
    -> next_nrcvd = nrcvd + 1;        -> next_nrcvd = nrcvd + 1;
  :: next_nrcvd = nrcvd;             :: next_nrcvd = nrcvd;
  fi                                 fi
  /* compute */                      /* compute */
  /* send    */                      /* send    */
  }; goto step;                      }; goto step;
}                                  }


/* N > 2T ∧ T ≥ F ≥ 0 */          /* N ≥ T ∧ T ≥ Fc ≥ Fnc ≥ 0 */
active[N] proctype OmitI() {       active[N] proctype CleanI() {
step: atomic {                     step: atomic {
  if                                 if
  :: (next_nrcvd < nsnt) ->          :: next_nrcvd < nsnt - Fnc
    next_nrcvd = nrcvd + 1;           -> next_nrcvd = nrcvd + 1;
  :: next_nrcvd = nrcvd;             :: next_nrcvd = nrcvd;
  fi                                 fi
  /* compute */                      /* compute */
  /* send    */                      /* send    */
  }; goto step;                      }; goto step;
}                                  }
```

         Listing 1.   **Listing 2.**

Fig. 2. Modeling the effect of faults on correct processes: Byzantine (ByzI), symmetric (SymmI), omission (OmitI), and clean crashes (CleanI)

memory implementation of message passing. Note that in contrast to Figure 1, the processes in Figure 2 are *not* the faulty ones, but correct ones whose variable next_nrcvd is subject to non-deterministic updates that correspond to the impact of faulty process. For instance, in the Byzantine case, in addition to the messages sent by correct processes, a process can receive up to f messages more. This is expressed by the condition (next_nrcvd < nsnt + F).

For Byzantine and symmetric faults we only model correct processes explicitly. Thus, we specify that there are N-F copies of the process. Moreover, we can use Property (RelComm) to model reliable communication. Omission and crash faults, however, we model explicitly, so that we have N copies of processes. Without going into too much detail, the impact of faulty processes is modeled by relaxed fairness requirements: as some messages sent by these f faulty processes may not be received, this induces less strict communication fairness:

$$\mathbf{G}\,\mathbf{F}\,\neg\,[\exists i.\ rcvd_i + f < nsnt]$$

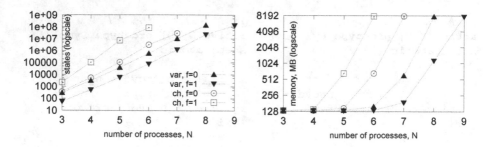

Fig. 3. Visited states (left) and memory usage (right) when modeling message passing with channels (ch) or shared variables (var). The faults are in effect only when $f > 0$. Ran with SAFETY, COLLAPSE, COMP, and 8GB of memory.

By similar adaptations one models, e.g., corrupted communication (e.g., due to faulty links) [72], or hybrid fault models [16] that contain different fault scenarios.

Comparing Promela Encodings: Channels vs. Shared Variables. Figure 3 compares the number of states and memory consumption when modeling message passing using both solutions. We ran SPIN to perform exhaustive state enumeration on the encoding of our case study algorithm in Listing 3. As one sees, the model with explicit channels and faulty processes ran out of memory on *six* processes, whereas the shared memory model did so only with *nine* processes. Moreover, the latter scales better in the presence of faults, while the former degrades with faults. This leads to the use the shared memory encoding based on *nsnt* variables. In addition, we have seen in the previous section that this encoding is very natural for defining abstractions.

Encoding the Control Flow. Recall Algorithm 1 on page 131, which is written in typical pseudocode found in the distributed algorithms literature. The lines 3–8 describe one step of the algorithm. Receiving messages is implicit and performed before line 3, and the actual sending of messages is deferred to the end, and is performed after line 8.

We encoded the algorithm in Listing 3 using custom PROMELA extensions to express notions of fault-tolerant distributed algorithms. The extensions are required to express a parameterized model checking problem, and are used by our tool that implements the abstraction methods introduced in [52]. These extensions are only syntactic sugar when the parameters are fixed: symbolic is used to declare parameters, and assume is used to impose resilience conditions on them (but is ignored in explicit state model checking). Declarations atomic <var> = all (...) are a shorthand for declaring atomic propositions that are unfolded into conjunctions over all processes (similarly for some). Also we allow expressions over parameters in the argument of active.

```
1   symbolic int N, T, F;   /* parameters */
2   /* the resilience condition */
3   assume(N > 3 * T && T >= 1 && 0 <= F && F <= T);
4   int nsnt;   /* number of echoes sent by correct processes */
5   /* quantified atomic propositions */
6   atomic prec_unforg = all(STBcast:sv == V0);
7   atomic prec_corr = all(STBcast:sv == V1);
8   atomic prec_init = all(STBcast@step);
9   atomic ex_acc = some(STBcast:sv == AC);
10  atomic all_acc = all(STBcast:sv == AC);
11  atomic in_transit = some(STBcast:nrcvd < nsnt);
12
13  active[N - F] proctype STBcast() {
14    byte sv, next_sv;            /* status of the algorithm */
15    int nrcvd = 0, next_nrcvd = 0; /* nr. of echoes received */
16    if  /* initialize */
17      :: sv = V0; /* v_i = FALSE */
18      :: sv = V1; /* v_i = TRUE */
19    fi;
20  step: atomic { /* an indivisible step */
21      if /* receive one more echo (up to nsnt + F) */
22        :: (nrcvd < nsnt + F) -> next_nrcvd = nrcvd + 1;
23        :: next_nrcvd = nrcvd; /* or nothing */
24      fi;
25      if /* compute */
26        :: (next_nrcvd >= N - T) ->
27          next_sv = AC;  /* accept_i = TRUE */
28        :: (next_nrcvd < N - T
29          && (sv == V1 || next_nrcvd >= T + 1)) ->
30          next_sv = SE; /* remember that <echo> is sent */
31        :: else -> next_sv = sv; /* keep the status */
32      fi;
33      if /* send */
34        :: (sv == V0 || sv == V1)
35          && (next_sv == SE || next_sv == AC) ->
36          nsnt++; /* send <echo> */
37        :: else;  /* send nothing */
38      fi;
39      /* update local variables and reset scratch variables */
40      sv = next_sv; nrcvd = next_nrcvd;
41      next_sv = 0; next_nrcvd = 0;
42      } goto step;
43  }
44  ltl fairness { []<>(!in_transit) } /* fairness -> formula */
45  /* LTL-X formulas */
46  ltl relay { [](ex_acc -> <>all_acc) }
47  ltl corr { []((prec_init && prec_corr) -> <>(ex_acc)) }
48  ltl unforg { []((prec_init && prec_unforg) -> []!ex_acc) }
```

Listing 3. Encoding of Algorithm 1 in parametric PROMELA

In the encoding in Listing 3, the whole step is captured within an atomic block (lines 20–42). As usual for fault-tolerant algorithms, this block has three logical parts: the receive part (lines 21–24), the computation part (lines 25–32), and the sending part (lines 33–38). As we have already discussed the encoding of message passing above, it remains to discuss the control flow of the algorithm.

Control state of the algorithm. Apart from receiving and sending messages, Algorithm 1 refers to several facts about the current control state of a process: "sent $\langle echo \rangle$ before", "if v_i", and "$accept_i \leftarrow$ TRUE". We capture all possible control states in a finite set SV. For instance, for Algorithm 1 one can collect the set $SV = \{V0, V1, SE, AC\}$, where:

- V0 corresponds to $v_i =$ FALSE, $accept_i =$ FALSE and $\langle echo \rangle$ is not sent.
- V1 corresponds to $v_i =$ TRUE, $accept_i =$ FALSE and $\langle echo \rangle$ is not sent.
- SE corresponds to the case $accept_i =$ FALSE and $\langle echo \rangle$ been sent. Observe that once a process has sent $\langle echo \rangle$, its value of v_i does not interfere anymore with the subsequent control flow.
- AC corresponds to the case $accept_i =$ TRUE and $\langle echo \rangle$ been sent. A process only sets accept to TRUE if it has sent a message (or is about to do so in the current step).

Thus, the control state is captured within a single *status variable sv* over SV with the set $SV_0 = \{V0, V1\}$ of initial control states.

Formalization. This paper is a hands-on tutorial on parameterized model checking. So we will use PROMELA to explain our methods in the following sections. Note that we presented the theoretical foundations of these methods in [52]. In this paper we will restrict ourselves to introduce some definitions that make it easier to discuss the central ideas of our abstraction.

In the code we use variables of different roles: we have parameters (e.g., n, t, and f), local variables ($rcvd$) and shared variables ($nsnt$). We will denote by Π, Λ, and Γ the sets of parameters, local variables, and shared variables, respectively. All these variables range over a *domain* D that is totally ordered and has the operations of addition and subtraction, e.g., the set of natural numbers $\mathbb{N}_0$. We have discussed above that fault-tolerant distributed algorithms can tolerate only certain fractions of processes to be faulty. We capture this using the *resilience condition* RC that is a predicate over the values of variables in Π. In our example, $\Pi = \{n, t, f\}$, and the resilience condition $RC(n, t, f)$ is $n > 3t \wedge f \leq t \wedge t > 0$. Then, we denote the set of *admissible parameters* by $\mathbf{P}_{RC} = \{\mathbf{p} \in D^{|\Pi|} \mid RC(\mathbf{p})\}$.

As we have seen, a system instance is a parallel composition of identical processes. The number of processes depends on the parameters. To formalize this, we define the size of a system (the number of processes) using a function $N : \mathbf{P}_{RC} \to \mathbb{N}$, for instance, in our example we model only correct processes explicitly, and so we use $n - f$ for $N(n, t, f)$.

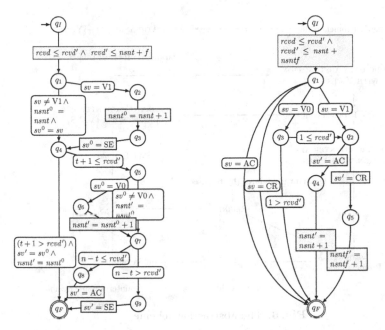

Fig. 4. CFA of our case study for Byzantine faults

Fig. 5. CFA of FTDA from [43] (if x' is not assigned, then $x' = x$)

To model how the system evolves, that is, to model a step of a process, we use control flow automata (CFA). They formalize fault-tolerant distributed algorithms. Figure 4 gives the CFA of our case study algorithm. The CFA uses the shared integer variable $nsnt$ (capturing the number of messages sent by non-faulty processes), the local integer variable $rcvd$ (storing the number of messages received by the process so far), and the local status variable sv, which ranges over a finite domain (capturing the local progress w.r.t. the FTDA).

We use the CFA to represent one atomic *step* of the FTDA: Each edge is labeled with a guard. A path from q_I to q_F induces a conjunction of all the guards along it, and imposes constraints on the variables before the step (e.g., sv), after the step (sv'), and temporary variables (sv^0). If one fixes the variables before the step, different valuations (of the primed variables) that satisfy the constraints capture non-determinism.

Recall that a system consists of $n - f$ processes that concurrently execute the code corresponding to the CFA, and communicate via $nsnt$. Thus, there are two sources of unboundedness: first, the integer variables, and second, the parametric number of processes.

4   Abstraction

In this section we demonstrate how one can apply various abstractions to reduce a parameterized model checking problem to a finite-state model checking

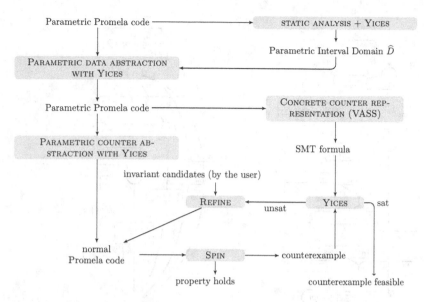

Fig. 6. The abstraction scheme

problem. An overview is given in Figure 6. We show how the abstraction works on the code level, that is, how the parametric PROMELA program constructed in Section 3 is translated to a program in standard PROMELA. Since we are interested in parameterized model checking, we need to ensure that the specifications are satisfied in concrete systems of all sizes. Hence, we need an abstract system that contains all behaviors that are experienced in concrete systems. Consequently, we use existential abstraction which ensures that if there exists a concrete system and a concrete run in that system, this run is mapped to a run in the abstract system. In that way, if there exists a system in which a specification is violated, the specification will also be violated in the abstract system. In other words, if we can verify a specification in the abstract system, the specification holds in *all* concrete systems; we say the verification method is sound. The formal exposition can be found in [52].

Usually abstractions introduce new behavior that is not present in the original system. Thus, a finite-state model checker might find a spurious run, that is, one that none of the concrete systems with fixed parameters can replay. In order to discard such runs, one applies abstraction refinement techniques [27].

In what follows, we demonstrate three levels of abstraction: parametric interval data abstraction, parametric interval counter abstraction, and parametric interval data abstraction of the local state space. The first two abstractions are used for reducing a parameterized problem to a finite-state one, while the third abstraction helps us to detect spurious counterexamples.

Throughout this chapter we are using the core part of asynchronous reliable broadcast by Srikanth&Toueg as our running example. Its encoding in parametric PROMELA is given in Listing 3. Our final goal is to obtain a PROMELA program that we can verify in SPIN.

4.1 Parametric Interval Data Abstraction

Let us have a look at the code on Listing 3. The process prototype STBcast refers to two kinds of variables, each of them having a special role:

- *Bounded variables.* These are local variables that range over a finite domain, the size of which is independent of the parameters. In our example, the variable of this kind are sv and next_sv.
- *Unbounded variables.* These are the variables that range over an unbounded domain. They may be local or shared. In our example, the variables nrcvd, next_nrcvd, and nsnt are unbounded. It might happen that the variables become bounded, when one fixes the parameters, as it is the case in our example with nsnt $\leq n - f$. However, we need a finite representation independent of the parameters, that is, the bounds on the variable values must be independent of the parameter values.

We can partition the variables into the sets B (bounded) and U (unbounded) by performing value analysis on the process body. Intuitively, one can imagine that the analysis iteratively computes the set B of variables that are assigned their values only using the following two kinds of statements:

- An assignment that copies a constant expression to a variable;
- An assignment that copies the value of another variable, which already belongs to B.

The variables outside of B, e.g., those that are incremented in the code, belong to U. As this can be done by a simple implementation of abstract interpretation [33], we omit the details here.

The data abstraction that we are going to explain below deals with unbounded variables by turning the operations over unbounded domains into operations over finite domains. The threshold-based fault-tolerant distributed algorithms give us a natural source of abstract values, namely, the threshold expressions. In our example, the variable next_nrcvd is compared against thresholds $t + 1$ and $n - t$. Thus, it appears natural to forget about concrete values of next_nrcvd. As a first try, we may replace the expressions that involve next_nrcvd with the expressions over the two predicates: p1_next_nrcvd $\equiv x < t + 1$ and p2_next_nrcvd $\equiv x < n - t$. Then, the following code is an abstraction of the computation block in lines (25)–(32) of Listing 3:

```
if /* compute */
  :: (!p2_next_nrcvd) -> next_sv = AC;
  :: (!p2_next_nrcvd && (sv == V1 || !p1_next_nrcvd)) ->
     next_sv = SE;
  :: else -> next_sv = sv;
fi;
```

Listing 4. Predicate abstraction of the computation block

In principle, we could use this kind of predicate abstraction for our purposes. However, we have seen that our modeling involves considerable amounts of arithmetics, e.g., code line 22 in our example contains comparison of two variables as well increasing the value of a variable. Such notions are not naturally expressed in terms of predicate abstraction. Rather, we introduce a parametric interval abstraction PIA, which is based on an abstract domain that represents intervals, whose boundaries are expressions to which variables are compared to; e.g., $t + 1$ and $n - t$. We then use an SMT solver to abstract expressions, e.g., comparisons.

Hence, instead of using several predicates, we can replace the concrete domain of every variable $x \in U$ with the abstract domain $\{I_0, I_{t+1}, I_{n-t}\}$. For reasons that are motivated by the counter abstraction — to be introduced later in Section 4.2 — we have to distinguish value 0 from a positive value. Thus, we are extending the domain with the threshold "1", that is, $\widehat{D} = \{I_0, I_1, I_{t+1}, I_{n-t}\}$.

The semantics of the abstract domain is as follows. We introduce an abstract version of x, denoted by $\hat{x}$; its values (from $\widehat{D}$) relate to the concrete values of x as follows: $\hat{x} = I_0$ iff $x \in [0; 1[$ and $\hat{x} = I_1$ iff $x \in [1; t + 1[$ and $\hat{x} = I_{t+1}$ iff $x \in [t + 1; n - t[$ and $\hat{x} = I_{n-t}$ iff $x \in [n - t; \infty[$. Having defined the abstract domain, we translate the computation block in lines (25)–(32) of Listing 3 as follows (we discuss below how the translation is done automatically):

```
1  if /* compute */
2    :: next_nrcvd == I_{n-t} -> next_sv = AC;
3    :: (next_nrcvd == I_0 || next_nrcvd == I_1 || next_nrcvd== I_{t+1})
4       && (sv == V1 || (next_nrcvd == I_{t+1} || next_nrcvd == I_{n-t}))
5       -> next_sv = SE;
6    :: else -> next_sv = sv;
7  fi;
```

Listing 5. Parametric interval abstraction of the computation block

The abstraction of the receive block (cf. lines 21–24 of Listing 3) involves the assignment next_nrcvd = nrcvd + 1 that becomes a *non-deterministic choice* of the abstract value of next_nrcvd based on the abstract value of nrcvd. Intuitively, next_nrcvd could be in the same interval as nrcvd or in the interval above. In the following, we provide the abstraction of lines 21–24, we will discuss later how this abstraction can be computed using an SMT solver.

```
8   if /* receive */
9     :: (/* abstraction of (next_nrcvd < nsnt + F) */) ->
10      if :: nrcvd == I_0 -> next_nrcvd = I_1;
11         :: nrcvd == I_1 -> next_nrcvd = I_1;
12         :: nrcvd == I_1 -> next_nrcvd = I_{t+1};
13         :: nrcvd == I_{t+1} -> next_nrcvd = I_{t+1};
14         :: nrcvd == I_{t+1} -> next_nrcvd = I_{n-t};
15         :: nrcvd == I_{n-t} -> next_nrcvd = I_{n-t};
16      fi;
17      :: next_nrcvd = nrcvd;
18   fi;
```

Listing 6. Parametric interval abstraction of the receive block

There are several interesting consequences of transforming the receive block as above. First, due to our resilience condition (which ensures that intervals do not overlap) for every value of nrcvd there are at most two values that can be assigned to next_nrcvd. For instance, if nrcvd equals I_{t+1}, then next_nrcvd becomes either I_{t+1}, or I_{n-t}. Second, due to non-determinism, the assignment is not anymore guaranteed to reach any value, e.g., next_nrcvd might be always assigned value I_1.

Formalization. In the following, we explain the mathematics behind the idea of parametric interval abstraction, and the intuition why it is precise for specific expressions. To do so, we start with some preliminary definitions, which allow us to define parameterized abstraction functions and the corresponding concretization functions. We then make precise what it means to be an existential abstraction and derive questions for the SMT solver whose response will provide us with the abstractions of the PROMELA code discussed above.

Consider the arithmetic expressions over constants and parameters that are used in comparisons against unbounded variables, e.g., next_nrcvd <= t+1. From this we get expressions, e.g., t+1 to which variables are compared. Let set $\mathcal{T}$ include all such expressions as well as the constants 0 and 1, and $\mu + 1$ be the cardinality of $\mathcal{T}$. We call the elements of $\mathcal{T}$ *thresholds*, and name them as as $e_0, e_1, \ldots, e_\mu$; with e_0 corresponding to the constant 0, and e_1 corresponding to 1.[1] Note that by evaluating threshold expressions for fixed parameters, we obtain a constant value of the threshold. Given a parameter evaluation **p** from $\mathbf{P}_{RC}$, we will denote by $e_i(\mathbf{p})$ the value of the ith threshold under **p**. Given $\mathcal{T}$, we define the domain of parametric intervals as: $\widehat{D} = \{I_j \mid 0 \le j \le \mu\}$. Observe that in our running example we actually write $\widehat{D} - \{I_0, I_1, I_{t+1}, I_{n-t}\}$, to make it more intuitive. This is an abuse of notation, and following the above definition strictly, one has to write the domain as $\{I_0, I_1, I_2, I_3\}$.

Our abstraction rests on an implicit property of many fault-tolerant distributed algorithms, namely, that the resilience condition RC induces an order on the thresholds used in the algorithm (e.g., $t + 1 < n - t$).

Definition 1. *The finite set $\mathcal{T}$ is uniformly ordered if for all $\mathbf{p} \in \mathbf{P}_{RC}$, and all $e_j(\mathbf{p})$ and $e_k(\mathbf{p})$ in $\mathcal{T}$ with $0 \le j < k \le \mu$, it holds that $e_j(\mathbf{p}) < e_k(\mathbf{p})$.*

Assuming such an order does not limit the application of our approach: In cases where only a partial order is induced by RC, one can simply enumerate all finitely many total orders. As parameters, and thus thresholds, are kept unchanged in a run, one can verify an algorithm for each threshold order separately, and then combine the results.

---

[1] We add 0 and 1 explicitly, because we will later see that these values precisely capture an existential quantifier, similar to [70]. However, in our setting, the abstract domain that distinguishes between 0, 1, and *more* [70] is too coarse to track whether variables have surpassed certain thresholds.

Definition 1 allows us to properly define the *parameterized abstraction function* $\alpha_{\mathbf{p}} \colon D \to \widehat{D}$ and the *parameterized concretization function* $\gamma_{\mathbf{p}} \colon \widehat{D} \to 2^D$.

$$\alpha_{\mathbf{p}}(x) = \begin{cases} I_j & \text{if } x \in [e_j(\mathbf{p}), e_{j+1}(\mathbf{p})[\text{ for some } 0 \le j < \mu \\ I_\mu & \text{otherwise.} \end{cases}$$

$$\gamma_{\mathbf{p}}(I_j) = \begin{cases} [e_j(\mathbf{p}), e_{j+1}(\mathbf{p})[& \text{if } j < \mu \\ [e_\mu(\mathbf{p}), \infty[& \text{otherwise.} \end{cases}$$

From $e_0(\mathbf{p}) = 0$ and $e_1(\mathbf{p}) = 1$, it immediately follows that for all $\mathbf{p} \in \mathbf{P}_{RC}$, we have $\alpha_{\mathbf{p}}(0) = I_0$, $\alpha_{\mathbf{p}}(1) = I_1$, and $\gamma_{\mathbf{p}}(I_0) = \{0\}$. Moreover, from the definitions of α, γ, and Definition 1 one immediately obtains:

Proposition 1. *For all $\mathbf{p}$ in $\mathbf{P}_{RC}$, for all a in D, it holds that $a \in \gamma_{\mathbf{p}}(\alpha_{\mathbf{p}}(a))$.*

Definition 2. *We define comparison between parametric intervals I_k and I_ℓ as $I_k \le I_\ell$ iff $k \le \ell$.*

Compared to the predicate abstraction approach initially discussed, Definition 2 is very naturally written in our parametric interval abstraction, and we can use it in the following. In fact, the central property of our abstract domain is that it allows to abstract comparisons against thresholds in a precise way. That is, we can abstract formulas of the form $e_j(\mathbf{p}) \le x_1$ by $I_j \le \hat{x}_1$ and $e_j(\mathbf{p}) > x_1$ by $I_j > \hat{x}_1$. This abstraction is precise in the following sense.

Proposition 2. *For all $\mathbf{p} \in \mathbf{P}_{RC}$ and all $a \in D$:
$e_j(\mathbf{p}) \le a$ iff $I_j \le \alpha_{\mathbf{p}}(a)$, and $e_j(\mathbf{p}) > a$ iff $I_j > \alpha_{\mathbf{p}}(a)$.*

We now discuss what is necessary to construct an existential abstraction of an expression that involves comparisons against unbounded variables using an SMT solver. Let Φ be a formula that corresponds to such an expression. We introduce notation for sets of vectors satisfying Φ. Formula Φ has two kinds of free variables: parameter variables from Π and data variables from $\Lambda \cup \Gamma$. Let $\mathbf{x}^p$ be a vector of parameter variables $(x_1^p, \ldots, x_{|\Pi|}^p)$ and $\mathbf{x}^d$ be a vector of variables $(x_1^d, \ldots, x_k^d)$ over D^k. Given a k-dimensional vector $\mathbf{d}$ of values from D, by

$$\mathbf{x}^p = \mathbf{p}, \mathbf{x}^d = \mathbf{d} \models \Phi$$

we denote that Φ is satisfied on concrete values $x_1^d = d_1, \ldots, x_k^d = d_k$ and parameter values $\mathbf{p}$. Then, we define:

$$\|\Phi\|_\exists = \{\hat{\mathbf{d}} \in \widehat{D}^k \mid \exists \mathbf{p} \in \mathbf{P}_{RC}\, \exists \mathbf{d} = (d_1, \ldots, d_k) \in D^k.$$

$$\hat{\mathbf{d}} = (\alpha_{\mathbf{p}}(d_1), \ldots, \alpha_{\mathbf{p}}(d_k)) \wedge \mathbf{x}^p = \mathbf{p}, \mathbf{x}^d = \mathbf{d} \models \Phi\}$$

Hence, the set $\|\Phi\|_\exists$ contains all vectors of abstract values that correspond to some concrete values satisfying Φ. Parameters do not appear anymore due to existential quantification. A PIA *existential abstraction* of Φ is defined to be a formula $\hat{\Phi}$ over a vector of variables $\hat{\mathbf{x}} = (\hat{x}_1, \ldots, \hat{x}_k)$ over $\widehat{D}^k$ such that $\{\hat{\mathbf{d}} \in \widehat{D}^k \mid \hat{\mathbf{x}} = \hat{\mathbf{d}} \models \hat{\Phi}\} \supseteq \|\Phi\|_\exists$. See Figure 7 for an example.

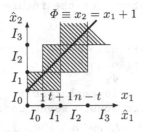

$$\hat{\Phi} \equiv \hat{x}_1 = I_0 \wedge \hat{x}_2 = I_1$$
$$\vee \; \hat{x}_1 = I_1 \wedge \hat{x}_2 = I_1$$
$$\vee \; \hat{x}_1 = I_1 \wedge \hat{x}_2 = I_2$$
$$\vee \; \hat{x}_1 = I_2 \wedge \hat{x}_2 = I_2$$
$$\vee \; \hat{x}_1 = I_2 \wedge \hat{x}_2 = I_3$$
$$\vee \; \hat{x}_1 = I_3 \wedge \hat{x}_2 = I_3$$

Fig. 7. The shaded area approximates the line $x_2 = x_1 + 1$ along the boundaries of our parametric intervals. Each shaded rectangle corresponds to one conjunctive clause in the formula to the right. Thus, given $\Phi \equiv x_2 = x_1 + 1$, the shaded rectangles correspond to $||\Phi||_{\exists}$, from which we immediately construct the existential abstraction $\hat{\Phi}$.

Computing the abstractions. So far, we have seen the abstraction examples and the formal machinery in the form of existential abstraction $||\Phi||_{\exists}$. Now we show how to compute the abstractions using an SMT solver. We are using the input language of Yices [38], but this choice is not essential. Any other solver that supports linear arithmetics over integers, e.g., Z3 [35], should be sufficient for our purposes. We start with declaring the parameters and the resilience condition:

```
1    (define n :: int)
2    (define t :: int)
3    (define f :: int)
4    (assert (and (> n 3) (>= f 0)
5                 (>= t 1) (<= f t) (> n (* 3 t)))))
```

Listing 7. The parameters and the resilience condition in YICES

Assume that we want to compute the existential abstraction of an expression similar to one found in line 22, that is,

$$\Phi_1 \equiv a < b + f.$$

According to the definition of $||\Phi_1||_{\exists}$, we have to enumerate all abstract values of a and b and check, whether there exist a valuation of the parameters n, t, and f and a concretization $\gamma_{n,t,f}$ of the abstract values that satisfies Φ_1. In the case of Φ_1 this boils down to finding all the abstract pairs $(\hat{a}, \hat{b}) \in \widehat{D} \times \widehat{D}$ satisfying the formula:

$$\exists a, b : \alpha_{n,t,f}(a) = \hat{a} \wedge \alpha_{n,t,f}(b) = \hat{b} \wedge a < b + f \qquad (1)$$

Given $\hat{a}$ and $\hat{b}$, Formula (1) can be encoded as a satisfiability problem in linear integer arithmetics. For instance, if $\hat{a} = I_1$ and $\hat{b} = I_0$, then we encode Formula (1) as follows:

```
6   (push)                    ;; store the context for the future use
7   (define a :: int)
8   (define b :: int)
9   (assert (and (>= a 1) (< a (+ t 1))))  ;; αn,t,f(a) = I₁
10  (assert (and (>= b 0) (< b 1)))        ;; αn,t,f(b) = I₀
11  (assert (< a (+ b f)))                 ;; Φ₁
12  (check)                                ;; is satisfiable?
13  (pop)                      ;; restore the previously saved context
```

Listing 8. Are there a and b with $a < b + f$, $\alpha_{n,t,f}(a) = I_1$, and $\alpha_{n,t,f}(b) = I_0$?

When we execute lines (1)–(13) of Listing 8 in YICES, we receive sat on the output, that is, formula 1 is valid for the values $\hat{a} = I_1$ and $\hat{b} = I_0$ and $(I_1, I_0) \in \|a < b + f\|_\exists$. To see concrete values of a, b, n, t, and f satisfying lines (1)–(13), we issue the following command:

```
14  (set-evidence! true)
15  ;; copy lines (1) – (13) here
```

YICES provides us with the following model:

```
(= n 7)
(= f 2)
(= t 2)
(= a 1)
(= b 0)
```

By enumerating all values from $\widehat{D} \times \widehat{D}$, we obtain the following abstraction of $a < b + f$ (this is an abstraction of line (22) in Listing 3):

```
   a == I_{n-t} && b == I_{n-t}  ||  a == I_{t+1} && b == I_{n-t}
|| a == I_1    && b == I_{n-t}  ||  a == I_0    && b == I_{n-t}
|| a == I_{n-t} && b == I_{t+1}  ||  a == I_{t+1} && b == I_{t+1}
|| a == I_1    && b == I_{t+1}  ||  a == I_0    && b == I_{t+1}
|| a == I_{t+1} && b == I_1    ||  a == I_1    && b == I_1
|| a == I_0    && b == I_1    ||  a == I_1    && b == I_0  ||  a == I_0 && b== I_0
```

Listing 9. Parametric interval abstraction of $a < b + f$

By applying the same principle to all expressions in Listing 3, we abstract the process code. As the abstract code is too verbose, we do not give it here. It can be obtained by running the tool on our benchmarks [1], as described in Section 6.1.

Specifications. As we have seen in Section 3.2, we use only specifications that compare status variable sv against a value from SV. For instance, the unforgeability property **U** (cf. p. 130) is referring to atomic proposition $[\forall i. \, sv_i \neq \text{V1}]$. Interval data abstraction does neither affect the domain of sv, nor does it change expressions over sv. Thus, we do not have to change the specifications when applying the data abstraction.

However, the specifications are verified under justice constraints, e.g., the reliable communication constraint (cf. RelComm on p. 134): $\mathbf{G}\,\mathbf{F} \neg [\exists i. \, rcvd_i < nsnt]$.

Our goal is that the abstraction preserves fair (i.e., just) runs, that is, if each state of a just run is abstracted, then the resulting sequence of abstract states is a just run of the abstract system. Intuitively, when we verify a property that holds on all *abstract* just runs, then we conclude that the property also holds on all *concrete* just runs. In fact, we apply existential abstraction to the formulas that capture just states, e.g., we transform the expression $\neg\,[\exists i.\ rcvd_i < nsnt]$ using existential abstraction $||\neg\,[\exists i.\ rcvd_i < nsnt]\,||_\exists$.

Let ψ be a propositional formula that describes just states, and $[\![\psi]\!]_\mathbf{p}$ be the set of states that satisfy ψ in the concrete system with the parameter values $\mathbf{p} \in \mathbf{P}_{RC}$. Then, by the definition of existential abstraction, for all $\mathbf{p} \in \mathbf{P}_{RC}$, it holds that $[\![\psi]\!]_\mathbf{p}$ is contained in the concretization of $||\psi||_\exists$. This property ensures justice preservation. In fact, we implemented a more general approach that involves *existential* and *universal* abstractions, but we are not going into details here. The interested reader can find formal frameworks in [56,74].

Remark on the precision. One may argue that domain $\widehat{D}$ is too imprecise and it might be helpful to add more elements to $\widehat{D}$. By Proposition 2, however, the domain gives us a *precise* abstraction of the comparisons against the thresholds. Thus, we do not lose precision when abstracting the expressions like $next\_nrcvd < t+1$ and $next\_nrcvd \geq n-t$, and we cannot benefit from enriching the abstract domain $\widehat{D}$ with expressions different from the thresholds.

4.2   Parametric Interval Counter Abstraction

In the previous section we abstracted a process that is parameterized into a finite-state process. In this section we turn a system parameterized in the number of finite-state processes into a one-process system with finitely many states. First, we fix parameters $\mathbf{p}$ and show how one can convert a system of $N(\mathbf{p})$ processes into a one-process system by using a counting argument.

Counter representation. The structure of the PROMELA program after applying the data abstraction from Section 4.1 looks as follows:

```
int nsnt: 2 = 0;            /* 0 ↦ I₀ , 1 ↦ I₁ , 2 ↦ I_{t+1} , 3 ↦ I_{n-t} */
active[n - f] proctype Proc() {
   int pc: 2 = 0;           /* 0 ↦ V0 , 1 ↦ V1 , 2 ↦ SE , 3 ↦ AC */
   int nrcvd: 2 = 0;        /* 0 ↦ I₀ , 1 ↦ I₁ , 2 ↦ I_{t+1} , 3 ↦ I_{n-t} */
   int next_pc: 2 = 0, next_nrcvd: 2 = 0;
   if  :: pc = 0; /* V0 */
       :: pc = 1; /* V1 */
   fi;
loop: atomic {
   /* receive */
   /* compute */
   /* send */ }
   goto loop;
}
```

Listing 10. Process structure after data abstraction

Observe that a system consists of $N(\mathbf{p})$ identical processes. We may thus change the representation of a global state: Instead of storing which process is in which local state, we just count for each local state how many processes are in it. We have seen in the previous section that after the PIA data abstraction, processes have a fixed number of states. Hence, we can use a fixed number of counters. To this end, we introduce a global array of counters k that keeps the number of processes in every potential local state. We denote by L the set of local states and by L_0 the set of initial local states. In order to map the local states to array indices, we define a bijection: $h \colon L \to \{0, \dots, |L| - 1\}$.

In our example, we have 16 potential local states, i.e., $L_{ST} = \{(pc, nrcvd) \mid pc \in \{V0, V1, SE, AC\}, nrcvd \in \widehat{D}\}$. In our PROMELA encoding, the elements of $\widehat{D}$ and SV are represented as integers; we represent this encoding by the function $val \colon \widehat{D} \cup SV \to \{0, 1, 2, 3\}$ so that no two elements of $\widehat{D}$ are mapped to the same number and no two elements of SV are mapped to the same number. We allocate 16 elements for k and define the mapping $h_{ST} \colon L_{ST} \to \{0, \dots, |L_{ST}| - 1\}$ as $h_{ST}((pc, nrcvd)) = 4 \cdot val(pc) + val(nrcvd)$. Then $k[h_{ST}(\ell)]$ stores how many processes are in local state ℓ. Thus, a global state is given by the array k, and the global variable $nsnt$.

It remains to define the transition relation. As we have to capture interleaving semantics, intuitively, if a process is in local state ℓ and goes to a different local state ℓ', then $k[h_{ST}(\ell)]$ must be decreased by 1 and $k[h_{ST}(\ell')]$ must be increased by 1. To do so in our encoding, we first *select* a state ℓ to move away from, perform a step as above, that is, calculate the successor state ℓ', and finally update the counters. Thus, the template of the counter representation looks as follows (we will discuss the select, receive, etc. blocks below):

```
int k[16]; /* number of processes in every local state */
int nsnt: 2 = 0;
active[1] proctype CtrAbs() {
  int pc: 2 = 0, nrcvd: 2 = 0;
  int next_pc: 2 = 0, next_nrcvd: 2 = 0;
  /* init */
loop: /* select */
    /* receive */
    /* compute */
    /* send */
    /* update counters */
  goto loop;
}
```

Listing 11. Process structure of counter representation

The blocks *receive*, *compute*, and *send* stay the same, as they were in Section 4.1. The new blocks have the following semantics: In *init*, an initial combination of counters is chosen such that $\sum_{\ell \in L_0} k[\ell] = N(\mathbf{p})$ and $\sum_{\ell \in L \setminus L_0} k[\ell] = 0$. In *select*, a local state ℓ with $k[\ell] \neq 0$ is non-deterministically chosen; In *update counters*, the counters of ℓ and a successor of ℓ are decremented and incremented respectively.

We now consider the blocks in detail and start with *init*. Each of $n-f$ processes start in one of the two initial states: $(V0, I_0)$ with $h_{ST}((V0, I_0)) = 0$ and $(V1, I_0)$ with $h_{ST}((V1, I_0)) = 3$. Thus, the initial block non-deterministically chooses the values for the counters $k[0]$ and $k[3]$, so that $k[0] + k[3] = n - f$ and all the other indices are set to zero. The following code fragment encodes this non-deterministic choice. Observe that the number of choices needed is $n - f + 1$, so the length of this code must depend on the choices of these parameters. We will get rid of this requirement in the counter abstraction below.

```
1  if  /* 0 ↦ (pc = V0, nrcvd = I₀);  3 ↦ (pc = V1, nrcvd = I₀) */
2    :: k[0] = n - f; k[3] = 0;
3    :: k[0] = n - f - 1; k[3] = 1;
4    ...
5    :: k[0] = 0; k[3] = n - f;
6  fi;
```

In the *select* block we pick non-deterministically a non-zero counter $k[\ell]$ and set *pc* and *nrcvd* so that $h_{ST}(pc, nrcvd) = \ell$. Again, here is a small fragment of the code:

```
7  if
8    :: k[0] != 0  -> pc = 0 /* V0 */; nrcvd = 0 /* I₀ */;
9    :: k[1] != 0  -> pc = 0 /* V0 */; nrcvd = 1 /* I₁ */;
10   ...
11   :: k[15] != 0 -> pc = 3 /* AC */; nrcvd = 3 /* Iₙ₋ₜ */;
12 fi;
```

Finally, as the *compute* block assigns new values to *next_pc* and *next_nrcvd*, which correspond to the successor state of $(pc, nrcvd)$, we update the counters to reflect the fact that one process moved from state $(pc, nrcvd)$ to state $(next\_pc, next\_nrcvd)$:

```
13 if
14   :: pc != next_pc || nrcvd != next_nrcvd ->
15      k[4 * pc + nrcvd]--; k[4 * next_pc + next_nrcvd]++;
16   :: else; /* do not update the counters */
17 fi;
```

This representation might look inefficient in comparison to the one with explicit processes; e.g., SPIN cannot use partial order reduction on this representation. However, this representation is only an intermediate step.

Specifications. In the original presentation of the system it is obvious how global states are linked with atomic propositions of the form $[\exists i.\ \Phi(i)]$ and $[\forall i.\ \Phi(i)]$; a process i must satisfy $\Phi(i)$ or all processes must do so, respectively. In the counter representation we do not "have" processes in the system anymore, and we have to understand which states to label with our atomic propositions.

In the counter representation, we exploit the fact that our properties are all quantified, which naturally translates to statements about counters: Let $[\![\Phi]\!]$ be the set of local states that satisfy Φ. In our example we are interested in the

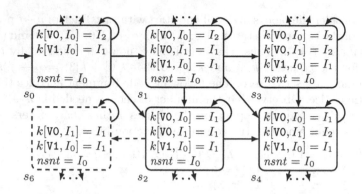

Fig. 8. A small part of the transition system obtained by counter abstraction

local states that satisfy $sv = \mathrm{AC}$, as it appears in our specifications. There are several such states (not all reachable, though) depending on the different values of $nsnt$. Then, a global state satisfies $[\exists i.\ \varPhi(i)]$ if $\bigvee_{\ell \in \llbracket \varPhi \rrbracket} k[\ell] \neq 0$. Similarly, a global state satisfies $[\forall i.\ \varPhi(i)]$ if $\bigwedge_{\ell \notin \llbracket \varPhi \rrbracket} k[\ell] = 0$.

As we are dealing with counters, instead of using disjunctions and conjunctions, we could also use sums to evaluate quantifiers: the universal quantifier could also be expressed as $\sum_{\ell \in \llbracket \varPhi \rrbracket} k[\ell] = N(\mathbf{p})$. However, in the following counter abstraction this formulization has drawbacks, due to the non-determinism of the operations on the abstract domain, while the abstraction of 0 is precise.

Counter abstraction. The counter representation encodes a system of $n - f$ processes as a single process system. When, n, t, and f are fixed, the elements of array k are bounded by n. However, in the parameterized case the elements of k are unbounded. To circumvent this problem, we apply the PIA abstraction from Section 4.1 to the elements of k.

In the counter abstraction, the elements of k range over the abstract domain $\widehat{D}$. Similar to Section 4.1, we have to compute the abstract operations over k. These are the operations in the *init* block and in the *update* block.

To transform the *init* block, we first compute the existential abstraction of $\sum_{\ell \in L_0} k[\ell] = N(\mathbf{p})$. In our example, we compute the set $||k[0] + k[3] = n - f||_{\exists}$ and non-deterministically choose an element from this set. Again, we can do it with YICES. We give the initialization block after the abstraction (note that the number of choices is fixed and determined by the size of the abstract domain):

```
1  if /* 0 ↦ (pc = V0, nrcvd = I₀); 3 ↦ (pc = V1, nrcvd = I₀) */
2    :: k[0] = 3 /* I_{n-t} */; k[3] = 0 /* I₀ */;
3    :: k[0] = 3 /* I_{n-t} */; k[3] = 1 /* I₁ */;
4    ...
5    :: k[0] = 0 /* I₀ */;   k[3] = 3 /* I_{n-t} */;
6  fi;
```

Listing 12. Initialization of the counters

In the *update* block we have to compute the abstraction of k[4 * pc + nrcvd]-- and k[4 * next_pc + next_nrcvd]++. We have already seen how to do this with the data abstraction. The update block looks as follows after the abstraction:

```
18  if
19    :: pc != next_pc || nrcvd != next_nrcvd ->
20    if /* decrement the counter of the previous state */
21      :: (k[((pc * 4) + nrcvd)] == 3) ->
22        k[((pc * 4) + nrcvd)] = 3;
23      :: (k[((pc * 4) + nrcvd)] == 3) ->
24        k[((pc * 4) + nrcvd)] = 2;
25      ...
26      :: (k[((pc * 4) + nrcvd)] == 1) ->
27        k[((pc * 4) + nrcvd)] = 0;
28    fi;
29    if /* increment the counter of the next state */
30      :: (k[((next_pc * 4) + next_nrcvd)] == 3) ->
31        k[((next_pc * 4) + next_nrcvd)] = 3;
32      :: (k[((next_pc * 4) + next_nrcvd)] == 2) ->
33        k[((next_pc * 4) + next_nrcvd)] = 3;
34      ...
35      :: (k[((next_pc * 4) + next_nrcvd)] == 0) ->
36        k[((next_pc * 4) + next_nrcvd)] = 1;
37    fi;
38    :: else; /* do not update the counters */
39  fi;
```

Listing 13. Abstract increment and decrement of the counters

In contrast to the counter representation, the increment and decrement of the counters in the array k are now non-deterministic. For instance, the counter k[((pc * 4) + nrcvd)] can change its value from I_{n-t} to I_{t+1} or stay unchanged. Similarly, the value of k[((next_pc * 4) + next_nrcvd)] can change from I_1 to I_{t+1} or stay unchanged.

Observe that this non-determinism adds behaviors to the abstract systems:

- both counters could stay unchanged, which leads to stuttering
- the value of k[((pc * 4) + nrcvd)] decreases, while at the same time the value of k[((next_pc * 4) + next_nrcvd)] stays unchanged, that is, we lose processes, and finally
- k[((pc * 4) + nrcvd)] stays unchanged and k[((next_pc * 4) + next_nrcvd)] increases, that is, processes are added.

Some of these behaviors lead to spurious counterexamples we deal with in Section 5. Figure 8 gives a small part of the transition system obtained from the counter abstraction. We omit local states that have the counter value I_0 to facilitate reading. The state s_0 represents the initial states with $t + 1$ to $n - t - 1$ processes having $sv = V0$ and 1 to t processes having $sv = V1$. Each transition corresponds to one process taking a step in the concrete system. For instance, in the transition (s_0, s_2) a process with local state $[\text{VO}, I_0]$ changes its state to $[\text{VO}, I_1]$. Therefore, the counter $\kappa[\text{VO}, I_0]$ is decremented and the counter $\kappa[\text{VO}, I_1]$ is incremented.

Specifications. Similar to the counter representations, quantifiers can be encoded as expressions on the counters. Instead of comparing to 0, we compare to the abstract zero I_0: A global state satisfies $[\exists i.\ \Phi(i)]$ if $\bigvee_{\ell \in [\![\Phi]\!]} k[\ell] \neq I_0$. Similarly, a global state satisfies $[\forall i.\ \Phi(i)]$ if $\bigwedge_{\ell \notin [\![\Phi]\!]} k[\ell] = I_0$.

4.3 Soundness

We do not focus on the soundness proofs here, the details can be found in [52]. The soundness is based on two properties:

First, between every concrete system and the abstract system, there is a simulation relation. The central argument to prove this comes from Proposition 2, from which follows that if a threshold is satisfied in the concrete system, the abstraction of the threshold is satisfied in the abstract systems. Intuitively, this means that if a transition is enabled in the concrete system, then it is enabled in the abstract system, which is required to prove simulation.

Second, the abstraction of a fair path (with respect to our justice properties) in the concrete system is a fair path in the abstract system. This follows from construction: we label an abstract state with a proposition if the abstract state satisfies the existential abstraction of the proposition, in other words, if there is a concretization of the abstract state that satisfies the proposition.

5 Abstraction Refinement

In Sections 4.1 and 4.2, we constructed approximations of the transition systems: First, we transformed parameterized code of a process into finite-state non-parameterized code; Second, we constructed a finite-state process that approximates the behavior of $n - f$ processes. Usually, abstraction introduces new behavior that is not present in the concrete system. As a result, specifications that hold in the concrete system, may be violated in the abstract system. In this case, a model checker returns an execution of the abstract system that cannot be replayed in the concrete system; such an execution is called a *spurious counterexample*.

As it was suggested in Proposition 2, PIA data abstraction does not lose precision for the comparisons against threshold expressions. In fact, in our experiments we have not seen spurious counterexamples caused by the PIA data abstraction. So, we focus on abstraction refinement of the PIA counter abstraction, where we have identified three sources of spurious behavior (a) the run contains a transition where the number of processes is decreasing or increasing; (b) the number of messages sent by processes deviates from the number of processes who have sent a message; (c) unfair loops.

Given a run of the counter abstraction, we have to check that the run is spurious for all combinations of parameters from $\mathbf{P}_{RC}$. This problem is again parameterized, and we are not aware of techniques to deal with it in the general case. Thus, we limit ourselves to detecting the runs that have a *uniformly spurious transition*, that is, a transition that does not have a concretization for all the parameters from $\mathbf{P}_{RC}$.

We check for spurious transitions using SMT solvers. To do so, we have to encode the transition relation of all concrete systems (which are defined by different parameter values) in SMT. We explain our approach in three steps: first we encode a single PROMELA statement. Based on this we encode a process step that consist of several statements. Finally, we use the encoding of a step to define the transition relation of the system.

5.1   Encoding the Transition Relation

Encoding a single statement. As we want to detect spurious behavior, the SMT encoding must capture a system on a less abstract level than the counter abstraction. One first idea would be to encode the transition relation of the concrete systems. However, as we do parameterized model checking, we actually have infinitely many concrete systems, and the state space and the number of processes in these systems is not bounded. Hence, we require a representation whose "degree of abstraction" lies between the concrete systems and the counter abstraction. In principle, the counter representation from Section 4.2 seems to be a good candidate. Its state is given by finitely many integer counters, and finitely many shared variables that range over the abstract domain. Although there are infinitely many states (the counters are not bounded), the state space and transition relation can be encoded as an SMT problem. Moreover, threshold guards and the operations on the process counters can be expressed in linear integer arithmetic, which is supported by many SMT solvers.

However, experiments showed that we need a representation closer to the concrete systems. Hence, we use a system whose only difference to the counter representation from Section 4.2 is that the shared variables are not abstracted. The main difficulty in this is to encode transitions that involve abstract local as well as concrete global variables. For that, we represent the parameters in SMT. Then, instead of comparing global variables against abstract values, we check whether the global variables are within parametric intervals. Here we do not go into the formal details of this abstraction. Rather, we explain it by example. The most complicated case is the one where an expression involves the parameters, local variables, and shared variables. For instance, consider the code on page 146, where a is a local variable and b is a shared one. In this new abstraction a is abstract and b is concrete. Thus, we have to encode constraints on b as inequalities expressing which interval b belongs to. Specifically, we replace $b = I_k$ with either $e_k \leq b < e_{k+1}$ (when k is not the largest threshold e_μ), or $e_\mu \leq b$ (otherwise):

$$
\begin{aligned}
&a == I_{n-t} \ \&\& \ n - t \leq b \ || \ a == I_{t+1} \ \&\& \ n - t \leq b \\
&|| \ a == I_1 \ \&\& \ n - t \leq b \ || \ a == I_0 \ \&\& \ n - t \leq b \\
&|| \ a == I_{n-t} \ \&\& \ t + 1 \leq b < n - t \ || \ a == I_{t+1} \ \&\& \ t + 1 \leq b < n - t \\
&|| \ a == I_1 \ \&\& \ t + 1 \leq b < n - t \ || \ a == I_0 \ \&\& \ t + 1 \leq b < n - t \\
&|| \ a == I_{t+1} \ \&\& \ 1 \leq b < t + 1 \ || \ a == I_1 \ \&\& \ 1 \leq b < t + 1 \\
&|| \ a == I_0 \ \&\& \ 1 \leq b < t + 1 \ || \ a == I_1 \ \&\& \ 0 \leq b < 1 \\
&|| \ a == I_0 \ \&\& \ 0 \leq b < 1
\end{aligned}
$$

Apart from this, statements that depend solely on shared variables are not changed. Finally, statements that consist of local variables and parameters are abstracted as in Section 4.1. This level of abstraction allows us to detect spurious transitions of both types (a) and (b).

Encoding a single process step. Our PROMELA code defines a transition system: A single iteration of the loop expresses one step (or transition) which consists of several expressions executed indivisibly. The code before the loop defines the constraints on the initial states of the transition system. Recall that we can express PROMELA code as a control flow automaton (cf. Section 3.3 and Figure 4). Formally, a *guarded control flow automaton* (CFA) is an edge-labeled directed acyclic graph $A = (Q, q_I, q_F, E)$ with a finite set Q of nodes called locations, an initial location $q_I \in Q$, and a final location $q_F \in Q$. Edges are labeled with simple PROMELA statements (assignments and comparisons). Each transition is defined by a path from q_I to q_F in a CFA. Our goal is to construct a formula that encodes the transition relation. We are doing this by translating a statement on every edge from E into an SMT formula in a way similar to [17][Ch. 16]. What we show below is not the most efficient encoding, but we omit optimizations to keep presentation clear.

First, we have to take care of multiple assignments to the same variable, as they can overwrite previously assigned values. Consider the following sequence of PROMELA statements S: x=1; y=x; x=2; z=x corresponding to a path of some CFA. If we naively encode it as $x = 1 \land y = x \land x = 2 \land z = x$, then the formula is immediately unsatisfiable due to the conflicting constraints on x. We thus need multiple versions of such variables, that is, we turn sequence S into S1: x1=1; y1=x1; x2=2; z1=x2. Now we can construct formula $x^1 = 1 \land y^1 = x^1 \land x^2 = 2; z^1 = x^2$ that treats the assignments correctly. Such a form is known as static single assignment (SSA); it can be computed by an algorithm given in [34].

We assume the following notation for the multiple copies of a variable x in SSA: x denotes the *input* variable, that is, the copy of x at location q_I; x' denotes the *output* variable, that is, the copy of x at location q_F; x^i denotes a *temporary* variable, that is, a copy of x that is overwritten by another copy before reaching q_F.

From now on we assume that the CFA in given in SSA form, and we can thus encode the transition relation. This requires us to capture all paths of the CFA. Our goal is to construct a single formula T over the following vectors of free variables:

- **p** is the vector of integer parameters from Π, which is not changed by a transition;
- **x** is the vector of integer input variables from $\Lambda \cup \{sv\}$;
- **x′** is the vector of integer output variables of **x**;
- **g** is the vector of integer input variables from Γ;
- **g′** is the vector of integer output variables of **g**;
- **t** is the vector of integer temporary variables of **x** and **g**;
- **en** is the vector of boolean variables, one variable en_e per an edge $e \in E$, which means that edge e lies on the path from q_I to q_F.

Let $form(s)$ be a straightforward translation of a PROMELA statement s into a formula as discussed above. Assignments are replaced with equalities and relations (e.g., $\leq$, $>$) are kept as they are. Then, for an edge $e \in E$ labeled with a statement s, we construct a formula $T_e(\mathbf{p}, \mathbf{x}, \mathbf{x}', \mathbf{g}, \mathbf{g}', \mathbf{t}, \mathbf{en})$ as follows:

$$T_e \equiv en_e \rightarrow form(s),$$

Now, formula T is constructed as the following conjunction whose subformulas are discussed in detail below:

$$T \equiv start \wedge follow \wedge mux \wedge \bigwedge_{e \in E} T_e$$

Intuitively, $start$ is saying that at least one edge outgoing from q_I is activated; $follow$ is saying that whenever a location has an incoming activated edge, it also has at least one outgoing activated edge; mux is expressing the fact that at most one outgoing edge can be picked. Formally, the formulas are defined as follows:

$$start \equiv \bigvee_{(q,q') \in E:\ q=q_I} en_{(q,q')}$$

$$follow \equiv \bigwedge_{(q,q') \in E} \left(en_{(q,q')} \rightarrow \bigvee_{(q',q'') \in E} en_{(q',q'')} \right)$$

$$mux \equiv \bigvee_{(q,q'),(q,q'') \in E} \neg en_{(q,q')} \vee \neg en_{(q,q'')}$$

We have to introduce formula mux, because the branching operators in PROMELA allow one to pick a branch non-deterministically, whenever the guard of the branch evaluates to true. To pick exactly one branch, we have to introduce the mutual exclusion constraints in the form of mux. In contrast, programming languages like C do not need this constraint, as the conditions of the if-branch and the else-branch cannot both evaluate to true simultaneously.

Having constructed formula T, we say that a process can make a transition from state $\mathbf{x}$ to state $\mathbf{x}'$ under some combination of parameters if and only if the formula $T(\mathbf{p}, \mathbf{x}, \mathbf{x}', \mathbf{g}, \mathbf{g}', \mathbf{t}, \mathbf{en}) \wedge RC(\mathbf{p})$ is satisfiable.

Transition relation of the counter representation. Now we show how to encode the transition relation R of the counter representation using the process transition relation T. The transition relation connects counters k and global variables g before a step with their primed versions k' and g' after the step. Recall that in Section 4.2, we introduced bijection h that maps states to numbers. In the following, by abuse of notation, by $h(x)$ we denote an SMT expression that encodes the bijection h. We will use the formulas *dec* and *inc*: Informally, *dec* ensures that the counter that corresponds to $h(x)$ is not equal to zero and decrements the counter, while *inc* increments the counter $k[h(x')]$. Formula R is the following conjunction

$$R \equiv dec \wedge T \wedge inc \wedge keep,$$

and we define *dec*, *inc*, and *keep* as follows:

$$dec \equiv \bigwedge_{0 \le \ell < |L|} h(x) = \ell \to k[\ell] > 0 \wedge k'[\ell] = k[\ell] - 1$$

$$inc \equiv \bigwedge_{0 \le \ell < |L|} h(x') = \ell \to k'[\ell] = k[\ell] + 1$$

$$keep \equiv \bigwedge_{0 \le \ell < |L|} (h(x) \ne \ell \wedge h(x') \ne \ell) \to k'[\ell] = k[\ell]$$

Now we can say that a counter representation of a system makes a step from (k, g) to (k', g') if and only if $R(p, x, x', k, k', g, g', t, en) \wedge RC(p)$ is satisfiable. In what follows, we denote the latter formula by *Step*.

In order to encode operations on k, we are using arrays. In our case, however, each array may be replaced with $|L|$ integer variables. Thus, we do not actually use important properties of array theory.

5.2   Spurious Behavior

Losing and introducing processes. We start with the first type of spurious behavior, where a transition "loses" or "introduces" processes. Consider the following sequence of abstract states, which introduces new processes due to nondeterminism of the counter updates:

```
1   k = {0, 0, 0, 0, 3, 0, 0, 0, 0, 0, 0, 0, 0, 0, 0, 0}, nsnt =0
2   k = {0, 0, 0, 0, 3, 0, 0, 0, 1, 0, 0, 0, 0, 0, 0, 0}, nsnt =1
3   k = {0, 0, 0, 0, 3, 0, 0, 0, 2, 0, 0, 0, 0, 0, 0, 0}, nsnt =2
```

Here we represent the abstract states in the format similar to the one used in our tool (Section 6). The assignment "$k = \{\dots\}$" shows the contents of the array k in C format, that is, the position $i = h(\ell)$ gives the abstract number of processes in local state ℓ. The assignment "$nsnt = \dots$" shows the value of $nsnt$.

As one can see, counter k[8] changes its value from I_0 to I_1 and then to I_{t+1}. The combination of k[8] $= I_{t+1}$ and k[4] $= I_{n-t}$ indicates that the transition from state 2 to state 3 is spurious. In fact, we can detect this kind of spurious behavior with YICES:

```
1  (set-evidence! true)
2  (set-verbosity! 3)
3  (define n::int)
4  (define t::int)
5  (define f::int)
6  (assert (and (> n (* 3 t)) (> t f) (>= f 0)))
7  (define k :: (-> (subrange 0 15) nat))
8  (assert+ (and (<= (- n t) (k 4))))
9  (assert+ (and (<= (+ t 1) (k 8)) (< (k 8) (- n t))))
10 ;; -> copy the assertion below for the indices 1-3, 5-7, 9-15
11 (assert+ (and (<= 0 (k 0)) (< (k 0) 1)))
12 (assert (= (- n f) (+
13   (k 0) (k 1) (k 2) (k 3) (k 4) (k 5) (k 6) (k 7)
14   (k 8) (k 9) (k 10) (k 11) (k 12) (k 13) (k 14) (k 15))))
15 (check)
```

Listing 14. Constraints on state 3 encoded in YICES

In lines $(8) - (11)$, we constrain the values of process counters to reside within the parametric intervals as defined by the abstract values of state 3. In lines $(12) -$ (14), we assert that the total number of processes equals $n - f$. YICES reports that the constraints are unsatisfiable, which means that state 3 cannot be an abstraction of a system state with $n - f$ processes. We conclude that the transition from state 2 to state 3 is uniformly spurious, and we eliminate it.

In fact, YICES also reports that it did not use all the assertions to come up with unsatisfiability. An unsatisfiable core — a minimal set of assertions that leads to unsatisfiability — consists of the assertions in lines $(8) - (9)$. Thus, we can remove every transition leading to a state with $k[4] = I_{n-t}$ and $k[8] = I_{t+1}$.

Now consider a sequence of abstract states, which is losing processes:

```
1  k = {0, 0, 0, 0, 3, 0, 0, 0, 0, 0, 0, 0, 0, 0, 0, 0}, nsnt =0
2  k = {0, 0, 0, 0, 2, 0, 0, 0, 1, 0, 0, 0, 0, 0, 0, 0}, nsnt =1
3  k = {0, 0, 0, 0, 1, 0, 0, 0, 1, 0, 0, 0, 0, 0, 0, 0}, nsnt =1
```

As with the case of introducing processes, we can detect with YICES that the transition from state 2 to state 3 is uniformly spurious, and eliminate all the transitions captured with an unsatisfiable core.

Losing messages. In our case study (cf. Figure 4) processes increase the global variable *nsnt* by one, when they transfer to a state where the value of the status variable is in $\{SE, AC\}$. Hence, in concrete system instances, *nsnt* should always be equal to the number of processes whose status is in $\{SE, AC\}$, while due to phenomena similar to those discussed above, we can "lose messages" in the abstract system. When checking safety properties, this kind of spurious behavior does not produce counterexamples. However, it generates spurious counterexamples for liveness. Consider the following example:

```
1  k = {0, 0, 0, 0, 3, 0, 0, 0, 0, 0, 0, 0, 0, 0, 0, 0}, nsnt =0
2  k = {0, 0, 0, 0, 3, 0, 0, 0, 1, 0, 0, 0, 0, 0, 0, 0}, nsnt =1
3  k = {0, 0, 0, 0, 2, 0, 0, 0, 2, 0, 0, 0, 0, 0, 0, 0}, nsnt =1
```

Consider state 3. Here, the number of processes with $sv = \mathrm{SE}$ is at least $t+1$ (as $k[8] = 2$ corresponding to I_{t+1}), while the number of messages is always strictly less than $t+1$ (as $nsnt = 1$ corresponding to I_1). We can try to check, whether the transition from state 2 to state 3 is spurious. This time, we also add the constraints by *Step*:

```
1   (set-evidence! true)
2   (set-verbosity! 3)
3   (define n::int)
4   (define t::int)
5   (define f::int)
6   (assert (and (> n (* 3 t)) (> t f) (>= f 0)))
7   (define k :: (-> (subrange 0 15) nat))
8   (define k' :: (-> (subrange 0 15) nat))
9   (assert+ (and (<= (+ t 1) (k 4)) (<= (k 4) (- n t)) ))
10  (assert+ (and (<= 1 (k 8)) (< (k 8) (+ t 1))))
11  (assert+ (and (<= 1 (k' 4)) (<= (k' 4) (+ t 1)) ))
12  (assert+ (and (<= 1 (k' 8)) (< (k' 8) (+ t 1))))
13  ;; copy the assertions below for the indices 1-3, 5-7, 9-15
14  (assert+ (and (<= 0 (k 0)) (< (k 0) 1)))
15  (assert+ (and (<= 0 (k' 0)) (< (k' 0) 1)))
16  ;; -> copy Step here <-
17  (check)
```

Listing 15. Concretization of transition from state 2 to state 3 in YICES

This time YICES reports that the constraints are satisfiable. Indeed, it is possible to pick the number of processes that satisfy the constraints in lines $(9) - (12)$ in Listing 15 and still do not increase $nsnt$ so that it reaches $t+1$. As we know that this example represents spurious behavior, the user can introduce an invariant candidate in PROMELA:

```
atomic tx_inv =
    ((card(Proc:pc == SE) + card(Proc:pc == AC)) == nsnt);
```

Then we can automatically test, whether the invariant candidate tx_inv is an invariant by checking that the following formula is unsatisfiable (tx_inv' is a copy of tx_inv with x replaced by x', and *Init* is a formula encoding the initial states):

$$\neg((Init \rightarrow tx\_inv) \wedge ((tx\_inv \wedge Step) \rightarrow tx\_inv'))$$

As soon as we know that tx_inv is an invariant, we can add the following assertion to the previous query in YICES:

```
18  (assert (= nsnt (+
19    (k 8) (k 9) (k 10) (k 11) (k 12) (k 13) (k 14) (k 15)))))
```

Listing 16. Constraint expressed by the invariant tx_inv

With this assertion in place, we discover that the transition from state 2 to states 3 is uniformly spurious.

5.3 Removing Transitions in Promela

So far, we have been concerned with detecting uniformly spurious transitions. Now we discuss how one can remove spurious transitions from the counter abstraction that we introduced in Section 4.2 (cf. code on p. 148).

Whenever we detect a uniformly spurious transition, we extract two sets of constraints from the SMT solver: The constraints on the abstract state before the transition (precondition), and the constraints on the abstract state after the transition (postcondition). Consider the following uniformly spurious transition:

```
1   k = {1, 0, 0, 0, 3, 0, 0, 0, 0, 0, 0, 0, 0, 0, 0, 0}, nsnt =0
2   k = {1, 1, 0, 0, 3, 0, 0, 0, 0, 0, 0, 0, 0, 0, 0, 0}, nsnt =1
```

Here we extract the following constraints from an unsatisfiability core given to us by the SMT solver (written in PROMELA notation):

```
pre = (nsnt == 0);
post = (k[0] == 1) && (k[1] == 2)
       && (k[4] == 3) && (k[15] == 0) && (nsnt == 0);
```

In order to remove the spurious transition, we have to enforce SPIN to prune the executions that include the transition. To this end, we introduce a boolean variable is_spur that turns true, whenever the current execution has at least one spurious transition. Then for each refinement iteration $K \geq 1$ we introduce a boolean variable pK_pre that turns true, whenever the current state satisfies the precondition of the spurious transition detected in iteration K. We modify PROMELA code as follows:

```
bool is_spur = 0; /* is the current execution spurious */
bool p1_pre = 0;  /* detected at refinement iteration 1 */
...
bool pK_pre = 0;  /* detected at refinement iteration K */
...
active[1] proctype CtrAbs() {
  ...
  /* init */
loop:
  ...
  pK_pre = (nsnt == 0);
  /* select */
  /* receive */
  /* compute */
  /* send */
  /* update counters */
  ...
  /* is the current transition spurious? */
  spur = spur || pK_pre && k[0] == 1 && k[1] == 2
         && k[4] == 3 && k[15] == 0 && nsnt == 0;
  goto loop;
}
```

Listing 17. Counter abstraction with detection of spurious transitions

Finally, we prune the spurious executions by modifying each LTL\X formula φ in PROMELA specifications as follows:

```
[]!is_spur -> φ
```

5.4 Detecting Unfair Loops

There is a third kind of spurious behavior that is not present in our case study, but it occurs in the experiments with omission faults (cf. Section 6). Modeling omission faults introduces 12 local states instead of 16. Here is a counterexample showing the violation of liveness property R (cf. Section 3):

```
 3  k = {2, 0, 0, 2, 0, 0, 0, 0, 0, 0, 0, 0}, nsnt = 0
 4  k = {2, 0, 0, 2, 0, 0, 1, 0, 0, 0, 0, 0}, nsnt = 1
 5  k = {2, 0, 0, 2, 0, 0, 1, 1, 0, 0, 0, 0}, nsnt = 2
 6  k = {2, 0, 0, 2, 0, 0, 1, 2, 0, 0, 0, 0}, nsnt = 2
 7  k = {1, 0, 0, 2, 0, 0, 1, 2, 0, 0, 0, 0}, nsnt = 2
 8  k = {0, 0, 0, 2, 0, 0, 1, 2, 0, 0, 0, 0}, nsnt = 2
 9  k = {0, 0, 0, 1, 0, 0, 1, 2, 0, 0, 0, 0}, nsnt = 2
10  k = {0, 0, 0, 0, 0, 0, 1, 2, 0, 0, 0, 0}, nsnt = 2
11  k = {0, 0, 0, 0, 0, 0, 0, 2, 0, 0, 0, 0}, nsnt = 2
12  k = {0, 0, 0, 0, 0, 0, 0, 2, 0, 0, 0, 1}, nsnt = 2
13  k = {0, 0, 0, 0, 0, 0, 0, 2, 0, 0, 0, 2}, nsnt = 2
14  k = {0, 0, 0, 0, 0, 0, 0, 1, 0, 0, 0, 2}, nsnt = 2
15  <<<<<START OF CYCLE>>>>>
16  k = {0, 0, 0, 0, 0, 0, 0, 1, 0, 0, 0, 2}, nsnt = 2
```

Listing 18. A counterexample with a spurious (unfair) loop

Here state (16) is repeated in a loop, but it violates the following fairness constraint saying that up to $nsnt - F$ messages must be eventually delivered:

```
atomic in_transit = some(Proc:nrcvd < nsnt - F);
ltl fairness { []<>(!in_transit) && (...) }
```

Again, using the SMT solver we can check, whether the loop is unfair, that is, no state within the loop satisfies the fairness constraint, e.g., !in_transit.

```
 1  (set-evidence! true)
 2  (set-verbosity! 3)
 3  (define n::int)
 4  (define t::int)
 5  (define f::int)
 6  (assert (and (> n (* 2 t)) (> t f) (>= f 0)))
 7  (define k :: (-> (subrange 0 11) nat))
 8  ;; the constraints by the state 14:
 9  (assert+ (and (<= 1 (k 7)) (< (k 4) (+ t 1) )))
10  (assert+ (and (<= (+ t 1) (k 11))))
11  ;; -> repeat the assertion below for the indices 0-6, 7-10
12  (assert+ (and (<= 0 (k 0)) (< (k 0) 1)))
13  (assert+ (>= nsnt (+ t 1)))
```

```
14  ;; constraints by !in_transit
15  (assert+ (not (or
16   (and (>= (- nsnt f) (+ t 1))
17    (or (/= (k 1) 0) (/= (k 4) 0) (/= (k 7) 0) (/= (k 10) 0)))
18   (and (>= (- nsnt f) (+ t 1))
19    (or (/= (k 0) 0) (/= (k 3) 0) (/= (k 6) 0) (/= (k 9) 0)))
20   (and (>= (- nsnt f) 1) (< (- nsnt f) (+ t 1))
21    (or (/= (k 0) 0) (/= (k 3) 0) (/= (k 6) 0) (/= (k 9) 0)))
22  )))
23  (check)
```

Listing 19. Does state 16 have a concretization that meets justice constraints?

This query is unsatisfiable and YICES gives us an unsatisfiable core that we track in PROMELA as we did with the spurious transitions:

```
/* update counters */
...
r0 = k[0] == 0 && k[1] == 0
    && k[2] == 0 && k[3] == 0 && k[4] == 0
    && k[5] == 0 && k[7] == 1 && k[10] == 0;
```

and modify each specification φ to avoid infinite occurrences of r0:

```
(<>[]r0) || φ
```

6 Experiments

In this section we describe the tool chain BYMC implementing the approach presented in Sections 3–5. We also demonstrate the results of experiments on finite-state as well as parameterized model checking of fault-tolerant distributed algorithms. The tool and the benchmarks are available at [1].

6.1 Running the Tool

In what follows, we use the tool on the running example bcast-byz.pml available in the set of benchmarks benchmarks-sfm14 at [1]. We also assume that the tool resides in the directory ${bymc}.

The tool chain supports two modes of operation:

- **Concrete model checking.** In this mode, the user fixes the values of the parameters p. The tool instantiates code in standard PROMELA and performs finite-state model checking with SPIN. This step is very useful to make sure that the user code operates as expected without abstraction involved.
- **Parameterized model checking.** In this mode, the tool applies data and counter abstractions (cf. Section 4), and performs finite-state model checking of the abstract model with SPIN.

For concrete-state model checking of the relay property, one issues command verifyco-spin as follows:

```
$ ${bymc}/verifyco-spin "N=4,T=1,F=1" bcast-byz.pml relay
```

The tool instantiates the model checking problem in directory
"./x/spin-bcast-byz-relay-N=4,T=1,F=1". The directory contains file
concrete.prm that differs from the source code as follows: The parameters N,
T, and F in the PROMELA code are replaced with the values 4, 1, 1 respectively.
The process prototype is replaced with $N - F = 3$ active processes.

In order to run parameterized model checking, one issues verifypa-spin
as follows:

```
$ ${bymc}/verifypa-spin bcast-omit.pml relay
```

The tool instantiates the model checking problem in a directory, whose name
follows the pattern "./x/bcast-byz-relay-yymmdd-HHMM.*". The directory contains the following files of interest: abs-interval.prm is the result of
the data abstraction; abs-counter.prm is the result of the counter abstraction; abs-vass.prm is the auxiliary abstraction for the abstraction refinement;
mc.out contains the last output by SPIN; cex.trace contains the counterexample (if there is one); yices.log contains communication log with YICES.

6.2   Concrete Model Checking for Small System Sizes

Listing 3 provides the central parts of the code of our case study. For the experiments we have implemented four distributed algorithms that use threshold-
guarded commands, and differ in the fault model. We have one algorithm for
each of the fault models discussed. In addition, the algorithms differ in the
guarded commands. The following list is ordered from the most general fault
model to the most restricted one. The given resilience conditions on n and t are
the ones we expected from the literature, and their tightness was confirmed by
our experiments:

BYZ. tolerates t Byzantine faults if $n > 3t$,
SYMM. tolerates t symmetric (identical Byzantine [11]) faults if $n > 2t$,
OMIT. tolerates t send omission faults if $n > 2t$,
CLEAN. tolerates t clean crash faults for $n > t$.

In addition, we verified a folklore reliable broadcasting algorithm that tolerates crash faults, which is given, e.g., in [23]. Further, we verified a Byzantine
tolerant broadcasting algorithm from [20]. For the encoding of the algorithm
from [20] we were required to use two message types and thus two shared variables — opposed to the one type of the ⟨echo⟩ messages in Algorithm 1. Finally, we implemented the asynchronous condition-based consensus algorithm
from [67]. We specialized it to binary consensus, which resulted in an encoding
which requires four shared variables.

The major goal of the experiments was to check the adequacy of our formalization. To this end, we first considered the four well-understood variants of [76],
for each of which we systematically changed the parameter values. By doing so,
we verify that under our modeling the different combination of parameters lead

Table 1. Summary of experiments related to [76]

# parameter values	spec	valid	Time	Mem.	Stored	Transitions	Depth
			Byz				
B1 N=7,T=2,F=2	(U)	✓	3.13 sec.	74 MB	$193 \cdot 10^3$	$1 \cdot 10^6$	229
B2 N=7,T=2,F=2	(C)	✓	3.43 sec.	75 MB	$207 \cdot 10^3$	$2 \cdot 10^6$	229
B3 N=7,T=2,F=2	(R)	✓	6.3 sec.	77 MB	$290 \cdot 10^3$	$3 \cdot 10^6$	229
B4 N=7,T=3,F=2	(U)	✓	4.38 sec.	77 MB	$265 \cdot 10^3$	$2 \cdot 10^6$	233
B5 N=7,T=3,F=2	(C)	✓	4.5 sec.	77 MB	$271 \cdot 10^3$	$2 \cdot 10^6$	233
B6 N=7,T=3,F=2	(R)	✗	0.02 sec.	68 MB	$1 \cdot 10^3$	$13 \cdot 10^3$	210
			OMIT				
O1 N=5,To=2,Fo=2	(U)	✓	1.43 sec.	69 MB	$51 \cdot 10^3$	$878 \cdot 10^3$	175
O2 N=5,To=2,Fo=2	(C)	✓	1.64 sec.	69 MB	$60 \cdot 10^3$	$1 \cdot 10^6$	183
O3 N=5,To=2,Fo=2	(R)	✓	3.69 sec.	71 MB	$92 \cdot 10^3$	$2 \cdot 10^6$	183
O4 N=5,To=2,Fo=3	(U)	✓	1.39 sec.	69 MB	$51 \cdot 10^3$	$878 \cdot 10^3$	175
O5 N=5,To=2,Fo=3	(C)	✗	1.63 sec.	69 MB	$53 \cdot 10^3$	$1 \cdot 10^6$	183
O6 N=5,To=2,Fo=3	(R)	✗	0.01 sec.	68 MB	17	135	53
			SYMM				
S1 N=5,T=1,Fp=1,Fs=0	(U)	✓	0.04 sec.	68 MB	$3 \cdot 10^3$	$23 \cdot 10^3$	121
S2 N=5,T=1,Fp=1,Fs=0	(C)	✓	0.03 sec.	68 MB	$3 \cdot 10^3$	$24 \cdot 10^3$	121
S3 N=5,T=1,Fp=1,Fs=0	(R)	✓	0.08 sec.	68 MB	$5 \cdot 10^3$	$53 \cdot 10^3$	121
S4 N=5,T=3,Fp=3,Fs=1	(U)	✓	0.01 sec.	68 MB	66	267	62
S5 N=5,T=3,Fp=3,Fs=1	(C)	✗	0.01 sec.	68 MB	62	221	66
S6 N=5,T=3,Fp=3,Fs=1	(R)	✓	0.01 sec.	68 MB	62	235	62
			CLEAN				
C1 N=3,Tc=2,Fc=2,Fnc=0	(U)	✓	0.01 sec.	68 MB	668	$7 \cdot 10^3$	77
C2 N=3,Tc=2,Fc=2,Fnc=0	(C)	✓	0.01 sec.	68 MB	892	$8 \cdot 10^3$	81
C3 N=3,Tc=2,Fc=2,Fnc=0	(R)	✓	0.02 sec.	68 MB	$1 \cdot 10^3$	$17 \cdot 10^3$	81

to the expected result. Table 1 and Figure 9 summarize the results of our experiments for broadcasting algorithms in the spirit of [76]. Lines B1–B3, O1–O3, S1–S3, and C1–C3 capture the cases that are within the resilience condition known for the respective algorithm, and the algorithms were verified by SPIN. In Lines B4–B6, the algorithm's parameters are chosen to achieve a goal that is known to be impossible [69], i.e., to tolerate that 3 out of 7 processes may fail. This violates the $n > 3t$ requirement. Our experiment shows that even if only 2 faults occur in this setting, the relay specification (R) is violated. In Lines O4–O6, the algorithm is designed properly, i.e., 2 out of 5 processes may fail ($n > 2t$ in the case of omission faults). Our experiments show that this algorithm fails in the presence of 3 faulty processes, i.e., (C) and (R) are violated.

Table 2 summarizes our experiments for the algorithms in [23], [20], and [67]. The specification (F) is related to agreement and was also used in [43]. Properties (V0) and (V1) are non-triviality, that is, if all processes propose 0 (1), then 0 (1) is the only possible decision value. Property (A) is agreement and similar to (R), while Property (T) is termination, and requires that every correct process eventually decides. In all experiments the validity of the specifications was as expected from the distributed algorithms literature.

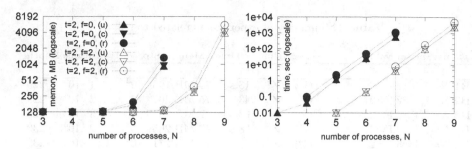

Fig. 9. SPIN memory usage (left) and running time (right) for BYZ

For slightly bigger systems, that is, for $n = 11$ our experiments run out of memory. This shows the need for parameterized verification of these algorithms.

6.3   Parameterized Model Checking

To show feasibility of our abstractions, we have implemented the PIA abstractions and the refinement loop in OCaml as a prototype tool BYMC. We evaluated it on different broadcasting algorithms. They deal with different fault models and resilience conditions; the algorithms are: (BYZ), which is the algorithm from Figure 4, for t Byzantine faults if $n > 3t$, (SYMM) for t symmetric (identical Byzantine [11]) faults if $n > 2t$, (OMIT) for t send omission faults if $n > 2t$, and (CLEAN) for t clean crash faults [80] if $n > t$. In addition, we verified the folklore broadcasting algorithm FBC — formalized also in [43] — whose CFA is given in Figure 5.

From the literature we know that we cannot expect to verify these FT-DAs without restricting the environment, e.g., without communication fairness, namely, every message sent is eventually received. To capture this, we use justice requirements, e.g., $J = \{[\forall i.\ rcvd_i \geq nsnt]\}$ in the Byzantine case.

Table 3 summarizes our experiments run on 3.3GHz Intel® Core™ 4GB. In the cases (A) we used resilience conditions as provided by the literature, and verified the specification. The model FBC is the folklore reliable broadcast algorithm also considered in [43] under the resilience condition $n \geq t \geq f$. In the bottom part of Table 3 we used different resilience conditions under which we expected the algorithms to fail. The cases (B) capture the case where more faults occur than expected by the algorithm designer ($f \leq t + 1$ instead of $f \leq t$), while the cases (C) and (D) capture the cases where the algorithms were designed by assuming wrong resilience conditions (e.g., $n \geq 3t$ instead of $n > 3t$ in the Byzantine case). We omit (CLEAN) as the only sensible case $n = t = f$ (all processes are faulty) results into a trivial abstract domain of one interval $[0, \infty)$. The column "#R" gives the numbers of refinement steps. In the cases where it is greater than zero, refinement was necessary, and "Spin Time" refers to the SPIN running time after the last refinement step. Finally, column $|\widehat{D}|$ indicates the size of the abstract domain.

Table 2. Summary of experiments with algorithms from [23,20,67]

#	parameter values	spec	valid	Time	Mem.	Stored	Transitions	Depth
		FOLKLORE BROADCAST [23]						
F1	N=2	(U)	✓	0.01 sec.	98 MB	121	$7 \cdot 10^3$	77
F2	N=2	(R)	✓	0.01 sec.	98 MB	143	$8 \cdot 10^3$	48
F3	N=2	(F)	✓	0.01 sec.	98 MB	257	$2 \cdot 10^3$	76
F4	N=6	(U)	✓	386 sec.	670 MB	$15 \cdot 10^6$	$20 \cdot 10^6$	272
F5	N=6	(R)	✓	691 sec.	996 MB	$24 \cdot 10^6$	$370 \cdot 10^6$	272
F6	N=6	(F)	✓	1690 sec.	1819 MB	$39 \cdot 10^6$	$875 \cdot 10^6$	328
		ASYNCHRONOUS BYZANTINE AGREEMENT [20]						
T1	N=5,T=1,F=1	(R)	✓	131 sec.	239 MB	$4 \cdot 10^6$	$74 \cdot 10^6$	211
T2	N=5,T=1,F=2	(R)	✗	0.68 sec.	99 MB	$11 \cdot 10^3$	$465 \cdot 10^3$	187
T3	N=5,T=2,F=2	(R)	✗	0.02 sec.	99 MB	726	$9 \cdot 10^3$	264
		CONDITION-BASED CONSENSUS [67]						
S1	N=3,T=1,F=1	(V0)	✓	0.01 sec.	98 MB	$1.4 \cdot 10^3$	$7 \cdot 10^3$	115
S2	N=3,T=1,F=1	(V1)	✓	0.04 sec.	98 MB	$3 \cdot 10^3$	$18 \cdot 10^3$	128
S3	N=3,T=1,F=1	(A)	✓	0.09 sec.	98 MB	$8 \cdot 10^3$	$42 \cdot 10^3$	127
S4	N=3,T=1,F=1	(T)	✓	0.16 sec.	66 MB	$9 \cdot 10^3$	$83 \cdot 10^3$	133
S5	N=3,T=1,F=2	(V0)	✓	0.02 sec.	68 MB	1724	9835	123
S6	N=3,T=1,F=2	(V1)	✓	0.05 sec.	68 MB	3647	$23 \cdot 10^3$	136
S7	N=3,T=1,F=2	(A)	✓	0.12 sec.	68 MB	$10 \cdot 10^3$	$55 \cdot 10^3$	135
S8	N=3,T=1,F=2	(T)	✗	0.05 sec.	68 MB	$3 \cdot 10^3$	$17 \cdot 10^3$	135

7 Discussions

Input languages for software model checkers are designed to capture limited degrees of non-determinism that are required to check, e.g., C/C++ industrial software. However, distributed algorithms typically show higher degrees of non-determinism, which makes them challenging for such existing tools. PROMELA, the input language of the SPIN model checker [2], was designed to simulate and validate network protocols. Consequently, PROMELA contains several primitives for concurrent and distributed systems, and we consider it the most suitable language for our purposes. Still, as we discussed, the semantics of the constructs do not match the ones required by distributed algorithms, and straight-forward implementations do not scale well. Similarly, PlusCal [60] is a high-level language to describe algorithms that can be translated to TLA+. It contains constructs to specify concurrent systems with shared variables. The UPPAAL model checker [14] has channels that model synchronous communications similar to rendezvous. Besides, it contains a broadcast primitive that is more closely related to hardware than to broadcasts in distributed systems. The input for the SMV model checker is also oriented towards hardware and provides rather low-level communication and coordination primitives. Lustre [48] is the input language for the SCADE tool set, and is limited to tightly coupled synchronous systems.

There have been two major undertakings of formalization that gained acceptance within the distributed algorithms community. Both were initiated by

Table 3. Summary of experiments in the parameterized case

$M \models \varphi$?	RC	Spin Time	Spin Memory	Spin States	Spin Depth	$|\hat{D}|$	#R	Total Time
BYZ $\models U$	(A)	2.3 s	82 MB	483k	9154	4	0	4 s
BYZ $\models C$	(A)	3.5 s	104 MB	970k	20626	4	10	32 s
BYZ $\models R$	(A)	6.3 s	107 MB	1327k	20844	4	10	24 s
SYMM $\models U$	(A)	0.1 s	67 MB	19k	897	3	0	1 s
SYMM $\models C$	(A)	0.1 s	67 MB	19k	1113	3	2	3 s
SYMM $\models R$	(A)	0.3 s	69 MB	87k	2047	3	12	16 s
OMIT $\models U$	(A)	0.1 s	66 MB	4k	487	3	0	1 s
OMIT $\models C$	(A)	0.1 s	66 MB	7k	747	3	5	6 s
OMIT $\models R$	(A)	0.1 s	66 MB	8k	704	3	5	10 s
CLEAN $\models U$	(A)	0.3 s	67 MB	30k	1371	3	0	2 s
CLEAN $\models C$	(A)	0.4 s	67 MB	35k	1707	3	4	8 s
CLEAN $\models R$	(A)	1.1 s	67 MB	51k	2162	3	13	31 s
FBC $\models U$	—	0.1 s	66 MB	0.8k	232	2	0	1 s
FBC $\models F$	—	0.1 s	66 MB	1.7k	333	2	0	1 s
FBC $\models R$	—	0.1 s	66 MB	1.2k	259	2	0	1 s
FBC $\not\models C$	—	0.1 s	66 MB	0.8k	232	2	0	1 s
BYZ $\not\models U$	(B)	5.2 s	101 MB	1093k	17685	4	9	56 s
BYZ $\not\models C$	(B)	3.7 s	102 MB	980k	19772	4	11	52 s
BYZ $\not\models R$	(B)	0.4 s	67 MB	59k	6194	4	10	17 s
BYZ $\models U$	(C)	3.4 s	87 MB	655k	10385	4	0	5 s
BYZ $\models C$	(C)	3.9 s	101 MB	963k	20651	4	9	32 s
BYZ $\not\models R$	(C)	2.1 s	91 MB	797k	14172	4	30	78 s
SYMM $\not\models U$	(B)	0.1 s	67 MB	19k	947	3	0	2 s
SYMM $\not\models C$	(B)	0.1 s	67 MB	18k	1175	3	2	4 s
SYMM $\models R$	(B)	0.2 s	67 MB	42k	1681	3	8	12 s
OMIT $\models U$	(D)	0.1 s	66 MB	5k	487	3	0	1 s
OMIT $\not\models C$	(D)	0.1 s	66 MB	5k	487	3	0	2 s
OMIT $\not\models R$	(D)	0.1 s	66 MB	0.1k	401	3	0	2 s

researchers with a background in distributed algorithms and with a precise understanding of what needs to be expressed. These approaches are on the one hand, the I/O Automata by Lynch and several collaborators [63,55,66], and on the other hand, TLA by Lamport and others [59,54,60]. IOA and TLA are general frameworks that are based on labeled transition systems and a variant of linear temporal logic, respectively. Both frameworks were originally developed at a time when automated verification was out of reach, and they were mostly intended to be used as formal foundations for handwritten proofs. Today, the tool support for IOA is still in preliminary stages [3]. For TLA [4], the TLC model checker is a simple explicit state model checker, while the current version of the TLA+ Proof System can only check safety proofs.

In all these approaches, specifying the semantics for fault-tolerant distributed algorithms is a research challenge, and we believe that this research requires an interdisciplinary effort between researchers in distributed algorithms and model checking. In this tutorial we presented our first results towards this direction.

The automatic verification of state-of-the-art distributed algorithm such as Paxos [58], or even more importantly, their implementations are currently out of reach, except possibly for very small system sizes. To be eventually able to verify such algorithms, we have to find efficient means to address the many problems these distributed algorithms pose to verification, for instance, large degrees of non-determinism due to faults and asynchrony, parameterization, and the use of communication primitives that are non-standard to the verification literature. The work that is presented here provides first steps in this direction. We focused on a specific class of fault-tolerant distributed algorithms, namely, threshold-based algorithms and derived abstraction methods for them.

The only way to evaluate the practical use of an abstraction is to conduct experiments on several case studies, and thus demonstrate that the abstraction is sufficiently precise to verify correct distributed algorithms, and find counterexamples in buggy ones. Hence, understanding implementations is crucial to evaluate the theoretical work and they are thus of highest importance. This motivates this tutorial that discussed the abstraction methods from an implementation point of view.

In more detail, we first added mild additions to the syntax of PROMELA to be able to express the kind of parameterized systems we are interested in. We also showed by experimental evaluation that the standard language constructs for interprocess communication do not scale well, and do not naturally match the required semantics for fault-tolerant distributed algorithms. We thus introduced an efficient encoding of a fault-tolerant distributed algorithm in the extended PROMELA. This representation builds the input for our tool chain, and we discussed in detail how it can be automatically translated into abstract models. We have introduced several levels of abstractions. As our abstractions are over-approximations, the model checker returned spurious counterexamples, such that we were led to counter example guided abstraction refinement (CEGAR) [27]. In contrast to the classic CEGAR setting, in the parameterized case we have an infinite number of concrete systems which poses new challenges. In this paper we discussed several of them and presented the details of the abstraction refinement approach that was sufficient to verify some of our case studies.

When taking a close look at our experiments, one observes that there are several algorithms that we verified for small instances, while we could not verify them in the parameterized setting. Developing new methods that allow us to also verify them is subject to ongoing work.

Acknowledgments. We are grateful to Francesco Spegni whose constructive comments helped us to improve the presentation.

References

1. ByMC 0.4.0: Byzantine model checker (2013),
   http://forsyte.tuwien.ac.at/software/bymc/ (accessed March 2014)
2. Spin 6.2.7 (2014), http://spinroot.com/ (accessed March 2014)

3. Tempo toolset. Web page, http://www.veromodo.com/
4. TLA – the temporal logic of actions. Web page, http://research.microsoft.com/en-us/um/people/lamport/tla/tla.html
5. Yices 1.0.40 (2013), http://yices.csl.sri.com/yices1-documentation.shtml (accessed March 2014)
6. Abdulla, P.A.: Regular model checking. International Journal on Software Tools for Technology Transfer 14, 109–118 (2012)
7. Abdulla, P.A., Jonsson, B.: Verifying programs with unreliable channels. Inf. Comput. 127(2), 91–101 (1996)
8. Aguilera, M.K., Delporte-Gallet, C., Fauconnier, H., Toueg, S.: Consensus with Byzantine failures and little system synchrony. In: DSN, pp. 147–155 (2006)
9. Alberti, F., Ghilardi, S., Pagani, E., Ranise, S., Rossi, G.P.: Universal guards, relativization of quantifiers, and failure models in model checking modulo theories. JSAT 8(1/2), 29–61 (2012)
10. Apt, K., Kozen, D.: Limits for automatic verification of finite-state concurrent systems. Inf. Process. Lett. 15, 307–309 (1986)
11. Attiya, H., Welch, J.: Distributed Computing, 2nd edn. John Wiley & Sons (2004)
12. Baier, C., Katoen, J.P., Larsen, K.G.: Principles of Model Checking. MIT Press (2008)
13. Ball, T., Majumdar, R., Millstein, T.D., Rajamani, S.K.: Automatic predicate abstraction of c programs. In: PLDI, pp. 203–213 (2001)
14. Behrmann, G., David, A., Larsen, K.G.: A tutorial on uppaal 4.0 (2006)
15. Biely, M., Charron-Bost, B., Gaillard, A., Hutle, M., Schiper, A., Widder, J.: Tolerating corrupted communication. In: PODC, pp. 244–253 (August 2007)
16. Biely, M., Schmid, U., Weiss, B.: Synchronous consensus under hybrid process and link failures. Theoretical Computer Science 412(40), 5602–5630 (2011)
17. Biere, A.: Handbook of satisfiability, vol. 185. IOS Press (2009)
18. Biere, A., Cimatti, A., Clarke, E.M., Fujita, M., Zhu, Y.: Symbolic model checking using SAT procedures instead of BDDs. In: DAC, pp. 317–320 (1999)
19. Bokor, P., Kinder, J., Serafini, M., Suri, N.: Efficient model checking of fault-tolerant distributed protocols. In: DSN, pp. 73–84 (2011)
20. Bracha, G., Toueg, S.: Asynchronous consensus and broadcast protocols. J. ACM 32(4), 824–840 (1985)
21. Browne, M.C., Clarke, E.M., Grumberg, O.: Reasoning about networks with many identical finite state processes. Inf. Comput. 81, 13–31 (1989)
22. Chambart, P., Schnoebelen, P.: Mixing lossy and perfect fifo channels. In: van Breugel, F., Chechik, M. (eds.) CONCUR 2008. LNCS, vol. 5201, pp. 340–355. Springer, Heidelberg (2008)
23. Chandra, T.D., Toueg, S.: Unreliable failure detectors for reliable distributed systems. J. ACM 43(2), 225–267 (1996)
24. Charron-Bost, B., Debrat, H., Merz, S.: Formal verification of consensus algorithms tolerating malicious faults. In: Défago, X., Petit, F., Villain, V. (eds.) SSS 2011. LNCS, vol. 6976, pp. 120–134. Springer, Heidelberg (2011)
25. Charron-Bost, B., Pedone, F., Schiper, A. (eds.): Replication: Theory and Practice. LNCS, vol. 5959. Springer, Heidelberg (2010)
26. Chou, C.T., Mannava, P., Park, S.: A simple method for parameterized verification of cache coherence protocols. In: Hu, A.J., Martin, A.K. (eds.) FMCAD 2004. LNCS, vol. 3312, pp. 382–398. Springer, Heidelberg (2004)
27. Clarke, E., Grumberg, O., Jha, S., Lu, Y., Veith, H.: Counterexample-guided abstraction refinement for symbolic model checking. J. ACM 50(5), 752–794 (2003)

28. Clarke, E., Talupur, M., Veith, H.: Proving Ptolemy right: the environment abstraction framework for model checking concurrent systems. In: Ramakrishnan, C.R., Rehof, J. (eds.) TACAS 2008. LNCS, vol. 4963, pp. 33–47. Springer, Heidelberg (2008)

29. Clarke, E., Talupur, M., Touili, T., Veith, H.: Verification by network decomposition. In: Gardner, P., Yoshida, N. (eds.) CONCUR 2004. LNCS, vol. 3170, pp. 276–291. Springer, Heidelberg (2004)

30. Clarke, E.M., Emerson, E.A.: Design and synthesis of synchronization skeletons using branching-time temporal logic. In: Kozen, D. (ed.) Logic of Programs 1981. LNCS, vol. 131, pp. 52–71. Springer, Heidelberg (1982)

31. Clarke, E.M., Grumberg, O., Peled, D.A.: Model Checking. MIT Press (1999)

32. Clarke, E., Talupur, M., Veith, H.: Environment abstraction for parameterized verification. In: Emerson, E.A., Namjoshi, K.S. (eds.) VMCAI 2006. LNCS, vol. 3855, pp. 126–141. Springer, Heidelberg (2006)

33. Cousot, P., Cousot, R.: Abstract interpretation: a unified lattice model for static analysis of programs by construction or approximation of fixpoints. In: POPL, pp. 238–252. ACM (1977)

34. Cytron, R., Ferrante, J., Rosen, B.K., Wegman, M.N., Zadeck, F.K.: Efficiently computing static single assignment form and the control dependence graph. ACM Trans. Program. Lang. Syst. 13(4), 451–490 (1991)

35. de Moura, L., Bjørner, N.S.: Z3: An efficient SMT solver. In: Ramakrishnan, C.R., Rehof, J. (eds.) TACAS 2008. LNCS, vol. 4963, pp. 337–340. Springer, Heidelberg (2008)

36. De Prisco, R., Malkhi, D., Reiter, M.K.: On k-set consensus problems in asynchronous systems. IEEE Trans. Parallel Distrib. Syst. 12(1), 7–21 (2001)

37. Dolev, D., Lynch, N.A., Pinter, S.S., Stark, E.W., Weihl, W.E.: Reaching approximate agreement in the presence of faults. J. ACM 33(3), 499–516 (1986)

38. Dutertre, B., de Moura, L.: A fast linear-arithmetic solver for DPLL(T). In: Ball, T., Jones, R.B. (eds.) CAV 2006. LNCS, vol. 4144, pp. 81–94. Springer, Heidelberg (2006)

39. Dwork, C., Lynch, N., Stockmeyer, L.: Consensus in the presence of partial synchrony. J. ACM 35(2), 288–323 (1988)

40. Emerson, E.A., Kahlon, V.: Reducing model checking of the many to the few. In: McAllester, D. (ed.) CADE 2000. LNCS, vol. 1831, pp. 236–254. Springer, Heidelberg (2000)

41. Emerson, E., Namjoshi, K.: Reasoning about rings. In: POPL, pp. 85–94 (1995)

42. Fischer, M.J., Lynch, N.A., Paterson, M.S.: Impossibility of distributed consensus with one faulty process. J. ACM 32(2), 374–382 (1985)

43. Fisman, D., Kupferman, O., Lustig, Y.: On verifying fault tolerance of distributed protocols. In: Ramakrishnan, C.R., Rehof, J. (eds.) TACAS 2008. LNCS, vol. 4963, pp. 315–331. Springer, Heidelberg (2008)

44. Fuegger, M., Schmid, U., Fuchs, G., Kempf, G.: Fault-Tolerant Distributed Clock Generation in VLSI Systems-on-Chip. In: EDCC 2006, pp. 87–96 (October 2006)

45. German, S.M., Sistla, A.P.: Reasoning about systems with many processes. J. ACM 39, 675–735 (1992)

46. Graf, S., Saïdi, H.: Construction of abstract state graphs with pvs. In: Grumberg, O. (ed.) CAV 1997. LNCS, vol. 1254, pp. 72–83. Springer, Heidelberg (1997)

47. Grumberg, O., Veith, H. (eds.): 25 Years of Model Checking. LNCS, vol. 5000. Springer, Heidelberg (2008)

48. Halbwachs, N., Lagnier, F., Ratel, C.: Programming and verifying real-time systems by means of the synchronous data-flow language lustre. IEEE Trans. Softw. Eng. 18, 785–793 (1992)
49. Holzmann, G.: The SPIN Model Checker: Primer and Reference Manual. Addison-Wesley Professional (2003)
50. Ip, C., Dill, D.: Verifying systems with replicated components in murϕ. In: Alur, R., Henzinger, T.A. (eds.) CAV 1996. LNCS, vol. 1102, pp. 147–158. Springer, Heidelberg (1996)
51. John, A., Konnov, I., Schmid, U., Veith, H., Widder, J.: Starting a dialog between model checking and fault-tolerant distributed algorithms. arXiv CoRR abs/1210.3839 (2012)
52. John, A., Konnov, I., Schmid, U., Veith, H., Widder, J.: Parameterized model checking of fault-tolerant distributed algorithms by abstraction. In: FMCAD, pp. 201–209 (2013)
53. John, A., Konnov, I., Schmid, U., Veith, H., Widder, J.: Towards modeling and model checking fault-tolerant distributed algorithms. In: Bartocci, E., Ramakrishnan, C.R. (eds.) SPIN 2013. LNCS, vol. 7976, pp. 209–226. Springer, Heidelberg (2013)
54. Joshi, R., Lamport, L., Matthews, J., Tasiran, S., Tuttle, M.R., Yu, Y.: Checking cache-coherence protocols with TLA$^+$. Formal Methods in System Design 22(2), 125–131 (2003)
55. Kaynar, D.K., Lynch, N.A., Segala, R., Vaandrager, F.W.: The Theory of Timed I/O Automata. Synthesis Lectures on Computer Science. Morgan & Claypool (2006)
56. Kesten, Y., Pnueli, A.: Control and data abstraction: the cornerstones of practical formal verification. STTT 2, 328–342 (2000)
57. Konnov, I., Veith, H., Widder, J.: Who is afraid of Model Checking Distributed Algorithms? (2012)
58. Lamport, L.: The part-time parliament. ACM Trans. Comput. Syst. 16, 133–169 (1998)
59. Lamport, L.: Specifying Systems, The TLA+ Language and Tools for Hardware and Software Engineers. Addison-Wesley (2002)
60. Lamport, L.: The pluscal algorithm language. In: Leucker, M., Morgan, C. (eds.) ICTAC 2009. LNCS, vol. 5684, pp. 36–60. Springer, Heidelberg (2009)
61. Lincoln, P., Rushby, J.: A formally verified algorithm for interactive consistency under a hybrid fault model. In: FTCS-23, pp. 402–411 (June 1993)
62. Lynch, N.: Distributed Algorithms. Morgan Kaufman, San Francisco (1996)
63. Lynch, N., Tuttle, M.: An introduction to input/output automata. Tech. Rep. MIT/LCS/TM-373, Laboratory for Computer Science, MIT (1989)
64. McMillan, K.: Symbolic model checking. Kluwer (1993)
65. McMillan, K.L.: Parameterized verification of the flash cache coherence protocol by compositional model checking. In: Margaria, T., Melham, T.F. (eds.) CHARME 2001. LNCS, vol. 2144, pp. 179–195. Springer, Heidelberg (2001)
66. Mitra, S., Lynch, N.A.: Proving approximate implementations for probabilistic I/O automata. Electr. Notes Theor. Comput. Sci. 174(8), 71–93 (2007)
67. Mostéfaoui, A., Mourgaya, E., Parvédy, P.R., Raynal, M.: Evaluating the condition-based approach to solve consensus. In: DSN, pp. 541–550 (2003)
68. O'Leary, J.W., Talupur, M., Tuttle, M.R.: Protocol verification using flows: An industrial experience. In: FMCAD, pp. 172–179 (2009)
69. Pease, M., Shostak, R., Lamport, L.: Reaching agreement in the presence of faults. J. ACM 27(2), 228–234 (1980)

70. Pnueli, A., Xu, J., Zuck, L.D.: Liveness with $(0, 1, \infty)$-counter abstraction. In: Brinksma, E., Larsen, K.G. (eds.) CAV 2002. LNCS, vol. 2404, pp. 107–111. Springer, Heidelberg (2002)
71. Powell, D.: Failure mode assumptions and assumption coverage. In: FTCS-22, Boston, MA, USA, pp. 386–395 (1992)
72. Santoro, N., Widmayer, P.: Time is not a healer. In: Cori, R., Monien, B. (eds.) STACS 1989. LNCS, vol. 349, pp. 304–313. Springer, Heidelberg (1989)
73. Schmid, U., Weiss, B., Rushby, J.: Formally verified Byzantine agreement in presence of link faults. In: ICDCS, July 2-5, pp. 608–616 (2002)
74. Shoham, S., Grumberg, O.: 3-valued abstraction: More precision at less cost. Inf. Comput. 206(11), 1313–1333 (2008)
75. Srikanth, T.K., Toueg, S.: Optimal clock synchronization. Journal of the ACM 34(3), 626–645 (1987)
76. Srikanth, T., Toueg, S.: Simulating authenticated broadcasts to derive simple fault-tolerant algorithms. Distributed Computing 2, 80–94 (1987)
77. Suzuki, I.: Proving properties of a ring of finite-state machines. Inf. Process. Lett. 28(4), 213–214 (1988)
78. Tsuchiya, T., Schiper, A.: Verification of consensus algorithms using satisfiability solving. Distributed Computing 23(5-6), 341–358 (2011)
79. Widder, J., Biely, M., Gridling, G., Weiss, B., Blanquart, J.P.: Consensus in the presence of mortal Byzantine faulty processes. Distributed Computing 24(6), 299–321 (2012)
80. Widder, J., Schmid, U.: Booting clock synchronization in partially synchronous systems with hybrid process and link failures. Distributed Computing 20(2), 115–140 (2007)
81. Wöhrle, S., Thomas, W.: Model checking synchronized products of infinite transition systems. LMCS 3(4) (2007)

Verification of Concurrent Systems with VerCors

Afshin Amighi, Stefan Blom, Saeed Darabi, Marieke Huisman,
Wojciech Mostowski, and Marina Zaharieva-Stojanovski

University of Twente, The Netherlands

Abstract. This paper presents the VerCors approach to verification of
concurrent software. It first discusses why verification of concurrent software is important, but also challenging. Then it shows how within the
VerCors project we use permission-based separation logic to reason about
multithreaded Java programs. We discuss in particular how we use the
logic to use different implementations of synchronisers in verification,
and how we reason about class invariance properties in a concurrent setting. Further, we also show how the approach is suited to reason about
programs using a different concurrency paradigm, namely kernel programs using the Single Instruction Multiple Data paradigm. Concretely,
we illustrate how permission-based separation logic is suitable to verify functional correctness properties of OpenCL kernels. All verification
techniques discussed in this paper are supported by the VerCors tool set.

1 Introduction

The quest for software correctness is as old as software itself, and as the complexity of software is steadily increasing, also the challenges to guarantee software correctness are increasing. In the 60-ies, Floyd and Hoare for the first time
proposed static techniques to guarantee that a program functioned as it was
supposed to do [28,24]. For a long time, their ideas remained mainly theoretical,
but during the last decade or so, we have seen a dramatic increase in the applicability of software verification tools for sequential programs. Several successful
tools and techniques in this area are Dafny [39], Spec# [6], ESC/Java2 [14],
OpenJML [17], KeY [7], and KIV [54].

However, this development is not sufficient to guarantee correctness of all
modern software. In particular, most modern software is inherently multithreaded – as this is often necessary to efficiently exploit the underlying multi-core
hardware – and often also distributed. This shift in software development has
also led in a shift of software verification technology: several groups are working
on tools and techniques to reason about multithreaded software. However, at the
moment, many of these techniques are still difficult to apply and require expert
knowledge about the underlying theory.

In this paper, we describe the current results of the VerCors project. Goal
of the VerCors project is to use the advance in program verification technology
for multithreaded programs to develop a practical and usable verification technology, that can also be used by non-verification-experts, and in particular by
experienced software developers.

M. Bernardo et al. (Eds.): SFM 2014, LNCS 8483, pp. 172–216, 2014.
© Springer International Publishing Switzerland 2014

The basis for the VerCors approach to the verification of multithreaded programs is the use of *permission-based separation logic*. Separation logic [55] is an extension of Hoare logic that was originally developed to reason about pointer programs. In contrast to classical Hoare logic, separation logic explicitly distinguishes between the heap and the store. In particular, this means that one can explicitly express that one has a pointer into a certain location at the heap. In addition, separation logic uses the *separating conjunction* $\star$ to combine formulas. A formula $\phi_1 \star \phi_2$ is valid for a heap h, if the heap h can be separated into two *disjoint* parts h_1 and h_2, such that ϕ_1 is valid for the heap h_1, and ϕ_2 is valid for the heap h_2.

It was soon realised that separation logic is also suitable to reason about multithreaded programs. If threads operate on disjoint parts of the heap, they can be verified in isolation, and there is no need to explicitly consider interferences between the two threads [46]. However, classical separation logic in itself is not flexible enough to verify all interesting multithreaded programs. In particular, classical separation logic does not allow two threads to simultaneously read a shared location, even though this is perfectly acceptable for a multithreaded program. Therefore, we combine separation logic with the notion of *access permissions* [12]. Within the logic, one can express that a thread has *read* or *write* permission on a location. Permissions can be transferred between threads at synchronisation points, including thread creation and joining (i.e., waiting for a thread to terminate). Soundness of permission-based separation logic ensures that (1) there always is at most one thread that has write permission on a location, and (2) if a thread has read permission, then all other threads also only can have read permission. This implies that if a program can be verified with this logic, it is free of data races. Moreover, it also allows each thread to be verified in isolation, because when a thread has permission to access a location, its value is *stable*. If a thread has write permission, it is only this thread that can change this location. If a thread has read permission, all other threads also only have read permissions, and thus the value stored in this location cannot be changed. As a consequence, there is no need to explicitly check for non-interference freedom (in contrast to classical verification methods for concurrent programs, such as Owicki-Gries [48]).

The concrete program annotation language that we use is an extension of the JML annotation language [13]. JML, the Java Modeling Language, is a behavioural interface specification language for Java programs. It allows to specify methods by pre- and postconditions (**requires** and **ensures** clauses, respectively). Additionally, it also supports class level specifications, such as class invariants and history constraints. JML is widely supported for sequential Java, with tools for static and run-time verification [13], annotation generation [23], etc. To make sure that all this work for sequential Java can be easily reused in a concurrent setting, the VerCors annotation language combines JML with support for permissions and separation.

This paper introduces the full details of our logic and our Java program annotation language, and illustrates this on several examples. All examples are verifiable using the VerCors tool set, which underlies all our work. The on-line version of the tool set as well as our library of examples are reachable through the project's home page [58]. The VerCors tool set encodes the verification problem of programs annotated with our specification language, into verification problems of existing verification tools, such as Chalice [37] and Boogie [38]. This allows us to leverage existing verification technology, instead of rebuilding everything from scratch.

Compared to other projects working on verification techniques for concurrent programs, the VerCors project distinguishes itself because it provides support to reason about different synchronisation mechanisms in a uniform way. Moreover, it also provides support to reason about functional properties. In a concurrent setting, it becomes more difficult to specify functional behaviour, because properties that hold for a thread in one state, might be invalidated by another thread in the next state. Only properties for which a thread holds sufficient permissions cannot be invalidated. This impacts what sort of properties can be specified for multithreaded programs. However, we show that it is possible to reason about class invariants in a concurrent setting. In particular, class invariants may be temporarily broken, provided no thread is able to observe that the invariant is broken. This technique allows one to specify and verify many meaningful reachability properties of objects in concurrent programs.

The last part of this paper discusses how permission-based separation logic also can be used to verify programs in a different concurrency paradigm: we show how it is used to verify OpenCL kernels [47]. These are a typical example of vector programs, where multiple threads execute the same instruction but on different data. Essentially, the approach distinguishes two levels of specifications: for each vector program a complete collection of permissions used by the program is specified. Additionally, for each thread the permissions necessary for that thread are specified, and it should be shown that the permissions used by the different threads together are no more than the permissions available for the complete vector program. Synchronisation between the threads in a vector program is done by a barrier; the specifications specify how at each barrier, the permissions can be redistributed between the threads. Finally, for this kind of programs, it is also possible to prove functional correctness, i.e., one can specify and verify what is computed by the program.

Overview of the Paper. The remainder of this paper is organised as follows. Section 2 presents our version of permission-based separation logic, illustrates how one can reason with it, and how this is supported by the VerCors tool set. Next, Sect. 3 discusses how we can specify different synchronisation mechanisms, while Sect. 4 discusses class invariants in a concurrent setting. Then, Sect. 5 discusses how the approach is used to reason about kernel programs. Finally, Sect. 6 discusses related work, while Sect. 7 concludes and sketches our ideas for future work.

Origins of the Material. More information about the details of our logic (described in Section 2 is published in LMCS [27]. An overview and architecture of the VerCors tool set is published at FM'2014 [10]. Our uniform specifications of the different synchronisation mechanisms have appeared in PDP'14 [2]. The modular specification and verification technique for concurrent class invariants is published in FASE'14 [60]. Finally, the verification approach for OpenCL kernels is published in Bytecode'13 and in SCP [30,11].

2   Permission-Based Separation Logic for Concurrent Programs

Before precisely defining the VerCors property specification language, we first give some background on separation logic and permissions in general. This description is mainly intuitive, and serves as background information.

2.1   Classical Separation Logic

The two main ingredients of formulas in classical separation logic are the points-to predicate $\mathsf{PointsTo}(x, v)$ (often written as $x \mapsto v$), and the separating conjunction $\star$. In the remainder of this paper, however, we will be using a different symbol for the separating conjunction, namely a double star $\ast\ast$. This is necessary to distinguish it from the multiplication operator of Java, whose meaning we want to retain in our JML-compatible specification language. A formula $\mathsf{PointsTo}(x, v)$ intuitively is valid for a heap h if the variable x points to a location that is in the domain of this heap h, and this location contains the value v. As explained above, a separating conjunction is valid for a heap h if the two conjuncts are valid for disjoint parts of this heap.

The verification rules in classical separation logic for look-up and update of a location on the heap contain an explicit precondition $\mathsf{PointsTo}(x, v)$, as follows:

$$\frac{\text{local variable } y}{\{\mathsf{PointsTo}(x, v)\}y := x\{\mathsf{PointsTo}(x, v) \ast\ast y = v\}} \text{(look-up)}$$

$$\frac{}{\{\mathsf{PointsTo}(x, \_)\}x := v\{\mathsf{PointsTo}(x, v)\}} \text{(update)}$$

This means that the $\mathsf{PointsTo}$ predicate also serves as an access permission: the location on the heap can only be read or written if the program fragment actually has a reference to it. This is in contrast to classical Hoare logic, where any variable can be read or written.

2.2   Concurrent Separation Logic

When separation logic was introduced to reason about programs with pointers, it was quickly realised that it would also be suitable to reason about concurrent programs. In particular, since separation logic requires explicit access to the fields on the heap that it reads and updates, the *footprint* of each thread is known. If two threads have disjoint footprints, they work on different parts of the heap, and thus their behaviours do not interfere.

O'Hearn was the first to use this idea, and to propose *Concurrent Separation Logic (CSL)*. A major ingredient of CSL was a rule for reasoning about concurrent programs [46]. Given a collection of n parallel threads,

- if each thread i can be specified (and verified) with a pre- and postcondition P_i and Q_i, respectively,
- if all preconditions are disjoint (w.r.t. the heap), and
- all postconditions are disjoint,

then they can be combined to verify the complete parallel program. This is expressed by the following rule:

$$\frac{\{P_1\}S_1\{Q_1\} \quad \ldots \quad \{P_n\}S_n\{Q_n\}}{\{P_1 \ast\ast \ldots \ast\ast P_n\}S_1 \parallel \ldots \parallel S_n\{Q_1 \ast\ast \ldots \ast\ast Q_n\}} \quad \begin{array}{l} \forall ij.i \neq j.\mathsf{var}(P_i) \cup \mathsf{var}(Q_i) \\ \text{not modified in } S_j \end{array}$$

O'Hearn calls this the *disjoint concurrency rule*.

For concurrent programs, an important property is that a program is free of *data races*. A data race occurs when two threads potentially might access the same location simultaneously, and at least one of the two accesses is a write. Clearly, when a program is verified using the rule for disjoint concurrency, it is free of data races.

2.3   Permissions and Resources

However, it is also easy to see that the rule is overly restrictive. Any program where two threads might *read* the same variable simultaneously cannot be verified with this rule.

To solve this problem, *fractional permissions* are introduced to specify the access that a thread requires to a location in a more fine-grained way. A fractional permission is a fraction in the interval (0,1] [12]. A permission with value 1, i.e., a full permission is understood as a permission to *write* a location; any permission with a value less than 1, i.e., a fractional permission, only gives access to *read* a location.

In the specifications, permissions are explicitly added to the assertions. In particular, the PointsTo operator is decorated with a fractional permission in the interval $(0, 1]$, such that $\mathsf{PointsTo}(x, v, \pi)$ means that the variable x has access permission π to a location on the heap, and this location contains the value v.

Once permissions are introduced, the PointsTo predicate can be separated into two parts:

$$\mathsf{PointsTo}(x, v, \pi) \equiv \mathsf{Perm}(x, \pi) \ast\ast x = v$$

Thus, $\mathsf{Perm}(x, \pi)$ means that a thread holds an access permission π on location x. In our approach, we use the Perm operator as the primitive operator. As a consequence, in our annotation language, it has to be checked explicitly that all formulas are *self-framed*, i.e., only properties can be expressed for which one has appropriate access conditions. This is crucial to maintain soundness of the approach. The essential feature of fractional permissions that enables the flow of permissions between the different threads is that they can be split and combined. Concretely, $\mathsf{Perm}(x, \pi)$ can be exchanged for $\mathsf{Perm}(x, \pi/2) \mathbin{**} \mathsf{Perm}(x, \pi/2)$ and vice versa.

In the verification rules for update and look-up, the permissions are explicitly added to the precondition (and returned in the postcondition). Then, in the context of Java that we are slowly moving to, memory locations are referred to by a combination of object references and field expressions, i.e., they are of the form $e.f$ (cf. Parkinson's separation logic for Java [49]). Furthermore, in Java objects can be dynamically allocated with the **new** operator. In this case, the allocation command returns an initial full write permission of 1 on all fields of the newly created object. Thus, in permission-based separation logic for Java, one has the following rules for update, look-up, and allocation, respectively:

$$\frac{}{\{\mathsf{Perm}(e.f, 1)\}e.f := v\{\mathsf{Perm}(e.f, 1) \mathbin{**} e.f = v\}} \text{ (update)}$$

$$\frac{\text{local variable } y}{\{\mathsf{Perm}(e.f, \pi) \mathbin{**} e.f = v\}y := e.f\{\mathsf{Perm}(e.f, \pi) \mathbin{**} y = v\}} \text{ (look-up)}$$

$$\frac{}{\{\mathsf{true}\}e := \textbf{new } \mathsf{C}()\{\mathsf{Perm}(e.f_1, 1) \mathbin{**} \ldots \mathsf{Perm}(e.f_n, 1)\}} \text{ (allocate)}$$

where $f_1, \ldots, f_n$ are the fields of class C.

The soundness proof of the verification rules ensures an additional global property on the permissions in the system, namely that the total number of permissions to access a location simultaneously *never* exceeds 1. This ensures that any program that can be verified is free of data races. If a thread holds a full permission to access a location, there can never be any other thread that holds a permission to access this location simultaneously. If a thread holds a read permission to access a location, then any other thread that holds a permission simultaneously must also have a read permission only. Thus, there can never be conflicting accesses to the same location, where one of the accesses is a write, thus a verified program is free of data races.

Abstract Predicates. Another commonly-used extension of separation logic are *abstract predicates* [50]. An important purpose of abstract predicates is to add inductive definitions to separation logic formulas, making it possible to define and reason about permissions on linked data structures. Abstract predicates can also be used to provide control over the visibility of specifications, which allows one to encapsulate implementation details. Another feature of abstract predicates is that they can be declared without providing a definition (similar to abstract methods in Java). This allows one to use abstract predicates as a token in specifications. This feature is used for example to specify behaviour of a program as an abstract state machine, e.g., to specify mutual exclusion.

Since abstract predicates can be a token, without a predicate body, they define more than just a set of access permissions. Therefore, we will use the term *resource* when referring to abstract predicates and/or access permissions.

```
public class Point {
  private int x, y;
  //@ invariant (x >= 0 && y >= 0) || (x <= 0 && y <= 0);

  //@ requires Perm(this.x, 1) ** Perm(this.y, 1);
  //@ ensures Perm(this.x, 1) ** Perm(this.y, 1);
  public void set(int xv, int yv){ this.x = xv; this.y = yv; }
}
```

Lst. 1. Class Point

Abstract predicates can have parameters, which can be program variables or (fractional) permissions. The latter can be used for example to specify different access permissions to different parts of a data structure. However, many separation logic tools do not support reasoning about abstract predicates with arbitrary parameters.

2.4   The VerCors Property Specification Language

As mentioned above, the property specification language that we use in the VerCors tool set combines separation logic with features from the Java Modeling Language (JML).

Example 1. Lst. 1 shows a simple example of a Java class **Point**. Below, we will use this class with extensions and variations as a running example. The class **Point** encapsulates values for a point in a 2D Cartesian coordinate. The contract of the method **set** specifies that write permissions on both x and y are required to execute this method. Moreover, when the method is finished, the same permission will be given back to the caller. As a functional property we add a requirement that every point is always in the first or the third quarter of the Cartesian space, we do this with the **invariant** clause.

More formally, in our VerCors property specification language we distinguish between *resource expressions* (R, typical elements r_i) and *functional expressions* (E, typical elements e_i), with the subset of logical expressions of type boolean (B, typical elements b_i). The grammar for our specification language is the following:

$$
\begin{aligned}
R ::= \; & b \\
| \; & \mathsf{Perm}(e.f, \pi) \\
| \; & (\backslash\mathsf{forall*} \; \mathsf{T} \; v; b; r) \\
| \; & r_1 \; ** \; r_2 \\
| \; & r_1 \; -* \; r_2 \\
| \; & b_1 \; ==\!> r_2 \\
| \; & e.\mathsf{P}(e_1, \ldots, e_2) \\
E ::= \; & \text{any } pure \text{ expression} \\
B ::= \; & \text{any } pure \text{ expression of type boolean}
\end{aligned}
$$

where T is an arbitrary type, v is a variable name, P is an abstract predicate of a special type **resource**, f is a field reference, and π denotes a fractional permission in the range $(0, 1]$.

The permission property Perm and the separating conjunction ** have been discussed above. Additionally, in our specifications, we use the separating implication −*. A formula ϕ_1 −* ϕ_2 is valid for a heap h if for any heap h' for which ϕ_1 is valid, the formula ϕ_2 is valid for the heap h ** h' (where h ** h' denotes the heap composed of h and h'. Thus, in other words, given a heap that satisfies the formula ϕ_1, this can be exchanged for a combined heap that satisfies the formula h'. Then, we also allow the separating quantification \forall*, which is essentially an iterative separating conjunction. We have the standard logical connectives to combine first-order formulas, and guarded resource expressions denoted by ==>. This is used to state conditional resource properties, the most typical condition being non-nullness of an object reference that is used in the following resource formula, for example, x != null ==> Perm(x, 1). Finally, we can refer to any predicate P declared and/or defined inside any Java classes.

The grammar above defines the language that can be used in all specification clauses of a Java program annotated with JML. As we already mentioned, JML allows one to state pre- and postconditions for methods with the **requires** and **ensures** keywords, respectively, or class invariants with the **invariant** keyword. Additionally, we extend the syntax of JML to allow one to declare and define predicates. Each predicate is declared and defined by its signature, name and an optional body in a class-level JML comment. Below, we will also use a special class of predicates, called *groups*. Group predicates are splittable over their permission predicates; why we need them and a more precise definition are discussed in Section 2.5 below, when discussing the specification of thread joining. Additionally, our syntax also allows one to declare *ghost class and method parameters*, i.e., specification-only class and method parameters. Ghost class and method parameters are specified using a **given** clause (for input parameters), and a **yields** clause for result values. Classes can only have ghost input parameters, methods can have both ghost input and output parameters.

Example 2. Lst. 2 extends the example from Lst. 1 with a predicate to encapsulate the permissions on the fields. Additionally, it adds two methods, which given any permission on the fields read the values and perform their defined tasks.

The annotations for methods plot and getQuarter express that given any fractional permission p on both x and y, the object can plot and identify the quarter, respectively. Additionally, the method specifications ensure that the required permissions are returned. Clearly, given any fraction $0 < p \leq \frac{1}{2}$, two threads can simultaneously execute plot and getQuarter on the same point object. However, two threads cannot execute set on the same point object simultaneously.

2.5   Reasoning about Dynamic Threads

As mentioned above, permissions are transferred between threads upon synchronisation. In the next section we will look at how we specify different

```
public class Point{
  //@ resource state(frac p) = Perm(this.x, p) ** Perm(this.y, p);
  private int x, y;

  //@ requires state(1); ensures state(1);
  public void set(int xv, int yv){ this.x = xv; this.y = yv; }

  //@ given frac p; requires state(p); ensures state(p);
  public void plot(){ /* plot the point on the screen */ }

  //@ given frac p; requires state(p); ensures state(p);
  public int getQuarter(){ /* return 1..4 to show the quarter. */ }
}
```

Lst. 2. Extended class of Point

synchronisation mechanisms in a uniform way. Here we discuss one special kind of synchronisation between threads, namely thread start and thread termination.

In Java, threads are objects. When the native **start** method is invoked on a thread object, the virtual machine will create a new thread of execution. This new thread will execute the run method of the thread object. The new thread will remain alive until it reaches the end of its run method. Other threads can wait for a thread to terminate. They do this by invoking the join method on a thread object. This will block the calling thread until the joined thread has terminated.

In Java, the correct way of using a thread is to first call **start** precisely once and then call join as many times as one would like. To enforce this order, the constructor of the **Thread** class ensures a **start** token that is required by the **start** method. The start method in turn ensures a join token. This join token has a fraction as argument and is defined as a group, so it can be shared between threads. To specify what permissions are transferred when threads are created and joined, we use the specification of the run method: the precondition of a thread is the precondition of the run method; the postcondition of a thread is the postcondition of the run method. For this purpose, we specify predicates **preFork** and **postJoin** that denote this pre- and postcondition, respectively. These predicates have trivial definitions to be extended in the thread implementing classes. Thus, we specify that the **start** method requires both the **start** token and the resources specified in **preFork** and gives them all up, i.e., it has postcondition join(1). Finally, the specification of the join method ensures that the resources specified in the **postJoin** predicate are obtained by executing this method. Notice that the **postJoin** predicate should be a group. Below, we give the definition of a group and describe the extended role of the join predicate in the precondition. This results in the following specification for class **Thread** in Lst. 3.

Every class that defines a thread extends class **Thread**. It can extend the predicates **preFork** and **postJoin** to denote extra permissions that are passed to

```
   class Thread implements Runnable {
2
      //@ resource start();
4     //@ resource preFork() = true;
      //@ group resource postJoin(frac p) = true;
6     //@ group resource join(frac p);

8     //@ requires true; ensures start();
      public Thread();
10
      //@ requires preFork(); ensures postJoin(1);
12    void run();

14    //@ requires start() ** preFork(); ensures join(1);
      public void start();
16
      //@ given frac p;
18    //@ requires join(p); ensures postJoin(p);
      public void join();
20 }
```

Lst. 3. Specification of class Thread

the newly created thread. To verify that the thread functions correctly, the run method is verified w.r.t. its specification. When verifying the thread that creates or joins this thread, the calls to start and join are verified using the standard verification rule for method calls.

Example 3. To illustrate how we reason about dynamic thread creation, we use a common pattern of signal-processing applications in which a chain of threads are connected through a shared buffer, in which we store several instances of class Point defined in Lst. 2. In addition, this example also demonstrates how the join predicate is used in case multiple threads join the same thread.

The complete application uses one shared buffer and four threads: a sampler, filter processes A and B, and a plotter. The buffer encapsulates an input field and two points, see Lst. 4. First, the sampler thread assigns a value to the input field of the buffer. Next, it passes the buffer to processes A and B, which are executed in parallel. Based on the value that the sampler thread stored in the inp field of Buffer, each process calculates a point and stores its value in the

```
public class Buffer {
   //@ resource state(frac p) = Perm(inp, p) ** Perm(outa, p) ** Perm(outb, p);
   public int inp;
   public Point outa, outb;
}
```

Lst. 4. Class Buffer

shared buffer. Finally, the computation results of both processes are displayed by the plotter.

What makes this example interesting is that both processes A and B join the sampler thread, i.e., they wait for the sampler thread to terminate, and in this way retrieve read permission on the input data that was written by the sampler thread.

In addition, the plotter waits for the two processing threads to terminate (by joining them), to retrieve their permissions on the shared buffer, and then combines these into full write permissions on all fields of the shared buffer.

Lst. 5 shows the sampler thread, Lst. 6 shows the AFilter class (class BFilter is similar and not shown here), Lst. 7 shows the Plotter class and finally Lst. 8 shows the main application. In the examples we sketch an outline of the correctness proof as comments in the code. We also indicate when predicates are **fold**-ed and **unfold**-ed, to encapsulate predicate definitions and expand them, respectively.

To understand the annotations, we need to explain the meaning of the join predicate, and why the postJoin predicate should be a group. In Example 3, both processes A and B join the sampler thread. If both joining threads would obtain the full set of permissions specified in postJoin, this would lead to unsoundness, because multiple threads would obtain a write permission on the same location simultaneously.

Instead, the full permission on the input field from the buffer must be split between these two processes. Therefore, a special join token predicate is introduced, which holds a fractional permission p. This permission specifies which part of the postJoin predicate can be obtained by the thread invoking the join method. The actual fraction of the join token that the joining thread currently holds is passed as an extra parameter to the join method, via the **given** clause.

However, to make this work, both predicates postJoin and join have to be splittable w.r.t. this permission. Splittable predicates are called *groups* and are declared with the **group** keyword. Formally, a predicate P, parametrised by permission q is a group if it respects the following equivalence $P(q)$ *-* $P(q/2)$ ** $P(q/2)$. That is, the group property transitively extends the splittability of atomic permissions over fractions to predicates.

The thread that creates the thread object obtains the join token, containing a full permission. Formally, the join token is defined as an abstract predicate without a body. It can be split and distributed as any other permission. The join token is created and returned upon thread construction, see line 14 in Lst. 3.

Example 3 continued. Inside the **main** method (Lst. 8), for each thread a Join token is created upon initialisation. The **main** method splits the ticket to join the sampler thread, and transfers each half to the processing threads, as specified by their preFork predicates. Additionally, the join tokens for the processing threads are transferred to the plotter.

Thus, the processing thread A (Lst. 6) uses a half join token to join the sampler thread, and to obtain half the resources released by the sampler thread.

```
public class Sampler extends Thread {
  //@ resource preFork = Perm(buffer.inp, 1);
  //@ group resource postJoin(frac p) = Perm(buffer.inp,p);
  Buffer buffer;

  // constructor

  //@ requires preFork(); ensures postJoin(1); // inherited from thread
  public void run(){
    //@ unfold preFork;
    // { Perm(buffer.inp,1) }
    sample();
    // { Perm(buffer.inp,1) }
    //@ fold postJoin(1) ;
  }

  //@ requires Perm(buffer.inp, 1); ensures Perm(buffer.inp, 1);
  private void sample(){
    // fill buffer.inp
  }
}
```

Lst. 5. Class Sampler

```
public class AFilter extends Thread {
  private Sampler sampler;
  private Buffer buffer;

  //@ resource preFork() = Perm(buffer.outa, 1) ** sampler.join(1/2);
  //@ group resource postJoin(frac p)=Perm(buffer.outa,p)**Perm(buffer.inp,p/2);

  // constructor

  //@ requires preFork(); ensures postJoin(1);
  public void run(){
    //@ unfold preFork; // { Perm(buffer.outa, 1) ** Join(sampler, 1/2) }
    sampler.join(); // { Perm(buffer.outa, 1) ** sampler.postJoin(1/2) }
    //@ unfold sampler.postJoin(1/2);
    // { Perm(buffer.outa, 1) ** Perm(buffer.inp, 1/2) }
    processA(); // { Perm(buffer.outa, 1) ** Perm(buffer.inp, 1/2) }
    //@ fold this.postJoin(1);
  }

  //@ requires Perm(buffer.outa, 1) ** Perm(buffer.inp, 1/2);
  //@ ensures Perm(buffer.outa, 1) ** Perm(buffer.inp, 1/2);
  private void processA(){/* reading buffer.inp and fill buffer.outa. */}
}
```

Lst. 6. Class AFilter

```
public class Plotter extends Thread {
    private Buffer buffer; private AFilter ta; private BFilter tb;
    //@ resource preFork() = ta.join(1) ** tb.join(1);
    //@ group resource postJoin(frac p) = buffer.state(p);

    //@ ensures start() ** Perm(buffer, 1) ** Perm(ta, 1) ** Perm(tb, 1);
    public Plotter(Buffer buf, AFilter fa, BFilter fb){ buffer=buf; ta=fa; tb=fb; }

    //@ requires preFork(); ensures postJoin(1);
    public void run(){
        //@ unfold preFork // { ta.join(1) ** tb.join(1) }
        ta.join(); // { ta.postJoin(1) ** tb.join(1) }
        tb.join(); // { ta.postJoin(1) ** tb.postJoin(1) }
        //@ unfold ta.postJoin(1); unfold tb.postJoin(1); fold buffer.state(1);
        // { buffer.state(1) }
        plot(); // { buffer.state(1) }
        //@ fold this.postJoin(1);
    }

    //@ requires buffer.state(1); ensures buffer.state(1);
    private void plot(){ /* plots the calculated points from the buffer */ }
}
```

Lst. 7. Class Plotter

```
//@ requires buf.state(1); ensures buf.state(1);
void main(){
    Sampler s=new Sampler(buf); // { s.join(1) ** buf.state(1) }
    //@ unfold buf.state(1); fold s.preFork()
    //{ s.preFork()**s.join(1)**Perm(buf.outa, 1)**Perm(buf.outb, 1) }
    AFilter a = new AFilter(buf, s);
    //{ s.preFork**s.join(1)**a.join(1)**Perm(buf.outa, 1)**Perm(buf.outb, 1) }
    //@ fold a.preFork;
    //{ s.preFork**a.preFork**s.join(1/2)**a.join(1)**Perm(buf.outb, 1) }
    BFilter b = new BFilter(buf, s);
    //{ s.preFork**a.preFork**s.join(1/2)**a.join(1)**b.join(1)**Perm(buf.outb, 1) }
    //@ fold b.preFork;
    //{ s.preFork**a.preFork**b.preFork**a.join(1)**b.join(1) }
    Plotter p = new Plotter(buf, a, b);
    //{ s.preFork**a.preFork**b.preFork**a.join(1)**b.join(1)**p.join(1) }
    //@ fold p.preFork; //{ s.preFork**a.preFork**b.preFork**p.preFork**p.join(1) }
    s.start(); a.start(); b.start(); p.start(); // { p.join(1) }
    p.join(); /* { p.postJoin(1) } */ //@ unfold p.postJoin(1);
    //@ fold buf.state(1);
}
```

Lst. 8. The main thread for the sampler, filters, and the plotter

Similarly, the plotter thread obtains a 1/2 read permission on inp and a write permission on outa by joining process A, and another 1/2 read permission on inp and a write permission on outb by joining process B. It then combines the read permissions into a write permission on inp to invoke its plot method.

2.6 Architecture of the VerCors Tool Set

The whole verification approach as outlined above is supported by our VerCors tool set. Rather than building yet another verifier, the VerCors tool leverages existing verifiers. That is, it is designed as a compiler that translates specified programs to a simpler language. These simplified programs are then verified by a third-party verifier. If there are errors then the error messages are converted to refer to the original input code.

Figure 1 shows the overall architecture of the tool. Its main input language is Java. For prototyping, we use the toy language PVL, which is a very simple object-oriented language that can express specified GPU kernels too. The C language family front-end is work-in-progress, but will support OpenCL in the near future. We mainly use Chalice [37], a verifier for an idealised concurrent programming language, as our

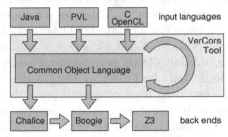

Fig. 1. VerCors tool architecture

back-end, but for sequential programs we also use the intermediate program verification language Boogie [38].

The implementation of the tool is highly modular. Everything is built around the Common Object Language data structure for abstract syntax trees. For Java and C, parsing happens in two passes. In the first pass an existing ANTLR4 [52] grammar is used to convert the programs into an AST while keeping all comments. In the second pass those comments that contain specifications are parsed using a separate grammar. This prevents us from having to maintain heavily modified grammars and makes it much easier to support multiple specification languages. The transformations to encode the program consist of many simple passes. Obviously, this impacts performance, but it is good for reusability and checkability of the passes. Our back-end framework allows switching between different versions, by setting up their command line execution using environment modules, a system for dynamic access to multiple versions of software modules[1].

3 Synchroniser Specifications

3.1 Reasoning about Synchronisers

Another way for threads to synchronise their behaviour is by using a lock. Locks provide a way to protect access to shared data. Only one thread at a time can

---

[1] http://modules.sourceforge.net

hold a lock, thus if threads only access the protected data while holding the lock, this means that there cannot be simultaneous access to the protected data. In Java, there are two ways to declare locks: any object can function as a lock, and be used via the **synchronized** statement. Alternatively, one can also define a lock object, and use the lock and unlock methods, declared in the Lock interface.

To reason about locks, we follow OHearn's approach for CSL and we associate a *resource invariant* with each lock, which specifies access to the data protected by the lock [46]. That is, the resource invariant makes the information about which data is protected by the lock explicit by naming the corresponding memory locations. A thread that acquires the lock, obtains the permissions specified in the resource invariant; when it releases the lock, it also has to release the permissions specified in the resource invariant. A particular challenge for Java is that locks might be *reentrant* [26], i.e., if a thread already holds a lock, it can obtain it once more. This does not change anything in the behaviour, except that to release the lock, it should be unlocked twice as well. Formally, a reentrancy level is maintained for the thread holding the lock. To ensure soundness, a thread should only obtain permissions when it acquires a lock for the first time, and it should only be forced to give up the permissions when it releases the lock for the last time. To manage this properly, the multi-set of locks that a thread holds has to be maintained in the specifications.

Originally, we added explicit verification rules for locks as primitives to the specification language (see [26]). However, this has the drawback that for every synchronisation mechanism, new rules have to be added to the logic. When looking into this in more detail, we realised that also for other synchronisation mechanisms, the notion of resource invariant is crucial to specify what resources can be redistributed between threads upon synchronisation.

Therefore, we took an alternative approach and we lifted the specification of synchronisation mechanisms to the API level of Java, i.e., we provide a *specification-based* approach to reason about locks. To make the approach applicable to different synchronisation mechanisms, we generalise the notion of a lock, i.e., we consider any routine that uses synchronisation to transfer a set of permissions as a *locking routine*. With our approach, we can specify arbitrary synchronisation mechanisms from the Java API in a similar way, and provide the ability to reason with these specifications modularly. We illustrate how our synchroniser specifications are used to verify code using the synchroniser.

In a separate line of work, we have derived program logic rules for atomic operations set, get and compareAndSwap as a synchronisation primitive [1]. We can use these specifications to show that (simplified versions of) Java's reference implementations of the various synchronisers indeed respect our specifications. For more information about these verifications, we refer to our PDP 2014 paper about synchroniser specifications [2].

3.2   Initialisation of Resource Invariants

A lock can only be used when it has been initialised, i.e., the access permissions specified in the resource invariant are stored "into" the lock. This ensures that

```
  //@ ghost boolean initialized = false;
2 //@ group resource initialized(frac p) = PointsTo(initialized, p/2, true);
  //@ requires inv(1) ** PointsTo(initialized, 1, false);
4 //@ ensures initialized(1);
  public void commit();
```

Lst. 9. Specifications for lock initialisation

the resources can be passed to a user upon synchronisation without introducing new resources. Initialisation of the resource invariant is done in the same way for all synchronisation mechanisms: class Object declares a ghost boolean field initialized that tracks information about the initialisation state of the resource invariant. Newly created locks are not initialised; the specification-only method commit, see Lst. 9, can be used by the client code to irreversibly initialise the lock. This means that the resources protected by the lock, as specified in the resource invariant predicate inv, become shared. To achieve this, commit requires the client to provide the complete resource invariant inv(1), together with an exclusive permission to change initialized (line 3). The method consumes the invariant ("stores it into the lock"). Moreover, it ensures that initialized cannot be changed any more by consuming part of the permission to access this field, effectively making it read-only (lines 2 and 4). For convenience, the result of commit is encapsulated in a single resource predicate initialized, which can be passed around and used as a permission ticket for locking operations, see below. The default location for the call to commit is at the end of the constructor of the synchronisation object. More complex lock implementations (which are not discussed in this paper) may require moving this call to another location in the program.

The actual resource invariant is typically decided by the user of the synchronisation class, therefore it is passed as a class parameter with the type (frac -> resource). For example, given a two-point coordinate class, such as in Lst. 1, using a ReentrantLock, the resource invariant that protects the x coordinate (only) is specified with xInv, which is passed both as a type parameter and during instantiation of the lock. By adding it as a type parameter it is specified that the declared local variable or field can only contain lock that use this particular invariant. By adding the argument during instantiation and object that has this particular invariant is created. For example:

```
//@ resource xInv(frac p) = Perm(x, p);
Lock/*@<xInv, ...>@*/ xLock=new ReentrantLock/*@< xInv >@*/();
```

As mentioned in Sect. 2, in our specifications such parameters (of which there will be more, hence the "..." above) are received through parameters specified with the **given** keyword.

3.3 Lock Hierarchy Specification

The synchronisation classes in the Lock hierarchy in the concurrency package are devoted to resource locking scenarios where either full (write) access is given

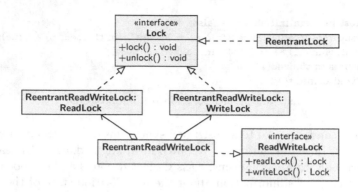

Fig. 2. The hierarchy of locks in the java.util.concurrent package

to one particular thread or partial (read) access is given to an indefinite number of threads. The complete hierarchy of locks is depicted in Fig. 2. We first discuss the specification of the Lock interface, and then we proceed with specifications of different lock implementations.

Lock Interface Specification. As explained above, our specification approach of the synchronisation mechanisms is inspired by the logic of Haack et al. [26]. However, we cannot just translate the rules from [26] into method specifications of the Lock interface, because the Lock interface can be used in different and wider settings than considered by Haack et al. In particular, Lock implementations may be non-reentrant; they may be used to synchronise non-exclusive access; and they may be used in *coupled* pairs to change between shared and exclusive mode (see the read-write lock specification below). Therefore, as an extension to the work of Haack et al., for the specification given in Lst. 10 the following aspects are considered:

- The locks use boolean parameters isExclusive and isReentrant, which can be correspondingly instantiated by implementations (line 2).
- To allow non-exclusive synchronisation, resource invariants have to be groups (line 1), see Sect. 2.5.
- For the non-exclusive locking scenarios, the client program has to record the amount of the resource fraction that was obtained during locking, so that the lock can reclaim the complete resource fraction upon unlocking. This information is passed around in the held predicate, which holds this fraction (line 5) (similar in spirit to the join predicate, as discussed in Section 2.5. This is purposely not declared as a group, so that clients are obliged to return their whole share of resources. The held predicate is returned during locking in exchange for the initialized predicate which is temporarily revoked for the time that the lock is acquired.

```
   //@ given group (frac -> resource) inv;
 2 //@ given boolean isExclusive, isReentrant;
   public interface Lock {
 4    //@ group resource initialized(frac p);
      //@ resource held(frac p);

 6

      //@ ghost public final Object parent;

 8

      /*@ given bag<Object> S, frac p;
10       requires LockSet(S) ** !(S contains this) ** initialized(p);
         requires parent != null ==> !(S contains parent);
12       ensures LockSet(this::parent::S) **
           inv(isExclusive ? 1 : p) ** held(p);
14    also
         requires isReentrant ** LockSet(S) **
16         (S contains this) ** held(p);
         ensures LockSet(this::S) ** held(p); @*/
18    void lock();

20    /*@ given bag<Object> S, frac p;
         requires LockSet(this::S) ** (S contains this) ** held(p);
22       ensures LockSet(S) ** held(p);
       also
24       requires held(p) ** inv(isExclusive ? 1 : p);
         requires LockSet(this::parent::S) ** !(S contains this);
26       ensures LockSet(S) ** initialized(p); @*/
      void unlock();
28 }
```

Lst. 10. Specification of the Lock interface

- For situations where several locks share the same resource and are effectively coupled as one lock, we need to ensure that only one lock is locked at a time. The coupling itself is realised by holding a reference to the parent object that maintains the coupled locks (line 7). The exclusive use of coupled locks is ensured by storing and checking this parent object in the set of currently held locks.
- A separate specification case is given for reentrant locking (when isReentrant is true).

As a result, in the specification of method lock() in Lst. 10, given the multi-set of locks, i.e., **bag<Object>** S, when the lock is acquired for the first time (lines 9–13), the locking thread gets permissions from the lock. If the lock is reentrant, and the thread already holds the lock (lines 15–17), then no new permission is gained, only the multi-set of locks held by the current thread is extended with this lock (where :: denotes bag addition). For coupled locks (where the parent is not null) the presence of the parent in the lock set is also checked and recorded, to

```
   //@ given group (frac -> resource) inv;
2  //@ given boolean reentrant;
   interface ReadWriteLock {
4    //@ group resource initialized(frac p);

6    //@ given frac p;
     //@ requires initialized(p);
8    //@ ensures \result.parent == this ** \result.initialized(p);
     /*@ pure @*/ Lock /*@< inv, false, reentrant >@*/ readLock();
10
     //@ given frac p;
12   //@ requires initialized(p);
     //@ ensures \result.parent == this ** \result.initialized(p);
14   /*@ pure @*/ Lock /*@< inv, true, reentrant >@*/ writeLock();
   }
```

Lst. 11. Specification of the ReadWriteLock interface

prevent parallel use of the coupled locks. The specification of method unlock()
in Lst. 10 describes the reverse process: if the multi-set of locks contains the
specific lock only once (lines 24–26), then this means the return of permissions
to the lock (i.e., inv does not hold in the postcondition) according to the held
predicate; otherwise (lines 20–22), the thread keeps the permissions, but one
occurrence of the lock is removed from the multi-set.

ReentrantLock Specification. Class ReentrantLock implements the Lock interface as an exclusive, reentrant lock. Thus, it inherits all specifications from
Lock and appropriately instantiates the two class parameters isReentrant and
isExclusive both to **true**:

```
//@ given group (frac -> resource) inv;
class ReentrantLock implements Lock /*@< inv, true, true >@*/ {
```

ReadWriteLock Specification. The ReadWriteLock is not a lock itself, but
a wrapper of two coupled Lock objects: one of them provides exclusive access for writing (WriteLock), while the other allows concurrent reading by several threads (ReadLock). The two classes are commonly implemented as inner
classes of the class that implements the ReadWriteLock interface (see Fig. 2 on
page 188). The two locks are intended to protect the same memory resources.
Hence our specifications in Lst. 11 state that the two getter methods (declared
as **pure**) for obtaining the two locks return a lock object with the same resource
inv, but which are non-exclusive (line 9) and exclusive (line 14), respectively. The
aggregate read-write lock has to be initialised itself (lines 7 and 12). Further,
using the return value keyword \result, we state in the respective postconditions
of the getter methods (lines 8 and 13) that the obtained locks are initialised and

hence can be acquired, and that they have the same parent object, which is an instance of the class implementing the ReadWriteLock interface.

Example 4. In this example we show how the specification of ReadWriteLock helps us to reason about a single-producer multiple-consumer application. Assume an application where one single producer produces data to be used by two separate consumer threads. The producer implemented as a Producer class obtains the write lock and then exclusively accesses the shared data field:

```
//@ given group (frac -> resource) pcinv;
public class Producer extends Thread {
    private final Lock/*@<pcinv, true, true>@*/ lock;
    private final SProdMCons example;

    //@ given frac p; requires lock.initialized(p); ensures lock.initialized(p);
    public void produce(){
        // { lock.initialized(p) }
        lock.lock(); // { lock.inv(1) ** lock.held(p) }
        //@ unfold lock.inv(1);
        // { Perm(example.data, 1) ** lock.held(p) } // from pcinv
        sample(); // { Perm(example.data, 1) ** lock.held(p) }
        //@ fold lock.inv(1);
        lock.unlock(); // { lock.initialized(p) }
    }
    // method run
}
```

Then, each consumer is trying to obtain a fractional permission of the shared data to use the value written by the producer:

```
//@ given group (frac -> resource) pcinv;
public class Consumer extends Thread {
    private final Lock/*@<pcinv, false, true>@*/ lock;
    private final SProdMCons example;
    private boolean flag; private int value;

    //@ given frac p; requires lock.initialized(p) ** Perm(this.value,1);
    //@ ensures lock.initialized(p) ** Perm(this.value,1);
    public void consume(){
        // { lock.initialized(p) }
        lock.lock(); // { lock.inv(p) ** lock.held(p) }
        //@ unfold lock.inv(p);
        // { Perm(example.data, p) ** lock.held(p) } // from pcinv
        this.value = example.data;
        if( flag == this.example.PRINT) print( );
        if( flag == this.example.LOG) log( );
        //@ fold lock.inv(p); // { lock.held(p) ** lock.inv(p) }
        lock.unlock(); // { lock.initialized(p) }
    }
    // methods run, print and log
}
```

The producer and consumers are then combined together in the following class:

```
public class SProdMCons {
  //@ group resource pcinv(frac p) = Perm(data, p);
  public final boolean PRINT = true, LOG = false;
  public int data;
  private ReadWriteLock/*@<pcinv, true>@*/ rwl;

  void main(){
    rwl = new ReentrantReadWriteLock/*@< pcinv >@*/();

    Producer producer =
        new Producer/*@< pcinv >@*/(this, rwl.writeLock());
    Consumer printer =
        new Consumer/*@< pcinv >@*/(this, PRINT, rwl.readLock());
    Consumer log =
        new Consumer/*@< pcinv >@*/(this, LOG, rwl.readLock());

    producer.start(); printer.start(); log.start();
    producer.join(); printer.join(); log.join();
  }
}
```

3.4   Semaphore Specification

To illustrate that similar specifications can be used to describe the behaviour of other synchronisers as well, we briefly discuss the specification of class **Semaphore**, which represents a *counting semaphore*. It is used to control threads' accesses to a shared resource, by restricting the number of threads that can access a resource simultaneously. Each semaphore is provided with a property *permits*, that represents the maximum number of threads that can access the protected resource. Accessing the resource must be preceded by acquiring a permit from the semaphore. A semaphore with n permits allows a maximum of n threads to access the same resource simultaneously. If n threads are holding a permit, a new thread that tries to acquire a permit blocks until it is notified that a permit is released.

When initialised with more than 1 permit, a semaphore closely corresponds to a non-reentrant **ReadLock**, but with the number of threads accessing the shared resource explicitly stated and controlled. When initialised with 1 permit, it provides exclusive access, and behaves the same as a non-reentrant **WriteLock**. Therefore, the specification of the semaphore is a stripped-down version of the **Lock** specification, see Lst. 12. In particular, semaphores are never reentrant, and they are not used in coupled combinations. Moreover, since the maximum number of threads that can access the shared resource is predefined with the **permits** field, we can also limit ourselves to simply providing each acquiring thread with an equal split of 1/**permits** of the resource invariant (lines 11 and 14). Note also that there is no access permission required for the **permits** field as it is declared to be final and hence can never change after initialisation.

```
   //@ given group (frac -> resource) inv;
2  public class Semaphore {
       //@ resource held(frac p) = initialized(p);
4      //@ ghost final int permits;

6      //@ requires inv(1) ** permits > 0;
       //@ ensures initialized(1) ** this.permits == permits;
8      public Semaphore(int permits);

10     //@ given frac p; requires initialized(p);
       //@ ensures inv(1/permits) ** held(p);
12     public void acquire();

14     //@ given frac p; requires inv(1/permits) ** held(p);
       //@ ensures initialized(p);
16     public void release();
   }
```

Lst. 12. Specification of the Semaphore class

4   Reasoning about Concurrent Class Invariants

In addition to proving the absence of data races and that data is correctly protected by a synchroniser, we also wish to show properties about the state of the program. In a concurrent setting, many program state properties become *unstable*, i.e., they can be invalidated by other threads. However, this section shows that also in a concurrent setting it is possible to reason about class invariants, restricting the reachable states of an object.

4.1   Concurrent Class Invariants

In essence, a class invariant expresses a property that should always hold for every object of a given class. Concretely, it is defined as a boolean predicate that should be continuously maintained. Consider class Point in Lst. 1 with the two fields x and y. As mentioned, we specified an invariant property that the point object always is in the first or third quarter of the Cartesian space:

//@ invariant ((x >= 0 && y >= 0) || (x <= 0 && y <= 0));

We could also specify different invariant properties, such as that the relation x + y >= 0 should always hold for every live Point object in the program:

//@ invariant I: (x + y >= 0);

Notice that we allow to explicitly name invariants (here the invariant is named I) as we later need to refer to them symbolically. Although the primary definition of a class invariant is a property that holds *always*, in practice this is impossible, unless the invariant expresses a relation over non-mutable locations. Otherwise, any change of a location might *break* the invariant, i.e., invalidate the correctness of the invariant predicate. Therefore, a verification technique should allow temporarily breaking of a class invariant at certain *invisible* program states.

In a sequential setting, the standard verification technique suggests that class invariants must hold in every pre- and poststate of a public method [43]. The verifier may assume that the class invariant holds at the beginning of every method, and has an obligation to prove that it still holds at the end of the method. In particular, only these states are *visible* states in a program, and any *breaking* (invalidating) of the invariant in a method's internal state is allowed. Therefore, a class invariant specified for a given class is treated as if it is implicitly added in the pre- and postcondition of every method in this class.

However, in a concurrent program, this approach can not be directly applied. An internal method's state in which a thread invalidates an invariant, might be a prestate of a method (a *visible state*) for another thread. Therefore, assuming the validity of a class invariant at the entrance of a method would be unsound. A technique for verifying concurrent class invariants should allow a thread to break a class invariant only in a state that is *invisible* for the other program threads, so that they would not be able to observe the invalidated state of the object.

To get an intuition of *visible states* in a concurrent program, consider the move method in the Point class in which both properties x and y are modified.

```
void move(){
    lockx.lock(); // lockx protects the location x
      x--;
    lockx.unlock();
    locky.lock(); // locky protects the location y
      y++;
    locky.unlock();
}
```

Clearly, having both updates protected by a lock, the scenario is data-race free. However, in the state after the release of the lock lockx, the invariant I may be invalidated, while both x and y are accessible by another thread: the invalidated state of the Point object is then observable/visible. This problem is sometimes called a *high-level data race* [4]. A class invariants verifier should detect an error in this scenario, reporting a visible state in which an invariant can be broken. The correct scenario could be protecting both updates with a single lock:

```
 lock.lock();
    x--;
    y++;
 lock.unlock();
```

In this way, the invalidated state is *hidden* for the other active program threads.

Further, we discuss the *class invariant protocol* for verifying concurrent class invariants. The protocol explains the conditions under which a class invariant may be safely broken, conditions that allow to assume that an invariant holds, and the obligations when the invariant's validity must be proved. The technique is modular and is built on top of our permission-based separation logic.

4.2   Class Invariant Protocol

We consider that class invariants express properties over instance class fields only. Therefore, we refer to an invariant I defined in a class C through a specific object v of class C, and we write $v.I$. The set of locations referred to by an invariant $v.I$ is called a *footprint of $v.I$*, denoted $\mathsf{fp}(v.I)$.

To define a class invariant, special *state formulas* are used: these formulas express only properties over the shared state and are free of permission expressions. Note that the class invariant I defined in the Point class contains neither PointsTo nor Perm predicate. This contrasts standard permission-based separation logic, where every location in a formula must be *framed* by a positive permission.

Assuming a Class Invariant. The control of the validity of a class invariant $v.I$ is kept by a predicate/token $\mathsf{holds}(v.I, 1)$. The token is produced after the creation of the valid object v, and afterwards it might be distributed among different threads. Thus, the holds token is a group, i.e., the equivalence mentioned in Sect. 4 holds:

$$\mathsf{holds}(v.I, \pi) \mathbin{*\!\!-\!\!*} \mathsf{holds}(v.I, \pi/2) \mathbin{**} \mathsf{holds}(v.I, \pi/2)$$

The intuitive meaning of this predicate is the following: when a thread holds (part of) this token, it may assume that the invariant $v.I$ holds. This means that at the same time several threads may rely on the validity of the invariant (each of them holding part of the invariant's holds token). The invariant is then *stable* and no other thread may break it. The following verification rule states that the property expressed by a class invariant can be used under the condition that (part of) the holds token is held:

$$\frac{\{\mathsf{holds}(v.I, \pi) \mathbin{**} v.I\}c\{F\}}{\{\mathsf{holds}(v.I, \pi)\}c\{F\}}$$

Example 5. Lst. 13 shows how a class invariant may be used for verifying a client code. The main thread creates initially a valid Point object s, for which the invariant s.I holds (s.x + s.y >=0), and obtains the token $\mathsf{holds}(s.I, 1)$ (line 3). Then, a set of new threads are forked (lines 5, 6), and each thread gets a reference to s and part of the holds token. Each forked thread has a task to create a sequence of new points at specific locations calculated from the location of s (lines 19–23). To prove that each new Point p is a valid object (p.x + p.y >=0) (line 21), each thread uses the class invariant s.I, which is guaranteed by the token $\mathsf{holds}(s.I, \pi)$.

```
   class DrawPoints {
2    void main(){
       Point s = new Point(0, 0); // holds(s.I, 1) token is produced
4      for (int k = 1; k<=10; k++) {
         Task t = new Task(s, k);
6        t.fork(); // each t gets part of holds token
       }
8      // join all Task threads
     }
10 }

12 class Task {
     Point s; int k;
14   // ... constructors

16   //@ given frac p; requires holds(s.I. p) ** ... ;
     //@ ensures holds(s.I. p) ** ... ;
18   void run(){
       for (int i = 1; i < 10; i ++) {
20       // s.I holds (because of the holds token)
         Point p = new Point(s.x + i, s.y + k); // use s.I to verify p.I
22       draw(p);
       }
24   }
   }
```

Lst. 13. Using a class invariant for verifying a client class

Breaking a Class Invariant. A class invariant may be temporarily broken by a specific thread, under the condition that the invalid state of the object is not observable by any other thread. To this end, breaking is allowed in explicitly specified parts of the program. The developer is expected to mark the program segment where breaking of an invariant might happen with two specification commands: the command **unpack**(v.I) indicates the start of the segment, while the **pack**(v.I) specification command is required to specify the end of the segment. We call this *an unpacked segment*. In the example of the Point class, both updates should be wrapped in an unpacked segment.

All changes in the unpacked segment should stay hidden for the other program threads. To ensure that no other thread might assume the validity of the invariant $v.I$ within the unpacked segment, the unpack($v.I$) command consumes the full holds($v.I, 1$) token, which ensures that no part of this token is still owned by another thread. The unpack($v.I$) command at the same time produces a new predicate, the unpacked($v.I, 1$) token, which serves as a license for the thread to break the invariant $v.I$. Holding the unpacked token is a required condition for assigning to any location that appears in the footprint of the invariant.

```
//@requires holds(this.I, 1); ensures holds(this.I, 1);
void move() {
    lock.lock(); // { Perm(x, 1) ** Perm(y, 1); }
    // { Perm(x, 1) ** Perm(y, 1) ** holds(this.I, 1) }
    // { Perm(x, 1) ** Perm(y, 1) ** holds(this.I, 1) ** this.I }
    // { Perm(x, 1) ** Perm(y, 1) ** holds(this.I, 1) ** x + y >= 0 }
    //@ unpack(this.I);
    // { Perm(x, 1) ** Perm(y, 1) ** unpacked(this.I, 1) ** x + y >= 0 }
    x--;
    // { Perm(x, 1) ** Perm(y, 1) ** unpacked(this.I, 1) ** x + y >= -1 }
    y++;
    // { Perm(x, 1) ** Perm(y, 1) ** unpacked(this.I, 1) ** x + y >= 0 }
    // { Perm(x, 1) ** Perm(y, 1) ** unpacked(this.I, 1) ** this.I }
    //@ pack(this.I);
    //@ { Perm(x, 1) ** Perm(y, 1) ** holds(this.I, 1) }
    lock.unlock();
    // { holds(this.I, 1); }
}
```

Lst. 14. An unpacked segment

Once all updates are done, the running thread must reestablish the validity of $v.I$ and call the pack($v.I$) command, which trades the unpacked($v.I$, 1) token for the holds($v.I$, 1) token. The unpack($v.I$) command is always followed by pack($v.I$) within the same method and executed by the same thread. This thread is called *a holder* of the unpacked segment. Lst. 14 shows the specified move method with the proof outline.

Restrictions to Unpacked Segments. As explained above, the unpacked segment may contain states in which a certain object is invalidated. Therefore, all changes in the segment must not be publicly exposed, i.e., they should not be observable for any thread except for the *holder* of the segment. Because of this, within an unpacked segment it is forbidden for the running thread to release permissions and to make them accessible to other threads. In particular, only safe commands are allowed, i.e., commands that exclude any lock-related operation (acquiring, releasing or committing a lock). Note that in the example in Lst. 14, the lock is acquired and released outside the unpacked segment. A call to a method m is a safe command if the called method m itself is safe, i.e., a method composed of safe commands only. A safe method should be specified with the optional modifier **safe**.

Forking a safe thread, i.e., a thread with a /*@safe@*/run() method, within an unpacked segment is also allowed, under the condition that the thread must be joined before the unpacked segment ends. These threads are called *local to the segment*. A safe thread may further fork other safe threads. The breaking token might then be shared among all local threads of the unpacked segment, and thus, they might all update different locations of the invariant footprint in parallel. For this purpose, the unpacked token is also a splittable token. This

```
void move(){
  //@ unpack(this.I);
  lock.lock(); // invalid call (must happen before unpacking)
  t.fork(); // allowed if t is a safe thread
  updateY(); // allowed if updateY is a safe method
  lock.unlock(); // invalid call, must happen after packing
  t.join(); // t is a safe thread, thus joining must be before packing
  //@ pack(this.I);
}
```

Lst. 15. Restrictions to an unpacked segment

means that breaking an invariant $v.I$ does not require full unpacked token, but for any $\pi > 0$, the predicate unpacked$(v.I, \pi)$ is valid breaking permission. The example on Lst. 15 shows the restrictions in an unpacked segment.

Object Initialisation. Object initialisation (the object constructor) is divided into two phases: (1) *object construction* creates an *empty* object v (all v's fields get a default value), and gives the running thread write permission for each of v's fields. (2) the init method follows mandatorily after object construction, where object fields are initialised. After this phase, the object may be used.

For every invariant $v.I$ the unpacked$(v.I, 1)$ token is produced for the first time at the end of the first phase of v's initialisation: the created object v is then still empty and might be in an invalid state in which some of its invariants are broken. This means that after this first phase, every invariant of the object v is in an unpacked state.

After the second phase and the initialisation of all v's object fields, the object v should be in a valid state. For every invariant $v.I$, the pack$(v.I)$ specification command is called by default at the end of the init method. Hence, at the end of v's initialisation, the invariant $v.I$ is in a packed state. We show the initialisation of a Point object in Lst. 16.

To conclude, we summarise the rules that define the invariant protocol:

R1. (*Assuming*) A thread t may assume (use) a class invariant $v.I$ if t holds the predicate holds$(v.I, \pi)$, $\pi > 0$.

R2. (*Breaking*) A thread t may write on a location $p.f$ if apart from holding a write permission to $p.f$, it holds a breaking token unpacked$(v.I, \pi)$, $\pi > 0$ for each invariant $v.I$ that refers to $p.f$, i.e., $p.f \in$ fp$(v.I)$.

R3. (*Reestablishing*) An invariant $v.I$ must have been reestablished when pack$(v.I)$ is executed.

R4. (*Exchanging tokens*) The token unpacked$(v.I, 1)$ is produced at v's construction; commands unpack$(v.I)$ and pack$(v.I)$ exchange the holds$(v.I, 1)$ token for the unpacked$(v.I, 1)$ token, and vice versa.

```
class Point {
    int x, y;
    Lock lock;
    //@ invariant I: (x + y >= 0);

    //@ ensures Perm(x, 1) ** Perm(y, 1) ** unpacked(I, 1);
    public Point() { /* effectively calls init */ }

    //@ requires Perm(x, 1) ** Perm(y, 1) ** unpacked(I, 1);
    //@ ensures holds(I, 1);
    void init() {
        x = 0; y = 0;
        //@ resource rinv = Perm(x, 1) ** Perm(y, 1);
        lock = new Lock/*@< rinv >@*/();
        //@ pack(I);
        // { Perm(x, 1) ** Perm(y, 1) ** holds(I, 1) }
        lock.commit(); // permissions are transferred to the lock
        // { holds(I, 1) }
    }
}
```

Lst. 16. Object Initialisation

4.3   Modular Verification

To be practically useful, the verification technique should be *modular*. Rule **R2**, listed above, requires a breaking token for all invariants that refer to $p.f$. However, in the context (class) where the assignment happens, not all invariants in the program are known. Therefore, it is impossible for the verifier to check modularly whether rule **R2** is properly satisfied.

Consider the example in Lst. 17: the class Line contains references of two Point objects (the **rep** modifiers in lines 2 and 3 are discussed later). The invariant I1 in the class Line refers to fields in p1 and p2. This means that assigning to a field x or y of a Point object may break an invariant of an existing Line object: therefore, this assignment should be allowed if the invariant I1 is also unpacked. When verifying the Point class, the verifier should be aware of the Line class, and possibly other classes that refer to the fields x and y in the Point class. Thus, it is impossible to verify the Point class in isolation.

This problem with modularity is not typical for concurrent programs, but also manifests itself when verifying class invariants in sequential programs. Several solutions are suggested for modular verification of sequential invariants [44,5,42,20]. Mostly they use the restrictions from Müller's *ownership type system* [19].

Using the restrictions of the ownership type system can also help to provide modular verification of concurrent class invariants. Below we first shortly discuss the ownership-type system and then we explain the verification technique for concurrent class invariants based on this type system. In general, in rule **R2**, to assign a location $p.f$, only the invariants of the object p are explicitly checked,

```
   class Line {
2    /*@ rep @*/ Point p1;
     /*@ rep @*/ Point p2;
4
     //@ invariant I1: (p1.x + p2.x <= 10 ** p1.y + p2.y <= 10);
6
     //@ requires unpacked(I1, 1) ** ... (permissions) ...;
8    //@ ensures holds(I1, 1) ** holds(p1.I, 1) ** holds(p2.I, 1);
     //@ ensures ... (permissions) ...;
10   void init(){
       p1 = new /*@ rep @*/ Point(0, 0);
12     p2 = new /*@ rep @*/ Point(0, 5);
       //@ pack(this.I1);
14   }

16   //@ requires holds(this.I1, 1) ** holds(p1.I, 1);
     //@ requires Perm(p1.x, 1) ** Perm(p1.y, 1);
18   //@ ensures holds(this.I1, 1) ** holds(p1.I, 1);
     //@ ensures Perm(p1.x, 1) ** Perm(p1.y, 1);
20   void moveP1() {
       //@ unpack(this.I1);
22     p1.move();
       //@ pack(this.I1); // trades the unpacked token for holds token
24   }

26 class Point{
     int x;
28   int y;
     //@ invariant I: (x + y >= 0);
30
     //@ given frac p;
32   //@ requires Perm(x, 1) ** Perm(y, 1) ** holds(I, p);
     //@ ensures Perm(x, 1) ** Perm(y, 1) ** holds(I, p);
34   /*@ safe @*/ void move() {
       //@ unpack(this.I);
36     x--;
       y++;
38     //@ pack(this.I);
     }
40 }
```

Lst. 17. Modular verification

while the technique guarantees that the unpacked token is implicitly held for all other necessary class invariants.

Ownership-Based Types. The ownership type system forces all objects in the heap to be organised in a structural way and it applies certain restrictions to the operations applicable to each object reference. In particular, each object is required to respect the concept of ownership topology, where objects are organised in a hierarchy. Each object has one owner, either the root of the tree, or another object in the heap. Each ancestor of an object p in the tree is p's *transitive owner*. The developer decides the position of an object in the tree by attaching an appropriate modifier from the set {**rep**, **peer**, **rd** } when the object is created. This modifier becomes a part of the type of the object reference, which shows the relation between the object and the **this** object. For example, if a new Point object is created with the **rep** modifier,

/*@ **rep** @*/ Point point = new /*@ **rep** @*/ Point();

the type **rep** indicates that the new object is owned by **this** object. The type **peer** is used when creating an object that should have the same owner as the **this** object, while **rd** is used for any other object. The type is actually attached to the object reference, because it shows the relation of the object in the context of the **this** object. If another reference of the same Point object is used in a different context, that reference would have another modifier, calculated appropriately according to the new context. For example, if the object a owns b, while b owns c, the type of a reference of c in the context of the object b is **rep**, while the type of a reference of c in the context of a is **rd**.

Having all objects in the heap structurally organised, the ownership type system imposes certain restrictions: writing to a field $p.f$ or a call to a *non-pure* method (a method with side-effects) with a receiver p is not allowed if the ownership type of the reference p is **rd**. In this way, each object controls all updates that happen in its transitively owned objects. This guarantees the following rule:

> **RO** If a field $p.f$ is modified in a method m, for each transitive owner o of p, the call stack contains a method invocation where o is a receiver.

Verification Technique via Ownership Types. To use the ownership-type system for modular verification of class invariants, additionally, the definition of a class invariant is restricted such that:

> **RCI** A class invariant $v.I$ may only express properties over fields of the object v, or fields of object that is transitively owned by v.

From the rule **RCI**, we can observe the following: a location $p.f$ may be referred to by an invariant of the object p or of an object v that is a transitive owner of p. Moreover, according to **RO**, the assignment of $p.f$ is preceded by a method call where v is a receiver. These two observations give the right to define the following: when assigning to a location $p.f$, it is enough to require the unpacked token only for the invariants of the object p ($p.I$) that refer to $p.f$. If any other invariant $v.I$ refers to $p.f$, then v is a transitive owner of p and the check that the actual thread holds the unpacked token for $v.I$ is a requirement of the method call where object v is a receiver.

More precisely, rule **R2** listed above is replaced with the following two rules:

R2.1. A precondition for assigning a value to a field $p.f$ requires a token unpacked($p.I, \pi$), $\pi > 0$, for each invariant I of the object p that refers to $p.f$.

R2.2. A precondition for invoking a method m that assigns a field $p.f$ requires the token unpacked(this.I, π), $\pi > 0$, for each invariant I of the **this** object that refers to $p.f$.

Example 6. In the example in Lst. 17 on page 200, each Line object line owns the objects line.p1 and line.p2. This hierarchy allows the invariant I1 in the Line class to express properties over fields in p1 and p2. The updates in the move method in the Point class (line 34) might break the invariant I defined in the class Point, as well as the invariant I1 in the Line class. Therefore, before these updates happen, both I and I1 have to be in an unpacked state. The invariant I is required to be unpacked in the method move, before the updates of x and y (line 35), while I1 has to be unpacked before the call to the move method in the Line class (line 21).

It is important to note that permissions for the updating fields, p1.x and p1.y, must be obtained outside the unpacked segments of both invariants I and I1. No locks are then acquired in the move method, and thus the method is safe (line 34). If these permissions were obtained through a lock inside the move method in the Point class (as in Lst. 14), the Line class could not be verified: the unpacked segment in the moveP1 method would then contain a method call to an unsafe method.

With this approach the verifier may perform both **R2.1** and **R2.2** having only the knowledge of the context where the assignment happens. This makes the approach modular. Although the method is applicable to ownership-based type systems only, this is not considered as a serious restriction, because ownership is a common and natural concept for organisation of objects in a program.

5   Reasoning about GPU Kernels

Above, we have considered how to reason about multithreaded Java programs, running on one or multiple CPUs. However, to achieve an increase in performance, modern hardware also uses different computing paradigms. GPUs, graphical processing units, which were initially designed to support computer graphics, are more and more used also for other programming tasks, leading to the development of the area of GPGPU (General Purpose GPU) programming.

```
kernel demo {
  global int[gsize] a,b;
  void main(){
    a[tid]:=tid;
    barrier(global);
    b[tid]:=a[(tid+1) mod gsize];
  }
}
```

Lst. 18. Basic example kernel

Until 2006 GPGPU programming was mainly done in CUDA [34], a proprietary GPU programming language from NVIDIA. However, recently a new platform-independent, low-level programming language standard for GPGPU programming, OpenCL [47], emerged. As a result, GPUs are now used in many different fields, including media processing [18], medical imaging [57] and eye-tracking [45].

The main characteristic of GPU kernels is that each kernel constitutes a massive number of parallel threads. All threads execute the same instruction, but each thread operates on its own share of memory. Barriers are used as the main synchronisation primitive between threads in a kernel.

This section shows how permission-based separation logic also can be used to reason about OpenCL kernels.

5.1 GPU Architecture

Before presenting our verification technique, we first briefly discuss the main characteristics of the GPU architecture (for more details, see the OpenCL specification [35]).

A GPU runs hundreds of threads simultaneously. All threads within the same *kernel* execute the same instruction, but on different data: the *Single Instruction Multiple Data (SIMD)* execution model. GPU kernels are invoked by a *host* program, typically running on a CPU. Threads are grouped into *work groups*. GPUs have three different memory regions: *global*, *local*, and *private* memory. Private memory is local to a single thread, local memory is shared between threads within a work group, and global memory is accessible to all threads in a kernel, and to the host program. Threads within a single work group can synchronise by using a *barrier*: all threads block at the barrier until all other threads have also reached this barrier. A barrier instruction comes with a flag to indicate whether it synchronises global or local memory, or both. Notice that threads within different work groups cannot synchronise.

Example 7. Lst. 18 shows the code of a kernel that initialises a global array b in such a way that position i contains $i + 1$ modulo the length of the array. It does so in a complicated way. Each thread first assign its thread id tid to position i

of a temporary array a. Then all threads wait for each other (which means that this code can only run for a single working group) and then position i of array b is assigned by reading position $i + 1$ modulo the working group size of array a. If the barrier would be removed, there would be a data race on a[i].

5.2 Verification of GPGPU Kernels

As mentioned, permission-based separation logic also is suitable to reason about kernel programs. When reasoning about kernel programs, we can prove that a kernel (i) does not have data races, and (ii) that it respects its functional behaviour specification. Kernels can exhibit two kinds of data races: (i) parallel threads within a work group can access the same location, either in global or in local memory, and this access is not ordered by an appropriate barrier, and (ii) parallel threads within different work groups can access the same locations in global memory. With our logic, we can verify the absence of both kinds of data races.

Concretely, for each kernel we specify all the permissions that are needed to execute the kernel. Upon invocation of the kernel, these permissions are transferred from the host code to the kernel. Within the kernel, the available permissions are distributed over the threads. Every time a barrier is reached, a barrier specification specifies how the permissions are redistributed over the threads (similar to the barrier specifications of Hobor et al. [29]). The barrier specification also specifies functional pre- and postconditions for the barrier. Essentially this specifies how knowledge about the global state upon reaching the barrier is spread over the different threads.

Traditionally, separation logic considers a single heap for the program. However, to reason about kernels, we make an explicit distinction between global and local memory. To support our reasoning method, kernels, work groups and threads are specified as follows:

- The *kernel specification* is a triple $(K_{res}, K_{pre}, K_{post})$. The resource formula K_{res} specifies all resources in global memory that are passed from the host program to the kernel, while K_{pre} and K_{post} specify the functional kernel pre- and postcondition, respectively. K_{pre} and K_{post} have to be framed by K_{res}. An invocation of a kernel by a host program is correct if the host program holds the necessary resources and fulfils the preconditions.
- The *group specification* is a triple $(G_{res}, G_{pre}, G_{post})$, where G_{res} specifies the resources in global memory that can be used by the threads in this group, and G_{pre} and G_{post} specify the functional pre- and postcondition, respectively, again framed by G_{res}. Notice that locations defined in local memory are only valid inside the work group and thus the work group always holds write permissions for these locations.
- Permissions and conditions in the work group are distributed over the work group's threads by the *thread specification* $(T_{pre}^{res}, T_{pre}, T_{post}^{res}, T_{post})$. Because threads within a work group can exchange permissions, we allow the resources before (T_{pre}^{res}) and after execution (T_{post}^{res}) to be different.

The functional behaviour is specified by T_{pre} and T_{post}, which must be framed by T_{pre}^{res} and T_{post}^{res}, respectively.

- A *barrier specification* $(B_{res}, B_{pre}, B_{post})$ specifies resources, and a pre- and postcondition for each barrier in the kernel. B_{res} specifies how permissions are redistributed over the threads (depending on the barrier flag, these can be permissions on local memory only, on global memory only, or a combination of global and local memory). The barrier precondition B_{pre} specifies the property that has to hold when a thread reaches the barrier. It must be framed by the resources that were specified by the previous barrier (considering the thread start as an implicit barrier). The barrier postcondition B_{post} specifies the property that may be assumed to continue verification of the thread. It must be *framed* by B_{res}.

Notice that it is sufficient to specify a single permission formula for a kernel and a work group. Since work groups do not synchronise with each other, there is no way to redistribute permissions over kernels or work groups. Within a work group, permissions are redistributed over the threads only at a barrier, the code between barriers always holds the same set of permissions.

Given a fully annotated kernel, verification of the kernel w.r.t. its specification essentially boils down to verification of the following properties:

- Each thread is verified w.r.t. the thread specification, i.e., given the thread's code T_{body}, the Hoare triple $\{T_{res} ** T_{pre}\}\ T_{body}\{T_{post}\}$ is verified using the permission-based separation logic rules defined in Sect. 5.4. Each barrier is verified as a method call with precondition $R_{cur} ** B_{pre}$ and postcondition $B_{res} ** B_{post}$, where R_{cur} specifies all current resources.
- The kernel resources are sufficient for the distribution over the work groups, as specified by the group resources.
- The kernel precondition implies the work group's preconditions.
- The group resources and accesses to local memory are sufficient for the distribution of resources over the threads.
- The work group precondition implies the thread's preconditions.
- Each barrier redistributes only resources that are available in the work group.
- For each barrier the postcondition for each thread follows from the precondition in the thread, and the fenced conjuncts of the preconditions of all other threads in the work group.
- The universal quantification over all threads' postconditions implies the work group's postcondition.
- The universal quantification over all work groups' postconditions implies the kernel's postcondition.

The first condition is checked by the Hoare logic rules discussed below; the other conditions are encoded as additional checks in the VerCors tool set.

We will illustrate our approach on the kernel program discussed in Example 7.

Example 8. Consider the kernel in Lst. 18. For simplicity, it has a single work group, so the kernel level and group level specification are the same.

```
kernel demo {
  global int[gsize] a;
  global int[gsize] b;

  requires Perm(a[tid],100) ** Perm(b[tid],100);
  ensures Perm(b[tid],100) ** b[tid] = (tid+1) mod gsize;
  void main(){
    a[tid]:=tid;
    barrier(global) {
      requires a[tid]=tid;
      ensures Perm(a[(tid+1) mod gsize],10) ** Perm(b[tid],100);
      ensures a[(tid+1) mod gsize]=(tid+1) mod gsize; }
    b[tid]:=a[(tid+1) mod gsize];
  }
}
```

Lst. 19. VerCors tool annotated version of the code in Lst. 18

At the kernel level, the required resources K_{res} are write permissions on arrays a and b. The kernel precondition K_{pre} states that the length of both arrays should be the same as the number of threads (denoted as *gsize* for work group size). The kernel postcondition expresses that afterwards, for any i in the range of the array, $b[i] = (i + 1)\%gsize$. Each thread i initially obtains a write permission at a[i]. When thread i reaches the barrier, the property a[i] = i holds; this is the barrier precondition. After the barrier, each thread i obtains a write permission on b[i] and a read permission on a[$(i + 1)\%gsize$], and it continues its computation with the barrier postcondition that a[$(i + 1)\%gsize$] = $(i + 1)\%gsize$. From this, each thread i can establish the thread's postcondition b[i] = $(i + 1)\%gsize$, which is sufficient to establish the kernel's postcondition. See Lst. 19 for a tool-verified annotated version.

Notice that the logic contains many levels of specification. However, typically many of these specifications can be generated, satisfying the properties above by construction. As discussed in Section 5.5 below, for the tool implementation it is sufficient to provide the thread and the barrier specifications.

5.3   Kernel Programming Language

This section defines a simple kernel language. The next section defines the logic over this simplified language, however we would like to emphasise that our tool can verify real OpenCL kernels.

Our language is based on the Kernel Programming Language (KPL) of Betts et al. [9]. However, the original version of KPL did not distinguish between global and local memory, while we do. As kernel procedures cannot recursively call themselves, we restrict the language to a single block of kernel code, without loss of generality. Fig. 3 presents the syntax of our language. Each kernel is merely

Reserved global identifiers (constant within a thread):

tid	Thread identifier with respect to the kernel
gid	Group identifier with respect to the kernel
lid	Local thread identifier with respect to the work group
tcount	The total number of threads in the kernel
gsize	The number of threads per work group

Kernel language:

b ::= boolean expression over global constants and private variables

e ::= integer expression over global constants and private variables

S ::= v := e $|v :=$ rdloc(e) $|v :=$ rdglob(e) $|$wrloc(e_1, e_2) $|$wrglob(e_1, e_2)
   $|$ nop $|S_1; S_2$ $|$if b then S_1 else S_2 $|$while b do S $|bid$: barrier(F)

F ::= $\emptyset$ $|$ {local} $|$ {global} $|$ {local, global}

Fig. 3. Syntax for Kernel Programming Language

a single statement, which is executed by all threads, where threads are divided into one or more work groups. For simplicity, but without loss of generality, global and local memory are assumed to be single shared arrays (similar to the original KPL presentation [9]). There are 4 memory access operations: read from location e_1 in local memory ($v :=$ rdloc(e_1)); write e_2 to location e_1 in local memory (wrloc(e_1, e_2)); read from global memory ($v :=$ rdglob(e)); and write to global memory (wrglob(e_1, e_2)). Finally, there is a barrier operation, taking as argument a subset of the flags local and global, which describes which of the two memories are fenced by the barrier. Each barrier is labelled with an identifier *bid*.

5.4 Kernel Program Logic

This section formally defines the rules to reason about OpenCL kernels. As explained above, we distinguish between two kinds of formulas: resource formulas (in permission-based separation logic), and property formulas (in first-order logic).

Syntax of Resource Formulas. Before presenting the verification rules, we first define the syntax of resource formulas. Section 2 on page 175 defined the syntax of resource formulas. However, our kernel programming language uses a very simple form of expressions only, and the syntax explicitly distinguishes between access to global and local memory. Therefore, in our kernel specification language we follow the same pattern, and we explicitly use different permission statements for local and global memory.

As mentioned above, the behaviour of kernels, groups, threads and barriers is defined as tuples $(K_{res}, K_{pre}, K_{post})$, $(G_{res}, G_{pre}, G_{post})$, $(T_{pre}^{res}, T_{pre}, T_{post}^{res}, T_{post})$, and $(B_{res}, B_{pre}, B_{post})$, respectively, where the resource formulas are defined by the following grammar:

$$\frac{}{\{R, P[v := e]\}v := e\{R, P\}} \text{ (assign)}$$

$$\frac{}{\{R \ast\ast \text{LPerm}(e, \pi), P[v := L[e]]\}v := \text{rdloc}(e)\{R \ast\ast \text{LPerm}(e, \pi), P\}} \text{ (read-local)}$$

$$\frac{}{\{R \ast\ast \text{LPerm}(e_1, \text{rw}), P[L[e_1] := e_2]\}\text{wrloc}(e_1, e_2)\{R \ast\ast \text{LPerm}(e_1, \text{rw}), P\}} \text{ (write-local)}$$

$$\frac{}{\{R_{\text{cur}}, B_{pre}(bid)\}bid : \text{barrier}(F)\{B_{res}(bid), B_{post}(bid)\}} \text{ (barrier)}$$

Fig. 4. Hoare logic rules

$E ::=$ expressions over global constants, private variables, $\text{rdloc}(E)$, $\text{rdglob}(E)$
$R ::= \text{true} \mid \text{LPerm}(E, p) \mid \text{GPerm}(E, p) \mid E ==> R$
$\quad \mid R_1 \ast\ast R_2 \mid (\backslash \text{forall} \ast \text{ T } v; E(v); R(v))$

Resource formulas can *frame* first-order logic formulas. For this purpose, we define the footprint of a resource formula as all global and local memory locations that are accessed to evaluate the formula (see [11] for more details).

Hoare Triples for Kernels. Since in our logic we explicitly separate the resource formulas and the first-order logic properties, we first have to redefine the meaning of a Hoare triple in our setting, where the pre- and the postcondition consist of a resource formula, and a first-order logic formula, such that the pair is properly framed.

$\{R_1, P_1\}S\{R_2, P_2\} =$
$\quad \forall \mathcal{R} \, \gamma.(\Gamma \vdash \mathcal{R}; \gamma \models R_1 \ast\ast P_1) \wedge (S, (\mathcal{R}_{\text{mg}}, \mathcal{R}_{\text{ml}}, \gamma), \text{R}) \rightarrow^* (\epsilon, (\sigma, \delta, \gamma'), F) \Rightarrow$
$\quad \forall \mathcal{R}'.\mathcal{R}'_{\text{mg}} = \sigma \wedge \mathcal{R}'_{\text{ml}} = \delta.\Gamma \vdash \mathcal{R}'; \gamma' \models R_2 \ast\ast P_2$

Fig. 4 summarises the most important Hoare logic rules to reason about kernel threads; in addition there are the standard rules for sequential compositional, conditionals, and loops. Rule (assign) applies for updates to local memory. Rules (read-local) and (write-local) specifies look-up and update of local memory (where $L[e]$ denotes the value stored at location e in the local memory array, and substitution is as usually defined for arrays, cf. [3]):

$$L[e][L[e_1] := e_2] = (e = e_1)?e_2 : L[e]$$

Similar rules are defined for global memory (not given here, for space reasons).

The rule (barrier) reflects the functionality of the barrier from the point of view of one thread. First, the resources before (R_{cur}) are replaced with the barrier resources for the thread ($B_{res}(bid)$). Second, the barrier precondition ($B_{pre}(tid)$) is replaced by the post condition ($B_{post}(tid)$). The requirement that the preconditions within a group imply the postconditions is not enforced by this rule; it must be checked separately.

5.5   Example: Binomial Coefficient

Finally we discuss the verification of a more involved kernel, to illustrate the power of our verification technique. The full example is available on-line and can be tried in the on-line version of our tool set [58].

The kernel program in Lst. 20 computes the binomial coefficients

$$\binom{N-1}{0} \cdots \binom{N-1}{N-1}$$

using N threads forming a single work group. Due to space restrictions, only the critical parts of the specifications have been given. The actual verified version has longer and more tedious specifications.

The intended output is the global array bin. The local array tmp is used for exchanging data between threads. The algorithm proceeds in $N-1$ iterations and in each iteration bin contains a row from Pascal's triangle as the first part, and ones for the unused part.

On line 10 the entire bin array is initialised to 1. This satisfies the invariants on line 11/12 that states that the array bin contains the Nth row of Pascal's triangle, followed by ones. The loop body first copies the bin array to the tmp array, then using a barrier that fences the local variable. These values are then transmitted to the next thread and the write permission on tmp is exchanged for a read permissions. Then, for the relevant subset of threads, the equation

$$\binom{N}{k} = \binom{N-1}{k-1} + \binom{N-1}{k}$$

is used to update bin, and the second barrier returns write permission on tmp.

Note that the first barrier fences the local variables, which is necessary to ensure that the next thread can see the values. The second barrier does not fence any variables because it is only there to ensure that the value has been read and processed, making it safe to write the next value in tmp.

6   Related Work

To conclude this paper, we briefly give some pointers to related work. We do not intend this discussion to be complete; for this we refer to the related work sections of our individual papers.

6.1   Tools for Verification of Java Programs

The examples in this paper are specified in a dialect of separation logic that extends the JML [36] specification language with concurrent features. Many different verification tools for JML already exist [13]. Also tools for separation logic exist, such as VeriFast [33], SmallFoot [8], and jStar [21]. We also mention Chalice [37] here. Strictly speaking this is not a separation logic tool, however its

```
   kernel binomial {
2      global int[gsize] bin;
       local int[gsize] tmp;
4
       requires gsize > 1 ** Perm(bin[tid],1) ** Perm(tmp[tid],100);
6      ensures Perm(bin[tid],100) ** bin[tid]=binom(gsize-1,tid);
       void main(){
8        int temp;
         int N:=1;
10       bin[tid]:=1;
         invariant Perm(bin[tid],100) ** Perm(tmp[tid],100);
12       invariant tid<N ? bin[tid]=binom(N,tid) : bin[tid]=1;
         while(N<gsize-1){
14         tmp[tid]:=bin[tid];
           barrier(1,{local}){
16           ensures Perm(bin[tid],100) ** Perm(tmp[(tid-1) mod gsize],10);
             ensures 0<tid & tid<=N -> tmp[(tid-1) mod gsize]=binom(N,tid-1);
18         }
           N := N+1;
20         if(0<tid & tid<N){
             temp:=tmp[(tid-1) mod gsize];
22           bin[tid]:=temp+bin[tid];
           }
24         barrier(2,{}){
             ensures Perm(bin[tid],100) ** Perm(tmp[tid],100);
26         }
         }
28     }
   }
```

Lst. 20. Kernel program for binomial coefficients

specification language (implicit dynamic frames [56]) is equivalent to separation logic [51].

SmallFoot and jStar support basic separation logic, without fractional permissions. The Chalice specification language is quite similar to ours, but more restricted. For example, it does not allow predicates with parameters and it does not support the magic wand. Moreover, its programming language does not have inheritance. The VeriFast tool supports both C and Java. The main difference with the VerCors tool is that it uses a pure version of separation logic rather than our free form.

One of the core components of a specification language for concurrent software is the access permission model, which determines how flexible the specification languages for access permissions is. Separation logic is not the only one available. One of the simplest models is the permission model of the Spec# programming system for C# [6]. This model organises access permissions as a forest of trees. It is also used in the VCC verifier for C code [15].

6.2   Synchronisers

As mentioned, our synchroniser specifications extend our earlier formalisation of reentrant locks [26]. Several other built-in formalisations of locks and synchronisation primitives exist. Chalice [37] formalises simple non-reentrant locks built into the Chalice language. The work of Gotsman et al. [25] is similar to our earlier formalisation, and we believe that our high-level approach could also be easily applied there to treat a wider range of synchronisation primitives.

Similarly, the work of Hobor and Gherghina on formalising Pthread-style barriers in Separation Logic [29] follows very similar principles. This work was the basis for our barrier specifications for OpenCL kernels. However, since OpenCL barriers are simpler, our barrier specifications for kernel programs also are much simpler. We are currently working on specifying and verifying also a Java API version of a cyclic barrier.

Finally, the VeriFast tool [33] adopts an approach similar to ours – locking is also specified on the API level, but only for simple and non-reentrant locks, and so-called higher-order abstract predicates are functionally similar to our class level specification parameters.

6.3   Class Invariants

The early developed techniques for verification of class invariants in sequential programs [43,41] support invariants with restricted definition only. This work is unsound for more complex data structures, for example if an invariant captures properties over different objects. Later, Poetzsch-Heffter [53] and Huizing et al. [31] developed sound techniques that do not restrict the invariant definition or the program itself; however, both approaches are not modular.

Müller et al. [44] propose two sound techniques for modular reasoning: the *ownership technique* and the less restrictive *visibility technique*. Both concepts, as well as Lu et al.'s modular technique [42], are designed for ownership-based type systems. All these techniques are captured in Drossopoulou et al.'s abstract unified framework [22].

Weiß models class invariants with a boolean model field *inv* [59]. Their validity is checked only on demand. Specifications use *inv* explicitly where needed, while this.*inv* is implicitly generated in each method pre- and postcondition.

Jacobs et al. [32] suggest a technique for verifying multithreaded programs with class invariants, using the *Boogie methodology* [5] for sequential programs. With this approach, a thread is allowed to break a class invariant of an object only if it completely owns the object, i.e., no other thread can access any field of this object. This is in contrast with the approach presented in this paper, where breaking a class invariant is independent of permissions on heap memory.

A different approach for modular verification of object invariants in concurrent programs is proposed by Cohen [16], implemented in VCC [15]. Each object is assigned a two-state invariant expressing the required relation between any two consecutive states of execution that has to be respected by every state update in the program.

6.4   GPUs

There already exists some work on the verification of GPU kernels. However, these approaches mainly focus on the verification of data race freedom of the interleaving of two arbitrary threads, whereas we verify an arbitrary single thread, and also consider functional correctness.

Li and Gopalakrishnan [40] verify CUDA programs by symbolically encoding thread interleavings. They focus on data race freedom, and were the first to observe that to ensure data race freedom it was sufficient to verify the interleavings of two arbitrary threads.

Betts et al. [9] verify GPU programs by encoding their behaviour as a BoogiePL program. The GPUVerify tool is highly efficient at automatically verifying data race freedom and absence of barrier divergence. However, it abstracts away from all data and cannot easily prove functional correctness.

7   Summary and Directions for Future Work

This paper illustrated the VerCors approach to verification of concurrent software. The approach uses permission-based separation logic as the underlying logic to handle the concurrency-related features. However, compared to other projects handling verification of concurrent software, the VerCors project focuses on making verification practical. It achieves this by using an easily accessible specification language, that reuses important aspects of the JML specification language, and by concentrating on also verifying functional program properties.

We discussed some distinguishing features of the VerCors project in more detail. First of all, we showed how different synchronisers can be specified uniformly in the specification language, and how these specifications are used to verify other programs. Moreover, (simplified versions of) Java's reference implementations of these synchronisers have been proven correct w.r.t. these specifications. This verification has not been discussed in detail in this paper, but it is important to know that the specifications are indeed correct. Second, we also discussed how an important class of functional correctness properties, namely that of class invariants can be specified and verified in a modular way in a concurrent setting. Key ingredient of the approach is that the annotator explicitly can control when the invariant may be broken, but that it has to be ensured that the broken invariant is not visible to other threads (until it is reestablished again). Last, we also showed how the approach can be used to verify other concurrency paradigms, and in particular how it is used to verify vector programs, following the Single Instruction Multiple Data paradigm. Concretely, we apply this technique to prove data race freedom and functional correctness of OpenCL kernel programs.

Future Work. The work described in this paper is part of an ongoing project and much more work remains to be done. In particular, the tool support needs to be improved and tested further, and on larger applications. At the moment, a user has to add many proof hints and annotations by hand. To make the approach scale to larger applications and usable for other software developers, a large effort is needed on generating annotations and proof hints automatically.

Additionally, we also plan to expand the application domain of the VerCors tool set. We would like to study what effort is needed to extend the verification techniques to other programming languages, e.g., C and Scala. We are also developing techniques to study more advanced functional properties; in particular to be able to verify that an application eventually computes an expected result.

For the GPU verification, we plan to study parallellisation and optimisations in more detail. When a sequential program is verified, and then parallellised to a vector program by a parallellising compiler, how can we make sure that the resulting vector program is also correct? And when the vector program is further optimised, to increase performance, how can we make sure that correctness of the optimised program is maintained?

Acknowledgments. This work was supported by ERC grant 258405 for the Ver-Cors project (Amighi, Blom, Huisman, Mostowski, and Zaharieva-Stojanovski), and EU STREP project 287767 CARP (Blom, Darabi, and Huisman).

References

1. Amighi, A., Blom, S., Huisman, M.: Resource protection using atomics: Patterns and verifications. Technical Report TR-CTIT-13-10, CTIT, University of Twente (2013)
2. Amighi, A., Blom, S., Huisman, M., Mostowski, W., Zaharieva-Stojanovski, M.: Formal specifications for Java's synchronisation classes. In: Lafuente, A.L., Tuosto, E. (eds.) 22nd Euromicro International Conference on Parallel, Distributed, and Network-Based Processing, pp. 725–733. IEEE Computer Society (2014)
3. Apt, K.R.: Ten years of Hoare's logic: A survey – Part I. ACM Trans. Program. Lang. Syst. 3(4), 431–483 (1981)
4. Artho, C., Havelund, K., Biere, A.: High-level data races. Softw. Test., Verif. Reliab. 13(4), 207–227 (2003)
5. Barnett, M., DeLine, R., Fähndrich, M., Leino, K.R.M., Schulte, W.: Verification of object-oriented programs with invariants. Journal of Object Technology 3(6), 27–56 (2004)
6. Barnett, M., Leino, K.R.M., Schulte, W.: The Spec# programming system: An overview. In: Barthe, G., Burdy, L., Huisman, M., Lanet, J.-L., Muntean, T. (eds.) CASSIS 2004. LNCS, vol. 3362, pp. 49–69. Springer, Heidelberg (2005)
7. Beckert, B., Hähnle, R., Schmitt, P.H. (eds.): Verification of Object-Oriented Software. LNCS (LNAI), vol. 4334. Springer, Heidelberg (2007)
8. Berdine, J., Calcagno, C., O'Hearn, P.: Smallfoot: Modular automatic assertion checking with separation logic. In: de Boer, F.S., Bonsangue, M.M., Graf, S., de Roever, W.-P. (eds.) FMCO 2005. LNCS, vol. 4111, pp. 115–137. Springer, Heidelberg (2006)
9. Betts, A., Chong, N., Donaldson, A., Qadeer, S., Thomson, P.: GPUVerify: A verifier for GPU kernels. In: Proceedings of the ACM International Conference on Object Oriented Programming Systems Languages and Applications, OOPSLA 2012, pp. 113–132. ACM, New York (2012)

10. Blom, S., Huisman, M.: The VerCors Tool for verification of concurrent programs. In: Jones, C., Pihlajasaari, P., Sun, J. (eds.) FM 2014. LNCS, vol. 8442, pp. 127–131. Springer, Heidelberg (2014)
11. Blom, S., Huisman, M., Mihelčić, M.: Specification and verification of GPGPU programs. Accepted to appear in Science of Computer Programming (2013)
12. Boyland, J.: Checking interference with fractional permissions. In: Cousot, R. (ed.) SAS 2003. LNCS, vol. 2694, pp. 55–72. Springer, Heidelberg (2003)
13. Burdy, L., Cheon, Y., Cok, D.R., Ernst, M.D., Kiniry, J.R., Leavens, G.T., Leino, K.R.M., Poll, E.: An overview of JML tools and applications. Software Tools for Technology Transfer 7, 212–232 (2005)
14. Chalin, P., Kiniry, J.R., Leavens, G.T., Poll, E.: Beyond assertions: Advanced specification and verification with JML and ESC/Java2. In: de Boer, F.S., Bonsangue, M.M., Graf, S., de Roever, W.-P. (eds.) FMCO 2005. LNCS, vol. 4111, pp. 342–363. Springer, Heidelberg (2006)
15. Cohen, E., Dahlweid, M., Hillebrand, M.A., Leinenbach, D., Moskal, M., Santen, T., Schulte, W., Tobies, S.: VCC: A practical system for verifying concurrent C. In: Berghofer, S., Nipkow, T., Urban, C., Wenzel, M. (eds.) TPHOLs 2009. LNCS, vol. 5674, pp. 23–42. Springer, Heidelberg (2009)
16. Cohen, E., Moskal, M., Schulte, W., Tobies, S.: Local verification of global invariants in concurrent programs. In: Touili, T., Cook, B., Jackson, P. (eds.) CAV 2010. LNCS, vol. 6174, pp. 480–494. Springer, Heidelberg (2010)
17. Cok, D.R.: OpenJML: JML for Java 7 by extending OpenJDK. In: Bobaru, M., Havelund, K., Holzmann, G.J., Joshi, R. (eds.) NFM 2011. LNCS, vol. 6617, pp. 472–479. Springer, Heidelberg (2011)
18. Cowan, B., Kapralos, B.: GPU-based acoustical occlusion modeling with acoustical texture maps. In: Proceedings of the 6th Audio Mostly Conference: A Conference on Interaction with Sound, AM 2011, pp. 55–61. ACM, New York (2011)
19. Dietl, W., Müller, P.: Universes: Lightweight ownership for JML. Journal of Object Technology 4(8), 5–32 (2005)
20. Dietl, W., Müller, P.: Object ownership in program verification. In: Clarke, D., Noble, J., Wrigstad, T. (eds.) Aliasing in Object-Oriented Programming. LNCS, vol. 7850, pp. 289–318. Springer, Heidelberg (2013)
21. DiStefano, D., Parkinson, M.: jStar: Towards practical verification for Java. In: ACM Conference on Object-Oriented Programming Systems, Languages, and Applications, pp. 213–226. ACM (2008)
22. Drossopoulou, S., Francalanza, A., Müller, P., Summers, A.J.: A unified framework for verification techniques for object invariants. In: Vitek, J. (ed.) ECOOP 2008. LNCS, vol. 5142, pp. 412–437. Springer, Heidelberg (2008)
23. Ernst, M.D., Cockrell, J., Griswold, W.G., Notkin, D.: Dynamically discovering likely program invariants to support program evolution. IEEE Transactions on Software Engineering 27(2), 99–123 (2001)
24. Floyd, R.W.: Assigning meanings to programs. Proc. Symp. Appl. Math. 19, 19–31 (1967)
25. Gotsman, A., Berdine, J., Cook, B., Rinetzky, N., Sagiv, M.: Local reasoning for storable locks and threads. In: Shao, Z. (ed.) APLAS 2007. LNCS, vol. 4807, pp. 19–37. Springer, Heidelberg (2007)
26. Haack, C., Huisman, M., Hurlin, C.: Reasoning about Java's reentrant locks. In: Ramalingam, G. (ed.) APLAS 2008. LNCS, vol. 5356, pp. 171–187. Springer, Heidelberg (2008)
27. Haack, C., Huisman, M., Hurlin, C., Amighi, A.: Permission-based separation logic for Java. Submitted to Logical Methods in Computer Science

28. Hoare, C.: An axiomatic basis for computer programming. Commun. ACM 12(10), 576–580 (1969)
29. Hobor, A., Gherghina, C.: Barriers in concurrent separation logic. In: Barthe, G. (ed.) ESOP 2011. LNCS, vol. 6602, pp. 276–296. Springer, Heidelberg (2011)
30. Huisman, M., Mihelčić, M.: Specification and verification of GPGPU programs using permission-based separation logic. In: BYTECODE 2013 (2013)
31. Huizing, K., Kuiper, R.: Verification of object oriented programs using class invariants. In: Maibaum, T. (ed.) FASE 2000. LNCS, vol. 1783, pp. 208–221. Springer, Heidelberg (2000)
32. Jacobs, B., Piessens, F., Leino, K.R.M., Schulte, W.: Safe concurrency for aggregate objects with invariants. In: Software Engineering and Formal Methods, pp. 137–147 (2005)
33. Jacobs, B., Smans, J., Philippaerts, P., Vogels, F., Penninckx, W., Piessens, F.: VeriFast: A powerful, sound, predictable, fast verifier for C and Java. In: Bobaru, M., Havelund, K., Holzmann, G.J., Joshi, R. (eds.) NFM 2011. LNCS, vol. 6617, pp. 41–55. Springer, Heidelberg (2011)
34. Jason Sanders, E.K.: CUDA by Example: An Introduction to General-Purpose GPU Programming. Addison-Wesley Professional (2010)
35. Khronos OpenCL Working Group. The OpenCL specification (2008-2013)
36. Leavens, G., Poll, E., Clifton, C., Cheon, Y., Ruby, C., Cok, D.R., Müller, P., Kiniry, J., Chalin, P.: JML Reference Manual. Dept. of Computer Science, Iowa State University (February 2007), http://www.jmlspecs.org
37. Leino, K., Müller, P., Smans, J.: Verification of concurrent programs with Chalice. In: Aldini, A., Barthe, G., Gorrieri, R. (eds.) FOSAD 2009. LNCS, vol. 5705, pp. 195–222. Springer, Heidelberg (2009)
38. Leino, K.R.M.: This is Boogie 2. Technical report, Microsoft Research (June 2008)
39. Leino, K.R.M.: Dafny: An automatic program verifier for functional correctness. In: Clarke, E.M., Voronkov, A. (eds.) LPAR-16 2010. LNCS, vol. 6355, pp. 348–370. Springer, Heidelberg (2010)
40. Li, G., Gopalakrishnan, G.: Scalable SMT-based verification of GPU kernel functions. In: SIGSOFT FSE 2010, Santa Fe, NM, USA, pp. 187–196. ACM (2010)
41. Liskov, B., Guttag, J.: Abstraction and specification in program development. MIT Press, Cambridge (1986)
42. Lu, Y., Potter, J., Xue, J.: Validity invariants and effects. In: Ernst, E. (ed.) ECOOP 2007. LNCS, vol. 4609, pp. 202–226. Springer, Heidelberg (2007)
43. Meyer, B.: Object-Oriented Software Construction, 2nd edn. Prentice-Hall (1997)
44. Müller, P., Poetzsch-Heffter, A., Leavens, G.T.: Modular invariants for layered object structures. Sci. Comput. Program. 62(3), 253–286 (2006)
45. Mulligan, J.B.: A GPU-accelerated software eye tracking system. In: Proceedings of the Symposium on Eye Tracking Research and Applications, ETRA 2012, pp. 265–268. ACM, New York (2012)
46. O'Hearn, P.W.: Resources, concurrency and local reasoning. Theoretical Computer Science 375(1-3), 271–307 (2007)
47. The OpenCL 1.2 specification (2011)
48. Owicki, S., Gries, D.: An axiomatic proof technique for parallel programs. Acta Informatica Journal 6, 319–340 (1975)
49. Parkinson, M.: Local reasoning for Java. Technical Report UCAM-CL-TR-654, University of Cambridge (2005)
50. Parkinson, M.J., Bierman, G.M.: Separation logic and abstraction. In: Palsberg, J., Abadi, M. (eds.) Proceedings of the 32nd ACM SIGPLAN-SIGACT Symposium on Principles of Programming Languages, pp. 247–258. ACM (2005)

51. Parkinson, M.J., Summers, A.J.: The relationship between separation logic and implicit dynamic frames. Logical Methods in Computer Science 8(3:01), 1–54 (2012)
52. Parr, T.: The Definitive ANTLR 4 Reference. Pragmatic Bookshelf (2013)
53. Poetzsch-Heffter, A.: Specification and Verification of Object-Oriented Programs. PhD thesis, Habilitation thesis, Technical University of Munich (1997)
54. Reif, W., Schellhorn, G., Stenzel, K., Balser, M.: Structured specifications and interactive proofs with KIV. In: Bibel, W., Schmitt, P. (eds.) Automated Deduction—A Basis for Applications, vol. II.1, pp. 13–39. Kluwer (1998)
55. Reynolds, J.: Separation logic: A logic for shared mutable data structures. In: 17th IEEE Symposium on Logic in Computer Science (LICS 2002), pp. 55–74. IEEE Computer Society (2002)
56. Smans, J., Jacobs, B., Piessens, F.: Implicit dynamic frames. ACM Trans. Program. Lang. Syst. 34(1) (2012)
57. Stone, S.S., Haldar, J.P., Tsao, S.C., Hwu, W.-M.W., Liang, Z.-P., Sutton, B.P.: Accelerating advanced MRI reconstructions on GPU-s. In: Proceedings of the 5th Conference on Computing Frontiers, CF 2008, pp. 261–272. ACM, New York (2008)
58. VerCors project homepage (2014), http://www.utwente.nl/vercors/
59. Weiß, B.: Deductive Verification of Object-Oriented Software: Dynamic Frames, Dynamic Logic and Predicate Abstraction. PhD thesis, Karlsruhe Institute of Technology (2011)
60. Zaharieva-Stojanovski, M., Huisman, M.: Verifying class invariants in concurrent programs. In: Gnesi, S., Rensink, A. (eds.) FASE 2014 (ETAPS). LNCS, vol. 8411, pp. 230–245. Springer, Heidelberg (2014)

Combining Monitoring
with Run-Time Assertion Checking

Frank S. de Boer[1,2] and Stijn de Gouw[1,2]

[1] CWI, Amsterdam, The Netherlands
[2] Leiden University, The Netherlands

Abstract. According to a study in 2002 commisioned by a US Department, software bugs annually costs the US economy an estimated $59 billion[1]. A more recent study in 2013 by Cambridge University estimated that the global cost has risen to $312 billion globally[2].

There exists various ways to prevent, isolate and fix software bugs, ranging from lightweight methods that are (semi)-automatic, to heavyweight methods that require significant user interaction. Our own method described in this tutorial is based on automated run-time checking of a combination of protocol- and data-oriented properties of object-oriented programs.

1 Run-Time Checking of Object-Oriented Programs

Given a program and a specification, a run-time verifier inserts checks in the code that determine whether the specification is satisfied. The checks are triggered during an actual execution of the program. In contrast to static verification, where properties are checked with respect to *all* executions (possibly there are infinitely many), run-time checkers only consider a single execution of the program. There is a wide range of specification languages used in run-time verification. They can be partitioned into two categories: languages that focus on the control-flow (these approaches are also called "monitoring"), and those focussing on data-flow.

As an example, one can use regular expressions to specify the order in which functions or methods in a program should be called [18]. Such specifications describe the control-flow of the program. Other formalisms for specifying control-flow are temporal logics, various kinds of automata and context-free grammars. For these formalisms, checking whether a given property holds of the current execution involves parsing a word (where the word is some representation of the trace of method calls in the current execution) in an automata. Generally only formalisms are chosen with a decidable parsing problem (in particular, this is the case for regular expressions, context-free grammars and most automata), so

---

[1] http://web.archive.org/web/20090610052743/
  http://www.nist.gov/public_affairs/releases/n02-10.htm
[2] http://www.prweb.com/releases/2013/1/prweb10298185.htm

M. Bernardo et al. (Eds.): SFM 2014, LNCS 8483, pp. 217–262, 2014.

that everything can be automated. Specification languages for monitoring are discussed in more detail in the next section.

Approaches that specify data-flow usually do so by annotating the source code with assertions: logical formulas that must be true whenever control passes them. The formulas constrain the values of the program variables. If assertions are expressed in first-order logic with arithmetic, it is in general undecidable due to unbounded quantification (i.e. ranging over an infinite number of values) whether the assertion is true, thus usually the assertions are restricted in some way. For instance, Java contains an **assert**-statement which restricts to quantifier-free formulas (i.e. Boolean expressions). *Design by Contract* [53] provides a systematic way of using assertions to specify classes, interfaces and methods with respectively class invariants and pre- and postconditions. It was first used in the programming language Eiffel, and subsequently has also been applied to many other programming languages. For example, JML [14] is one of the most popular specification languages for Java and supports Design by Contract. JML also supports unbounded quantification, though assertions containing unbounded quantifiers are not checked by the JML run-time assertion checker.

While type checking for the most used imperative languages is done fully automatically at compile-time, run-time checking is done (also fully automatically) during execution, and properties are only checked for the current execution. This generally allows more expressive specifications compared to type checkers. Static verification cannot be automated. In particular, even if one restricts pre- and postconditions to just the formulas *true* and *false*, the resulting specification language is still undecidable (such assertions suffice to express the halting problem).

> Our own proposal is a method for run-time checking of object-oriented programs. We discuss below in more detail how run-time checking applies to the specific context of object-oriented programming, focussing first on single-threaded Java, and then describe an extension to concurrency.

Two of the basic features of object-oriented programming are data abstraction and encapsulation. In the design of software, these features support the methodology of *programming to interfaces* [31]. This methodology allows the developer of client code to abstract from irrelevant implementation details. Combined with the *design by contract* principle [53], programming by interfaces is one of the main approaches to mastering the complexity of software today.

One of the main formal behavioral interface specification languages for Java, the Java Modeling Language (JML) [14], is inherently *state-based*; i.e., JML mainly provides support for the specification of classes in terms of their fields, including so-called *model* fields that represent certain aspects of the data structures underlying the implementation. JML does not provide explicit support for the specification of the *interaction* between objects, in contrast to other formalisms such as message sequence charts and UML sequence diagrams [23,41].

On the other hand, the very semantic foundations of object-oriented programming are defined in terms of sequences of messages. In [43], a *fully abstract* trace semantics for a core Java-like language is given, where traces (or *communication histories*) are (finite) sequences of messages. A fully abstract semantics in general captures the observable behavior abstracting from implementation details. Such an abstraction is required in for example a proper semantic definition of *behavioral subtyping* as is illustrated by the *fragile base class problem* [54]: According to the initial/final state semantics the class B (Figure 1) and its revised version in Figure 2 below are behaviorally equivalent.

```
class B {
  int x = 0;

  void m() {
    x = x+1;
  }

  void n() {
    x = x+1
  }
}
```

Fig. 1. First version of a base class B

```
class B {
  int x = 0;

  void m() {
    this.n();
  }

  void n() {
    x = x+1;
  }
}
```

Fig. 2. New version of a base class B

However the behavior of the subclass M defined in Figure 3 is clearly different for the two versions of the base class. In particular, when using the revised version of the base class, the definitions of the methods m and n in the subclass M are mutually recursive, giving rise to a non-terminating loop.

```
class M extends B {
  void n() {
    this.m();
  }
}
```

Fig. 3. Subclass of the base class

It is worthwhile to observe the analogy between this anomaly with repect to the substitutivity of (behaviorally) equivalent classes and the following basic counter-example to the compositionality of the initial/final state semantics for *multi-threaded* programs. Both threads T_1 and T_2 of Figure 4 have the same initial/final state semantics, however the initial/final state semantics of the *interleaving* of T_1 and thread T clearly differs from that of T_2 and T, if assignments are treated atomically.

```
thread T_1 { x=x+1; x=x+1 }
thread T_2 { x= x+2; }
thread T { x=0 }
```

Fig. 4. Multi-Threaded Programs

This counter-example shows that for a compositional semantics of multi-threaded programs we need more specific information about the underlying implementation, namely information about *how* the final state is generated from the initial state. The *minimal* information needed is captured by a fully abstract semantics (see [55] for a definition of the *full abstraction problem*). In general fully abstract semantics of concurrent systems are based on some form of *trace* semantics. Of interest here is that the above work on fully abstract semantics for a core Java-like language shows that some form of trace semantics is needed even for sequential (single threaded) programs. More specifically, [43] shows that a form of trace semantics for object-oriented programs indeed guarantees substitutivity assuming encapsulation of the object state. Consequently, also the fragile base class problem, as shown above, can only be resolved by some form of trace semantics of behavioral subtyping. In this case, the sequences of internal communication distinguishes the classes in Figure 1 and Figure 2. Fischer and Wehrheim [28] further investigate behavioral subtyping based on histories for object-oriented languages.

The following question arises: how to bridge the gap between the semantic foundations of Java based on traces and the abstraction level of formal behavioral interface specification state-based languages like JML? To this end we aim to find a formalism and corresponding tool support which:

1. Integrates properties of the control-flow and data-flow.
2. Is at the same abstraction level as the object-oriented programming model.
3. Is sufficiently expressive.
4. Is user-friendly, i.e., fairly close to the familiar surface syntax of the programming language.
5. Supports automated run-time checking.
6. Adds as little overhead as possible.
7. Contains some form of error reporting.

1.1   Outline

Section 2 contains a survey of existing formalisms and tools for specifying object-oriented programs.

Section 3 presents our own formalism for single-threaded object-oriented programs. The basic notions of a communication view, attribute grammars and assertions in attribute grammars are introduced. The section concludes with a motivation for the design choices that were taken during the development of the specification language.

Section 4 describes the architecture of SAGA, a tool for run-time checking the previously presented formalism. First, the components of a generic tool architecture are identified. Second, each component is instantiated with different tools which are then evaluated.

Section 5 contains two case studies. First we specify a small but very common Java library: a `Stack`. Subsequently we consider a larger industrial case from the e-commerce company Fredhopper. The section finishes with an evaluation based on the two cases.

2   Specifying Object-Oriented Programs: Formalisms and Tools

In this section we give an overview of existing specification languages for object-oriented programs. The specification languages can be roughly partitioned into those which focus on formalizing protocol-oriented properties (all but the last three categories listed below), and those focussing on data. All specification languages for protocol properties are based on some form of histories (also known as traces): sequences of method calls or returns. Languages focussing on data restrict the values of variables and fields in a program by means of logical formulas. We describe whether the specification languages are used in actual tools for static verification or run-time checking.

Sequence Diagrams. A sequence diagram[3] shows how multiple objects interact with each other over time. The diagram depicts the messages exchanged between

---

[3] See http://www.omg.org/spec/UML/ for the latest UML specification of sequence diagrams.

the objects, and the order in which they are sent. In the context of object-oriented programs, the messages in a sequence diagram correspond to method calls. Since sequence diagrams visualize a single interaction, one could select a set of sequence diagrams as a specification of the behaviour of an object-oriented program, by requiring that the methods in the program are executed in the order specified by one of the sequence diagrams in the set. The resulting specification language describes properties of the protocol of the program.

While sequence diagrams have been used in theoretical studies for verification purposes [24,50], to the best of our knowledge, sequence diagrams as a specification language have not been used in actual tools for static or run-time verification. There are several reasons for this. First, any specification based on visualization tends to become unclear and even infeasible for describing large interactions. Second, the number of interactions exhibited in programs are often unbounded due to loops and recursion. Thus one would need an additional language for characterizing infinite sets of sequence diagrams.

Regular Expressions. A regular expression [44] is a declarative notation for a regular language. A language is a set of words. The words are usually (finite) strings of characters, though more complex objects can be used as well. The regular languages are those that can be obtained from a finite language by union, concatenation and Kleene star (an infinite union of finite concatenations of a language). If r_1 and r_2 are regular expressions, the notation for these three operations is respectively $r_1 + r_2$ (union), $r_1 r_2$ (concatenation) and r_1* (Kleene star). As an example, the regular expression $(ab)*$ denote the language of all words starting with "a" in which "a" and "b" alternate. The formal properties of regular languages have been widely studied in the field of formal languages and theory of computation, see for example the books [65,51].

As a specification language for object-oriented programs, regular expressions can be used to denote valid histories [18]. In this setting, the alphabet symbols correspond to method names, histories are represented as sequences of such alphabet symbols, and the valid histories are the words of the regular language. Note that in contrast to the previous sequence diagrams, regular expressions support a convenient notation for an infinite set of histories with the Kleene star.

There are various tools for run-time checking which support regular expressions: JmSeq [58], Tracematches [2] and JavaMOP [17]. The run-time check corresponds to solving the word problem (or parsing problem): decide whether the history is a word of the language denoted by a given regular expression. This can be done efficiently. In particular, if a history is valid according to a given regular expression, then parsing algorithms exist that decide in constant time whether the history resulting from appending a single call is also valid according to the regular expression (for the full history, this leads to parsing algorithms which are linear in the size of the history), see [32]. Moreover one does not need to store the full history, only the "state" of the parser for the previous history, and the method call which is added to the previous history are needed to determine validity of the new history.

Context-Free Grammars. A context-free grammar G is a quadruple $G = \langle V, \Sigma, P, S \rangle$ where V is a set of non-terminals, Σ is a set of terminal symbols, S is the start-symbol of the grammar (a non-terminal), and P is a set of production rules. The production rules specify how each non-terminal (independent of the context in which that non-terminal occurs, hence the name context-free) is allowed to be rewritten into a sequence of terminals and non-terminals. The grammar generates a context-free language, namely the set of all strings of terminal symbols that can be obtained by repeatedly applying the production rules of the grammar, starting from the start symbol of the grammar. For example, the grammar below (the used notation for the grammar is BNF [4]) with the non-terminal S as its start symbol, and "a" and "b" as terminal symbols generates all words of the form $a^k b^k$, $k \geq 0$ (in words: k a's, followed by k b's). The symbol ϵ denotes the empty word.

$$
\begin{array}{l}
S ::= a\ S\ b \\
\quad |\quad \epsilon
\end{array}
$$

Context-free grammars are strictly more expressive than regular expressions. Using the so-called pumping lemma [65], one can prove that there is no regular expression which denotes the same language as the grammar above. However it is more complex to parse a string in a given context-free grammar, than in a regular expression. The currently best known practical algorithms can parse a string of length n in (worst case) $\mathcal{O}(n^3)$ time.

When used as a specification language for object-oriented programs, the terminal symbols are the method names, and the grammar specifies the valid orderings in which these methods are allowed to be called (in other words, the context-free grammar generates the valid histories). The run-time check which decides whether a history is valid consists of parsing the current history in the given grammar. PQL [52] and JavaMOP [17] are examples of tools that support run-time checking based on context-free grammars.

Automata. There are too many kinds of automata too list them here exhaustively, but all of them contain at least two things: a notion of a state, and a transition function between states. A finite automaton, one of the simplest automata, contains additionally a set of accepting states and a start state, with the requirement that the set of states must be finite. Finite automata are equivalent in expressive power to regular expressions. A push-down automaton is an extension of a finite automaton with a stack of infinite size. Push-down automata are equivalent in expressive power to context-free grammars.

In general, automata can be seen as a representation of a formal language: it takes a string as input, and accepts or rejects it based on an acceptance condition (the specific acceptance condition varies greatly between the different kinds of automata). However, unlike the above declarative formalisms of regular expressions and context-free grammars, automata tend to have an imperative flavor, focussing on *how* to parse a formal language, as opposed to directly specifying the language itself.

As a specification language for object-oriented programs, JavaMOP [17] supports finite automata. LARVA [22] supports a kind of automata called timed automata with stopwatches.

Temporal Logics. Temporal logic [60] is a variant of *Modal Logic* [30]. As the name indicates, the basis for temporal logics is a notion of time on which the truth of a formula may depend. In particular, as the system described a temporal logic formula evolves from one state to the next, the truth value of the formula *can* change. There are many kinds of temporal logics, but they can roughly be classified as being linear-time or branching-time. In linear-time logics, time is viewed as a set of paths (the paths being sequences of "time instances"). LTL [60] is a widely used linear-time logic. Branching-time logics represent time as a tree in which the current time is the root, and the branches are considered as "possible futures". CTL [20] is the main branching-time logic.

Temporal logics have been used extensively in model checking [21], for example in the tools (there are too many others to fully list here): BLAST [37] Java Pathfinder [70] NuSMV [19] PRISM [48] SPIN [40] UPPAAL [9]. Temporal logics have also been used in run-time checking, even for the functional language Haskell [66]. Examples of run-time checkers of temporal logic formulas for Java are JavaMOP [17] and Java Pathfinder [3].

Process Algebras. Process algebras [5,36] have been used to formally model concurrent systems. There exist a wide variety of process algebras (or process calculi), but all approaches share some basic characteristics.

Each approach has a notion of a basic process from which larger processes are built using various operators (for example, for parallel composition, sequential composition and recursion). Message passing is used as the only way two different actors or processes can interact (instead of for example, shared variable concurrency). Finally, all approaches come with a set of algebraic laws (hence the name "process algebra") which for example can be used to show that syntactically different processes are semantically equal (i.e. have the same behavior).

For reference we list some of the most used process algebras here: CSP [39,1], LOTOS [69], CCS [56], ACP [12] and the more recent π-calculus [57,64]. CSP has been used in the tool Jass [6] for run-time checking object-oriented programs.

First-Order Logic. First-order logic is a formal system for specifying and reasoning about formulas about objects (or values) that range over some domain of discourse. All variables and terms in a first-order formula range over objects of the domain of discourse.

First-order logic can be used to specify programs by means of assertions: a logical formula in which the free variables (i.e. all variables not bound by $\forall$ and $\exists$) are program variables. Assertions are written in the source code of the program and must be true whenever control passes over them. Floyd describes in [29] a method for proving properties using first-order assertions. His work was extended by Hoare in [38]. First-order logic also forms the basis for dynamic logic and second- and higher-order logic described below.

The popular tool-suite for JML [14] supports first-order assertions for both static verification and run-time checking of Java programs. The run-time checker for JML only checks formulas involving bounded quantifiers: quantified variables that range over a finite set of values. Validity of formulas involving unbounded quantifiers is in general undecidable, as already noted in the previous section.

Dynamic Logic. Like temporal logic, Dynamic Logic (DL) [62,33] is a variant of *modal logic* [30] which allows the direct expression of program equivalence and weakest preconditions. DL extends full first-order logic with two additional (mix-fix) relations: < . > . (diamond) and [.]. (box). In both cases, the first argument is a *statement*, whereas the second argument is another DL formula. A formula $< s > p$ is true if there exists a terminating execution of s after which the formula p is true. A formula $[s]p$ is true after all terminating executions of s, the formula p is true. For example, the formula $<\texttt{x=x-1;}> (x == 0)$ is equivalent to $x = 1$. Dynamic logic has been used as a specification language in the static verifiers KeY [8] and KIV [35].

Second- and Higher-Order Logic. Second-Order logic is a highly expressive formalism which allows quantification over predicates and functions over the values of the underlying domain. This contrasts with first-order logic, in which only quantification over values of the domain is allowed. The expressiveness comes at a price: no sound and complete proof systems (with decidable proof rules and axioms) can exist for full second-order logic. Higher-Order logic is a generalization of second-order and first-order logic which allows quantification over objects of an arbitrary higher type (i.e. quantification over predicates of predicates, and so on). There exist various theorem provers for programs that support higher-order logic: Isabelle/HOL [45], Why3 [27], PVS [68] and Coq [13].

Another relatively recent approach is Separation Logic [63], which extensively uses inductively defined predicates (i.e. second-order logic), but adds several non-standard logical connectives to reason about heap properties, such as the separating conjunction and the points-to predicate. These connectives support modularity, though they complicate proof theory (they cannot be axiomatized [15]). Tools that support separation logic for static verification of programs include: VeriFAST [42], jStar [26], Slayer [11] and Smallfoot [10].

3   Trace Specifications for Control- and Data-Flow

The formalisms described in the previous section for specifying object-oriented programs can be categorized in roughly two categories: those focussing on the control-flow of the program, and those focussing on the data-flow of the program. Formalisms focussing on the control-flow specify the allowed orderings between method calls, for example using regular expressions, context-free grammars or temporal logics. Formalisms for describing the data-flow generally use assertions to restrict the values of fields, parameters or local variables, possibly enhanced by constructs such as pre-post conditions and class invariants for supporting design by contract. But none of described specification languages were developed to *combine* the specification of the control-flow with the data-flow in a single formalism. In contrast, the behavior of almost all Java programs depends on both control-flow and data-flow: for example, the behavior of a stack is fully characterized by the sequence of method calls to `push` and `pop` it receives (the control-flow), together with the parameter and return values (the data-flow). For Java programs that encapsulate their internal state[4] an execution can be represented by the *global communication history* of the program: the sequence of *messages* corresponding to the invocation and completion of (possibly static) methods, including actual parameters and return values. Similarly, the execution of a single object can be represented by its *local communication history*, which consists of all messages sent and received by that object. The behavior of a program (or object) can then be defined as the set of its allowed histories. Jeffrey and Rathke [43] develop a fully abstract semantics based on histories which coincides with the standard operational semantics.

Let us call the orderings between method-calls and returns the *control-flow* of a history, and the actual parameters and return values the *data-flow* of the history. In this section we develop a single formalism which allows combining data-oriented properties of the history with protocol-oriented properties. To be of practical use, such a formalism should be *user-friendly*, amenable to (at least) *automated run-time verification* and sufficiently *expressive*. Below we propose attribute grammars extended with assertions and conditional productions for the specification of histories, and compare several alternatives approaches with respect to expressiveness, usability and automation.

Specifications can be used in two different ways: as a description of how an API (in our case, a set of Java classes and interfaces) must be used by a client (this can be seen as a kind of formalized user manual), or as an internal specification for developers of a class to test the class which is being developed. In the first case, only methods visible to clients can be used in the specification (i.e. public methods and no self-calls, since the user has no control over private methods and self-calls), in the second case for internal use we must also monitor self-calls and calls to private methods.

3.1   Modeling Framework

The modeling framework consists of three basic ingredients: communication views, grammars with conditional productions, and assertions. We use the interface of the Java `BufferedReader` (Figure 5) as a running example to explain these modeling concepts. In particular, we formalize the following property of the `BufferedReader`:

---

[4] Encapsulation means that objects do not have direct access to the fields of other objects. If access to a field x is needed, the programmer instead adds two methods `T getx()` and `void setX(T val)`.

The `BufferedReader` may only be closed by the same object which created it, and read actions may only occur between the creation and closing of the `BufferedReader`.

Note that the above property constrains the clients that use the `BufferedReader`; in other words, it is a kind of "user manual" for the reader, but does not guarantee that the reader itself works properly (since this property does not restrict the behavior of the reader itself). The property is a little unusual in that the reader actually cannot even detect whether a client uses it according to the above specification, since the reader has no way to detect whether the caller of `close` is the same object that constructed it. This last part can be seen as a form of dynamically checked ownership: the client which created the reader owns it, and the above property can serve as a first step to ensure that no information about the reader is leaked to other clients.

```
interface BufferedReader {
  void close();
  void mark(int readAheadLimit);
  boolean markSupported();
  int read();
  int read(char[] cbuf, int off, int len);
  String readLine();
  boolean ready();
  void reset();
  long skip(long n);
}
```

Fig. 5. Methods of the BufferedReader Interface

As a naive first step one might be tempted to define the behavior of `BufferedReader` objects simply in terms of 'call-m($\overline{T}$)' and 'return-m($\overline{T}$)' messages of all methods 'm' in its interface, where the parameter types $\overline{T}$ are included to distinguish between overloaded methods (such as `read`). However, interfaces in Java contain only signatures of provided methods: methods where the `BufferedReader` is the callee. Calls to these methods correspond to messages received by the object. In general the behavior of objects also depends on messages sent by that object (i.e. where the object is the caller), and on the particular constructor (with parameter values) that created the object. Moreover it is often useful to select a particular subset of method calls or returns, instead of using calls and returns to all methods (a partial or incomplete specification). Finally in referring to messages it is cumbersome to explicitly list the parameter types. A *communication view* addresses these issues.

Communication View. A communication view is a partial mapping which associates a name to each message. Partiality makes it possible to filter irrelevant events and message names are convenient in referring to messages.

Suppose we wish to formally specify the property on page 227. This is a property which must hold for the local history of all instances of `java.util.BufferedReader`. The communication view in Figure 6 selects the relevant messages and associates them with intuitive names: *open, read* and *close.*

```
local view BReaderView specifies java.util.BufferedReader {
  BufferedReader(Reader in) open,
  BufferedReader(Reader in, int sz) open,
  call void close() close,
  call int read() read,
  call int read(char[] cbuf, int off, int len) read
}
```

Fig. 6. Communication view of a BufferedReader

All return messages and call messages methods not listed in the view are filtered. Note how the view identifies two different messages (calls to the overloaded `read` methods) by giving them the same name *read*. Though the above communication view contains only provided methods (those listed in the `BufferedReader` interface), required methods (e.g. methods of other interfaces or classes) are also supported. Since such messages are sent to objects of a different class (or interface), one must include the appropriate type explicitly in the method signature. For example consider the following message:

`call void C.m() out`

If we would additionally include the above message in the communication view, all call-messages to the method m of class C sent by a `BufferedReader` would be selected and named *out*. In general, incoming messages received by an object correspond to calls of provided methods and returns of required methods. Outgoing messages sent by an object correspond to calls of required methods and returns of provided methods. Incoming call-messages of local histories never involve static methods, as such methods do not have a callee.

Besides normal methods, communication views can contain signatures of constructors (i.e. the messages named *open* in our example view). As such, the set of signatures that occur in a communication view is not necessarily a subset of the signatures in the interface it specifies (since Java interfaces do not contain constructors). In this case, the view selects all calls/returns to an object of a class that implements that interface.

Incoming calls to provided constructors raise an interesting question: what would happen if we select such a message in a local history? At the time

of the call, the object has not even been created yet, so it is unclear which
BufferedReader object receives the message. We therefore only allow return-
messages of provided constructors (clearly constructors of other objects do not
pose the same problem, consequently we allow selecting both calls and returns to
required constructors), and for convenience omit **return**. Alternatively one could
treat constructors like static methods, disallowing incoming call-messages to constructors in local histories altogether. However this makes it impossible to express
certain properties (including the desired property of the **BufferedReader**) and
has no advantages over the approach we take.

Java programs can distinguish methods of the same name only if their parameter types are different. Communication views are more fine-grained: methods can
be distinguished also based on their return type or their access modifiers (such
as **public**). For instance, consider a scenario with suggestively named classes
Base and three subclasses **Sub1**, **Sub2** and **Sub3**, all of which provide a method
m. The return type of m in the **Base**, **Sub1** and **Sub2** classes is the class itself
(i.e. **Sub1** for m provided by **Sub1**). In the **Sub3** class the return type is **Sub1**.
To monitor calls to m only with return type **Sub1**, simply include the following
event in the view:

call Sub1 C.m() messagename

One may ask: why allow private methods to appear in specifications? After all,
private methods cannot be used by an outside client of the class. The same question arises when considering whether to monitor self-calls or not. By allowing
to monitor private methods and self-calls, the modeling framework and corresponding tool support can also be used by developers of the class, to test the
current implementation of the class in development. Communication views include an optional **excludeSelfCalls** keyword which indicates per event whether
self-calls must be tracked (for self-calls, the caller and the callee are the same).
While typically developers do not want to exclude self-calls for the purpose of
internal tests, this keyword is especially useful in public specifications for other
clients, that describe how the class must be used by the client.

Local communication views, such as 6, selects messages sent and received by *a single object* of a particular class, indicated by 'specifies
java.util.BufferedReader'. In contrast, global communication views select
messages sent and received by *any* object during the execution of the Java program. This is useful to specify global properties of a program. In addition to instance methods, calls and returns of static methods can also be selected in global
views. Figure 7 shows a global view which selects all returns of the method m of
a class or interface (or any of its subclasses) called **Ping**, and all calls to m on a
subtype of a class or interface called **Pong**. Note that communication views do
not distinguish instances of the same class (e.g. calls to 'Ping' on two different
objects of class 'Ping' both get mapped to the same terminal 'ping'). Different instances *can* be distinguished in the grammar using the built-in attributes
'caller' or 'callee', see the next two sections.

```
global view PingPong {
  return void Ping.m() ping,
  call void Pong.m() pong
}
```

Fig. 7. Global communication view

In contrast to interfaces of the programming language, communication views can contain constructors, required methods, static methods (in global views) and can distinguish methods based on return type or method modifiers such as 'static', or 'public'. See table 1 for a list of supported features which require special care. For example, to support dynamic binding, the actual run-time type of the callee must be used, instead of the static type of the variable or field in which the callee is stored. This means that the correspondence between the messages named in the communication view, and actual method calls in the program source code must be made at run-time. The other features listed in the table have been discussed above.

Table 1. Supported Java features that require special care

Constructors
Inheritance
Dynamic Binding
Overloading
Static Methods
Required Methods
Access Modifiers

Context-Free Grammars. Now that we have identified the basic messages using the communication view, the question arises how we can specify the valid orderings between these messages: *the protocol*. More specifically, we want to find a notation for the set of the valid histories (where a history is a finite sequence of messages). While the histories in this set will be finite (since at any point during execution, the then current history is finite), the set itself usually contains an infinite number of histories due to recursion or loops, so we cannot simply write it down explicitly. We can consider the set to be a language in which each history is a word, and each message is an alphabet symbol. This suggests we can use existing formalisms for defining languages, in particular the ones surveyed in Section 2. We use context-free grammars to specify the protocol behavior of histories.

Definition 1. *A history is valid with respect to a given context-free grammar if and only if all prefixes of the history (including the history itself) are generated by the grammar.*

The discussion in Section 3.3 provides a motivation for choosing grammars over the other formalisms, and a justification for our definition of a valid history.

The grammar below specifies the valid histories of the `BufferedReader`:

$$
\begin{aligned}
S &::= open\ C \\
&\quad |\quad \epsilon \\
C &::= read\ C \\
&\quad |\quad close\ S \\
&\quad |\quad \epsilon
\end{aligned}
$$

Fig. 8. Context-Free Grammar which specifies that 'read' may only be called in between 'open' and 'close'

This grammar describes the prefix closure of sequences of the terminals 'open', 'read' and 'close' as given by the regular expression $((open\ read * close)*)$. In general, the message names given by a communication view form the terminal symbols of the grammar, whereas the non-terminal symbols specify the structure of valid sequences of messages (in particular, the start symbol S generates the valid histories).

3.2 Attribute Grammars and Assertions

While context-free grammars provide a convenient way to specify the *protocol structure* of the valid histories, they do not take data such as parameters and return values of method calls and returns into account. Thus the question arises how to specify the *data-flow* of the valid histories. To that end, we first extend the above context-free grammars with so-called attributes.

Definition 2. *Terminal Attributes. Given a terminal T, an attribute of T assigns a value to each instance[5] of T (i.e. to each token of T).*

For example, consider a terminal INT_LITERAL, and suppose the string "33" is an instance of INT_LITERAL. One could define an attribute *val* for INT_LITERAL, which assigns the number 33 to the string "33". Note that terminal attributes can assign different values to different instances of the same terminal.

In the previous section we saw that (instances of) terminals correspond to call or return messages. The question arises: what are sensible attributes for such terminals? Several objects are involved in the sending of the messages: the

---

[5] A token is a string of symbols. A terminal can be seen as a token type, whose tokens are considered to be syntactically "similar".

caller, the *callee*, and the actual data being sent in the form of actual parameters or a return value *result*. We define *built-in* attributes (named *callee*, *caller*, and so on) to capture precisely those objects involved in the message. In summary, attributes of terminals are determined (i.e., built-in) from the method signatures given in the communication view.

Next we define attributes for non-terminals. Unlike attributes for terminals, they are defined by the user in the grammar. Given a context-free grammar G and a non-terminal V, let us denote by $L(V)$ the language generated from the non-terminal V by using the productions of G.

Definition 3. *Non-terminal Attributes. Given a set of values D and a context-free grammar with a non-terminal V, an attribute for V is a function $f : L(V) \to D$.*

Intuitively the above definition states that a non-terminal attribute assigns values to all of the words generated by that non-terminal. The value of non-terminal attributes is user-defined: the user must associate with each production, source code that computes the attribute values of all non-terminals involved in the production. There are two kinds of non-terminal attributes: synthesized attributes and inherited attributes. In each production the user defines the value of the synthesized attributes of the non-terminal on the left-hand side of the production, and the values of the inherited attributes of the non-terminals appearing on the right-hand side of the production. In general this does not rule out circular attribute definitions The seminal paper [47] in which Knuth first introduced attribute grammars contains an algorithm which detects circular definitions. Using actual source code for the attribute definitions ensures that all attribute values of non-terminals are computable. Of course this source code may not terminate, we rely on the user to make sure that it does.

In our setting, the grammar non-terminals generate sequences of call/return messages. Hence, a non-terminal attribute can be seen as a property of the data-flow of that sequence and hence, as an important special case, the attributes of the start symbol of the grammar can be considered as properties of the data-flow of the history. We are now ready to define attribute grammars:

Definition 4. *An attribute grammar is a pair (G, F), where G is a context-free grammar, and F is a set of attributes for G.*

Note that the attributes themselves do not alter the language generated by the attribute grammar, they only *define* properties of data-flow of the history. We extend the attribute grammar with assertions to specify properties of attributes. For example, in the attribute grammar in Figure 9 a user-defined synthesized attribute 'c' for the non-terminal 'C' is defined to store the identity of the object which closed the `BufferedReader` (and is `null` if the reader was not closed yet). Synthesized attributes define the attribute values of the non-terminals on the left-hand side of each grammar production, thus the 'c' attribute is not set in the productions of the start symbol 'S'. The extension of context-free grammars to attribute grammars with assertions and conditional productions (next called "extended attribute grammars") naturally gives rise to the following modification in the definition of a valid history.

Definition 5. *A history is valid with respect to a given extended attribute-grammar if and only if all prefixes of the history (including the history itself) are generated by the grammar, and all assertions in the grammar were true for every prefix of the history.*

The assertion in the attribute grammar of the `BufferedReader` allows only those histories in which the object that opened (created) the reader is also the object that closed it. Throughout the paper the start symbol in any grammar is named 'S'. For clarity, attribute definitions are written between parentheses '(' and ')' whereas assertions over these attributes are surrounded by braces '{' and '}'.

$$
\begin{aligned}
S ::= &\ open\ C_1\ \{\texttt{assert (open.caller == null ||}\\
      &\qquad\qquad\quad\ \texttt{open.caller ==} C_1\texttt{.c ||}\\
      &\qquad\qquad\quad\ C_1\texttt{.c == null);}\}\\
   |\ &\ \epsilon\\
C ::= &\ read\ C_1\ (C\texttt{.c =} C_1\texttt{.c;})\\
   |\ &\ close\ S\ (C\texttt{.c = close.caller;})\\
   |\ &\ \epsilon \qquad\ (C\texttt{.c = null;})
\end{aligned}
$$

Fig. 9. Attribute Grammar which specifies that 'read' may only be called in between 'open' and 'close', and the reader may only be closed by the object which opened it

Assertions can be placed at any position in a production rule and are evaluated at the position they were written. Note that assertions appearing directly before a terminal can be seen as a precondition of the terminal, whereas post-conditions are placed directly after the terminal. This is in fact a generalization of traditional pre- and post-conditions for methods as used in design-by-contract: a single terminal 'call-m' can appear in multiple productions, each of which is followed by a different assertion. Hence different preconditions (or post-conditions) can be used for the same method, depending on the context (grammar production) in which the event corresponding to the method call/return appears. Traditional pre- and post-conditions are still useful if in every context, the same assertion must be used: in that case, the assertions in the grammar would be duplicated at every occurence of the appropriate terminal. In Section 5.1 we show an example which uses traditional pre- and post-conditions.

It is important to note that for a meaningful semantics we have to restrict the attribute grammars to those grammars which are side-effect free (with respect to the heap) so that they don't affect the flow of control of the tested program, and which do not involve dereferencing of the built-in attributes of the grammar terminal (the formal parameters of the corresponding methods as specified by the communication view) because these refer to the *current* heap (and not to the past one corresponding to the occurrence of the message). This latter restriction is a fairly natural requirement as the method call which generated the grammar terminal only passed the the object identities of the actual parameters, but not the values of the fields of these objects. Note also that this requirement is automatically satisfied by using encapsulation.

Attribute grammars in combination with assertions cannot express *protocol that depend on data*. To express such protocols we consider attribute grammars enriched by *conditional productions* [59]. In such grammars, a production is chosen only when the given condition (a `boolean` expression over the inherited attributes) for that production is true. Hence conditions are evaluated before any of the symbols in the production are parsed, before synthesized attributes of the non-terminals appearing in the production are set and before assertions are evaluated. In contrast to assertions, conditions in productions affect the parsing process. The Worker grammar in Figure 30 in the case study contains a conditional production for the 'T' non-terminal.

In summary, a communication view selects and names the relevant messages. Selection allows to focus just on the relevant messages while names allow the identification of different messages, and enable the user to refer to the messages in a user-friendly manner. Context-free grammars specify the allowed orderings of the messages. The terminals of the grammars are the names as introduced by the communication view. These names are not just simple strings, but also contain various attributes such as the sender, receiver and the data sent in the message. The non-terminals are user-defined and generate sets of sequences of messages (i.e. histories), as given by the grammar productions. The start symbol of the grammar generates the valid histories. A context-free grammar can thus be seen as specifying a kind of invariant of the control-flow. Attribute grammars allow defining data properties of sequences of terminals, and in particular of the whole history. To this end, the user defines attributes of the grammar non-terminals in terms of the attributes of the grammar terminals. The values of non-terminal attributes are defined by Java code, which ensures that the attribute definitions are computable. The extension of attribute grammars with assertions makes it possible to specify data-oriented properties of the history, by constraining the value of the non-terminal attributes.

Finally, conditional productions can be used for protocols that *depend* on data. In general, it is possible to specify a single interface or class with multiple communication views (and corresponding grammars). This increases expressiveness: it makes it possible to specify the intersection of two context-free languages (if the user specifies two grammars, the history must satisfy both), and context-free languages are not closed under intersection. Furthermore multiple communication views and grammars can be used as partial specifications for the class or interface, to focussing on a particular behavioral aspect. If it is possible to decompose a single complete specification into multiple partial specifications, the resulting specifications are often simpler. This stems from the fact that a complete specification formalizes various properties, and care must be taken to avoid unwanted interference between these properties. In contrast, partial specifications can be used to formalize each property individually.

3.3 Discussion

We now briefly motivate our choice of attribute grammars extended by assertions as specifications and discuss its advantages over alternative formalisms.

Instead of context-free grammars, we could have selected push-down automata to specify protocol properties (formally these have the same expressive power). Unfortunately push-down automata cannot handle attributes. An extension of push-down automata with attributes results in a kind of Turing machine. From a user perspective, the declarative nature and higher abstraction level of grammars (compared to the imperative and low-level nature of automata) makes them much more suitable than automata as a *specification* language. In fact, a push-down automaton which recognizes the same language as a given grammar is an *implementation* of a parser for that grammar.

Both the BufferedReader above and the case study use only regular grammars. Since regular grammars simplify parsing compared to context-free grammars, the question arises if we can reasonably restrict to regular grammars. Unfortunately this rules out many real-life use cases. For instance, the following grammar in EBNF[6] specifies the valid protocol behavior of a stack:

$$S ::= (push\ S\ pop\ ?)^*$$

It is well-known that the language generated by the above grammar is not regular (apply the pumping lemma for regular languages [65]), so regular grammars (without attributes) cannot be used to enforce the safe use of a stack. It is possible to specify the stack using an attribute which counts the number of pushes and pops:

```
S ::= S₁ push (S.cnt = S_1.cnt+1;)
    |   S₁ pop  (S.cnt = S_1.cnt-1;)
               {assert S.cnt >=0;}
    |   ε       (S.cnt = 0;)
```

The resulting grammar is clearly less elegant and less readable: essentially it encodes (instead of directly expresses, as in the grammar above) a protocol-oriented property as a data-oriented one. The same problem arises when using regular grammars to specify programs with recursive methods. Thus, although theoretically possible, we do not restrict to regular grammars for practical purposes.

---

[6] EBNF is an extension of the usual BNF notation for context-free grammars which allows using the operators on regular expressions (such as the Kleene star '*' and the '?' operator standing for an optional occurrence, i.e., 'r?' stands for 'r + ε') directly inside grammars.

Ultimately the goal of run-time checking safety properties is to prevent unsafe ongoing behavior. To do so, errors must be detected as soon as they occur; this is known as *fail-fast*, and the monitor must *immediately* terminate the system: it cannot wait until the program ends to detect errors. In other words, the monitor must decide *after every event* whether the current history is still valid. The simplest notion of a valid history (one which should not generate any error) is that of a word generated by the grammar. One way of fulfilling the above requirement, assuming this notion of validity, is to restrict to prefix-closed grammars. Unfortunately it's not possible to decide whether a context-free grammar is prefix-closed. The following lemmas formalize this result:

Lemma 1. *Let L_M be the set of all accepting computation histories[7] of a Turing Machine M. Then the complement $\overline{L_M}$ is a context-free language.*

Proof. See [65].

Lemma 2. *It is undecidable whether a context-free language is prefix-closed.*

Proof. We show how the halting problem for M (which is undecidable) can be reduced to deciding prefix-closure of $\overline{L_M}$. To that end, we distinguish two cases:

1. M does not halt. Then L_M is empty so $\overline{L_M}$ is universal and hence prefix-closed.
2. M halts. Then there is an accepting history $h \in L_M$ (and $h \notin \overline{L_M}$). Extend h with an illegal move (one not permitted by M) to the configuration C, resulting in the history $h\#C$. Clearly $h\#C$ is not a valid accepting history, so $h\#C \in \overline{L_M}$. But since $h \notin \overline{L_M}$, $\overline{L_M}$ is not prefix-closed.

Summarizing, M halts if and only if $\overline{L_M}$ is not prefix-closed. Thus if we could decide prefix-closure of the context-free language (lemma 1) $\overline{L_M}$, we could decide whether M halts.

Since prefix-closure is not a decidable property of grammars (not even if they don't contain attributes) we propose the following alternative definition for the valid histories. A communication history is valid if and only if all its prefixes are generated by the grammar. Note that this new definition naturally fulfills the above requirement of detecing errors after every event. And furthermore this notion of validity is decidable assuming the assertions used in the grammar are decidable. As an example of this new notion of validity, consider the following modification of the above grammar:

$$
\begin{array}{lll}
T ::= S & \{\texttt{assert S.cnt >=0;}\} \\
S ::= S_1 \; push & (\texttt{S.cnt = S\_1.cnt+1;}) \\
\quad | \quad S_1 \; pop & (\texttt{S.cnt = S\_1.cnt-1;}) \\
\quad | \quad \epsilon & (\texttt{S.cnt = 0;})
\end{array}
$$

---

[7] A computation history of a Turing Machine is a sequence $C_0\#C_1\#C_2\#\ldots$ of configurations C_i. Each configuration is a triple consisting of the current tape contents, state and position of the read/write head. Due to a technicality, the configurations with an odd index must actually be encoded in reverse.

Note that the history *push pop* is a word generated by this grammar, but not its prefix *pop*, which as such will generate an error (as required). Note that thus in general invalid histories are guaranteed to generate errors. On the other hand, if a history generates an error all its extensions are therefore also invalid.

Observe that our approach monitors only safety properties ('prevent bad behavior'), not liveness ('something good eventually happens'). This restriction is not specific to our approach: liveness properties in general cannot be rejected on any finite prefix of an execution, and monitoring only checks finite prefixes for violations of the specification. Most liveness properties fall in the class of the non-monitorable properties [61,7]. However it *is* possible to ensure liveness properties for terminating programs: they can then be reformulated as safety properties. For instance, suppose we want to guarantee that a method void m() is called before the program ends. Introduce the following global view

```
global view livenessM {
  call void C.m() m,
  return static void C.main(String[]) main
}
```

The occurence of the 'main' event (i.e. a return of the main method of the program) signifies the program is about to terminate. Define the EBNF grammar

$S ::= \epsilon$
$\quad | \quad m$
$\quad | \quad m+ main$

(where '+' stands for one or more repetitions). This grammar achieves the desired effect since the only terminating executions allowed are those containing m. In local views a similar effect is obtained by including the method finalize (which is called once the object will be detroyed) instead of main.

4 Implementation

Given a Java interface specified with an attribute grammar, we would like to test whether an object implementing the interface satisfies the properties defined in the grammar at every point in its lifetime. In this section we first describe the generic architecture of our tool SAGA [25] which achieves this. Four different components are combined: a state-based assertion checker, a parser generator, a debugger and a general tool for meta-programming. Traditionally these tools are used for very diverse purposes and don't need to interact with each other. We therefore investigate requirements needed to achieve a seamless integration of these components, motivated by describing the workflow of the run-time checker. In the next section we instantiate the four components with concrete state-of-the-art tools.

Suppose that during execution of a Java program, a method of a class (subsequently referred to as CUT, the 'class under test') which implements an interface specified by an attribute grammar is called. The new history of the object on which the method was called should be updated to reflect the addition of

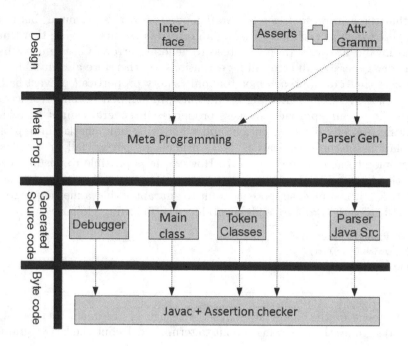

Fig. 10. Generic Tool Architecture

the method call. To represent the history of an object of CUT, the **Meta-Programming** tool generates for each method m in CUT two classes `call-m` and `return-m`. These classes contain the following fields: the object identitity of the *callee*, the identity of the *caller* and the actual parameters. Additionally `return-m` contains a field `result` containing the return value. A Java `List` containing instances of `call-m` and `return-m` then stores the history of an object of CUT.

The meta-programming tool further generates code for a wrapper class which replaces the original main class. We will refer to this class as the "history class". This history class contains a field H, a Java `map` containing pairs (`id`, `h`) of an object identity `id` and its local history `h`. Moreover it stores the current values of the synthesized attributes of the start symbol, these can be used in assertion languages supporting design by contract (See Section 5.1 for an example of this usage). The history class executes the original program inside the **Debugger**. The Debugger is responsible for monitoring execution of the program. It must be capable of temporarily 'pausing' the program whenever a call or return occurs, and execute user-defined code to update H appropriately . Moreover the Debugger must be able to read the identity of the callee, caller and parameters/return-value.

After the history is updated the run-time checker must decide whether it still satisfies the specification (the attribute grammar). Observe that a communication history can be seen as a sequence of tokens (in our setting: communication events). Since the attribute grammar together with the assertions generate the language of all valid histories, checking whether a history satisfies the specification reduces to deciding whether the history can be parsed by a parser for the attribute grammar, where moreover during parsing the assertions must evaluate to true. Therefore the **Parser Generator** creates a parser for the given attribute grammar. Since the history is a heterogenous list of `call-m` and `return-m` objects, the parser must support parsing streams of tokens with user-defined types. Assertions in general describe properties of Java objects, and the grammar contains assertions over attributes, the attributes must be normal Java variables. Consequently the parser generator must allow arbitrary user-defined java code (to set the attribute value) in rule actions. The use of Java code ensures the attribute values are computable. Since assertions are allowed in-between any two (non)-terminals, the parser generator should support user-defined actions between arbitrary grammar symbols. At run-time, the parser is triggered whenever the history of an object is updated. The result is either a parse error, which indicates that the current communication history has violated the protocol structure specified by the attribute grammar, or a parse tree with new attribute values. During parsing, the **Assertion Checker** evaluates the assertions in the grammar on the newly computed attribute values. To avoid parsing the whole history of a given object each time a new call or return is appended, ideally the parser should support incremental parsing [34]. An incremental parser computes a parse tree for the new history based on the parse trees for prefixes of the history. In our setting, the attribute grammar specifies invariant properties of the ongoing behavior. Hence the parser constructs a new parse tree after each call/return, consequently parse trees for all prefixes of the current history can be exploited for incremental parsing.

To illustrate how the tools described above interact with each other at run-time, the UML sequence diagram in Figure 11 shows the run-time environment of a successful method invocation of a (single-threaded) Java program, containing a class Class Under Test (CUT) whose local history is specifed by an attribute grammar. The actors in the sequence diagrams are:

- 'User Prog': A client class that instantiates and uses CUT.
- 'Debugger': Java debugger that intercepts all method calls and corresponding returns from 'User Prog' to CUT.
- 'History (instance)': an instance of the history class. This class stores the local history of each object of CUT.
- 'Parser': an instance of a parser for the given attribute grammar. The source code of the Parser was generated by the Parser Generator.
- 'Assertion Checker': provides facilities to check assertions at run-time.
- 'Class Under Test (CUT)': The class which was specified using an attribute grammar.
- 'stderr': the standard error stream of the system. Error reports (such as an assertion failure or protocol violation) can be sent to this stream.

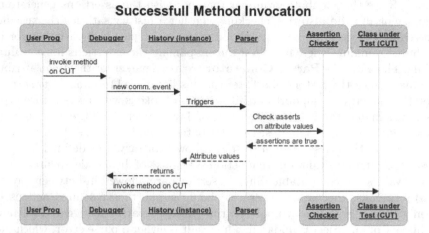

Fig. 11. Run-time environment of successfull method invocation

Figure 12 shows a scenario in which a method return causes the updated history to violate the grammar rules. In this case, the parser detects a parse error and outputs a protocol violation to 'stderr'. The scenario in which parsing is successfull, but the assertions cause an error, is not shown but very similar.

4.1   Instantiating the Tool Architecture

The previous section introduced the generic tool architecture, which was based on four different components: meta-programming, debugger, parser generator and state-based run-time assertion checker. Here we instantiate these four components with particular (state of the art) tools, and report our experiences to what extent the requirements stated in the previous section are satisfied by these current tools. The main overhead of the run-time checker is caused by the parser, hence we discuss performance (both theoretical and in practice) in the paragraph on parser generators.

Meta-Programming. Rascal [46] is a tool-supported domain specific language for meta programming. We use its parsing, source code analysis, source-to-source transformation and source code generation features. A ± 1000 line Rascal program[8] takes care of:

- parsing and analyzing the Java method signatures in the communication view.
- generating Java source for a debugger. The debugger should intercept any method call and return, and inform the History class that an event occured.

---

[8] Excluding the grammar for Java.

Method Return: protocol violation

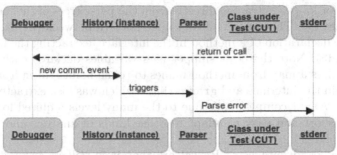

Fig. 12. Run-time environment of successfull method invocation

- generating the token classes `call-m` and `return-m` for each call and return event in the view.
- generating the History class, which specifically accepts new events from the provided methods in the interface and acts as a token stream for the generated parser.

The full source code which Rascal generates for the above tasks contains about 50 times the number of events + 100 lines of code, in other words, the size of the generated code depends mainly on the number of events in the communication view.

Note that we require general meta programming features for several input languages, not just Java. This application of Rascal has three languages as input (ANTLR grammars, View declarations and Java), and one output language (Java). Rascal runs on a JVM, such that it integrates into any Java environment.

In the following Rascal snippet we generate update methods in the history class which are called whenever a method returns.

```
return "
<for ('<mods> <return> <id> (<formals>)' <- methods) {
  r = "return_<id>";>
public void update(return_<id> e) {
<if (r in tokens){>
  e.setType(<grammarName>Lexer.<tokens[r]>);
  addAndParse(e);<}>
}
<}>";
```

This return statement contains three levels. The Rascal language level (in bold-face) provides the return statement, the string, and embedded in the string expressions marked by <...> angular brackets. The string that is generated represent an (unparsed) Java fragment. The fragments embedded in back ticks (') represent parsed Java fragments from the input interface. Inside those fragments Rascal expressions occur again between angular brackets.

The string template language of Rascal allows us to instantiate a number of methods called `update` using a `for` loop and an `if` statement. The data that is used in the for loop is extracted directly from the parse trees of the methods in a Java interface file. The concrete Java source pattern between the back ticks (') matches the declaration of a method in the interface, extracting the name of the method (`<id>`). Note that this snippet uses variables declared earlier, such as `tokens` which is a map from method names to token names taken from the view declaration in the interface and `grammarName` which was also extracted from the view earlier. Albeit complex code due to the many levels required for this task, the code is short and easy to adapt to other kinds of analysis and generation patterns.

The main disadvantages of Rascal are that it is still in an alpha stage, it is not fully backwards compatible and we discovered numerous bugs in Rascal during development of the Rascal program. However overall our experience was quite positive. The identified bugs were fixed quickly by the Rascal team, and its powerful parsing, pattern matching and transforming concrete syntax features proved indispensable.

Debugger. We evaluated Sun's implementation of the Java Debugging Interface for the debugger component. It is part of the standard Java Development Kit, hence maintenance of the debugger is practically guaranteed. The Sun debugger starts the original user program in separate a virtual machine which is monitored for occurences of `MethodEntryEvent` (method calls) and `MethodExitEvent` (method returns). It allows defining event handlers which are executed whenever such events occur. It also allows retrieving the caller, callee, parameters values and return value of events using `StackFrames`. No actual Java source code for the class under test is needed for the debugging. The approach is safe in that no source code nor bytecode is modified for the monitoring. The Sun debugger meets all requirements for the debugger stated above. As the main disadvantage, we found that the current implementation of the debugger is very slow. In fact it was responsible for the majority of the overhead of the run-time checker. This is not necessarily problematic: as testing is done during development, the debugger will typically not be present in performance critical production code. Moreover, one usually wants to test only up to a certain bound (for instance, in time, or in the number of events), and report on results once the bound is exceeded. Nonetheless, for testing up to huge bounds, a different implementation for the debugger is needed.

As an alternative we have also tested AspectJ, a Java compiler which supports aspect-oriented programming. Aspect-oriented programming is tailored for monitoring. AspectJ can intercept method calls and returns conveniently with pointcuts, and weave in user-defined code (advices) which is executed before or after the intercepted call. In our case the pointcuts correspond to the calls and returns of the messages listed in the communication view. The advice consists of code which updates the history. The code for the aspect is generated from the communication view automatically by the Rascal meta-program. Advice can either be woven into Java source code, byte code or at class load-time fully automatically by AspectJ. Note that in contrast to the above Java Debugger approach this step involves changing the source or bytecode, which may be deemed as less safe. We use the inter-type declarations of AspectJ to store the local history of an object as a field in the object itself. This ensures that whenever the object goes out of scope, so does its history and consequently reduces memory usage. Clearly the same does not hold for global histories, which are stored inside a separate Aspect class. Figure 13 shows a generated aspect. The second and third line specify the relevant method, in this case **BufferedReader.read**. The fourth line binds variables ('clr', 'cle', ...) to the appropriate objects. Note that to support dynamic binding, it is not possible to statically match method calls to in the Java source to the below pointcut: the dynamic type of the callee, which is determined at run-time, determines whether the pointcut matches. The fifth line ensures that the aspect is applied only when Java assertions are turned on. Assertions can be turned on or off for each communication view individually. The fifth line contains the advice that updates the history. Note that since the event came was defined in a local view, the history is treated as a field of the callee and will not persist in the program indefinitely but rather is garbage collected as soon as callee object itself is.

```
    /* call int read(char[] cbuf, int off, int len); */
before(Object clr, BufferedReader cle,
        char[] cbuf, int off, in len):
 (call( int *.read(char[], int, int))
  && this(clr) && target(cle) && args(cbuf, off, len)
  && if(BReaderHistoryAspect.class.desiredAssertionStatus() ))
 {
   cle.h.update(new call_push(clr, cle, cbuf, off, len));
 }
```

Fig. 13. Aspect for the event 'call int read(char[] cbuf, int off, int len)'

As a third alternative, we also tested the meta-programming tool Rascal to generate code which intercepts the method calls and returns appropriately. This can be done by defining a transformation on the actual Java source code of the class under test, which requires a full Java grammar (which must be kept in sync with the latest updates to Java). To capture the identity of the callee, parameter values and return value of a method, one only needs to transform that particular method (i.e. locally). But inside the method there is no way to access the identity of the caller. Java does offer facilities to inspect stack frames, but these frames contain only static entities, such as the name of the method which called the currently executing method, or the type of the caller, but not the caller itself. To capture the caller, a global transformation at all call-sites is needed (and in particular one needs to have access to the source code of *all* clients which call the method). The same problem arises in monitoring calls to required methods.

Finally it proved to quickly get very complex to handle all Java features listed in Table 1. We wrote an initial version of a weaver in Rascal which already took over 150 lines (over half of the full checker at the time) without supporting method calls appearing inside expressions, inheritance, dynamic binding, constructors and overloading. Moreover the meta-programming approach is also unsuitable if the Java source code is not available (which happens frequently for libraries) ing where only byte code is available, limiting the applicability of the tool. In summary, while it is possible to implement monitoring by defining a code transformation in Rascal, this rules out bytecode only libraries, and quickly gets complex due to the need for a full (up to date) Java grammar and the complexity of the full Java language.

Parser Generator. For the the parser generator component we tested ANTLR v3, a state of the art parser generator. It generates fast recursive descent parsers for Java and allows grammar actions and custom token streams. It even supports conditional productions: productions which are only chosen during parsing whenever an associated Boolean expression (the condition) is true and allow for a degree of context-senstitiveness. Attribute grammars with conditional productions express protocols that depend on data which are typically not context-free. ANTLR also supports EBNF, a notation grammars which extends context-free grammars with the operations from regular expressions, for example the Kleene star. Though EBNF does not strictly increase expressiveness (the language generated by such grammars is still context-free), it is convenient for practical purposes: sometimes a regular expression is simpler and more natural than a full-fledged grammar.

Due to the power of general context-free grammars extended with attributes (as introduced in the seminal paper [47] by Knuth), they can be quite expensive to parse. In particular, the currently best known algorithm [67] to parse context-free grammars has a time complexity of $\mathcal{O}(n^{2.38})$ (with very huge constants), where n is the number of terminals to parse. The current best practical algorithms (with reasonably sized constants) require cubic time. Clearly parsing n tokens cannot be done in less than $\mathcal{O}(n)$ steps, since the entire input must be read. Besides this trivial linear lower bound, no non-trivial lower bounds are known [32], though Lee [49] showed that multiplication of two square Boolean matrices can be reduced at a certain cost to parsing context-free grammars. In particular, she showed that if parsing n tokens can be done in $\mathcal{O}(n^{3-\epsilon})$ steps, then we can multiple two n by n Boolean matrices in $\mathcal{O}(n^{3-(\epsilon/3)})$ steps, with small constants. This means that any practical (i.e. small constants) sub-cubic parsing algorithm also can be used as a practical sub-cubic matrix multiplication algorithm. However no such fast practical algorithm is known for matrix multiplication.

ANTLR avoids the cubic-time parsing inefficiency by only supporting LL(*) grammars[9]. Due to the restriction, the parsing algorithm used by ANTLR is for most grammars linear, and quadratic in the worst case. A major disadvantage of

---

[9] A strict subset of the context-free grammars. Left-recursive grammars are not LL(*).

ANTLR is that it lacks support for incremental parsing: each time the history is updated (i.e. a single terminal is added), the full history has to be reparsed. Additionally the full history has to be saved. Support for incremental parsing is planned by the ANTLR developers. We have not been able to find any Java parser generator which supports incremental parsing of attribute grammars.

Assertion Checker. We tested two state-based assertion languages: standard Java assertions and the Java Modeling Language (JML). Both languages suffice for our purposes. A Java assertions is a statement `assert b;` where b is a standard `boolean` expressions. As a consequence, note that Java assertions can contain calls to methods that return a `boolean`. Though Java assertions can not contain quantifiers, it is to some degree possible to simulate those using a method containing a loop. Java does not enforce assertions to be side-effect free: one needs to check manually that only 'pure' assertions are used.

JML is far more expressive than the standard Java assertions. It allows unbounded quantification, in general any first-order formula can be expressed in JML, and supports Design by Contract (see also Section 5.1). JML also ensures that assertions are side-effect free. Unfortunately the JML tool support is not ready yet for industrial usage. In particular, the last stable version of the JML run-time assertion checker dates back over 8 years, when for instance generics were not supported yet. The main reason is that JML's run-time assertion checker only works with a proprietary implementation of the Java compiler, and unsurprisingly it is costly to update the proprietary compiler each time the standard compiler is updated. This problem is recognized by the JML developers [16]. OpenJML, a new alpha version of the JML run-time assertion checker integrates into the standard Java compiler, and initial tests with it provided many valuable input for real industrial size applications. See the Sourceforge tracker of Open-JML at `http://sourceforge.net/tracker/?group_id=65346&atid=510629` for the kind of issues we have encountered when using OpenJML.

5 Case Studies

In this section we use the formalism described in Section 3 and the extension to design by contract described in Section 4 to specify a Java library, and an industrial-sized case from the e-commerce company Fredhopper. The Java library we consider is a (last-in-first-out) Stack. The Stack example illustrates how the *Design by Contract* methodology as supported by JML can be used to specify the **push** and **pop**-methods purely in terms of histories in an elegant manner. In particular, this example shows how synthesized attributes of the start-symbol can be used conveniently inside method pre- and postconditions. Based on the case study, we discuss our experiences with SAGA.

5.1 Design by Contract: Stack

A Stack is an abstract data type which has only two operations **push** and **pop**. The operation **push** adds an object to the stack, while **pop** returns and removes

```
public interface Stack {
    void push(Object item);
    Object pop();
}
```

Fig. 14. Stack Interface

the last element from the stack which was pushed but not yet removed. The operation **pop** is not allowed on an empty Stack. Figure 14 shows an interface for the Stack in Java.

Our task is to find a specification for the Stack which ensures that **pop** is never called by the user on an empty stack, and moreover that **pop** returns the right object when called on a non-empty stack. The communication view in Figure 15 selects three events. The returns of push are needed to keep track of the elements which have been pushed onto the Stack. Note that it would incorrect be to consider the calls to **push** instead: suppose some strange implementation of **push** would itself call **pop** as its first action, before restoring the removed element and adding the element which was passed to **push**. Then calling **push** on an empty stack would fail (since that results in calling **pop** on an empty stack), but the history would be 'PUSH POP' (which seemingly looks valid for a Stack). Selecting returns of push avoids this problem. The calls to **pop**, which are referred to by the terminal 'POP', are needed to ensure that **pop** is never called on an empty Stack. In this case it would not suffice to track only returns of **pop**, since whenever **pop** is executed on an empty stack, the run-time checker would only detect the failure after executing of **pop** (which fails), and thus does not *prevent* unsafe behavior.

The protocol behavior of this view can be defined in terms of sequences of the *terminals* 'PUSH' and 'POP' generated by the context-free grammar given in Figure 16, where 's' is the start symbol.

The non-terminal 's' generates the *prefix closure* of the standard grammar for *balanced* sequences of 'PUSH' and 'POP' (which are generated by the non-terminal 'b'). This ensures that **pop** is never called on an empty stack.

In order to specify the relation between the actual parameters of calls to the **push** method and the return values of the **pop** method, we introduce a synthesized attribute 'stack' of type JMLListValueNode for the non-terminal 's'. JMLListValueNode is a JML class for a singly-linked list with *side-effect free* implementations of the methods JMLListValueNode append(Object item) , which appends an item to the list, and JMLListValueNode concat(JMLListValueNode ls2) which concatenates two lists. The intended value of the 'stack' attribute is a list of the elements which are pushed but have not yet been popped. Since balanced Stacks are empty, associating the 'stack' attribute also to the b-non-terminal would be redundant. Figure 17 shows how 'stack' is updated in each production of the non-terminal s. Intuitively the value of 'stack' at the root of the parse-tree

```
local view StackHistory specifies Stack {
    return push PUSH;
    call pop POP;
}
```

Fig. 15. Communication View of a Stack

$$s ::= \text{PUSH } s$$
$$| \quad s\ s$$
$$| \quad b$$
$$b ::= \text{PUSH } b \text{ POP}$$
$$| \quad \epsilon$$
$$| \quad b\ b$$

Fig. 16. Abstract Stack Behavior

$$s ::= \text{PUSH } s_1 \quad (\text{stack } =s_1.\text{stack.append(PUSH.item)};)$$
$$| \quad s_1\ s_2 \quad (\text{stack } =s_1.\text{stack.append}(s_2.\text{Stack});)$$
$$| \quad b \qquad (\text{stack } = \text{stack.clear()};)$$
$$b ::= \text{PUSH } b \text{ POP}$$
$$| \quad \epsilon$$
$$| \quad b\ b$$

Fig. 17. Attribute Grammar Stack Behavior

(i.e. an occurence of the start-symbol s) is a list containing the current contents of the Stack. Figure 18 shows the parse tree for the history resulting from the program s.push(5); s.push(7); s.pop();. Note that this does not mean that an actual implementation of the stack interface works correctly: the attribute grammar can be considered as a 'reference implementation' of the stack, but we still need to ensure that an actual implementation of the Stack matches (in the sense that calling pop returns the right value) this reference implementation.

In order to specify the method contracts for the Stack, the JML implementation of SAGA (described in Section 4.1) allows referring to the synthesized attributes of the root of the parse tree. Since the start symbol in the parse tree generates the whole history, intuitively the synthesized attributes of the start symbol can be thought of as a property of the entire history. In order to use the attribute 'stack' of this grammar in assertions for specifying the contracts of the push and pop methods of the 'Stack' interface (Figure 14) in terms of communication histories, the modeling framework provides a class StackHistory which corresponds to the communication view of Figure 15. This class contains a 'getter' method JMLListValueNode stack() which retrieves the value of the attribute 'stack' of the root of the parse tree of the current history.

Figure 19 illustrates how the StackHistory class can be used to specify the desired contracts. The JML keyword model indicates that history (of type StackHistory) can be used only in specifications. The keyword instance

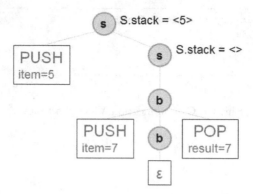

Fig. 18. Parse tree annotated with attribute values for the history push(5) push(7) pop() in the grammar of Figure 17 (irrelevant attributes ommitted)

```
interface Stack {
  //@ public model instance StackHistory history;

  //@ ensures history.stack().equals(
  //@              \old(history.stack()).append(item));
  void push(Object item);

  //@ ensures history.stack().equals(
  //@              \old(history.stack()).tail());
  //@ ensures \result == \old(history.stack()).head();
  Object pop();
}
```

Fig. 19. JML Specification Stack Interface

specifies that `history` will be added as a (non-static) field to any class that implements the `Stack` interface. The `ensures` and `requires` clauses specify the method contracts in terms of the 'stack' attribute (whose value is defined in the attribute grammar). Summarizingly, the property that `pop` may not be called on an empty stack is ensured by the productions of the grammar (the grammar productions can be considered to be an interface invariant for the protocol behavior), and the property that `pop` returns the right object is guaranteed by the method contracts and the definition of the attribute 'stack'.

Note that alternatively we could have avoided the method contracts by instead adding appropriate assertions in the attribute grammar before and after *every* occurence of 'PUSH' and 'POP' in the grammar. This leads to duplication since 'PUSH' occurs multiple times in the grammar. Moreover, for this alternative solution, we should also have added to the communication view that we intend to capture returns of `pop`: otherwise there would be no way to check that `pop` returned the right value. For the above example, we favour the above

design-by-contract solution over the assertions-in-grammar, since it avoids duplication of specifications and additionally avoids adding the extra terminal for
returns of **pop**. This increases readability of the grammar, and results in less
overhead for the run-time check since the sequence of tokens to parse is shorter.

5.2 Fredhopper Case-Study

Fredhopper[10] is a search, merchandising and personalization solution provider,
whose products are tailored to the needs of online businesses. Fredhopper operates behind the scenes of more than 100 of the largest online shops[11]. It provides
the Fredhopper Access Server (FAS), which is a distributed concurrent object-
oriented system that provides search and merchandising services to eCommerce
companies. Briefly, FAS provides to its clients structured search capabilities
within the client's data. Each FAS installation is deployed to a customer according to the FAS deployment architecture (See Figure 20).

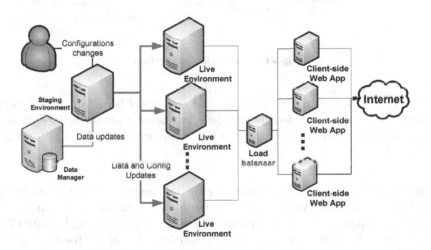

Fig. 20. An example FAS deployment

FAS consists of a set of live environments and a single staging environment. A
live environment processes queries from client web applications via web services.
FAS aims at providing a constant query capacity to client-side web applications.
A staging environment is responsible for receiving data updates in XML format, indexing the XML, and distributing the resulting indices across all live
environments according to the *Replication Protocol*. The Replication Protocol is
implemented by the *Replication System*. The Replication System consists of a

---

[10] http://www.sdl.com/products/fredhopper/
[11] http://www.sdl.com/campaign/wcm/gartner-maqic-quadrant-wcm-2013.html?
    campaignid=70160000000fSXu

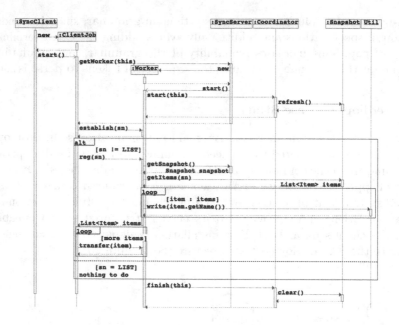

Fig. 21. Replication interaction

SyncServer at the staging environment and one *SyncClient* for each live environment. The SyncServer determines the schedule of replication, as well as its content, while SyncClient receives data and configuration updates according to the schedule.

Replication Protocol. The SyncServer communicates to SyncClients by creating *Worker* objects. Workers serve as the interface to the server-side of the Replication Protocol. On the other hand, SyncClients schedule and create *ClientJob* objects to handle communications to the client-side of the Replication Protocol. When transferring data between the staging and the live environments, it is important that the data remains *immutable*. To ensure immutability without interfering the read and write accesses of the staging environment's underlying file system, the SyncServer creates a *Snapshot* object that encapsulates a snapshot of the necessary part of the staging environment's file system, and periodically *refreshes* it against the file system. This ensures that data remains immutable until it is deemed safe to modify it. The SyncServer uses a *Coordinator* object to determine the safe state in which the Snapshot can be refreshed. Figure 21 shows a UML sequence diagram concerning parts of the replication protocol with the interaction between a SyncClient, a ClientJob, a Worker, a SyncServer, a Coordinator and a Snapshot. the diagram also shows a *Util* class that provides static methods for writing to and reading from `Stream`. The figure assumes that SyncClient has already established connection with a SyncServer and shows how a ClientJob from the SyncClient and a Worker from a SyncServer

```
interface Snapshot {
 void refresh();
 void clear();
 List<Item> items(String sn);
}

interface Worker {
 void establish(String sn);
 List<Item> reg(String sn);
 void transfer(Item item);
 SyncServer server();
}
```

Fig. 22. SnapShot and Worker interfaces of Replication System

```
interface SyncServer {
 Snapshot snapshot();
}

interface Coordinator {
 void start(Worker t);
 void finish(Worker t);
}

class Util {
 static void write(String s) { .. }
}
```

Fig. 23. SyncServer and Coordinator interfaces of Replication System

are instantiated for interaction. For the purpose of this paper we consider this part of the Replication Protocol as a *replication session*.

In this section we show how to modularly decompose object interaction behavior depicted by the UML sequence diagram in Figure 21 using SAGA. Figures 22 and 23 shows the corresponding interfaces and classes, note that we do not consider SyncClient as our interest is in object interactions of a replication session, that is after ClientJob.start() has been invoked.

The protocol descriptions and specifications considered in this case study have been obtained by manually examining the behavior of the existing implementation, by formalizing available informal documentations, and by consulting existing developers on intended behavior. Here we first provide such informal descriptions of the relevant object interactions:

```
local view SnapshotHistory
grammar Snapshot.g
specifies Snapshot {
 call void refresh() rf,
 call void clear() cl
}
```

Fig. 24. Snapshot Communication View

```
local view CoordinatorHistory
grammar Coordinator.g
specifies Coordinator {
 call void start(Worker t) st,
 call void finish(Worker t) fn
}
```

Fig. 25. Coordinator Communication View

- Snapshot: at the initialization of the Replication System, `refresh` should be called first to refresh the snapshot. Subsequently the invocations of methods `refresh` and `clear` should alternate.
- Coordinator: neither of methods `start` and `finish` may be invoked twice in a row with the same argument, and method `start` must be invoked before `finish` with the same argument can be invoked.
- Worker: `establish` must be called first. Furthermore `reg` may be called *if* the input argument of `establish` is not "LIST" but the name of a specific replication schedule, and that `reg` must take that name as an input argument. When the `reg` method is invoked and before the method returns, the Worker must obtain the replication items for that specific replication schedule via method `items` of the Snapshot object. The Snapshot object must be obtained via method `snapshot` of its SyncServer, which must be obtained via the method `server`. It must notify the name of each replication item to its interacting SyncClient. This notification behavior is implemented by the static method `write` of the class `Util`. The method `reg` also checks for the validity of each replication item and so the method must return a subset of the items provided by the method `items`. Finally `transfer` may be invoked after `reg`, one or more times, each time with a unique replication item, of type `Item`, from the list of replication items, of type `List<Item>`, returned from `reg`.

Figures 24 to 27 specifies communication views. They provide partial mappings from message types (method calls and returns) that are local to individual objects to grammar terminal symbols. Note that the specification of the Worker's behavior is modularly captured by two views: `WorkerHistory` and

```
local view WorkerHistory grammar Worker.g
specifies Worker {
 call void establish(String sn) et,
 call List<Item> reg(String sn) rg,
 return List<Item> reg(String sn) is,
 call void transfer(Item item) tr
}
```

Fig. 26. Worker Communication View

```
local view WorkerRegHistory grammar WorkerReg.g
specifies Worker {
 call List<Item> reg(String sn) rg,
 return List<Item> reg(String sn) is,
 return Snapshot SyncServer.snapshot() sp,
 call List<Item> Snapshot.items(String sn) ls,
 return List<Item Snapshot.items(String sn) li,
 call static void Util.write(String s) wr
}
```

Fig. 27. WorkerReg Communication View

WorkerRegHistory. The view WorkerHistory exposes methods establish, reg
and transfer. Using this view we would like to capture the overall valid interaction in which Worker is the callee of methods, and at the same time the view
helps abstracting away the implementation detail of individual methods. The
view WorkerRegHistory, on the other hand, captures the behavior inside reg.
According to the informal description above, the view projects incoming method
calls and returns of reg, outgoing method calls to server and items, and as
well as the outgoing static method calls to write.

We now define the abstract behavior of the communication views, that
is, the set of allowable sequences of interactions of objects restricted to
those method calls and returns mapped in the views. Each local view also
defines the file containing the attribute grammar, whoses terminal symbols the view maps method invocations and returns to. Specifically, Figures 28 to 31 shows the attribute grammars Snapshot.g, Coordinator.g,

$$S ::= \epsilon \mid rf\ T$$
$$T ::= \epsilon \mid cl\ S$$

Fig. 28. Snapshot Attribute Grammar

$$
\begin{aligned}
S ::=\quad & T \ (T.\texttt{ts} = \texttt{new HashSet();}) \\
T ::=\ \epsilon\ |\ & st \ \{\texttt{assert ! } T.\texttt{ts.contains}(st.\texttt{t});\} \\
& (T.\texttt{ts.add}(st.\texttt{t});)\ T_1 \ (T_1.\texttt{ts} = T.\texttt{ts};) \\
& |\ fn \ \{\texttt{assert } T.\texttt{ts.contains}(fn.\texttt{t});\} \\
& (T.\texttt{ts.remove}(fn.\texttt{t});)\ T_1 \ (T_1.\texttt{ts} = T.\texttt{ts};)
\end{aligned}
$$

Fig. 29. Coordinator Attribute Grammar

$$
\begin{aligned}
S ::=\ \epsilon\ |\ & et\ T \ (T.\texttt{d} = et.\texttt{sn};) \\
T ::=\ \epsilon\ |\ & \{!\,\texttt{"LIST".equals}(T.\texttt{d});\}? \\
& rg \ \{\texttt{assert } rg.\texttt{sn.equals}(T.\texttt{d});\}\ U \\
U ::=\ \epsilon\ |\ & is\ V \ (V.\texttt{m} = \texttt{new ArrayDeque}(is.\texttt{result});) \\
V ::=\ \epsilon\ |\ & tr \quad \{\texttt{assert } V.\texttt{m.peek().equals}(tr.\texttt{item});\} \\
& (V.\texttt{m.pop}();)\ V_1 \ (V_1.\texttt{m} = V.\texttt{m};)
\end{aligned}
$$

Fig. 30. Worker Attribute Grammar

`Worker.g` and `WorkerReg.g` for views `SnapshotHistory`, `CoordinatorHistory`, `WorkerHistory` and `WorkerRegHistory` respectively.

The simplest grammar `Snapshot.g` specifies the interaction protocol of Snapshot. It focuses on invocations of methods `refresh` and `clear` per Snapshot object. The grammar essentially specifies the (prefix-closure of the) regular expression (`refresh clear`)∗.

The grammar `Coordinator.g` specifies the interaction protocol of Coordinator. It focuses on invocations of methods `start` and `finish`, both of which take a Worker object as the input parameter. These method calls are mapped to terminal symbols st and fn, while their inherited attribute is a `HashSet`, recording the input parameters, thereby enforcing that for each unique Worker object as an input parameter only the set of sequences of method invocations defined by the regular expression (`start finish`)∗ is allowed.

The grammar `Worker.g` specifies the interaction protocol of Worker It focuses on invocations and returns of methods `establish`, `reg` and `transfer`. The grammar specifies that for each Worker object, `establish` must be first invoked, then followed by `reg` and then zero or more `transfer`, that is, the regular expression (`establish reg transfer`∗). We use the attribute definition of the grammar to ensure the following:

– The input argument of `establish` and `reg` must be the same;
– `reg` can only be invoked if the input argument of `establish` is not "LIST";
– The return value of `reg` is a list of `Item` objects such that `transfer` is invoked with each of `Item` in that list from position 0 to the size of that list.

The grammar `WorkerReg.g` specifies the behavior of the method `reg` of Worker. It focuses on the invocations and returns of method `reg` of Worker as well as the outgoing method calls and returns of `Util.write` and `SyncServer.snapshot` and `Snapshot.items`. At the protocol level the grammar

```
/*S accepts call to Worker.reg() and, records */
/*the input schedule name, also S allows */
/*arbitary calls to SyncServer.snapshot() */
/*and Util.write() */
S ::= ε | wr S | sp S | rg T (T.d = et.sn;)

/*T accepts and stores the return */
/*snapshot object from SyncServer.snapshot() */
T ::= ε | sp V (V.d = T.d; U.s = sp.result;)

/*U ensures call items() is called on the same */
/*snapshot object, and the replication items */
/*for the correct schedule are retrieved */
U ::= ε | ls {assert ls.callee.equals(U.s);
             assert ls.sn.equals(U.d);}
         V (V.s = U.s;)

/*V records replication items and their name */
/*returned from item() */
V ::= ε | li W (W.is = new HashSet(li.result);
               W.ns = new HashSet();
               for (Item i :W.is) {
                   W.ns.add(i.name()); })

/*W ensures all replication */
/*items are processed */
W ::= ε | wr (W.ns.remove(wr.s);)
         W₁ (W₁.ns =W.ns; W₁.is =W.is;)
         | is {assert W.is.containsAll(is.result);
              assert W.ns.isEmpty();}
         X

X ::= ε | sp X | rg X
```

Fig. 31. WorkerReg Attribute Grammar

specifies the regular expression (`snapshot items write*`) inside the invocation method `reg`. We use attribute definition to ensure the following:

- `Snapshot.items` must be called with the input argument of `reg` and it must be called on the Snapshot object that is identical to the return value of `SyncServer.snapshot`;
- The static method `Util.write` must be invoked with the value of `Item.name` for each `Item` object in the Collection returned from `Snapshot.items`;

– The returned list of Item objects from reg must be a subset of that returned from Snapshot.items.

Notice that methods Util.write and SyncServer.snapshot may be invoked outside of the method reg. However, this particular behavioral property does not specify the protocol for those invocations. The grammar therefore abstracts from these invocations by allowing any number of calls to Util.write and SyncServer.snapshot before and after reg.

5.3   Experiment

We applied SAGA to the Replication System. The current Java implementation of FAS has over 150,000 lines of code, and the Replication System has approximately 6400 lines of code, 44 classes and 5 interfaces.

We have successfully integrated SAGA into the quality assurance process at Fredhopper. The quality assurance process includes automated testing that includes automated unit, integration and system tests as well as manual acceptance tests. In particular system tests are executed twice a day on instances of FAS on a server farm. Two types of system tests are scenario and functional testing. Scenario testing executes a set of programs that emulate a user and interact with the system in predefined sequences of steps (scenarios). At each step they perform a configuration change or a query to FAS, make assertions about the response from the query, etc. Functional testing executes sequences of queries, where each query-response pair is used to decide on the next query and the assertion to make about the response. Both types of tests require a running FAS instance and as a result we may leverage SAGA by augmenting these two automated test facilities with runtime assertion checking using SAGA.

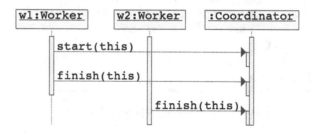

Fig. 32. Violating histories

To integrate of SAGA with the system tests, we employ Apache Maven tool[12], an open source Java based tool for managing dependencies between applications and for building dependency artifacts. Maven consists of a project object model (POM), a set of standards, a project lifecycle, and an extensible dependency

---

[12] maven.apache.org

```
class WKImpl extends Thread
implements Worker {
 final Coordinator c;
 WKImpl(Coordinator c) {
   this.c = c; }
 public void run() {
  try { .. c.start(this); ..
  } finally {
    c.finish(this); .. }}}
```

Fig. 33. Incorrect behavior of WKImpl

management and build system via plug-ins. We use its build system to automatically generate and package the parser/lexer of attribute grammars as well as aspects from views and grammars. We expose the packaged aspects, parser and lexer to FAS instance on the server farm and employ Aspectj using load-time weaver for monitoring method calls/returns during the execution of FAS instances on the server farm. Table 2 shows the number of join point matches during the execution of 766 replication sessions over live client data. Figure 34 shows the exection time of the 766 replication sessions with and without the integration of SAGA in milliseconds. At some points (for example, around 261 events), the figure seemingly indicates that the system runs faster with SAGA than without. In reality this is not the case: the dependence of the case study on user input (i.e., to start replication sessions) means that it is impossible to replicate an execution exactly (with the only difference being SAGA turned on and off respectively) and leads to small errors in the measurements. However, despite the fact that we cannot control the exact flow of control of the replication sessions (due to this dependence on user input), the graph clearly shows that the integration of SAGA has minimal performance impact on the execution time.

During this session we have found an assertion error at join point call finish due to the condition $T.\text{ts.contains}(fn.t)$ not being satisfied at non-terminal T of the grammar Coordinator.g. Specifically, the implementation of Worker (WKImpl) that invoke finish before start. Figure 32 shows the sequence diagram of an invalid history causing the error, fully automatically generated from the output of SAGA. Figure 33 shows part of the implementation of WKImpl. It turns out that in the run method of WKImpl, the method start is invoked inside a try block while the method finish is invoked in the corresponding finally block. As a result when there is an exception being thrown by the execution preceding the invocation of start inside the try block, for example a network disruption, finish would be invoked without start being invoked.

Table 2. Join point matches in 766 replication sessions

Join point	Terminal	Match
call static write	wr	247446
return snapshot	sp	3061
call transferItem	tr	1101
return reg (WorkerHistory)	is	765
return reg (WorkerRegHistory)	is	765
call establish	et	766
call reg (WorkerHistory)	rg	765
call reg (WorkerRegHistory)	rg	765
return items	li	765
call start	st	766
call finish	fn	766
call items	ls	765
call refresh	rf	766
call clear	cl	766

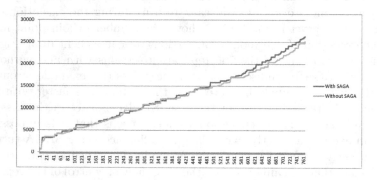

Fig. 34. Comparison of the execution time (milliseconds) of the replication sessions with and without the integration of SAGA

References

1. Abdallah, A.E., Jones, C.B., Sanders, J.W. (eds.): Communicating Sequential Processes. LNCS, vol. 3525. Springer, Heidelberg (2005)
2. Allan, C., Avgustinov, P., Christensen, A.S., Hendren, L.J., Kuzins, S., Lhoták, O., de Moor, O., Sereni, D., Sittampalam, G., Tibble, J.: Adding trace matching with free variables to AspectJ. In: OOPSLA, pp. 345–364 (2005)
3. Artho, C., Drusinksy, D., Goldberg, A., Havelund, K., Lowry, M., Păsăreanu, C.S., Roşu, G., Visser, W.: Experiments with test case generation and runtime analysis. In: Börger, E., Gargantini, A., Riccobene, E. (eds.) ASM 2003. LNCS, vol. 2589, pp. 87–107. Springer, Heidelberg (2003)
4. Backus, J.W.: The syntax and semantics of the proposed international algebraic language of the Zurich ACM-GAMM conference. In: IFIP Congress, pp. 125–131 (1959)

5. Baeten, J.C.M., Basten, T., Reniers, M.A.: Process Algebra: Equational Theories of Communicating Processes, 1st edn. Cambridge University Press, New York (2009)
6. Bartetzko, D., Fischer, C., Möller, M., Wehrheim, H.: Jass - Java with assertions. Electr. Notes Theor. Comput. Sci. 55(2) (2001)
7. Bauer, A., Leucker, M., Schallhart, C.: Comparing LTL semantics for runtime verification. J. Log. Comput. 20(3), 651–674 (2010)
8. Beckert, B., Hähnle, R., Schmitt, P.H. (eds.): Verification of Object-Oriented Software. LNCS (LNAI), vol. 4334. Springer, Heidelberg (2007)
9. Bengtsson, J., Larsen, K.G., Larsson, F., Pettersson, P., Yi, W.: Uppaal — a tool suite for automatic verification of real–time systems. In: Alur, R., Sontag, E.D., Henzinger, T.A. (eds.) HS 1995. LNCS, vol. 1066, pp. 232–243. Springer, Heidelberg (1996)
10. Berdine, J., Calcagno, C., O'Hearn, P.W.: Smallfoot: Modular Automatic Assertion Checking with Separation Logic. In: de Boer, F.S., Bonsangue, M.M., Graf, S., de Roever, W.-P. (eds.) FMCO 2005. LNCS, vol. 4111, pp. 115–137. Springer, Heidelberg (2006)
11. Berdine, J., Cook, B., Ishtiaq, S.: sLAYER: Memory safety for systems-level code. In: Gopalakrishnan, G., Qadeer, S. (eds.) CAV 2011. LNCS, vol. 6806, pp. 178–183. Springer, Heidelberg (2011)
12. Bergstra, J.A., Klop, J.W.: Act_{tau}: A universal axiom system for process specification. In: Algebraic Methods, pp. 447–463 (1987)
13. Bertot, Y., Castéran, P., Huet, G., Paulin-Mohring, C.: Interactive theorem proving and program development: Coq'Art: the calculus of inductive constructions. Texts in theoretical computer science. Springer, Berlin (2004)
14. Burdy, L., Cheon, Y., Cok, D.R., Ernst, M.D., Kiniry, J.R., Leavens, G.T., Leino, K.R.M., Poll, E.: An overview of JML tools and applications. International Journal on Software Tools for Technology Transfer 7(3), 212–232 (2005)
15. Calcagno, C., Yang, H., O'Hearn, P.W.: Computability and complexity results for a spatial assertion language for data structures. In: Hariharan, R., Mukund, M., Vinay, V. (eds.) FSTTCS 2001. LNCS, vol. 2245, pp. 108–119. Springer, Heidelberg (2001)
16. Chalin, P., James, P.R., Karabotsos, G.: JML4: Towards an industrial grade IVE for java and next generation research platform for JML. In: Shankar, N., Woodcock, J. (eds.) VSTTE 2008. LNCS, vol. 5295, pp. 70–83. Springer, Heidelberg (2008)
17. Chen, F., Rosu, G.: MOP: an efficient and generic runtime verification framework. In: OOPSLA, pp. 569–588 (2007)
18. Cheon, Y., Perumandla, A.: Specifying and checking method call sequences of Java programs. Software Quality Journal 15(1), 7–25 (2007)
19. Cimatti, A., Clarke, E., Giunchiglia, F., Roveri, M.: Nusmv: A new symbolic model verifier. In: Halbwachs, N., Peled, D.A. (eds.) CAV 1999. LNCS, vol. 1633, pp. 495–499. Springer, Heidelberg (1999)
20. Clarke, E.M., Emerson, E.A.: Design and synthesis of synchronization skeletons using branching-time temporal logic. In: Kozen, D. (ed.) Logic of Programs. LNCS, vol. 131, pp. 52–71. Springer, Heidelberg (1981)
21. Clarke, E.M., Grumberg, O., Peled, D.: Model checking. MIT Press (2001)
22. Colombo, C., Pace, G.J., Schneider, G.: LARVA — safer monitoring of real-time java programs (tool paper). In: SEFM, pp. 33–37 (2009)
23. Damm, W., Harel, D.: LSCs: Breathing life into message sequence charts. Formal Methods in System Design 19(1), 45–80 (2001)

24. de Boer, F.S., Bonsangue, M.M., Steffen, M., Ábrahám, E.: A fully abstract semantics for UML components. In: de Boer, F.S., Bonsangue, M.M., Graf, S., de Roever, W.-P. (eds.) FMCO 2004. LNCS, vol. 3657, pp. 49–69. Springer, Heidelberg (2005)
25. de Gouw, S., de Boer, F.S., Johnsen, E.B., Wong, P.Y.H.: Run-time checking of data- and protocol-oriented properties of Java programs: an industrial case study. In: SAC, pp. 1573–1578 (2013)
26. Distefano, D., Parkinson, M.J.: jStar: towards practical verification for Java. In: OOPSLA, pp. 213–226 (2008)
27. Filliâtre, J.-C., Marché, C.: The Why/Krakatoa/Caduceus platform for deductive program verification. In: Damm, W., Hermanns, H. (eds.) CAV 2007. LNCS, vol. 4590, pp. 173–177. Springer, Heidelberg (2007)
28. Fischer, C., Wehrheim, H.: Behavioural subtyping relations for Object-Oriented formalisms. In: Rus, T. (ed.) AMAST 2000. LNCS, vol. 1816, pp. 469–483. Springer, Heidelberg (2000)
29. Floyd, R.W.: Assigning meanings to programs. In: Schwartz, J.T. (ed.) Mathematical Aspects of Computer Science, Providence, Rhode Island. Proceedings of Symposia in Applied Mathematics, vol. 19, pp. 19–32. American Mathematical Society (1967)
30. Gabbay, D.M., Kurucz, A., Wolter, F., Zakharyaschev, M.: Many-Dimensional Modal Logics: Theory and Applications. Elsevier (2003)
31. Gamma, E., Helm, R., Johnson, R., Vlissides, J.: Design Patterns. Elements of Reusable Object-Oriented Software. Addison-Wesley (1995)
32. Grune, D., Jacobs, C.J.: Parsing Techniques - A Practical Guide, 2nd edn. Springer (2008)
33. Harel, D., Kozen, D., Tiuryn, J.: Dynamic Logic. MIT Press, Cambridge (2000)
34. Hedin, G.: Incremental attribute evaluation with side-effects. In: Hammer, D. (ed.) CCHSC 1988. LNCS, vol. 371, pp. 175–189. Springer, Heidelberg (1989)
35. Heisel, M., Reif, W., Stephan, W.: Implementing verification strategies in the KIV-system. In: Lusk, E.'., Overbeek, R. (eds.) CADE 1988. LNCS, vol. 310, pp. 131–140. Springer, Heidelberg (1988)
36. Hennessy, M.: Algebraic theory of processes. MIT Press series in the foundations of computing. MIT Press (1988)
37. Henzinger, T.A., Jhala, R., Majumdar, R., Sutre, G.: Software verification with BLAST. In: Ball, T., Rajamani, S.K. (eds.) SPIN 2003. LNCS, vol. 2648, pp. 235–239. Springer, Heidelberg (2003)
38. Hoare, C.A.R.: An axiomatic basis for computer programming. Commun. ACM 12(10), 576–580 (1969)
39. Hoare, C.A.R.: Communicating Sequential Processes. Prentice-Hall (1985)
40. Holzmann, G.J.: The model checker SPIN. IEEE Trans. Software Eng. 23(5), 279–295 (1997)
41. International Telecommunication Union. ITU-T Recommendation Z.120: Message Sequence Chart (MSC). Technical report, ITU, Geneva (2001)
42. Jacobs, B., Smans, J., Philippaerts, P., Vogels, F., Penninckx, W., Piessens, F.: VeriFast: a powerful, sound, predictable, fast verifier for C and Java. In: Bobaru, M., Havelund, K., Holzmann, G.J., Joshi, R. (eds.) NFM 2011. LNCS, vol. 6617, pp. 41–55. Springer, Heidelberg (2011)
43. Jeffrey, A., Rathke, J.: ava Jr: Fully abstract trace semantics for a core Java language. In: Sagiv, M. (ed.) ESOP 2005. LNCS, vol. 3444, pp. 423–438. Springer, Heidelberg (2005)
44. Kleene, S.C.: Representation of events in nerve nets and finite automata. Automata Studies (1956)

45. Klein, G., Nipkow, T.: A machine-checked model for a Java-like language, virtual machine, and compiler. ACM Trans. Prog. Lang. Syst. 28(4), 619–695 (2006)
46. Klint, P., van der Storm, T., Vinju, J.J.: Rascal: a domain specific language for source code analysis and manipulation. In: Walenstein, A., Schupp, S. (eds.) Proceedings of the IEEE International Working Conference on Source Code Analysis and Manipulation (SCAM 2009), pp. 168–177 (2009)
47. Knuth, D.E.: Semantics of context-free languages. Mathematical Systems Theory 2(2), 127–145 (1968)
48. Kwiatkowska, M., Norman, G., Parker, D.: PRISM: Probabilistic symbolic model checker. In: Field, T., Harrison, P.G., Bradley, J., Harder, U. (eds.) TOOLS 2002. LNCS, vol. 2324, pp. 200–204. Springer, Heidelberg (2002)
49. Lee, L.: Fast context-free grammar parsing requires fast boolean matrix multiplication. J. ACM 49(1), 1–15 (2002)
50. Li, X., Liu, Z., Ile, J.: A formal semantics of UML sequence diagram. In: Australian Software Engineering Conference, pp. 168–177 (2004)
51. Martin, J.C.: Introduction to Languages and The Theory of Computation. McGraw-Hill (2010)
52. Martin, M., Livshits, B., Lam, M.S.: Finding application errors and security flaws using PQL: a Program Query Language. In: OOPLSLA (2005)
53. Meyer, B.: Object-Oriented Software Construction, 2nd edn. Prentice-Hall (1997)
54. Mikhajlov, L., Sekerinski, E.: A study of the fragile base class problem. In: Jul, E. (ed.) ECOOP 1998. LNCS, vol. 1445, pp. 355–382. Springer, Heidelberg (1998)
55. Milner, R.: Fully abstract models of typed λ-calculi. Theoretical Comput. Sci. 4, 1–22 (1977)
56. Milner, R.: A Calculus of Communication Systems. LNCS, vol. 92. Springer, Heidelberg (1980)
57. Milner, R.: Communicating and Mobile Systems: The π-Calculus. Cambridge University Press, New York (1999)
58. Nobakht, B., Bonsangue, M.M., de Boer, F.S., de Gouw, S.: Monitoring method call sequences using annotations. In: Barbosa, L.S., Lumpe, M. (eds.) FACS 2010. LNCS, vol. 6921, pp. 53–70. Springer, Heidelberg (2012)
59. Parr, T.J., Quong, R.W.: Adding semantic and syntactic predicates to LL(k): pred-LL(k). In: Fritzson, P.A. (ed.) CC 1994. LNCS, vol. 786, pp. 263–277. Springer, Heidelberg (1994)
60. Pnueli, A.: The temporal logic of programs. In: 18th Annual Symposium on Foundations of Computer Science, pp. 46–57 (1977)
61. Pnueli, A., Zaks, A.: PSL model checking and run-time verification via testers. In: Misra, J., Nipkow, T., Sekerinski, E. (eds.) FM 2006. LNCS, vol. 4085, pp. 573–586. Springer, Heidelberg (2006)
62. Pratt, V.R.: Semantical considerations on Floyd-Hoare logic. In: FOCS, pp. 109–121 (1976)
63. Reynolds, J.C.: Separation logic: A logic for shared mutable data structures. In: LICS, pp. 55–74 (2002)
64. Sangiorgi, D., Walker, D.: The Pi-Calculus - a theory of mobile processes. Cambridge University Press (2001)
65. Sipser, M.: Introduction to the theory of computation. PWS Publishing Company (1997)
66. Stolz, V., Huch, F.: Runtime verification of concurrent Haskell programs. Electr. Notes Theor. Comput. Sci. 113, 201–216 (2005)
67. Valiant, L.G.: General context-free recognition in less than cubic time. J. Comput. Syst. Sci. 10(2), 308–315 (1975)

68. van den Berg, J., Jacobs, B.: The LOOP Compiler for Java and JML. In: Margaria, T., Yi, W. (eds.) TACAS 2001. LNCS, vol. 2031, pp. 299–312. Springer, Heidelberg (2001)
69. van Eijk, P.H.J., Vissers, C., Diaz, M. (eds.): Formal Description Technique Lotos: Results of the Esprit Sedos Project. Elsevier Science Inc., New York (1989)
70. Visser, W., Havelund, K., Brat, G.P., Park, S., Lerda, F.: Model checking programs. Autom. Softw. Eng. 10(2), 203–232 (2003)

Test Case Generation by Symbolic Execution: Basic Concepts, a CLP-Based Instance, and Actor-Based Concurrency

Elvira Albert[1], Puri Arenas[1], Miguel Gómez-Zamalloa[1],
and Jose Miguel Rojas[2]

[1] DSIC, Complutense University of Madrid (UCM), Spain
[2] Department of Computer Science, University of Sheffield, UK

Abstract. The focus of this tutorial is white-box test case generation (TCG) based on symbolic execution. Symbolic execution consists in executing a program with the contents of its input arguments being symbolic variables rather than concrete values. A symbolic execution tree characterizes the set of execution paths explored during the symbolic execution of a program. Test cases can be then obtained from the successful branches of the tree. The tutorial is split into three parts: (1) The first part overviews the basic techniques used in TCG to ensure termination, handling heap-manipulating programs, achieving compositionality in the process and guiding TCG towards interesting test cases. (2) In the second part, we focus on a particular implementation of the TCG framework in constraint logic programming (CLP). In essense, the imperative object-oriented program under test is automatically transformed into an equivalent executable CLP-translated program. The main advantage of CLP-based TCG is that the standard mechanism of CLP performs symbolic execution for free. The PET system is an open-source software that implements this approach. (3) Finally, in the last part, we study the extension of TCG to actor-based concurrent programs.

1 Introduction

A lot of research has been devoted in the last years to the problem of generating test cases automatically. A recent survey [6] describes some of the most prominent approaches to TCG, namely *model-based TCG*, *combinatorial TCG*, *(adaptive) random TCG*, *search-based TCG* and *structural (white-box) TCG*. This tutorial focuses on *structural (white-box) TCG*, an approach in which the availability of the code of the program under test is assumed and test cases are obtained from the concrete program (e.g., using its control flow graph) in contrast to *black-box* testing, where they are deduced from a specification of the program. Also, our focus is on *static* testing, since we assume no knowledge about the input data, in contrast to *dynamic* approaches [17,24] which execute the program under test using concrete input values.

Symbolic execution [11,13,15,23,31,35,36,46] is arguably the most widely used enabling technique for structural white-box TCG. It has received a renewed

M. Bernardo et al. (Eds.): SFM 2014, LNCS 8483, pp. 263–309, 2014.

interest in recent years, thanks in part to the increased availability of computational power and decision procedures [9]. Structural white-box TCG is among the most studied applications of symbolic execution, with several tools available [10]. Symbolic execution consists in executing a program with the contents of its input arguments being symbolic variables rather than concrete values. A symbolic execution *tree* characterizes the set of execution paths explored during the symbolic execution of a program. Test cases are obtained from the successful branches of the tree. The set of obtained test cases forms a test suite.

The first part of the tutorial is devoted to review the basic concepts of TCG by symbolic execution. We start by explaining the challenges to efficiently handle heap-manipulating programs [38] in symbolic execution. The presence of dynamic memory operations such as object creation and read/write field accesses requires special treatment during symbolic execution. Moreover, in order to ensure reliability, symbolic execution must consider all possible shapes these dynamic data structures can take. We proceed next to see how one can go to symbolic execution to the actual production of test cases. An important issue that is discussed afterwards is the compositionality of the TCG process. Finally, we overview a practical issue to efficiently generate more relevant test cases. In particular, guided TCG is a methodology that aims at steering symbolic execution towards specific program paths in order to generate relevant test cases and filter out less interesting ones.

The second part of the tutorial introduces CLP-based Test Case Generation. CLP-based TCG advocates the use of CLP technology to perform test case generation of imperative object-oriented programs. The process has two phases. In the first phase, the imperative object-oriented program under test is automatically transformed into an equivalent executable *CLP-translated* program. Instructions that manipulate heap-allocated data are represented by means of calls to specific *heap operations*. In the second phase, the CLP-translated program is symbolically executed using the standard CLP execution and constraint solving mechanisms. The above-mentioned heap operations are also implemented in standard CLP, in a suitable way in order to support symbolic execution. We will see the advantages of the CLP-based framework and, in particular, why it is very relevant to implement guided TCG and an efficient heap solver. In this context, we present the PET system, a system that implements the CLP-based TCG framework described in this part and which is available online.

The last part of the tutorial is focused on TCG of actor-based concurrent programs. It is known that writing correct concurrent programs is harder than writing sequential ones, because with concurrency come additional hazards not present in sequential programs such as race conditions, data races, deadlocks, and livelocks. However, due to the non-deterministic interleavings of processes, traditional testing for concurrent programs is not as effective as for sequential programs. Systematic and exhaustive exploration of all interleavings is typically too time-consuming and often computationally intractable (see, e.g., [45] and its references). Furthermore, the fact that different scheduling policies can be implemented affects the order in which tasks are selected for execution and, thus, the initial state when resuming a task can be different by adopting one policy or another. As a result, computation is often non-deterministic and multiple (possibly different) solutions can be produced depending on the interleaved tasks and the scheduler.

The adoption of actor systems has some advantages in the regard. Very briefly, actors [1, 25] constitute a model of concurrent programming that has been gaining popularity and that it is being used in many systems (such as ActorFoundry, Asynchronous Agents, Charm++, E, ABS, Erlang, and Scala). Actor programs consist of computing entities called actors or objects, each with its own local state and thread of control, that communicate by exchanging messages asynchronously. An object configuration consists of the local state of the objects and a set of pending messages (or *tasks*). In response to receiving a message, an object can update its local state, send messages, or create new objects. At each step in the computation of an object system, an object from the system is scheduled to process one of its pending messages. The advantage of using actor-systems in testing is that, as objects do not share their states, one can assume [41] that the evaluation of all statements of a task takes place serially (without interleaving with any other task) until it releases the processor (gets to a return instruction). This assumption alleviates already a lot the scalability issues mentioned above. We will discuss a basic algorithm and the main challenges in TCG of actor systems.

2   Test Case Generation by Symbolic Execution

This section provides a general overview of TCG by symbolic execution and the main challenges that currently the method poses.

2.1   Basic Concepts in Symbolic Execution

A symbolic execution *tree* characterizes the set of execution paths explored during the symbolic execution of a program. During the course of symbolic execution, the values of the program's variables are represented as symbolic expressions over the input symbolic values and a *path condition* is maintained. Such a path condition is updated whenever a branch instruction is executed. For instance, for each conditional statement in the program, symbolic execution explores both the "then" and the "else" branch, refining the path condition accordingly. The satisfiability of each of these branches is checked and symbolic execution stops exploring any path whose path condition becomes unsatisfiable, hence only feasible paths are followed. Test cases are obtained from the successful branches of the tree. The set of obtained test cases forms a test suite.

In this context, the quality of a test suite is usually assessed by using code coverage criteria. A coverage criterion aims at measuring how well the program under test is exercised by a test suite. Some popular coverage criteria are: *statement coverage* which requires that every statement of the code is executed; *branch coverage* which requires all conditional statements in the program to be evaluated both to true and false; and *path coverage* which requires that every possible trace through a given part of the code is executed. These criteria are however not *finitely applicable* [49]. That is, they can not always be satisfied by a *finite* test suite, due to infinite paths and infeasible statements in the program under test (i.e., dead code). An alternative to path coverage, which is *finitely applicable* is the *loop-k* coverage criterion, which requires traversing all paths in the program except those with more than k iterations on any loop.

Observe that by construction symbolic execution achieves the *path coverage* criterion above described. However, since the symbolic execution tree is in general infinite, a termination criterion must be imposed to ensure its finiteness. Such a termination criterion can be expressed in different forms. For instance, a computation time budget can be established, or an explicit bound on the depth of the symbolic execution tree can be imposed. We adopt a more code-oriented termination criterion. Concretely, we impose an upper bound k on the number of times each loop is iterated. By doing so, the finitely applicable (feasible) version of the *path coverage* criterion, i.e., the *loop-k* coverage, is achieved.

```
1 int intExp(int a,int n) {
2   if (n < 0)
3     throw new ArithmeticException();
4   else {
5     int out = 1;
6     while (n > 0) {
7       out = out*a;
8       n--;
9     }
10    return out;
11  }
12 }
```

Fig. 1. Java source code

Example 1. Figure 1 shows the Java source code for method `intExp` which takes two integer input arguments `a` and `n` and computes a^n by successive multiplications. If the value of the input argument `n` is less than 0, an arithmetic exception is thrown. For simplicity, we assume that the method cannot receive values 0 for both of its arguments (undefined 0^0). Figure 2 shows the symbolic execution tree of method `intExp` for *loop-1* termination criterion (*loop-k* with $k=1$). That is to say, we require all paths that do not exercise the loop body (zero times) and those that exercise the loop body one time. Nodes in the tree denote symbolic states, and the edges are labeled with the line number of the instruction that is executed. Observe that symbolic execution starts with the empty path condition (PC: *true*). At each branching point, PC is updated with different conditions over the input arguments. For instance, when the `if` statement is executed, both **then** (*true*) and **else** (*false*) alternatives are feasible, therefore symbolic execution forks and the PC is updated accordingly in each of the resulting paths.

In the tree, solid squares denote intermediate symbolic states, solid double squares denote successful (terminating) symbolic execution paths, and the only dashed square denotes an unfinished path, i.e., a path that is about to enter the loop body a second time and hence is pruned by the *loop-1* criterion.   □

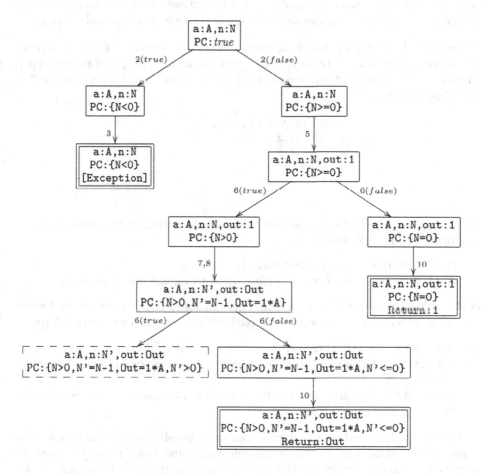

Fig. 2. Symbolic execution tree

2.2 Handling Heap-Manipulating Programs

One of the main challenges in symbolic execution is to efficiently handle heap-manipulating programs [38]. As will be illustrated later through an intuitive example, these kind of programs often create and use complex dynamically heap-allocated data structures. The presence of dynamic memory operations such as object creation and read/write field accesses requires special treatment during symbolic execution. Moreover, in order to ensure reliability, symbolic execution must consider all possible shapes these dynamic data structures can take. In trying to do so, however, scalability issues arise since high (often exponential) numbers of shapes may be built due to the *aliasing* of references.

In practice, symbolic execution assumes no knowledge about the heap shape (unless explicitly provided in advance via e.g., preconditions), in contrast to standard execution, where a program runs on concrete and fully-known initial heap (as part of the execution context). Let us motivate the importance of special treatment for heap operations and aliasing of references on a simple example.

Example 2. Consider the following method `mist`. It receives as input arguments two references `r1` and `r2` to objects of type `C` (contains a field `f` of integer type), checks the value of `r1.f` and writes `r2.f` in the **then** branch or writes `r1.f` in the **else** branch.

```
1 void mist(C r1, C r2) {
2   if (r1.f > 0)
3     r2.f = 1;
4   else
5     r1.f = 0;
6 }
```

Seemingly, the method contains only two feasible paths, each corresponding to one branch of the **if** statement:

1. If `r1.f>0`, then write `r2.f=1` (line 3).
2. If `r1.f<=0`, then write `r1.f=0` (line 5). Nothing is learned about `r2`.

However, these cases fall short to cover all possible executions of method `mist`. There are other unapparent execution paths that must also be explored. Namely:

3. If `r1` points to *null*, then a null pointer exception is thrown at line 2.
4. If `r1.f>0` and `r2` points to *null*, then a null pointer exception is thrown at line 3.
5. If `r1` and `r2` point to the same object o and `o.f>0`, then write `o.f=1` (line 3). We say that `r1` and `r2` are *aliased*.

Notice that only by exhaustive exploration of all possible heap configuration can symbolic execution generate these "hidden" paths and hence reveal the presence of potential runtime errors for this rather simple method. Furthermore, let this example also serve to see the relevance of the *loop-k* coverage criterion. Observe that the set of the first two cases above, while not being sufficient to exercise the complete behavior of method `mist`, would still be enough to achieve 100% branch and statement coverage, which may convey an illusory sense of confidence on the correctness of a *possibly* buggy program.   □

Lazy Initialization. Lazy initialization [30] is the *de facto* standard technique to enable symbolic execution to systematically handle arbitrary input data structures, and to explore all possible heap shapes that can be generated during the process, including those produced due to aliasing of references. The main idea is that symbolic execution starts with no knowledge about the program's input arguments and, as the program symbolically executes and accesses object fields, the components of the program's inputs are initialized on an "as-needed" basis. The intuition is as follows. To symbolically execute method m of class C, a new object o of class C with all its fields uninitialized is created (the this object in Java). When an unknown field of primitive type is read, a fresh unconstrained variable is created for that field. When an unknown reference field is accessed, all possibilities are explored non-deterministically choosing among the following values: (a) null; (b) any existing symbolic object whose type is compatible with the field's type and might *alias* with it; and (c) a fresh symbolic object. Such non-deterministic choices are materialized into branches in the symbolic execution tree. As a result, the heap associated with any particular execution path is built using only the constraints induced by the visited code.

The practicality and effectiveness of lazy initialization has been proved with its use by existing symbolic execution engines such as PET and SPF. However, the very nature of the technique, i.e., producing branching due to *aliasing* choices at *every* heap operation point, hampers the overall efficiency of symbolic execution and its applicability to real-world programs.

A Heap Solver. The observation that branching due to *aliasing* choices can be made "more lazily" than in lazy initialization by delaying such choices as much as possible lead to the development of a *heap solver* [4] which enables a more efficient symbolic execution of heap-manipulating programs. The key features of the heap solver are the treatment of reference aliasing by means of *disjunctive reasoning*, and the use of advanced *back-propagation* of heap related constraints. In addition, the heap solver supports the use of *heap assumptions* to avoid aliasing of data that, though legal, should not be provided as input.

Let us further illustrate the benefits of the heap solver over lazy initialization by symbolically executing method m from Figure 3 using both approaches. For simplicity, let us assume that the executions of methods a and b do not modify the heap. The symbolic execution tree computed using lazy initialization (as in, e.g., PET and SPF) is shown in Figure 4a. Note that before a field is accessed, the execution branches if it can alias with previously accessed fields. For example, the second field access z.f branches in order to consider the possible aliasing with the previously accessed x.f. Similarly, the write access to y.f must consider all possible aliasing choices with the two previous accessed fields x.f and z.f. This ensures that the effect of the field access is known within each branch. For example, in the leftmost branch the statement y.f=x.f+1 assigns -4 to x.f, y.f and z.f, since in that branch all these objects are aliased. The advantage of this approach is that by the time we reach the if statement we know the result of the test, since each variable is fixed. However, such early branching creates a combinatorial explosion problem since, for example, method a is symbolically executed in two branches and method b in five.

```
 1 void m(Ref x, Ref y, Ref z) {
 2    x.f=1;
 3    z.f=-5;
 4    a();
 5    y.f=x.f+1;
 6    b();
 7    if (x==z)
 8       c(y.f);
 9    else
10       d(y.f);
11 }
```

Fig. 3. Heap Solver: Motivating example

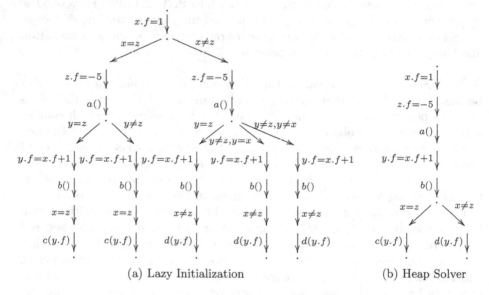

(a) Lazy Initialization   (b) Heap Solver

Fig. 4. Symbolic Execution Trees: Lazy Initialization and Heap Solver

On the other hand, the heap solver enables symbolic execution to perform as shown in Figure 4b, where branching only occurs due to explicit branching in the program, rather than to aliasing. For this purpose, the heap solver handles non-determinism due to aliasing of references by means of *disjunctions*. In particular, at instruction 5 the solver will carry the following conditional information for x.f' (the current value of field f of x): $x = z \rightarrow x.f' = z.f \wedge x \neq z \rightarrow x.f' = x.f$ indicating that if x and z are aliased, then x.f' will take its value from z.f and, otherwise, from x.f. Once the conditional statement at line 7 is executed and we learn that x and z are aliased (in the **then** branch), we need to look up *backwards* in the heap and propagate this unification so that instruction 5 can be fully executed. This allows the symbolic execution of d(y.f) with a known value for y.f. The heap solver works on a novel internal representation of the heap that encodes the disjunctive information and easily allows looking up backwards in the heap. In addition, it is possible to provide *heap assumptions* on non-aliasing, non-sharing and acyclicity of heap-allocated data in the initial state. The heap solver can take these assumptions into account to discard aliasing that is known not to occur for some input data. Importantly, the heap solver can be used by any symbolic execution tool for imperative languages through its interface heap operations.

Backwards Propagation, Arrays, and Heap Assumptions. As described in the previous section, the heap solver uses information about equality and disequality of references to determine equality among the heap cells. This is done by propagating such information forwards in the rules of attributes. A straightforward extension to the solver allows propagating information backwards as well. In doing so, the heap solver is capable of further refining disjunctive information and variables' domains, which in turn can lead to promptly pruning unfeasible symbolic execution branches.

Example 3. Consider the method m but with the condition of the if (in instruction 7) changed to "if (x.f == 1)". Thanks to backwards propagation, the solver can infer that in the if branch, variables x, y and z do not alias, and therefore the call call_c is performed with a 2 value.   □

Another straightforward extension to the heap solver allows to handle arrays in a similar fashion to how object fields are handled, with the difference being that array indices play the role of object references that point to the heap-allocated data.

The last important feature of the heap solver is the support for heap assumptions. As we have seen so far, symbolic execution assumes feasible all possible kinds of aliasing among heap-allocated (reference) input data of the same type. However, it may be the case that while some of these aliasings might indeed occur, others might not (consider, for instance, aliased data structures that cannot be constructed using the public methods in the Java class). In order to avoid generating such inputs, the heap solver provides support for *heap assumptions*, that is, assertions describing reachability, aliasing, separation and sharing conditions in the heap. Concretely, the following heap assumptions are supported:

- *non-aliasing(a,b):* specifies that memory locations a and b are not the same.
- *non-sharing(a,b):* specifies disjointness, i.e., that references a and b do not share any common region in the heap.
- *acyclic(a):* specifies that a is an acyclic data structure.

2.3   From Symbolic Execution to TCG

The outcome of symbolic execution is a set of *path conditions*, one for each symbolic execution path. Each *path condition* represents the conditions over the input variables that characterize the set of feasible concrete executions of the program that take the same path. In a next step, off-the-shelf constraint solvers can be used to solve such path conditions and generate concrete instantiations for each of them. This last step provides actual test inputs for the program, amenable to further validation by testing frameworks such as JUnit, which execute such test inputs and check that the output is as expected.

Example 4. Let us look at the symbolic execution tree of Figure 2 again. Intuitively, the union of the three successful paths denoted with solid double squares make up the symbolic test suite for method `intExp` that optimally satisfies the *loop-1* criterion:

# Input	Output	Path condition
1 A, N	[exception]	{N<0}
2 A, N	1	{N=0}
3 A, N	Out	{N>0,N'=N-1,Out=1*A,N'<=0}

The following are *concrete* test cases that can be derived from the above symbolic ones.

# Input	Output
1 -10, -10	[Exception]
2 -10, 0	1
3 -10, 1	10

And from these concrete test cases, the JUnit tests shown in Figure 5 can be obtained.

It is important to note that imposing a larger k would allow to continue the exploration through the unfinished, pruned path (dashed square) thus generating test cases corresponding to further loop unrollings.   □

2.4   Compositionality

Compositional reasoning is a general purpose methodology that has been successfully applied in the past to scale up static analysis and software verification techniques and that has also proved effective for scaling up symbolic execution and TCG [5, 7, 19, 40]. The overall goal of compositionality is to alleviate the inter-procedural path explosion problem. That is, in the context of symbolic execution and TCG, the path explosion caused by repeatedly conjoining the symbolic execution trees of methods when their invocations occur. The main idea is that symbolic execution and TCG of large programs can be done more effectively, and more efficiently, by first performing symbolic execution and TCG of their individual components separately. In the context of object-oriented programming, a method is the basic code component.

In symbolic execution for TCG, compositionality means that when a method m invokes another method p, for which TCG has already been performed, the

```
public void test_1(){
  int input0 = -10;
  int input1 = -10;
  try{
    int output = Test.intExp(input0,input1);
  }
  catch(Exception ex){
    assertEquals("exception","java.lang.ArithmeticException",
                 ex.getClass().getName());
    return;
  }
  fail("Fail");
}
public void test_2(){
  int input0 = -10;
  int input1 = 0;
  int output = Test.intExp(input0,input1);
  int expected = 1;
  assertEquals("OK",expected,output);
}
public void test_3(){
  int input0 = -10;
  int input1 = 1;
  int output = Test.intExp(input0,input1);
  int expected = -10;
  assertEquals("OK",expected,output);
}
```

Fig. 5. JUnit tests generated for introductory example

execution can *compose* the *test cases* available for p (also known as *method summary* for p) with the current execution state and continue the process, instead of having to symbolically execute p again. By test cases (or method summary), we refer to the set of path conditions obtained by symbolically executing p. As a result of this composition step, a method summary for m is created. Then, larger portions of the system under test (components, modules, libraries, etc.) are incrementally executed, following a bottom-up traversal of its call graph, composing previously computed components results (*summaries*) until finally whole-program results can be computed. Let us recall that since the symbolic execution tree is in general infinite, a *termination criterion* is essential to ensure finiteness of the process. Then, a method summary is a *finite* set of *summary cases*, one for each terminating path through the symbolic execution tree of the method. Intuitively, a summary can be regarded as a complete specification of the method for a certain termination criterion, but it is still a partial specification of the method in general.

Intuitively, compositional TCG has several advantages over traditional non-compositional TCG. First, it avoids repeatedly performing TCG of the same method. Second, components can be tested with higher precision when they are chosen small enough. Third, since separate TCG is done on parts and not on the whole program, total memory consumption may be reduced. Fourth, separate TCG can be performed in parallel on independent computers and the global TCG time can be reduced as well. Furthermore, having a compositional TCG approach in turn provides a practical solution to handle *native code*, i.e., code which is implemented in a different programming language and may be unavailable. This is achieved by modeling the behavior of native code as a method summary which can be composed with the current state during symbolic execution in the same way as the test cases inferred automatically by the testing tool are. By treating native code, we overcome one of the inherent limitations of symbolic execution (see [38]).

Approaches to Compositional TCG. In order to perform compositional TCG, two main approaches can be considered:

Context-sensitive. Starting from an entry method m (and possibly a set of pre-conditions), TCG performs a top-down symbolic execution such that, when a method call p is found, its code is executed from the actual state ϕ. In a context-sensitive approach, once a method is executed, we store the summary computed for p in the context ϕ. If we later reach another call to p within a (possibly different) context ϕ', we first check if the stored context is sufficiently general. In such case, we can adapt the existing summary for p to the current context ϕ'. At the end of each execution, it can be decided which of the computed (context-sensitive) summaries are stored for future use.

Context-insensitive. Another possibility is to perform the TCG process in a context-insensitive way. This strategy comprises the following steps. First, the call graph for the entry method $m_\mathcal{P}$ of the program under test is computed, which gives us the set of methods that must be tested. Then, the strongly connected components (SCCs for short) for such graph are computed. SCCs are traversed in reverse topological order starting from those which do not depend on any other. The idea is that each SCC is symbolically executed from its entry m_{scc} w.r.t. the most general context (i.e., *true*). If there are several entries to the same SCC, the process is repeated for each of them. Hence, it is guaranteed that the obtained summaries can always be adapted to more specific contexts.

In general terms, the advantages of the context-insensitive approach are that composition can always be performed and that only one summary needs to be stored per method. However, since no context information is assumed, summaries can contain more test cases than necessary and can be thus more expensive to obtain. In contrast, the context-sensitive approach ensures that only the required information is computed, but it can happen that there are several invocations to the same method that cannot reuse previous summaries (because the associated contexts are not sufficiently general). In such case, it is more efficient to obtain the summary without assuming any context. A context-insensitive approach is used in what follows.

Method Summaries. A *method summary* for m is a finite set of *summary cases*, each of which mainly consists of the path condition for a particular symbolic execution path of m. Each element in a summary is said to be a *summary case* of the summary. Intuitively, a method summary can be seen as a *complete specification* of the method for the considered coverage criterion, so that each summary case corresponds to the *path constraints* associated to each finished path in the corresponding (finite) execution tree. Note that, though the specification is complete for the criterion considered, it will be, in general, a *partial specification* for the method, since the finite tree may contain incomplete branches which, if further expanded, may result in (infinitely) many execution paths.

When the method does not include any heap-related operation, the path condition alone sufficiently characterizes the symbolic execution path (as in [7, 19]). However, in the presence of heap-manipulating methods, special mechanisms must be employed. We adopt an intuitive alternative which consists in explicitly encoding the input and output heaps and store them along with the path condition. Doing so, requires the implementation of two operations, a heap compatibility check and a heap composition operation.

Compatibility and Composition of Summaries. Let us assume that during the symbolic execution of a method m, there is a method invocation to another method p within a current state ϕ. The challenge is to define a composition operation so that, instead of symbolically executing p, its previously computed summary $\mathcal{S}_p$ can be reused. As a result, TCG for m should produce the same results regardless of whether we use a summary for p or we inline symbolical execution of p within TCG for m, in a non-compositional way. Roughly speaking, the state ϕ_c stored in a summary case is *compatible* with the current state ϕ if: 1) the path condition stored in the summary case can be conjoined to the current path condition, and 2) the structure of the input heap in the summary case match with the structure of the current heap. Note that compatibility of a summary case is checked on the fly, so that if ϕ is not compatible with ϕ_c, the composition will fail, the summary case will be discarded, and symbolic execution will proceed to attempt to compose the next summary case in $\mathcal{S}_p$.

Example 5. Table 1 shows the summary obtained by symbolically executing method `simplify` using the *loop-1* coverage criterion: The summary contains 5 cases, which correspond to the different execution paths induced by the calls to methods `gcd` and `abs`. For the sake of clarity, we adopt a graphical representation for the input and output heaps. Heap locations are shown as arrows labeled with their reference variable names. Split-circles represent objects of type R and fields n and d are shown in the upper and lower part, respectively. Exceptions are shown as starbursts, like in the special case of the fraction "0/0", for which an arithmetic exception (AE) is thrown due to a division by zero. In the method summary examples of Tables 2 and 3, split-rectangles represent arrays, with the length of the array in the upper part and its list of values in the lower one. Assume that method `arraycopy` is native. This means that its code is not available

```
class Arithmetics {
    static int abs(int a) {
        if (a >= 0) return a;
        else return -a;
    }
    static int gcd(int a,int b) {
        int res;
        while (b != 0) {
            res = a%b;  a = b;   b = res;
        }
        return abs(a);
    }
}
class Rational {
    int n; int d;
    void simplify() {
        int gcd = Arithmetics.gcd(n,d);
        n = n/gcd;  d = d/gcd;
    }
    Rational[] simp(Rational[] rs) {
        int length = rs.length;
        Rational[] oldRs = new Rational[length
            ];
        arraycopy(rs,oldRs,length);
        for (int i = 0; i < length; i++)
            rs[i].simplify();
        return oldRs;
    }
}
```

Fig. 6. Example for Compositional TCG.

Table 1. Summary of method simplify

A_{in} A_{out}	$Heap_{in}$	$Heap_{out}$	EF	$Constraints$
r(A)	A → (F/0)	A → (M/0)	ok	F<0, N=-F, M=F/N
r(A)	A → (F/0)	A → (1/0)	ok	F>0
r(A)	A → (0/0)	A → (0/0) B → AE	exc(B)	
r(A)	A → (F/G)	A → (M/N)	ok	G<0, F mod G=0, K=-G, M=F/K, N=G/K
r(A)	A → (F/G)	A → (M/1)	ok	G>0, F mod G=0, M=F/G

Table 2. Summary of method `arraycopy`

A_{in}	A_{out}	$Heap_{in}$	$Heap_{out}$	EF	Constraints
[X,Y,0]	H	H	H	ok	∅
[r(A),null,Z]	A→[L|[V|_]]		A→[L|[V|_]] B→NPE	exc(B)	Z>0, L>0
[null,Y,Z]	H		A→NPE	exc(A)	Z>0
[X,Y,Z]	H		A→AE	exc(A)	Z<0
[r(A),r(B),1]	A→[L1|[V|_]] B→[L2|[V2|_]]		A→[L1|[V|_]] B→[L2|[V|_]]	ok	L1>1, L2>0

Table 3. Summary of method `simp`

A_{in}	A_{out}	$Heap_{in}$	$Heap_{out}$	EF	Constraints
r(A)	r(B)	A→[0|[]]	A→[0|[]] B→[0|[]]	ok	∅
null	X	H	A→NPE	exc(A)	∅
r(A)	r(C)	A→[1|[r(B)]] B→(F/0)	A→[1|[r(B)]] B→(M/0) C→[1|[r(B)]]	ok	F<0, K=-F, M=F/K
r(A)	r(C)	A→[1|[r(B)]] B→(F/0)	A→[1|[r(B)]] B→(1/0) C→[1|[r(B)]]	ok	F>0
r(A)	X	A→[1|[r(B)]] B→(0/0)	A→[1|[r(B)]] B→(0/0) C→[1|[r(B)]] D→AE	exc(D)	∅
r(A)	r(C)	A→[1|[r(B)]] B→(F/G)	A→[1|[r(B)]] B→(M/N) C→[1|[r(B)]]	ok	G<0, F mod G=0, K=-G, M=F/K, N=G/K
r(A)	r(C)	A→[1|[r(B)]] B→(F/G)	A→[1|[r(B)]] B→(M/1) C→[1|[r(B)]]	ok	G>0, F mod G=0, M=F/G
r(A)	X	A→[1|[null]]	A→[1|[null]] C→[1|[null]] B→NPE	exc(B)	∅

and we cannot symbolically execute it. A method summary for `arraycopy` can be provided, as shown in Table 2, where we have (manually) specified five cases: the first one for arrays of length zero, the second and third ones for null array references, the fourth one for a negative length, and finally a normal execution on non-null arrays. Now, by using our compositional reasoning, we can continue symbolic execution for `simp` by composing the specified summary of `arraycopy` and the one computed for `simplify`. The result of compositional symbolic execution is presented in Table 3, that is, the entire summary of method `simp` for a *loop-1* coverage criterion.   □

2.5 Guided TCG

A common limitation of symbolic execution in the context of TCG is that it tends to produce an unnecessarily large number of test cases for all but tiny programs. This limitation not only hinders scalability but also complicates human reasoning on the generated test cases. Guided TCG is a methodology that aims at steering symbolic execution towards specific program paths in order to efficiently generate more relevant test cases and filter out less interesting ones with respect to a given structural *selection criterion*. The goal is thus to improve on scalability and efficiency by achieving a high degree of control over the coverage criterion and hence avoiding the exploration of unfeasible paths. This has potential applicability for industrial software testing practices such as unit testing, where units of code (e.g. methods) must be thoroughly tested in isolation, or *selective testing*, in which only specific paths of a program must be tested.

Example 6. Let us consider the unit-testing for method `simplify` (see Figure 6). A proper set of unit-tests should include one test to exercise the exceptional behavior arising from the division by zero, and another test to exercise the normal behavior. Ideally, no more tests should be provided since there is anything else to be tested in method `simplify`. This methodology works well under the assumption that called methods are tested on their own, in this case method `gcd`. Standard TCG by symbolic execution would consider all possible paths including those arising from the different executions of method `gcd`, in this case 5 paths. The challenge in Guided TCG is to generate only the two test-cases above, avoiding as much as possible traversing the rest of the paths (which for this criterion can be considered redundant). As another example, let us consider selective testing for method `simplify`. E.g., one could be interested in generating a test-case (if any) that makes method `simplify` produce an exception due to a division by zero. The challenge in Guided TCG is again to generate such a test avoiding traversing as much as possible the rest of the paths.   □

The intuition of Guided TCG is as follows: (1) A heuristics-based *trace-generator* generates possibly partial traces, i.e., partial descriptions of paths, according to a given selection criterion. This can be done by relying on the control-flow graph of the program. (2) Bounded symbolic execution is guided by the obtained traces. The process is repeated until the selection criterion is satisfied or until no more traces are generated. Section 3.6 presents a concrete CLP-based methodology for guided TCG and formalizes a concrete guided TCG scheme to support the criteria for unit testing considered in the above example.

3   CLP-Based TCG

We present a particular instance of TCG based on symbolic execution, and an implementation, in which CLP is used as enabling technology.

3.1 Constraint Logic Programming

We assume certain familiarity with Logic Programming (LP) [33] and Constraint Logic Programming (CLP) [27, 34]. Hence we only briefly overview both paradigms.

Logic Programming. Logic Programming is a programming paradigm based on the use of formal logic as a programming language. A logic program is a finite set of predicates defining relationships between logical terms. An atom (or call) A is a syntactic construct of the form $p(t_1, \ldots, t_n)$, with $n \geq 0$, where p/n is a predicate signature and $t_1, \ldots, t_n$ are terms. A clause is of the form $H : -B_1, \ldots, B_m.$, with $m \geq 0$, where its head H is an atom and its body $B_1, \ldots, B_m$ is a conjunction of m atoms (commas denote conjunctions). When $m = 0$ the clause is called a fact and is written "H.". The standard syntactic convention is that names of predicates and atoms begin with a lowercase letter. A goal is a conjunction of atoms. We denote by $\{X_1 \rightarrow t_1, \ldots, X_n \rightarrow t_n\}$ the substitution σ with $\sigma(X_i) = t_i$ for $i = 1, \ldots, n$ (with $X_i \neq X_j$ if $i \neq j$), and $\sigma(X) = X$ for all other variables X. Given an atom A, $\theta(A)$ denotes the application of substitution θ to A. Given two substitutions θ_1 and θ_2 , we denote by $\theta_1 \theta_2$ their composition. An atom A' is an instance of A if there is a substitution σ with $A' = \sigma(A)$.

SLD (Selective Linear Definite clause)-resolution is the standard operational semantics of logic programs. It is based on the notion of derivations. A derivation step is defined as follows. Let G be $A_1, \ldots, A_R, \ldots, A_k$ and $C = H : -B_1, \ldots, B_m.$ be a renamed apart clause in P (i.e., it has no common variables with G). Let A_R be the selected atom for its evaluation. As in Prolog, we assume the simple leftmost selection rule. Then, G' is derived from G if θ is a *most general unifier* between A_R and H, and G' is the goal $\theta(A_1, \ldots, A_{R-1}, B_1, \ldots, B_m, A_{R+1}, \ldots, A_k)$.

As customary, given a program P and a goal G, an SLD derivation for $P \cup \{G\}$ consists of a possibly infinite sequence $G = G_0, G_1, G_2, \ldots$ of goals, a sequence $C_1, C_2, \ldots$ of properly renamed apart clauses of P (i.e. C_i has no common variables with any G_j nor C_j with $j < i$), and a sequence of computed answer substitutions $\theta_1, \theta_2, \ldots$ (or most-general unifiers, *mgus* for short) such that each G_{i+1} is derived from G_i and C_{i+1} using θ_{i+1}. Finally, we say that the SLD derivation is composed of the subsequent goals $G_0, G_1, G_2, \ldots$

A derivation step can be non-deterministic when A_R unifies with several clauses in P, giving rise to several possible SLD derivations for a given goal. Such SLD derivations can be organized in SLD trees. A finite derivation $G = G_0, G_1, G_2, \ldots, G_n$ is called successful if G_n is the empty goal, denoted ϵ. In that case $\theta = \theta_1 \theta_2 \ldots \theta_n$ is called the computed answer for goal G. Such a derivation is called failing if it is not possible to perform a derivation step with G_n.

Executing a logic program P for a goal G consists in building an SLD tree for $P \cup \{G\}$ and then extracting the computed answer substitutions from every non-failing branch of the tree.

Constraint Logic Programming. Constraint Logic Programming is a programming paradigm that extends Logic programming with *Constraint solving*. It augments the LP expressive power and application domain while maintaining its semantic properties (e.g., existence of a fixpoint semantics).

In CLP, the bodies of clauses may contain constraints in addition to ordinary literals. CLP integrates the use of a constraint solver to the operational semantics of logic programs. As a consequence of this extension, whereas in LP a computation state consists of a goal and a substitution, in CLP a computation state also contains a *constraint store*. The special *constraint* literals are stored in the *constraint store* instead of being solved according to SLD-resolution. The satisfiability of the constraint store is checked by a constraint solver. Then, we say that a CLP computation is successful if there is a derivation leading from the initial state $S_0 = \langle G_0 \mid true \rangle$ (initially the constraint store is empty, i.e., *true*) to the final state $S_n = \langle \epsilon \mid S \rangle$ such that ϵ is the empty goal and S is satisfiable.

The CLP paradigm can be instantiated with many constraint domains. A constraint domain defines the class of constraints that can be used in a CLP program. Several constraint domains have been developed (e.g., for terms, strings, booleans, reals). A particularly useful constraint domain is CLP(FD) (Constraint Logic Programming over Finite Domains) [47]. CLP(FD) constraints are usually intended to be arithmetic constraints over finite integer domain variables. It has been applied to constraint satisfaction problems such as planning and scheduling [14,34]. Some features of CLP(FD) that make it suitable for TCG of programs working with integers are:

- It provides a mechanism to define the initial finite domain of variables as an interval over the integers and operations to further refine this initial domain.
- It provides a built-in *labeling* mechanism, which can be applied on a list of variables to find values for them such that the current constraint store is satisfied.

As we will see in the next section, our CLP-based TCG framework will rely on CLP(FD) to translate conditional statements over integer variables into CLP constraints. Moreover, the labeling mechanism is essential to concretize the obtained test cases in order to obtain concrete input data amenable to be used and validated by testing tools.

3.2   CLP-Based Test Case Generation

CLP-based Test Case Generation advocates the use of CLP technology to perform test case generation of imperative object-oriented programs. The process has two phases. In the first phase, the imperative object-oriented program under test is automatically transformed into an equivalent executable *CLP-translated* program. Instructions that manipulate heap-allocated data are represented by means of calls to specific *heap operations*. In the second phase, the CLP-translated program is symbolically executed using the standard CLP execution and constraint solving mechanism. The above-mentioned heap operations

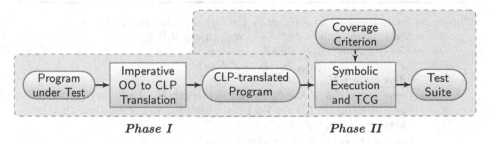

Fig. 7. CLP-based Test Case Generation Framework

are also implemented in standard CLP, in a suitable way in order to support symbolic execution. The next two sections overview these two phases, which are also shown graphically in Figure 7.

The Imperative Object-Oriented Language. Although our approach is not tied to any particular imperative object-oriented language, we consider as the source language a subset of Java. For simplicity, we leave out of such subset features like concurrency, bitwise operations, static fields, access control (i.e., the use of public, protected and private modifiers) and primitive types besides integers and booleans. Nevertheless, these features can be relatively easy to handle in practice by our framework, except for concurrency, which is well-known to pose further challenges to symbolic execution and its scalability.

CLP-Translated Programs. The translation of imperative object-oriented programs into equivalent CLP-translated programs has been subject of previous work (see, e.g., [2, 21]). Therefore, we will recap the features of the translated programs without going into deep details of how the translation is done. The translation is formally defined as follows:

Definition 1 (CLP-translated program). *The CLP-translated program for a given method m from the original imperative object-oriented program consists of a finite, non-empty set of predicates $m, m_1, \ldots, m_n$. A predicate m_i is defined by a finite, non-empty set of mutually exclusive rules, each of the form $m_i^k(In, Out, H_{in}, H_{out}, E) : -[g,]b_1, \ldots, b_j.$, where:*

1. *In and Out are, resp., the (possibly empty) list of input and output arguments.*
2. *H_{in} and H_{out} are, resp., the input and (possibly modified) output heaps.*
3. *E is an exception flag that indicates whether the execution of m_i^k ends normally or with an uncaught exception.*
4. *If m_i is defined by more than one rule, then g is the constraint that guards the execution of m_i^k, i.e., it must hold for the execution of m_i^k to proceed.*
5. *$b_1, \ldots, b_j$ is a sequence of instructions including arithmetic operations, calls to other predicates and built-ins to operate on the heap, etc., as defined in Figure 8. As usual, an SSA transformation is performed [12].*

$$Clause ::= Pred(Args_{in}, Args_{out}, H_{in}, H_{out}, ExFlag) :- [G,]B_1, B_2, \ldots, B_n.$$
$$G ::= Num^* \ ROp \ Num^* \mid Ref_1^* \ \backslash== \ Ref_2^* \mid type(H, Ref^*, T)$$
$$B ::= Var \ \#= \ Num^* \ AOp \ Num^*$$
$$\mid Pred(Args_{in}, Args_{out}, H_{in}, H_{out}, ExFlag)$$
$$\mid \mathsf{new\_object}(H_{in}, C^*, Ref^*, H_{out})$$
$$\mid \mathsf{new\_array}(H_{in}, T, Num^*, Ref^*, H_{out}) \mid \mathsf{length}(H_{in}, Ref^*, Var)$$
$$\mid \mathsf{get\_field}(H_{in}, Ref^*, FSig, Var) \mid \mathsf{set\_field}(H_{in}, Ref^*, FSig, Data^*, H_{out})$$
$$\mid \mathsf{get\_array}(H_{in}, Ref^*, Num^*, Var)$$
$$\mid \mathsf{set\_array}(H_{in}, Ref^*, Num^*, Data^*, H_{out})$$

$Pred ::= Block \mid MSig$	$ROp ::= \ \#> \mid \#< \mid \#>= \mid \#=< \mid \#= \mid \#\backslash=$	
$Args ::= [\ ] \mid [Data^* \mid Args]$	$AOp ::= \ + \mid - \mid * \mid / \mid mod$	
$Data ::= Num \mid Ref \mid ExFlag$	$T ::= bool \mid int \mid C \mid array(T)$	
$Ref ::= null \mid r(Var)$	$FSig ::= C{:}FN$	
$ExFlag ::= ok \mid exc(Var)$	$H ::= Var$	

Fig. 8. Syntax of CLP-translated programs

Specifically, CLP-translated programs adhere to the grammar in Figure 8. As customary, terminals start with lowercase (or special symbols) and non-terminals start with uppercase; subscripts are provided just for clarity. Non-terminals *Block*, *Num*, *Var*, *FN*, *MSig*, *FSig* and *C* denote, resp., the set of predicate names, numbers, variables, field names, method signatures, field signatures and class names. A clause indistinguishably defines either a method which appear in the original source program (*MSig*), or an additional predicate which correspond to an intermediate block in the control flow graph of original program (*Block*). A field signature *FSig* contains the class where the field is defined and the field name *FN*. An asterisk on a non-terminal denotes that it can be either as defined by the grammar or a (possibly constrained) variable (e.g., *Num**, denotes that the term can be a number or a variable). Heap references are written as terms of the form $r(Ref)$ or *null*. The operations that handle data in the heap are translated into built-in heap-related predicates.

Let us observe the following:

- There exists a one-to-one correspondence between blocks in the control flow graph of the original program and rules in the CLP-translated one.
- Mutual exclusion between the rules of a predicate is ensured either by means of mutually exclusive *guards*, or by information made explicit on the heads of rules, as usual in CLP. This makes the CLP-translated program deterministic, as the original imperative one is (point 4 in Definition 1).
- The global memory (or heap) is explicitly represented by means of logic variables. When a rule is invoked, the input heap H_{in} is received and, after executing the body of the rule, the heap might be modified, resulting in H_{out}. The operations that modify the heap will be shown later.
- Virtual method invocations are resolved at compile-time in the original imperative object-oriented language by looking up all possible runtime

```
   new_object(H,C,Ref,H') :- build_object(C,Ob), new_ref(Ref),
                             H' = [(Ref,Ob)|H].
   new_array(H,T,L,Ref,H') :- build_array(T,L,Arr), new_ref(Ref),
                             H' = [(Ref,Arr)|H].

            type(H,Ref,T) :- get_cell(H,Ref,Cell), Cell = object(T,_).
          length(H,Ref,L) :- get_cell(H,Ref,Cell), Cell = array(_,L,_).

    get_field(H,Ref,FSig,V) :- get_cell(H,Ref,Ob), FSig = C:FN,
                             Ob = object(T,Fields), subclass(T,C),
                             member_det(field(FN,V),Fields).
     get_array(H,Ref,I,V) :- get_cell(H,Ref,Arr), Arr = array(_,_,Xs),
                             nth0(I,Xs,V).

set_field(H,Ref,FSig,V,H') :- get_cell(H,Ref,Ob), FSig = C:FN,
                             Ob = object(T,Fields), subclass(T,C),
                             replace_det(Fields,field(FN,_),field(FN,V),
                                    Fields'),
                             set_cell(H,Ref,object(T,Fields'),H').
   set_array(H,Ref,I,V,H') :- get_cell(H,Ref,Arr), Arr = array(T,L,Xs),
                             replace_nth0(Xs,I,V,Xs'),
                             set_cell(H,Ref,array(T,L,Xs'),H').
```

```
 get_cell([(Ref',Cell')|_],Ref,Cell) :- Ref == Ref', !, Cell = Cell'.
       get_cell([_|RH],Ref,Cell) :- get_cell(RH,Ref,Cell).
  set_cell([(Ref',_)|H],Ref,Cell,H') :- Ref == Ref', !,
                             H' = [(Ref,Cell)|H].
set_cell([(Ref',Cell')|H'],Ref,Cell,H) :- H = [(Ref',Cell')|H'],
                             set_cell(H',Ref,Cell,H').
```

Fig. 9. Heap operations for ground execution [22]

instances of the method. In the CLP-translated program, such invocations are translated into a choice of type instructions which check the actual object type, followed by the corresponding method invocation for each runtime instance.

– Exceptional behavior is handled explicitly in the CLP-translated program.

These observations will become more noticeable later on Example 7.

Note that the above definition proposes a translation to CLP as opposed to a translation to pure logic (e.g. to predicate logic or even to propositional logic, i.e., a logic that is not meant for "programming"). This is because we then want to execute the resulting translated programs to perform TCG and this requires, among other things, handling a constraint store and then generating actual data from such constraints. CLP is a natural paradigm to perform this task.

Heap Operations. Figure 9 summarizes the CLP implementation of the operations to create heap-allocated data structures (new_object and new_array) and to read and modify them (getfield , set_array, etc.) [22]. These operations rely on some auxiliary predicates (like deterministic versions of member member_det, of replace replace_det, and nth0 and replace_nth0 for arrays) which are quite standard and hence their implementation is not shown. For instance, a new object is created through a call to predicate new_object(H_{in},Class,Ref,H_{out}), where H_{in} is the current heap, Class is the new object's type, Ref is a unique reference in the heap for accessing the new object and H_{out} is the new heap after allocating the object. Read-only operations do not produce any output heap. For example, get_field(H_{in},Ref,FSig,Var) retrieves from H_{in} the value of the field identified by *FSig* from the object referenced by *Ref*, and returns its value in *Var* leaving the heap unchanged. Instruction set_field(H_{in},Ref,FSig,Data,H_{out}) sets the field identified by *FSig* from the object referenced by *Ref* to the value *Data*, and returns the modified heap H_{out}. The remaining operations are implemented likewise.

The Heap term. Our CLP-translated programs manipulate the heap as a black-box through its associated operations. The heaps generated and manipulated by using these operations adhere to this grammar:

$$
\begin{aligned}
Heap &::= [\,] \mid [Loc|Heap] \\
Cell &::= object(C^*,Fields^*) \mid array(T^*,Num^*,Args^*) \\
Loc &::= (Num^*,Cell) \\
Fields &::= [\,] \mid [field(FN,Data^*)|Fields^*]
\end{aligned}
$$

The heap is represented as a list of locations which are pairs formed by a unique reference and a cell. Each cell can be an object or an array. An object contains its type and its list of fields, each of which is made of its signature and data content. An array contains its type, its length and its list of elements.

Example 7. Figure 10a shows the Java source code of class List, which implements a singly-linked list. The class contains one field first of type Node. As customary, Node is a recursive class with two fields: data of type int and next of type Node. Method remAll takes as argument an object l of type List, traverses it (outer while loop) and for each of its elements, traverses the this object and removes all their occurrences (inner loop). Figure 10b shows the equivalent (simplified and pretty-printed) CLP-translated code for method remAll. Let us observe some of the main features of the CLP-translated program. The if statement in line 23 is translated into two mutually exclusive rules (predicate if1) guarded by an arithmetic condition. Similarly, the if statement in line 25 is translated into predicate if2, implemented by two rules whose mutual exclusion is guaranteed by terms null and r(_) appearing in each rule head. Observe that iteration in the original program (while constructions) is translated into recursive predicates. For instance, the head of the inner while loop is translated into predicate loop2, its condition is guarded by the rules of predicate cond2 (null or r(_)), and recursive calls are made from predicates if1 (first rule) and if2 (both rules). Finally, exception handling is made explicit in the CLP-translated program; the second rule of predicate block1 encodes the runtime null pointer exception ('NPE') that raises if the input argument l is null.　　□

```
1 class Node {
2   int data;
3   Node next;
4 }
5 class List {
6   Node first;
7   void remAll(List l) {
8     // block1
9     Node lf = l.first;
10    // loop1
11    while (lf != null) {
12      // block2
13      Node prev = null;
14      Node p = null;
15      Node next = first;
16      // loop2
17      while (next != null) {
18        // block3
19        prev = p;
20        p = next;
21        next = next.next;
22        // if1
23        if (p.data == lf.data)
24          // if2
25          if (prev == null) {
26            first = next;
27            p = null;
28          } else {
29            prev.next = next;
30            p = prev;
31          }
32      }
33      // block4
34      lf = lf.next;
35    }
36  }
37 }
```

```
remAll([r(Th),L],[],Hi,Ho,E) :-
  block1([Th,L],Hi,Ho,E).
block1([Th,r(L)],Hi,Ho,E) :-
  get_field(Hi,L,first,LfR),
  loop1([Th,L,LfR],Hi,Ho,E).
block1([Th,null],Hi,Ho,exc(E)) :-
  create_object(Hi,'NPE',E,Ho).
loop1([Th,L,null],H,H,ok).
loop1([Th,L,r(Lf)],Hi,Ho,E) :-
  block2([Th,L,Lf],Hi,Ho,E).
block2([Th,L,Lf],Hi,Ho,E) :-
  get_field(Hi,Th,first,FR),
  loop2([Th,L,Lf,null,null,FR],Hi,Ho,E).
loop2([Th,L,Lf,Prev,P,null],Hi,Ho,E) :-
  block4([Th,L,Lf],Hi,Ho,E).
loop2([Th,L,Lf,Prev,P,r(F)],Hi,Ho,E) :-
  block3([Th,L,Lf,P,F],Hi,Ho,E).
block3([Th,L,Lf,P,F],Hi,Ho,E) :-
  get_field(Hi,F,next,FRN),
  get_field(Hi,F,data,A),
  get_field(Hi,Lf,data,B),
  if1([A,B,Th,L,Lf,P,F,FRN],Hi,Ho,E).
if1([A,B,Th,L,Lf,Prev,P,FRN],Hi,Ho,E) :-
  #\=(A,B),
  loop2([Th,L,Lf,Prev,P,FRN],Hi,Ho,E).
if1([A,A,Th,L,Lf,Prev,P,FRN],Hi,Ho,E) :-
  if2([Th,L,Lf,Prev,P,FRN],Hi,Ho,E).
if2([Th,L,Lf,r(F),P,N],Hi,Ho,E) :-
  set_field(Hi,F,next,N,H2),
  loop2([Th,L,Lf,F,F,N],H2,Ho,E).
if2([Th,L,Lf,null,P,N],Hi,Ho,E) :-
  set_field(Hi,Th,first,N,H2),
  loop2([Th,L,Lf,null,null,N],H2,Ho,E).
block4([Th,L,Lf],Hi,Ho,E) :-
  get_field(Hi,Lf,next,LfRN),
  loop1([Th,L,LfRN],Hi,Ho,E).
```

(a) Java source code   (b) CLP-translation

Fig. 10. CLP-based TCG example

3.3 Semantics of CLP-Translated Programs

The standard CLP execution mechanism suffices to execute the CLP-translated programs. Let us focus on the concrete execution of CLP-translated programs by assuming that all input parameters of the predicate to be executed (i.e., In and H_{in}) are fully instantiated in the initial input state.

Let M be a method in the original imperative program, m be its corresponding predicate in the CLP-translated program P, and P' be the union of P and the predicates in Figure 9. As explained in the previous section, the operational semantics of the CLP program P' can be defined in terms of *derivations*. A derivation is a sequence of reductions between states $S_0 \rightarrow_p S_1 \rightarrow_P \ldots \rightarrow_P S_n$, also denoted $S_0 \rightarrow_P S_n$, where a *state* $\langle G \mid \theta \rangle$ consists of a goal G and a constraint store θ. The concrete execution of m with input θ is the derivation $S_0 \rightarrow S_n$, where $S_0 = \langle m(In, Out, H_{in}, H_{out}, ExFlag) \mid \theta \rangle$ and θ initializes In and H_{in} to be fully ground. If the derivation successfully terminates, then $S_n = \langle \epsilon \mid \theta' \rangle$ and θ' is the *output constraint store*.

This definition of concrete execution relies on the correctness of the translation algorithm, which must guarantee that the CLP-translated program captures the same semantics of the original imperative one [2, 21].

Example 8. The following is a *correct* input state for predicate remAll/5:

```
⟨remAll([r(1),null],Out,
  [(1,object('List',[field('Node':first,null)]))],Hout,E) I true⟩
```

Observe that the list of input arguments and the input heap (both underlined) are fully instantiated. Argument r(1) corresponds to the implicit reference to the *this* object, which appears in the input heap term with its field first being instantiated to null. Concrete execution on this input state yields a final state in which:

```
Out  = [ ]∧
Hout = [(1,object('List',[field('Node':first,null)])),
        (2,object('NPE',[ ]))]∧
E    = exc(2)
```

Notice that in this final state, a new object of type NPE (Null Pointer Exception) is created in the heap. The fact that the execution ends with an uncaught exception is indicated in flag E.   □

3.4   Symbolic Execution

When the source imperative language does not support dynamic memory, symbolic execution of the CLP-translated programs is attained by simply using the standard CLP execution mechanism to run the main goal (i.e., the predicate name after the method under test) *with all arguments being free variables*. The inherent constraint solving and backtracking mechanisms of CLP allow to keep track of path conditions (or constraint stores), failing and backtracking when unsatisfiable constraints are hit, hence discarding such execution paths; and succeeding when satisfiable constraints lead to a terminating state in the program, which in the context of TCG implies that a new test case is generated.

However, in the case of heap-manipulating programs, the heap-related operations presented in Figure 9 fall short to generate arbitrary heap-allocated data structures and all possible heap shapes when accessing symbolic references. This is a well-known problem in TCG by symbolic execution. A naive solution to this problem could be to fully initialize all the reference parameters prior to symbolic execution. However, this would require imposing bounds on the size of input data structures, which is highly undesirable. Doing so would circumscribe the symbolic search space, hence jeopardizing the overall effectiveness of the technique.

Lazy Initialization. A straightforward generalization of predicate get_cell in Figure 9 provides a simple and flexible solution to the problem of handling arbitrary input data structures during symbolic execution, and constitutes a quite natural implementation of the *lazy initialization* technique in our CLP-based framework. Figure 11 shows the new implementation of the get_cell operations; observe that we have added just two new rules to the implementation shown in Figure 9.

```
        get_cell(H,Ref,Cell) :- var(H), !, H = [(Ref,Cell)|_].
get_cell([(Ref',Cell')|_],Ref,Cell) :- Ref == Ref', !, Cell = Cell'.
get_cell([(Ref',Cell')|_],Ref,Cell) :- var(Ref), var(Ref'), Ref = Ref',
                                        Cell = Cell'.
      get_cell([_|RH],Ref,Cell) :- get_cell(RH,Ref,Cell).
```

Fig. 11. Redefining get_cell operations for symbolic execution [22]

The intuitive idea is that the heap during symbolic execution contains two parts: the *known part*, with the cells that have been explicitly created during symbolic execution appearing at the beginning of the list, and the *unknown part*, which is a logic variable (tail of the list) in which new data can be added. Importantly, the definition of get_cell/3 distinguishes two situations when searching for a reference: (i) It finds it in the known part (second clause), meaning that the reference has already been accessed earlier (note the use of syntactic equality rather than unification, since references at execution time can be variables); or (ii) It reaches the unknown part of the heap (a logic variable), and it allocates the reference (in this case a variable) there (first clause). The third clause of get_cell/3 allows to consider all possible aliasing configurations among references. In essence, get_cell/3 is therefore a CLP implementation of *lazy initialization*.

Let us illustrate the use of lazy initialization in symbolic execution with an example.

Example 9. Figure 12 shows the CLP-translated program for method mist from Example 2. Let mist(In,Out,Hin,Hout,E) be the initial goal for symbolic execution. Observe that the input heap Hin is a free variable (i.e., fully unknown). Let us choose rule mist[1]. By doing so, the list of input arguments In gets instantiated to [r(A),R2], which indicates that the first argument is a reference to an existing object in the heap, as opposed to the null reference in rule mist[2]. The execution of the get_field instruction imposes new constraints on the shape of the input heap. Namely, Hin is partially instantiated to [(A,object('C',[field(f,F)|M]))|N]. Observe that there is still an unknown part in the heap (variable N). Also, observe that the list of fields for object A is also represented by an open list, meaning that there might be other fields in this object, but nothing has been learned about them yet.

Now, let us assume that the execution proceeds with rules if[1] and then[1]. At this point, the second argument is also set to be a valid reference r(B). The execution of the set_field will internally reach predicate get_cell (Figure 11), leading to consider two possibilities:

- References R1=r(A) and R2=r(B) point to two different objects in the heap. In this case, the resulting output heap is

$$\text{Hout} = [\ (\text{A,object('C',[field(f,D1)|M])),} \\ \text{(B,object('C',[field(f,1)|P]))|N],}$$

  and the constraint store is $\theta = \{D1 > 0\}$.
- References R1=r(A) and R2=r(A) point to the same object in the heap, i.e., they are aliased. Here, the resulting output heap is
  Hout=[(A,object('C',[field(f,D1)|M]))|N], with $\theta = \{D1 > 0\}$.   □

```
mist¹([r(A),R2],[],Hin,Hout,E) :-
    get_field(Hin,A,f,D1),
    if([D1,A,R2],Hin,Hout,E).
mist²([null,R2],[],Hin,Hout,exc(Exc)) :-
    create_object(Hin,'NPE',Exc,Hout).
if¹([D1,A,R2],Hin,Hout,E) :-
    #>(D1,0),
    then([R2],Hin,Hout,E).
if²([D1,A,R2],Hin,Hout,ok) :-
    #<=(D1,0),
    set_field(Hin,A,f,0,Hout),
then¹([r(B)],Hin,Hout,ok) :-
    set_field(Hin,B,f,1,Hout).
then²([null],Hin,Hout,exc(Exc)) :-
    create_object(Hin,'NPE',Exc,Hout).
```

Fig. 12. CLP-translated program for method mist (Example 2)

To conclude this section, let us now provide a definition for symbolic execution in terms of the CLP derivation tree of the CLP-translated program extended with built-in operations to handle dynamic memory:

Definition 2 (Symbolic Execution). *Let M be a method, m be its corresponding predicate from its associated CLP-translated program P, and P' be the union of P and the set of predicates in Figure 9. The symbolic execution of m is the CLP derivation tree, denoted as $\mathcal{T}_m$, with root $m(In, Out, H_{in}, H_{out}, E)$ and initial constraint store $\theta = \{\}$ obtained using P'.*

3.5 Test Case Generation

When handling realistic programs, it is well-known that the symbolic execution tree to be explored is in general infinite. This is because iterative constructs such as loops and recursion, whose number of iterations depend on input arguments, usually induce an infinite number of execution paths when executed with symbolic input values. It is therefore essential to establish a *termination criterion*. Such a termination criterion can be expressed in different forms. For instance, a computation time budget can be established, or an explicit bound on the depth of the symbolic execution tree can be imposed (called *depth-k* criterion). In this thesis, we adopt a more code-oriented termination criterion. Specifically, we impose an upper bound k on the number of times each loop is iterated. As a byproduct of imposing such a bound, the *loop-k* structural coverage criterion below is satisfied.

Finite symbolic execution tree, test case, and TCG. Let us now establish definitions for key concepts of our approach:

Definition 3 (Finite symbolic execution tree, test case, and TCG). *Let m be the corresponding predicate for a method M in a CLP-translated program P, and let $\mathcal{C}$ be a termination criterion.*

- *$\mathcal{T}_m^{\mathcal{C}}$ is the finite and possibly incomplete symbolic execution tree of m with root $m(In, Out, H_{in}, H_{out}, EF)$ w.r.t. $\mathcal{C}$.*
- *Let b be a successful (terminating) path in $\mathcal{T}_m^{\mathcal{C}}$. A test case for m w.r.t. $\mathcal{C}$ is a 6-tuple of the form: $\langle \sigma(In), \sigma(Out), \sigma(H_{in}), \sigma(H_{out}), \sigma(EF), \theta \rangle$, where σ and θ are, resp., the substitution and the constraint store associated to b.*
- *TCG is the process of generating the set of test cases obtained for all successful (terminating) paths in $\mathcal{T}_m^{\mathcal{C}}$.*

In the remainder of this dissertation, we comply with the above abstract (symbolic) definition of *test case*, hence adopting a non-standard use of the term "test case". Standard test cases are concrete, i.e., actual input values on which the program under test can be run. In contrast, in this thesis a *test case* represents the class of inputs that will follow the same execution path, characterized by a path condition (and symbolic expressions for variables). A *test suite* is hence a set of test cases that characterizes all symbolic execution paths explored by symbolic execution using a particular termination criterion. Nevertheless, it is possible to produce actual values from the obtained *symbolic* test cases. This can be done in a straightforward subsequent stage in our framework. Namely, we can

Table 4. Test cases for method `remAll`

N	Input Heap	Output Heap	Constraint Store	EF
1	this l.first = null	this l.first = null	$\emptyset$	ok
2	this.first = null l.first→(A)→ null	this.first = null l.first→(A)→ null	$\emptyset$	ok
3	this.first →(A)→ null l.first →(B)→ null	this.first →(A)→ null l.first →(B)→ null	$\{A \neq B\}$	ok
4	this.first →(A)→ null l.first →(A)→ null	this.first = null l.first →(A)→ null	$\emptyset$	ok
5	this l ——→ null	-	$\emptyset$	exc
6	this.first →(A)→ null l = this	this.first = null l = this	$\emptyset$	ok
7	this.first→(A)→ null l.first	this.first = null l.first →(A)→ null	$\emptyset$	ok

use the *labeling* mechanisms of standard *clpfd* domains to assign concrete values to all variables which satisfy the path condition, thus solving it. As a result of this last step, concrete and executable test cases are obtained.

Example 10. The test suite generated for method `remAll` for a *loop-1* coverage criterion is shown in Table 4. The first 5 cases are generated without considering aliasing of references. By doing so, the last two cases are also generated. Let us explain in detail three of the obtained test cases:

- **Case 3.** Corresponds to the path in which both the `this` list and the input list l contain just one element. The constraint $\{A \neq B\}$ indicates that fields `this.first.data` and `l.first.data` must have different values. The output heap is the same as the input heap, which means that the heap remains unchanged at the end of the execution path represented by this test case (although it may have suffered changes in intermediate derivations).
- **Case 4.** The input heap is the almost same as in case 3, but here, the symbolic variables corresponding to `this.first.data` and `l.first.data` are unified (variable A), meaning that their values are the same. In the output heap, notice that the first node from the `this` list has been removed.
- **Case 7.** Reference fields `this.first` and `l.first` are aliased. That is, they point to the same `Node` object in the heap. Removing element A from the `this` list boils down to setting reference `this.first` to `null`, leaving the object in the heap intact.

Finally, as mentioned before, by solving the constraint system and applying labeling on the variables involved, concrete inputs can be obtained. A concrete instantiation for this test case would consist of the following input heap {this.first $\rightarrow$ 1 $\longrightarrow$ null, l.first $\longrightarrow$ 2 $\longrightarrow$ null} where variables A and B have been assigned concrete values 1 and 2, respectively, such that the constraint store $A \neq B$ is satisfied. As the test case specifies, the heap in the concrete output state remains unchanged. $\qquad \square$

The PET System. PET (Partial Evaluation-based Test case generator) is a system that implements the CLP-based TCG framework described in this chapter. It is is fully implemented in SWI-Prolog [48] and uses the CLP(FD) library [47] (Constraint Logic Programming over Finite Domains) as constraint solver. Some of the important features of the PET system are:

- It is generic. Provided that appropriate CLP translations are available, PET can work with other imperative object-oriented languages. That is, once the CLP translation is done, the language features are abstracted away. That is to say, the TCG phase of the approach implemented in PET is language independent. In this way, we elude the difficulties of explicitly dealing with features like recursion, procedure calls, dynamic memory allocation, exceptions, etc., whose treatment may differ from one language to another.
- It is flexible. Different termination (coverage) criteria can be easily incorporated to the PET system. These criteria are written in PET as predicates which are permanently checked during TCG. Adding new criteria consists in implementing such a predicate, which requires only basic knowledge of logic programming.
  It is incremental. One of the artifacts that the PET system generates is a test case generator. To the best of our knowledge, this is a unique feature in a TCG tool nowadays. Namely, PET allows to extend test suites by exploring further in the symbolic execution tree in an on-demand fashion. In other words, PET allows to incrementally relax the imposed termination criterion to explore symbolic execution paths that were initially pruned by the termination criterion.

The PET system is available for download as open-source software and for online use through its web interface at http://costa.ls.fi.upm.es/pet. Furthermore, an Eclipse plugin called jPET [3] is available. jPET supports full sequential Java and some of its interesting features are:

- Interactive test case visualization. jPET integrates a test case viewer to allow an intuitive, interactive visualization of the information contained in test cases. This includes objects and arrays involved in the input and output heap terms.
- Trace highlighting. On selection of a particular test case, jPET highlights the sequence of instructions in the original Java source code that the test case exercises. Alternatively, a *trace debugging* feature allows for a step-by-step highlighting of the source code, as in the traditional style of code debugging.

- Parsing of method preconditions written in JML [28]. jPET enables the specification of conditions on the input arguments of methods. These conditions are written in a subset of JML (Java Modeling Language), the standard specification language within software verification of Java. Using preconditions allows steering symbolic execution towards interesting parts of the program under test, ignoring others that are less interesting.
- Generation of JUnit. JUnit is a Unit Testing Framework for Java, which provides a set of classes to support writing, executing and reusing test cases. jPET generates self-contained JUnit test cases, as shown in Example 4. Whereas those unit tests therein are rather simple, the generation of JUnit code for heap-manipulating programs is much more challenging, as it often involves the need to synthesize the input and output heaps and compare the output heap stored in the test case with the resulting heap after the execution of the test.

3.6   Guided CLP-Based TCG

Whereas standard TCG by symbolic execution aims to cover *all* feasible paths of the program under test w.r.t. a termination criterion, in guided TCG, the termination criterion is combined with a *selection criterion*. To that end, the concept of *coverage criterion* is redefined to be a pair of two components $\langle TC, SC \rangle$. TC is a *termination criterion* that, as discussed earlier, ensures finiteness of symbolic execution. This can be done either based on execution steps or on loop iterations. Again, let us adhere to *loop-k*, which limits to a threshold k the number of allowed loop iterations and/or recursive calls (of each concrete loop or recursive method). SC is a *selection criterion* that determines which test cases the TCG must produce. In guided TCG this will steer symbolic execution towards the paths that should be explored. In particular, we consider the following two coverage criteria:

- all-local-paths: It requires that all *local* execution paths within the method under test are exercised up to a *loop-k* limit. This has a potential interest in the context of unit testing, where each method must be tested in isolation.
- program-points(P): Given a set of program points P, it requires that all of them are exercised by at least one test case up to a *loop-k* limit. This criterion is the most appropriate choice for bug-detection and reachability verification purposes. A particular case of it is *statement coverage* (up to a limit), where all statements in a program or method must be exercised.

This section develops a concrete methodology to incorporate selection criteria into the CLP-based TCG framework. To that end, we could employ a post-processing phase where only the test cases that are sufficient to satisfy the selection criterion are selected by looking at their traces. This is however not an appropriate solution in general due to the exponential explosion of the paths that have to be explored in symbolic execution. Instead, we now aim at using the selection criterion to drive the TCG process towards satisfying paths, stressing to avoid as much as possible the exploration of irrelevant and redundant ones. The key idea that allows us to guide the TCG process is to pass *trace terms* as input arguments to symbolic execution. These trace terms can be complete or partial, which allows guiding completely or partially, the symbolic execution towards specific paths.

First, let us define the notion of *trace term* and update Definition 1 to add a trace term as an additional argument to each rule of the CLP-translated program, which enables us to keep track of the sequence of rules that are symbolically executed. Notice that trace terms are not cardinal components in the translated program, but rather a supplementary argument with a central role in this chapter.

Definition 4 (CLP translated program with traces). *Given the rule of Definition 1, its CLP-translation with trace is:* $m(In, Out, H_{in}, H_{out}, EF, T) : - g, b'_1, \ldots, b'_n."$ *where:*

- *In, Out, H_{in}, H_{out} and EF remain as in Definition 1.*
- *T is the trace term for m of the form $m(k, P, \langle T_{c_i}, \ldots, T_{c_m} \rangle)$, where*
  - *P is the (possibly empty) list of trace parameters, i.e., the subset of the variables in rule m^k on which the resource consumption depends.*
  - *$c_i, \ldots, c_m$ is the (possibly empty) subsequence of method calls in $b_1, \ldots, b_n$.*
  - *T_{c_j} is a free logic variable representing the trace term associated to the call c_j.*
- *Calls in the body of the rule are extended with their corresponding trace terms, i.e., for all $1 \leq j \leq n$, if $b_j \equiv p(I_p, O_p, H_{in_p}, H_{out_p})$, then $b'_j \equiv p(I_p, O_p, H_{in_p}, H_{out_p}, T_{c_j})$; otherwise $b'_j \equiv b_j$.*

Now, let us revisit the definition of test case and TCG (Definition 3) to incorporate the notion of *trace* as an input argument for symbolic execution.

Definition 5 (Test case with trace and TCG). *Given a method m, a termination criterion C and a successful (terminating) path b in the symbolic execution tree T_m^C with root $m(In, Out, H_{in}, H_{out}, EF, T)$, a test case with trace for m w.r.t. C is a 6-tuple of the form: $\langle \sigma(In), \sigma(Out), \sigma(H_{in}), \sigma(H_{out}), \sigma(EF), \sigma(T), \theta \rangle$, where σ and θ are, resp., the set of bindings and the constraint store associated to b. TCG generates the set of test cases with traces obtained for all successful paths in T_m^C.*

Trace-Guided TCG. Given a method m, a coverage criterion $C = \langle TC, SC \rangle$, and a (possibly partial) trace π, trace-guided TCG generates the set tgTCG of test cases obtained for all successful branches of m using π as a guiding input argument for symbolic execution. Observe that the TCG guided by one trace π generates: (a) exactly one test case if π is complete and corresponds to a feasible path; (b) none if π is unfeasible; or (c) possibly several test cases if π is partial. In the latter case the traces of all test cases are instantiations of the partial trace.

For convenience, let us also define firstOf-tgTCG(m, TC, π) to be the unary set containing the leftmost successful branch of the symbolic execution tree of m.

Now, by relying on the existence of a trace generator $TraceGen$ that generates, on demand and one by one, (possibly partial) traces according to C, we define in Algorithm 1 a generic scheme for guided TCG.

Algorithm 1. Generic scheme for guided TCG

```
Input: M, and ⟨TC,SC⟩
TestCases = {}
while TraceGen has more traces and TestCases does not satisfy SC
    Ask TraceGen to generate a new trace in Trace
    TestCases = TestCases ∪ firstOf-tgTCG(M,TC,Trace)
Output: TestCases
```

The intuition is as follows: the trace generator generates a trace, possibly using for that SC, TC and the current $TestCases$. If the generated trace is feasible, then the first solution of its trace-guided TCG is added to the set of test cases. The process finishes either when SC is satisfied, or when the trace generator has already generated all traces up to TC. If the trace generator is complete (see below), this means that SC cannot be satisfied within the limit imposed by TC. Observe that for some selection criteria, e.g., all-local-paths, the calls to firstOf-tgTCG can be computed in parallel.

Example 11. Figure 13a shows a Java program made up of three methods: lcm calculates the least common multiple of two integers, gcd calculates the greatest common divisor of two integers, and abs returns the absolute value of an integer. Figure 13b shows the equivalent CLP-translated program. Method lcm is translated into predicates lcm, cont, try and div. As per Section 3.2, the translation preserves the control flow of the program and transforms iteration into recursion (e.g. method gcd). Note that the example has been chosen deliberately small and simple to ease comprehension. Let us consider the TCG for method lcm with program-points for points μ and κ as selection criterion. Let us assume that the trace generator starts generating the following two traces:

$$t_1 : \text{lcm}(1,[\text{cont}(1,[\text{G},\text{check}(1,[\text{A},\text{div}(2,[])])])])$$
$$t_2 : \text{lcm}(2,[\text{cont}(1,[\text{G},\text{check}(1,[\text{A},\text{div}(2,[])])])])$$

The first iteration does not add any test case since trace t_1 is unfeasible. Trace t_2 is proved feasible and a test case is generated. The selection criterion is now satisfied and therefore the process finishes. The following test case is obtained for the program-points criterion for method lcm and program points ⓤ and ⓚ. This particular case illustrates specially well how guided TCG can reduce the number of produced test cases through adequate control of the selection criterion.

Constraint store	Trace
{A=B=0,Out=-1}	lcm(1,[cont(1,[gcd(1,[loop(1,[abs(1,[])])]),
	try(1,[abs(1,[]),div(2,[])])])])

□

(a) Java source code

```
int lcm(int a,int b) {
  if (a < b) {
    int aux = a;
    a = b;
    b = aux;
  }
  int d = gcd(a,b);
  try {
    return abs(a*b)/d;
  } catch (Exception e) {
    return -1;                    (μ)
  }
}

int gcd(int a,int b) {
  int res;
  while (b != 0) {
    res = a%b;
    a = b;
    b = res;
  };
  return abs(a);
}

int abs(int a) {
  if (a >= 0)
    return a;                     (κ)
  else
    return -a;
}
```

(b) CLP-translation

```
lcm([A,B],[R],_,_,E,lcm(1,[T])) :-
  A #>= B,
  cont([A,B],[R],_,_,E,T).
lcm([A,B],[R],_,_,E,lcm(2,[T])) :-
  A #< B,
  cont([B,A],[R],_,_,E,T).
cont([A,B],[R],_,_,E,cont(1,[T,V])) :-
  gcd([A,B],[G],_,_,E,T),
  try([A,B,G],[R],_,_,E,V).
try([A,B,G],[R],_,_,E,try(1,[T,V])) :-
  M #= A*B,
  abs([M],[S],_,_,E,T),
  div([S,G],[R],_,_,E,V).
try([A,B,G],[R],_,_,exc,try(2,[])).
div([A,B],[R],_,_,ok,div(1,[])) :-
  B #\= 0,
  R #= A/B.
div([A,0],[-1],_,_,catch,div(2,[])).       (μ)
gcd([A,B],[D],_,_,E,gcd(1,[T])) :-
  loop([A,B],[D],_,_,E,T).
loop([A,0],[F],_,_,E,loop(1,[T])) :-
  abs([A],[F],_,_,E,T).
loop([A,B],[E],_,_,G,loop(2,[T])) :-
  B #\= 0,
  body([A,B],[E],_,_,G,T).
body([A,B],[R],_,_,E,body(1,[T])) :-
  B #\= 0,
  M #= A mod B,
  loop([B,M],[R],_,_,E,T).
body([A,0],[R],_,_,exc,body(2,[])).
abs([A],[A],_,_,ok,abs(1,[])) :-
  A #>= 0.                                  (κ)
abs([A],[-A],_,_,ok,abs(2,[])) :-
  A #< 0.
```

Fig. 13. Guided TCG Example: Java (left) and CLP-translated (right) programs

There are two properties of high importance in guided TCG, *completeness* and *effectiveness*. Intuitively, a concrete instantiation of the guided TCG scheme is *complete* if it never reports that the coverage criterion is not satisfied when it is indeed satisfiable. *Effectiveness* is related to the number of iterations the algorithm performs. These two properties depend completely on the trace generator. A trace generator is *complete* if it produces an over-approximation of the set of traces satisfying the coverage criterion. Its *effectiveness* depends on the number of redundant and/or unfeasible traces it generates: the larger the number, the less effective the trace generator.

Trace Generators for Structural Coverage Criteria. Let us now describe a general approach to build complete and effective trace generators for structural coverage criteria by means of program transformations. Then, we describe in detail an instantiation for the all-local-paths coverage criteria.

The *trace-abstraction* of a program can be defined as follows. Given a CLP-translated program with traces P, its trace-abstraction is obtained as follows: for every rule of P, (1) remove all atoms in the body of the rule except those corresponding to rule calls, and (2) remove all arguments from the head and from the surviving atoms of (1) except the last one (i.e., the trace term).

Example 12. Figure 14 shows the trace-abstraction for the CLP-translated program of Figure 13b. Observe that the trace-abstraction basically corresponds the control-flow graph of the CLP-translated program.   □

The trace-abstraction can be directly used as a trace generator as follows: (1) Apply the termination criterion in order to ensure finiteness of the process. (2) Select, in a post-processing, those traces that satisfy the selection criterion. Such a trace generator produces on backtracking a superset of the set of traces of the program satisfying the coverage criterion. Note that, this can be done as long as the criteria are structural. The obtained trace generator is by definition complete. However, it can be very ineffective and inefficient due to the large number of unfeasible and/or unnecessary traces that it can generate.

In the following, we propose a concrete, and more effective, instantiation for the all-local-paths coverage criteria. As we will see, this is done by taking advantage of the notion of partial traces and the implicit information on the concrete coverage criteria. A concrete instantiation for the program-points coverage criteria is described at [39].

```
lcm(lcm(1,[T])) :- cont(T).
lcm(lcm(2,[T])) :- cont(T).
cont(cont(1,[T,V])) :- gcd(T), try(V).
try(try(1,[T,V])) :- abs(T), div(V).
try(try(2,[])).
div(div(1,[])).
div(div(2,[])).
gcd(gcd(1,[T])) :- loop(T).
loop(loop(1,[T])) :- abs(T).
loop(loop(2,[T])) :- body(T).
body(body(1,[T])) :- loop(T).
body(body(2,[])).
abs(abs(1,[])).
abs(abs(2,[])).
```

Fig. 14. Trace-abstraction

An Instantiation for the all-local-paths Coverage Criterion. Let us start from the trace-abstraction program and apply a syntactic program slicing which removes from it the rules that do not belong to the considered method.

Definition 6 (slicing for all-local-paths coverage criterion). *Given a trace-abstraction program P and an entry method M:*

1. *Remove from P all rules that do not belong to method M.*
2. *In the bodies of remaining rules, remove all calls to rules which are not in P.*

The obtained sliced trace-abstraction, together with the termination criterion, can be used as a trace generator for the all-local-paths criterion for a method. The generated traces will have free variables in those trace arguments that correspond to the execution of other methods, if any.

```
lcm(lcm(1,[T])) :- cont(T).
lcm(lcm(2,[T])) :- cont(T).
cont(cont(1,[G,T])) :- try(T).
try(try(1,[A,T])) :- div(T).
try(try(2,[])).
div(div(1,[])).
div(div(2,[])).
```
```
lcm(1,[cont(1,[G,try(1,[A,div(1,[])])])])
lcm(1,[cont(1,[G,try(1,[A,div(2,[])])])])
lcm(1,[cont(1,[G,try(2,[])])])
lcm(2,[cont(1,[G,try(1,[A,div(1,[])])])])
lcm(2,[cont(1,[G,try(1,[A,div(2,[])])])])
lcm(2,[cont(1,[G,try(2,[])])])
```

Fig. 15. Slicing of method lcm for all-local-paths criterion

Example 13. Figure 15 shows on the left the sliced trace-abstraction for method lcm. On the right is the finite set of traces that is obtained from such trace abstraction for any *loop-k* termination criterion. Observe that the free variables G, resp. A, correspond to the sliced away calls to methods gcd and abs.   □

Let us define the predicates: computeSlicedProgram(M), that computes the sliced trace-abstraction for method M as in Definition 6; generateTrace(M,TC, Trace), that returns in its third argument, on backtracking, all partial traces computed using such sliced trace-abstraction, limited by the termination criterion TC; and traceGuidedTCG(M,TC,Trace,TestCase), which computes on backtracking the set tgTCG (definition of Trace-guided TCG above), failing if the set is empty, and instantiating on success TestCase and Trace (in case it was partial). The guided TCG scheme in Algorithm 1, instantiated for the all-local-paths criterion, can be implemented in Prolog as follows:

```
(1) guidedTCG(M,TC) :-
(2)     computeSlicedProgram(M),
(3)     generateTrace(M,TC,Trace),
(4)     once(traceGuidedTCG(M,Trace,TC,TestCase)),
(5)     assert(testCase(M,TestCase,Trace)),
(6)     fail.
(7) guidedTCG(_,_).
```

Intuitively, given a (possibly partial) trace generated in line (3), if the call in line (4) fails, then the next trace is tried. Otherwise, the generated test case is asserted with its corresponding trace which is now fully instantiated (in case it was partial). The process finishes when `generateTrace/3` has computed all traces, in which case it fails, making the program exiting through line (7).

Example 14. The following test cases are obtained for the all-local-paths criterion for method `lcm`:

Constraint store	Trace
{A>=B}	lcm(1,[cont(1,[gcd(1,[loop(1,[abs(1,[])])]), try(1,[abs(1,[]),div(1,[])])])])
{A=B=0,Out=-1}	lcm(1,[cont(1,[gcd(1,[loop(1,[abs(1,[])])]), try(1,[abs(1,[]),div(2,[])])])])
{B>A}	lcm(2,[cont(1,[gcd(1,[loop(1,[abs(1,[])])]), try(1,[abs(1,[]),div(1,[])])])])

This set of 3 test cases achieves full code and path coverage on method `lcm` and is thus a perfect choice in the context of unit-testing. In contrast, the original, non-guided, TCG scheme with *loop-2* as termination criterion produces 9 test cases.   □

A thorough experimental evaluation was performed in [39] which demonstrates the applicability and effectiveness of guided TCG.

4   TCG of Concurrent Programs

The focus of this section is on the development of automated techniques for testing *concurrent objects*.

4.1   Concurrent Objects

The central concept of the concurrency model is that of *concurrent object*. Concurrent objects live in a *distributed* environment with asynchronous and unordered communication by means of asynchronous method calls, denoted $y \mathbin{!} m(\overline{z})$. Method calls may be seen as triggers of concurrent activity, spawning new tasks (so-called *processes*) in the called object. After an asynchronous call of the form $x = y \mathbin{!} m(\overline{z})$, the caller may proceed with its execution without blocking on the call. Here x is a *future variable* which allows synchronizing with the completion of task $m(\overline{z})$. In particular, the instruction `await` x? allows checking whether m has finished. In this case, execution of the current task proceeds and x can be used for accessing the return value of m via the instruction x.get. Otherwise, the current task releases the processor to allow another available task to take it.

A synchronous call of the form $x = y.m(\overline{z})$, is internally transformed into the statement sequence $w = y \mathbin{!} m(\overline{z})$; if (*this* == y) `await` w?; $x = w$.get,

```
class A(Int n, Int ft) {                    Int fact(Int k, A ob){
Int sumFacts(A ob) {                            Fut <Int> f; Int res = 1;
    Fut<Int> f; Int res=0;                      if (k <= 0) res = 1;
    Int m = this.n;                             else { f = ob ! fact(k - 1,this);
    await this.ft >= 0;                             await f ?; res = f.get;
    while (m > 0) {                                 res = k * res;
        f =ob ! fact(this.ft, this);            }
        await f ?;                              return res;
        Int a = f.get;                      }
        res = res + a;                      Int setN(Int a)  { this.n=a; return 0; }
        this.ft = this.ft + 1;              Int setFt(Int b) { this.ft=b; return 0; }
        m = m - 1;                          Int set(Int a, Int b){
    }                                           this.setN(a); this.setFt(b);
    return res;                                 return 0;
}                                           }
```

Fig. 16. ABS running example

where w is a fresh future variable. This is because when the synchronous call is executed on the same object *this* we do not want to block this object (this would lead to a deadlock on the object *this*). Instead, we use an `await` instruction that will allow that the execution of the synchronous call to m can start to execute. The statement $x = w.\texttt{get}$ blocks the execution of the current object until $m(\overline{z})$ on y returns a value. The if statement avoids a deadlock when the object y is equal to *this*. For simplicity we assume that all methods return a value.

Example 15. Fig. 16 shows the implementation of class A, which contains two integer fields and five methods. Method sumFacts computes $\sum_{k=ft}^{ft+(n-1)} k!$ by asynchronously invoking fact on object ob. The `await` instruction before entering the loop allows releasing the processor if ft is negative. Once ft takes a non-negative value, the task can resume its execution and enter the loop. For instance, the asynchronous call f = ob ! fact(3, this); in sumFacts will add the task fact(3, this) to the queue of ob. When this task starts executing, it will add the task fact(2, ob) on the object this, which in turn will add fact(1, this) on ob and so on, in such a way that the factorial is computed in a distributed way between the two objects. Note that the calls are synchronized on future variables. This means that until the recursive call fact(1, this) is not completed the other tasks are suspended on their corresponding `await` conditions.   □

Let us briefly present the semantics for the concurrency instructions. An *object* is a term $ob(o, t, h, \mathcal{Q})$ where o is the object identifier, t is the identifier of the *active task* that holds the object's lock or $\bot$ if the object's lock is free, h is its local heap and $\mathcal{Q}$ is the set of tasks in the object. A *task* is a term $tk(t, m, l, s)$ where t is a unique task identifier, m is the method name executing in the task,

$$(\text{MSTEP})\ \frac{selectObject(S) = \text{ob}(o, \bot, h, \mathcal{Q}), \mathcal{Q} \neq \emptyset, selectTask(\mathcal{Q}) = t, S \overset{o \cdot t}{\leadsto^*} S'}{S \overset{o \cdot t}{\longrightarrow} S'}$$

$$(\text{NEWOB})\ \frac{t = tk(t, m, l, x = \text{new } D(\bar{y}); s), \text{fresh}(o'), h' = newhp(D), l' = l[x \rightarrow o'], \text{class } D(\bar{f})}{\text{ob}(o, t, h, \mathcal{Q} \cup \{t\}) \leadsto \text{ob}(o, t, h, \mathcal{Q} \cup \{tk(t, m, l', s)\}) \cdot \text{ob}(o', \bot, h'[\bar{f} \mapsto l(\bar{y})], \{\})}$$

$$(\text{ASYNC})\ \frac{t = tk(t, m, l, y = x \,!\, m_1(\bar{z}); s), l(x) = o_1, \text{fresh}(t_1), l_1 = buildLocals(\bar{z}, m_1, l)}{\text{ob}(o, t, h, \mathcal{Q} \cup \{t\}) \cdot \text{ob}(o_1, \_, \_, \mathcal{Q}') \leadsto}{\text{ob}(o, t, h, \mathcal{Q} \cup \{tk(t, m, l[y \mapsto t_1], s)\}) \cdot \text{ob}(o_1, \_, \_, \mathcal{Q}' \cup \{tk(t_1, m_1, l_1, body(m_1))\})}$$

$$(\text{AWAIT1})\ \frac{t = tk(t, m, l, \langle \text{await } y?; s \rangle), l(y) = t_1,\ tk(t_1, \_, \_, s_1) \in \text{Objects}, s_1 = \epsilon(v)}{\text{ob}(o, t, h, \mathcal{Q} \cup \{t\}) \leadsto \text{ob}(o, t, h, \{tk(t, m, l, s)\} \cup \mathcal{Q})}\ \bullet$$

$$(\text{AWAIT2})\ \frac{t = tk(t, m, l, \langle \text{await } y?; s \rangle), l(y) = t_1,\ tk(t_1, \_, \_, s_1) \in \text{Objects}, s_1 \neq \epsilon(v)}{\text{ob}(o, t, h, \mathcal{Q} \cup \{t\}) \leadsto \text{ob}(o, \bot, h, \{tk(t, m, l, \langle \text{await } y?; s \rangle)\} \cup \mathcal{Q})}$$

$$(\text{GET})\ \frac{t = tk(t, m, l, \langle x = \text{get}.y; s \rangle), l(y) = t_1,\ tk(t_1, \_, \_, s_1) \in \text{Objects}, s_1 = \epsilon(v)}{\text{ob}(o, t, h, \mathcal{Q} \cup \{t\}) \leadsto \text{ob}(o, t, h, \{tk(t, m, l[x \mapsto v], s)\} \cup \mathcal{Q})}$$

$$(\text{RETURN})\ \frac{t = tk(t, m, l, \text{return } x; s)}{\text{ob}(o, t, h, \mathcal{Q} \cup \{t\}) \leadsto \text{ob}(o, \bot, h, \{tk(t, \_, \_, \epsilon(l(x)))\} \cup \mathcal{Q})}$$

Fig. 17. Summarized Semantics for Distributed and Concurrent Execution

l is a mapping from local variables to their values, and s is the sequence of instructions to be executed or ϵ if the task has terminated.

A *state* or *configuration* S has the form $o_0 \cdot o_1 \cdots \cdot o_n$, where $o_i \equiv \text{ob}(o_i, t_i, h_i, \mathcal{Q}_i)$. The execution of a program from a method m starts from an initial state $S_0 = \{\text{ob}(0, 0, \bot, \{tk(0, m, l, body(m))\}$. Here, l maps parameters to their initial values (null in case of reference variables), $body(m)$ is the sequence of instructions in method m, and $\bot$ stands for the empty heap.

Fig. 17 presents the semantics of the concurrent objects. As objects do not share their states, the semantics can be presented as a macro-step semantics [41] (defined by means of the transition "$\longrightarrow$") in which the evaluation of all statements of a task takes place serially (without interleaving with any other task) until it gets to a *release point*, i.e., a point in which the object's processor becomes idle $\bot$ (due to an **await** or **return** instruction). In this case, we apply rule MSTEP to select an available task from an object, namely we apply the function $selectObject(S)$ to select non-deterministically one object in the state with a non-empty queue $\mathcal{Q}$ and $selectTask(\mathcal{Q})$ to select non-deterministically one task of $\mathcal{Q}$.

The transition $\leadsto$ defines the evaluation within a given object. We sometimes label transitions with $o \cdot t$, the name of the object o and task t selected (in rule MSTEP) or evaluated in the step (in the transition $\leadsto$). The notation $h[\bar{f} \mapsto l(\bar{y})]$ (resp. $l[x \mapsto v]$) stands for the result of storing $l(\bar{y})$ in the fields $\bar{f}$ (resp. v in x).

The remaining sequential instructions are standard and thus omitted. In NEWOB, an active task t in object o creates an object o' of class D which is introduced to the state with a free lock. Here h' stands for a default mapping on the fields of class D initialized with the values of $l(\bar{y})$. ASYNC spawns a new task (the initial state is created by $buildLocals$) with a fresh task identifier t_1 which is associated to the corresponding future variable y in l. We have assumed that $o \neq o_1$, but the case $o = o_1$ is analogous, the new task t_1 is simply added to $\mathcal{Q}$ of o_1.

The remaining rules define the concurrent execution within each distributed object. In AWAIT1, the future variable we are awaiting for points to a finished task and the await can be completed. The finished task t_1 is looked up in all objects in the current state (denoted Objects). Otherwise, AWAIT2 yields the lock so that any other task of the same object can take it. GET blocks the object until the task is finished. When RETURN is executed, the return value is stored in v so that it can be obtained by the future variable that points to that task. Besides, the lock is released and will never be taken again by that task. Consequently, that task is *finished* (marked by adding the instruction $\epsilon(v)$) but it does not disappear from the state as its return value may be needed later on in an await. In what follows, a *derivation* $S_0 \longrightarrow \cdots \longrightarrow S_n$ from an initial state S_0 of an object system is a sequence of macro-steps (applications of rule MSTEP). Since the execution is non-deterministic, multiple derivations are possible from an initial state.

Example 16. For instance, let us consider the following code corresponding to some method m of some class B.

     (a) A x = new A(5,10);
     (b) Fut<Int> f;
     (c) f = x ! fact(2,x);
     (d) await f?;
     (e) z = f.get;

where class A is that in Ex. 15. We start from the initial state $S_0 = \{\mathsf{ob}(0,0,\perp, \{tk(0,m,l_0,(a)\cdots(e)))\}$. By applying consecutively rules NEWOB, ASYNC and AWAIT2 to (a), (c) and (d) respectively we get:

$$S_1 = \{\mathsf{ob}(0,0,\perp,\{tk(0,m,l_0,(d)\cdot(e))\}), \mathsf{ob}(1,\perp,h_1,\{tk(2,\mathsf{fact},l_2,body(\mathsf{fact}))\})\}$$

where $l_0(f) = 2$, $l_2(k) = 2$, $l_2(\mathsf{ob}) = 1$ and $h_1(n) = 5$, $h_2(\mathsf{ft}) = 10$. We apply now a macro step on object 1, by reducing task 2. In this case the macro step stops when executing await f? of method fact, and the state is modified as follows:

$$S_2 = \{\ \mathsf{ob}(0,0,\perp,\{tk(0,m,l_0,(d)\cdot(e))\}),$$
$$\mathsf{ob}(1,2,h_1,\{tk(2,\mathsf{fact},l_2,\mathsf{await}\ \mathsf{f?};\ldots),tk(3,\mathsf{fact},l_3,body(\mathsf{fact}))\})\}$$

where $l_2(f) = 3$, $l_3(k) = 1$, $l_3(\mathsf{ob}) = 1$. Similarly as done before, task with identifier 3 is now reduced, stopping the derivation when we reach await f?:

$$S_3 = \{\ \mathsf{ob}(0,0,\perp,\ \{tk(0,m,l_0,(d)\cdot(e))\}),$$
$$\mathsf{ob}(1,2,h_1,\{tk(2,\mathsf{fact},l_2,\mathsf{await}\ \mathsf{f?};\ldots),$$
$$tk(3,\mathsf{fact},l_3,\mathsf{await}\ \mathsf{f?};\ldots),tk(4,\mathsf{fact},l_4,body(\mathsf{fact}))\})\}$$

where $l_3(f) = 4$, $l_4(k) = 0$, $l_4(\mathsf{ob}) = 1$. Now only task 4 can be reduced and applying rule RETURN we get:

$$S_4 = \{ \ \mathsf{ob}(0,0,\bot, \ \{tk(0,m,l_0,(d)\cdot(e))\}),$$
$$\mathsf{ob}(1,2,h_1, \{tk(2,\mathsf{fact},l_2,\mathsf{await} \ \mathsf{f?};\ldots),$$
$$tk(3,\mathsf{fact},l_3,\mathsf{await} \ \mathsf{f?};\ldots), tk(4,\bot,l_4,\epsilon(1))\})\}$$

Now, task 3 can be reduced by applying first AWAIT1 and after RETURN:

$$S_5 = \{ \ \mathsf{ob}(0,0,\bot, \ \{tk(0,m,l_0,(d)\cdot(e))\}),$$
$$\mathsf{ob}(1,2,h_1, \{tk(2,\mathsf{fact},l_2,\mathsf{await} \ \mathsf{f?};\ldots),$$
$$tk(3,\bot,l_3,\epsilon(1)), tk(4,\bot,l_4,\epsilon(1))\})\}$$

Similarly we reduce task 2 and after task 0 from object 0 and we finally get:

$$S_6 = \{ \ \mathsf{ob}(0,0,\bot, \ \{tk(0,m,l_0,\epsilon)\}),$$
$$\mathsf{ob}(1,2,h_1, \{tk(2,\bot,l_2,\epsilon(2)),$$
$$tk(3,\bot,l_3,\epsilon(1)), tk(4,\bot,l_4,\epsilon(1))\})\}$$

where $l_0(z) = 2$. □

Given an initial state, a naïve exploration of the search space to reach all possible system configurations does not scale. The challenge is then in avoiding the exploration of redundant states which lead to the same configuration. Partial-order reduction (POR) [16,20] is a general theory that helps mitigate the state-space explosion problem by exploring the subset of all possible interleavings which lead to a different configuration. A concrete algorithm (called DPOR) was proposed by Flanagan and Godefroid [18] which maintains for each configuration a backtrack set, which is updated during the execution of the program when it realizes that a non-deterministic choice must be tried. Recently, TransDPOR [45] extends DPOR to take advantage of the transitive dependency relations in actor systems to explore fewer configurations than DPOR. As noticed in [32,45], their effectiveness highly depend on the actor selection order.

In our semantics in Fig. 16, functions *selectObject* and *selectTask* can be implemented with novel strategies and heuristics to further prune redundant state exploration, and they can be easily integrated within the aforementioned algorithms. For instance, *selectObject* could try to find a *stable object*, i.e., an object to which no other actor will post messages. Basically, this means that the object is autonomous since its execution does not depend on any other actor and thus no backtracking is required from that point. Furthermore, when temporal stability of any object cannot be proved, it is possible to look for heuristics that assign a weight to the messages according to the error that the object-selection strategy may make when proving stability w.r.t. them. Finally, function *selectTask* can be defined to select independent tasks according to the independence notion defined in [8], which basically establishes that two tasks are independent if they access disjoint parts of the shared memory. Note that this would avoid non determinism reordering among tasks.

4.2   Coverage and Termination Criteria for Concurrent Objects

As commented in Sec. 2.1, an important problem in symbolic execution is that, since the input data is unknown, the execution tree to be traversed is in general infinite. Hence it is required to integrate a *termination criterion* which guarantees that the length of the paths traversed remains finite while at the same time an interesting set of test cases is generated, i.e., certain code *coverage* is achieved.

Task-Level Coverage and Termination Criteria. Given a task executing on an object, we aim at ensuring its local termination by leveraging existing Coverage Criteria (CC for short) developed in the sequential setting to the context of concurrent objects. We focus on the *loop-k* coverage criteria [26] described in Sec. 2.1, which limits the number of times we iterate on loops to a threshold K_l (other existing criteria would pose similar problems and solutions). However applying the task-level CC to all tasks *does not guarantee termination*. This is because we can switch from one task to another an infinite number of times. For example, consider the symbolic execution of ob_1 ! $fact(n, ob_2)$, where method fact is defined in Ex. 15. We circularly switch from object ob_1 to object ob_2 an infinite number of times because each asynchronous call in one object adds another call on the other object (see Ex. 16). This is not detected by the task-level CC because each method invocation is a new task. Intuitively, we get the following situation, where we show in each state the value of the queues in both objects. In each step the corresponding call to fibo is always selected.

$$\{ob_1, ob_2\}, Q_{ob_1} = \{fact(n, ob_2)\}, Q_{ob_2} = \{\} \qquad \longrightarrow$$
$$\{ob_1, ob_2\}, Q_{ob_1} = \{await\ f?; \ldots\}, Q_{ob_2} = \{fact(n_1, ob_1)\} \qquad \overset{n_1 = n-1}{\longrightarrow}$$
$$\{ob_1, ob_2\}, Q_{ob_1} = \{fact(n_2, ob_2), await\ f?; \ldots\}, Q_{ob_2} = \{await\ f?; \ldots\} \overset{n_2 = n_1 - 1}{\longrightarrow}$$
$$\ldots \qquad \ldots \qquad \longrightarrow \ldots$$

The same problem can happen even with a single object, e.g., in method sumFacts when executing `await (ft >= 0)`, there is an infinite branch in the evaluation tree, corresponding to the case `ft < 0` which can be re-tried forever. I.e., we can apply infinitely the rule AWAIT2 in Fig. 17 on the task `await (ft >= 0)`, whose effect is to extract the task from the queue, to prove that the task does not hold, and to put again the task in the queue.

Task-Switching Coverage and Termination Criteria. In both examples above we can observe that the problem, in presence of concurrency relies, not only on loops, but also on the number of task switches allowed per object. Thus, the number of task switches can be limited by simply allowing a fixed and global number of task switching. However, it might happen that, due to excessive task switching in certain objects, others are not properly tested (i.e., their tasks exercised) because the *global* number of allowed task switches has been exceeded. For example, suppose that we add the instructions `B ob_2 = new B(); ob_2 ! q();` before the return in method sumFacts, where B is a class that implements method q but whose code is not relevant. Then, as the evaluation for the *while* loop generates an infinite number of task switches (because of the `await` instruction in the loop), the evaluation of the call `ob_2 ! p();` is not reached. Thus, in order to have fairness in the process and guarantee proper coverage from the concurrency point of view, we propose to *limit the number of task switches* per *object* (i.e., per concurrency unit).

4.3   Task Interleavings in TCG

An important problem in TCG of concurrent languages is that, when a task t suspends, there could be other tasks on the same object whose execution at this point could interleave with t and modify the information stored in the heap. It is essential to consider such task interleavings in order not to lose any important path. For example, let us consider a class C with two fields int n, f, and a method p in C defined as: int p(){n = 0; await (f > 0); if(n>=0) return 1; else return 2; }. Suppose a call of the form x = o ! p(); await x?; y = x.get. The symbolic execution of p, will in principle consider just one path (the one that goes through the if branch), giving as result always y = 1. There can be however another task (suspended in the queue of the object o) which executes when p suspends in await (f > 0) and writes a negative value on n. This would exercise the else branch when p resumes, giving as result y = 2. For example, suppose that the method void set(){n = −1; } belongs to class C and that set() is in the queue when executing await (f > 0), and that is executed before f > 0 holds. Then the execution of p() will try the else branch.

The questions that we solve in this section are: (a) is it possible to consider all interleavings that affect the method's coverage? (b) do we have means to discard useless interleavings? (i.e., those which do not add new paths). As regards (a), it is not enough to assume that there is one instance of each method call in the queue as further coverage is possible by introducing multiple instances of the same method. Even though termination is guaranteed by the limit imposed on the number of task switches in Sec. 4.2 (i.e., the length of the queue is finite), it is more appropriate to define an additional coverage criteria in this new dimension by fixing the maximum length of a queue in order to achieve a more meaningful coverage.

In order to answer question (b), we start by characterizing the notion of useless interleaving. Starting from the set of all methods in the class of the method under test, we propose a sequence of *prunings* which ensure that only useless interleavings are eliminated. The objective is to over-approximate, for each method m, the set related(m), which contains all methods whose interleaved execution with m can lead to a solution not considered before. The remaining ones are useless interleavings. Starting from the set of all methods in the class of the method under test, we propose a sequence of *prunings* which ensure that only useless interleavings are eliminated.

(Pruning 1). The first refinement is to discard methods which do not modify the heap, i.e., *pure* methods. Purity can be syntactically proved by checking that the method does not contain any instruction of the form *this.f* $= x$ and that methods (transitively) invoked from it are pure. Using this pruning on Ex. 15, we get related(sumFacts) = {sumFacts, set, setN, setFt}.

(Pruning 2). The second pruning amounts to considering only *directly impure* methods (ignoring transitive calls), i.e., those which write directly on fields. Let p be the method under test, m be a directly impure method and q a method that invokes m. The intuition is that by considering m alone, we execute it from a more general context, while its execution from q will be just more specific (since q will have added additional constraints). Hence, it will not add additional local traces for p. With this pruning, related(sumFacts) = {sumFacts, setN, setFt}.

(Pruning 3). The third pruning consists in considering only the interleavings with those methods that write (directly) on fields which are used (read or written) before an `await` , *and* read after an `await`. These sets are easily computed by just looking for instructions *this.f = x* and *x = this.f* in the corresponding program fragments. Given a field f, the intuition for this condition is that, if f has not been accessed before the `await` then there is no information about the field. Thus, related(sumFacts) = {sumFacts, setFt}.

4.4 Related Work on TCG of Thread-Based Concurrency

As it happens with actor-based systems, the main difficulties in TCG of thread-based systems are related to the scalability when considering thread interleavings. In thread-based systems, this problem is exacerbated. In [37], a symbolic execution framework which combines symbolic execution with model checking is presented to detect safety violations. Safety properties are represented by using logical formalisms understood by the model checker or that can be inserted in the code as annotations. The model checker, when doing symbolic execution, is able to report counterexamples which violate the correctness safety criterion. Furthermore, when generating test cases, the model checker generates the paths that fulfill the safety property. To reduce the number of thread interleavings, the model checker uses partial order reduction techniques [20] as we do. An advantage on this technique is the possibility of handling native calls through mixed concrete-symbolic solving. The main drawback of this framework is that satisfiability of constraints is checked at the end of each branch of the symbolic tree, what it might be unfeasible. Thus, they use preconditions on the symbolic input values in order to avoid the exploration of branches which violate the precondition. In contrast to [37], our CLP-approach is able to discard a branch in the symbolic tree once the associated constraint are unsatisfiable.

Other approaches that use techniques different from ours are [29, 43, 44]. The work [29] combines dynamic symbolic execution (concolic testing) with unfoldings. The unfolding approach allows constructing a compact representation of the interleavings and thus the new testing algorithm may use this information to guide the symbolic execution, avoiding irrelevant interleavings. This new approach achieves in some cases an exponential gain when compared with existing dynamic partial-order reduction based approaches [18, 45]. Basically, the point is that in the previous approaches, the number of explored interleavings depends on the order in which processes are executed, but in this new approach it does not, since interleavings are computed a priory.

In [43,44], a runtime algorithm to monitor executions for multithreaded Java and possibly detect safety violations is presented. From a concrete execution, they automatically extract a partial order causality from a sequence of read-/write events on shared variables. Basically they extract, for a shared variable, the sequence of write/reads/write to that variable in the execution. Thus any permutation of these events can be considered an execution of the program if and only if it does not contradict the partial order. The main drawbacks is the state explosion since a large number of unreachable branches may be explored.

As an improvement of the previous work, in [42], a novel approach uses concolic execution (a combination of symbolic and concrete execution) to test shared-memory in multithreaded programs by using an algorithm based on race-detection and flipping. From a concrete execution, they determine the partial order relation or the exact race conditions between the processes in the execution path. Afterwards, such processes involved in races are flipped by generating new thread schedules and generating new test inputs. Hence, differently to the previous conservative approaches, in this work they explore one path from each partial order, avoiding possible warnings that could never occur in a real execution.

5   Conclusions

This tutorial summarizes the basic principles used in TCG by symbolic execution. It first discusses the main challenges that TCG currently poses: the efficient handling of heap-manipulating programs, compositionallity, and guiding the process. It then overviews a particular instantiation of the generic TCG framework that uses CLP as enabling technology. We will review the main features, advantages and implementation of this CLP-approach. Finally, we discuss the extension of the basic framework to handle concurrent actor systems.

Acknowledgments. This work was funded partially by the EU project FP7-ICT-610582 ENVISAGE: Engineering Virtualized Services (http://www.envisageproject.eu) and by the Spanish projects TIN2008-05624 and TIN2012-38137.

References

1. Agha, G.A.: Actors: A Model of Concurrent Computation in Distributed Systems. MIT Press, Cambridge (1986)
2. Albert, E., Arenas, P., Genaim, S., Puebla, G., Zanardini, D.: Cost Analysis of Java Bytecode. In: De Nicola, R. (ed.) ESOP 2007. LNCS, vol. 4421, pp. 157–172. Springer, Heidelberg (2007)
3. Albert, E., Cabañas, I., Flores-Montoya, A., Gómez-Zamalloa, M., Gutiérrez, S.: jPET: an Automatic Test-Case Generator for Java. In: WCRE 2011, pp. 441–442. IEEE Computer Society (2011)
4. Albert, E., de la Banda, M.G., Gómez-Zamalloa, M., Rojas, J.M., Stuckey, P.: A CLP Heap Solver for Test Case Generation. Theory and Practice of Logic Programming 13(4-5), 721–735 (2013)

5. Albert, E., Gómez-Zamalloa, M., Rojas, J.M., Puebla, G.: Compositional CLP-Based Test Data Generation for Imperative Languages. In: Alpuente, M. (ed.) LOPSTR 2010. LNCS, vol. 6564, pp. 99–116. Springer, Heidelberg (2011)
6. Anand, S., Burke, E.K., Chen, T.Y., Clark, J.A., Cohen, M.B., Grieskamp, W., Harman, M., Harrold, M.J., McMinn, P.: An orchestrated survey of methodologies for automated software test case generation. Journal of Systems and Software 86(8), 1978–2001 (2013)
7. Anand, S., Godefroid, P., Tillmann, N.: Demand-Driven Compositional Symbolic Execution. In: Ramakrishnan, C.R., Rehof, J. (eds.) TACAS 2008. LNCS, vol. 4963, pp. 367–381. Springer, Heidelberg (2008)
8. Andrews, G.R.: Concurrent Programming: Principles and Practice. Benjamin/Cummings (1991)
9. Cadar, C., Sen, K.: Symbolic Execution for Software Testing: Three Decades Later. Commun. ACM 56(2), 82–90 (2013)
10. Cadar, C., Godefroid, P., Khurshid, S., Păsăreanu, C.S., Sen, K., Tillmann, N., Visser, W.: Symbolic Execution for Software Testing in Practice: Preliminary Assessment. In: ICSE 2011, pp. 1066–1071. ACM (2011)
11. Clarke, L.A.: A System to Generate Test Data and Symbolically Execute Programs. IEEE Transactions on Software Engineering 2(3), 215–222 (1976)
12. Cytron, R., Ferrante, J., Rosen, B.K., Wegman, M.N., Kenneth Zadeck, F.: Efficiently Computing Static Single Assignment Form and the Control Dependence Graph. ACM Trans. Program. Lang. Syst. 13(4), 451–490 (1991)
13. Degrave, F., Schrijvers, T., Vanhoof, W.: Towards a Framework for Constraint-Based Test Case Generation. In: De Schreye, D. (ed.) LOPSTR 2009. LNCS, vol. 6037, pp. 128–142. Springer, Heidelberg (2010)
14. Dovier, A., Formisano, A., Pontelli, E.: A Comparison of CLP(FD) and ASP Solutions to NP-Complete Problems. In: Gabbrielli, M., Gupta, G. (eds.) ICLP 2005. LNCS, vol. 3668, pp. 67–82. Springer, Heidelberg (2005)
15. Engel, C., Hähnle, R.: Generating Unit Tests from Formal Proofs. In: Gurevich, Y., Meyer, B. (eds.) TAP 2007. LNCS, vol. 4454, pp. 169–188. Springer, Heidelberg (2007)
16. Esparza, J.: Model checking using net unfoldings. Sci. Comput. Program. 23(2-3), 151–195 (1994)
17. Ferguson, R., Korel, B.: The Chaining Approach for Software Test Data Generation. ACM Trans. Softw. Eng. Methodol. 5(1), 63–86 (1996)
18. Flanagan, C., Godefroid, P.: Dynamic partial-order reduction for model checking software. In: POPL, pp. 110–121. ACM (2005)
19. Godefroid, P.: Compositional Dynamic Test Generation. In: POPL 2007, pp. 47–54. ACM (2007)
20. Godefroid, P.: Using partial orders to improve automatic verification methods. In: Larsen, K.G., Skou, A. (eds.) CAV 1991. LNCS, vol. 575, pp. 176–185. Springer, Heidelberg (1992)
21. Gómez-Zamalloa, M., Albert, E., Puebla, G.: Decompilation of Java Bytecode to Prolog by Partial Evaluation. Information and Software Technology 51(10), 1409–1427 (2009)
22. Gómez-Zamalloa, M., Albert, E., Puebla, G.: Test Case Generation for Object-Oriented Imperative Languages in CLP. Theory and Practice of Logic Programming, ICLP 2010 Special Issue 10(4-6), 659–674 (2010)
23. Gotlieb, A., Botella, B., Rueher, M.: A CLP Framework for Computing Structural Test Data. In: Palamidessi, C., et al. (eds.) CL 2000. LNCS (LNAI), vol. 1861, pp. 399–413. Springer, Heidelberg (2000)

24. Gupta, N., Mathur, A.P., Soffa, M.L.: Generating Test Data for Branch Coverage. In: ASE 2000, pp. 219–228. IEEE Computer Society (2000)
25. Haller, P., Odersky, M.: Scala actors: Unifying thread-based and event-based programming. Theor. Comput. Sci. 410(2-3), 202–220 (2009)
26. Howden, W.E.: Symbolic Testing and the DISSECT Symbolic Evaluation System. IEEE Transactions on Software Engineering 3(4), 266–278 (1977)
27. Jaffar, J., Maher, M.J.: Constraint Logic Programming: A Survey. Journal of Logic Programming 19/20, 503–581 (1994)
28. The Java Modelling Language homepage (2013),
    http://www.eecs.ucf.edu/~leavens/JML//index.shtml
29. Kähkönen, K., Saarikivi, O., Heljanko, K.: Using unfoldings in automated testing of multithreaded programs. In: Goedicke, M., Menzies, T., Saeki, M. (eds.) ASE, pp. 150–159. ACM (2012)
30. Khurshid, S., Păsăreanu, C.S., Visser, W.: Generalized Symbolic Execution for Model Checking and Testing. In: Garavel, H., Hatcliff, J. (eds.) TACAS 2003. LNCS, vol. 2619, pp. 553–568. Springer, Heidelberg (2003)
31. King, J.C.: Symbolic Execution and Program Testing. Commun. ACM 19(7), 385–394 (1976)
32. Lauterburg, S., Karmani, R.K., Marinov, D., Agha, G.: Evaluating Ordering Heuristics for Dynamic Partial-Order Reduction Techniques. In: Rosenblum, D.S., Taentzer, G. (eds.) FASE 2010. LNCS, vol. 6013, pp. 308–322. Springer, Heidelberg (2010)
33. Lloyd, J.W.: Foundations of Logic Programming, 2nd ext. edn. Springer (1987)
34. Marriott, K., Stuckey, P.J.: Programming with Constraints: an Introduction. MIT Press (1998)
35. Meudec, C.: ATGen: Automatic Test Data Generation using Constraint Logic Programming and Symbolic Execution. Softw. Test., Verif. Reliab. 11(2), 81–96 (2001)
36. Müller, R.A., Lembeck, C., Kuchen, H.: A Symbolic Java Virtual Machine for Test Case Generation. In: IASTEDSE 2004, pp. 365–371. ACTA Press (2004)
37. Pasareanu, C.S., Visser, W., Bushnell, D.H., Geldenhuys, J., Mehlitz, P.C., Rungta, N.: Symbolic pathfinder: integrating symbolic execution with model checking for java bytecode analysis. Autom. Softw. Eng. 20(3), 391–425 (2013)
38. Păsăreanu, C.S., Visser, W.: A Survey of New Trends in Symbolic Execution for Software Testing and Analysis. Int. J. Softw. Tools Technol. Transf. 11(4), 339–353 (2009)
39. Rojas, J.M., Gómez-Zamalloa, M.: A Framework for Guided Test Case Generation in Constraint Logic Programming. In: Albert, E. (ed.) LOPSTR 2012. LNCS, vol. 7844, pp. 176–193. Springer, Heidelberg (2013)
40. Rojas, J.M., Păsăreanu, C.S.: Compositional Symbolic Execution through Program Specialization. In: 8th Workshop on Bytecode Semantics, Verification, Analysis and Transformation, BYTECODE 2013 (March 2013)
41. Sen, K., Agha, G.: Automated Systematic Testing of Open Distributed Programs. In: Baresi, L., Heckel, R. (eds.) FASE 2006. LNCS, vol. 3922, pp. 339–356. Springer, Heidelberg (2006)
42. Sen, K., Agha, G.: A race-detection and flipping algorithm for automated testing of multi-threaded programs. In: Bin, E., Ziv, A., Ur, S. (eds.) HVC 2006. LNCS, vol. 4383, pp. 166–182. Springer, Heidelberg (2007)
43. Sen, K., Roşu, G., Agha, G.: Online efficient predictive safety analysis of multithreaded programs. In: Jensen, K., Podelski, A. (eds.) TACAS 2004. LNCS, vol. 2988, pp. 123–138. Springer, Heidelberg (2004)

44. Sen, K., Roşu, G., Agha, G.: Detecting errors in multithreaded programs by generalized predictive analysis of executions. In: Steffen, M., Zavattaro, G. (eds.) FMOODS 2005. LNCS, vol. 3535, pp. 211–226. Springer, Heidelberg (2005)
45. Tasharofi, S., Karmani, R.K., Lauterburg, S., Legay, A., Marinov, D., Agha, G.: TransDPOR: A Novel Dynamic Partial-Order Reduction Technique for Testing Actor Programs. In: Giese, H., Rosu, G. (eds.) FORTE 2012 and FMOODS 2012. LNCS, vol. 7273, pp. 219–234. Springer, Heidelberg (2012)
46. Tillmann, N., de Halleux, J.: Pex–White Box Test Generation for.NET. In: Beckert, B., Hähnle, R. (eds.) TAP 2008. LNCS, vol. 4966, pp. 134–153. Springer, Heidelberg (2008)
47. Triska, M.: The Finite Domain Constraint Solver of SWI-Prolog. In: Schrijvers, T., Thiemann, P. (eds.) FLOPS 2012. LNCS, vol. 7294, pp. 307–316. Springer, Heidelberg (2012)
48. Wielemaker, J., Schrijvers, T., Triska, M., Lager, T.: SWI-prolog. Theory and Practice of Logic Programming 12(1-2), 67–96 (2012)
49. Zhu, H., Hall, P.A.V., May, J.H.R.: Software Unit Test Coverage and Adequacy. ACM Comput. Surv. 29(4), 366–427 (1997)

Model-Based Testing

Malte Lochau[1], Sven Peldszus[1], Matthias Kowal[2], and Ina Schaefer[2]

[1] TU Darmstadt, Germany
{malte.lochau,sven.peldszus}@es.tu-darmstadt.de
[2] TU Braunschweig, Germany
{kowal,schaefer}@isf.cs.tu-bs.de

Abstract. Software more and more pervades our everyday lives. Hence, we have high requirements towards the trustworthiness of the software. Software testing greatly contributes to the quality assurance of modern software systems. However, as today's software system get more and more complex and exist in many different variants, we need rigorous and systematic approaches towards software testing. In this tutorial, we, first, present model-based testing as an approach for systematic test case generation, test execution and test result evaluation for single system testing. The central idea of model-based testing is to base all testing activities on an executable model-based test specification. Second, we consider model-based testing for variant-rich software systems and review two model-based software product line testing techniques. Sample-based testing generates a set of representative variants for testing, and variability-aware product line testing uses a family-based test model which contains the model-based specification of all considered product variants.

1 Introduction

Software more and more pervades our everyday lives. It controls cars, trains and planes. It manages our bank accounts and collects our personal information for salary or tax purposes. It comes to our homes with smart home technology in our fridges or washing machines which get increasingly connected with the Internet and personal mobile devices. Because of the ubiquity and pervasiveness of modern software systems, we have high requirements towards their trustworthiness.

Software testing greatly contributes to the quality assurance of modern software systems [55,41]. In general, testing is a partial verification technique as it only checks a software system on a selected set of inputs, while formal methods, such as model checking or program verification, allow a complete verification by considering all possible system runs. One major advantage of software testing over formal methods, however, is that testing can be performed in the actually runtime environment of the software, including all hardware and peripheral devices, while formal methods usually abstract from certain details. However, today's software system get more and more complex. They exist in many different variants in order to satisfy changing environment conditions,

M. Bernardo et al. (Eds.): SFM 2014, LNCS 8483, pp. 310–342, 2014.

such as user, technical or legal requirements. Hence, in order to ensure safety-critical, business-critical or mission-critical requirements, we need rigorous and systematic approaches for software testing.

In this tutorial, we, first, present model-based testing as an formal approach for dynamic functional testing of single systems [54]. The central idea of model-based testing is to base all testing activities on an executable formal test model of the expected system behavior. The test model can be used for test case generation, for test case execution and and for test result evaluation. In main advantages of model-based testing over classical manual testing activities is that test cases can be derived in a systematic and automatic fashion from the test models with defined coverage metrics. Furthermore, model-based testing allows the automation of test execution and test result evaluation by comparing the actual test results with the expected results expressed in the test model. When software evolves, the test models allow regression test selection by automatic change impact analysis on the test models. After an introduction of the general notions of model-based testing, we introduce the formal notions of model-based input/output conformance testing.

Second, we consider model-based testing for variant-rich software systems [50], in form of software product lines. Testing software product lines is particularly complex because the number of possible product variants is exponential in the number of product features. Hence, it is generally infeasible to test all product variants exhaustively. We review two model-based software product line testing techniques which can be used in combination to facilitate efficient testing of variant-rich software systems. First, sample-based testing allows to automatically generate a set of representative variants which should be tested instead of testing all possible product variants. Second, we present variability-aware product line testing which uses a family-based test model which contains the model-based specification of all considered product variants and define the notion of product line conformance testing.

This tutorial is structured as follows. In Sect. 2, we introduce the key notions and concepts of (software) testing. In Sect. 3, the principles of model-based testing techniques are described together with a formalization of model-based input/output conformance testing following Tretmans [54]. In Sect. 4, we extend the model-based testing principles to software product lines and describe two recent techniques for variability-aware product line testing. Sect. 5 concludes the tutorial.

2   Foundations of Software Testing

Generally speaking, (software) testing deals with the quality assurance of a (software) product. The IEEE defines the purpose of *testing* as

> [...] an activity performed for evaluating product quality, and for improving it, by identifying defects and problems [17].

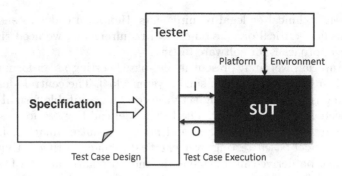

Fig. 1. General Setting of Software Testing

It characterizes the testing activity itself as

> [...] the process of operating a system or component under specified
> conditions, observing or recording the results, and making an evaluation
> of some aspects of the system or component [17].

Thus, the notion of testing comprises any kind of activity explicitly aiming at
ensuring quality requirements a software product must meet. This includes arbitrary activities *and* properties somehow relevant for the product quality goals.
Hence, a wide range of testing approaches exists, differing in the methods applied and the test aims pursued. For instance, a testing method may be either
static, e.g., systematic code inspections, or *dynamic* by means of experimental
executions of the *system under test* (SUT).

The general setting for conducting (dynamic) tests on an SUT is illustrated in
Fig. 1. In each test case execution, the SUT is run by a *Tester* under controlled
environmental/platform conditions by stimulating accessible inputs I and ob-
serving the expected output behaviors O of the SUT. The *Tester* might be a
real person, a virtual process, e.g., a test script for test automation etc. The
category of dynamic testing is often further subdivided into *active* testing, i.e.,
real executions are enforced under experimental input sequences I and *passive*
testing, e.g., by just monitoring output behaviors of the system under operation.
According to Tretmans, the actual aspects to be observed as outputs during test
case execution depend on the charateristics under considertion.

> (Software) testing is an activity for checking or measuring some qual-
> ity characteristics of an executing object by performing experiments in
> a controlled way w.r.t. a specification [54].

Therefore, the *design* principles for appropriate test cases depend on those aspects under consideration. In particular, characteristics to be investigated by
testing may be

- *functional*, i.e., related to some *behavioral* aspect expected from the system,
  e.g., by means of (visible) actions,

- *extra-functional*, i.e., concerning robustness, performance, reliability, availability etc. of (software) functions as well as
- *non-functional*, i.e., massively depending on the (hardware) platform, e.g., energy consumption, resource consumption etc.

We concentrate on test case design for finding *functional* errors. This may include finding errors in all parts of the system potentially interacting with the software. Test case *executions* perform determined sequences of input actions (stimuli) together with sequences of output actions expected from the SUT as defined by the system *specification* The resulting test verdict denotes whether the actual product reaction conforms to this expected behavior. The following notions are used in the literature for situations in which a test case execution fails [55].

- A *failure* is an undesired observable behavior of an SUT.
- A *fault* in an SUT causes a failure, e.g., by reaching a human/software error, hardware defects etc., during test execution.
- A (software) *error* is a logical error in the implementation of a requirement thus potentially leading to a fault.

A software is erroneous if it fails to satisfy its requirements. Hence, an implementation is tested against the requirements, which are either represented in an informal, e.g., textual, or in a formal way, e.g., a formal specification such as a *test model* [55].

Depending on the development phase in which test cases are applied onto an implementation, test cases are to be defined according to the current representation of the implementation available. For instance, test cases may be applied to an abstract implementation model, to implementation code fragments running on a hardware emulator, as well as to the final software fully deployed onto the target platform. Summarizing, we use the following characterization of (dynamic) software testing.

Definition 1 (Software Testing). *Software testing consists of the dynamic validation/verification of the behavior of a program on a finite set of test cases suitably selected from the usually infinite input/execution domain against the expected behavior.*

This definition essentially reflects the notion proposed in [55]. Applying testing as a verification technique is often considered as a counter part to *formal* verification techniques such as model checking. Both approaches can be opposed as follows. *Testing* allows a *partial*, i.e., incomplete verification of the correctness of an implementation with respect to a specification and thus constituting a heuristic verification method. The implementation can be tested at any level of abstraction as long as it is executable. In particular, tests can be applied to the final system implementation including any factor potentially influencing the software such as hardware components etc. Furthermore, testing can be performed by engineers at any skill level in a totally informal and pragmatic way. In contrast, *formal verification* permits a *complete* verification of the correctness of an implementation with respect to a specification. The implementation must be represented by means of a formal abstraction of the real implementation. Hence, the major challenges when applying formal methods like model checking are (1) to ensure an implementation to be a valid refinement of the verified abstraction, (2) scalability issues, and (3) ensuring correctness of the verification tools. Both methods have advantages and disadvantages, thus complementing rather than excluding each other.

The goal of software testing is to design and apply *test suites* for a software product under test. Test suites contain a set of *test case specifications*. In practice, the design of a test suite consists of selecting sample input data for the SUT, where the concrete test derivation techniques and test case representation depend on several factors, e.g., the *test method*, e.g., static, dynamic testing, the *test aim*, e.g., functional, non-functional tests, the *test scale*, e.g., unit, component, integration, system tests, and the *information base*, e.g., black box, white box, gray box tests. The test scale corresponds to the level of abstraction considered in particular development phases where the test cases are applied. In addition, the actual testing technique heavily depends on the information base available for the system under test, e.g., accessibility to the implementation source code and platform details. Thus, black box tests comprise, e.g., combinatorial testing strategies and model-based testing as both solely consider the I/O interface of the system under test. In white box testing, the source code and further implementation details are fully accessible, whereas in gray box testing only some of those details, e.g., an architectural description, are available.

The *quality* of a test suite, e.g., with respect to the reliability of the verification results obtainable from a test suite execution is estimated by means of *adequacy criteria*. Those criteria define metrics not only to measure the suitability of a test suite, but also to guide the test case selection process, e.g., by constituting test end criteria for test case generation algorithms. For instance, *structural coverage criteria* constitute the most widespread notion for measuring test suite adequacy. Those criteria require test cases of a test suite to sufficiently traverse structural elements, i.e., *test goals*, either located in a (test) model representation, or in the code under test. Therefore, either an explicit coverage of control flow constructs like statements, decision structures, loops, and entire paths, or implicit coverage of data flows, e.g., by means of *def-use* coverage is enforced. Closely related to structural coverage criteria are data coverage criteria requiring appropriate coverage of the input data space, e.g., one-value, boundaries, equivalence classes, random-value, and all-values. Furthermore, combinatorial coverage criteria over input value domains are frequently used, e.g., pairwise, T-wise for a constant T and N-wise coverage for a variable N. Further adequacy and test selection criteria are based, e.g., on fault-models capturing well-known typical implementation faults, on mappings of test cases to requirements and scenarios, on explicit test case specification languages, and statistical methods for random generation of test data.

For further details on principles and practices of (software testing), we refer to interested reader, amongst others, to the classical text books on software testing of Myers [41] and Beizer [6], to the Dagstuhl Tutorial on formal foundations of model-based testing by Broy et al. [9] and recent standardizations from industries [17,18,56]. Here, we limit our considerations to dynamic testing of functional characteristics at component-level based on model-based black-box knowledge in the following. This testing discipline is usually referred to as *model-based input/output conformance testing*.

3 Model-Based Testing

In this section, we provide an introduction into the fundamental concepts of model-based testing and review a formal approach to model-based input/output conformance testing initially introduced by Tretmans [54].

3.1 Fundamentals and Concepts

In model-based testing, a *test model* serves as a specification of the implementation under test (cf. Fig. 1). Depending on the model-based testing practices applied, test models may provide a comprehensive basis for any activity during the testing processes including test case derivation, test coverage measurement, test case execution, test result evaluation, and test reporting [55]. In combination with appropriate test interfaces and tool support, model-based software testing campaigns are executable in a more or less fully automated way once a (validated) test model specification, as well as a well-defined testing interface are available.

Definition 2 (Model-Based Testing [55]). *Model-based testing is the automation of black box tests.*

The implementation under test to constitutes a *black box* solely offering predefined input/output interfaces for the tester to interact with the system during testing. Beyond that, nothing is known about the internal implementation details and the computational states, data structures, hardware usage etc., during (test) executions.

In model-based testing, the test model constitutes an explicit, but usually highly abstracted representation of all behavioral aspects being relevant for the system implementation to behave correctly. Therefore, formalisms used for test modeling should offer natural notions and artifacts apparent in the testing method, e.g., a concept for test case specifications that makes distinctions between input and output behaviors and that allows the identification of test goals covered by test executions. Concerning functional testing, we are, in particular, interested in capturing the dynamics of a system, i.e., in test models that define the *behavior* of a system under test. Therefore, a test model should provide a finite representation of the potentially infinite execution domain of a software system under test, e.g., by means of high-level modeling languages such as state machines and other behavioral models as, e.g., defined by the UML [55]. Thereupon, the modeling language under consideration must incorporate a rigorous, accurate formalization together with a precise operational semantics that allows for a clear definition of *behavioral conformance* of experimental executions of an SUT with respect to the expected behavior.

Testing in general constitutes a semi-formal, pragmatic approach for software verification/validation. The representative executions performed on the SUT may be designed ad hoc. In contrast, model-based conformance testing relies on formal specifications by means of formalized test models. Hence, the purpose of behavioral conformance testing is to compare the intended and the actually implemented behaviors and to decide whether they differ only up to some degree of confidence [55]. Recent literature on the formal foundations of conformance testing provides corresponding conceptual frameworks to denote testing principles by means of notions known from formal operational semantics and behavioral equivalences [54]. In general, verifying the correctness of a (software) system implementation i with respect to a formal behavioral specification s requires to verify an *implementation relation*

$$i \simeq s$$

to hold between both, where $\simeq$ denotes the particular equivalence relation under consideration for behavioral conformance [16]. Intuitively, this notation denotes the implementation i to be correct if it shows the same set of behaviors as permitted by the specification s. The formal semantics $[\![\cdot]\!]$ for characterizing those *sets of behaviors* depends on the representation and comparability of the specification s and the implementation i as well as the relation $\simeq$ under consideration. In many cases, it is sufficient, or even only possible, to establish a *preorder* relation

$$i \sqsubseteq s$$

to hold between an implementation and a specification, i.e., requiring the set of behaviors of the implementation to be included in the set of specified behaviors. In that sense, implementation i is *correct* if it shows *at most* the sets of (visible) behaviors as specified in s. When applying model-based testing as a verification technique, the specification s is given as a test model, e.g., represented as a state machine model. Correspondingly, a *conformance relation*

$$i \textbf{ conforms } s \ :\Leftrightarrow\ [\![i]\!] \subseteq [\![s]\!]$$

is established between the implementation and test model specification in the context of model-based testing.

Considering model-based testing, i constitutes a black box, i.e., the internal structure of the implementation under test is unknown to the tester. Thus, the verification of the behavioral conformance requires to relate a black box, i.e., a monolithic object solely offering an I/O interface that hides any internal details of the system under test, with a formal test model represented by abstract modeling entities, e.g., in terms of algebraic objects. In addition, even if an exhaustive testing campaign has been successfully executed on the implementation under test, no guaranteed statements about the correctness of the implementation can be stated as test result confidence and reproducibility depends on the internal properties of the implementation, e.g., whether non-deterministic behaviors are potentially apparent. To overcome this mismatch, Bernot was the first to propose i to represent an (imaginary) *implementation model* i to be assumed for establishing a conformance relation **conforms** between a test model and a black box SUT [7]. This way, both the implementation i and the specification s share the same semantic domain defined by $[\![i]\!]$ and $[\![s]\!]$, respectively. Based on Bernot's abstract framework, this idea was later adopted, amongst others, by Tretmans for formalizing model-based testing frameworks with concrete test modeling formalisms under consideration [54].

The definition of behavioral conformance by means of (implicit) behavioral inclusion relation **conforms** between SUT i and specification s constitutes an *intentional* characterization of model-based testing. In contrast, *extensional* descriptions make use of the class $\mathcal{U}$ of all possible external observers (tester) explicitly comparing particular observable behaviors of i with those of s, i.e.,

$$i \text{ \bf conforms } s \;:\Leftrightarrow\; \forall u \in \mathcal{U} : obs(u, i) \approx obs(u, s).$$

We now give instantiations of both kinds of characterizations of behavioral conformance in terms of the **ioco** relation and a respective test case derivation algorithm as proposed by Tretmans [54].

3.2   A Formal Approach to Model-Based Testing

Formal approaches to I/O conformance testing abstract from the concrete syntax of (high-level) test modeling languages. Instead, labeled transition systems (LTS) are used constituting a well-established semantic model for discrete, event-driven reactive control systems. To serve as test model specification for I/O conformance testing, the special sub class of *input/output labeled transition systems* is considered in the following [9]. A labeled transition system specifies system behaviors by means of a transition relation $\rightarrow\, \subseteq Q \times act \times Q$ defined over a set Q of states and a label alphabet act of actions. In case of I/O labeled transition systems, the set $act = I \cup U \cup \{\tau\}$ of actions is subdivided into disjoint subsets of controllable input actions I, observable output actions U and internal actions summarized under the special symbol $\tau \notin (I \cup U)$.

Definition 3 (I/O Labeled Transition System). *An* I/O *labeled transition system is a tuple* $(Q, q_0, I, U, \longrightarrow)$*, where* Q *is a countable set of states,* $q_0 \in Q$ *is the initial state,* I *and* U *are disjoint sets of* input actions *and* output actions*, respectively, and* $\longrightarrow\, \subseteq Q \times act \times Q$ *is a labeled transition relation.*

By $\mathcal{LTS}(act)$ we denote the set of LTS defined over label alphabet act. Each *computation* of a system specified by an LTS refers to some *path*

$$q_0 \xrightarrow{\mu_1} s_1 \xrightarrow{\mu_2} s_2 \xrightarrow{\mu_3} \cdots \xrightarrow{\mu_{n-1}} s_{n-1} \xrightarrow{\mu_n} s_n$$

of the state-transition graph starting from the initial state q_0. Please note that we often identify an LTS s with its initial state q_0 in the following. The *behavior* of a computation is defined by the *trace* $\sigma = \mu_1\mu_2\cdots\mu_n \in act^*$, i.e., the respective sequence of actions occurring as transition labels in the computation. The following notations for LTS trace semantics are frequently used in the literature [54].

Definition 4 (LTS Trace Semantics). *Let s be an I/O LTS, $\mu_i \in I \cup U \cup \{\tau\}$ and $a_i \in I \cup U$.*

$$s \xrightarrow{\mu_1 \cdots \mu_n} s' := \exists s_0, \ldots, s_n : s = s_0 \xrightarrow{\mu_1} s_1 \xrightarrow{\mu_2} \cdots \xrightarrow{\mu_n} s_n = s'$$

$$s \xrightarrow{\mu_1 \cdots \mu_n} := \exists s' : s \xrightarrow{\mu_1 \cdots \mu_n} s'$$

$$\neg s \xrightarrow{\mu_1 \cdots \mu_n} := \nexists s' : s \xrightarrow{\mu_1 \cdots \mu_n} s'$$

$$s \xRightarrow{\epsilon} s' := s = s' \ or \ s \xrightarrow{\tau \cdots \tau} s'$$

$$s \xRightarrow{a} s' := \exists s_1, s_2 : s \xRightarrow{\epsilon} s_1 \xrightarrow{a} s_2 \xRightarrow{\epsilon} s'$$

$$s \xRightarrow{a_1 \cdots a_n} s' := \exists s_0, \ldots, s_n : s = s_0 \xRightarrow{a_1} s_1 \xRightarrow{a_2} \cdots \xRightarrow{a_n} s_n = s'$$

$$s \xRightarrow{\sigma} := \exists s' : s \xRightarrow{\sigma} s'$$

$$\neg s \xRightarrow{\sigma} := \nexists s' : s \xRightarrow{\sigma} s'$$

The set of traces of an LTS s is defined as

$$Tr(s) := \{\sigma \in (I \cup U)^* \mid \exists s' \in Q : q_0 \xRightarrow{\sigma} s'\}.$$

To illustrate the notions and concepts of I/O conformance testing based on LTS, we consider as our running example a simple *vending machine*.

Example 1. The graphical representation of an LTS is illustrated in Fig. 2 denoting different behavioral specifications of a vending machine for beverages, where $I = \{1\text{€}, 2\text{€}\}$ and $U = \{coffee, tea\}$. By convention, transition labels referring to input actions are prefixed by " ? " and outputs actions by " ! ". Each vending machine accepts different types of coins as inputs and (optionally) returns a cup of coffee and/or tea. The trace semantics of the different specifications are given as

- $Tr(q_1) = \{?1\text{€}, ?1\text{€·!}coffee, ?1\text{€·!}tea\}$,
- $Tr(q_2) = \{?1\text{€}, ?2\text{€}, ?1\text{€·!}coffee, ?1\text{€·!}tea, ?2\text{€·!}coffee, ?2\text{€·!}tea\}$,
- $Tr(q_3) = \{?1\text{€}, ?2\text{€}, ?1\text{€·!}coffee, ?2\text{€·!}coffee\}$,
- $Tr(q_4) = \{?1\text{€}, ?2\text{€}, ?1\text{€·!}coffee, ?2\text{€·!}tea\}$,
- $Tr(q_5) = \{?1\text{€}, ?2\text{€}\}$,
- $Tr(q_6) = \{?1\text{€}, ?1\text{€·!}coffee\}$,
- $Tr(q_7) = \{?1\text{€}, ?1\text{€·!}coffee\}$,
- $Tr(q_8) = \{\}$,

where · denotes concatenation as usual.

According to the test assumption formulated by Bernot [7], we require both a test model specification s as well as an implementation i, i.e., the SUT, to be represented by LTS models, i.e., $s, i \in \mathcal{LTS}(act)$. We further restrict our considerations to LTS being image finite and with finite τ-sequences [54].

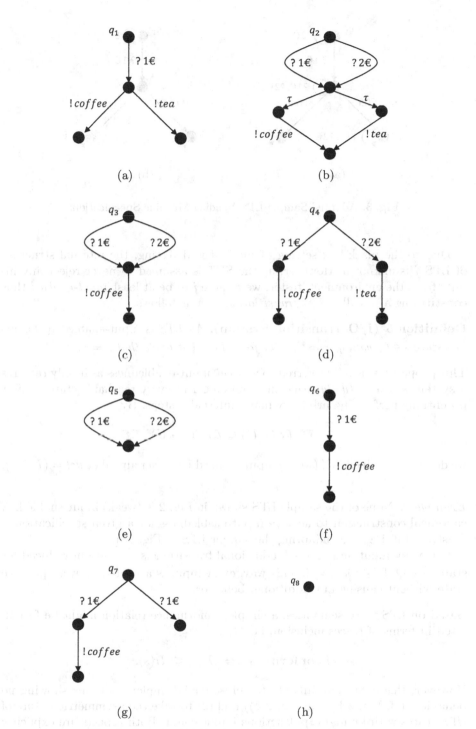

Fig. 2. Sample LTS Vending Machine Specifications

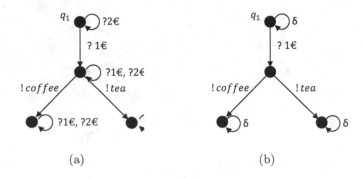

Fig. 3. Adapted Sample LTS Vending Machine Specifications

Due to the black-box setting of model-based testing, the internal structure of LTS i is unknown. However, as the SUT is assumed to never reject any inputs from the environment/tester, we require i to be at least *input-enabled* thus constituting a so-called *I/O transition system* as follows.

Definition 5 (I/O Transition System). *An LTS is* input-enabled *iff for every state* $s \in Q$ *with* $q_0 \Longrightarrow^* s$ *and for all* $a \in I$ *it holds that* $s \xrightarrow{a}$.

This property is usually referred to as *weak* input-enabledness as it only requires a system s to *eventually* react on inputs $a \in I$ in every reachable state s' after potentially performing arbitrary many internal τ-steps. By

$$\mathcal{IOTS}(I, U) \subseteq \mathcal{LTS}(I \cup U)$$

we denote the sub class if (weak) input-enabled LTS over alphabet $act = (I \cup U)$.

Example 2. None of the sample LTS shown in Fig. 2 is (weak) input enabled. A canonical construction to achieve input-enabledness for a given specification is illustrated in Fig. 3(a) adapting the sample LTS in Fig. 2(a).

For every input action $a \in I$, additional transitions $s \xrightarrow{a} s$ are introduced for states $s \in Q$ if $\nexists s' : s \xrightarrow{a} s'$. This way, every input is accepted in every possible state without causing any additional behavior.

Based on LTS trace semantics, a simple conformance relation might be formulated in terms of traces inclusion, i.e.,

$$i \textbf{ conforms } s :\Leftrightarrow Tr(i) \subseteq Tr(s).$$

However, this definition fails (1) to refuse trivial implementations showing no behaviors (cf. Fig. 2(h) and Fig. 2(e)) and (2) to take the asymmetric nature of LTS traces with input/output actions into account. Both aspects are explicitly addressed by the concept of observational *input/output conformance* (ioco).

The intentional characterization of observational conformance is based on the notion of *suspension traces* [54]. For an implementation i to conform to a specification s, the observable output behaviors of i after any possible sequence of inputs must be permitted by s. For this to hold, the set $out(P)$ of output actions enabled in any possible state $p' \in P$ of i reachable via a sequence σ, denoted $P = p$ **after** σ, must be included in the corresponding set of s. To further rule out trivial implementations i never showing any outputs, the concept of *quiescence* by means of a special output action δ is introduced to explicitly permit the absence (suspension) of any outputs after an input.

Definition 6. *Let s be an LTS, $p \in Q$, $P \subseteq Q$ and $\sigma \in (I \cup U)^*$.*

- $init(p) := \{\mu \in (I \cup U) \mid p \xrightarrow{\mu}\}$,
- p is quiescent, *denoted* $\delta(p)$, *iff* $init(p) \subseteq I$,
- p **after** $\sigma := \{q \in Q \mid p \xRightarrow{\sigma} q\}$,
- $out(P) := \{\mu \in U \mid \exists p \in P : p \xrightarrow{\mu}\} \cup \{\delta \mid \exists p \in P : \delta(p)\}$,
- $Straces(p) := \{\sigma' \in (I_S \cup U_S \cup \{\delta\})^* \mid p \xRightarrow{\sigma'}\}$ *where* $q \xrightarrow{\delta} q$ *iff* $\delta(p)$.

If not stated otherwise, we assume a given LTS to be implicitly enriched by transitions $q \xrightarrow{\delta} q$ for all quiescent states q with $\delta(p)$. Action δ may be interpreted as observational quiescence, i.e., if δ is observed, then the system awaits some input to proceed. We write $act_\delta = (act \setminus \{\tau\}) \cup \{\delta\}$ as a short hand for the set of visible actions including quiescence.

Example 3. By adding δ-transitions to quiescent states in the sample LTS specifications in Fig. 2, we are able to define the specified behaviors in terms of their suspension traces. For instance, in Fig. 3(b) the resulting LTS for q_1 is shown, where we have

$$Straces(q_1) = \{\delta, ?1\text{€}, \delta \cdot ?1\text{€}, ?1\text{€} \cdot !coffee, ?1\text{€} \cdot !coffee \cdot \delta, \ldots\}.$$

This way, we are now able to further discriminate the behaviors of the different specifications, e.g., $?1\text{€} \cdot \delta \notin Straces(q_6)$, whereas $?1\text{€} \cdot \delta \in Straces(q_7)$

As described in Sect. 3.1, A behavioral conformance relation **conforms** to hold between implementation i and specification s requires the inclusion of all observable behaviors of i in those of s. When applying a conformance relation **conforms** the input/output conformance relation **ior** by means of suspension trace inclusion, we obtain the following definition.

Definition 7 (I/O Conformance). *Let $s \in \mathcal{LTS}(I \cup U)$ and $i \in \mathcal{IOTS}(I, U)$.*

$$i \text{ ior } s :\Leftrightarrow \forall \sigma \in act_\delta^* : out(i \text{ after } \sigma) \subseteq out(s \text{ after } \sigma).$$

Thus, input/output conformance i **ior** s ensures for every state reachable in i via a trace σ to (1) show *at most* those outputs as permitted by respective states in s reachable via σ and (2) to be *quiescent* iff a quiescent state is reachable in s via σ. Note that in case of deterministic behaviors, p **after** σ contains at most one element for all traces σ.

As a direct consequence of the definition of I/O conformance, we obtain a preorder correspondence between i and s as follows.

Lemma 1. *Let $s \in \mathcal{LTS}(I \cup U)$ and $i \in \mathcal{IOTS}(I, U)$. Then it holds that*

$$i \; \textbf{ior} \; s \; \Leftrightarrow \; Straces(i) \subseteq Straces(s).$$

Hence, input/output conformance requires that the reaction of i to every possible environmental behavior σ is checked against those of s independent of the fact whether a proper reaction to σ is actually specified in s. In practice, conformance testing is usually limited to *positive* cases. I.e., only for those behaviors which are explicitly specified in s, the corresponding reaction of i has to be checked for behavioral input/output conformance (ioco).

Definition 8 (IOCO [54]). *Let $s \in \mathcal{LTS}(I \cup U)$ and $i \in \mathcal{IOTS}(I, U)$.*

$$i \; \textbf{ioco} \; s \; :\Leftrightarrow \; \forall \sigma \in Straces(s) : out(i \; \textbf{after} \; \sigma) \subseteq out(s \; \textbf{after} \; \sigma).$$

Again, from i **ioco** s it follows that i shows at most the behaviors that are specified in s. But, in contrast to **ior**, i may show arbitrary reactions for those behaviors not specified in s. As a consequence, Lemma 1 does not hold for **ioco** and we obtain the following correspondence.

Lemma 2. ior $\subset$ ioco.

Example 4. Again, consider the sample LTS specifications in Fig. 2 assuming δ-transitions to be added to quiescent states. Investigating the observable behavior for the possible environmental stimuli $\sigma = ?1\text{\euro}$ and $\sigma' = ?2\text{\euro}$, this leads to

- $out(q_1 \; \textbf{after} \; \sigma) = \{coffee, tea\}$, $out(q_1 \; \textbf{after} \; \sigma') = \{\}$
- $out(q_2 \; \textbf{after} \; \sigma) = \{coffee, tea\}$, $out(q_2 \; \textbf{after} \; \sigma') = \{coffee, tea\}$,
- $out(q_3 \; \textbf{after} \; \sigma) = \{coffee\}$, $out(q_3 \; \textbf{after} \; \sigma') = \{coffee\}$,
- $out(q_4 \; \textbf{after} \; \sigma) = \{coffee\}$, $out(q_4 \; \textbf{after} \; \sigma') = \{tea\}$
- $out(q_5 \; \textbf{after} \; \sigma) = \{\delta\}$, $out(q_5 \; \textbf{after} \; \sigma') = \{\delta\}$
- $out(q_6 \; \textbf{after} \; \sigma) = \{coffee\}$, $out(q_6 \; \textbf{after} \; \sigma') = \{\}$
- $out(q_7 \; \textbf{after} \; \sigma) = \{coffee, \delta\}$, $out(q_7 \; \textbf{after} \; \sigma') = \{\}$
- $out(q_8 \; \textbf{after} \; \sigma) = \{\}$, $out(q_8 \; \textbf{after} \; \sigma') = \{\}$.

For instance, assume that q_6 is adapted to be weak input-enabled, then it holds that q_6 **ioco** q_7, but not vice versa due to the additional quiescent state of q_7. Similarly, we have q_2 **ioco** q_1 as no behavior for $!2\text{\euro}$ in q_2 is specified in q_1, thus, leaving open implementation freedom in q_2. In contrast, q_1 **ioco** q_2 does not hold as q_1 shows quiescent behavior for $!2\text{\euro}$ which is not permitted by q_2.

Although the set of suspension traces which has to be verified on i for establishing **ioco** to some s is now limited to $Straces(s)$, this set is, however, still potentially infinite making input/output conformance verification impracticable. The set of suspension traces under consideration is further restricted to (finite) sub sets $\mathcal{F} \subseteq act_\delta^*$ and the resulting restricted **ioco**-relation is denoted as

$$i \; \textbf{ioco}_{\mathcal{F}} \; s \; :\Leftrightarrow \; \forall \sigma \in \mathcal{F} : out(i \; \textbf{after} \; \sigma) \subseteq out(s \; \textbf{after} \; \sigma),$$

where **ior** = **ioco**$_{act_\delta^*}$ and **ioco** = **ioco**$_{Straces(s)}$ holds.

The notions considered so far constitute *intentional* characterizations of behavioral input/output conformance. In addition, an *extensional* characterization of **ioco** is given by means of test cases t, i.e., observer processes derivable from a specification s and applicable to SUT i such that

$$i \text{ passes } t :\Leftrightarrow obs(i, t) \approx obs(s, t).$$

In order to define the interaction of a test case t with SUT i during test case execution in a formal way, test cases are also represented as I/O labeled transition systems. In particular, considering a specification $s \in \mathcal{LTS}(I, U)$ and a corresponding SUT $i \in \mathcal{IOTS}(I, U)$, the domain $\mathcal{TEST} \subseteq \mathcal{LTS}(U, I)$ contains those *test cases* derived from s and applied to i for verifying input/output conformance of i with respect to s. Due to the asymmetric nature of communication between I/O-labeled LTS, the input and output alphabets are reversed in $t \in \mathcal{TEST}$ compared to those of s and i. In addition, the special input action $\Theta \notin U \cup I$ represents the counterpart of δ, i.e., when observed during test case execution, Θ denotes the occurrence of a quiescent state in i.

Definition 9 (Test Case). *A test case t is an LTS such that*

- *t is deterministic and has a finite set of traces,*
- *Q contains terminal states **pass** and **fail** with $init(\textbf{pass}) = init(\textbf{fail}) = \varnothing$ and*
- *for each non-terminal state $q \in Q$ either (1) $init(q) = \{a\}$ for $a \in I$ or (2) $init(q) = U \cup \{\Theta\}$*

holds.

Thus, each test case corresponds to a suspension trace of s such that in every test step, i.e., a transition in t, either (1) one particular input is stimulated in i, or (2) every possible output potentially emitted by i is accepted (including quiescence). If an unexpected output is observed, termination state **fail** is immediately entered and, otherwise, termination state **pass** is eventually reached after a finite sequence of (alternating) test steps. An algorithm for deriving test cases t from specifications s after a transformation into a respective *suspension automaton* can be found in [54].

Example 5. Consider the test case in Fig. 4(a) derived from specification q_1 in Fig. 2(a). For an implementation i to pass this test case, it has to accept the input !1€ and then either to return a *coffee*, or a *tea* as output, whereas no output, i.e., quiescence Θ, is an erroneous behavior. In contrast, the test case in Fig. 4(b) is derived from q_7 in Fig. 8(c) permitting *coffee* as well as *nothing* as outputs after inserting 1€ as input. Thus, this test case is, e.g., capable to distinguish implementations complying q_7 from those complying q_6 for which no quiescence is allowed after inserting 1€.

A test suite $T \subseteq \mathcal{TEST}$ is a finite set of test cases. The following properties have been proven to hold for input/output conformance testing based test suites T designed on the basis of suspension traces [54].

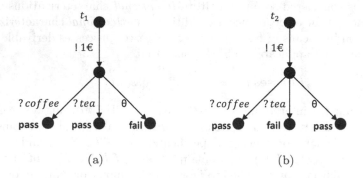

(a)   (b)

Fig. 4. Sample Test Cases for the Vending Machine

Theorem 1. *Let $s \in \mathcal{LTS}(I \cup U)$, $i \in \mathcal{IOTS}(I \cup U)$ and $\mathcal{F} \subseteq Straces(s)$. Then it holds that*

1. *any derivable test case $t \in \mathcal{TEST}$ is sound, i.e., i **ioco** o implies that i passes t and*
2. *the set $\mathcal{TEST}$ of all derivable test cases is exhaustive, i.e., i **ioco** o if i passes all $t \in \mathcal{TEST}$.*

Based on this fundamental concept of formal input/output conformance, various enhanced results, e.g., concerning compositionality properties of **ioco** [8], as well as extensions to **ioco** concerning advanced system characteristics, e.g., real time [52] and hybrid behaviors [43] have been proposed.

4   Model-Based Testing of Software Product Lines

Until now, we assumed an SUT to constitute a monolithic software system with predefined and fixed amount of functionality. However, modern software systems usually expose various kinds of *diversity*, e.g., due to extensible configurability [50]. The corresponding software implementations comprise *families* of similar, yet well-distinguished software product *variants*. Software product line engineering [12] is a well-established paradigm for concisely engineering those kinds of variant-rich software implementations including strategies for efficiently testing families of similar product variants under test.

4.1   Software Product Line Engineering and Testing

A software product line constitutes a configurable software system built upon a common core platform [12]. Product implementation variants are derivable from those generic implementations in an automated way by selecting a set of domain *features*, i.e., user-visible product characteristics, to be assembled into a customized product variant. Software product line engineering defines a comprehensive process for building and maintaining a product line. During domain engineering, a product line is designed by (1) identifying the set of relevant domain features within the problem space and (2) by developing corresponding engineering artifacts within the solution space associated with a feature (combination) for assembling implementation variants for feature selections. During domain engineering, logical dependencies between features further refine the *valid configuration space* by restricting combinations of features. For instance, domain feature models provide an intuitive, visual modeling language for specifying the configuration space of a product line [27] (cf. Sect. 4.2).

Features not only correspond to configuration parameters within the problem space of a product line, but also refer (to assemblies of) engineering artifacts within the solution space at any level of abstraction. For instance, concerning the behavioral specification of variable software systems at component level, modeling approaches such as state machines are equipped with feature parameters denoting well-defined variation points within a generic product line specification including any possible model variant [11]. This way, explicit specifications of common and variable parts among product variants within the solution space allow for a systematic reuse of engineering artifacts among the members of a product family.

Also testing is considered an integral part of software product line engineering. *Reusable test artifacts*, e.g., variable test models and test cases designed during domain engineering are applied to those SUT assembled for the respective *product variants under test* during application engineering. McGregor was one of the first to provide a systematic overview of how to adopt recent testing notions and activities to product line engineering [37]. He identified different *scopes* under consideration in SPL testing, namely the entire SPL, a particular product, as well as individual assets, i.e., feature components and their integration. In order to facilitate large-scale reuse of test artifacts among product variants when testing an SPL, common test artifacts can be organized as SPL artifacts as well. In [38], McGregor et al. further elaborate reuse potentials in SPL testing by proposing SPL testing approaches explicitly taking variability among *products under test* into account. A first survey on product family testing approaches is given by Tevanlinna et al. [53]. The authors focus on the adoption of regression testing principles for variability-aware testing collections of similar products. The application of model-based testing principles to SPL testing was first mentioned in [42] as well as in [49]. In [46], Oster et al. provide a survey on SPL testing approaches focusing on model-based testing. Further comprehensive surveys on recent SPL testing approaches can be found in [20] and in the mapping study provided in [40].

The general setting for the (model-based) testing of a product line is illustrated in Fig. 5 extending the previous setting for single system testing in Fig.1. Testing a product line implementation with n possible product variants against a product line specification essentially requires to verify that

$$i_k \text{ conforms } s_k, 1 \leqslant k \leqslant n,$$

holds, i.e., to test every individual product implementation variant i_k against its corresponding specification variant s_k. As the number n of product variants

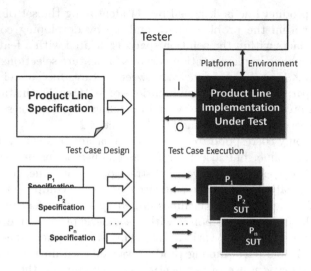

Fig. 5. General Setting of Product Line Testing

grows exponentially with the number of features, this product-by-product approach is, in general, infeasible. In addition, due to the high degree of similarity and corresponding (specification and implementation) artifact reuse potentials among the different variants, repetitive exhaustive test modeling, test suite derivation and test execution for every particular variant causes lots of redundant efforts. To cope with those challenges, different product line testing strategies have been proposed in the literature and are explained in the following.

Reusable Product Line Test Model. In contrast to (re-)modeling every product variant test model specification anew from scratch, a *reusable* product line test model is built that (virtually) comprises every possible model variant. Those model elements that are common to all members of the product line become part of every test model variant, whereas variable elements are only mapped into those model variants for which they are relevant. One of the most common approaches for reusable product line test modeling are so-called 150% specifications, where all common and variable elements are part of one model whose set of elements constitutes a superset of the test model variants. The projection of a particular test model variant from a 150% model is done, e.g., by adding explicit annotations to the variable elements by means of selection conditions over feature parameters [14], or by defining implicit behavioral restrictions by means of modal specifications combined with deontic logics [4,3,2]. Hence, a product line test model comprises two parts, i.e., (1) a configuration model, e.g., given by a domain feature model (cf. Sect. 4.2) defining the valid product space of the product line under test and (2) a 150% test model, e.g., by means of a modal I/O labeled transition system (cf. Sect.4.3). Based on a 150% test model, a product line may be tested product-by-product without re-modeling every variant anew.

However, to also reduce the efforts for test suite derivations and executions, further strategies have been proposed.

Sample-based Product Line Testing. In this strategy, only a *representative subset* of variants is considered for which product-specific test suites are generated, whereas those variants that are unselected remain untested. Various coverage criteria and subset selection heuristics have been proposed, e.g., inspired by combinatorial testing [33,25,44,13,47,23,29,24].

Regression-based Product Line Testing. In this strategy, only those test cases are generated anew for a variant under test that are not reusable from a previously tested variant. The required test case reuse analysis is similar to change impact analysis techniques known from regression testing [53,19,34]. Again, every single variant has to be considered to guarantee a complete product line test coverage.

Family-based Product Line Testing. In this strategy, a test suite is derived from a 150% test model rather than from the test model variants. This way, each test case is connected to the subset of product variants for which it is valid. A complete test coverage of a product line is achievable without considering any particular product variant [11].

In this tutorial, we will focus on two approaches for model-based product line testing. In Sect. 4.2, we present a technique for sample-based product line testing using a domain feature model for selecting a representative product subset under test, and in Sect. 4.3, a family-based approach for variability-aware product line test modeling and test suite design is presented based on modal input/output LTS specifications.

4.2   Sample-Based Software Product Line Testing

The *domain model* (sometimes referred to as variability model) plays a pivotal role in software product line engineering plays, because it contains information about the product features and its dependencies. A common representation for the domain model are feature models (FM), which are usually created during a (feature-oriented) domain analysis [15,27]. In Fig. 6, we show an exemplary feature model of a vending machine where features refer to different drinks or payment methods. A *feature model* is a hierarchical structure, where features can be selected in a top-down manner. Different constraints can be modeled for the contained features: First, each feature can be optional (denoted by the white bullet, e.g. **Tea**) or mandatory (denoted by the black bullet, e.g. **Coffee**). Second, features may be used for grouping (e.g. feature **Beverage**) and contain no functionality themselves. Additionally, we can specify group constraints on sibling features, like *alternative* and *or* groups. Alternative-features are mutually exclusive and cannot be selected for the same variant, whereas or-features have no upper bound. Finally, we can express dependencies between features using *cross-tree constraints*, which are expressed by propositional formulas.

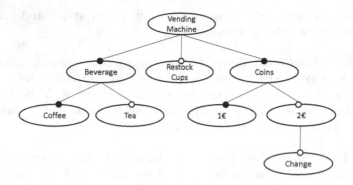

Fig. 6. Domain Feature Model of Vending Machine SPL

In most cases, features are developed and tested separately by several teams. But even if we assume that they work without errors for themselves, it is not assured that they still work error-free after an integration of several features into a larger system. Such erroneous and unexpected behavior is referred to as *feature interaction (FI)*. One of the most promising techniques to detect feature interactions is *sample-based combinatorial interaction testing (CIT)*, because is uses the domain feature model to derive a small number of variants which have to be tested. This set of product variants is supposed to cover relevant combinations of features. The sample-based product line testing technique is subdivided into three steps:

1. Create the feature model
2. Generate a subset of variants based on the FM, covering relevant combinations of features
3. Apply single system testing to the selected variants

One method for CIT is *pairwise testing*, which tries to cover all combinations of two features by the selected set of variants and is able find FIs between two features. To this end, both features must be present, not present and only one must be present in at least one tested variant to fulfill the pairwise testing criterion. It is possible to cover combinations of one, three, four, five and six features as well, but there exists a trade-off between computation time and test coverage. The higher t (where t is the number of features), the higher is the test coverage, but also the computation time to find a corresponding set of product variants [30] and the resulting number of product variants to be tested. Pairwise testing detects about 70% of all errors in a system (3-wise 95% error detection).

The selected set of products to be tested is also called *covering array*. Generating covering arrays is equivalent to the set covering problem which is a NP-complete decision problem in combinatorics. We explain the problem in the following by means of a small example. Given a set S with $S = \{a, b, c, d, e\}$. S is divided into several subsets $M = \{\{a, b, c\}, \{b, d\}, \{c, d\}, \{d, e\}\}$, which represent valid product configurations. The challenge of the set covering problem is to find the minimal number of sets in M that cover the complete set of S. In our example, the solution is $L = \{\{a, b, c\}, \{d, e\}\}$.

However, this approach requires that all product variants are already known. Since, the number possible solutions in a FM grows exponentially with the number of features, it is almost impossible to compute all valid variants before [25]. Even finding a single valid variant in a large feature model is equal to the NP-complete Boolean Satisfiability Problem (SAT). Luckily, we are mostly dealing with realistic FMs. Actual customers should be able to configure the FM of the SPL in a decent amount of time. No company would introduce a FM, where a customer needs thousands of years to select a valid variant. Mendonca et al. [39] proved the efficient satisfiability of realistic FMs with additional cross-tree constraints.

Chvátal's Algorithm (1979). One of the first heuristic greedy algorithms to solve the set covering problem was developed in 1979 by Chvátal [10]. The algorithm does not calculate the optimal solution. It is also not yet specialized for product variant selection.

The algorithm is divided into four separate steps. The solution, i.e., the set cover, is stored in the set L which is empty at the beginning. The set M contains the set of possible subsets M_i. The algorithm selects the set M' with the highest number of uncovered elements. This set is added to the solution L and removed from all sets M_i. The algorithm terminates if there are no more elements to select.

1. Step: Set $L = \emptyset$
2. Step: **If** $M_i = \emptyset, \forall i, i \in \{1, 2, ..., n\}$ **Stop. Else** find M', where number of uncovered elements is maximised
3. Step: Add M' to L and replace each M_i by $M_i - M'$
4. Step: Jump to Step 2

The worst case is if M only consists of subsets with different elements so that the algorithm must add each subset to L and $L = M$ holds at the end.

Adaptation of Chvátal's Approach to FMs. Johansen et al. [25,26] have done an extensive amount of research in adapting and improving the original algorithm of Chvátal for product variant selection on the basis of FMs. In the following, we explain their algorithm shown as Algorithm 1.

Initially, the algorithm needs an FM as input. All possible t-tuple combinations of features are generated and written into the set S. This set includes invalid tuples as well. For, e.g. $t = 2$, all combinations of two features are present in S after the first step. After the creation of a new empty product configuration k (line 3), the algorithm iterates through all tuples in S and tries to add the tuple $p \in S$ to the configuration k. This is only possible, if the configuration stays valid with the selected tuple with respect to the feature model. The validity check is done by a standard SAT-Solver. As a result, the configuration grows, and the set S shrinks, since covered tuples are removed from S. A configuration k is added

```
input  : arbitrary FM
output: t-wise covering array
1   S ← all t-tuples
2   while S ≠ ∅ do
3   |   k ← new and empty configuration
4   |   counter ← 0
5   |   foreach tuple p in S do
6   |   |   if FM is satisfiable with k ∪ p then
7   |   |   |   k ← k ∪ p
8   |   |   |   S ← S\{p}
9   |   |   |   counter ← counter + 1
10  |   |   end
11  |   end
12  |   if counter > 0 then
13  |   |   L ← L ∪ (FM satisfy with {k})
14  |   end
15  |   if counter < # of features in FM then
16  |   |   foreach tuple p in S do
17  |   |   |   if FM not satisfiable with p then
18  |   |   |   |   S ← S\{p}
19  |   |   |   end
20  |   |   end
21  |   end
22  end
```

Algorithm 1. Adaptation of the algorithm for FMs

to the final solution L (line 13) in case that at least one tuple is contained. A configuration is extended with other features, e.g., mandatory features, in order to generate a valid product variant for the feature model based on the tuples in k (cf. "FM is satisfiable with k").

The variable *counter* in the last loop makes sure that all invalid t-tuples are removed from S at some point during computation. This point has been identified by empirical studies. It would be inefficient, e.g., to remove the invalid feature tuples at he beginning, because the SAT-Solver must check too many valid tuples [25].

The vending machine example (see Fig.6) has exactly 12 valid configurations. The covering array for $t = 2$ contains only six variants (see Table 1). Even in such small FMs, we are able to save 50% time for tests with the help of sample-based product line testing.

Improved algorithm ICPL. ICPL is one of the most advanced and efficient algorithms for computing a t-wise covering array. It is based on the above algorithm with several logical and technical improvements. The main goal is to find all valid tuples to be covered by the t-wise covering array as fast as possible since checking invalid tuples slow the whole process down. Single satisfiability checks

Table 1. Covering array for the vending machine

Feature\Product	0	1	2	3	4	5
Coffee	X	X	X	X	X	X
Beverage	X	X	X	X	X	X
2€		X	X	X	X	
Change		X			X	
Tea		X	X			X
Restock Cups		X		X		X
1€	X	X	X	X	X	X
Coins	X	X	X	X	X	X
Vending Machine	X	X	X	X	X	X

for each tuple are not efficient to identify invalid tuples. ICPL takes advantage of the property that a covering array of strength t is a subset of an array with strength $t + 1$, which is proved in [26]. The algorithm calculates all t-wise covering arrays $1 \leqslant n < t$, where $n, t \in \mathbb{N}$, at first. This step improves the overall tuple covering process and provides an earlier identification of invalid tuples (see [25] for more detailed information). In one iteration, one t-tuple is covered after the other. ICPL uses the knowledge that an already covered tuple cannot be added to the current configuration with another assignment of the features which means that t-tuples with other assignments for the contained features can be skipped instantly. The skipped tuples must not be deleted from the set, since they may be valid in another configuration. Likewise, if all features of the FM are already contained in the current configuration, it is not possible to add any other tuple. All remaining tuples can be skipped for this iteration.

The parallelization of the algorithm allows shortening the computation time significantly. With respect to the number of CPU cores, the original t-sets are split up and equally divided over the cores. It is done in several points in ICPL, e.g., for finding invalid t-tuples. The whole computation time of ICPL is almost inversely proportional with the number of cores due to high parallelism.

To provide an impression of the computation time of ICPL and the size of the computed covering array, Table 2 shows the results for four larges FMs in terms of the number of features and the number of constraints. The largest FM with nearly 7000 features is one version of the popular Linux kernel. Instead of testing millions or billions of variants, we only need to test the 480 product configurations, which are calculated by the ICPL algorithm for the Linux kernel. The computation time with roughly nine hours is quite fast.

Further Improvements to Feature Interaction Coverage. The main goal of sample-based software product line testing is to identify errors caused by feature interactions. The standard CIT methods, as decried above, use all t-tuple combinations for features to ensure a 100% coverage of the FM. It is possible to be more efficient at this point, since not all features interact with each other. Feature interactions usually occur via shared resources or communication. These

Table 2. ICPL Evaluation [25]

Feature Model	Features	Constraints	2-wise size	2-wise time (s)
2.6.28.6-icse11.dimacs	6,888	187,193	480	33,702
freebsd-icse11.dimacs	1,396	17,352	77	240
ecos-icse11.dimacs	1,244	2,768	63	185
Eshop-fm.xml	287	22	21	5

two interaction types are identified as the most crucial ones [35,21]. The information about such interactions is present in development documents, such as system specifications or architectural descriptions. Based on such specifications, we can annotate FMs with the respective information about shared resources and communication between features. Annotating the FM with this additional information provides us with the advantage of reducing the t-tuple input set for the CIT algorithm. We generate only the most important tuples, where interactions are most likely to occur with regard to the specification. Less tuples have to be covered, which results in a faster computation time and a smaller covering array [29].

4.3   Variability-Aware Software Product Line Testing

Interface theories provide formal approaches for the definition of the observable behaviors which a component implementation is allowed to show by abstracting from the concrete implementation details [48,5]. Modal interface specifications further distinguish between *optional* and *mandatory* behaviors by means of *may/must* modality in order to leave open implementation freedom up to a certain degree. In a *modal transition system* (MTS) each transition is either a *may*, or a *must* transition [32,48,5,36]. The set of valid implementations of a modal specification correspond to the set of modal *refinements* of that specification each comprising at least all must behaviors and at most all may behaviors. In addition, a *compatibility* notion defines criteria for valid compositions of components with respect to their modal specifications.

Various approaches for applying modal specifications as product line modeling formalism have been proposed [22,31,4]. By interpreting *must* behaviors as commonality and *may* behaviors as variability among the product line variants, each implementation corresponds to one particular product configuration. Hence, modal refinement corresponds to component implementation variant derivation within the solution space. Those sets of variants may be further restricted in terms of compatibility to other components and/or the environment/user [31]. Recent approaches focus on family-based product line model checking based on modal specifications [4,3,2]. In contrast, we consider MTS to denote variable test model specifications as a basis for an intentional characterization of model-based input/output conformance testing for a software product line implementations under test.

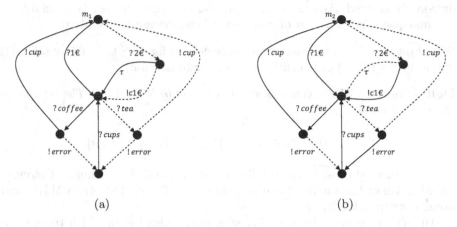

(a)   (b)

Fig. 7. Sample MTS Vending Machine Product Line Specifications

Formally, modal transition systems extend LTS by incorporating two transition relations to distinguish two different transition modalities, namely (possible) *may* and (mandatory) *must* transitions.

Definition 10 (Modal I/O Transition System). *A* model I/O transition system *is a tuple* $(Q, q_0, I, U, \longrightarrow_\diamond, \longrightarrow_\square)$, *where Q is a countable set of states,* $q_0 \in Q$ *is the* initial state, *I and U are disjoint sets of* input actions *and* output actions, *respectively,* $\longrightarrow_\diamond \subseteq Q \times act \times Q$ *is a may-transition relation, and* $\longrightarrow_\square \subseteq Q \times act \times Q$ *is a must-transition relation such that* $\longrightarrow_\square \subseteq \longrightarrow_\diamond$ *holds.*

Requiring $\longrightarrow_\square \subseteq \longrightarrow_\diamond$ ensures an MTS to be *syntactically consistent*, i.e., mandatory behaviors are always also allowed. By $\mathcal{MTS}(act)$ we denote the set of modal transition systems labeled over alphabet *act*. Again, we often use an MTS *m* and its initial state q_0 as synonyms in the subsequent definitions and examples.

Example 6. The graphical representation of an MTS is illustrated in Fig. 7 specifying two modal versions of a vending machine extending the simple vending machines from Sect. 3. We now have $I = \{1\text{€}, 2\text{€}, coffee, tea, cups\}$ and $U = \{c1\text{€}, cup, error\}$, respectively. Transitions with *may* modality are denoted by dashed arrows, whereas those with *must* modality are denoted by solid arrows. Hence, a vending machine implementing specification m_1 in Fig. 7(a) must accept 1€ coins as inputs and may optionally also accept 2€ coins. As each beverage costs 1€, the vending machine may further output 1€ change (output action *c1€*) if 2€ have been thrown in. The machine offers coffee per default but may also allow for choosing tea via inputs *coffee* and *tea*. A cup containing the selected beverage is dispensed as long as cups are available within the machine. Otherwise, an (optional) error output may be given and new cups may be inserted. The alternative specification m_2 alters m_1 in two ways: (1) providing change after inserting 2€ must be implemented whereas omitting *c1€* is optionally allowed via the τ-transition and (2) whenever tea is selectable and the machine is running out of cups, error handling must take place.

We adapt the notion of traces previously defined for LTS to MTS by taking the modality $\gamma \in \{\Box, \Diamond\}$ of transitions $s \xrightarrow{\mu}_\gamma s'$ into account.

Definition 11 (MTS Trace Semantics). *Let m be an MTS. The set of modal traces is defined as*

$$Tr_\gamma(m) := \{\sigma \in (I \cup U)^* \mid \exists s \in Q : q_0 \xRightarrow{\sigma}_\gamma s\}.$$

From syntactical consistency, it follows that $Tr_\Box(s) \subseteq Tr_\Diamond(s)$ holds. Thereupon, an adaption of the further trace notations for LTS (cf. Def. 4) to MTS can be done, correspondingly.

An MTS m constitutes a *partial* system specification in which those behaviors corresponding to *may*-traces are considered *optional* leaving open implementation freedom within well-defined bounds. Retrieving an implementation variant from a modal specification by selecting/neglecting optional behaviors corresponds to the concept of *modal refinement*. A modal specification m_1 is a *refinement* of a modal specification m_2 if (1) the mandatory behaviors of m_2 are preserved by m_1 and (2) the possible behaviors of m_1 are permitted by m_2.

Definition 12 (Modal Refinement). *Let s, t be two MTS with $act = act_s = act_t$. A relation $R \subseteq Q_s \times Q_t$ is a (weak) modal refinement iff whenever sRt and $a \in act \setminus \{\tau\}$ it holds that*

1. *if $t \xrightarrow{a}_\Box t'$ then $\exists s' : s \xrightarrow{\tau}{}^*_\Box \xrightarrow{a}_\Box s'$ and $(s', t') \in R$,*
2. *if $s \xrightarrow{a}_\Diamond s'$ then $\exists t' : t \xrightarrow{\tau}{}^*_\Diamond \xrightarrow{a}_\Diamond t'$ and $(s', t') \in R$, and*
3. *if $s \xrightarrow{\tau}_\Diamond s'$ then $\exists t' : t \xrightarrow{\tau}{}^*_\Diamond t'$ and $(s', t') \in R$.*

The largest (weak) modal refinement relation is denoted by $\leq_m$ and s is a (weak) model refinement of t iff there is weak modal refinement containing (s_0, t_0).

A modal refinement s is *complete* if $\longrightarrow_\Box = \longrightarrow_\Diamond$ holds. A complete refinement s of t is an *implementation* of t.

Example 7. Consider the complete refinements in Fig. 8 referring to the modal vending machine specifications in Fig. 7. Please note that we assume an (implicit) pruning of the state-transition removing those transitions becoming unreachable after a modal refinement. We observe the following (complete) refinements.

- $s_1 \leq_m m_1$ and $s_1 \leq_m m_2$
- $s_2 \leq_m m_1$ and $s_2 \not\leq_m m_2$
- $s_3 \not\leq_m m_1$ and $s_3 \leq_m m_2$
- $s_4 \leq_m m_1$ and $s_4 \not\leq_m m_2$
- $s_5 \leq_m m_1$ and $s_5 \leq_m m_2$
- $s_6 \not\leq_m m_1$ and $s_6 \not\leq_m m_2$

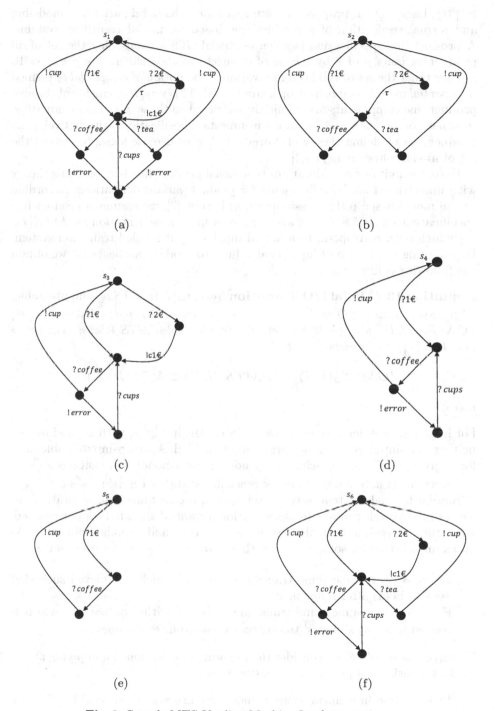

Fig. 8. Sample MTS Vending Machine Implementations

In [31], Larsen et al. proposed an approach for behavioral variability modeling and formal verification of a product line based on modal transition systems. A product line specification is given as modal LTS s comprising the set of all product variants p of s by means of complete modal refinements $p \leqslant_m s$. To further tailor the set of valid product variants, the notion of *compatibility* defined by a *partial* modal composition operator is used. This way, refinements of variable product line components are implicitly restricted to those which are compatible to other components and/or an environmental specification. Alternatively, the product line modeling theory of Asirelli et al. uses deontic logics to restrict the set of modal refinements [4,3,2].

Here, we limit our considerations to a modal product line test modeling theory with unrestricted modal refinements for product variant derivations. According to the model-based testing assumption of Bernot [7], we assume a product line specification $s \in \mathcal{MTS}(I \cup U)$ and a product line implementation $i \in \mathcal{MTS}(I \cup U)$ which both correspond to a modal input/output labeled transition system. By adopting the notion of input-enabledness to modal specifications, we obtain the following definition.

Definition 13 (Modal I/O Transition System). *An MTS is γ-input-enabled iff for every state $s \in Q$ with $q_0 \Longrightarrow^*_\gamma s$ and for all $a \in I$ it holds that $s \overset{a}{\Longrightarrow}_\gamma$. By $\mathcal{IOMTS}_\gamma(I, U)$ we denote the set of γ-input-enabled MTS labeled over act $= (I \cup U \cup \{\tau\})$ and conclude that*

$$\mathcal{IOMTS}_\square(I, U) \subset \mathcal{IOMTS}_\diamond(I, U) \subset \mathcal{MTS}(I \cup U)$$

holds.

For instance, considering the sample MTS models in Fig. 7, both m_1 and m_2 are neither *may*-input-enabled, nor *must*-input-enabled. Again, γ-input-enabledness for a given MTS may be achieved by adding corresponding transitions $s \overset{a}{\to}_\gamma s$ for every input action $a \in I$ to every reachable state s with $\nexists s' : s \overset{a}{\Longrightarrow}_\gamma s'$.

Similar to single system testing, we require a product line implementation i as well as all derivable product implementation variants $i' \leqslant_m i$ to be input-enabled. Unfortunately, γ-input-enabledness is not preserved under modal refinement. As an example, consider some state s with $q_0 \Longrightarrow^*_\gamma s$ and $s \overset{a}{\to}_\gamma$ for every $a \in I$.

- For $\gamma = \diamond$, assume some transition $s \overset{a}{\to}_\diamond s'$ which is removed such that $\neg s \overset{a}{\to}_\diamond$ holds after refinement.
- For $\gamma = \square$, assume some transition $s \overset{a}{\to}_\diamond s'$ with $\neg q_0 \Longrightarrow^*_\square s'$ which is refined to $s \overset{a}{\to}_\square s'$ and s' to obstruct *must*-input-enabledness.

To solve this problem, we consider the following assumptions for applying modal LTS as a basis for a product line testing theory.

- Product line implementations i under test are *may*-input-enabled, i.e., $i \in \mathcal{IOMTS}_\diamond(I, U)$, whereas for product line specification we only require $s \in \mathcal{MTS}(I \cup U)$ as usual.

– Derivations of product implementation variants i' are restricted to those preserving may-input-enabledness denoted $i' \leqslant_m^\Diamond i$ such that

$$\leqslant_m^\Diamond \subseteq \mathcal{IOMTS}_\Diamond(I, U) \times \mathcal{IOMTS}_\Diamond(I, U) \subset \leqslant_m .$$

As a result, it holds that $i' \in \mathcal{IOMTS}_\Box(I, U)$ for every complete refinement i' of i. Similar to the notions of traces and input-enabledness, also the auxiliary definitions for defining input/output conformance relations on LTS are adaptable to MTS as follows.

Definition 14. *Let s be an MTS, $p \in Q$, $P \subseteq Q$, $\sigma \in (I \cup U)^*$, and $\gamma \in \{\Box, \Diamond\}$.*

1. *$init_\gamma(p) := \{\mu \in (I \cup U) \mid p \xrightarrow{\mu}_\gamma\}$,*
2. *p is may-quiescent, denoted by $\delta_\Diamond(p)$, iff $init_\Box(p) \subseteq I$, p is must-quiescent, denoted by $\delta_\Box(p)$, iff $init_\Diamond(p) \subseteq I$,*
3. *p after$_\gamma$ $\sigma := \{q \in Q \mid p \xRightarrow{\sigma}_\gamma q\}$,*
4. *$Out_\gamma(P) := \{\mu \in U \mid \exists p \in P : p \xrightarrow{\mu}_\gamma\} \cup \{\delta_\gamma \mid \exists p \in P : \delta_\gamma(p)\}$, and*
5. *$Straces_\gamma(p) := \{\sigma' \in (I \cup U \cup \{\delta\})^* \mid p \xRightarrow{\sigma'}_\gamma\}$ where $q \xrightarrow{\delta}_\gamma q$ iff $\delta_\gamma(p)$.*

Again, if not stated otherwise, we assume a given MTS to be implicitly enriched by transitions $q \xrightarrow{\delta}_\gamma q$ for γ-quiescent states q.

Example 8. Considering the sample MTS specifications in Fig. 7 and $\sigma = ?1\text{€} \cdot ?tea$ it holds that

– $Out_\Diamond(m_1 \text{ after}_\Diamond \sigma) = \{cup, error\}$
– $Out_\Diamond(m_2 \text{ after}_\Diamond \sigma) = \{cup, error\}$
– $Out_\Box(m_1 \text{ after}_\Diamond \sigma) = \{\}$
– $Out_\Box(m_2 \text{ after}_\Diamond \sigma) = \{error\}$
– $Out_\Box(m_1 \text{ after}_\Box \sigma) = \{\}$
– $Out_\Box(m_2 \text{ after}_\Box \sigma) = \{\}$

whereas for $\sigma' = ?2\text{€}$

– $Out_\Diamond(m_1 \text{ after}_\Diamond \sigma') = \{c1\text{€}, \delta\}$
– $Out_\Diamond(m_2 \text{ after}_\Diamond \sigma') = \{c1\text{€}, \delta\}$
– $Out_\Box(m_1 \text{ after}_\Diamond \sigma') = \{\delta\}$
– $Out_\Box(m_2 \text{ after}_\Diamond \sigma') = \{c1\text{€}\}$
– $Out_\Box(m_1 \text{ after}_\Box \sigma') = \{\}$
– $Out_\Box(m_2 \text{ after}_\Box \sigma') = \{\}$

holds.

According to the intuition of modal consistency, we observe the following correspondences.

Proposition 1. *Let s be an MTS, $p \in Q$, $P \subseteq Q$, $\sigma \in (I \cup U)^*$.*

1. *$init_\Box(p) \subseteq init_\Diamond(p)$,*
2. *$\delta_\Box \subseteq \delta_\Diamond$,*

3. p **after**$_\square$ $\sigma \subseteq p$ **after**$_\diamond$ σ,
4. $Out_\square(P) \subseteq Out_\diamond(P)$, and
5. $Straces_\square(p) \subseteq Straces_\diamond(p)$.

Testing a modal implementation $i \in \mathcal{IOMTS}_\diamond(I, U)$ against a modal specification $s \in \mathcal{MTS}(I, U)$ aims at verifying that every derivable product implementation variant $i' \leqslant_m^\diamond i$ conforms to a corresponding product specification variant $s' \leqslant_m s$. For this to hold, an intuitive notion of modal input/output conformance should ensure that

— all *possible* behaviors of a product line implementation are *allowed* and that
— all *mandatory* behaviors of a product line implementation are *required*

by the respective product line specification. Hence, for a model I/O conformance relation i **mior** s to hold, it requires trace inclusion of both *may*-suspension-traces and *must*-suspension-traces, respectively.

However, if we interpret the set of *must*-behaviors specified by s as the product line *core* behavior to be shown by all product variants, this notion of I/O conformance fails to fully capture this intuition. Similar to the non-modal version, suspension trace inclusion solely ensures *some* behavior of the specified behaviors to be actually implemented (if any), but it does not differentiate within the set of allowed behaviors between mandatory and optional ones. To overcome this drawback, we consider an alternative definition for modal I/O conformance, i **mior**$_\leqslant$ s, that is closer to the very essence of modal refinement requiring *alternating* suspension trace inclusions as follows.

Definition 15 (Modal I/O Conformance). *Let* $s \in \mathcal{MTS}(I, U)$ *and* $i \in \mathcal{IOMTS}_\diamond(I, U)$.

i **mior** s $:\Leftrightarrow$

1. $\forall \sigma \in act_\delta^* : Out_\diamond(i$ **after**$_\diamond$ $\sigma) \subseteq Out_\diamond(s$ **after**$_\diamond$ $\sigma)$ *and*
2. $\forall \sigma \in act_\delta^* : Out_\square(i$ **after**$_\square$ $\sigma) \subseteq Out_\square(s$ **after**$_\square$ $\sigma)$.

i **mior**$_\leqslant$ s $:\Leftrightarrow$

1. $\forall \sigma \in act_\delta^* : Out_\diamond(i$ **after**$_\diamond$ $\sigma) \subseteq Out_\diamond(s$ **after**$_\diamond$ $\sigma)$ *and*
2. $\forall \sigma \in act_\delta^* : Out_\square(s$ **after**$_\square$ $\sigma) \subseteq Out_\square(i$ **after**$_\square$ $\sigma)$.

Hence, the **mior**$_\leqslant$ relation requires a product line implementation i to show

— *at least* all mandatory behaviors and
— *at most* the allowed behaviors

of a product line specification s. The respective modal versions of the **ioco** relation can be defined, accordingly.

Definition 16 (Modal IOCO). *Let* $s \in \mathcal{MTS}(I, U)$ *and* $i \in \mathcal{IOMTS}_\diamond(I, U)$.

i **mioco** s $:\Leftrightarrow$

1. $\forall \sigma \in Straces_\diamond(s) : Out_\diamond(i \text{ after}_\diamond \sigma) \subseteq Out_\diamond(s \text{ after}_\diamond \sigma)$ and
2. $\forall \sigma \in Straces_\square(i) : Out_\square(i \text{ after}_\square \sigma) \subseteq Out_\square(s \text{ after}_\square \sigma)$.

$i \text{ mioco}_\leqslant s :\Leftrightarrow$

1. $\forall \sigma \in Straces_\diamond(s) : Out_\diamond(i \text{ after}_\diamond \sigma) \subseteq Out_\diamond(s \text{ after}_\diamond \sigma)$ and
2. $\forall \sigma \in Straces_\square(i) : Out_\square(s \text{ after}_\square \sigma) \subseteq Out_\square(i \text{ after}_\square \sigma)$.

Based on the previous observations, we conclude the following notion of soundness for modal **ioco**.

Theorem 2 (Soundness). *Let Let $s \in \mathcal{MTS}(I, U)$, $i \in \mathcal{IOMTS}_\diamond(I, U)$ and $i \text{ mioco}_\leqslant s$. Then it holds that $\forall i' \leqslant_m^\diamond i : i' \text{ mioco}_\leqslant s$.*

Hence, family-based product line conformance testing in terms of the presented intentional characterization of modal I/O conformance ensures (1) safety as it permits implementation variants to only show allowed behaviors and (2) liveness as it enforces implementation variants to at least show all core behaviors. Further results, e.g., concerning completeness and exhaustiveness notions, as well as an extensional characterization of modal **ioco** is open for future work. Concerning the latter, two main adaptations with respect single system testing are required.

1. The modality $\gamma \in \{\diamond, \square\}$ of an action a (including quiescence) occurring at a transition $s \xrightarrow{a}_\gamma s'$ is *observable*, e.g., by defining two separate alphabets $act_\square = act \times \{\square\}$ and $act_\diamond = act \times \{\diamond\}$, respectively.
2. The definition of a test case (cf. Fig. 4) is to be adopted for modal testing to require *every* must-behavior to be observed before giving the verdict **pass**, therefore, potentially requiring multiple test runs.

Clause 2. reflects that verifying the inclusion of all *must*-behaviors of the specification to be contained in the respective set of the implementation literally requires the specification to be (implicitly) tested against the implementation.

5   Conclusion

In this tutorial, we have presented the foundations of model-based testing. We have considered dynamic testing of functional characteristics at component-level based on model-based black-box knowledge for single system testing. This testing discipline is usually referred to as model-based input/output conformance testing. Furthermore, we have presented model-based testing techniques for variant-rich software systems, such as software product lines. We have explained sample-based product line testing based on variant selection techniques and a theory for variability-aware product line conformance testing.

References

1. Alur, R., Henzinger, T.A., Kupferman, O., Vardi, M.Y.: Alternating Refinement Relations. In: Sangiorgi, D., de Simone, R. (eds.) CONCUR 1998. LNCS, vol. 1466, pp. 163–178. Springer, Heidelberg (1998)
2. Asirelli, P., ter Beek, M.H., Fantechi, A., Gnesi, S.: A Model-Checking Tool for Families of Services. In: Bruni, R., Dingel, J. (eds.) FMOODS/FORTE 2011. LNCS, vol. 6722, pp. 44–58. Springer, Heidelberg (2011)
3. Asirelli, P., ter Beek, M.H., Gnesi, S., Fantechi, A.: Formal Description of Variability in Product Families. In: SPLC 2011, pp. 130–139 (2011)
4. Asirelli, P., ter Beek, M.H., Fantechi, A., Gnesi, S.: A Logical Framework to Deal with Variability. In: Méry, D., Merz, S. (eds.) IFM 2010. LNCS, vol. 6396, pp. 43–58. Springer, Heidelberg (2010)
5. Bauer, S.S., Hennicker, R., Janisch, S.: Interface Theories for (A)synchronously Communicating Modal I/O-Transition Systems. Electronic Proceedings in Theoretical Computer Science 46, 1–8 (2011)
6. Beizer, B.: Software Testing Techniques, 2nd edn. Van Nostrand Reinhold Co., New York (1990)
7. Bernot, G.: Testing against Formal Specifications: A Theoretical View. In: Abramsky, S. (ed.) TAPSOFT 1991, CCPSD 1991, and ADC-Talks 1991. LNCS, vol. 494, pp. 99–119. Springer, Heidelberg (1991)
8. van der Bijl, M., Rensink, A., Tretmans, J.: Compositional testing with ioco. In: Petrenko, A., Ulrich, A. (eds.) FATES 2003. LNCS, vol. 2931, pp. 86–100. Springer, Heidelberg (2004)
9. Broy, M. (ed.): Model-Based Testing of Reactive Systems: Advanced Lectures, 1st edn. Springer, Heidelberg (2005)
10. Chvatal, V.: A Greedy Heuristic For The Set-Covering Problem. Mathematics of Operations Research (1979)
11. Cichos, H., Oster, S., Lochau, M., Schürr, A.: Model-Based Coverage-Driven Test Suite Generation for Software Product Lines. In: Whittle, J., Clark, T., Kühne, T. (eds.) MODELS 2011. LNCS, vol. 6981, pp. 425–439. Springer, Heidelberg (2011)
12. Clements, P.C., Northrop, L.: Software Product Lines: Practices and Patterns. SEI Series in Software Eng. Addison-Wesley (2001)
13. Cohen, M.B., Dwyer, M.B., Shi, J.: Coverage and Adequacy in Software Product Line Testing. In: ISSTA, pp. 53–63. ACM (2006)
14. Czarnecki, K., Antkiewicz, M.: Mapping Features to Models: A Template Approach Based on Superimposed Variants. In: Glück, R., Lowry, M. (eds.) GPCE 2005. LNCS, vol. 3676, pp. 422–437. Springer, Heidelberg (2005)
15. Czarnecki, K., Eisenecker, U.W.: Generative Programming: Methods, Tools, and Applications. ACM Press/Addison-Wesley (2000)
16. De Nicola, R.: Extensional Equivalence for Transition Systems. Acta Informatica 24, 211–237 (1987), http://portal.acm.org/citation.cfm?id=25067.25074
17. of Electrical, I., Engineers, E.: IEEE Standard Glossary of Software Engineering Technology 610.121990 (1990)
18. of Electrical, I., Engineers, E.: IEEE Standard for Software Test Documentation IEEE Std 829-1998 (1998)
19. Engström, E.: Exploring Regression Testing and Software Product Line Testing - Research and State of Practice. Lic dissertation, Lund University (May 2010)
20. Engström, E., Runeson, P.: Software Product Line Testing – A Systematic Mapping Study. Information and Software Technology 53(1), 2–13 (2011)

21. Ferber, S., Haag, J., Savolainen, J.: Feature Interaction and Dependencies: Modeling Features for Reengineering a Legacy Product Line. In: Chastek, G.J. (ed.) SPLC 2002. LNCS, vol. 2379, p. 235. Springer, Heidelberg (2002)

22. Fischbein, D., Uchitel, S., Braberman, V.A.: A Foundation for Behavioural Conformance in Software Product Line Architectures. In: Hierons, R.M., Muccini, H. (eds.) ISSTA 2006, pp. 39–48. ACM (2006)

23. Gustafsson, T.: An Approach for Selecting Software Product Line Instances for Testing. In: SPLiT (2007)

24. Henard, C., Papadakis, M., Perrouin, G., Klein, J., Traon, Y.L.: Multi-objective Test Generation for Software Product Lines. In: SPLC (2013)

25. Johansen, M.F., Haugen, O., Fleurey, F.: An Algorithm for Generating t-wise Covering Arrays from Large Feature Models. In: SPLC, pp. 46–55. ACM (2012)

26. Johansen, M.F., Haugen, Ø., Fleurey, F.: Properties of Realistic Feature Models Make Combinatorial Testing of Product Lines Feasible. In: Whittle, J., Clark, T., Kühne, T. (eds.) MODELS 2011. LNCS, vol. 6981, pp. 638–652. Springer, Heidelberg (2011)

27. Kang, K.C., Cohen, S.G., Hess, J.A., Novak, W.E., Peterson, A.S.: Feature-Oriented Domain Analysis (FODA) Feasibility Study. Tech. rep., Carnegie-Mellon University Software Engineering Institute (November 1990)

28. Kim, C.H.P., Batory, D., Khurshid, S.: Reducing Combinatorics in Testing Product Lines. In: AOSD, pp. 57–68. ACM (2011)

29. Kowal, M., Schulze, S., Schaefer, I.: Towards Efficient SPL Testing by Variant Reduction. In: VariComp, pp. 1–6. ACM (2013)

30. Kuhn, D.R., Wallace, D.R., Gallo, J. A.M.: Software fault interactions and implications for software testing. IEEE Trans. Softw. Eng. 30(6), 418–421 (2004)

31. Larsen, K.G., Nyman, U., Wąsowski, A.: Modal I/O Automata for Interface and Product Line Theories. In: De Nicola, R. (ed.) ESOP 2007. LNCS, vol. 4421, pp. 64–79. Springer, Heidelberg (2007)

32. Larsen, K.G., Thomsen, B.: A Modal Process Logic. In: LICS, pp. 203–210 (1988)

33. Lochau, M., Oster, S., Goltz, U., Schürr, A.: Model-based Pairwise Testing for Feature Interaction Coverage in Software Product Line Engineering. Software Quality Journal, 1–38 (2011)

34. Lochau, M., Schaefer, I., Kamischke, J., Lity, S.: Incremental Model-Based Testing of Delta-Oriented Software Product Lines. In: Brucker, A.D., Julliand, J. (eds.) TAP 2012. LNCS, vol. 7305, pp. 67–82. Springer, Heidelberg (2012)

35. Lochau, M., Goltz, U.: Feature Interaction Aware Test Case Generation for Embedded Control Systems. Electron. Notes Theor. Comput. Sci. 264, 37–52 (2010)

36. Lüttgen, G., Vogler, W.: Modal Interface Automata. In: Baeten, J.C.M., Ball, T., de Boer, F.S. (eds.) TCS 2012. LNCS, vol. 7604, pp. 265–279. Springer, Heidelberg (2012)

37. McGregor, J.D.: Testing a Software Product Line. Tech. Rep. CMU/SEI-2001-TR-022, Carnegie Mellon, Software Engineering Inst. (2001)

38. McGregor, J.D., Sodhani, P., Madhavapeddi, S.: Testing Variability in a Software Product Line. In: Proceedings of the Software Product Line Testing Workshop (SPLiT), pp. 45–50. Avaya Labs, Boston (2004)

39. Mendonca, M., Wąsowski, A., Czarnecki, K.: SAT-based Analysis of Feature Models is Easy. In: Proc. Int'l Software Product Line Conference, pp. 231–240 (2009)

40. da, M.S., Neto, P.A., Carmo Machado, I.D., McGregor, J.D., de Almeida, E.S., de Lemos Meira, S.R.: A Systematic Mapping Study of Software Product Lines Testing. Inf. Softw. Technol. 53, 407–423 (2011)

41. Myers, G.J.: The Art of Software Testing. Wiley, New York (1979)
42. Olimpiew, E.M.: Model-Based Testing for Software Product Lines. Ph.D. thesis, George Mason University (2008)
43. van Osch, M.: Hybrid input-output conformance and test generation. In: Havelund, K., Núñez, M., Roşu, G., Wolff, B. (eds.) FATES 2006 and RV 2006. LNCS, vol. 4262, pp. 70–84. Springer, Heidelberg (2006)
44. Oster, S., Lochau, M., Zink, M., Grechanik, M.: Pairwise Feature-Interaction Testing for SPLs: Potentials and Limitations. In: 3rd International Workshop on Feature-Oriented Software Development (FOSD) (2011)
45. Oster, S., Zorcic, I., Markert, F., Lochau, M.: MoSo-PoLiTe - Tool Support for Pairwise and Model-Based Software Product Line Testing. In: VaMoS (2011)
46. Oster, S., Wübbeke, A., Engels, G., Schürr, A.: Model-Based Software Product Lines Testing Survey. In: Model-based Testing for Embedded Systems. CRC Press Taylor & Francis (2010) (to appear)
47. Perrouin, G., Sen, S., Klein, J., Le Traon, B.: Automated and Scalable T-wise Test Case Generation Strategies for Software Product Lines. In: ICST, pp. 459–468 (2010)
48. Raclet, J.B., Badouel, E., Benveniste, A., Caillaud, B., Legay, A., Passerone, R.: Modal Interfaces: Unifying Interface Automata and Modal Specifications. In: EMSOFT 2009, pp. 87–96. ACM (2009)
49. Reuys, A., Kamsties, E., Pohl, K., Reis, S.: Model-Based System Testing of Software Product Families. In: Pastor, Ó., Falcão e Cunha, J. (eds.) CAiSE 2005. LNCS, vol. 3520, pp. 519–534. Springer, Heidelberg (2005)
50. Schaefer, I., Rabiser, R., Clarke, D., Bettini, L., Benavides, D., Botterweck, G., Pathak, A., Trujillo, S., Villela, K.: Software diversity: state of the art and perspectives. STTT 14(5), 477–495 (2012)
51. Scheidemann, K.: Verifying Families of System Configurations. Ph.D. thesis, TU Munich (2007)
52. Schmaltz, J., Tretmans, J.: On Conformance Testing for Timed Systems. In: Cassez, F., Jard, C. (eds.) FORMATS 2008. LNCS, vol. 5215, pp. 250–264. Springer, Heidelberg (2008)
53. Tevanlinna, A., Taina, J., Kauppinen, R.: Product Family Testing: A Survey. ACM SIGSOFT Software Engineering Notes 29, 12–18 (2004)
54. Tretmans, J.: Testing concurrent systems: A formal approach. In: Baeten, J.C.M., Mauw, S. (eds.) CONCUR 1999. LNCS, vol. 1664, p. 46. Springer, Heidelberg (1999)
55. Utting, M., Legeard, B.: Practical Model-Based Testing: A Tools Approach. Morgan Kaufmann, San Francisco (2007)
56. van Veenendaal, E. (ed.): ISTQB-Glossary-of-Testing-Terms-2-0. Glossary Working Party (2007)

Author Index